Winning the Third World

The New Cold War History

Odd Arne Westad, editor

This series focuses on new interpretations of the Cold War era made possible by the opening of Soviet, East European, Chinese, and other archives. Books in the series based on multilingual and multiarchival research incorporate interdisciplinary insights and new conceptual frameworks that place historical scholarship in a broad, international context.

A complete list of books published in The New Cold War History is available at www.uncpress.unc.edu.

Winning the Third World

Sino-American Rivalry during the Cold War

GREGG A. BRAZINSKY

The University of North Carolina Press
Chapel Hill

© 2017 The University of North Carolina Press

Set in Adobe Text Pro by codeMantra
The University of North Carolina Press has been a member of the
Green Press Initiative since 2003.

Cover illustration: *Red and Blue Rising*, © simon2579; Chinese Dragon,
© exxorian. istockphoto.com

Library of Congress Cataloging-in-Publication Data
Names: Brazinsky, Gregg, author.
Title: Winning the Third World : Sino-American rivalry during the Cold War /
    Gregg A. Brazinsky.
Other titles: New Cold War history.
Description: Chapel Hill : University of North Carolina Press, [2017] | Series: The
    new Cold War history | Includes bibliographical references and index.
Identifiers: LCCN 2016042808 | ISBN 9781469631707 (cloth : alk. paper) |
    ISBN 9781469668642 (pbk. : alk. paper) | ISBN 9781469631714 (ebook)
Subjects: LCSH: United States—Foreign relations—China. | United States—
    Foreign relations—1945–1989. | China—Foreign relations—United States. |
    China—Foreign relations—20th century. | Cold War.
Classification: LCC E183.8.C5 B679 2017 | DDC 327.73051—dc23 LC record
    available at https://lccn.loc.gov/2016042808

This book is dedicated to the loving memory of five people
who would very much have liked to see its completion:

Herbert Brazinsky

Sol Brazinsky

Rebecca Brazinsky

Murray Brodsky

Ella Brodsky

Contents

Figures

Acknowledgments

I am grateful to the individuals and organizations that provided me with the resources and guidance that I needed to write this book. During 2010–11, I was privileged to be a visiting scholar at the Woodrow Wilson International Center for Scholars. I made significant progress on the manuscript during this year not only because the center enabled me to take time off from teaching but also because of the outstanding environment that it provided for thinking and writing. I am also grateful to the Smith Richardson Foundation for providing me with a Junior Faculty Research Grant in 2008. Though my research during the grant period took a different direction than initially intended, the support of the foundation and the interest of its grant officers in my work were invaluable to the completion of this book. I received several research and travel grants from the Sigur Center for Asian Studies at The George Washington University and the university's History Department while working on this book. Former Dean of the Elliott School of International Affairs Mike Brown also provided me with a small research grant in one critical instance when I needed to spend more time in Beijing. Without this financial support I would not have been able to gather the necessary materials from Chinese archives. Last, the LBJ Presidential Library provided me with a grant to conduct research on this book in 2009; like many other scholars, I am grateful to the library for its generosity and splendid staff.

I am indebted to several individuals for their help with research and writing. I was fortunate that the University of North Carolina Press chose Lorenz Lüthi as a reader for this manuscript. Lorenz transcended the bias of friendship and pointed out important issues and sources that I had missed in the initial draft. I have also learned a great deal from my conversations with him in Beijing and elsewhere. When I first started learning Mandarin so that I could work on China as well as Korea, nobody offered me more encouragement than Chen Jian. He set an example with his own scholarship, the influence of which can be seen very easily in this manuscript, and gave me an opportunity to present my work in an early stage at Cornell University. Shen Zhihua shared his great knowledge and experience with Chinese sources and continues to foster a highly collegial atmosphere in which Chinese and American scholars working on the Cold War can interact. Conversations with several other scholars working on Chinese Cold War diplomacy helped me sharpen my ideas for this book. Among them are Niu Jun, Yang Kuisong, Dai Chaowu, Yafeng Xia, Li Danhui, Jiang Huajie, Li Qianyu, Sergey Radchenko, and Jeremy Friedman. I especially thank Niu Jun for sending copies of some of his books.

During my year at the Wilson Center, I was fortunate to have Sunny Yiqian Xu and Zhu Zhang as interns. They both did outstanding work. At George Washington University, Qingfei Yin served as my research assistant for one year with the support of the Sigur Center and helped with some of the more difficult documents. Kelley Qiuyun Shang, one of the best undergraduate students I have taught, also worked as a short-term research assistant on two occasions. A number of Chinese graduate students (some of whom are now faculty) also served as short-term research assistants, including Tian Wuxiong, Zhang Jing, Zheng Shuai, Wang Bo, Yuan Jing, Melanie Leung, Bai Xiaoyu, and Sun Xiu.

It has been a great pleasure to work once again with the University of North Carolina Press. I would like to thank series editor Odd Arne Westad, whose scholarship has been a beacon for other scholars writing about the Cold War in the Third World, as well as Chuck Grench, Jay Mazzocchi, and Jad Adkins for shepherding the manuscript through the different stages necessary for publication.

Many other friends and colleagues have also encouraged and supported me. The History Department and the Elliott School of International Affairs at The George Washington University have been highly collegial environments to work in. I especially thank Bill Becker, whose support as department chair is greatly appreciated, and Ed Berkowitz, Jim Hershberg, Hope M. Harrison, Jisoo Kim, Ed McCord, Leo Ribuffo, Ron Spector, and Andrew Zimmerman for being constant sources of friendship, ideas, and encouragement. The staff at GW's Gelman Library has also been superb and helpful in tracking down hard-to-find Chinese volumes through interlibrary loan. Though my years as a student are increasingly distant, my work still bears the intellectual imprint of past mentors at Amherst College and Cornell University, especially Gordie Levin, Sherman Cochran, and Tim Borstelmann. At the Wilson Center, I was grateful to Christian Ostermann for facilitating both my stay at the center and my contacts with Chinese scholars working on the Cold War. Before and after my year at the center, I was especially grateful to have the friendship and support of my former doctoral student, James F. Person. His work at the center has helped scholars around the world gain a better understanding of the Cold War in Asia. He and his wife, Jooeun Kim, offered valuable camaraderie and encouragement throughout the time that I worked on this project.

Last, as always, I thank my family for its patience and encouragement, especially my mother and stepfather, Carol and Harry Weiner. They have stood by me through all of the vicissitudes of life that I faced while writing this book, and I owe them the deepest gratitude.

A Note on Romanization

All Chinese words were romanized according to the pinyin system. During the 1950s and 1960s American officials often used the Wade-Giles system to romanize Chinese names. Thus they wrote "Peiping" instead of Beijing or "Chou En-lai" instead of Zhou Enlai. For the sake of consistency, I have converted these Wade-Giles romanizations to pinyin but bracketed the pinyin word. Therefore, where it said "Peiping" in the original document I wrote it as [Beijing].

Winning the Third World

Introduction

No two countries will have greater influence over the destiny of humanity in the twenty-first century than the United States and the People's Republic of China. Their size, wealth, and power enable them to expand their influence around the world, arousing a combination of admiration and resentment. Although the two nations can and in fact must cooperate on many global issues, their different histories, values, and conceptions of world order make competition in at least some areas inevitable. In the early twenty-first century, Sino-American competition has been especially prevalent in parts of Asia and Africa that were once dominated by European colonialism and today struggle to achieve economic development. Many observers fear that a rising China will sweep American influence out of these regions and thus challenge or replace American ascendancy in world politics. They worry that China will spread a model of political and economic development that will fundamentally undermine the liberal international order that the United States seeks to uphold.[1]

These fears are not completely new, and neither is China's determination to establish itself as an important power in what used to be called the Third World. This book tells the story of an intense and enduring competition that prevailed between Beijing and Washington in the region during an earlier but not so distant era—the Cold War. It demonstrates that this competition was an important priority for both the United States and China and that it played a pivotal role in shaping the Cold War's evolution. This competition spread across diverse regions of the globe and encompassed the diplomatic, political, cultural, and economic realms. It shaped the destinies of some Asian and African countries and helped to define the global agendas of both the People's Republic of China (PRC) and the United States.

What fueled such an expansive competition? I argue that status was the most important driving force behind this struggle. A powerful nationalistic tide that sought to avenge China's humiliation at the hands of European colonialism was at the heart of Chinese politics through much of the twentieth century. It helped to inspire the creation of the Chinese Communist Party (CCP) and had a profound effect on the worldview of the party's leaders. Through much of the Cold War, Beijing found itself alienated from the Free World and relegated to a subordinate position vis-à-vis

Moscow within the Communist Bloc. It viewed the Afro-Asian world as the one region where it could play a leadership role and thus reassert its importance in world affairs.

The period between 1949 and 1972 was one of unremitting American hostility toward almost all Chinese objectives, however. American officials believed that if China succeeded it would threaten their ambitions to integrate newly independent countries into a U.S.-led international order. Washington mobilized its political and economic resources in a long-standing effort to prevent Beijing from attaining the status it craved. It pressured Afro-Asian nations to shun the PRC diplomatically, it targeted Communist China in its propaganda campaigns, it helped to suppress China's allies in many newly independent countries, and it tried to minimize the impact of Chinese economic and military assistance programs.

In the end, China did not—at least during the Cold War period—ever gain the status and influence in the Third World to which it aspired. Yet this was by no means a result of the wisdom or efficacy of American policies. During the 1950s and 1960s, there were numerous instances where China gained the respect and admiration of other Afro-Asian countries despite Washington's efforts. Often China's own zealotry or refusal to compromise doomed its quest to be viewed as a leader by other Third World nations. And of course, the vagaries and unpredictability of politics in newly independent nations proved just as frustrating to China's efforts to establish its influence as it did to those of its rivals.

Reframing the Cold War

In recent years, historians have almost entirely demolished the myth that the Cold War was simply an East-West conflict dominated by the two superpowers. American officials were never as completely focused on the Soviet Union as the first generation of Cold War historians made them out to be. Matthew Connelly has demonstrated that although Washington viewed the conflict with communism as an important priority, it was equally horrified by the prospect of a North-South conflict that would divide the world along racial and religious lines.[2] Other scholars have shown that, despite their preponderant military power, the Americans and the Soviets did not always play a determinative role in shaping events and outcomes. Tony Smith argues that the "fundamental features" of the Cold War cannot be understood without "seeing the governments of countries such as North Korea and China, East and West Germany, Great Britain and Israel, Egypt and Cuba . . . as having had principal roles to play that gave the Cold War the character it came to have."[3]

China's quest for ascendance in the Third World is one of the most prominent examples of how other players made their impact felt and shaped America's agenda. Although the PRC putatively shared a common ideology with the Soviet Union, the motives, objectives, and strategies guiding Beijing's involvement in Afro-Asian countries differed in many ways from those of Moscow—a fact that would eventually foster Sino-Soviet as well as Sino-American competition in the region.[4] As a non-Western nation that succeeded at state building despite its own history as a victim of colonialism, China had an appeal to other newly independent societies that its Great Power rivals did not. And it was precisely these characteristics that made the PRC such a vexing problem for American officials. China's Afro-Asianism constituted an independent, militant force that threatened to realize America's two worst fears: the spread of communism and the triumph of revolution in the Global South. Thus, when it came to crafting policy toward the Third World, Americans sometimes viewed Beijing as an even greater threat than Moscow.

It is no secret that the PRC and the United States were adversaries during the Cold War, but rivalry between the two in the Third World has received little attention from scholars.[5] Since the late 1960s political scientists and diplomatic historians have devoted a great deal of attention to China's relationships with different parts of Asia and Africa, with some of the most recent literature taking advantage of new Chinese archival materials.[6] But the focus of most of these studies has been Chinese policies and, to a lesser degree, the response that these policies engendered. The literature on America's relations with the Third World is far more voluminous. During the past twenty years in particular, diplomatic historians have broadened our understanding of American involvement in Asia, Africa, and Latin America, often through multinational, multiarchival research. Even so, this scholarship has focused largely on U.S. relations with specific countries and regions rather than how the United States contested specific adversaries.[7]

Through bringing Sino-American competition into focus, this book contributes to a more complex and multifaceted understanding of the Cold War. It sheds new light on American and Chinese objectives in Asia and Africa and how the clash between them affected the political development of newly independent nations. At the same time, however, it is not my intention to argue that Sino-American competition provides the best or most comprehensive framework for understanding the Cold War in the Third World. Indeed, a number of players competed for influence in Asia, Africa, and Latin America through a broad array of different tactics and methods during this period. Historians have profitably explored U.S.-Soviet, Sino-Soviet, and U.S.-Cuban competition.[8] Work remains to be done on East-West German and

North-South Korean competition in the region. A focus on Sino-American competition offers a valuable window into a much larger house that might be called the Cold War in the Third World. But it remains one of many windows through which the subject needs to be viewed.

Understanding how Communist China could pose such an important challenge to the United States requires an appreciation not only of the many actors who shaped the Cold War but also of how different forms of power were used to wage it. The PRC could never match the United States or the Soviet Union when it came to deploying military power or dispensing economic aid. But these were not the only means of projecting influence. As John Lewis Gaddis has noted, power can exist in multiple forms, and nonmilitary kinds of power, including economic, cultural, ideological, and moral power, often played an important role in shaping the contours of the Cold War. Even if the United States and the Soviet Union were preponderant militarily, these other forms of power were more evenly distributed.[9] Aside from the Korean War, where American and Chinese forces confronted each other directly on the battlefield, it was in these nonmilitary theaters where China most often challenged American influence.

Of course, these nonmaterial forms of power had their limitations. They could not protect the PRC from attack or raise its people's standard of living. They could, however, bolster China's status internationally. And it was the pursuit of status that, for a variety of reasons, became a critical objective of the PRC's policy in the Third World from the moment of its establishment.

Status and Sino-American Competition in the Third World

The central argument of this book is that Sino-American rivalry in the Third World was, in essence, a competition over status. Status, however, is a somewhat slippery concept, and there is no clear consensus on its meaning. Achieving a high status can mean different things to different nations and actors. Unlike military power and economic prosperity, status is not easily measured or quantified. Unlike territory or armaments, status is not acquired unilaterally; others must perceive and recognize it, and such perceptions are invariably subjective.[10] How, then, can we define status? And what did status mean to China?

Influenced by the renowned sociologist Max Weber, international relations theorists have often understood status as a state's relative standing within a hierarchy. William C. Wohlforth calls status "a recognized position within a social hierarchy, implying relations of dominance and deference."[11] But this definition does not quite fit Cold War China's aspirations in the Third World. Beijing staked its appeal to other Afro-Asian peoples on the idea that it did not seek the same dominance that its Great Power rivals were ostensibly pursuing. Party leaders wanted nationalists and revolutionaries to admire and emulate the People's Republic but claims to a higher standing in a formal hierarchy would undercut the basis of its appeal. At the same time, the idea that China was a middle kingdom that deserved a central position in international affairs continued to inform the outlook of Chinese officials. They believed that the PRC had a special role to play in liberating and championing the oppressed peoples of the globe. Paradoxically, Beijing sought to create an informal, antihierarchical hierarchy, subtly promoting itself as the first among equals without commanding formal deference. Achieving status in the Afro-Asian world meant enjoying a special position in the absence of a formal hierarchy. It is in this sense that I use the term "status" throughout this book in order to convey more accurately China's aspirations.

In describing the Sino-American competition for "status," this book frequently refers to related terms, including "prestige," "legitimacy," and "honor." In general, I view status as the larger objective sought by the PRC and gaining prestige, legitimacy and other attributes as important subcomponents of this goal. Prestige and honor generally describe the degree of admiration accrued by states or leaders through their actions. They help a state to gain a more important position in international politics, but they do not—as status does—describe the position itself. Legitimacy refers to a state's legal standing in international institutions and, like prestige, may help a state to improve its status, but nevertheless it usually does not convey any formal or informal leadership position.[12] At the same time, the boundaries between these concepts are fuzzy; neither American nor Chinese officials usually drew such fine distinctions. Nevertheless, I attempt to use each term where it seemed most appropriate for describing the specific policy, initiative, or objective that Beijing was trying to pursue.

Despite the difficulties inherent in defining and assessing status, its relevance to Chinese diplomacy—both past and present—has been widely noted.[13] David C. Kang has argued persuasively that a more traditional status hierarchy governed China's relations with the rest of East Asia for the five centuries before it came into extensive contact with the West.[14] Other political scientists have used the concept of status to understand China's rising political and economic influence in the present era. They have been interested in such questions as whether and how China will pursue greater status as the global distribution of military strength and wealth shifts in its favor.[15] Some have also been concerned about whether China's current efforts to attain greater status will cause international conflicts.[16] This literature has rarely if ever touched on the Cold War period, but it has demonstrated the enduring significance of status in China's foreign policy.

Historians have generally not focused on status as an overarching explanation of Chinese diplomacy as often as political scientists, but they have nevertheless noted its importance. Chen Jian, who is perhaps the leading scholar of Chinese Cold War diplomacy, has been the most explicit. In his books *Mao's China and the Cold War* and *China's Road to the Korean War*, Chen notes in several places that erasing China's history of victimization and changing its "weak power status" were important objectives for Mao and his colleagues.[17] In Chen's work, Beijing's determination to raise its international stature is seen as a function of Mao's revolutionary nationalist ideology and his desire to carry out a "continuous revolution" at home.[18] My goal in emphasizing status instead of ideology is not to turn Chen's analysis on its head; I agree that status and ideology were deeply interrelated. I am mainly seeking to frame things in a way that is most appropriate for a study of Sino-American competition in the Third World. The United States could do little to change Mao's thinking or the ideological underpinnings of China's policies. It could, however, seek to prevent the PRC from gaining status. And I discovered abundant evidence in U.S. archives that this was an important American priority.

During the Cold War, achieving status in world affairs was important to Chinese officials for two key reasons: the historical memory of China's past humiliation at the hands of the Great Powers and Mao Zedong's cult of personality. These two factors worked in tandem to create a sense of urgency about the PRC's international standing. The idea that China once stood at the center of world civilization but was robbed of its rightful position by predatory Westerners and Japanese has been critical to the modern Chinese national consciousness. During the late nineteenth and early twentieth centuries, as Chinese first began to imagine themselves as a nation, they also began to look on their recent past as a period when their country had been exploited, divided, and bullied by Western imperialists. As China struggled for unity during the years between 1911 and 1949, both the Chinese Communist Party (CCP) and its rival party, the Guomindang (GMD), claimed to be at the helm of a grand national awakening that would one day end China's history of victimization. Once the CCP triumphed it staked its legitimacy in part on its ability to liberate China from the indignities of its past and restore its central position in world affairs.[19] Achieving greater status, especially among other postcolonial societies, came to be viewed as a means of ending China's history of humiliation and regaining the honor and glory that had been stolen from it.

At the center of Chinese decision-making was Mao Zedong. Historians focusing on China's Cold War foreign policy are in broad agreement that Chairman Mao was the pivotal figure in shaping the PRC's relations with the outside world.[20] Although the urbane diplomat Zhou Enlai often represented

China on the world stage, Mao was deeply involved in all of the PRC's most critical decisions, and his influence on the tone and content of Chinese diplomacy was unmistakable.[21] Yet Mao was even more than this. He was the guiding spirit and voice behind the Chinese Revolution. His ideas and writings gave Chinese communism its distinctive characteristics and mobilized a generation of his compatriots to support drastic social, economic, and political change. When China sought to expand its influence abroad, it was also seeking to spread the influence of Maoist ideas about guerrilla warfare, peasant mobilization, and economic development. Mao's personal prestige and Communist China's status in world affairs were inextricably intertwined. The chairman's longing to enhance his own stature as a theoretician and fortify his rule at home strengthened his determination to raise Chinese status in world affairs.

The key question that Mao and his comrades faced was *how* to increase China's status. The CCP found two overlapping answers to this question. One of these was revolutionary evangelism. The provenance of the PRC lay in anticolonial revolution, and this shaped the core of its national identity.[22] Chinese leaders were convinced that their revolution would have great international as well as national ramifications, and they eagerly encouraged others seeking to overthrow imperialism or foreign domination to emulate their experience. They pursued this objective through disseminating Mao Zedong's writings on guerrilla warfare and providing weapons and material support for wars of national liberation. But the PRC sought greater status not only among those engaged in violent struggle but also among Afro-Asian nations that had recently achieved national independence and shared with China a history of colonial exploitation. Through diplomacy, economic aid, cultural exchange, and propaganda, Beijing promoted itself as a successful example of postcolonial nation-building and sought a position of leadership for itself in the Third World. It rarely attempted to subvert the newly independent governments in countries like Egypt, Ghana, or Tanzania; instead, it aimed to persuade them that the PRC understood and could help them in a way that the Americans or the Soviets could not. Yet Beijing used diplomacy in different ways at varying times. In some instances (such as between 1954 and 1962 and after 1972), it emphasized coexistence with Afro-Asian nations of all political orientations. In other instances (especially between 1962 and 1966), it more actively sought to organize the Third World politically around a militant and radical agenda. Beijing sometimes alternated between these strategies and sometimes pursued a combination of them, tailoring its approach to constantly shifting domestic and international circumstances.

Regardless of how Beijing sought to enlarge its status, it was always met with strong resistance from Washington. The United States emerged from

World War II with the confidence that went with being the wealthiest and mightiest nation in the world. It generally felt secure about its own standing among newly independent countries. Despite this confidence, the United States tended to take a greatly exaggerated view of how quickly and substantially the PRC would be able to expand its influence. It was the perception and fear that China would succeed rather than the underlying reality that often determined American policy—a fact that in many ways accounts for the intensity and scope of the competition.

In contending that Sino-American competition was driven by status, I by no means argue that such other considerations as security or economic interests were irrelevant. Instead, I argue that Beijing and Washington viewed status in the Third World as critical precisely because it could facilitate the achievement of other more tangible objectives. Max Weber argued that "social honor, or prestige, may even be the basis of political and economic power and frequently has been."[23] Political scientist Robert Jervis applied this insight directly to the arena of international politics when he noted that "prestige and saving face" are not "ephemeral goals pursued by . . . foolish statesmen unappreciative of the vital role of power." They are "aspects of a state's image that greatly contribute to the pursuit of other goals."[24] This was particularly true of PRC diplomacy. Beijing generally did not—and, for the most part, could not—build military bases or create informal economic controls. Instead, it sought to persuade others to support its political agenda through diplomacy, cultural exchange, and limited but symbolic economic aid. Even when the PRC did use military force or support insurgencies, considerations of status figured into Chinese decision-making.

Ultimately, the rivalry between Beijing and Washington in the Third World demonstrated that it is far easier to seek status than to attain it. Ironically, both sides often ended up weakening rather than enhancing their status through competing with each other. When American officials pressured newly independent nations to avoid contacts with the PRC, they inevitably came across as domineering and elicited accusations of neocolonialism. At the same time, the revolutionary zeal that inspired Beijing's diplomacy in the Third World could be a double-edged sword. On the one hand, nationalists in other Afro-Asian countries were attracted to the PRC's devout anticolonialism and willingness to support allies despite its own hardships. On the other hand, this same revolutionary zeal sometimes turned into a fanaticism that alienated more moderate Afro-Asian states and led to conflicts between the PRC and its neighbors.

It is difficult to make lasting gains in status because status is subject to shifting and sometimes highly individual perceptions. Chinese leaders constantly tried to construct a unifying Afro-Asian imaginary that placed the PRC at the center of a community of postcolonial nations. China sometimes succeeded in getting other Afro-Asian peoples to invest in its vision. But in the end this imagined community was just that—imagined and not real.[25] The PRC oversimplified the complex and shifting motives and ideas that caused Asian and African leaders to seek solidarity. Leaders in newly independent Afro-Asian countries could be swift to adjust their views based on changing circumstances. When they did so, they often gave lie to the vision of unity that China's quest for status in the Third World hinged on. Moreover, political instability prevailed in much of the Global South during the Cold War often confounding the efforts of both Americans and Chinese to cultivate particular leaders or elites. Military coups, successful insurgencies, or other power plays could swiftly realign politics in developing countries, altering relations with and perceptions of outside powers. The degree to which Beijing or Washington could influence subjective perceptions of their relative status in the Third World was limited by many unpredictable exogenous factors.

Despite the difficulties inherent in accruing status, Beijing was not entirely unsuccessful. In some instances, China proved adept at finding the right message to assuage doubts about its ambitions and fire the enthusiasm of its closest sympathizers. But the PRC often proved to be its own worst enemy. Even when American efforts to undermine Beijing proved almost fruitless, Communist China sometimes managed to snatch defeat from the jaws of victory through its uncompromising stances and poor policy choices. In the end, the United States did not triumph in its competition with the PRC. The complexities and unpredictability of the Third World made it a difficult place for selling visions. And the PRC simply could never have the kind of transformative influence that it somewhat immodestly hoped for.

Organization

The organization of this book is both chronological and thematic. The chapter layout is designed to capture the evolution and multiple forms of Sino-American competition in the Third World. Chapter 1 traces the emergence of Sino-American rivalry in the Third World from 1919 to 1950, when the CCP endured a myriad of hardships before gaining political control over the mainland. Long before they were a significant force in world politics, the CCP's leaders believed that China would naturally come to play a leadership role in a world revolution against colonialism and that this would help to redeem the country's past humiliation. During the same period, Americans slowly came to perceive the CCP as a threat to their ambitions to integrate all of Asia into a liberal international order. Chapter 2 focuses on 1950 to 1954, when China's quest for status incurred many new obligations. Beijing felt compelled to assist other Asian Communist movements in Korea and Indochina and paid a hefty price to do so. Washington, in contrast, often cited the need to prevent China from gaining prestige in Asia as a reason for its deep involvement in both of these conflicts. Moreover, American officials were alarmed by the growth of China's international status during the Korean War. They therefore implemented new policies designed to weaken the PRC, most notably stronger support for Taiwan and a punishing trade embargo.

After waging a costly and protracted war in Korea and supporting a violent insurgency in Vietnam, the PRC looked for less costly means to extend its influence during the mid- and late 1950s. Chapters 3, 4, and 5 look at how Beijing sought to promote a new image of itself as a peaceful, anticolonial power. In 1954–55, Beijing seized the opportunity presented by two major international conferences at Geneva and Bandung to enhance its status among Afro-Asian states. Chapter 3 looks at Chinese diplomacy at these conferences and how the United States tried to contest it. After Bandung, the PRC continued to court its neighbors in South and Southeast Asia by pursuing summitry and, in some instances, offering limited economic aid. In Chapter 4, I examine both China's expanding diplomatic activities in the region and American efforts to block them. The fifth chapter surveys how the United States and the PRC used cultural diplomacy to strengthen their own status and undermine each other's.

During the early 1960s, the contours of Sino-American competition in the Third World shifted because of other significant developments in world politics—notably, the Sino-Soviet split and the Sino-Indian border conflict of 1962. Chapter 6 explains how these changes intensified competition between Beijing and Washington. Conflict with Moscow and India drove the PRC to promote a more radical, militant version of Afro-Asian unity, provoking American fears that Beijing would unite subaltern peoples throughout the globe against a liberal world order. Washington therefore ramped up its efforts to counter Chinese influence. Chapters 7, 8, and 9 examine three key strategies used by the PRC: diplomacy, support for insurgencies, and economic aid. Chapter 7 explores China's diplomatic offensive in Asia and Africa during the years 1963–65. Beijing aligned itself with other Afro-Asian states that were, for different reasons, frustrated with Great Power hegemony. Together, they promoted such events as the Second Afro-Asian Conference, which encouraged unity while inciting hostility toward the United States and the Soviet Union. Washington countered by advocating more moderate versions of nonalignment and by mobilizing public opinion against Chinese officials when they traveled abroad. Chapter 8 examines China's support for insurgencies in Southeast Asia and Africa during the 1960s. Beijing supported these insurgencies because they promised to validate Mao's writings on guerrilla warfare and revolution, fostering greater admiration for the Chinese Revolution internationally. At the same time, the possibility that these wars for national liberation would strengthen Chinese prestige was a key reason that the Kennedy and Johnson administrations became so committed to counterinsurgency. Chapter 9 shows how Beijing used its aid programs in Africa to showcase the benefits of Sino-African cooperation and raise its profile in the region. In response, the United States began tailoring its own aid projects to undercut the political impact of those launched by Beijing.

Sino-American competition in the Third World began to wind down during the late 1960s. Chapter 10 shows how limited cooperation in the region slowly replaced competition as relations between Washington and Beijing thawed during the Nixon and Carter administrations. President Richard M. Nixon had a relatively unique understanding of the importance of status in international affairs. He was far more sympathetic to China's deeply rooted desire for status than his predecessors and was careful not to embarrass the CCP leadership during negotiations. America's new willingness to support rather than undermine Beijing's status in international affairs enabled the two countries to shift from competition to limited cooperation against the Soviets in the Third World.

Sources, Scope, and Limitations

This book is based on extensive research in American and Chinese archives. Those I visited in the United States—the presidential libraries, the National Archives, and the Library of Congress, among others—will be well known to students of foreign affairs. The bulk of the Chinese materials are from the PRC's Foreign Ministry Archive. In 2004, the PRC Foreign Ministry began to release a portion of its records dealing with the period between 1949 and 1965. Although these materials contained significant gaps, they represented a definite advance in our knowledge of China's Cold War diplomacy, and they have been used in several recent studies.[26] In 2012, the ministry reversed course and reclassified many documents, leaving only a small percentage of its materials available to researchers.[27] By then, however, the horse had already been let out of the stable. Thousands of documents have been copied and are now in the possession of scholars who spent time in the archive when it was relatively open. I plan to make the vast majority of Chinese archival materials cited in this book available to other researchers through the Cold War International History Project at the Woodrow Wilson Center for Scholars.

The scope of this book is nevertheless limited by the kinds of materials that were available in China and the United States. Although I make extensive use of Chinese materials, many of which have never been used before, some subjects could not be treated as fully as they deserved owing to a lack of available evidence. Documents pertaining to Chinese foreign policy after 1965, the last date covered by the Foreign Ministry Archive, are rare, with the exception of a few published sources.[28] Even when the Foreign Ministry Archive was open, few documents about aspects of Chinese policy that are still considered sensitive were declassified. For example, although some materials about China's support for insurgencies in Asia and Africa (covered in Chapter 8) were available, the documentary record was far from complete. Thus, although I detail the strategies and motives behind Beijing's policies as much as possible, in certain places the lack of sources prevents me from telling the entire story.

Other limitations in this study are deliberate. This book looks at Sino-American competition in the Third World primarily from the perspectives of Beijing and Washington. I largely did not gather source materials from countries whose loyalties Beijing and Washington were vying for, and I do not examine how Chinese or American policies were received in detail. There are several reasons for this. First, Sino-American competition spanned an area far too diverse—both linguistically and geographically—to cover in one book. Moreover, in such countries as Cambodia and Pakistan where Sino-American competition was especially vigorous, archives that could shed light on the subject are extremely limited, inaccessible, or destroyed.[29] Preliminary investigations into English-speaking countries that hold archival records from the period yielded few significant results. Further, the scope and nature of Sino-American competition, as well as the indigenous response, varied greatly from country to country. A complete exploration of the varied reactions to Chinese and American influence would easily have required another book. *Winning the Third World* is therefore a starting point toward understanding the full impact of the foreign policy of Beijing and Washington on the region. Scholars researching in Indonesian, Swahili, Laotian, and other languages might one day shed light on other dimensions of the subject.

In the book's title and throughout the text I use the now somewhat anachronistic term "Third World." Although this term is understandably considered derogatory when used in certain contexts today, I employ it as it was used during the Cold War: to refer to developing nations in Asia, Africa, and Latin America that did not align with either the Free World or the Communist Bloc. Readers will notice that I do not devote equal attention to all parts of the Third World. Latin America in particular receives relatively little attention. I focus on issues and regions where the United States clearly saw the PRC as a threat and took measures to contest it. Beijing was not without ambitions to extend its influence and gain prestige in the Western Hemisphere. In their official rhetoric, Chinese officials often depicted the peoples of Latin America as linked with those of Asia and Africa in a shared struggle against Great Power hegemony. The PRC targeted the region with propaganda broadcasts, welcomed its leaders for visits, maintained contacts with Communist parties throughout the continent, and provided special training for Latin American revolutionaries.[30] Yet even though American intelligence agencies reported on these activities, Washington was far more concerned with the Cuban and Soviet influence in the Western Hemisphere and did not mount vigorous efforts to undermine Chinese influence there. By a similar token, Beijing did what it could to support the Palestinian Liberation Organization and its Arab allies in their conflict with Israel.[31] I have not devoted significant attention to this topic because Washington was far more concerned with other actors in the Arab-Israeli conflict.[32]

Telling the story of Sino-American competition in the Third World brings to the fore some understudied aspects of the Cold War while offering a new perspective on such well-studied events as the Korean War and the Indochina conflict. Sino-American competition factored into key decisions made in Beijing and Washington in ways that have thus far not been fully appreciated. The history of the PRC's policy toward the Third World during the Cold War, moreover, offers a new way of understanding the origins of contemporary Chinese globalism. The concerns of Cold War–era Chinese officials are not as removed from those that guide current PRC policy as many think. In the twenty-first century, as America's status as a hyperpower seems to be waning and other countries—foremost among them the PRC—seem more prone to challenge the United States, the ironies and complexities of Sino-American competition during the Cold War become all the more relevant. The past lies not only behind us but also before us.

Chapter 1

The Emergence of a Rivalry, 1919–1950

The origins of Sino-American rivalry in the Third World can be traced to the thought and actions of two men at the end of World War I: Woodrow Wilson and Mao Zedong. In 1919, Wilson was at the center of world attention while Mao could not have been further from it. The American president led a relatively young nation that was wealthy and powerful enough to aspire to world leadership. The twenty-five-year-old Chinese revolutionary, by contrast, was an unknown figure in a relatively old nation that was too weak to prevent itself from being divided up and humiliated by the imperial powers. Despite the stark differences between the two men in wealth, fame, and power, they were not completely unalike. Both were visionaries who saw the world not as it was but as it should be. And both were charismatic leaders with a special aptitude for words that helped them persuade people around the globe of the validity of their respective visions.

In 1919, it was Wilson who had gained a unique opportunity to make his vision a reality. When an armistice concluding World War I on the basis of Wilson's "Fourteen Points" was signed in the fall of 1918, the president held an almost unparalleled influence in international politics. Cheering crowds greeted him when he arrived in France to negotiate the Versailles Treaty in December. During the closing months of the war, Wilson had kindled hopes throughout the world with his dramatic pronouncements calling for self-determination, the legal equality of all nations, and the peaceful resolution of international disputes. Many believed that the president would use America's growing might and influence to create a new world order that would be based on just principles and enable peace to endure. By the time treaty negotiations began in Paris, it was readily apparent that what one scholar has called "The Wilsonian Moment" was transforming the thinking of people around the world in unexpected ways.[1]

Wilson almost certainly never envisioned the galvanizing effect of his ideas on the colonial world. He had only the haziest conception of how his notion of self-determination would be applied. But by the end of World War I, a generation of indigenous elites, some of them educated in the metropole, seized on this concept. A number of nationalist leaders from areas under European or Japanese colonial control traveled to Paris and petitioned the Great Powers to make good on Wilson's promises by ending imperial rule. But they were greeted with indifference if not outright hostility by the assembled statesmen. The ensuing disillusionment sparked nationalistic convulsions in colonial societies around the globe.[2]

China was among the countries most deeply affected by the wave of protest that swept through the colonial world in 1919. During the nineteenth century the European powers and Japan had carved out spheres of influence in China and forced the emperor to sign a series of unequal treaties giving foreigners special privileges. Compounding the emperor's difficulties were China's humiliating defeats in wars against France in 1884–85 and Japan in 1894–95. At Versailles, a Chinese delegation led by the eloquent diplomat Wellington Koo petitioned the convening powers to return former German concessions in Shandong province to China. But France and Britain had already promised that these concessions would be awarded to Japan and stood fast against Wilson's preference to see them returned. Fueled by popular indignation at the conference's decision, massive nationwide protests began to spread throughout China on 4 May 1919. Hundreds of thousands of Chinese students and intellectuals across the country and around the world mobilized— launching a movement to boycott Japanese products, forming new patriotic societies, and calling for the rejection of the Versailles Treaty.[3]

Mao Zedong was among the most strident voices in the chorus of young activists. The events of May 1919 played a critical role in shaping his thinking. The future CCP chairman followed developments in Paris from his native province, Hunan, and shared his compatriots' disillusionment when the conference denied China's petition. In June, he became a founding member of the United Students Association, which lobbied the government in Beijing to reject the Versailles Treaty and annul the unequal treaties. Mao contributed to the national awakening that blossomed in China in the aftermath of the May Fourth demonstrations by editing a new journal, the *Xiang River Review*.[4] The review provided an outlet for the young revolutionary to express his views about world affairs and the destiny of his country.

Some of Mao's earliest writings made clear his bitter disappointment with Wilson and the European powers. One editorial penned in July and entitled "Poor Wilson" heaped scorn on the once admired American president: in Paris, Wilson had been "like an ant on a hot skillet. He didn't know what to do." He was "surrounded by thieves like [Georges] Clemenceau, Lloyd George, [Japanese foreign minister] Makino [Nobuaki], and [Vittorio] Orlando" and "did nothing except to attend various kinds of meetings where he could not speak his mind." Mao "felt sorry for him."[5] Whereas the *Xiang River Review* attacked the United States and Europe, it was sympathetic toward other peoples suffering under colonialism. Mao lamented in one editorial that "the demands of the Indian people have not been granted."

The British, he continued, sought to "suppress the political movement of the Indian people with military might."[6] He expressed a similar feeling of kinship with the Koreans, whose appeal for independence had—much like China's—been turned away at the Versailles Conference. "Korea," he wrote, "bewails the loss of its independence; so many people have died . . . but it was simply ignored by the Peace Conference." Mao concluded with disgust: "So much for national self-determination! I think it is really shameless!"[7]

For Mao, the outcome of the Versailles Conference was an object lesson in power politics. He became convinced that the weakness and backwardness of China and other colonies enabled imperialists to maintain their dominance. He made it his purpose to reverse the humiliations China had suffered at Versailles and to restore his country's status in world affairs. But how to achieve this objective? China could have attempted to build up its own military and become an imperialist power. Mao's disillusionment with Wilson, however, led him to more greatly admire the revolution that had been completed two years earlier in Russia with its more radical opposition to colonialism.[8] Rather than emulating the West, the future chairman would promote a revolution that could liberate both China and the world from imperialism.

Mao's grand ambitions did not immediately draw the attention of the United States. To Americans, Mao and other Chinese radicals who shared his objectives represented little more than a fringe group in a distant part of the world. But after helping to found the Chinese Communist Party in 1921, Mao led a long and improbable struggle against foreign and domestic opponents that ended in a stunning victory in 1949. In the course of this struggle Mao's view of China's role in the world continued to develop. He came to believe that the Chinese Revolution would play a special role in international affairs. It would restore China's status as a great nation by standing at the forefront of a broader revolution that would unite Asia and liberate all colonial societies.

Americans never fully understood the appeal of revolutionary ideals like those espoused by Mao in China. Initially, they had difficulty believing that most Chinese would want anything other than the continuation of their so-called special relationship with the United States. During the 1920s, they rarely saw Mao and his followers as a threat because they believed that it would simply be impossible for genuine communism to take root in China. They repeatedly argued that members of the CCP were not real Communists. As the CCP came closer to its goal of helping China to, as Mao would one day claim, "stand up," however, it became clear that its agenda for Asia was incompatible with Washington's. By the end of World War II, American officials were increasingly concerned about how a revolutionary China could threaten or undermine their own vision for a postwar international order. When the CCP triumphed in 1949 and made clear its intention to spread revolution throughout the colonial world, Washington could only acknowledge that it had a new rival.

The May Fourth Movement, the Founding of the CCP, and the United Front

The May Fourth uprisings occurred against a background of political turmoil and civil strife within China. No unified government existed, and coalitions of warlords struggled for control over different provinces. Japan and the Western powers held extraterritorial privileges derived from the unequal treaties that they had forced China to sign during the nineteenth century. American, European, and Japanese citizens living in China were virtually exempt from Chinese law, whereas Chinese citizens residing in British or French settlements were subject to foreign jurisdiction. This disunity and inequality were sources of great frustration to young Chinese nationalists. Nie Rongzhen, who would become one of the ten marshals in the People's Liberation Army (PLA), remembered passing through the infamous treaty ports on a trip to France, where he intended to study, in 1919. During the trip he could not help but feel that "a Chinese moving around on his own territory can unexpectedly come under foreign jurisdiction is really outrageous."[9]

Even as Chinese nationalists viewed achieving unity and ending foreign domination as their most pressing tasks, they were deeply aware that China was not the only country suffering under Western imperialism. The writings of Mao and other future CCP leaders exhibited a strong identification with Egyptians, Koreans, Indians, and other peoples who had lost their independence. They conceptualized themselves as part of what historian Michael H. Hunt has called a "community of the weak and oppressed."[10] At the same time, Chinese revolutionaries saw this "community" not only as a group that could sympathize with their plight but also as a venue to redeem China's status. They expected that, given China's historic centrality in world affairs, its revolution would naturally become an example for and influence on other revolutionary movements. China would gain prestige among other indigenous nationalists by helping them to wage revolution.

These ideas were plainly evident in Mao Zedong's writings from the May Fourth period, which frequently expressed the conviction that the influence of the Chinese revolution would spread throughout Asia. Mao was perhaps most explicit on this point in a letter that he wrote to several close friends in the New People's Study Society, one of several nationalist student groups that he founded or cofounded. "Our activities should in no way be limited to

China," Mao argued. Revolution needed to first be waged at home, but "there should be people helping Russia complete her social revolution, helping Korea gain independence, helping the countries of Southeast Asia become independent, and helping Mongolia, Xinjiang, Tibet and Qinghai to become autonomous and enjoy self-determination." The ultimate goal of their society would be "to reform China and the world."[11]

In a letter to Zhang Guoji, a member of the New People's Study Society who was living in Singapore, Mao even had the temerity to talk about Chinese nation-building in Southeast Asia. He wrote that if people from Hunan province who traveled to the region could "introduce the new culture recently generated within China, the inhabitants of Southeast Asia (not only the overseas Chinese) will be greatly benefitted." Mao thought that the society needed "to get a great number of members to live in Southeast Asia to engage in educational and cultural movements." He continued: "Once there are some results, they should then organize overseas Chinese as well as the natives, from all sectors and walks of life to launch nation building. Worldwide universal harmony [*datong*] must be built on the foundation of national self-determination."[12] At the time that Mao wrote these words, China was still fractured, weak, and divided, yet the future chairman foresaw the possibility that the Chinese Revolution would one day transform the Asian continent.

Mao was not the only one calling for China to join a broader revolution against imperialism. His fervent animosity toward colonialism and determination to restore China's international standing was shared by others who convened secretly in Shanghai in July 1921 when the First Party Congress establishing the CCP was held. Initially, the party remained a small and fairly insignificant force in Chinese politics. By 1924 it still had fewer than five hundred members.[13] Although party members had some liberty to conduct activities and express their views freely, the organization needed to remain secret.[14] Even during the party's embryonic phase, however, its members were encouraged to think about the connection between China's anticolonial revolution and uprisings occurring elsewhere in the East.

Often, this encouragement came from Moscow and the Comintern. Scholars disagree about the extent of Moscow's influence over the CCP during its formative years, but it is difficult to deny that the Comintern played an important role in the party's formation and guided its leadership on some key issues.[15] In 1913, Vladimir Lenin had written enthusiastically about the "Awakening of Asia" and argued that the 1905 Russian Revolution was exerting a broad democratizing influence on China, India, and Persia.[16] After the Bolsheviks gained power in October 1917, he continued to believe that Russia could inspire revolutionary changes in the region. Meetings of the Comintern (called Congresses) brought together members of different

Communist parties from throughout Europe and Asia and gave CCP members some of their first opportunities to interact with other revolutionaries. The Comintern's leadership viewed China as a particularly important locus for the spread of the world anti-imperial revolution. Grigory Zinoviev, the chairman of the Comintern, wrote in 1925: "The events in China will doubtless have a tremendous revolutionizing significance for other colonies and the countries dependent on imperialist England." He anticipated that "the enormous contingents of oppressed humanity who live in the East, numbering hundreds of millions, will greedily seize on every item of news from revolutionary China and will concentrate their thoughts on how they themselves can organize and revolt against the oppressors on the imperialists."[17] Such expressions of faith in China by the Comintern's leaders undoubtedly encouraged the fledgling CCP in its aspirations to lead a revolution in Asia.

Yet the CCP and the Comintern were not always in agreement about the best course for the Chinese revolution. The Comintern's leadership believed that the newly created party was not strong enough to overthrow imperialism and destroy feudalism within China on its own. It therefore directed the CCP to form a united front with the party it would ultimately defeat in a protracted, bloody civil war—the Guomindang. Party leaders somewhat reluctantly accepted the Comintern's reasoning that China first needed to undergo a bourgeois nationalist revolution that would unify the country and eliminate foreign influence. In 1924, the party formally aligned with the GMD while maintaining quasi-independent status within the larger organization.[18] The first united front period would last until 1927.

Although the CCP's alliance with the GMD was short-lived, the Chinese Communists expanded their ranks significantly during this period. The May Thirtieth Movement (1925) was instrumental in this regard. The movement began during a mass protest against the owners of a Japanese mill in Shanghai. After a Japanese foreman killed a striking Chinese laborer who was protesting his horrific working conditions, Communist leaders organized an anti-imperialist demonstration. During the demonstration, police fired on the crowd, killing eleven protesters and sparking a series of rallies and strikes throughout China. Japanese and Western authorities dealt with this new wave of protests by declaring martial law in their concession areas, moving gunboats into Shanghai, and equipping volunteer forces. Chinese nationalists responded by organizing boycotts against British and Japanese goods and seizing factories.[19] These events greatly increased the appeal of the CCP's message. By the end of 1925, the party had twenty thousand members, and by the beginning of 1927 its ranks had swollen to nearly sixty thousand.[20]

As the CCP grew, so too did its sense of consanguinity with other revolutionaries and its conviction that China was becoming a leader in the global struggle against imperialism. In its weekly journal, the *Guide* (*Xiangdao*), the CCP published an article on 5 June calling on all people to "resist the great massacre of the cruel and savage imperialists." It argued that the Shanghai massacre was not an "unusual occurrence"; it was an "inevitable phenomenon under capitalist imperialist rule." The party asked: "Are the small, weak peoples of India, Egypt, and Africa as well as the oppressed classes of Europe and the United States not slaughtered regularly by the capitalist-imperialist robbers?"[21] Party leaders believed that the protests sweeping through China would bolster revolutionary forces worldwide. In October 1925, with demonstrations still occurring in major cities, the CCP passed a resolution confidently proclaiming that "the struggle of the Chinese people has opened a new front against imperialism and at the same time it has increased the strength of the global proletariat and the oppressed peoples of the East." The rise of revolutionary activity in Asia and Africa was already creating problems for the imperialists. The resolution noted, "It is no longer as easy for the imperialists to move forces to invade China as it was before." One reason for this was "the development of revolutionary movements in China, Morocco, Syria, and other places."[22]

Demands for revision of the infamous unequal treaties followed swiftly after the May Thirtieth protests.[23] For many Chinese revolutionaries, abrogation of the treaties was the key to restoring their country's lost status in world affairs. While both the GMD and CCP made the treaties a high priority, the CCP tended to be more radical on the issue. The party explicitly viewed protesting the treaties as a way to unite with other anticolonial movements and assert China's special role among them. When they made speeches or held rallies calling for treaty revisions, CCP officials also called for the unity of oppressed nations. Yun Daying, the secretary of the district party committee, gave an hour-long speech about the history of treaties that ended by arguing: "The Chinese anti-imperialist movement should assist anti-imperialist movements in other countries, and they in turn should assist the Chinese anti-imperialist movement."[24]

The revolutionary energies that drove the May Thirtieth protests and the demands for treaty revision were apparent to American officials. During the 1920s, however, Washington could not foresee that these energies would one day give rise to a major rival. Some U.S. diplomats on the ground in China demonstrated a keen understanding of the sentiments that produced the May Thirtieth Movement, although their analysis was at times informed by a sense of racial superiority. John V. MacMurray, the U.S. minister in China, bombarded the State Department with detailed analyses of the mood on the street in Shanghai and elsewhere during the months after the May Thirtieth demonstrations. He could sense how a yearning for respect had come to influence the ideas and behaviors of many Chinese. MacMurray believed that what he termed "the present crisis of feeling" resulted from "a revulsion against what the individual Chinese feels to be the offense to his personal dignity and self-esteem implicit in the overbearing attitude of the white man towards the Chinese." Demands for revision of the unequal treaties were a "manifestation of the discontent with a sense of inferiority which the Chinese have come to feel is symbolized by the special provisions in the treaties."[25] Although he understood the source of China's growing revolutionary fervor, MacMurray was not especially sympathetic. Like other American diplomats and businesspeople living in China, his primary concern was the protection of American property and rights, and he opposed concessions to Chinese nationalists.[26]

One reason that MacMurray saw so little need for concessions was his belief that the Communists could never become a significant force in Chinese politics. "The Communist Party finds in China only very limited scope for its special type of propaganda," he explained in 1926, "since the class of industrial workers is only a minute fraction of the total population."[27] MacMurray's view made sense at the time. The Maoist model of agrarian socialist revolution had yet to be invented, and it was difficult to imagine that a revolution led by the industrial proletariat could triumph in a society like China, which was still dominated by the countryside. Even if the party remained active, it seemed unlikely that it would become as significant a force as the GMD and almost unimaginable that it would develop the strength and organizational efficiency to unify a country dominated by competing warlords.

The State Department did not entirely share MacMurray's views. It did not see the Communists as an immediate threat, but it nonetheless believed that the causes of the rising antiforeign nationalism in China should be addressed. Secretary of State Frank B. Kellogg and other key officials in the Harding and Coolidge administrations hoped that through the right policies they could mitigate the radical component of Chinese nationalism and coopt China into a liberal, rule-based international order. The State Department therefore sought to appease Chinese sentiment on the unequal treaties and other key issues. In 1928, it negotiated a new tariff treaty with China that accorded the Chinese government a greater degree of autonomy.[28] Washington also expressed a willingness to surrender its special treaty privileges though negotiations.[29] The State Department's efforts to show American sympathy for Chinese aspirations were not completely successful. Ending the unequal treaties would prove a frustrating and protracted process because of China's ongoing political instability. Even so, the possibility that rising nationalist, anticolonialist sentiment would eventually contribute to the emergence of a Communist China never crossed the minds of Americans. Such a possibility would, in fact, seem even smaller during the next decade, when the CCP was pushed to the brink of extinction.

The CCP's Struggle for Survival, 1927–1937

The May Thirtieth Movement contributed to a surge in the popularity of the CCP after 1925, but this very expansion would soon create serious problems for the party. The larger and more influential the CCP became, the more the leaders in the Guomindang viewed the party as a threat to be eliminated. In 1926, the GMD launched the Northern Expedition, an effort to unify China under a single government and break the power of local warlords, with the CCP's full and enthusiastic cooperation. But in this campaign, the left's growing power and the CCP's skills at mass mobilization became more apparent. In April 1927, Jiang Jieshi, the leader of the GMD, decided that for his party's rule to be uncontested, the CCP would have to be destroyed. He unleashed the White Terror, a massive counterrevolutionary campaign in which thousands of Communists were massacred in Shanghai and other cities. Survivors were forced underground or to the remote countryside, where they sought desperately to regroup.[30] The CCP spent much of the so-called Nanjing Decade (1927–37) struggling for survival. But even when the leaders faced total destruction, they never saw themselves as a marginal group of radicals on society's fringes; they continued to believe that they were leading a revolution that would transform China and the world.

Mao Zedong was not the most important figure in the CCP at the beginning of this period, but his strategies would prove critical to the party's survival and his influence gradually expanded. Before the United Front collapsed, he had gained a deep interest in mobilizing the peasantry. Mao had begun organizing peasant associations in 1925 and subsequently wrote several essays describing the critical significance of the peasantry to revolution in China.[31] His work with the peasantry was geared toward the international as well as the domestic context. He explicitly taught the peasants about the threat that imperialism posed to China and other Afro-Asian countries. By June 1926, Mao had organized more than twenty "Associations to Erase Humiliation (*xuechihui*)." Using the slogan "Strike against the Great Powers, Wipe Clean the National Humiliation," these associations were public, mass-based revolutionary organizations designed, according to Mao Zedong's life chronicle, "to develop the anti-imperialist patriotic struggle." At association meetings Mao gave speeches about Western imperialism and the May Thirtieth protests. He explained the broader nationalist movement that was unfolding in Chinese cities and encouraged unity against the British and the Japanese.[32]

Mao continued these efforts after progressive members of the GMD helped him to secure an appointment as principal of the Peasant Movement Training Institute, where his job was to mobilize peasants in the countryside to support the United Front's military campaigns.[33] In this position, he continued teaching peasants that China must change its weak position in international politics, defeat imperialism, and connect with other revolutionary forces. He told one gathering in 1927: "Other countries are strong, our country is weak; other countries are rich, our country is poor; other countries are industrially developed and have airplanes and cannons; in our country there are still broadswords and long spears." The time had come for the Chinese people to unite and change the way their country was perceived: "If you want the nation to become strong and prosperous, the people should not bear oppression and exploitation. They should rise up in revolution, unite, strike against the Great Powers, and drive away the warlords."[34]

After the White Terror, Mao took his experiences in promoting rural activism with him to the countryside and applied his knowledge to building a new base area. He fled first to Jinggangshan, a remote, mountainous area, where he worked with Zhu De, the military leader who would eventually play a critical role in engineering the CCP's victory over the Nationalists in 1949, and Peng Dehuai, a former GMD military officer, to build a new Red Army and mobilize the peasants. Attacks by Nationalist (GMD) troops soon forced Mao to flee to Ruijin, a small, remote city in southeastern Jiangxi Province. There Mao established a new base area and formed the Jiangxi Soviet, a government set up by the CCP as a rival to the Guomindang-led regime in Nanjing.[35] In Jiangxi, Mao developed his strategic thinking about guerrilla warfare and its relation to the countryside. In particular, he came to see the potential of establishing rural base areas, incorporating peasants into the Red Army, and surrounding the cities—all of which would be key in the CCP's eventual military triumph.[36]

Mao's most important priority during these years was sheer survival. Even after Japanese forces occupied Manchuria in 1931 and threatened to take over more of the Chinese mainland, Jiang Jieshi remained obsessed with eliminating the Communist challenge and devoted a significant number of troops to the cause.[37] The Jiangxi Soviet was under constant siege by GMD forces, which carried out a series of encirclement campaigns designed to destroy the Red Army.[38] Although Mao and his comrades lacked time to write about world revolution at great length during these years, it is noteworthy that even as the Red Army fought off enemy attacks, party documents still professed faith in the global importance of the CCP's struggle. Months after Mao arrived in Jiangxi, some of the party's key committees were already making this point. In February 1930, when a new Front Committee was set up to unify command over several of the CCP's armies, the committee issued a notice proclaiming that the armed struggle in Jiangxi and other provinces "has worldwide significance as a powerful element providing armed support for the soviets and promoting the world revolution."[39]

Mao wrote in equally sweeping language when he prepared CCP forces to participate in specific battles and campaigns. In June 1930, he received orders from the CCP Central Committee to carry out an attack on Nanchang, the largest city in Jiangxi Province, as part of a broader offensive against the Nationalists. At the time, Mao's relationship with the Central Committee, which had gone underground in Shanghai, was strained, and he initially felt somewhat ambivalent about the plan. But he eventually embraced it as an opportunity to promote his own vision of mass-based revolution.[40] He exhorted peasants and workers to support the effort because the "victory of the Chinese revolution can assuredly raise the curtain on the world revolution." The revolution would "not only be the death of the Chinese reactionary warlords and rulers" but also "mark the eve of the collapse of imperialism." Ultimately, the CCP's "Red flag" would "fly throughout the entire world."[41]

Although Mao's adversaries within the CCP disagreed with his tactics, they often spoke of the world historical importance of the Chinese revolution with the same ardor. Many of his rivals were members of the senior leadership who maintained close ties with Moscow and the Comintern, from which Mao sought greater autonomy. Wang Ming, the head of the CCP delegation to the Comintern, was one of Mao's chief rivals during the 1930s, but he nevertheless sung the praises of the Jiangxi Soviet in much the same way that Mao did. During a lengthy address to the Thirteenth Plenum of the Executive Committee, Wang touted the soviet's radical experiments in agricultural reform and peasant mobilization as an example for revolutionaries in other colonial societies: "The People's Army and the establishment of a revolutionary base . . . has great meaning and use both in theory and practice." The Jiangxi Soviet had "already become a model for Annam [Vietnam], Taiwan, Cuba, Java, and all of the people's liberation struggles in the colonial and semicolonial areas." Last, he explained that "China's current revolution is the most important link in the chain of world revolution."[42] For Wang as for Mao, the significance of the Jiangxi Soviet ultimately lay not only in the experiences it provided for the CCP but also in its potential to give the party a glorious and noble standing among others suffering under colonialism.

Despite the CCP's pride in the Jiangxi Soviet, the experiment would not last. During the fall of 1933, the GMD launched its Fifth Encirclement

Campaign, which, after a year of fighting, finally broke through the CCP's defenses and dealt the party a significant blow. It cut the Red Army in half and forced much of the remnant to embark on the agonizing Long March.[43] During these dark days when the party's very existence was in jeopardy, Mao called on other revolutionaries to recognize the pivotal significance of the CCP and lend it support. In August 1933, when Jiangxi came under attack, he issued an appeal to the "oppressed peoples of the world" to unite and help the CCP in its struggle. The appeal claimed that the GMD was allied with bourgeois-imperialist classes and governments throughout the world and that its efforts to eradicate the CCP served the interests of imperialism. The Nationalists wanted to destroy the Jiangxi Soviet because it was "a powerful companion of the proletariat and toiling popular masses of the whole world in their struggle against imperialism." Mao exhorted oppressed peoples throughout the world to "call upon our brothers, the soldiers of your own countries, to oppose imperialist aggression against the colonies and refuse to slaughter the toiling popular masses of China in the interest of the imperialist bourgeoisie!"[44]

The next year would be a dark one for the CCP, but it did not shake Mao's determination to turn the Chinese Revolution into a force that would change the world. Unable to withstand the continuing GMD assault, the Red Army embarked on a harrowing and protracted military retreat in October 1934. Tens of thousands of Red Army troops and party supporters perished through GMD gunfire, famine, and disease during the Long March. When the march ended in northern Shaanxi Province roughly one year later, fewer than ten thousand were left alive.[45] The party had been shaken to its core, but Mao had strengthened his position by pinning the blame for the CCP's travails on his rivals and sidelining those who had maintained close ties with the Comintern.[46] Less than a year after the march ended, Mao gave his famous interviews to the American journalist Edgar Snow. He made it clear that despite the party's hardships he still foresaw the triumph of revolution in China and Asia. Snow asked Mao whether he anticipated that "revolution would occur in other Asiatic colonial or semicolonial countries" if the CCP prevailed. He responded boldly, "The Chinese Revolution is a key factor in the world situation, and its victory is heartily anticipated by the people of every country, and especially by the toiling masses of the colonial countries." When the CCP gained power "the masses of many colonial countries will follow the example of China and win a similar victory of their own."[47] Mao hinted that the CCP would eventually assist other anticolonial revolutions in Asia. If the Koreans wished to "break away from the chains of Japanese impe-rialism," Mao explained, "we will extend them our enthusiastic help in their struggle for independence."[48]

The resilience and ambition exhibited by the CCP during the Nanjing Decade were not sufficient to attract much interest or anxiety from American officials. The White House needed to concern itself chiefly with pulling the nation out of the Great Depression and resolving critical domestic issues. American diplomats whose responsibility was China and the Asian region were, in general, far more concerned about how to halt Japanese aggression than they were with the CCP's potential.[49] American officials became dimly aware of the CCP and its motives but seldom made an effort to understand the party or its leadership. For the most part, they continued to believe that the Chinese people had no natural affinity for communism and that members of the CCP were not real Communists like the ones in Moscow. Instead, they saw Mao and his comrades as rural bandits masquerading under the socialist banner. American officials were sometimes concerned by clashes between the CCP and GMD but continued to believe that the issues that contributed to the CCP's popularity could be addressed with reforms and that a radical turn in Chinese politics could be averted.

The views of Nelson T. Johnson, who served as the American minister (1929–35) and ambassador (1935–41) to China, were representative of how U.S. officials regarded the CCP during these years. Johnson was one of the most respected China experts in the State Department at the time of his appointment. Intelligent and amiable, he had served as deputy consul and consul in several Chinese cities during the years 1909–25 and then as chief of the Division of Far Eastern Affairs in the Department of State. By the time he returned to China in 1929, Johnson had acquired a broad expertise on Chinese politics and America's Asia policy.[50] Yet despite his long experience in China, Johnson consistently misjudged the motives and nature of the CCP. He based his assessments of the party on the flawed assumption that the Chinese people wanted to model their society on Western institutions and ideals. Thus, the Communists were not genuine revolutionaries with real grievances against the United States or its allies but miscreants and criminals using socialistic slogans to justify their actions.

Johnson expressed this view early during his tenure as minister. On 12 October 1930, after a series of clashes between the CCP and GMD, he voiced concerns about the violence but dismissed the Communist as "bandits" who had no guiding set of principles:

> In speaking of "Communists" or "Reds" in China, it must be borne in mind that the terms are rarely used in their technical sense, but rather loosely to denote lawless elements who have risen in various parts of the country against constituted authority. . . . It would be fallacious to ascribe too much importance to these activities and their possible connections

with Moscow. The number of Chinese intellectuals who professed Communism is negligible, and although the Soviet device of "Hammer and Sickle" is often used by the marauding bands who called themselves "Communists," it is intended—ludicrously enough—chiefly as a badge of respectability in the hope of being classed as something above the category of common brigands.[51]

Johnson couldn't believe that China with its agricultural economy could ever provide fertile ground for true communism to bloom. "Under normally peaceful conditions and with a reasonably efficient administration communist doctrines cannot take root in China," he explained in another report, approvingly citing one GMD member who contended that "only an idiot or a madman would deem communism workable in China."[52]

Not all American officials were as dismissive of the Communists as Johnson was. But those who argued that the Communists needed to be taken seriously found their views largely ignored in Washington. O. Edmund Clubb, the vice consul at Hankou, was among the few who thought that the Communists could become a significant political force. In 1932, Clubb wrote a 123-page report on the CCP, and he remained actively interested in the party's rise during the 1930s.[53] He argued: "Since 1927, the Reds have accomplished a considerable conquest and a considerable organization, . . . It behooves the political student in China to keep close tab[s] on the movement, even should he not yet be prepared to admit (what seems to me to be the probability) that this agrarian revolt will continue its development still further."[54] After reading the report, Ambassador Johnson remained unconvinced, however. He saw no indication that the "people affected by this movement have been seized with any prose-lytizing fervor or any desire to reform the country and their neighbors in their own interest." Moreover, it didn't appear that the movement's leaders—whom Clubb had identified, among others, as Mao Zedong and Zhu De—were "of sufficient caliber to become the leader statesmen of China's revolution."[55]

In Washington, officials working on the Far East were, if anything, even less concerned by Clubb's stern warnings. No high-ranking officers in the State Department appear to have read the report, and there was no official recommendation to take any action after it was received.[56] One other lengthy report on the CCP was filed by one of Clubb's colleagues, J. C. Huston, the American consul in Shanghai, in 1931, but it too failed to stir much interest. After the report was received, one officer in the Far East Division still believed that the CCP was "in reality far more closely resembling the Taiping or the 'Boxer' movements than anything 'made in Moscow.'"[57] Given the indifference of most American China specialists to the CCP, it is not surprising that the party did not become a priority in Washington during the 1930s. With the exception of a few officials who observed the CCP carefully and closely, Americans simply could not perceive the genuine appeal that the party's promises to restore China's integrity and promote social justice had for many Chinese. As the CCP endured the hardships of the Long March and came under continuous assaults by the GMD, it seemed to American officials like a desperate group of bandits trying to survive rather than an efficient organization that could inspire radical changes in Chinese consciousness. Yet within a few years of the time Clubb filed his report, it was becoming obvious that the party would play an important role in shaping China's future.

The Sino-Japanese War

The Sino-Japanese War (1937–45) was a catastrophe for China, but it unquestionably boosted the fortunes of the CCP. The party had barely survived the previous decade and remained a small, albeit resilient force when the war began. But the conflict with Japan created circumstances in which the CCP could flourish. It demanded the attention of the GMD, giving Mao and his comrades much-needed breathing space to rebuild the Red Army and expand into new territory. Just as important, the CCP fixed its ideological agenda more firmly during the war years, strengthening the role of Mao and eliminating dissenting voices. Mao wrote some of his most famous and influential treatises, and cadres began putting forward the idea that Mao Zedong's theories could serve as a guide for revolutionaries elsewhere. The CCP would emerge from the war stronger, more confident, and more convinced than ever that it was destined to reclaim China's lost status by helping the rest of Asia throw off the shackles of colonialism.

The Xi'an Incident of December 1936 played a particularly important role in strengthening the position of the CCP. After Japan invaded and occupied Manchuria in 1931, Mao had repeatedly attacked his rival Jiang Jieshi for persecuting the CCP while "humiliating" China by refusing to offer tougher resistance to the Japanese.[58] By 1936, some of Jiang's generals had come to sympathize with these arguments and demanded that the GMD put more emphasis on resisting Japan. Seeking to curb the renegade generals, Jiang traveled to their headquarters in Xi'an but was kidnapped by the very generals he had gone to silence. Jiang's captors, Zhang Xueliang and Yang Hucheng, forced him to agree to seek unity with the CCP and focus on defeating Japan.[59] Once he was released Jiang agreed to halt the fighting and the two rival parties began negotiating the terms for establishing a second united front.[60] In the meantime, Communist armies took advantage of the dissension within the GMD's ranks to gain control over new territories, including the city of Yan'an, which the CCP set as its capital.[61]

After the Xi'an Incident, CCP rhetoric focused more on the anti-Japanese struggle and how it would set an example for other anticolonial revolutions. During the period immediately before the Marco Polo Bridge Incident (July 1937), which marked the beginning of all-out war, Mao was already emphasizing that the war of resistance would have wide ramifications in Asia. In May 1937, he gave an interview to Helen Foster Snow, the wife of Edgar Snow working under the pseudonym Nym Wales. During the interview he explained, "China's war of resistance demands that we win the final victory. The scope of this victory is not limited to Shanhaiguan or to the Northeast but should include the liberation of Korea and Taiwan, and even the success of the people's revolutionary war of liberation within Japan."[62] Mao made it clear that he saw the anti-Japanese war as a struggle not only to drive imperialism from the mainland but also to achieve a broader triumph of revolutionary forces in Asia.

As the war with Japan intensified, the party's leading propagandists continued to stress the centrality of China's struggle. Zhang Hanfu, the editor-in-chief of *Xinhua Ribao* (New China Daily), China's first daily Communist newspaper, expressed these ideas forcefully in an essay he wrote in 1939 entitled "On Self-Reliance and Obtaining Foreign Aid."[63] Zhang explained:

> As for the people of the colonies and the semi-colonies, their fate is the same as China's. They see that the war of resistance in China is giving their own independence and liberation movement a glorious example. All the experience and lessons of the resistance war are a rich and powerful weapon for ways and means and prescriptions for their own struggle to achieve independence and liberation. The victory of the Chinese war will cause their victory to come more easily and more swiftly. They see the Chinese war of resistance as the harbinger and vanguard of their own resistance movement.[64]

For Zhang, the war of resistance against Japan, like the CCP's other significant endeavors, was something that other peoples in Asia were bound to emulate. As other colonial and semicolonial peoples looked to China, the country's special role in international affairs would be restored.

Somewhat ironically, despite the CCP's bold assertion that the war of resistance would be a model for other revolutionaries, Mao used CCP forces sparingly and allowed the GMD to bear the brunt of casualties. At the same time, he sought to assure that even though the CCP's actual role was not large, its perceived role was far more impressive. The cornerstone of Mao's strategy was guerrilla warfare, a subject he later wrote about brilliantly in essays that earned him an international reputation as a master tactician. The CCP set up guerrilla bases in territories occupied by Japanese forces and used them to inflict casualties on the enemy. These tactics had little chance of forcing a Japanese retreat, but they made the CCP look vigorous and active in comparison to Jiang's government, whose failures on the battlefield were clear.[65] As Stuart R. Schram, a leading scholar of the early history of the CCP, has noted, "Mao Zedong understood that expansion behind Japanese lines certified the patriotic credentials of the Chinese Communist Party while simultaneously vastly increasing the territory, population and resources of the Party."[66]

Invading Japanese forces may also have unintentionally contributed to the perception that the CCP, not the GMD, was the empire's most significant enemy. Seeking to legitimate an imperial project that much of the rest of the world viewed as a flagrant violation of international law, Japan often characterized all of its opponents in China as "communists," a term that it knew had deeply negative connotations in the United States and Europe. Ambassador Johnson could easily recognize Japan's strategy. He wrote in December 1935, "The new stereotype which the Japanese will use and which will justify Japanese intervention in China has been invented. It is the word 'communist.' Just as every man who armed and who offered any resistance to Japan in Manchuria was a bandit in 1931 and 1932, so all Chinese offering opposition to the Japanese in China will become 'communist.'"[67] Through such efforts to slander their opponents, however, Japan unwittingly validated the CCP propagandists' claim that the party was at the forefront of the anti-imperialist struggle.

When CCP forces did score real successes against the Japanese on the battlefield, the victories were immediately cast as beacons of hope for other colonial peoples. The controversial Battle of the Hundred Regiments, a series of engagements fought by the Eighth Route Army against Japanese forces between August and December 1940, provides a case in point. In the battle's initial phase, commander Peng Dehuai's forces destroyed railroads and bridges in Hebei and Shanxi Provinces, dealing a significant blow to the Japanese war industry. After the Japanese military launched a successful counterattack reasserting its control over the area and forcing the Eight Route Army to fold back into CCP bases, Mao became increasingly critical of Peng, claiming that he had recklessly shown the extent of CCP troop strength to the GMD. Praise for the Eight Route Army's exploits were sharply curtailed.[68] Initially, however, both Mao and other party leaders hailed the battle as a significant victory for anticolonial forces. In an interview conducted in August, when it appeared that Chinese forces had dealt Japan a significant setback, Peng Dehuai called the battle "a great inspiration for the struggles in Vietnam and other Pacific regions." The victory would "promote the further development of the international revolutionary movement and gain greater sympathy from the people of all countries for China's War of Resistance." It had demonstrated both "the Chinese people's strength in their struggle" and "the great strength and bright future" of the Chinese nation.[69] At a time when many other nations still viewed China as weak and helpless, Peng hoped that the CCP's military success would earn respect for both the party and the country it aspired one day to govern.

In part because it took credit for offering the strongest resistance to Japan, the CCP experienced a great resurgence between 1937 and 1940. During this short time, party membership rose from forty thousand to eight hundred thousand while the number of Red Army soldiers rose from ninety thousand to five hundred thousand.[70] But this rapid growth created problems. New party members needed to be indoctrinated and taught loyalty to the CCP and the distinctive version of socialism that it had come to espouse. This was accomplished primarily through a "rectification campaign" (*zhengfeng*) that lasted for over three years. The campaign was based on the premise that Marxism-Leninism needed to be adapted to local conditions in China. Emphasis was placed on the propagation of Mao Zedong Thought, which, it was argued, had brilliantly achieved this objective.[71] By the campaign's end, Mao's leadership of the party was unquestioned, and outside influences over the party—notably that of Moscow and the Comintern—had been diminished.[72]

The rectification campaign strengthened the CCP's ambitions to stand at the helm of Asia's revolutionary forces even as it gave these ambitions additional specificity and direction. As part of the campaign, party cadres were forced to engage in self-criticism and attend extended study sessions focused on Mao Zedong Thought.[73] Among the key points emphasized in these sessions was that CCP members had an obligation to advance the cause of revolution internationally as well as at home. In a speech that the CCP made part of the curriculum used during study sessions, future CCP vice chairman Liu Shaoqi explained the proper attitude for loyal party members: "They are deeply concerned with the bitter and difficult circumstances of their own class and the workers of the world. They are concerned with the liberation struggle of toilers everywhere and with news of their victories and defeats, knowing that no matter where the victory or defeat occurs, it is their own; thus they exhibit the greatest sympathy and show their solidarity [with their comrades]."[74] Liu was essentially trying to get all CCP members to internalize the party's oft-repeated mantra that the Chinese Revolution was an important part of a larger world revolution that commanded sympathy.

As the rectification campaign established Mao Zedong Thought as the ideological basis for the CCP, a growing number of party propagandists began to argue that revolutionaries in other colonial areas could also benefit greatly from studying Mao's writings. Zhang Ruxin, one of the earliest proponents of Mao Zedong Thought, made this point explicitly in an essay entitled "Advance under the Banner of Comrade Mao Zedong," that he published in a party journal in 1941. Zhang claimed that Mao had made great contributions to both Marxist theory and the global struggle against imperialism:

> The many contributions of the Chinese Communist Party, and, in particular, Mao Zedong, on the questions of the Chinese Revolution are indisputably the creative development and enrichment of Marxism in China. All of these new creations and developments are not only of great significance for the Chinese revolution and the Chinese people's liberation struggle at the present time and in the future, but, in addition, one should earnestly point out, they are great contributions to the revolutionary movements of all colonial and semi-colonial states.[75]

Zhang went on to assert that the theory and tactics created by the CCP were "extremely valuable revolutionary capital" for "the great majority (if not all) of the colonial and semi-colonial states."[76]

Liu Shaoqi made a similar point in a 1945 report on the party's constitution. He explained: "As a pupil of Marx, Engels, Lenin and Stalin, Comrade Mao Zedong has exactly effected the integration of the Marxist-Leninist theories with the practice of the Chinese revolution. This has given rise to Chinese communism—Mao Zedong Thought—which has guided and still is guiding, the Chinese people towards complete emancipation and which has made [a] useful contribution to the cause of emancipation of the people all over the world, particularly people in the East."[77] Liu's statement simultaneously demarcated the exceptionalism of Chinese communism and Mao Zedong Thought while again emphasizing that they could provide a model for other revolutionaries.

During the early 1940s the CCP began to turn its lofty rhetoric about revolutionary leadership into more concrete action. In 1940, it started to offer aid to other revolutionary movements, and in October 1941, the party made a more ambitious effort to bring these movements together by holding the "Eastern Peoples Anti-Fascist Congress" in Yan'an. The congress drew more than 130 delegates from eighteen countries, including Korea, Vietnam, and Burma. At the conference, Mao appealed for regional unity against Japan.[78] Zhu De delivered an address calling on delegates to study "the valuable admonitions of China's united front and the struggle in the occupied areas." Delegates at the congress called for the establishment of a volunteer corps to fight alongside Communist armies and an "Eastern People's School" to help develop Communist cadres.[79]

Yan'an attempted to follow up on the congress by advocating further steps to reach out to other revolutionaries in the Asian region. Immediately after the bombing of Pearl Harbor in December 1941, Mao called a meeting of the Central Committee, and the party issued a new directive based on the chairman's guidance regarding the Pacific anti-Japanese united front.[80] "Efforts should be made," the directive mandated, "to develop anti-Japanese guerrilla warfare in the enemy-occupied regions of South China, Hainan Island, Vietnam and all regions in Southeast Asia occupied by Japan." In seeking to extend CCP operations to Southeast Asia, the Central Committee called for coordination with other Communist parties. "The work in all localities in Southeast Asia should be done in concert with the Communist Party of the given nation," it recommended, and help was to be extended "in developing united front work on a broad scale."[81] Although the CCP was still years away from gaining control over the mainland, it had already begun acting on its ambitions to extend its influence well beyond China's borders.

One would think that, given the CCP's growing size and influence, its increasing emphasis on conformity, its authoritarian methods of organization and indoctrination, and its ambitions to become the leader of revolutionary forces in Asia, American officials would have been deeply hostile toward it. But, at least during World War II, this was not always the case. Whether it was because the CCP was successful at pulling the wool over their eyes or because they were too naive to grasp the full scope of the party's ambitions, many key American diplomats in China often professed a great admiration for Mao and his comrades. They continued to believe that the Chinese Communists were fundamentally different from those in Russia and Eastern Europe and that the CCP was not intent on threatening or damaging American interests. Yet there was always an underlying tension between the goals of the CCP and those of the Franklin D. Roosevelt administration in Washington. Roosevelt envisioned a much greater role for China in the postwar world, but to achieve this, he believed, China needed to be unified and allied with the United States.[82] A divided or revolutionary China simply did not square with the president's vision for a new world order.

American assessments of the CCP became increasingly favorable after the outbreak of the Sino-Japanese War and the creation of the Second United Front. Often these assessments were based on the same assumption that had guided initial evaluations of the CCP during the late 1920s and early 1930s: that Mao and his comrades were somehow not real Communists. But rather than representing the CCP as a group of misguided bandits, American officials now tended to depict the party's leaders as agrarian reformers whose values were closer to those of the United States than to those of the Bolsheviks. This change in attitude could be seen plainly in Ambassador

Johnson's characterization of the CCP after 1937. "Chinese communism was a communism that grew out of agrarian discontent. It was essentially an agrarian movement, and in no sense an industrial proletarian movement such as the one which took over the cities and established communism in Russia," he wrote in a cable to the State Department in 1938.[83] Johnson also expressed deeper concerns and cynicism about the motives of the CCP's rivals in the GMD. He noted with that many of Jiang Jieshi's subordinates continued to talk about the need to remove the Communist threat once the conflict with Japan was over and warned, "It would be difficult to imagine anything that would be more calculated to alienate foreign opinion from the Chinese government than would recrudescence of internecine warfare in China."[84]

After the United States declared war against Japan in December 1941, the CCP began to take on a more generous and optimistic view of the United States, and this in turn led American officials toward an even more benign view of the CCP. Roosevelt's initial vision of the postwar international order was explicitly anticolonialist, and the president made it clear on different occasions that he wanted to see the end of empire in India, Southeast Asia, and elsewhere.[85] Though he saw the United States and not China as the driving force behind the demise of imperialism, FDR's objectives certainly had some overlap with those of Mao and his comrades. The Atlantic Charter and the formation of the Grand Alliance, joining together Great Britain, the Soviet Union, and the United States, kindled hopes among the CCP leadership that progressive forces opposing imperialism and seeking reform in China would predominate once the Axis Powers were defeated.[86] When Mao talked about the future of Asia with Western reporters, he increasingly emphasized commonalities rather than differences. During an interview with the German journalist Günther Stein in 1944, Mao contended that colonial peoples "should have the right of self-rule, like the Philippines." He added, "This is also true of India. It means putting into practice the Atlantic Charter."[87] Mao continued to call for the liberation of the oppressed, but in discussions with European and American journalists, he shrewdly represented it as a Western as well as a Chinese objective. American officials who read the interview concluded that Mao was not dangerous but "moderate and reasonable."[88]

A group of younger American diplomats stationed in China, who have sometimes been called China hands because of their extensive experience there, played the most significant role in propagating a more positive image of the CCP. Among the group's most prominent members were John Paton Davies and John S. Service, the second and third secretaries, respectively, at the American embassy. Service and Davies both believed that the CCP would inevitably play a critical role in shaping China's fate after World War II and warned about the dangers of not engaging with its leadership. Both met with Mao Zedong, Zhou Enlai, and other CCP leaders on different occasions and came away impressed with their honesty and zeal, especially in comparison to the GMD's leadership, which they viewed as weak and corrupt.

In their reporting, the China hands downplayed the possibility that the CCP would seek to spread communism internationally. Davies explained in one memorandum that the CCP had abandoned its previous commitment to world revolution and chosen a more reasonable course for itself. "As the Chinese Communists moved away from world revolution to nationalism," he contended, "they also moved in the direction of a more moderate internal political and economic policy." Foreign observers visiting the CCP base area found that it was "far removed from orthodox Communism" and called its administration "remarkably honest." Davies recommended that the United States establish a consulate in Chinese Communist territory as a means of both gaining more information about the CCP and reducing the chances of a war between the CCP and GMD that could hamper the larger war effort.[89]

Davies's recommendations led to the dispatch of the U.S. Army Observer Group (also called the Dixie Mission) to Yan'an in July 1944. The mission, which consisted primarily of a small group of U.S. military officers but also included Service, established a formal liaison with the Chinese Communists that would remain in place until 1947.[90] Americans who stayed with the CCP at its base continued to be impressed with the party and became strong advocates of closer ties between Washington and Yan'an. After meeting with Mao and his comrades in August 1944, Service even recommended providing direct assistance to the CCP: "We may well decide, on the basis of what the Chinese Communist military forces have achieved and their apparent potentialities for contributing to the defeat of Japan, that those military forces deserve our active support—probably in the form of military supplies." He realized that such support not only would be "interpreted as an indication of American approval" but also would improve the military effectiveness of CCP forces. American assistance would therefore "raise the prestige of the Communist Party and ultimately its influence in China." Service's view of the GMD was so negative that he did not view strengthening the Communists as dangerous or even undesirable. In fact, it "might swing the balance of political forces in China far enough so that the[Guomindang] would be forced to reform its policies."[91]

In Washington, however, the president showed no evidence that he shared the view that the CCP needed to be part of any postwar political arrangement. Many of FDR's decisions elevated Jiang's status as the leader of China with little regard to the reaction that it would arouse from the Communists or America's own diplomats. In 1943, the president invited Jiang to attend the Cairo Conference, where the GMD chairman could play the part of an eminent statesman through joining discussions with FDR and British prime minister Winston Churchill about the fate of Asia and the breakup of the Japanese empire. Although FDR also encouraged Jiang to shake hands with the CCP, the GMD chairman gained legitimacy by being seen alongside other influential world leaders.[92] The president had already told Jiang that he envisioned China as one of the "four policemen" that would be responsible for maintaining order after the war, with China playing a key role in Asia. He hoped that a moderate, unified China would help to administer trusteeships in Southeast Asia and elsewhere, thus allowing the rest of Asia to achieve independence over time.[93] Although Washington's relationship with the GMD was far from harmonious, FDR's efforts to work with Jiang on regional issues underscored important and ultimately irreconcilable differences between the United States and the CCP. The United States wanted to end colonialism in Asia, but it wanted to do so gradually and in a way that would serve American interests. China would be an important actor in the postwar world, but it would also follow Washington's guidance. It would not seek to lead revolutionary forces in Asia, swiftly overthrow colonialism, and undermine Western interests as the CCP aspired to do.

Seeking to steer China toward greater moderation and unity, FDR dispatched Patrick J. Hurley as his special envoy in August 1944. Hurley visited Yan'an in November 1944, somewhat naively assuming that he would be able to broker an agreement between the CCP and the GMD and maintain solidarity against Japan. He did manage to get Zhou Enlai to travel to Chongqing for negotiations, but when talks failed, he blamed the Communists and committed Washington to supporting Jiang.[94] In February 1945, Hurley cabled the State Department urging Washington to refuse pending CCP requests for aid. It would be "identical to supplying arms to the Communist armed party and would therefore be a dangerous precedent." Moreover, he cautioned the secretary of state, "The established policy of the United States to prevent the collapse of the National Government and to sustain [Jiang Jieshi] as President of the Government . . . would be defeated by acceptance of the Communist Party's plan or by granting the Lend Lease and monetary assistance requested by General [Zhu De]."[95] Stubborn in his views, Hurley would not tolerate dissent from Service, Davies, and other American diplomats sympathetic to the CCP. After the U.S. embassy's political officers sent a cable to Washington expressing concerns about Hurley's approach, the presidential envoy appealed personally to FDR and had most of the pro-CCP foreign service officers removed from China.[96]

American policies alienated the CCP and only strengthened the party's determination to establish China as the leader of anticolonial forces in Asia. In August 1944, the party's Southern Bureau published an analysis of the international situation that became influential within the party. The bureau argued that although Roosevelt was a "progressive figure," the United States was nevertheless likely to stand in the way of the CCP's ambitions to gain standing both in China and around the world. The American government, it claimed, "will never give up its leadership role over China's politics and economy; nor will it give up its influence on China's central government." Given Washington's proclivity toward supporting Jiang and the GMD, the Soviet government and people needed to be regarded as "the most reliable friends of China's democratic revolution." The CCP once again asserted that when the Japanese were defeated, a new China would reclaim an important position in world affairs. "We should emphasize that we will make a tremendous contribution to the securing of postwar world peace and world economic cooperation," the bureau argued.[97]

By the end of the war, the CCP increasingly viewed the United States as an obstacle not only to its ambitions in China but also to its grander vision of Eastern revolution. On 24 April 1945, roughly three weeks after Hurley had announced that the official U.S. position would be to support the GMD, Mao delivered a major address entitled "On Coalition Government" to the Seventh Party Congress, where he was designated the first chairman of the CCP Central Committee. Mao's tone was unquestionably more combative. The time had come, Mao proclaimed, for the Chinese people "to conquer all difficulties and achieve their fundamental demands, their great historic aspirations." Not only had the Chinese people played "a very great role in the war against Japan," but they would also "play a very great role in safeguarding peace in the postwar world and the decisive one in safeguarding peace in the East." He warned that "if any foreign government helps the Chinese reactionaries and opposes the Chinese people's democratic cause," it would be "committing a gross mistake." Last, Mao reasserted China's sense of kinship with other victims of imperialism. "The Chinese people should help the Korean people to win liberation," he stated. An "independent and democratic India" would be "essential for world peace," and it was also hoped that the people of Burma, Malaya, Indonesia, the Philippines, and Vietnam would "exercise their right to establish independent and democratic states of their own."[98]

By 1945 the agendas of Washington and the CCP were increasingly irreconcilable. They both wanted to see Japan defeated, but otherwise their visions of postwar Asia and China's role in it contrasted sharply. The key questions that remained to be answered were whether the CCP would one day lead

China and whether the United States would stand in the way of the party's victory. When World War II ended at last in September 1945, these questions took on a new urgency.

The Triumph of the CCP

Once the Axis Powers had been defeated, cooperation between Moscow and Washington quickly fell apart. The end of the mutually supportive relationship that had existed between the two emerging superpowers extinguished any hope of preventing civil war in China. It had taken pressure from both Washington and Moscow to preserve an uneasy truce between the CCP and GMD. But as Cold War tensions emerged, the two superpowers started to show greater favoritism toward their respective allies. In August 1945, Joseph Stalin signed a treaty of friendship with Jiang's government and pressured the CCP leadership to negotiate with the GMD. But tensions between Washington and Moscow over Japan at the London Conference of Foreign Ministers in September prompted the Soviets to take a more hard-line stance in their China policy. Soviet forces had occupied Manchuria at the end of the war, and they now started to bar GMD forces from the region while granting the CCP preferential access, ultimately enabling Mao and his comrades to establish a base area there.[99]

The Truman administration made one final effort to broker a compromise between the two parties by sending George C. Marshall to China in December 1945. Although Marshall got the two sides to agree to a truce in January 1946, he could never find satisfactory solutions for the most vexing issues: how political power would be shared and what would happen to the CCP's armed forces in a power-sharing arrangement.[100] In the meantime, American aid began to flow in increasing amounts to the Nationalists, including the sale of $1 billion in surplus war equipment at deep discounts and the provision of $178 million in goods through the United Nations Relief and Rehabilitation Administration.[101] Large-scale American assistance to the GMD led the CCP to believe that Washington was untrustworthy.

The Soviet's abrupt decision to withdraw from Manchuria in March 1946 ultimately precipitated an all-out military struggle for control of China. As Soviet forces departed, they facilitated the CCP's efforts to occupy the region's cities and towns. Both parties viewed the northeast as strategically important, and fighting between their forces intensified as the Soviets pulled out. By June the war was widening to north and central China, and it would soon encompass much of the mainland.[102]

Although the CCP's primary focus during this period was defeating the GMD, it continued to see its struggle against Jiang and his American supporters as one with global dimensions. Mao made this point most explicitly with the articulation of an "intermediate zone" theory in late 1946. During an interview with the American journalist Anna Louise Strong, the chairman squarely rejected the proposition that the emerging struggle between the United States and the Soviet Union was the most significant conflict in world affairs. Washington's anti-Soviet propaganda was actually a "smoke-screen" to cover other more pressing contradictions. These included "the contradictions between the U.S. reactionaries and the American people and the contradictions of U.S. imperialism with other capitalist countries and with the colonial and semi-colonial countries."[103] According to Mao, the intermediate zone consisted mostly of oppressed non-Western countries, including China, and it was in this zone that Washington was trying to gain dominance.[104] The chairman's purpose in identifying a zone of countries that were separate from both the United States and the Soviet Union was likely to encourage the anti-colonial struggle in China and in other areas still under the control of Western imperialism.[105]

Communist Party propagandists elaborated on Mao's idea during the months after the interview, drawing more explicit links between the CCP's struggle and those of other oppressed nations and asserting China's leadership in the global battle against the new imperial forces supported by the United States. An article that appeared in *Jiefang Ribao* (Liberation Daily) in January 1947 described how the international situation had changed during the prior year. It argued that the "American imperialist clique had replaced fascist Germany, Japan, and Italy to become the invader of the world." At the same time, the "progress of the world's peoples" was occurring much more rapidly than it had after World War I. The signs of this included the creation of "democratic" governments in eastern and southern Europe, the emergence of progressives in Germany, Japan, and Italy, and "the struggle under the leadership of China to win the independence and freedom of the colonial and semi-colonial nations."[106] The world was now divided between progressive and imperialist forces, and China, it boasted, was at the helm of a global war of liberation.

In a major essay published in 1947, Lu Dingyi, the director of the party's propaganda department, emphasized some of the same points. "The self-defense war now being waged by the Chinese people against Jiang Jieshi and the American imperialists is, in its nature, a war for the motherland." The same kind of war, he argued, "is breaking out in many colonial and semi-colonial countries including: the Philippines, Vietnam, Indonesia, Iran, and Greece." Lu called for the establishment of a new united front whose purposes would be "world peace and democracy and independence of all nations against the American imperialism and its running dogs in various countries." Ultimately, the creation of this new united front on a world scale would "characterize a new page in world history" in which the "stable and lasting peace of the world is insured," Lu predicted. He ended by reasserting, "The Chinese movement for independence, peace, and democracy is an important chapter in world history."[107]

Before the CCP could turn this new page in world history, however, one critical task remained: defeating the much larger forces of the GMD. The party achieved this objective far more quickly than most expected. Despite the numerical superiority of the Nationalist army, Mao proved a better tactician and CCP forces were often more dedicated and better organized.[108] Over the course of 1948, the Nationalists suffered a series of setbacks that caused thousands of GMD troops to desert and join the Communist side.[109] As victory neared, Mao sought to protect the revolution and sustain its momentum. He believed that these objectives could best be achieved by strengthening ties with the Soviet Union and looking for ways to expand the influence of the revolution internationally.

Through much of the Chinese civil war, Stalin had kept in communication with Mao, but Soviet support had been unreliable, with Moscow unwilling to take the risk of completely alienating the Nationalist government. As it started to become clear that the CCP would triumph, however, Stalin realized that improved relations between Moscow and the CCP would be just as beneficial to him as they were to Mao.[110] One of the major issues in the discussions between CCP and Communist Party of the Soviet Union (CPSU) that followed was the role of revolutionary China in Asia and the colonial world. Conversations on the issue began in February 1949 when Moscow dispatched Anastas Mikoyan, a prominent member of the Politburo, to China to hold discussions with the CCP leadership. While meeting with Mikoyan, Mao showed a great enthusiasm for expanding the CCP's ties with the other Communist parties of Asia. The two discussed the possibility of establishing an Asian Communist Information Bureau (Cominform) that would be similar to the one created by the Soviets in 1947 to coordinate the activities of European Communist parties.[111]

Although the Asian Cominform was never created, the Kremlin showed increasing sympathy for the CCP's grand ambitions. The gradual adjustment of Stalin's position became clear when Mao dispatched a delegation to Moscow led by Liu Shaoqi, the CCP's second in command, in June 1949. Liu's delegation delivered to Stalin an extensive report on the party's domestic and international activities. The report generally was highly respectful toward the Soviet Union but also boasted about the possibility of the CCP expanding its influence to other parts of the colonial world. The Chinese Communists had been successful at organizing a national anti-imperialist front, developing new tactics for carrying out guerrilla warfare, and creating a Marxist-Leninist party in a poor country, among other things. It noted that the "experience of the Chinese revolution may be of great utility to other colonial and semi-colonial countries."[112]

Stalin was eager to make up for wavering in his support for the CCP in previous years. The Soviet leader acknowledged that the Chinese Communists were likely to be more successful than Moscow in colonial areas. Liu and Stalin agreed that in the future, the Soviets would continue to bear primary responsibility for spreading communism in Europe and the West but that the CCP could take the lead in liberating African and Asian countries from colonialism.[113] Through this informal division of labor agreement, China emerged as a much more confident and determined actor in the colonial world. Having attained Moscow's endorsement for their objectives, CCP leaders showed a greater eagerness to gain influence over other revolutionary movements.

At roughly the same time that Liu and Stalin were exchanging views, the CCP's United Front Work Department had begun drawing up plans to instruct leaders from other Asian Communist parties in the revolutionary tactics developed by Mao Zedong. The department's secretary general took charge of a study group that included representatives from India, Vietnam, Indonesia, and several other Southeast Asian countries. High-ranking party officials such as Deng Xiaoping and Zhu De taught courses that used Mao's writings as study materials. These courses covered party building, armed struggle, and other subjects that could facilitate the spread of China's revolutionary model.[114] Through drawing revolutionaries from throughout the Asian region to China, the CCP looked to consolidate its status as an important center of world revolution. Party leaders likely hoped that making Maoist theory and the CCP's own experiences the key component of the curriculum would also imbue students with a lasting admiration for the Chinese version of communism.

After the CCP finally vanquished the GMD, consolidated its control of the Chinese mainland, and declared the formation of the People's Republic of China in October 1949, its conviction that China was destined to assume an important new role in world affairs could only continue to grow. Liu Shaoqi followed up his visit to the Soviet Union with another bold attempt to boost China's leadership position among Asian revolutionaries during the Trade Union Conference of Asian and Australasian Countries, which took place in Beijing in November 1949. The conference was held a mere six weeks after the formal inauguration of the PRC. The vice chairman gave an address that reflected the confidence gained by party leaders through years of long, hard struggle. Liu once again cited the Chinese Revolution and the CCP's use of armed struggle as a model for revolutionaries in other non-Western countries. The path of Mao Zedong was also "the path that people in many colonial and semi-colonial countries must adopt in order to pursue national independence and people's democracy."[115] The speech proved controversial because some delegations believed that Liu's discussion of armed struggle was inappropriate for a trade unions conference that included capitalist countries. Nevertheless, Moscow ultimately endorsed the speech and published it in the official Soviet newspaper, *Pravda*.[116]

In the United States, as the CCP came closer to conquering the mainland and seizing the opportunity to expand its influence abroad, the Truman administration faced vexing questions: Should it continue to support Jiang and hope that his regime managed to survive? Or should it cut its losses and pursue a reconciliation with the CCP? If it supported Jiang, how much more assistance should be given to a regime that continued to flounder despite already receiving large sums of aid? The administration had to take many factors into account, including public sympathy for Jiang and criticism from the Republican opposition that more needed to be done to support the GMD.[117]

Why did the United States aid Jiang despite fears that it was betting on a losing cause? The decision-making process was bureaucratic and complex, but American concerns that the CCP would expand its influence in Asia were an important part of the debate. The goodwill that had prevailed between American officials and the CCP during World War II was largely a distant memory, and Washington was swiftly coming to see Mao and his comrades as an unmitigated threat. In March 1948, the National Security Council (NSC) drafted a report on American assistance to China that made this clear: "China's propinquity to Southeast Asia means that if the Chinese Communists take over all of China, they would in turn strengthen communist movements in Indochina, Burma and areas further south." The report went on to advocate limited assistance for Jiang's government, although its recommendations reflected a disagreement among members of the NSC staff, with the army, navy, and air force members calling for military and economic aid and the State Department member arguing that only economic aid should be provided.[118] Congress ultimately passed an aid package that included $338 million in economic aid and $125 million in military aid.[119]

American aid was not enough to save Jiang, however, and as the CCP continued to gain ground Washington only became more worried about the party's influence on the rest of Asia. By early 1949, some U.S. officials voiced fears that the CCP would undermine the U.S. position in the Pacific through its propaganda campaigns. In March, one United States Information Service (USIS) officer in Nanjing explained that the CCP always depicted itself as part of "the Communist world revolution" while making the United States the "ultimate villain." Even worse, CCP propaganda had already "begun to take a brotherly interest in the activities of other Asiatic countries and Asiatic Communist parties in Japan, Korea, French Indo-China, Malaya and Indonesia." Once the Communists gained control over the Chinese mainland, the "Chinese Communist propaganda front" would "probably be extended to all such areas in the hope of securing all of East Asia."[120]

The Central Intelligence Agency (CIA) reached similar conclusions about the threat posed by Chinese communism in neighboring countries. In August, it prepared a report on "Communist Methods in Asia" that included an extensive section on the CCP and its foreign policy objectives. The report explained that the "CCP hopes to unite one billion Orientals in a Communist Asia, led by the CCP and oriented toward Moscow." The CIA seems to have either guessed or learned about the Sino-Soviet division of labor agreement that Liu Shaoqi and Stalin had made just a few months earlier. It noted that "the USSR has perhaps delegated to the CCP . . . at least some measure of responsibility for building in Mao's words 'a bulwark of Communism in Asia.'" Although the agency recognized that hostility toward communism within China could pose a problem for the CCP, it still feared the ramifications of the CCP victory. It reported: " In addition to the great encouragement which Chinese Communist success presumably has given to other Communist movements in Asia, there are likely to be material repercussions especially in those countries neighboring China which have large Chinese minorities, well-organized CCP branches or both." In the end the report ominously predicted, "As the CCP consolidates its control in China, there is no doubt that it will engage in more aggressive operations throughout Asia."[121]

Fears that the CCP would become more active in Asia once it gained control of the mainland led American officials to advocate increasingly desperate efforts to delay its triumph. By October 1949, Mao Zedong had declared the establishment of the People's Republic of China, but small pockets of GMD resistance survived in parts of southern and southwestern China. Even when the CCP's triumph appeared imminent, the Joint Strategic Survey Committee (JSSC), a group of high-ranking military officers who advised the Joint Strategic Committee (JCS), advocated doing everything possible to halt the Communists' advance. The committee reported in October that although the Communists could be expected to gain control over most of the mainland, there remained non-Communist areas in the south and southwest. "These areas," the JSSC explained, "now separate Southeast Asia from Communist controlled China." The committee believed that if communism could be contained "within north and east central China rather than at China's southern borders," it would "minimize Communist penetrations from the north into southeast Asia."[122] Ultimately, however, the JSSC's fears became a reality. The CCP could not be contained, and by the end of 1949 the GMD had been driven from the mainland and forced to take refuge in Formosa, which Americans guessed would also eventually fall.

The Question of Recognition and China's Role in Asia

By the end of 1949, the triumph of the CCP was a fait accompli. The Truman administration now had to decide whether to officially recognize the PRC or deny its legitimacy through nonrecognition. Although the CCP's victory horrified Jiang Jieshi's U.S. supporters, the China issue competed with numerous others for the president's attention. Many in the State Department favored extending recognition eventually because doing so might encourage the newly established PRC to be more independent from Moscow and salvage a part of the fabled China market for American businesses. Republican members of Congress and some high-ranking military officers, however, staunchly opposed any efforts to improve relations with the CCP, making recognition politically risky.[123] In this context, Secretary of State Dean Acheson chose to wait because he believed that the Communists would eventually capture Formosa, destroy the remnants of the GMD, and make recognition by the United States and the United Nations inevitable. Political pressures from Jiang's sympathizers and Truman's Republican opponents unquestionably swayed the administration toward this route. At the same time, the policy was consistent with the advice that the administration received from some diplomats and intelligence agencies. Several officials advised delaying recognition of the PRC because they wanted to prevent China from inspiring revolutionaries elsewhere in Asia and undermining U.S. interests.

Historians have debated whether China would have been willing to establish relations with the United States if American policy had been more accommodating.[124] The most recent documentary evidence suggests that Mao was willing to consider normal relations, but they had to be on the CCP's terms. China would not grovel before the United States or plead for recognition. Thus, in May 1949, when the U.S. ambassador in China, John Leighton Stewart, made contact with Huang Hua, director of the Foreign Affairs Office of the Nanjing Military Control Commission, Mao instructed Haung to be "cordial, but not enthusiastic." At the same time, Mao was more willing to discuss the possibility of mutual recognition if the United States agreed to respect the sovereign equality of Communist China. It would need to atone for its past imperialism by agreeing to "cut off its connections with the GMD remnants, and never interfere with China's internal affairs."[125] As the CCP saw it, if Washington accepted Mao's terms, recognition would elevate the status of the new Chinese government. If China agreed to anything less, the country's long-standing humiliation by the Western powers would continue.

From the time the PRC was inaugurated, however, many American officials were intent on preventing it from gaining legitimacy. On 5 November, a little more than a month after Mao Zedong had proclaimed the formation of the PRC, Troy L. Perkins, a longtime China hand working at the Office of Chinese Affairs, wrote a memorandum urging the State Department to delay recognition. He explained, "Recognition should not be extended before the Communist regime has concretely indicated that it is prepared to respect at least the minimum standards of international conduct and to assume the responsibilities of government in the treatment of foreign nationals and their interests." What would be the ramifications of extending recognition without receiving proper assurances from the new Chinese government? He continued, "Hasty recognition by any of the leading Western Powers would have immediate and far-reaching repercussions in Southeast Asia because of the indication of a break in the democratic ranks and the aid and comfort given to local Communist movements." The United States, Perkins believed, needed to consider the attitudes of Southeast Asian states that did not favor early recognition.[126]

Some American diplomats stationed in Southeast Asia had a similar view. Edwin F. Stanton, the U.S. ambassador in staunchly anti-Communist Thailand, wrote to Acheson in December arguing that Washington should "delay recognition [of the] Chinese Communist Government" and make recognition contingent on receiving assurances that the new government would "fully protect" American rights and interests in China, and "uphold [the] principles of international law." If the United States offered recognition without obtaining such safeguards, Stanton continued, other countries would be forced to follow suit. "This act," he contended, "will be followed by influx large Chinese Communist diplomatic, consular staffs who can confidently be expected make concerted effort to weld Chinese minorities in these countries into potent pro-Communist weapon which can and will be turned against government in power."[127]

As Truman and Acheson mulled over such advice, intelligence arguing that Mao and his comrades were intent on fomenting a broader revolution in Asia continued to surface. One widely circulated "Review of the World Situation" written by the CIA in January 1950 starkly spelled out the dangers that Communist China posed to American interests in other parts of Asia. The urgent question for the year, the review contended, was "whether Soviet-oriented China based Communism can continue to identify itself with nationalism, exploit economic privations and anti-Western sentiment, and sweep into power by one means or another elsewhere in Asia." The agency was sure that Moscow and Beijing were harboring aggressive intentions. It reported that the "USSR clearly proposes to use the China base in its drive to spread Communism in Asia." Moreover, the PRC was taking concrete measure toward this goal. According to the review, the Beijing Liaison Bureau had begun calling for Communist labor cadres to assist in the struggle for national liberation in what it considered "vulnerable 'colonial' areas" such as South Korea, Indonesia, and Indochina. The CIA believed that the French were likely to be forced to withdraw from Vietnam and that "once Indochina had succumbed, the fragile Thai and Burmese governments would orient themselves at least nominally toward China rather than toward the West."[128] By early 1950, this nightmare of a Communist Asia under the sway of Chinese influence had taken hold of the intelligence establishment.

The recommendations put forward by diplomats such as Stanton and the warnings issued by the intelligence community all weighed on the mind of Acheson and other high-ranking U.S. officials as they considered whether to recognize the PRC. The delay proved to be critical. When North Korean forces stormed across the thirty-eighth parallel in June 1950, the entire U.S. strategic calculus for Asia changed dramatically. The Truman administration shifted almost immediately from a grudging willingness to afford Communist China basic diplomatic courtesies to a firm refusal to make concessions to Asian communism. The outbreak of the Korean War and China's eventual intervention would also ensure that American suspicions of Chinese motives in Asia evolved into more concrete measures to prevent Beijing from enhancing its prestige in the region.

––––––––

The Korean War would turn the United States and the People's Republic of China into bitter adversaries on the battlefield. But the seeds for a long and enduring rivalry were already planted. Beijing viewed gaining a position of leadership among the revolutionary forces in the colonial world as the key to restoring China's status in the international community. The United States, for its part, feared that the expansion of Chinese prestige in Asia and elsewhere would undermine American interests and thus committed itself to stopping China's advances. Future conflict was all but inevitable.

Chapter 2

The Burdens of Status, 1950–1954

If great power comes with great responsibility, then great status comes with great obligations. As one group of scholars concluded, "When the community of states attributes major power status to a few of its members, such attribution comes with expectations that these states will exercise leadership on a variety of issues and conflicts central to international and regional politics."[1] China found this out the hard way between 1950 and 1954. From the time the PRC was established, it aspired to become the principal revolutionary force in Asia, and CCP officials often spoke as if this ambition was already a reality. The Soviets had quickly agreed that their Chinese comrades should bear responsibility for spreading anticolonial revolution in the Afro-Asian world.[2] But once the CCP secured control of the mainland, its ability to play this role was swiftly tested by developments in Indochina and Korea. If China really wanted to become a significant force in Asian politics, it needed to take on the obligation of supporting other revolutionaries in these neighboring countries.

For the newly created PRC, the stakes could not have been higher. Mao and his comrades repeatedly argued that aiding other Asian revolutionaries was China's "internationalist duty," and this became an important motive for Beijing's deep involvement in both the Vietnamese and Korean conflicts.[3] Party officials recognized that if the PRC successfully fulfilled its obligations in these struggles, China would consolidate its status as a major power in both Asia and the Communist Bloc. If it failed to take up these challenges, however, the PRC could no longer credibly claim leadership of a wider Asian revolution. Liu Shaoqi gave voice to these aspirations and fears in an internal party directive written in March 1950: "After the victory of our revolution, to assist in every possible way the Communist parties and people in all oppressed nations in Asia to win their liberation is an international obligation that the CCP and the Chinese people cannot shirk. It is also one of the most important methods to consolidate the victory of the Chinese revolution in the international arena."[4] Such ideas were critical in shaping Beijing's policies in Indochina and Korea during the PRC's first five years of existence.

The more the PRC championed North Korean and Vietnamese revolutionaries, the more menacing China became to American officials. Preventing Beijing from gaining prestige in Asia through victories on the battlefield in Korea became a prime U.S. motive for fighting on in the war. Moreover, after getting bloodied by PRC troops in Korea, Americans quickly succumbed to exaggerated fears that Communist China would dispatch troops to Indochina. The United States subsequently focused on weakening Chinese prestige in the eyes of other Asians. Its policy toward Taiwan evolved from strategically defending the island to actively using Taiwan to challenge the PRC's legitimacy and preclude Beijing's admission to international institutions. Americans also recognized that China's economic growth would be an important determinant of its standing in Asia. It therefore encouraged other nations to mount a sustained trade embargo against the PRC during and after the Korean War.

The Korean War

On 25 June 1950, Kim Il Sung ordered North Korean forces to carry out a full-scale invasion of South Korea in a bold effort to reunify the Korean peninsula. The Truman administration's swift, determined response to North Korea's offensive came as a surprise to Beijing, Pyongyang, and Moscow. They foresaw neither Washington's decision to immediately dispatch American forces to the peninsula nor the UN Security Council's rapid condemnation of North Korean aggression. [5] Within a week China faced not only the arrival of the first American forces on Korean soil but also the Truman administration's dispatch of the Seventh Fleet to the Taiwan Strait. At Washington's urging, the United Nations had made an irrevocable commitment to restoring the sovereignty and territorial integrity of South Korea. The PRC had regarded the United States as one of its main adversaries from its inception, but now the prospects of a direct confrontation with the world's most powerful military loomed large.

Washington's decision to take a stand in South Korea posed an urgent dilemma for China's new leaders. Mao and his colleagues had been deeply involved in the North Korean invasion during its planning stages. Before launching the attack, Pyongyang had engaged in extensive discussions about possible outcomes with Moscow. Stalin had told Kim Il Sung in May that if his forces faltered, they would need to rely on Chinese assistance. Russian sources suggest that Mao not only approved of the plan that Kim and Stalin had drawn up but also agreed to intervene if North Korean forces did not prevail.[6] But Mao had made this promise under the assumption that the United States was disinclined to intervene in the conflict. A potential military clash with the United States made Chinese involvement in Korea much riskier. It could, Chinese leaders feared, jeopardize domestic reconstruction and precipitate a broader American offensive against the Chinese mainland.[7]

Despite the enormous risks and costs of taking on the United States when it was still consolidating control over the mainland, the CCP dispatched more than 3 million volunteers to the Korean peninsula between 1951 and 1953.[8] Why was the CCP willing to wage such a costly war so soon after a long and arduous struggle to defeat the GMD? Historians have emphasized an array of different factors ranging from security concerns to domestic politics to ideology.[9] My emphasis here, however, hews closest to that of Chen Jian, who, in his seminal work *China's Road to the Korean War*, argues that "revolutionary nationalism became a persistent driving force for changing China's weak power status and pursuing a prominent position in the world." Beijing's yearning to regain its stature in world affairs "strongly" influenced "the PRC's foreign policy in general and Beijing leaders' management of the Korean crisis in particular."[10] Washington's perception of the war and China's role in it was in some ways the mirror image of Beijing's. Americans recognized that the war could provide a powerful boost to Chinese prestige in Asia, but rather than fighting for this, they were willing to wage war to prevent it. Truman administration officials often argued that only through continuing to prosecute the war would they be able to stop China from expanding its revolution.

Chinese Communist Party leaders paid a great deal of attention to how their actions would be perceived in Asia when they considered intervention in Korea. They repeatedly argued that the Korean War was a heroic struggle against imperialism and that by fighting alongside their brethren in the Democratic People's Republic of Korea (DPRK) they would gain the admiration of other revolutionaries. Mao made this point on several occasions after deciding to send Chinese People's Volunteers (CPV) to the peninsula. The critical decision came on 8 October, one day after American forces had crossed the thirty-eighth parallel and entered North Korean territory. The chairman's order proclaimed that volunteers were being sent to "assist the Korean people's war of liberation, repel the invasion launched by American imperialists and their running dogs, and to defend the interests of the Korean people, the Chinese people and the people of all Eastern countries." Fighting alongside the North Koreans, they were to "strive for a glorious victory."[11] From Mao's perspective, the war was about more than just Korea; it was about the fate of anticolonial revolution in the East and China's central role in it.

The chairman wrote about the decision in similar terms in another important telegram sent to Zhou Enlai five days later. In the brief interim, Moscow had reneged on an earlier promise to provide air cover for Chinese troops if they entered the war. The key question was whether CPV forces would still intervene in the absence of the promised Soviet support. Although Mao had hesitated and called for a temporary halt in military preparations, his ultimate answer was yes. Again he argued that intervention would be "very important to the interests of China, Korea, the East and the whole world." However, if American troops reached the Yalu River, which formed the border between North Korea and China, "the international and domestic reactionary bluster would surely become louder." Mao concluded, "In short, we believe that we should enter the war and that we must enter the war. Entering the war can be most rewarding; failure to do so may cause great harm."[12] Mao's message reflected a sense of both obligation and possibility. On the one hand, China "must" enter the war in part because it was expected of the PRC as the leader of the Eastern revolution. On the other hand, joining the war could be rewarding. Mao did not directly express what the rewards might be. But he again seemed to be pointing to the possibility of a new, enhanced stature for China in the region.

Party officials took care to be generous in their descriptions of the North Koreans and their struggle against the United States. They cast DPRK forces as heroic and argued that Beijing had a special relationship with North Korea that obliged it to support its fraternal neighbor. On 24 October, shortly after Chinese volunteers crossed the Yalu, Zhou Enlai emphasized these points in a speech to the Chinese People's Political Consultative Conference. The struggle of the North Korean people was "very courageous and moving to us," he stated. The Korean problem was an "international problem," and given the brave struggle that the DPRK was waging, other socialist countries (which he termed the "peace camp") had a moral and revolutionary obligation to support it. For China, an "Eastern" nation whose security and destiny were tied closely to that of the DPRK, the obligation was particularly pressing: "If we consider North Korea's position in the East, we cannot but offer it assistance; if we consider that our relationship is as close as lips and teeth we cannot but offer assistance." The premier also warned of dangerous consequences should the North Koreans be defeated. "Only if North Korea is victorious will there be no wedge driven into the peace camp," he argued.[13] From Zhou's perspective, the PRC would never be seen as a leader in Asia if it did not demonstrate solidarity with other heroic revolutionaries. If China was seen as unwilling to aid what was historically one of its closest allies, it would lead to criticism of China and a loss of respect among other members of the so-called peace camp.

Even after they decided to send Chinese volunteers to the Korean theater, CCP officials remained deeply concerned about how the war effort would be perceived in North Korea and elsewhere. Mao and his comrades did everything in their power to make sure that the comportment of CPV forces would reflect favorably on China. They understood that other revolutionaries in Asia would be more likely to respect Beijing's leadership if Chinese forces acted out the promises of CCP rhetoric. "When Chinese volunteers enter

Korean territory," Chairman Mao ordered on 18 October, "they must respect the North Korean people, the North Korean army, the Korean Workers Party, other democratic parties, and the North Korean leader, Kim Il Sung. This will be an important political basis for assuring that we accomplish our military obligation."[14] Mao issued a similar directive to Chinese forces on 15 January 1951, exhorting them to "not take even a single needle or a single thread from the Korean people, in the same way we feel about our own country and treat our own people."[15] By laying out strict standards for the behavior of Chinese volunteers on the battlefield, Mao hoped to garner admiration for the CPV as the heroic army of a new independent nation while dispelling any historical mistrust toward the PRC that may have lingered in Korea.

These concerns about national prestige carried over to the diplomatic realm. Chinese diplomats responsible for negotiating an end to the conflict received instructions to act in a way that demonstrated national pride and insisted on China's right to be treated as a legitimate power. In November 1950, a Chinese delegation that had initially been invited to the United Nations to take part in discussions of a resolution on American intervention in Taiwan arrived in New York. Inevitably, both Washington and representatives of non-Communist governments sought to engage the delegation in negotiations about ending the war.[16] In December, Zhou gave members of the delegation permission to talk about Korea but also ordered them to maintain their composure and dignity and not to compromise key principles: "You should talk about the North Korea issue and the Taiwan issue with great confidence, proving at every opportunity that the American imperialists are invading North Korea and Taiwan; the UN resolution is illegal, and not allowing us to participate in the UN is disregarding 475 million Chinese people."[17] Zhou's instructions reflected the PRC's view of the war as a struggle to restore not only Korea's sovereignty but also China's rightful position in world affairs. Members of the delegation strove to follow through on Zhou's orders, making their case through acting poised and refusing to be intimidated by American verbal assaults. Wu Xiuquan, the official envoy of the PRC in New York, delivered a highly publicized speech condemning the U.S. invasion of North Korea and Taiwan. He recalled Chinese efforts to demonstrate statesmanlike behavior that would stand in contrast to the sometimes hysterical Americans. The delegates relished the opportunity to prove that they were not "bandits," as their adversaries claimed, and to "let the people of the world see what kind of people we were." Wu recalled, "Our calm, composed attitude and dignified, upstanding bearing was a silent refutation and effective counterattack on our slanderers."[18]

The confident bearing of Chinese officials at the UN was strengthened in part by the CPV's initial successes on the battlefield. By mid-December

1950, Chinese and North Korean forces had recaptured the vast majority of North Korean territory. Mao subsequently decided to pursue a total victory and instructed Peng Dehuai, the commander of Chinese forces, to cross the thirty-eighth parallel. In early January 1951, Seoul fell to the new Sino–North Korean onslaught. Beijing was suddenly confident that the conflict in Korea would end on terms that were highly favorable to China and the Communist Bloc. But the PRC's faith in its military prowess was unwarranted, and some of these initial victories would soon be reversed. A counteroffensive initiated by UN forces on 25 January recaptured the South Korean capital and pushed the enemy back above the thirty-eighth parallel by spring. Beijing launched one last effort to destroy UN forces in April, but the offensive failed and the war remained stalemated along the thirty-eighth parallel for two years as complicated and arduous negotiations over an armistice agreement made halting progress.[19]

The changing situation on the battlefield did not necessarily influence how CCP leaders viewed the conflict, however. As it became clear during early 1951 that the war was likely to be protracted, they continued to emphasize that, by shouldering its international duty, the PRC would inspire other nationalist movements in the region. "We should earn a victory against the United States and strike a blow against the head of the world imperialist camp and crush its arrogance," Zhou Enlai proclaimed in January 1951.[20] According to Zhou, the liberation of Pyongyang by Chinese forces had "boosted the morale" of all of the people in the "peace camp" and was having a great impact on international politics: "The victory of the Chinese people has given rise to cheers throughout Europe; it has especially encouraged the revolutionary movements of other oppressed peoples and broadened the movement for world peace. . . . The influence of our victory in Korea is broad. It has created divisions, contradictions and confusion among our enemies. The revolutionary movement in the peace camp has become deep and firm."[21] Through continuing the struggle against the United States in Korea, the premier argued, China could gain a heroic stature among other revolutionaries fighting against the imperialist camp. The idea that the actions of Chinese volunteers were having a transformative effect not only on the battlefield but also on world politics was a big part of why CCP leaders could embrace the consequences of fighting a protracted war for the next three years.

In many ways, China's desire to enhance its prestige in Asia and among nations of the peace camp was a key reason that the war lasted so long. By the summer of 1952, the North Korean leadership had grown war-weary, owing to the Americans' almost incessant bombing of its territory. But the Chinese were reluctant to conclude an agreement ending the war if it reflected weakness and did not enhance the overall strength of revolutionary forces in Asia. When Pyongyang suggested that Beijing consider responding to an American proposal on the thorny prisoner of war issues, Mao sent a telegram to Kim Il Sung explaining why he was not ready to make concessions. He noted that although continuing the war would entail further sacrifices for the Chinese and Korean people, they were worth it because their war effort was "inspiring the peace-loving peoples of the whole world in the struggle against aggressive war and is facilitating the development of the movement for defense of peace throughout the world." By fighting on, the Chinese were thus not only protecting their own security but garnering the admiration of other countries and peoples who opposed imperialism. Were the PRC to accept American proposals, it would embolden the enemy and hurt China's standing. It would, in Mao's words, "make the enemy even more ambitious and undermine our prestige."[22]

As the PRC strove to achieve greater standing in Asia through fighting in Korea, Washington attempted to thwart these ambitions. When Chinese volunteers crossed the Yalu, they irrevocably changed the character and meaning of the Korean War for the United States and its allies. Before Beijing entered the war, the Truman administration had seen the conflict as a limited police action and hoped that American troops could return home swiftly. After the UN command weathered the Chinese onslaught in the winter of 1950, however, the administration found itself embroiled in a protracted war whose outcome would have wide ramifications. General Douglas MacArthur, the commander in chief of UN forces, famously termed the conflict "an entirely new war."[23] The early successes of the Chinese offensive in the battlefield rekindled the sense of crisis that the Truman administration had felt when the war broke out. Washington now confronted difficult policy decisions: What should American strategy be now that it faced a much stronger and more determined opponent? Should the war be expanded to China? Americans pondered these questions during the winter of 1950–51. As other scholars have demonstrated, the Truman administration decided to limit the war despite the objections of MacArthur and South Korean president Syngman Rhee. It did not try to recapture North Korean territory or to attack the PRC, but it did commit itself firmly to the survival of an independent South Korea.[24]

What did the Truman administration hope to achieve by fighting a limited war? American officials believed that even if they could not roll back communism, they could still minimize the gains in prestige made by Beijing if they successfully defended the Republic of Korea. They also sought to prevent the conflict's ambiguous outcome from being perceived as either a defeat for the United States or a victory for Communist China. As American officials determined U.S. strategy in the war, they laid out numerous objectives but often emphasized the need to prevent China from enlarging its status in Asia as a key reason for continuing to fight.

Concerns about growing Chinese prestige were present in the earliest discussions of how the United States should respond to the changing situation on the battlefield. On the day after Christmas in 1950, President Harry S. Truman held a long meeting with his top advisers and generals to discuss the war. At the time, UN forces had been pushed below the thirty-eighth parallel and Seoul had once again fallen to the enemy. The general consensus was that although Korea was not the right place to fight a major war, American forces should not withdraw from the peninsula. During the meeting Dean Acheson called for a rewriting of MacArthur's directives.[25] On 29 December the president signed off on a special message sent by the Joint Chiefs of Staff to MacArthur. Truman and his advisers made clear their disagreements with the general's calls for enlarging the war, but they nevertheless did want to prevent or, at a minimum, slow down China's conquest of the peninsula. They believed that "resistance to Chinese–North Korean aggression at some point in Korea and a deflation of the military and political prestige of the Chinese Communists would be of great importance to our national interests."[26]

Two weeks later, Truman sent another series of messages to the obdurate MacArthur detailing American objectives. The third of these described Washington's political considerations and discussed what the administration believed were the benefits of mounting a successful resistance to Chinese forces on the peninsula. Once again, preventing Mao and his comrades from achieving the "glorious victory" that they sought figured prominently in the president's thinking. Among the purposes that Truman believed a "successful resistance" in Korea would serve was to "deflate the dangerously exaggerated political and military prestige of Communist China which now threatens to undermine the presence of non-Communist Asia and to consolidate the hold of Communism on China itself."[27] For the president, China's entry into the Korean War had changed the political stakes. The United States now needed not only to protect its own credibility but also to curtail the expansion of Chinese influence into other Asian countries. Even if the president did not favor expanding the war as MacArthur did, he still believed that preventing the fall of South Korea would inhibit China's efforts to enlarge its standing.

General MacArthur's dismissal in April 1951 did not significantly change the Truman administration's thinking. The real disagreement between the president and the general had not been over the importance of deflating Communist China but over whether an all-out war against the PRC was necessary to achieve this objective. As American forces recaptured lost territory and pushed enemy forces back above the thirty-eighth parallel during the spring of 1951, Washington continued seeking to shape public perceptions of the conflict. Language that was quite similar to that used by Truman in his letters to MacArthur appeared repeatedly in American strategy papers and high-level official correspondence long after the general had been dismissed for insubordination.

In May 1951, the NSC redrafted its security policy toward Asia to reflect the changing situation in Korea. Washington remained committed to limiting the war to the peninsula, but even so, it hoped to inflict significant damage on Chinese forces. The first course of action that the new policy guidelines listed for dealing with Communist China was to "Continue strong efforts to deflate Chinese Communist political and military strength and prestige by inflicting heavy losses on Chinese forces in Korea through the present UN operation."[28] During the subsequent two years of war, destroying Chinese divisions, inflicting casualties, and taking Communist prisoners became important objectives for the UN Command. Indeed, at almost the same time that the NSC drafted these guidelines, UN forces were meting out heavy losses to CPV forces. In April, Mao had ordered the ill-fated Fifth Phase Offensive, an effort to reestablish Chinese superiority on the battlefield that mobilized more than six hundred thousand volunteers. In a series of hard-fought battles, the CPV suffered more than eighty-five thousand casualties while the UN Command took more than seventeen thousand prisoners of war.[29] These defeats forced CCP leaders to back away from their goal of total victory and agree to begin armistice negotiations.[30] From the American standpoint, devastating the CPV and forcing Beijing to compromise its objectives represented a significant victory.

When Dwight D. Eisenhower assumed the presidency in 1953, he brought with him both a new determination to end the increasingly unpopular war in Korea and a greater willingness to consider expanded military operations against the PRC. Initially, key officials in the Eisenhower administration were convinced that the Chinese would not agree to a fair settlement unless CPV forces were dealt another humiliating defeat. "I don't think we can get much out of a Korean settlement until we have shown—before all Asia—our clear superiority by giving the Chinese one hell of a licking," Secretary of State John Foster Dulles told White House aide Emmet John Hughes.[31] In the early months of the administration, various government agencies began to reassess the options for general U.S. strategy in Korea, paying particular attention to the ramifications of enlarging the conflict. On 2 April 1953, the NSC Planning Board circulated a new document, NSC 147, reflecting these efforts. The document considered the costs and benefits of removing existing restraints on military operations in the Korean theater and explored such possibilities as launching air attacks and a naval blockade against the Chinese mainland and undertaking a new coordinated offensive on the peninsula to capture more territory.[32] Despite the planning board's evolving strategic considerations, it maintained the Truman administration's commitment to weakening Chinese prestige. NSC 147 explained that "a substantial UN military success in Korea" of the kind Eisenhower was seeking "would deflate the present Communist Chinese military prestige and influence in Asia and enhance the position of the United States in Asia."[33]

Although armistice negotiations made significant progress in subsequent weeks, the administration did not immediately take the option of expanding the war off the table. During an NSC meeting held on 13 May, Eisenhower still spoke frankly about the possibility of a nuclear attack against the PRC.[34] When the council met again one week later, Omar Bradley, the chairman of the Joint Chiefs of Staff, argued that if the negotiations broke down, it would be necessary to expand the war beyond Korea and use atomic weapons.[35] Bradley's arguments served as the basis for NSC Action 794, which endorsed the chairman's approach. The State Department prepared a "political annex" to explain the rationale for this course of action.[36] If American actions were successful, the annex contended, "Chinese Communist prestige in the area [Asia] would be greatly diminished and fear of Chinese Communist military aggression reduced. U.S. prestige would correspondingly be increased, and with careful handling, U.S. influence in the area enhanced."[37] Guided in part by its belief that handing the Chinese a significant defeat in the Korean would hurt the PRC's stature, the Eisenhower administration continued to contemplate expanding the war until an armistice agreement was finally reached in July. Even after signing the armistice, Eisenhower kept some of the key elements of Action 794 as a backup plan in the event of renewed conflict.[38]

Ultimately, however, the extent to which the Eisenhower administration would have carried out its plans to expand the war can only be a matter of speculation. The road to the armistice was tortuous, but the key Communist concessions on POWs during the spring of 1953 enabled both sides to reach a final agreement on terms.[39] The war ended without either side having achieved a complete victory.

Despite the war's ambiguous outcome, however, Beijing took far greater pride in its role in Korea than did Washington. The PRC had fulfilled its revolutionary obligation to its ally, and CPV forces had fought to a draw with the world's most powerful military. Unsurprisingly, CCP officials were often celebratory in the way they talked about the war whereas Americans, for the most part, accepted the terms of the armistice with somber resignation. Party military leaders depicted China's performance as a stunning achievement. Peng Dehuai boasted that, thanks to the actions of the Chinese volunteers under his command, "the first-rate armed forces of the greatest industrial power of the capitalist world were forced to stop at where they began." These triumphs, Peng believed, marked a sharp break with the humiliations that China had suffered in the past and the dawn of a new era in which the world needed to respect Chinese military prowess. "Gone forever is the time when the western powers have been able to conquer a country in the [Far] East merely by mounting several cannons along the coast [as they had] in the past hundred years."[40] The general spoke in equally jubilant terms about the influence of China's "victory" abroad. He believed that the war would "undoubtedly . . . stimulate the confidence and aspiration of those people under colonial and semi-colonial rule in their struggle against imperialism."[41]

In Washington, perceptions of the net outcome of the war were not dissimilar to those in Beijing. Americans, too, recognized that the PRC had gained stature. After making a trip through Asia in December 1953, Vice President Richard M. Nixon explained during one NSC meeting that "Chinese prestige from the Korean incident has received a good boost throughout Asia."[42] The vice president was far more moderate in his policy prescriptions than most of his colleagues. He argued that containment was not likely to work and that the United States would need to come to terms with Communist China.[43] Most American officials, however, became more focused on preventing Beijing from strengthening its position. Before the Korean War had started, many in the Truman administration believed that the Soviets posed the greatest danger to American interests in Asia. But once Chinese volunteers stormed across the Yalu River, American officials increasingly came to see the PRC as the greater threat. Washington had begun taking measures to pressure Beijing outside Korea, such as bolstering the U.S. presence in the Philippines. But it was American policy toward Indochina that was perhaps most directly influenced by China's entry into the Korean War.[44]

Indochina

Vietnam and Korea were intimately related in the minds of both U.S. and Chinese officials. To the CCP leadership, the American role in Korea represented only part of a broader U.S. effort to establish its dominance in Asia at the expense of revolutionary forces. In June 1950, Zhou Enlai had labeled the dispatch of American troops to the Korean peninsula "a premeditated step whose purpose was to allow the United States to fabricate an excuse to invade Taiwan, North Korea, Vietnam, and the Philippines." He called on "all the people of the world who love peace, justice and freedom, especially the oppressed nations of the East, to rise up and stop the American invasion of the East."[45] Americans, too, believed that Korea and Vietnam were both part of a larger conflict, although they took a very different view of who the liberators and oppressors were. As President Truman told Jean de Lattre, the commander of French forces in Indochina, during de Lattre's visit to Washington in 1951, the Korean War and the French campaign in Indochina were part of "the same fight for liberty."[46]

Beijing and Washington both regarded Vietnam as essential to their interests. Although they sacrificed far more blood and treasure in Korea, they initially attached greater strategic value to Vietnam. Since the end of World War II, the country had been caught in a bitter struggle between America's ally, the French, and a nationalist insurgency under the leadership of Ho Chi Minh that sought independence from colonial rule and had gained Beijing's sympathy. Both sides foresaw devastating repercussions if their respective allies in Vietnam were defeated. "If we do not aid Vietnam and hold the enemy there then our hardships will be greater and our troubles will also be greater," Liu Shaoqi explained in a June 1950 meeting with other high-ranking CCP officials.[47] Although some American officials feared being associated with the colonialist French, they likewise predicted difficulties for the United States if their allies failed. The Joint Chiefs of Staff offered its view in April 1950 that the "fall of Indochina would undoubtedly lead to the fall of the other mainland states of Southeast Asia." This would "result in the virtually complete denial to the United States of the United States of the Pacific littoral of Asia." It considered the PRC one of the most significant potential causes of instability in Southeast Asia and called for "prompt and continuing measures" to "reduce the pressure from Communist China."[48]

High-ranking CCP officials embraced responsibility for the Vietnamese revolution from the earliest days of the PRC. They believed that aiding the Vietminh was, like aiding the DPRK, an internationalist duty that they needed to fulfill. Even before the party had consolidated its control of the Chinese mainland it had already become the most significant source of foreign aid and supplies for the Vietnamese insurgents.[49] In February 1950, Ho Chi Minh joined Stalin and Mao Zedong in Moscow, where the three held several meetings to discuss how the two Communist giants could assist the Vietminh cause. Stalin stated his preference that "the Chinese comrades take over the principal responsibility of supporting and supplying the Vietnamese comrades," and Mao promised to think about the best way this could be accomplished.[50] By the spring of 1950, the CCP had agreed to provide military advisers, weapons, and nonmilitary supplies such as clothes and medicine to succor the revolutionary cause in Vietnam.[51]

The most critical organization for funneling assistance to the Vietminh was the Chinese Military Advisory Group (CMAG), a group of seventy-nine advisers and their assistants organized by the CCP Central Military Commission in April 1950. The group was charged with helping the Vietnamese to build an army and plan combat operations against the French.[52] Because of CMAG's pivotal position in Beijing's policy toward Indochina, Mao and his comrades made a special effort to shape its outlook and tactics. The CCP leadership inculcated officers in this group with a sense of revolutionary mission and obligation. "Since our revolution has achieved victory, we have an obligation to help others. This is called internationalism," Mao told the group's senior members during a meeting on 27 June 1950. Zhu De gave CMAG a similar charge: "As internationalists we should regard assistance to Vietnam as an important international task and should spare no effort to help the Vietnamese achieve victory."[53] Ultimately, Mao and his colleagues hoped that CMAG's activities in Vietnam would bring glory to China throughout Asia much as the success of Chinese troops in Korea had done. When Luo Guibo, the head of the Chinese advisory delegation in Vietnam, returned to China for guidance during the fall of 1950, Mao explained to him that "regardless of whether it is aiding the Koreans against America or the Vietnamese against the French, they are both internationalist and patriotic. They both have a great meaning, and they are both glorious. Only the method of assistance differs."[54]

As in the Korean theater, Mao believed that Chinese personnel dispatched to Vietnam needed to act in a way that would reflect positively on the PRC. The chairman instructed Luo: "Vietnam is not China; you cannot mechanically copy the Chinese way. In front of the people you must genuinely and honestly introduce our successful experience of revolution but also explain the lessons of our failure."[55] Luo was proud of the efforts made by his group to implement Mao's commands. He later wrote, "In giving aid to Vietnam, the Chinese government never asked for money back or collected debt from Vietnam; it did not force them to sign unequal treaties; it did not set up any military bases or quarter even one soldier. Everything was at no cost and had no conditions attached. This amply illustrates Mao Zedong's great internationalism."[56] Beijing unquestionably sought to expand its influence in Indochina through CMAG, but it sought to do so in a way that would distinguish it from the colonialists who had dominated Asia in the past.

Motivated by a sense of revolutionary obligation, Luo and other Chinese advisers offered indispensable assistance to the Vietminh throughout their struggle with the French. In 1951, CMAG began providing extensive operational guidance to the People's Army of Vietnam (PAVN) and helping it to streamline its command structure. At the same time, the PRC dispatched a group of political advisers to Indochina who taught the Vietnamese Workers Party (VWP) to draft laws, organize finances, and, most importantly, raise revenues for military operations. Over the course of 1952, CMAG played a pivotal role in planning and executing the PAVN's highly successful Northwest Campaign. The CCP Central Military Commission carefully reviewed plans for the campaign before it was initiated, and Chinese advisers helped to direct PAVN forces on the ground. By December 1952, the campaign had helped drive the French out of a significant tract of territory in northwest Vietnam that could be used as a base.[57]

In the months after the Northwest Campaign, both Washington and Beijing stepped up support for their respective allies in Indochina. When General Henri Navarre assumed command of French forces, he drew up an ambitious plan to secure territories still held by the French and drive the Vietminh from the areas they had recently captured. The Eisenhower administration agreed to bankroll what would come to be known as the Navarre Plan with $385 million in military aid. Chinese advice was instrumental in crafting the strategy that the PAVN ultimately used to counter the French offensive. At Beijing's insistence, Ho Chi Minh decided that Vietminh forces should continue to concentrate on the northwest, thereby setting up a climactic showdown in Dien Bien Phu. During the fabled battle that precipitated the French withdrawal from Indochina, the PRC supplied antiaircraft guns, provided special training for Vietminh battalions, and dispatched army engineers with expertise in trench warfare. This support proved critical in helping the Vietminh slowly to gain the advantage on the battlefield and dealt Paris a humiliating defeat.[58]

Beijing represented the Vietminh victories as victories for the PRC while generally stressing two points: first, Ho Chi Minh and his comrades were following the Maoist example, and second, the Vietnamese and Chinese were joined in a common revolutionary struggle. Both points received a great deal of emphasis in the state run newspaper, the *People's Daily*. In January 1954, as the PAVN was readying itself for battle at Dien Bien Phu, the newspaper ran an article entitled "Chinese Revolutionary Materials Are Widely Disseminated among the Vietnamese People." It reported that VWP cadres were diligently studying Mao's political tracts and that Vietnamese army officers had taken a keen interest in the chairman's military writings.[59] After French forces were defeated, the *People's Daily* touted the victory as a triumph for Asia's war for liberation: "In the struggle to shatter the invasion schemes of the American imperialists and achieve peace, the liberation of Dien Bien Phu has given the peace-loving people in every country of the world and every country in Asia an increased faith in a great victory."[60] Through emulating the PRC in their successful war against imperialism, CCP officials believed, the Vietminh were cementing China's status as the leader of revolutionary forces in Asia.

Washington never completely understood Beijing's view of the Indochina conflict. The Chinese leadership believed that the PRC could gain prestige by helping the Vietminh to overcome the French. As long as PAVN forces continued to hold their own, Mao and his colleagues did not see the need to dispatch PLA divisions.[61] Washington, however, was obsessed with the possibility that Beijing would send troops. Although American officials knew that Chinese aid was vital to the Vietminh, they worried much more about the potential impact of Chinese boots on the ground in Indochina. When discussing China's role in Indochina, American officials often focused on how to stop the PRC from dispatching forces rather than on Chinese assistance to the Vietminh.

American intelligence agencies first contemplated the prospects of Chinese military intervention in Indochina during the months after People's Volunteers crossed the Yalu. If PRC forces drove the French out of Indochina, they concluded, the ramifications could be disastrous—in fact, they would be far worse than if the Vietminh themselves defeated France. One national intelligence estimate prepared in 1951 contended, "Large-scale participation of Chinese Communist forces in a Viet Minh victory would cause far greater repercussions in Southeast Asia than a victory by the Viet Minh alone." Such a victory "would be interpreted as a success for Chinese arms rather than as a victory for Indochinese nationalism." Moreover, the confidence of other Southeast Asian nations such as Burma and Thailand would be undermined, making them more likely to seek an accommodation with communism.[62] At a time when UN forces in Korea were struggling to overcome the initial Chinese offensive, Americans feared that another demonstration of China's martial prowess would enable the PRC to establish itself as the dominant power in Asia.

As the situation in Korea stabilized and armistice negotiations proceeded, albeit haltingly, the possibility that Chinese forces might join the fray in Indochina loomed as an ominous possibility in the minds of American officials. They worried in particular that the PRC troops fighting in Korea might suddenly become available for deployment in Vietnam if an armistice was attained. A study done by the NSC staff in February 1952 explained, "A cessation of hostilities in Korea would greatly increase the logistical capacity of the Chinese Communists to support military operations in Indochina." The staff also worried that Chinese intervention in Indochina would sway the psychological balance in Asia in favor of the PRC. The study warned, "Successful overt Chinese Communist aggression in this area, especially if achieved without encountering more than token resistance on the part of the United States or the United Nations, would have critical psychological and political consequences which would probably include the relatively swift alignment of the rest of Asia and thereafter the Middle East to communism, thereby endangering the stability and security of Europe."[63] Although Americans obviously did not want to see the Vietminh triumph, they sensed a far greater danger to their interests and the global balance of power if the PRC once again proved its willingness to make sacrifices for the sake of promoting revolution in Asia.

American officials sometimes disagreed on how likely the Chinese were to dispatch forces to Vietnam, but they all recognized that it could have disastrous consequences and tried to ensure that it did not happen. In 1953–54, the Eisenhower administration let the Chinese know that if they deepened their involvement in Indochina, there would be a harsh reprisal from the United States. In a speech given in Saint Louis in September 1953, Secretary of State John Foster Dulles explained bluntly that there was now "a risk that, as in Korea, Red China might send its own army into Indochina. The Chinese Communist regime should realize that such a second aggression could not occur without grave consequences which might not be confined to Indochina."[64] The administration also held wide-ranging discussions both internally and with other members of NATO about how PRC aggression could be deterred. Possible measures included the use of harassing tactics in the Taiwan Strait and the introduction of nuclear weapons. The administration tried but failed to assemble a coalition of interested states in Europe and Asia that might intervene collectively in support of the French in the hopes that a unified effort would persuade the Chinese that the costs of intervention were too high.[65] Ultimately, however, much of this discussion proved superfluous. The Vietminh handed the French a humiliating defeat at Dien Bien Phu without overt Chinese military involvement. In the aftermath, the French and other important U.S. allies wanted to pursue negotiations. At least in the short run, a political rather than military solution to the struggle would be sought.

In the end, America's worst fears about China and the First Indochina War were not realized. Nevertheless, Beijing's role in Indochina added to the considerable gains in stature it had made during the Korean War. China had strengthened its position as the leader of revolutionary forces in Asia by arming and guiding the Vietminh. At least according to Chinese accounts, Ho Chi Minh and his comrades expressed genuine gratitude for both Chinese assistance and the PRC's revolutionary model. "The biggest reason for this victory is that China and the Soviet Union gave us all out assistance," Ho Chi Minh wrote to Mao after the Vietminh's victory in the Northwest Campaign. "The victory was a victory of the Maoist line of revolutionary internationalism."[66] More important, aside from the United States, the other major powers considered the PRC's role in Indochina important enough for China to have a seat at the negotiating table when talks on a political settlement began in Geneva. This, too, would be a significant platform for the PRC to stand up as a significant and responsible actor (discussed in the next chapter). All of these gains for the PRC did not sit well with Washington. Having failed to prevent Beijing from enhancing its revolutionary credentials in Korea and Indochina, the United States began looking for other ways to take the PRC down a notch.

Punishing the PRC: Supporting Taiwan

The conflicts in Korea and Indochina most immediately affected American policy toward Taiwan. During the period between 1949 and 1954, U.S. policy toward Jiang Jieshi's government in Taipei was transformed. In 1949, American officials had grown wary of supporting Jiang; his failure to maintain control over the mainland despite hundreds of millions of dollars of American aid had embarrassed the Truman administration. Washington eventually came to believe, however, that keeping the island of Formosa out of Beijing's hands would reduce Chinese prestige in Asia. Moreover, supporting the Taiwanese Republic of China (ROC) as a rival government in international institutions served American purposes by fundamentally contesting the legitimacy of the PRC. As Sino-American frictions deepened over Korea and Indochina, American support for Taiwan grew much stronger and its determination to defend the island firmer.

For the PRC, of course, continuing GMD control of Taiwan stood as an ever-irksome reminder of both China's humiliations at the hands of the Great Powers and the one failure suffered by the PLA during the Chinese civil war. CCP forces had dispatched their Nationalist adversaries with ruthless efficiency in hard-fought battles leading to the conquest of the mainland in 1949, but they encountered surprisingly tough resistance when they tried to conquer Jinmen and Dengbu—small islands near the mainland that remained under Jiang Jieshi's control. The battle on Jinmen, where GMD forces captured or destroyed roughly ten thousand PLA troops with the aid of American weapons was especially embarrassing to Mao and his comrades. The fact that GMD troops owed much of their success to American-supplied airplanes and warships heightened the CCP's perception of the United States as a threat. As Chen Jian has noted, Mao and his colleagues now "viewed the liberation of Taiwan from the perspective of a long-range Sino-American confrontation in East Asia."[67]

At the time of these setbacks for the PRC, the Truman administration was wavering on how to handle the Taiwan issue. Truman and Acheson both believed that the island was likely to fall to the CCP eventually and did not want to stake American credibility on its future. In December 1949, the Joint Chiefs of Staff called for a stepped-up program of military and economic assistance to the Nationalist government, citing America's national security interests.[68] Acheson, however, thought that further assistance to the GMD would be futile, given the hostility of the indigenous population to Jiang and the incompetence of his government. If the United States followed through on the suggestions of the JCS, Acheson told chairman Omar Bradley, "we will have once more involved U.S. prestige in another failure for all to see."[69]

At the time, the administration believed that the greatest potential danger for the United States regarding Taiwan was linking its own credibility too greatly to the survival of the GMD.

The outbreak of the Korean War forced the Truman administration to reconsider its ambivalence about defending Taiwan. Two days after the DPRK invasion, Truman announced that he was moving the Seventh Fleet to the Taiwan Strait. He stopped far short of endorsing the GMD, but he did state that given the outbreak of war in Korea, a move by the PRC against Taiwan would constitute a serious threat to American forces in the Pacific. At the same time, he called on Jiang Jieshi's government to stop all air and sea operations against the mainland.[70] Beijing immediately denounced Truman's statement. Zhou Enlai called the dispatch of the Seventh Fleet "an invasion of China's territory." The premier added, "Regardless of any obstructive actions taken by the United States, the fact that Taiwan belongs to China can never be changed."[71]

The American security commitment to Taiwan would far outlive the wartime necessities that prompted the Truman administration to establish it. A key consideration guiding U.S. policy was the possibility that preserving the ROC could undermine Beijing's standing internationally. Briefly after Truman dispatched the Seventh Fleet, American intelligence analysts began to advance this argument. In July 1950, the CIA explained, "So long as Taiwan remains out of Chinese Communist hands, [Beijing] loses some political prestige, both at home and abroad." Although the agency noted that "such considerations of 'political face' probably are not sufficient in themselves to impel an immediate invasion," it worried that such an invasion might well be successful in the absence of effective American resistance.[72]

With such considerations in the background, the Truman administration gradually increased the level of America's commitment to Taiwan. In August 1950, the National Security Council approved NSC 37/10 on "Immediate U.S. Courses of Action with Respect to Formosa." The United States would "continue the present policy of denying Formosa to communist forces." The document recommended that the administration assess Chinese Nationalist forces and provide them with military equipment, supplies, and grant aid.[73] American economic assistance, some of which was aimed at bolstering the military aid program, also grew over the next few years. Although U.S. aid to the GMD government in Taiwan paled in comparison to what Jiang had received before losing the mainland, it still reached $81 million in 1952 and $115 million in 1953.[74]

In addition to increasing economic and military assistance to Taipei, the Truman administration began to exert American influence on other issues to strengthen the Republic of China's legitimacy at the expense of the PRC's.

In 1952, when Washington ended the U.S. occupation of Japan, the Truman administration barred the PRC from joining in the negotiation of the San Francisco Peace Treaty and sought instead to invite a delegation from the ROC. The right to negotiate and become a signatory to major international treaties has always been an important marker of legitimacy in world politics. If the ROC rather than the PRC sent a delegation to San Francisco, it would have made an important symbolic statement about whose sovereignty over the mainland was recognized by the international community. The United States did not completely get its way on the issue, however. Washington needed to compromise with London, which had established relations with the PRC in 1950 and wanted to invite Beijing. In the end, neither of the two Chinas was allowed to participate.[75]

Having failed to get its way in San Francisco, the Truman administration subsequently pressured Japan to sign a separate peace treaty with Jiang Jieshi's government in Taipei.[76] The signing of the Treaty of Taipei in 1952 represented a significant political victory for both the United States and the ROC. Although the treaty encompassed only Taiwan and the surrounding islands (thereby undermining the GMD's claims to have jurisdiction over all of China), it nevertheless aroused Beijing's ire because, according to its terms, Japan acknowledged the ROC as a legitimate sovereign entity while not signing any similar treaty with the PRC.[77] Even if China was gaining stature among the revolutionary forces in Asia through its roles in Korea and Indochina, the treaty was a reminder that Washington still had means at its disposal to diminish the PRC.

The Eisenhower administration was even more vigorous in its support for Taiwan. Eisenhower, too, looked at the island as a political tool that could be used to curtail China's political, social, and moral authority in Asia. Early in his administration, the NSC staff produced two studies—one on U.S. policy toward the PRC and the other on Taiwan—that eventually served as important bases for American policy. Both recommended a more robust American commitment to the island because of its political and symbolic significance.

The first of these two documents, NSC 166/1, provided a comprehensive framework for American China policy. It analyzed the PRC's prospects and motives while laying out a strategy for negating Chinese influence. The NSC acknowledged that Beijing had attained "a position of leadership among Asian Communist movements and regimes." The council ruled out overthrowing the current Chinese government through the use of armed force or seeking an accommodation with the regime via concessions. Instead, American policy would be "to seek, by means short of war to reduce the relative power position of Communist China in Asia." This meant isolating the PRC from both other Asian countries and the international community to the greatest degree possible. The United States could, through appropriate political measures, "impose impediments to [the] general international acceptance of the Chinese Communist regime thus reducing [Beijing's] effectiveness in rendering propaganda support to the USSR and forestalling an increase of Chinese Communist prestige." The council recommended the adoption of several policies that could weaken the PRC politically. These included fostering "strong and healthy non-Communist governments" in South Korea, Taiwan, and Indochina and developing the "political, military and economic strength of Japan."[78]

The NSC attached a particular importance to the ROC because its very existence posed a serious challenge to the PRC's status in the international community. The council recognized that Taiwan and the other territories that the PRC claimed rightfully belonged to China were important to its overall effort to achieve greater social recognition in Asia. "For both security and prestige reasons," it contended, "[Beijing] is anxious to restore Chinese sovereignty over all historically Chinese areas with the possible exception of Outer Mongolia." Although the CCP had, for the most part, accomplished this, the NSC noted, "Taiwan remains in the hands of the anti-Communist U.S.-supported National Government."[79] Jiang Jieshi's government in Taiwan could thus be considered an "asset to the U.S. position in the Far East." The council explained, "The existence of the Chinese government on Formosa offers an at least symbolic alternative to Communist control of the mainland, and helps to frustrate the Communist objective of gaining international acceptance as the sole representative of the Chinese people."[80] By 1953, Washington certainly recognized that Jiang Jieshi's chances of regaining control of the Chinese mainland were minimal. But the Eisenhower administration also realized that his government could be a powerful symbolic rallying point for Asians who opposed communism and wished to aid U.S. efforts to undermine Beijing.

These were powerful arguments for continuing American support for Taiwan, and the administration soon ratcheted up its commitment to the island. NSC 166/1 made it official U.S. policy to build up Taiwan as a symbolic alternative to the PRC and challenge to Beijing's legitimacy in Asia. The United States would "recognize and support the Chinese Nationalist Government on Formosa as the Government of China and the representative of China in the United Nations and other international bodies." Washington would also assist Taipei "in achieving increased support from all non-Communist groups" while helping to "increase the effectiveness of its armed forces for action in defense of Formosa, for raids against the Communist mainland and seaborne commerce with Communist China and for such offensive operations as may be in the U.S. interest."[81] The Eisenhower administration thus went far beyond providing for Taiwan's defense against an attack. It also sought to upgrade the ROC's offensive capacity in case a broader war between the United States and China erupted while increasing support for the GMD in the international community.

Although NSC 166/1 certainly denoted a more affirmative American policy toward Taiwan, it was short on specifics. The NSC Planning Board delineated these in greater detail in a study that it produced in March 1953 on American objectives and actions in Formosa. This report made much more explicit mention of the political significance of Taiwan and explained how the island could be used to contest the influence of the CCP. The first third of the report focused on the Nationalist government in Taipei as a political force. It began by noting that American security interests were "threatened not only by hostile military power on the China mainland but also by hostile and dynamic political power." Taiwan, it argued, was "an essential weapon in the continuing political struggle with the communist world, especially the Chinese segment of it."[82]

The study argued that for Taiwan to become an effective political counterweight to the PRC, its prestige in the international community needed to be increased. This could be accomplished in part through continuing ROC economic and political development. The report contended that many governments in the Free World were unaware of the positive changes that the GMD had made in its organization and governance since it had been driven from the mainland. Publicizing its progress would "go far toward increasing the [Nationalist] Chinese Government's prestige in the eyes of other noncommunist governments and would have a favorable effect upon its relations with such governments." Along similar lines, the report counseled continuing American support for Taipei at the United Nations. Seating Taipei rather than Beijing on the UN Security Council, it argued, would serve "not only to counteract the increase of communist influence in international counsels but also to preserve and enhance the Chinese National Government's prestige in the eyes of the Chinese people."[83] The report's analysis influenced the Eisenhower administration's official policy toward Taiwan, which it laid out most clearly in NSC 146/2. Drafted in November 1953, the top-secret policy paper covered "United States Objectives and Courses of Action with Respect to Formosa and the Chinese National Government." It called for robust political and military assistance to the ROC. American military aid would help to support an army of 350,000 as well as a small navy and an air force. Politically, Washington would both recognize and urge other governments to recognize Taipei as the government of China while supporting it as the representative of China at the United Nations. It would also try to increase the appeal of the GMD both in Taiwan and on the mainland.[84]

Undermining Chinese prestige was not the only reason that the United States increased its commitment to Taiwan. Many American officials genuinely believed that a strong Taiwan with a formidable military could serve as a deterrent against Chinese aggression elsewhere in Asia.[85] Taken together, these concerns gave the Eisenhower administration a powerful incentive to support Jiang Jieshi's government. The depths of this commitment would be demonstrated in 1954–55, when the United States hinted that it might use nuclear weapons in response to the PRC bombardment of two small islands (Jinmen and Mazu), which were controlled by Taipei.[86] The First Taiwan Strait Crisis helped to pave the way for the U.S.-ROC Mutual Security Treaty of December 1954. Concerned that Jiang might somehow maneuver the United States into a large-scale military confrontation with the PRC, Eisenhower had initially resisted such a treaty. Although the agreement did not cover Jinmen and Mazu, it removed any ambiguities about the administration's willingness to defend Taiwan. And of course, the treaty conferred greater legitimacy on Taipei, strengthening its international position and indirectly tying it together with other nations in America's Pacific alliance structure such as Japan and South Korea.[87] By 1954, strengthening Taiwan politically and militarily had become a cornerstone of America's broader effort to weaken Chinese prestige in Asia. American officials believed, however, that strengthening Taiwan was not sufficient to undermine Beijing's appeal. They would also need to find ways to weaken the PRC. In particular, they wanted to make sure that China could not thrive economically. The trade embargo was the chief weapon used to accomplish this objective.

Punishing China: The Trade Embargo

In the early twenty-first century it has become almost commonly received wisdom that sanctions and other forms of economic coercion don't work. They may diminish standards of living but almost never do enough damage to their intended targets to significantly change their behavior. The Truman and Eisenhower administrations were both well aware of this underlying reality when it came to the PRC. During the Korean War, they recognized that sanctions would probably not bring Beijing to the negotiating table any more quickly. After the Korean War, they realized that maintaining a trade embargo would do little to prevent the PRC from seeking to spread revolution. Nevertheless, Washington successfully pressured the United Nations to impose trade controls on China during the Korean War and maintained the embargo after the war ended even though most of its allies abandoned the policy. Why did the United States adhere to an apparently ineffective and possibly counterproductive policy? The main reason was that changing

Beijing's behavior was never the only goal. American officials hoped that the embargo would have a psychological impact as well as an economic one. The moral censure implied by sanctions could increase the PRC's isolation from the international community. Moreover, even if the embargo did not destroy the Chinese economy, it could hinder industrialization and recovery, thereby limiting the appeal of the PRC as a model for other Asian countries.

In the immediate aftermath of the CCP's triumph on the mainland, the Truman administration had been reluctant to impose a comprehensive embargo on the PRC. It opted to restrict trade only in strategic materials while keeping other forms of commerce open in the hopes of maintaining some influence and creating frictions between Beijing and Moscow. China's entry into the Korean War swiftly provoked a far more hostile American policy, however. Washington announced a comprehensive embargo on all American trade with the PRC in December 1950.[88] By that time, the United States had already joined with its Western European allies to establish the Consultative Group to develop controls on trade with the Eastern Bloc. A special Consultative Committee (COCOM) monitored the implementation of these controls. After Beijing's entry into the Korean War, COCOM placed restraints on trade with the PRC that went beyond those imposed on Eastern Europe and the Soviet Union, thereby creating the so-called China differential.[89] During and after the occupation of Japan (1945–52) the United States was also in a position to strongly influence Japanese trade policy. It had restricted Sino-Japanese trade after 1949, and after China entered the Korean War, it implemented new export control measures.[90]

The Truman administration was not satisfied with sanctioning the PRC through COCOM, however. Washington also wanted Asian, Middle Eastern, and other nations to join in limiting their commerce with the PRC. Aware that many UN members, including some U.S. allies, would resist instituting Washington's comprehensive embargo, the administration pushed for more limited controls on articles that could help Chinese volunteers on the battlefield. On 1 February, the UN General Assembly passed a resolution calling on members to refrain from giving any assistance to the "aggressors" in Korea and to "consider additional measures" that might be taken in response to the PRC invasion.[91] Over the next few months, the Truman administration lobbied persistently to have new economic controls included in these "additional measures." After much maneuvering and pressuring various allies, it finally persuaded the General Assembly to adopt a resolution calling for the embargo of arms, ammunition, and other strategic goods in May 1951.[92]

From the outset, many American officials advocated UN sanctions less as a means of damaging the Chinese economy than as a way to bring the moral force of world opinion against the PRC. In March, as the United States was considering economic sanctions, the State Department prepared a position paper that argued: "The major significance of sanctions may be to give concrete emphasis to the United Nations' disapproval and condemnation of Chinese Communist aggression rather than to accomplish important military or economic results." If all of the non-Communist members of the United Nations agreed to enforce sanctions, "certain psychological and political effects might be produced in China, in the United States, and among all United Nations countries which would equal and might surpass the economic or military value of sanctions."[93] From the American perspective, lining up countries to join in implementing trade controls would not only limit Chinese war making capabilities but establish an ongoing form of symbolic condemnation.

The Truman administration was particularly eager to have Asian and Arab nations join in imposing these economic controls. It recognized that Pakistan, Ceylon, and other countries seeking to maintain neutrality had trading relationships with China that they were reluctant to disrupt. Washington was disappointed when many Arab and Asian nations opposed the February 1951 UN General Assembly Resolution that called for consideration of further measures to address Beijing's intervention in Korea and laid the groundwork for instituting trade controls. The administration was eager to see neutralist Asian countries give more affirmative backing to any economic sanctions that were adopted. In fact, one of the reasons that the administration did not insist on a comprehensive UN embargo and settled for imposing controls on only strategic materials was that it hoped to "induce the Arab-Asian states to support or at least to abstain on rather than to oppose a resolution recommending its application."[94] Washington believed that compelling Asian and Middle Eastern nations to support an implicit moral censure of Beijing would weaken the PRC's claims to be their champion.

The resolution ultimately bore mixed results in part because some Asian countries were reluctant to completely endorse it. It was adopted by a vote of forty-seven to zero with eight abstentions coming mainly from Asian and Arab countries. The abstentions left Washington with a sense of incomplete victory, however. The reluctance of India, Egypt, and other influential Afro-Asian nations to go on the record in support of sanctions irked those in the Truman administration determined to see Asia strongly condemn the PRC.[95] The embargo had a definite economic impact, but it was short-lived. Exports to Communist China plummeted from $347 million in the first half of 1951 to $134.5 million in the second half of the year. Malaya, Pakistan, Egypt, and several other Afro-Asian nations reduced their trade with Communist China significantly. Yet by the first half of 1952, many of these countries had again expanded their trade with the PRC.[96] The UN resolution's vague language permitted individual states to determine "which commodities from its territory fall within the embargo."[97] Further, many neutral Asian and Arab countries were unwilling to overlook their economic interests for the sake of giving the United States moral vindication.

Growing ambivalence about economic controls targeting China in South Asia and the Middle East contributed to the failure of American efforts to garner support for more comprehensive sanctions in 1952. Exhausted by the war, some State Department officials wanted to make the case for a complete embargo, claiming that stricter sanctions might bring Beijing to the negotiating table. But others expressed caution about the mood in the Middle East and Asia and argued that pressing the issue could even embarrass the United States. Henry A. Byroade, assistant secretary of state for the Middle East, South Asia, and Africa, argued that a total embargo would "threaten the economic stability of India and Pakistan" and have adverse consequences for other countries in the region. He added that only a few of the most pro-U.S. countries in the Near East were likely to support Washington on the issue and that an attempt to persuade others to join "could only result in adversely affecting their attitude toward the United States."[98] In the end, these internal debates were rendered moot by the July 1953 armistice ending the Korean War.

When the war ended, the UN embargo was lifted, and members of COCOM saw little reason to persist with the embargo though Washington would have liked them to. The Eisenhower administration grudgingly accommodated allies that wanted to trade with the PRC, gradually acquiescing as they lobbied to eliminate the China differential. At the same time, Washington decided to hold the line.[99] With America's closest allies looking to drop sanctions, the State Department no doubt realized that staying the course would not likely cause the PRC serious economic harm. So why did Washington persist? Although a number of confused and sometimes contradictory arguments were advanced in support of the sanctions, it is clear that American officials remained convinced that they could somehow damage China's prestige in Asia. The NSC argued that although sanctions might not hobble the Chinese economy, they could slow its growth. Asian countries that were expectantly watching the PRC to see whether its socialist development programs were succeeding would quickly become disillusioned.

The NSC had delineated the relation between China's prestige in Asia and its economic development explicitly in NSC 166/1:

To promote its position and power from both the domestic and world (especially Asian) standpoints, [Beijing] apparently feels that it must convince Chinese and Asian opinion that Communist China is becoming a great and progressive nation. It appears to believe that expansion of Communism and of China's leadership in Asia, as well as the regime's internal popularity, depend to a considerable extent upon propagating the idea that Communist China is making dynamic progress in industrialization, popular welfare, and strength. The importance attached to these considerations is indicated in the tremendously organized efforts for self-advertisement to Asia that the regime is making, in its extreme concern of maintaining prestige, and its sensitivity to setbacks in its industrialization program from the standpoint of psychological consequences.[100]

If the PRC wanted to advertise its economic progress and industrialization programs to gain prestige among its Asian neighbors, the NSC reasoned, then hampering this progress would reduce its influence. Although the council reported that Western controls would not "of themselves prevent substantial Chinese Communist economic development," it also contended that such controls "might be expected to increase Chinese Communist difficulties in achieving anything approaching rapid industrialization."[101]

The U.S. embargo on China remained in place until Richard M. Nixon lifted it in 1971 as part of his broader effort to promote détente with Beijing. It endured because high-ranking American officials were convinced that it isolated the PRC despite its limited economic and strategic value. Sanctions foisted on China "the sense of ostracism—being treated as different and not morally the equal of other countries," Secretary of State John Foster Dulles explained.[102]

The Chinese response to the embargo confirmed the American view of its utility to some degree. Communist Party officials claimed that the PRC's economy had not suffered any serious ramifications from American and UN sanctions. "The American imperialists' blockade and embargo does not intimidate us," Zhou Enlai proclaimed in an address to the Chinese People's Political Consultative Conference in October 1951. "To the contrary, we have used it to eliminate reliance on semicolonialism in our economy, shorten the process of gaining complete economic independence, and accelerate progress toward eliminating the special privileges of the American imperialists in China."[103] At the same time, the Chinese government fought exclusion from trade with other Asian countries. In previous centuries, Chinese emperors had seen trade with tributary states not only as an economic relationship but also as a symbolic act that implied that the two parties respected each other's sovereignty and legitimacy.[104] These historical patterns may well have subtly informed the outlook of Mao and his colleagues.

During the early 1950s, Beijing readily accepted disadvantageous trade agreements with several of its neighbors in efforts to nullify the political impact of the embargo. China showed great eagerness to trade with neutralist countries whose loyalties remained up for grabs. The PRC offered especially generous terms to Ceylon, which had not formally recognized the PRC but preferred to remain as far detached from the Cold War as possible. When a trade delegation from Ceylon visited in October 1952, Zhou instructed the Ministry of Commerce to offer to sell rice to Ceylon at the market price while purchasing rubber above the market price. He explained that the reasons for this were to "smash the imperialist blockade and embargo and help the government of Ceylon solve its urgent difficulty with rice."[105] The premier hoped that trade would lead to stronger ties between Ceylon and the PRC, raising Beijing's profile among neutral Asian countries. "Our countries need cultural relations in addition to economic relations," Zhou urged the visiting Ceylonese delegation, and he proposed an exchange of cultural troupes. He also raised the possibility that eventually Beijing and Colombo could exchange diplomatic envoys.[106] In January 1953, China agreed to a similar barter arrangement with Indonesia."[107] Neither agreement was in the PRC's economic interests. But during the early Cold War, Beijing consistently attached a higher priority to gaining social recognition than it did to economic welfare—a mentality that would later be reflected in its willingness to offer aid to Afro-Asian countries despites its own dire poverty. If trade agreements could help the PRC gain legitimacy among wavering Asian states, then they were worth pursuing despite disadvantageous terms.

Ultimately, the Truman and Eisenhower administrations' trade controls cannot be said to have achieved their ostensible purposes. There is little evidence that the embargo had any influence on Beijing's strategic considerations in either Korea or Indochina. In Asia, the PRC worked with neighboring countries to negotiate its way around the embargo. PRC trade rebounded so quickly with Arab and Asian nations because most of them did not want to isolate China indefinitely, as Washington hoped they would. The embargo did not make China stronger, but it did little to weaken its influence.

———

During the first four years of its existence, the People's Republic of China fulfilled the onerous obligations that came with the status to which it aspired. Through intervening in Korea, where it held UN forces to a stalemate, and aiding its comrades in Indochina, China emerged as the unquestioned champion of revolutionary forces in Asia. The triumphs of the PRC and its allies in these conflicts drew the attention and often the admiration of Asian nations. Taiwan remained an unresolved irritant to the PRC that Washington continued to use to weaken Beijing's standing when it could, but China had weathered almost everything that the United States could bring on, including the trade embargo and other uniquely hostile policies. Beijing's resilience only made Washington more prone to take an exaggerated view of Chinese ambitions and the threat that the PRC posed to U.S. interests.

Defiant as the PRC was, however, fulfilling its revolutionary obligations had been exhausting. Struggling against the world's wealthiest and most powerful country on so many different levels took an enormous toll and could not continue indefinitely. With the ending of the Korean War and the French retreat from Indochina, the PRC increasingly looked for more peaceful means of enlarging its stature in Asia, even if it required a temporary abatement in revolutionary zeal. The United States, however, would come to see Beijing's campaign to enlarge its status peacefully as just as threatening and insidious as its efforts to do so militarily.

Chapter 3

From Geneva to Bandung

One of the most widely told stories of the 1954 Geneva Conference might, as it turns out, have been apocryphal. According to some accounts, as the delegations attending the conference opened discussions to find a peaceful resolution to the Indochina conflict, Zhou Enlai magnanimously offered to shake hands with Secretary of State John Foster Dulles. The secretary, however, brusquely walked past Zhou, scarcely acknowledging him. Several Chinese diplomats present at the conference later claimed that the story was a pure fabrication, although one American diplomat claims to have seen it occur.[1] How precisely the story came to be invented if it did not take place is a mystery. Nevertheless, it remained so prevalent in the minds of both American and Chinese political leaders that Nixon made a very deliberate effort to shake hands with Zhou Enlai when he visited the PRC eighteen years later in atonement for Dulles's purported misdeed.[2] Even if the story is a myth or an exaggeration, it is not difficult to see why it took on a life of its own. It was in many ways emblematic of how American and Chinese leaders approached the world at the time.

At Geneva, Zhou Enlai represented a country that was very deliberately trying to take advantage of the opportunities presented by major international conferences to elevate its global stature. The Geneva Conference and the Afro-Asian Conference held eight months later in Bandung, Indonesia, were crucial in this regard. During the time frame spanned by these two conferences the PRC sought, above all, to convince the world that it was committed to peace. Having encouraged revolutionaries in Vietnam and Korea, CCP leaders now believed that the best way to consolidate the PRC's status as an important global actor was to strengthen China's relations with its neighbors and improve its national security while deepening the revolution at home. Chinese diplomats at Geneva and Bandung made concerted efforts to win over leaders of neutral countries and foster divisions between the United States and its allies, some of whom were willing to adopt a more moderate stance toward China. Much like the PRC's leaders in the early twenty-first century, Zhou Enlai and his comrades strove to convince the world that China was committed to a "peaceful rise," although they did not use the same term. Nevertheless, like more recent Chinese leaders, Zhou claimed that China was a responsible world power seeking to improve the welfare of its people rather than engage in international adventurism.[3]

The fiercely anti-Communist Dulles, on the other hand, represented a government that would do everything in its power to deny the fundamental legitimacy of the PRC. Dulles was never much the charmer when dealing with Asians or nonwhite peoples in general, for that matter. The former prince of Cambodia Norodom Sihanouk once described him as an "acidy arrogant man."[4] But when it came to China, Dulles and his colleagues carried a special grudge. They stereotyped the Chinese as "hysterical" and "fanatical" and remained angry that China had rejected America's ally Jiang Jieshi.[5] They scoffed at the idea that China could be a peaceful power and wanted to isolate it from the international community.

The Eisenhower administration understood Beijing's strategy at these conferences and strove to undermine it. Even as the PRC represented Bandung and Geneva as important events that conferred legitimacy and prestige on their participants, Washington downplayed their significance and sought to belittle their achievements. While China seized the opportunity presented by Geneva and Bandung to raise its profile among both allies and adversaries, the United States consistently tried to prevent the Chinese from winning friends and gaining influence.

Creating a New Image of China

Between 1949 and 1953, the CCP had primarily sought to strengthen its global influence by exporting revolution to other parts of Asia and standing in bold defiance to the United States. By 1953, however, Chinese leaders recognized that this approach would alienate as many Asian countries as it attracted. Unrelenting advocacy of revolution could raise suspicions that China was intent on subverting neutral nations such as Burma and India, and it was now these neutralist Asian countries that Beijing believed it needed to win over. When armistice negotiations over the Korean War wound down in late 1952, Chinese officials sensed that a less militant approach would win greater approval from neighboring countries. Having established itself as a leader of revolutionary forces in Asia through its actions in Korea and Vietnam, Beijing now fostered an alternative image of itself that could be propagated in newly independent but nonrevolutionary societies. Rather than emphasizing its role as the progenitor of a violent global struggle against colonialism, the PRC increasingly represented itself as a force for world peace that challenged warmongering nations such as Japan and the United States. The goal was to win the trust of Indonesia, India, Pakistan and other nations in the region that claimed neutrality in the Cold War but were not without some history of acrimony toward China. This shift in Beijing's strategy was also a product of necessity. By the fall of 1952, the PRC had wearied of the heavy casualties suffered in Korea and recognized that there were limits to what could be accomplished on the battlefield. Moreover, the CCP's leaders were eager to get the country's much needed economic reconstruction under way. They had already drawn up an ambitious Five-Year Plan calling for rapid industrial growth and recognized that a more peaceful international environment would facilitate its implementation.[6]

Although Chinese volunteers continued to fight and die in large numbers in Korea, the PRC began to reorient its diplomacy in September and October 1952. It made plans to hold an Asia and Pacific Peace Conference in Beijing and became interested in the possibility of signing nonaggression pacts with India and Burma. It was Mao Zedong who first raised the possibility of such agreements in a letter to Zhou Enlai while Zhou was in Moscow to discuss economic and foreign policy issues with Stalin. The chairman explained that India and Burma had indicated that they wanted to sign nonaggression pacts and that Indian prime minister Jawaharlal Nehru wanted to visit China. Mao thought that if Delhi and Rangoon advanced such proposals publicly it would be "inconvenient for us to refuse."[7] Stalin not only supported Mao's opinion but encouraged the PRC to take a strong leadership position in the upcoming Asia peace conference. Echoing what he had told Liu Shaoqi in 1949 when the two had agreed to the Sino-Soviet division of labor, Stalin told Zhou that, though the Soviet Union would also attend the conference, China should play "the principal role" at such an Asia-centered event.[8]

With Stalin willing to defer to China's priorities, Beijing strove to demonstrate its eagerness for peaceful engagement with its neighbors. Shortly after his return from Moscow, Zhou met with the Indian ambassador in Beijing and discussed the possibility of Nehru visiting the PRC.[9] Moreover, the CCP did everything that it could to publicize the Asia and Pacific Peace Conference, which was held in early October and drew representatives from thirty-seven countries. Throughout the conference, Beijing emphasized peaceful coexistence and the need to reduce tensions. Mao expressed hope that the conference would make "a huge contribution to the great common task of the people of the whole Asian region and even the whole world of protecting stability and peace."[10]

Although the CCP's foreign policy rhetoric had initially been bellicose and focused on the antinomy between imperialism and revolution, after 1953 Chinese officials emphasized that the "central contradiction" in international affairs was between "war and peace." In a report to his colleagues in the Ministry of Foreign Affairs, Zhou divided the world into two camps: one, led by the Soviet Union, strove for peace while the other, led by the United

States and its allies, wanted war. "As the strength of the Soviet Union and the other people's democratic countries grows," he contended, "the opposition between the peace movement and the pro-war camp has deepened." The premier depicted the PRC as a nation striving for peace with its neighbors while the United States sought military confrontation. "We call for the resolution of all international disputes through peaceful negotiations. Our opponents only insist on war to resolve them," Zhou explained. "The basis of our policy is peaceful coexistence and peaceful competition between countries with different systems." American militarism on the other hand was creating a growing fissure between Washington and the nations of Europe, Asia, the Middle East and North Africa. Eventually, Zhou confidently predicted, "not even a few countries would be left on America's side."[11]

Zhou sought to codify these ideas in December 1953 when an Indian delegation visited China to discuss an agreement that would govern trade along the Tibetan borderland. After Beijing occupied Tibet in 1951, long-standing trade patterns that routinely traversed the Sino-Indian border had persisted, and the two countries wanted to allow this trade to continue peacefully.[12] During these discussions Zhou put forward the Five Principles of Peaceful Coexistence as broad guidelines for relations among Asian countries. The principles were: respect for sovereignty and territorial borders; nonaggression; no interference in the internal affairs of other nations; equality and mutual benefit; and peaceful coexistence.[13] They served the evolving purposes of Chinese diplomacy brilliantly. The principles gave formal expression to some of the CCP's new ideas about diplomacy and provided a unifying concept that the PRC could use to gain support among newly independent Asian nations.

Zhou's efforts to win support for the Five Principles were boosted immeasurably by the egotism and ambition of his key partner in this effort, Jawaharlal Nehru. Delhi shared Beijing's interest in promoting the principles as an important new model for Asian relations. Nehru saw this as an opportunity to strengthen India's status even if it also meant raising the prestige of a potential rival. By the spring of 1954, Chinese and Indian leaders were working together to sell the rest of Asia on the Five Principles (which Nehru called Pancha Sila). They portrayed the principles as a momentous development in international politics while emphasizing that India and China were both nations with a long history of peaceful development and a deep influence on the rest of Asia. It therefore made sense that they would take the lead in establishing the organizing ideals to govern the continent during an era of rapid decolonization.

The growing accord between Beijing and Delhi was readily apparent when Zhou Enlai made his first visit to India in June 1954. The visit occurred during a brief interlude in the Geneva Conference when the premier responded to an invitation from the Indian president on relatively short notice. The two leaders did everything possible to play up the significance of the visit and ensure that it attracted the notice of other Asian countries. Before the visit Nehru stressed the world historical importance of the Chinese Revolution and the critical need for Sino-Indian cooperation. In a speech to the Indian Parliament roughly one month before Zhou's visit, Nehru called the revolution "the greatest event in history since World War II."[14] When the Chinese premier arrived in Delhi, he was greeted with a grand reception. The former president of India K. R. Narayanan recalled, "Wherever he went there were hundreds and thousands of people greeting the Chinese Premier shouting the slogan 'Hind-China Bhai Bhai' Indians and Chinese are brothers."[15] By treating Zhou as an important world statesman, Nehru helped to foster respect for the premier and raise China's standing in Asia while underscoring India's central role in bringing China into the international community.

Over his four days in India, Zhou held six meetings with Nehru. Throughout these meetings, the two leaders emphasized that the Five Principles represented a significant contribution to world peace and discussed the prospects for persuading other Asian nations to follow them. "As to making the part of Asia an area of peace, we would like to see the relationship existing between India and China to be prevalent in this area," Zhou explained while talking about South and Southeast Asia. He thought that if the "principles are applied to all States of Asia that would be very beneficial." Nehru agreed enthusiastically and predicted that the Five Principles would "gladly be accepted by these States," with Indonesia and Burma especially eager to adopt them. He suggested that Zhou visit Rangoon and make a declaration on the principles and then follow up with Djakarta.[16] To assure that the Five Principles became influential, the two leaders planned to seize every opportunity to promote them among other world leaders. As Nehru saw it, "The more we refer to those principles—and other countries too—the better it is."[17] Doubtless, some utilitarian considerations existed in both Beijing and Delhi. Nehru likely saw the Five Principles in part as a means of temporarily reducing the threat of Chinese expansion, whereas the PRC wanted to ensure that no other countries were drawn into an American-led alliance in the region.[18] Nevertheless, Zhou's visit to India was an important step toward establishing the Five Principles as guidelines for relations among Asian countries and recasting the global image of the PRC.

With Nehru's encouragement, Zhou held discussions with Burmese prime minister U Nu before returning to Geneva. The main purpose of the premier's trip to Rangoon was to gain another endorsement for the principles. He got U Nu on board by pledging to seek peaceful solutions to the major issues plaguing Sino-Burmese relations. He claimed that the two most pressing problems—border disputes and the status of Chinese living in Burma—were a result of the failure of the CCP's predecessor, the Guomindang, to address them. The premier promised that the PRC would work with Burma to resolve the border issues and mentioned that Beijing had been hammering out an agreement with Indonesia to resolve the questions of overseas Chinese citizenship and migration. Zhou expressed hope that the same framework being developed to govern the rights of Chinese living in Indonesia could be applied to other countries, including Burma.[19] At the end of the visit, U Nu joined Zhou and Nehru in endorsing the Five Principles of Peaceful Coexistence as a basis for relations among Asian states.[20] Once again Zhou had scored a significant victory with his diplomacy. Another neutral Asian country had received the premier and endorsed his principles, reducing the PRC's isolation and gaining it trust and recognition.

American officials were deeply worried about the impact of Zhou's charm offensive, especially in India, whose leadership they saw as naive. Briefly after the Zhou-Nehru meeting, the American embassy in Delhi cabled the State Department that the premier had received an "enthusiastic reception" as he sought to "charm Nehru into believing he has nothing to fear from China."[21] A report on American programs in India circulated by the Operations Coordinating Board (OCB) several months later was even more blunt. It claimed that Zhou had "apparently flattered the Indian leaders by allowing them to believe they were exerting some influence on his thinking."[22] The OCB determined to counter what it termed "the Indian tendency to accept at face value Communist countries' protestations of anti-colonialism" through a USIS campaign of press broadcasts, radio and film.[23]

Washington was initially less concerned about Burma, whose leaders convinced American officials that they harbored "no illusions re permanency [of the Zhou]-Nu statement." Rangoon made it clear that, above all, it wanted to be left alone and would zealously guard its domestic politics against interference from either Beijing or Washington. In discussions with American officials, Burmese leaders claimed that they had agreed to a joint statement with Zhou only because it could be used as propaganda against domestic insurgents who anticipated support from the CCP. At the same time, the Burmese government warned American officials that they should not "embarrass" Burma by "public[ly] associating Burma with American policies."[24] Eventually, however, both Burma and India would frustrate Washington's efforts to isolate China by continuing to pursue engagement with the Communist giant.

Nehru and U Nu helped Beijing to consolidate its diplomatic gains by agreeing to visit the PRC in the fall of 1954. When Nehru traveled to China in October, his sense of self-importance once again redounded to the PRC's benefit. The prime minister was just as intent on demonstrating the significance of the Five Principles and Sino-Indian entente as Beijing was, and he consistently played up the importance of the trip. In a press conference held briefly before his departure, Nehru explained why his trip was much more important than the Southeast Asia Treaty Organization (SEATO), which Washington had recently formed: "Numerous conferences like SEATO are being held here, there and everywhere. But these two great nations—India and China have lived for 10,000 years and want to do it another 10,000 years or more. The meeting, therefore, between the Prime Ministers of India and China is a very big thing itself and a world event."[25] Such pronouncements not only served Delhi's purposes but also helped Beijing by affirming new China's critical importance in world politics and drawing attention to its peace campaign. Beijing of course made its own efforts to play up Nehru's visit and the legitimacy it seemed to confer on the PRC. The Indian prime minister was greeted by cheering crowds, with as many as one million people lining the streets of Beijing. He later reported that the reception he received could be "compared only with the warm and loving reception that I am given in my own country."[26]

Several weeks after Nehru's visit, the PRC scored another diplomatic coup when it welcomed Burma's U Nu for a state visit. Chinese officials again seized the opportunity to promote the Five Principles and strengthen the PRC's standing among neutralist Asian countries. Zhou offered assurances about China's intentions. He agreed to a joint communiqué pledging that Beijing and Rangoon would encourage their foreign nationals to respect the laws and customs of their host countries, calming Burmese fears about overseas Chinese.[27] Zhou also offered to provide economic aid to U Nu's government with no conditions attached.[28] Although the visit did not resolve all of the outstanding issues between the two countries—boundary issues in particular remained unsettled—the Burmese delegation left China favorably impressed. In subsequent conversations with American diplomats they reported being "surprised at [the] air of prosperity in Shanghai," and the president of the Burmese Supreme Court announced that, after being received by the head of the Communist Chinese Supreme Court, he was "satisfied Chinese Communist Courts dealt out justice evenly so far as private parties were concerned."[29]

Zhou's high-level diplomacy with India and Burma and the introduction of the Five Principles were important early achievements of China's peace campaign. Two of the most influential neutral leaders in Asia strengthened Beijing's credibility and standing by entering into major agreements with China and supporting it on such key issues as UN representation. Chinese successes on this front irked the Eisenhower administration, which insisted that Asian countries reject dealings with the Communists and take sides. Zhou's meetings with U Nu and Nehru were merely the first step in a much broader effort to realign Chinese diplomacy and build the PRC's profile in Asia, however. Even as Zhou was touring India and Burma, this larger campaign was being put to a much more difficult test in Geneva, where the United States contested virtually every aspect of China's participation.

Geneva

The shift in Beijing's diplomacy in 1953–54 coincided with a fleeting moment of hope for peace in the early Cold War. Stalin's death in March 1953 was followed by turmoil behind the Iron Curtain. In June, Moscow marched troops into East Berlin to suppress a massive uprising against Walter Ubricht's Communist regime. Just days later, Laverntiy Beria, the first deputy prime minister and second most powerful figure in the Soviet government, was arrested and removed from his official posts. When the dust settled, the Soviet Union's new leader, Georgi Malenkov, declared that his country was committed to peace and the resolution of the German conflict.[30] The Eisenhower administration responded enthusiastically to Moscow's changed rhetoric. The most immediate result was a foreign ministers' conference in Berlin in January 1954. Attended by representatives of the United States, the Soviet Union, Great Britain, and France, the Berlin Conference was a venue for wide-ranging discussions on issues such as arms limitations and the future of Germany. The ministers failed to agree on most of these issues, but they still believed that Cold War frictions in Asia might be eased through subsequent negotiations. Before adjourning they announced that a conference in Geneva would be held to discuss the problems of Korea and Indochina.[31]

The United States was, from the outset, the least enthusiastic of the powers about holding the proposed conference on Asia and wanted to prevent the PRC from playing a significant role. As the four nations worked to set the agenda for the conference, tensions flared between the Soviet Union and the United States over Chinese participation. The meeting in Berlin coincided with what might be considered the heyday of the Sino-Soviet alliance, and the Soviet foreign minister Vyacheslav Molotov labored to ensure that its ally would have a voice in deciding critical issues. He initially proposed a five-power conference to discuss "world problems," but the United States said that it "would have nothing to do with any conference including Communist China except as it related to the specific problems of a settlement in Korea and Indochina."[32] Dulles even questioned the legitimacy of holding a "five-power conference," given Beijing's official UN status. Molotov, of course, sharply disagreed. He insisted that "it was just as legitimate [to] hold [a] five-power conference as [the] present four-power meeting." He argued that the PRC was "a great power" and warned that those "failing to recognize this may find themselves in [a] difficult position."[33]

In the testy exchanges that ensued between Molotov and Dulles, the Russian minister insisted that China deserved to be treated as an important power while the secretary of state continued seeking to deny PRC recognition. Molotov complained that America's policy toward China was "dominated by emotion" and ignored "facts and the knowledge of what future prospects were." He thought that America's refusal to recognize Beijing might be understandable "if China was a small country or if there was any chance of the Government being replaced," but in fact the PRC was "the largest and most powerful country in all of Asia." Dulles responded curtly that American policy toward China was based on the simple precept that "one does not strengthen one's enemy by giving him increased authority or prestige, or any other sort of help."[34] He insisted that the Geneva Conference focus on specific issues and confer no new recognition or status on Beijing.

Owing in large part to American insistence, Molotov's original idea for a wide-ranging five-power conference was restricted to a more specific proposal to settle disputes over Korea and Indochina. The American delegation attempted to undermine even this narrower agenda, however, because it worried about any conference that invited the PRC as a participant. Dulles put particular pressure on the French, who still depended on American assistance for the war in Indochina. He instructed one member of the American delegation to "get word to the French that if they accepted a five-power conference on Southeast Asia and Indochina, they should bear in mind that the question of whether the United States could participate in such a conference was extremely dubious." Americans feared that if Paris involved itself in such negotiations, there would be an "adverse effect on the morale and will of the three Associated states [of Indochina] and their peoples." Such a development, they warned, "would be a cause for grave concern to the United States, which was pouring hundreds of millions of dollars of treasure and resources into the war."[35] Ultimately, however, Americans realized that, as the position of French forces in Indochina was declining, it would be difficult to prevent their ally from participating.[36]

In February, the four delegations meeting in Berlin finally agreed that the conference's two key objectives would be to unify the Korean peninsula and restore peace in Indochina. The United States, the Soviet Union, the People's Republic of China, Great Britain, and France were the only countries that would be represented at both the "Korea" and "Indochina" sessions. The two Koreas as well as the other countries that had fought in the Korean War were allowed to attend the first session, while the DRV and other "interested states" such as Laos and Cambodia were also scheduled to attend the latter session.[37]

Even after the Americans reconciled themselves to Beijing's presence in Geneva, they still sought to make sure the conference would not strengthen the CCP's international position or deepen its influence over neighboring Asian countries. If China did get to participate, Washington tried to make sure it would do so in a chastened mood rather than with an emboldened outlook. When the four powers in Berlin drew up the resolution to hold the conference, the American delegation initially lobbied for a clause stipulating that the Chinese Communists must give proof of their "spirit of peace" if they were to be allowed to join the talks in Geneva. Ultimately, Washington abandoned this proposal in an effort to be conciliatory toward Paris and Moscow.[38] Nevertheless, Washington would not forsake its broader effort to deny China equal standing at the conference by imposing special limitations on its participation.

Dulles stated plainly that during the actual conference, the United States would do everything that it could to diminish and isolate China. He explained that in Geneva, "the United States Government would not sit down with the Chinese Communist government except in those instances where there was a concrete case where the Chinese Communists because of their actual position must be dealt with." Moreover, Dulles emphasized, the United States "would only sit down with the Chinese Communists on the basis of a clear understanding that such discussions did not constitute recognition of the Chinese Communist regime."[39] Although Washington reluctantly agreed to send a delegation to Geneva, it determined long before dispatching its representatives that it would try to prevent the conference from becoming a significant international event.

Despite American churlishness, Beijing still looked at Geneva as a golden opportunity. Having been barred from the United Nations and most other international organizations since its founding, the PRC viewed the conference as a sort of coming-out party, and CCP leaders were not going to let the American imperialists spoil their fun. In contrast to Washington, which tended to paint the conference as a stillborn failure before it even started, Chinese leaders enthusiastically promoted Geneva as a critical opportunity to resolve difficult international issues. Beijing attached particular importance to its own participation; it viewed the conference as a venue to showcase the diplomatic skills of its leaders and broaden its interactions with other Asian nations.

In the run-up to Geneva, Zhou Enlai made the case for the conference's importance both at home and abroad. In February he prepared the Foreign Ministry's "Preliminary Opinions on the Assessment of and Preparation for the Geneva Conference," which was approved by the CCP Central Secretariat in early March. The premier wrote that the "People's Republic of China's participation in the conference alone has already marked a big step toward relaxing international tensions and therefore has won widespread support by peace-loving peoples and countries all over the world." China's policy, Zhou explained, would be one of "actively participating in the Geneva Conference" and "enhancing diplomatic and international activities." It was hoped that such a strategy would serve to "undermine the policy of blockade embargo and expanding armaments and war preparations by the U.S. imperialists" and promote "the relaxation of the tense international situation." The document also lambasted the United States and its allies for seeking to assure that the conference would fail. Zhou complained that "the bloc of imperialist aggressors and the U.S. government in particular, has been intentionally underestimating the significance of the Geneva Conference and predicting that it . . . will not achieve any result."[40]

Although Zhou's harsh criticisms of the United States may at first seem like standard Chinese Communist rhetoric, in reality they were not far off the mark. Washington, in fact, had little interest in seeing the conference succeed. This was especially true in the period immediately preceding the conference when France had yet to suffer its humiliating defeat at Dien Bien Phu and Americans still hoped that U.S. military assistance would be enough to defeat the Vietminh. One memo on U.S. policy explained that Secretary of State Dulles viewed the conference as "a holding action in order to provide time for the French to ratify the EDC [European Defense Community] and to permit a favorable military build-up and execution of the Navarre Plan." The United States was therefore not interested in approaching Britain and France so that it could settle procedural questions in advance but, at the time, was looking merely to "obtain the views" of those governments.[41] Going into Geneva, Americans were hoping to reverse the situation on the battlefield and nullify the conference's efforts to achieve peace through negotiation.

Despite America's efforts to diminish the conference, CCP officials devoted much time to preparing for what they envisioned as China's dramatic entrance onto the stage of international diplomacy. In February and March, Zhou's background reading included intelligence reports and exchanges between Washington and Moscow.[42] Other key CCP officials gathered information or talked with allies to prepare Beijing for the conference. Zhang Wentian, the PRC ambassador in Moscow, sought Soviet help in making sure that the Chinese delegation acquitted itself well in Geneva. In a conversation with Foreign Minister Molotov, he explained that his country was "intent on taking an active part in the Geneva Conference" and requested that "a competent USSR foreign ministry specialist be selected" to help the Chinese by "sharing experience in the organizational work of international conferences, the methods and techniques of bourgeois representatives, etc."[43]

As the conference approached, Beijing and Washington leaned on their allies to support their positions. American officials wanted to make sure that their North Atlantic Treaty Organization (NATO) partners—especially the French—remained firm and did not create opportunities for the PRC to expand its influence. In late March, Secretary of State Dulles wrote the American ambassador in France that "he was seriously concerned by what appear to be growing expectations in France that Geneva will produce a settlement for Indochina as a result of U.S. concessions to Communist China." Dulles reiterated that there was in fact "no possibility whatsoever of concessions by U.S. to Communist China." He instructed the ambassador to "lose no effective opportunity to make the foregoing points forcefully with French leaders and particularly those who show signs of wavering." The secretary also asked for the text of a speech that he made on "The Threat of Red Asia" to be distributed and "discreetly emphasized in France."[44] Washington hoped that by firming up support for its agenda among allies it could ensure that they took a hard line with the Chinese.

While Americans encouraged their allies to be rigid and unyielding in Geneva, the Chinese urged their allies to be flexible so that the conference could succeed. Chinese leaders recognized that cooperation between the CCP and the Democratic Republic of Vietnam (DRV) would be critical for any compromise on Indochina. In the month before the conference, Chinese leaders attempted to make sure that their Vietnamese allies approached the conference with the right frame of mind. In mid-March, Zhou Enlai sent a telegram to Ho Chi Minh explaining that, "regardless of the results, we should all participate enthusiastically in the Geneva Conference." The premier even encouraged Ho to make such preparations as gathering relevant materials and drafting proposals for discussion.[45] At the end of March, the DRV leader visited Beijing to discuss the issue.[46] By coordinating strategy with its allies, the PRC also likely hoped that it would be able to negotiate more effectively when the time came.

The United States and China remained committed to these competing objectives when the conference opened. The State Department continued seeking to isolate China and diminish the conference. Secretary of State Dulles himself did not stay in Geneva long. After sitting through several meetings with his "mouth drawn down at the corners, and his eyes on the ceiling, sucking his teeth," the secretary simply took off and left most of the negotiating to Under Secretary Walter Bedell Smith.[47] Dulles's behavior was undoubtedly his way of demonstrating American indifference toward the entire enterprise. Before he left, he instructed Smith to have as little as possible to do with the PRC: "You will not deal with the delegates of the Chinese Communist regime, or any other regime not now diplomatically recognized by the United States, on any terms which imply political recognition or which concede to that regime any status other than that of a regime with which it is necessary to deal on a de facto basis in order to end aggression or the threat of aggression, and to obtain peace."[48] Through their icy treatment of the Chinese delegates, Americans at the conference literally embodied the United States' larger effort to exclude the PRC from the realm of international diplomacy.

Zhou Enlai countered by continuously asserting China's legitimacy. In one conversation with Zhou, Anthony Eden, the British deputy undersecretary of foreign affairs, slipped and referred to the "four great powers" before correcting himself and speaking of the "five great powers" in which he included China. Nevertheless, Zhou eagerly pounced on the opportunity to assert that "China deserves the status of great power. This is an existing fact."[49] CCP officials also strove to sew mistrust between Washington and its allies by demonstrating that the PRC wanted the conference to be a success and the United States did not. Discussing Korea with a member of the French delegation, Wang Bingnan, a PRC Foreign Ministry official, insisted that "we only want the conference to be successful, and we do not want it to fail." On the other hand, it was obvious that the Americans attitude was "the opposite" of China's.[50] Zhou and his colleagues were keen to prove that they could be both strong and conciliatory while conducting diplomacy in a highly professional manner. They thus worked to dispel American accusations that the CCP was fanatical and committed to war while paving the way for China to play a more influential role in Asia.

Accounts written by some of the conferences attendees testify to Zhou's grace and skill when meeting with his peers. One memo written by the Australian representative in Geneva, Richard Gardiner Casey, recorded that "[Zhou] has quite a face, is about of middle height and with a good-looking eye. . . . He uses his hands a good deal in conversation. He made certain gestures from time to time, at each of which a Chinese servant in a smart white jacket appeared from nowhere with a tray of rather tart China tea, of which I felt myself obliged to drink many cups."[51] Other diplomats at the conference were impressed in similar ways by Zhou's confident demeanor. One British memo recorded that Zhou "had given the impression that he was very much the father of all of Asia and that it was his task to arrange matters accordingly."[52] Whatever their political disagreements with Zhou, many who met him could not but admire his professionalism. Of course, etiquette alone does not win arguments. Nevertheless, Zhou's manner, combined with his genuine interest in making sure the conference succeeded, discredited American depictions of the PRC, making it easier for Washington's allies to negotiate and ultimately strengthen China's input into the settlement.

The Geneva Conference itself was divided into two phases. Neither Beijing nor Washington had high expectations for the first phase, which sought a permanent settlement for the Korean peninsula. Dulles had already concluded during the Berlin Conference that it was "very unlikely" that it would "achieve a free and independent Korea."[53] In this rare instance the CCP agreed that Washington was correct. Having spent months in protracted armistice negotiations with the United States over the fate of the peninsula, the Chinese knew firsthand how difficult it would be to get the parties to come to an agreement. Zhou showed little surprise when the negotiations over Korea became deadlocked on 28 April—just two days after they had begun.[54] As could have been expected, the delegations attending the Korea session did not reach any agreed positions and did not even vote on any proposals.[55]

The session on Indochina appeared much more promising. Two critical developments in the ongoing conflict between Indochina and France greatly strengthened China's hand. The first occurred on 8 May, when Vietminh forces captured Dien Bien Phu. The second occurred on 12 June, when the French parliament turned out Prime Minister Joseph Laniel and replaced him with longtime critic of the war in Indochina Pierre Mendes-France.[56] CCP leaders saw an opportunity not only to strengthen their influence in the area but also to drive a wedge between Washington and Paris. Even as they sensed opportunity at Geneva, however, the Chinese were deeply worried that the United States would be able to draw Cambodia and Laos into a collective security arrangement directed against the PRC. Zhou proved willing to compromise with the Europeans on Vietnam in order to prevent Washington from enlisting Phnom Penh and Vientiane in what would eventually come to be known as SEATO.

Zhou's diplomacy at the conference during the crucial weeks of June 1954 amounted to an almost virtuoso performance. He moved back and forth between the European and Asian delegations exploring possible compromises and testing the limits of what each side could accept. The premier vied to convince all in attendance that the PRC was genuinely committed to achieving peace in Indochina, whereas the United States continued to harbor aggressive intentions. He did much to shape the final form of the Geneva Accords, making sure that the agreement protected China's security and limited American opportunities for expansion.

As he labored to broker an agreement that was acceptable to all parties, Zhou concentrated on two interrelated tasks. First, he worked to narrow the areas of disagreement between the Communist camp and America's allies. Second, he strove to convince the Vietminh that compromise was necessary to reach agreement. China's allies in the DRV were often more uncompromising than Beijing when it came to their nation's future. Zhou felt obliged to educate them about the complexities of the international situation. As they carried out this game of high-stakes diplomacy, CCP officials always strove to make the PRC indispensable to the conference's success.

Negotiations with London and Paris intensified after Mendes-France assumed the post of prime minister. Zhou quickly set up a meeting with the new head of the French government. On 23 June, the two held a frank exchange about their objectives and concerns regarding Indochina. The premier made it clear that an agreement needed to place constraints on U.S. actions in the region. He explained that "we don't want to see that these three countries [Laos, Cambodia, and Vietnam] become military bases of the United States or that the United States builds up a military pact with them." If America insisted on establishing a military base in the region, Zhou warned, "we have to check it out, and we can't just let it go without checking."[57] In later meetings, Zhou advocated the neutralization of Laos and Cambodia and sought to prevent them from joining a formal alliance with Washington. He raised the issue of American plans to set up a defense pact that would include Laos and Cambodia with both Mendes-France and Eden. If Washington formed such a pact, Zhou warned, "then peace would have no meaning other than the preparation for new hostilities."[58]

Even as Zhou remained vigilant against any U.S. effort to establish bases or alliances in Indochina, he demonstrated his willingness to compromise in order to achieve peace. In July he traveled to Liuzhou, a city in south-central China not far from the Sino-Vietnamese border, to discuss the conference proceedings with Ho Chi Minh and other DRV leaders. During these meetings, Zhou pressured his Vietminh comrades to compromise so that the conference would be a success. Once again, the United States figured prominently in the premier's arguments. He told his Vietnamese allies that they needed to be careful not to ask for too much in Geneva. If peace was not achieved, then it was "certain that the U.S. will intervene providing Cambodia, Laos and Bao Dai with weapons and ammunition, helping them train military personnel, and establishing military bases there." Only through diplomacy, Zhou believed, could the Communist camp "isolate the United States and break up its plans."[59] By the time Zhou returned to Geneva he had persuaded the DRV to go along with the PRC's plans for a compromise on several key issues, including the temporary division of Vietnam into separate zones controlled by the French and the Vietminh.

While China pushed its allies and the Europeans to compromise, the United States urged its NATO partners to stand firm. Much as the premier suspected, the Eisenhower administration did have plans to incorporate Cambodia and Laos into the future SEATO and was reluctant to be party to any agreement that would make this impossible. In mid-June, as Zhou was moving back and forth between European and Asian delegations, Dulles cabled the American representatives in Geneva that they should try to avoid surrendering on this point. He considered it "important that neither we nor other friendly delegations give any impression of agreement which would exclude possibility of bringing Laos and Cambodia into some collective security system in Southeast Asia or if this should be done making the military arrangements implicit in any such relationship."[60] The secretary fumed at London and Paris as the two moved toward compromising with Beijing on the neutralization of Laos and Cambodia in early July. When the French government asked him to return to Geneva to oversee the final part of the Indochina phase of the conference, Dulles declined, complaining that London and Paris were intent on concluding an armistice agreement "on terms substantially less favorable than those we could respect." He was disappointed because the two seemed willing to agree to "neutralizing and demilitarizing Laos, Cambodia and Vietnam so as to impair their capacity to maintain stable, non-Communist regimes."[61]

Washington opposed the neutralization of Laos and Cambodia so adamantly because it feared that this would ultimately mean opening them up to Chinese control. Even when the Communists took pains to show that they were being flexible, Americans remained suspicious. During one meeting with Molotov, Walter Bedell Smith noted that in some recent conversations Zhou "had taken an apparently reasonable view on Laos and Cambodia" by agreeing to recognize those states as long as they were not used as military bases by the United States. Nevertheless, Smith emphasized that "if we kept out the Chinese would have to keep out" and that the two new states "would have to be allowed to join whatever regional security arrangements would best protect their integrity." Americans, he explained, "wanted to be sure that these countries were not handed over to the Chinese." After the meeting, Smith worried privately that the Communists wanted to "get all they can in Laos now." Only the threat of U.S. intervention would "stop them from going ahead with their plans for taking all of it eventually through military conquest, French capitulation, or infiltration."[62] From the American perspective, the Chinese were really just using neutralization to promote their own objectives. They concluded that any agreement that improved Beijing's position in Laos and Cambodia wasn't worth signing.

But the United States was ultimately the odd man out at Geneva. France was eager to reach a compromise to extricate itself from Indochina, and the PRC believed that if it played a prominent role in achieving a settlement, it would strengthen its standing in Asia. Under these circumstances China was able to find common ground with Washington's allies while the United States remained at best aloof from and at worst hostile to the negotiations. On 20–21 July, the assembled delegates finally produced the Geneva Accords. Zhou had been highly influential in hammering out the final terms of these agreements. He had pressured the Vietminh to agree to the division of Vietnam along the seventeenth parallel and to acknowledge the presence of its forces in Laos and Cambodia.[63] By doing so he paved the way for the final agreements, which stipulated that Vietnam be divided into two zones, one governed by the Vietminh and the other by the French-supported Bao Dai. The Geneva Accords also contained provisions designed to protect the sovereignty and neutrality of Cambodia and Laos. All foreign troops were to be withdrawn from the two countries, and both were prohibited from entering alliances or allowing foreign troops on their soil.[64]

Chinese and American reactions to the Geneva Accords were diametrically opposed. Zhou Enlai viewed the agreements as a triumph for China's peace campaign. The PRC had agreed to accept a divided Vietnam and, in some instances, to sacrifice the interest of its revolutionary allies in Indochina, but it was ultimately willing to make compromises to ensure that the conference succeeded. In August, the premier reported on the Geneva Conference at a Central People's Government Committee meeting. He proudly explained, "During the time of the Geneva Conference the achievement of China's peaceful diplomacy was to move the tense international situation one step toward relaxation." Now China would have the responsibility to "make an effort along with the other participating countries to guarantee and thoroughly implement the various agreements to restore peace in Indochina."[65] For the PRC, contributing to a major peace agreement and assuming new responsibilities for preserving peace in Asia represented a significant accomplishment that conferred greater status.

Moscow also hailed the Geneva Conference as a major victory for their Chinese comrades. One protocol produced by the Communist Party Central Committee Plenum reported that at the conference "the People's Republic of China has finally taken its rightful place as one of the five great powers." It noted that China had "stepped out into the international arena with a consistently democratic position and, moreover, with unprecedented authority." Moscow ultimately deemed Beijing's successful diplomacy at the conference as "a victory for the entire democratic camp, headed by the Soviet Union."[66] It is quite possible that, privately, some Soviet officials viewed the leadership shown by the CCP in Geneva as a cause for concern as well as pride. Yet none could deny that the conference had been a stunning success for the Chinese.

Washington, of course, took a much dimmer view of what had happened at Geneva and was determined to limit the global impact of the conference. The Eisenhower administration refused to sign the Geneva Accords and instead issued a vaguely worded statement congratulating the parties for reaching an agreement but denying that the United States had an obligation to abide by its terms. The president explained that America's role in Geneva was "to be helpful where desired and to aid France, and Cambodia, Laos and Vietnam to obtain a just and honorable settlement." According to Eisenhower, the United States had "not been party to or bound by the decisions taken by the Conference," but it would "not use force to disturb the settlement."[67] Eisenhower wanted to maintain enough flexibility to guard against PRC encroachment in Southeast Asia while not appearing to discount completely the will of its allies.

The United States remained keen to prevent China from parlaying its role in the conference into a more permanent position of leadership in Asia. Walter Bedell Smith reported that the notion that the PRC had "combined the 'forces of peace'" was a strain that ran through nearly all Communist rhetoric at Geneva. In fact, the Communists had often attempted to represent peace as their "private property." According to Smith, "Not only [the] weakness of this argument but also the affrontery [sic] of it should be obvious." The Americans hoped that France, which the CCP often rhetorically included in its "forces of peace," would help to "rebut this premise." At the same time, the United States needed to "pick up everything . . . which helps knock down that inadmissible although not by any means new, Communist reasoning."[68] Smith predicted that a robust American presence in Asia would pressure the Chinese into abandoning its facade of goodwill toward its neighbors. He wrote that Zhou had seemed "most concerned over U.S. activities in Asia" and argued that "the more active we are, on all fronts, . . . the more anxious we can make him."[69] Provoking Chinese anxieties, Americans hoped, might elicit angry, impulsive actions and rhetoric that would discredit Beijing's claims to be contributing to regional peace.

For Beijing, Zhou's diplomacy at Geneva no doubt demonstrated what could be achieved through demonstrating moderation and playing up the PRC's commitment to peace. But the CCP leadership was also convinced that the United States would by no means sit back and allow the PRC to strengthen its standing. Several days after the accords were signed, the CCP Central Committee sent a telegram to Zhou "concerning policies and measures in the struggle against the United States and Jiang Jieshi after the Geneva Conference." The Central Committee predicted that the United States would be "unwilling to accept its failure at the Geneva Conference, and will inevitably continue to carry out a policy of creating international tension for the purpose of taking over more spheres of influence from Britain and France, of expanding military bases for preparing for war, and remaining hostile to our Organization of Defense and rearming Japan." The United States, it forecast, would also use Taiwan "to carry out pirate-style robberies of ships" bound for China from other Asian countries. Even worse, Washington was considering a mutual defense treaty with Taiwan, which had the potential to "make things tense for a long period." In this context, China's main goals would be "break up the U.S.-Jiang treaty of defense and the Southeast Asian treaty of defense."[70] Beijing embraced the idea that the best way to counter American efforts to stir up tensions was to persuade other Asian nations that it was sincere when it talked about peaceful coexistence. By the time the Geneva Conference ended, a unique opportunity to do this was already on the horizon. A number of newly independent Asian nations had begun discussing the possibility of holding a grand conference of Afro-Asian nations, and China was intent on playing a major role in the proceedings.

Beijing, Washington, and the Bandung Conference

Hosted by Indonesian president Sukarno in April 1955, the Bandung Conference was a critical event in the history of the Cold War. At Bandung, twenty-nine nations and colonies convened to promote cooperation among Afro-Asian peoples, marking the first time that so many leaders from postcolonial societies gathered to discuss common problems and goals. By banding together, they hoped to strengthen the influence of Afro-Asian countries in world politics and avoid further entanglement in Cold War rivalries.[71] The conference would prove a stunning triumph for Zhou Enlai's diplomacy. Zhou captured the attention of other delegations with his tact and composure and paved the way for broader contacts between the PRC and Afro-Asian countries.

It was Indonesian prime minister Ali Sastroamidjojo who first called for a conference of Afro-Asian nations to promote anticolonial solidarity and discuss common problems. Ali's idea received an initial hearing at the Colombo Meeting in April 1954. The other four countries in attendance—India, Burma, Ceylon, and Pakistan—did not immediately become strong supporters of Ali's proposal, but their attitudes changed over the next few months.[72] Nehru, for several reasons, reversed his initial ambivalence and became a strong proponent. The Indian prime minister viewed the creation of SEATO in September 1954 as a worrisome development and came to believe that an Afro-Asian Conference might shift regional politics away from Cold War rivalries.[73] Sino-Indian entente also played a role in Nehru's decision-making. Having formally announced the Five Principles after Zhou Enlai's June visit, he now saw an Afro-Asian conference as a venue where they could be promoted.[74]

Beijing realized that an Afro-Asian conference would present an opportunity to showcase its diplomacy and therefore monitored discussions among the Colombo countries closely in the months before the conference was announced. At the same time, it waited expectantly for an invitation.

The Foreign Ministry's Asia Department reported in December: "If we can strive for participation and enthusiastically employ our influence within and without the conference; strive to have the Five Principles of Peaceful Coexistence as the political foundation of the Afro-Asian conference; then the Afro-Asian conference can be pushed toward a direction beneficial to peace."[75] When Nehru and U Nu visited the PRC in late 1954, CCP officials lobbied for China's inclusion in the conference. Zhou told Nehru that Beijing was "willing to participate in the conference because the purpose of the conference is peace in Asia and Africa and peace in the world."[76] Mao brought up the issue with U Nu in December. "We feel a great interest in the Afro-Asian conference," he told the Burmese leader, and promised that if China attended, it would work for regional peace.[77] Encouraged by their interactions with Zhou, Nehru and U Nu both became strong supporters of China's inclusion. "I feel that it would be out of the question for us to leave out China," Nehru explained in a note. "It would also be a little absurd for Asian countries to meet and the biggest Asian country to be left out."[78] Given Nehru's view, it is not surprising that the PRC was on the list of invitees set at the Bogor Conference in December 1954. Beijing received an invitation on 15 January and sent a letter to Prime Minister Sastroamidjojo accepting on 10 February.[79]

The Afro-Asian Conference aroused suspicions in the Eisenhower administration, and the PRC's invitation was especially troubling. On 31 December, Secretary of State Dulles sent a circular telegram to American consular offices in more than twenty countries expressing his apprehensions. Dulles worried that "Chinese Communist[s] would utilize [the] conference as [a] sounding board for propaganda and might succeed in creating appearance of unity between Communist and non-Communist Asian and African states and appearance of division between Asian and African non-Communist states and the West." Doubtless remembering Zhou Enlai's highly adept performance in Geneva just a few months earlier, the secretary also warned that Zhou would likely exhibit a "formidable capacity for dominating [the] conference and utilizing others for own ends."[80]

American intelligence reports filed in late January echoed Dulles's concerns. The Office of Intelligence Research (OIR) noted that in the wake of the Geneva Conference the PRC had decided to "pursue world recognition more actively . . . and consider seriously opportunities outside Asia to play upon colonial problems."[81] The OIR added that, at Bandung, Zhou and his cohort would likely "miss no opportunities to turn conference emotions against the U.S. and to present subtly its own case as a leader and liberator of colonial peoples."[82] For American policy makers, this raised the prospect not only that Communist China would expand its influence but that the entire postcolonial world would grow more hostile toward the United States.

Months before the conference got under way, China and the United States were already strategizing about how to handle it. For Washington, whose very notion of a world divided into Free and Communist zones the conference was intended to question, this task posed a daunting challenge. Nevertheless, American officials wanted to do all that they could to prevent Beijing from turning Bandung into a soapbox for its criticisms of the United States. Although China had scored a minor victory simply by garnering an invitation, CCP leaders recognized that they too would face some obstacles at Bandung. One Chinese Foreign Ministry report estimated that of "the invited countries, four-fifths have not established diplomatic relations with us" and some had "diplomatic relations with the Jiang [Jieshi] bandits." Moreover, the "traditional biases" of some Afro-Asian peoples would require the PRC to "make great reverses."[83] Nevertheless, China was determined to use the conference to build new relationships. In the three months before the conference began, both Beijing and Washington considered the best methods for shaping the tone of the conference, with each eager to make sure that its own view prevailed.

Zhou Enlai doubtless recognized that he would need another virtuoso performance for Beijing to achieve its objectives. The PRC Foreign Ministry made extensive preparations during the weeks before the premier and his team departed, drafting detailed reports on several key issues. From the outset these reports argued that China should "work hard to win over the 'peaceful and neutral' countries and attempt to divide the countries that follow the United States and are hostile to us."[84] These objectives were elaborated in a draft proposal for attending the conference that Premier Zhou presented to all members of the Political Bureau of the CCP Central Committee for study on 4 April.[85] By that time, Mao had announced that Zhou would lead the delegation to Bandung and be accompanied by Vice Premier Chen Yi and the diplomat Huang Hua among others.[86]

The proposal began by praising some of the prior achievements of China's peace offensive, noting that the "Sino-Indian and Sino-Burmese joint declarations are exerting a great influence upon the Asian region." At the same time, however, it warned that the United States continued to threaten China and sought to undermine the conference. The proposal accused the United States of "organizing an invasive bloc, trying to strengthen its control over Afro-Asian countries and preparing for a new war." Moreover, it reported, Washington intended "to sabotage the conference through the use of servile countries." Nevertheless, most of the countries slated to attend shared the "common wishes of seeking peace, independence, economic and cultural development." The Foreign Ministry believed that "for this reason we have conditions beneficial to our work of expanding the forces of peace in the Afro-Asian region and even the whole world."[87] Chinese leaders were confident that by deploying the rhetoric of peaceful coexistence as they had done at Geneva they would again be able to counter American efforts to isolate them.

Cultivating an image of a new China that was genuinely committed to peace was to be the focal point of Premier Zhou's activities. "Our direction at the Afro-Asian conference," the draft proposal stated, "should be attempting to expand the united front of peace, and stimulate movements of national liberation." In Bandung, China would "strive to have more countries of the Afro-Asian region accept the Five Principles and thus expand the peace zone."[88] Through enshrining the Five Principles as a basis for peace and solidarity, Chinese diplomats also aimed to establish a special role for the PRC as the nation whose ideas had engendered a new regional order.

The PRC was keenly aware that not all of the delegations attending the conference would be equally receptive to its persuasions. The Foreign Ministry divided the other nations attending Bandung into four groups: "peaceful and neutral countries" such as India and Burma; "countries close to peaceful and neutral" such as Egypt, Sudan, Cambodia, and Laos; "countries close to opposition to peace and neutrality" such as Japan, South Vietnam, and Iran; and finally "countries that oppose peace and neutrality," which included Thailand, Turkey, and the Philippines. The Foreign Ministry's plan called for efforts to "unify" countries in the first group, "win over" those in the second, "influence" those in the third, and "isolate" America's allies in the fourth group. It would achieve this by making contacts with the different delegations outside of the conference. These contacts would afford opportunities to "explain our positions and attempt to solve some specific issues."[89] By approaching neutralist countries that were not overtly hostile, CCP officials aimed to convince other Afro-Asian nations to recognize the PRC and establish basic trade and cultural relations with it. Ultimately, this could enhance China's legitimacy and advance its peace campaign.

Zhou's delegation was also to take advantage of the content, purpose, and tone of the conference to criticize the United States. With such issues as imperialism and racism on the docket, the CCP anticipated that Washington would be highly vulnerable. In discussion of colonialism, for instance, the Foreign Ministry recommended that the delegation "oppose all forms of colonialism and have the United States as the main target." By pointing out "the imperialistic nature of military blocs, military alliances, policies of embargo and disruption, etc.," the PRC could channel the anti-imperialist discourse that was bound to be salient at Bandung into a penetrating critique of U.S. policy in Asia.[90] On 4 April, Zhou Enlai presented these reports for formal discussion and approval at a meeting of the Political Bureau of the CCP Central Committee. When the premier's plans were approved on 6 April, the agenda was set.[91]

As CCP leaders prepared assiduously for the conference, the Eisenhower administration concentrated on limiting any gains that Beijing might make. In February the Operations Coordinating Board (OCB) assembled a special working group, which drew up a series of working papers describing the objectives of both the United States and the PRC at Bandung. The OCB believed that Beijing's main goals would be to gain prestige and influence and to seek a propaganda advantage. On both of these points, it argued, "Chinese Communist and U.S. interests run counter to each other." One OCB working paper predicted, "The ChiComs can be expected to make statements or speeches designed to embarrass the U.S. or its friends." It argued that the United States "should be prepared not only to meet these, but also take the initiative on them." Washington would try to use the PRC's calls for peace against it; for instance, the United States could "embrace the 'Five Principles' . . . and show how the ChiComs have violated them."[92]

The Eisenhower administration seized on a Manila Pact meeting held in Bangkok in late February to discuss American concerns about Bandung. The Afro-Asian Conference Working Group prepared a special briefing paper for Secretary of State Dulles with a list of points that he might raise with America's allies during the meeting. It claimed that even though Washington did "not regard the Bandung Conference as of direct concern," it realized that the United States would likely be "the target of the Chinese Communists at the Conference." Dulles should also mention that it was "in the interests of all of the non-Communist nations represented at the Bandung Conference to do everything possible to frustrate the efforts of the Chinese Communists" and not allow Bandung to become a tool for undermining "the resistance of non-Communist Asia to Communist subversion and aggression."[93]

Seeking to reinforce the secretary's activities in Bangkok, the State Department prepared instructions for the American missions in friendly countries that would be attending the conference. Washington remained fixated on the possibility that Beijing would exploit the conference for its own ends. Acting Secretary of State Herbert Hoover Jr. warned, "Chinese Communists may be expected [to] exert disproportionate influence and make every effort [to] utilize [the] Conference [to] enhance [its] own prestige and discredit U.S. and its allies in [the] eyes [of] Asian-African nations." Beijing would also seek to "create [a] psychology which would make it difficult for Asian-African countries, particularly those under Communist threat, [to] accept essential aid from [the] U.S." To undermine the CCP's plan, the State Department provided a list of useful points that American allies might bring up. These included "unmistakable Communist aggression in Korea," "slave labor" in Communist China and the Soviet Union, and the PRC's belligerent actions in the Taiwan Strait.[94]

The Afro-Asian working group also prepared briefing papers to supply U.S. allies with intellectual ammunition that they could use to attack China. The State Department was particularly eager to turn the issue of colonialism—which it recognized would be a central theme of the conference—against Moscow and Beijing. It pointed to Communist expansion in Europe and Asia as a manifestation of neocolonialism and argued that the PRC and USSR were imperial powers. A paper entitled "The Chinese Communist Empire: [Beijing]'s New Imperialism" explained this idea. It contended that "the leading colonial and imperial powers in Asia today are the USSR and Communist China." Under CCP rule "minorities have been brought forcefully under the yoke of the imperial power, local cultures have been subverted, and claims have been levied against territory to which the regime does not have juridical rights."[95] Americans hoped that their allies in Asia, such as Turkey and the Philippines, would use these points at Bandung to prevent the PRC from promoting itself as a champion of anticolonial movements.

Although they were troubled by American scheming, CCP officials believed that U.S. activities could be successfully countered with the right strategy. The Foreign Ministry noted that many Afro-Asian nations remained suspicious of American aid and the "slave-like" conditions attached to it. At the same time, it was "impossible" that China's "achievements in economic development would have no influence and attraction for these countries." The CCP hoped that by maintaining its emphasis on peace and cooperation in the economic realm, it could find new trading partners and isolate the United States. The Foreign Ministry recommended that China's trade activities at the conference mirror its larger diplomatic campaign. The PRC should seek to "establish as well as develop our country's equal and cooperative relationship with various Afro-Asian countries on economic and trade matters" while opposing "the forceful addition of trade restrictions and regulations by American imperialists."[96] The purpose of this approach was to forge a new sphere of Afro-Asian economic cooperation in which American intervention would be limited and the PRC could play a significant role.

When the date for the conference finally arrived on 18 April, controversy and tensions continued to swirl around China's participation. As delegations assembled in Bandung, Chinese artillery cannons were shelling Jinmen and Mazu, two offshore islands that had remained under Taipei's control. Beijing had initiated the shelling in September 1954 in the hopes of calling attention to America's continuing military presence in Asia and mobilizing domestic support for socialist reconstruction at home.[97] But China's actions seemed to contradict the spirit of the Five Principles and

Zhou Enlai speaks at the Bandung Conference. (Xinhua News Agency)

created doubts about the PRC's intentions among many of the guests at Bandung. Taipei added to this tension and controversy through a desperate last-minute effort to prevent the premier from attending the conference.[98] Taiwan had not been invited and worried that a successful performance by Zhou would lead more emerging states to recognize Beijing. Seeking to prevent such a scenario, Guomindang agents sabotaged an Indian airliner known as the "Kashmir Princess," which exploded in midair while en route from Hong Kong to Djakarta on 11 April. Zhou had originally intended to travel to Indonesia on that very flight but changed his plans after deciding to visit Rangoon and New Delhi before the conference. The details surrounding how much Zhou had found out about the plot before it happened remain murky, but the premier had instructed several other high-ranking PRC officials who were scheduled to travel to Bandung to alter their travel arrangements and avoid the "Kashmir Princess."[99] When the airliner exploded, it carried Chinese journalists and members of the delegation's staff, but no high-ranking CCP officials were aboard. As the conference began, many wondered whether the incident would cause Zhou and his colleagues to take a combative tone against allies of the United States and Taiwan who were in attendance.

The premier realized, however, that China's interests and reputation would be better served if his delegation showed composure and restraint instead of launching into hysterics. He made this clear in a speech to the plenary session on 19 April, the second day of the conference. Zhou's biographers have widely cited this speech as one of the most stunning successes of his career and a defining moment at Bandung.[100] Before he gave the speech, the premier had been worried that the anti-Communist views espoused by some delegations would poison the atmosphere.[101] Zhou quickly decided that striking a conciliatory tone should be his top priority, so at the last minute, he modified his address.[102] The final version stressed common interests, mutual respect, and the PRC's goodwill toward its neighbors. Zhou explained that the Chinese delegation had "come to seek commonality rather than establish differences." The majority of Afro-Asian nations, he contended, "have suffered and still continue to suffer under the disaster and pain caused by colonialism." If the nations assembled at the conference "could find a common foundation" through their past sufferings, then they could "easily respect, sympathize with and support each other." Seeking to allay suspicions of communism, the premier stressed that while Afro-Asian nations should acknowledge "the differences in their social systems and ways of thinking," such differences "should not obstruct us from seeking commonality and uniting."[103]

Zhou's dramatic address thoroughly captured the attention of the other delegates. His translator at the conference, Pu Shouchang, who read the major portion of the speech in English, remembered that "throughout the speech it was so quiet in the hall that you could hear a pin drop."[104] Zhou received high praise from numerous Afro-Asian statesmen, including Gamel Abdel Nasser, Nehru, and U Nu, who told him that the address was a "great answer to those who attack China."[105] The speech was a turning point for China at Bandung. It dispelled a good deal—although not all—of the skepticism about Chinese intentions. Delegations that had been wavering in their views of the PRC now came to admire Zhou as a statesman committed to peace and restraint and were more willing to make contact with him. Zhou's address also made it far easier for the PRC delegation to turn its attention to improving China's image through other activities.

For the remainder of the conference, Zhou and the Chinese delegation strove to capitalize on the favorable impression left by the speech. The premier kept an extraordinarily busy schedule at Bandung—attending meetings and parties, attempting to negotiate agreements, and engaging in discussions of key issues late into the night. By the end of his second day at the conference, Zhou had made contact with the heads of all but three delegations.[106] Although there were hints of rivalry between Zhou and Nehru, the Indian prime minister played an important role in brokering the Chinese delegation's initial contacts with leaders of some countries that China had no relations with.[107] On 21 April, for instance, Nehru hosted a dinner to which he invited Zhou and the delegation chiefs of Thailand, the Philippines, and Saudi Arabia.[108] Such meetings gave Zhou a chance to demonstrate his reasonableness to those that had been urged by Washington to challenge the PRC as openly and loudly as possible.

The premier's tact and patience at dispelling criticisms from pro-Western delegations garnered admiration for both his delegation and the PRC. When disagreements arose, the premier preferred to handle them in private conversations rather than through a noisy airing of mutual grievances. According to Zhou's admittedly hagiographic official biography, one such incident occurred on the third day of the conference when the anti-Communist Ceylonese prime minister John Kotelawala spoke against communism and labeled China a "threat" during a meeting of the Political Committee. Zhou met privately with Kotelawala after the session to convey his concerns that such rhetoric would damage the conference and make it impossible to come to an agreement on the questions on the agenda. The next day both Zhou and Kotelawala downplayed their disagreement, disappointing some members of the media who had been eagerly waiting to see sparks fly.[109] Rather than seeking to defeat or shame his critic, Zhou tried instead to coopt him so that Afro-Asian unity would prevail and the conference would succeed. The ultimate objective was to raise the international profile of both Bandung and the PRC.

Yet as Zhou tried to persuade the other delegations that China wanted peace and stability, the ongoing Taiwan Strait Crisis remained an elephant in the room. To explain the PRC's position, the premier held special meetings outside of the normal conference sessions with leaders from Ceylon, Burma, India, Indonesia, Pakistan, the Philippines, and Thailand. Though he continued to blame Washington for the crisis and insist that Taiwan was a "question of China's domestic affair[s]," Zhou also expressed a readiness to ease tensions in the strait. Beijing, he explained, was "willing to sit down and enter into negotiations with the United States Government." After these discussions the premier made a statement on the relaxation of tensions in the Taiwan area and reiterated this position at the final session of the conference.[110] These statements seem to have found their mark. Although Zhou did not fully persuade him, the Filipino diplomat Carlos Romulo admitted that the premier's announcement on Taiwan had "electrified the conference."[111] Three days later Dulles agreed to hold cease-fire negotiations, ending the crisis. [112] Both Washington and Beijing claimed victory, but in the context of Bandung, the PRC scored the greater diplomatic coup. By offering to negotiate, Zhou disarmed America's allies, taking away one of their most potentially effective talking points. And China was able to explain the Taiwan issue to other Afro-Asian nations in a way that drew their sympathy—as a struggle against foreign imperialism.

In the weeklong conference, Beijing made significant strides not only at demonstrating its moderation but also at expanding its relations in the Middle East. In 1955, the PRC still lacked formal relations with any government in the region. Zhou systematically engaged with Arab countries at Bandung, offering support on the issue of Palestine and discussing the possibilities of greater economic and cultural ties. In return, China gained prestige by associating itself with independent governments that were strongly anticolonialist in their political orientation.

The key to China's efforts to engage with the Arab world was Egypt's charismatic and influential prime minister, Gamal Abdel Nasser. Zhou first met with Nasser in Rangoon on 15 April when both men were traveling to Djakarta.[113] They talked several more times during the conference, with Nasser inviting Zhou to dinner on 21 April and the premier responding in kind by inviting the Egyptian to a banquet at the Chinese delegation's villa.[114] Nasser, for his part, believed that Egypt's interests could be served through contacts with the PRC. With the Eisenhower administration unwilling to sell weapons to Egypt because of strong pro-Israel sentiment in the United States, Nasser hoped that the PRC might help to arrange arms sales from the Communist Bloc. He also viewed China as a potential market for Egypt's bumper cotton crop. Both sides got what they wanted from these meetings. China played a role—though the specifics are unclear—in mediating the 1955 arms deal that enabled Egypt to purchase Soviet weapons through Czechoslovakia, and Cairo's cotton exports to the PRC increased significantly in subsequent months.[115] Nasser put his formidable influence behind China's efforts to engage with the Arab world facilitating contacts between Beijing and other Arab countries during and after Bandung. By January 1956, Cairo and Beijing had agreed that a new Chinese commercial office would be set up in Egypt and that its representatives would have diplomatic immunity and other privileges.[116] This was an important step toward the establishment of normal relations, which occurred a few months later.

With Nasser's blessing, Beijing made other small but significant inroads into the Arab world at Bandung. The premier spoke with several leaders from the region who were relatively close to the United States. This included a meeting with the Syrian delegation on 21 April, a visit to the Saudi delegation's cocktail party on 22 April, and a ninety-minute meeting with the highly regarded Lebanese diplomat Charles Malik briefly after the conference ended.[117] Although Zhou was moderate in his personal statements on Palestine and Israel, the Chinese delegation participated in discussions of the issue and ultimately backed a resolution supporting Palestinian rights. Several Arab leaders expressed gratitude to the premier for his position.[118] These political gestures were complemented by efforts to demonstrate China's respect for the Muslim faith. Da Pusheng, a well-known eighty-one-year-old Imam, accompanied Zhou's delegation as representative of the Chinese Muslim community. Da presented Chinese-language versions of the Koran to several delegates, attended a prayer meeting at a new mosque built by the Indonesian government, and discussed Chinese Muslim participation in hajj pilgrimages to Mecca with delegates from Egypt and Saudi Arabia.[119]

Chinese contacts with Middle Eastern nations at Bandung immediately improved Sino-Arab economic and cultural relations. Within a year of the conference Beijing had concluded ten trade agreements with Arab countries, all giving China most-favored-nation status and providing for the exchange of trade representatives. In February 1956, the PRC dispatched a cultural troupe led by Burhan Shahidi, a Uyghur member of the CCP and chairman of the China Islamic Association. The delegation toured Saudi Arabia, Jordan, Lebanon, Syria, and other states that still had no formal relations with the PRC.[120] These new exchanges and agreements raised China's profile in the Middle East, giving it a de facto legitimacy in a region of the world where it had previously been little known or shunned.

To be sure, Beijing did not get everything that it wanted at Bandung. Before the proceedings began, Zhou hoped for the creation of a new liaison office that could coordinate future Afro-Asian conferences but no permanent institutions were established.[121] Moreover, Washington's allies followed through on its guidance to talk about communism as a form of neocolonialism. Zhou Enlai reported from the conference that "pro-American countries such as Turkey, Pakistan, Lebanon and Iraq have used the debate on so called 'various forms of colonialism' to obstruct the conference from reaching a consensus."[122] In the end, he could not prevent a reference to "colonialism in all its forms" from being inserted in the final communiqué.[123] If Zhou was not omnipotent at Bandung, however, he was nonetheless influential. The ten principles that concluded the final communiqué produced at the conference might not have directly replicated the premier's Five Principles, but the two bore significant resemblance.[124] Ultimately, Beijing was more than willing to accept small defeats and compromises to ensure that the conference advanced the cause of Afro-Asian unity and strengthened China's position among newly independent states.

By most accounts, Zhou achieved exactly what he set out to do at Bandung: demonstrate professionalism, gain trust and respect for the PRC, and convince other Asian nations that Beijing was committed to peace. Even relatively pro-Western leaders praised Zhou's diplomacy. The Filipino diplomat Romulo wrote that the premier "comported himself as one who has taken a leaf from Dale Carnegie's tome on How to Win Friends and Influence People." Zhou had been "affable of manner, moderate of speech."[125] During a conversation held briefly after the conference ended, Lebanese diplomat Charles Malik praised the premier effusively for the role he had played:

> I think it can be said, Mr. Prime Minister, that you came out of this conference winning every important battle. . . . You had many pleasant and perhaps even fruitful contacts with important leaders of Asia and Africa. We have had a chance to see Chinese Communists in action and they appear to be human beings like the rest of us. . . . You made a good hit at the Conference, perhaps, as I say, the best hit of all. And you crowned all this magnificent performance with your offer the other day to negotiate your differences with the United States. Thus throughout, the Conference has been pure gain for you.[126]

The fact that Zhou elicited such admiration from respected conservative statesmen is clear evidence that he quieted fears of China while creating doubts about Washington's campaign to isolate the PRC.

Washington was troubled by its allies' embrace of Zhou at Bandung, though it did see some hopeful signs. A report published by the OIR shortly after the conference fretted that Zhou "apparently convinced most of his fellow-conferees that he is a reasonable statesman." Moreover, the premier's "characterization of China as itself an object of subversive operations—conducted by the United States—was probably convincing to many listeners." Ultimately, the OIR feared that "the efforts of the Communist Chinese to identify themselves with the causes that mean the most to Asians might blind some of the Asians to the threat the [Beijing] regime represents."[127] Yet the American perspective had not been completely ignored; instead, "the concept of Communist colonialism received a full hearing." More important, Americans hoped that Beijing was constraining itself with its emphasis on the Five Principles of Peaceful Coexistence. Washington reasoned that after Zhou's performance at the conference, China would want to avoid the seeming hypocrisy that would come with aggressive actions in the future: "The longer Communist China behaves in a manner calculated to support its pretensions, the higher the price it would have to pay among Asians were it to engage in new aggression."[128]

Beijing, however, did not see as great a contradiction between the more militant line it had adopted before 1954 and the Five Principles. From the CCP's perspective, the PRC's support for violent revolution was part of the same struggle against colonialism as its diplomacy in Geneva or Bandung. In both instances, Beijing perceived a special leadership role for itself in ridding the world of imperialism and paving the way for a peaceful postcolonial international order. Chinese leaders unsurprisingly sometimes used similar rhetoric in talking about the two. "Undoubtedly," Zhou said when reporting on Bandung, "the struggle against colonial aggression by the Chinese people together with the other peoples in Asia and Africa will be helpful to the great cause of opposing war and defending of peace for people throughout the world."[129] After Bandung, Zhou was certainly not without cause for such optimism.

————

The PRC had been established only in 1949, making its performance at Geneva and Bandung truly impressive. Within a two-year time frame it had transformed its image in Asia and created a new basis for its claims to Great Power status. Yet many issues between the PRC and its neighbors remained unresolved. The key question was whether the Five Principles and China's new approach would be sufficient to settle these issues and bring stability to Asia for the long term. American efforts to undermine Zhou's charismatic performances at Geneva and Bandung had mostly proven futile, but the United States still wielded a great deal of influence over the Afro-Asian nations whose friendship China sought. After Bandung, Washington and Beijing were thus set to vie even more determinedly for the loyalties of the vast parts of Asia and Africa that remained officially nonaligned.

Chapter 4

Advancing the Peace Offensive, 1955–1958

"The forces of colonialism still seek to destroy the independence of the Afro-Asian countries and to oppress the nationalist movements of the region," Zhou Enlai warned at a meeting of the CCP's Political Consultative Conference in March 1957, "but this cannot rescue colonialism from its demise, and it cannot stop the advance of Afro-Asian peoples." The premier boasted that the "Afro-Asian region, which was long the victim of colonial invasion, will definitely become a big family of independent nations, peaceful coexistence, and friendly cooperation."[1] Zhou was confident that the political situation in the Afro-Asian world favored China, and not without reason. The PRC's diplomatic foray after the Korean War was yielding positive results. As China's emissary, Zhou had stood tall at the Geneva and Bandung Conferences and Beijing had gained greater acceptance as significant player on the international stage. American efforts to build an alliance structure to contain China had, by contrast, been at best a partial success.[2] Although the long-standing mistrust of China that long prevailed in the region persisted to some degree, there could be no question that the PRC was gaining prestige.

After Bandung, the Chinese government continued to build its status as a peaceful Asian power through diplomacy. It established normal relations with more Afro-Asian countries and reached out to its neighbors in Asia by hosting state visits, dispatching prominent officials on highly visible tours, and offering limited economic assistance. The CCP arranged these diplomatic rituals with care to assure maximum political impact. Loath to see Beijing make diplomatic gains, Washington worked to disrupt and diminish even minor diplomatic initiatives launched by the PRC in the Third World. Throughout the 1950s, American officials pressured Asian and African leaders to ostracize the PRC. They discouraged high-level state visits between China and other Afro-Asian countries and lobbied neutralist leaders not to offer recognition to Beijing.

America's diplomatic maneuverings to counter China were largely futile. Newly independent nations in South and Southeast Asia wanted good relations with the United States but adamantly refused to allow Washington to dictate their policies. To Washington's chagrin, Asian leaders were often willing to establish normal diplomatic and economic ties with the PRC—especially when it served personal or national interests. Although such strongly pro-Western countries as South Korea, Thailand, and the Philippines followed America's lead, China's peace offensive was generally well received. By 1958, even American officials were acknowledging that the PRC would inevitably play an important role in shaping Asia's future.

State Visits

After the Bandung Conference, the PRC turned to routine diplomatic channels to develop its relations with other Afro-Asian states. In particular, Beijing looked to increase both the number of foreign dignitaries visiting the PRC and the number of visits to newly independent Asian and African nations made by Chinese officials. For the CCP, the purpose of arranging these state visits almost always went beyond the specific agenda for discussion. In a manner that was vaguely reminiscent of the rituals observed by China's dynastic emperors in previous centuries, the PRC often aimed to exploit these occasions to bolster its status.[3] The CCP went to great lengths to manage both the reception of its own officials abroad and the greeting of Afro-Asian dignitaries in China. It carefully arranged the details of both to make sure that they created a favorable image of the PRC as a strong, independent Asian country committed to peace and development. Communist Party officials hoped that other newly independent nations—socialist and capitalist alike—might see some aspects of the PRC's development as worthy of emulation.

When the CCP leadership welcomed foreign dignitaries, it devoted a great deal of attention to the image of new China that was presented. The PRC Ministry of Foreign Affairs wrote up detailed analyses of visiting officials, their possible objectives, and China's relation with their countries. Afro-Asian leaders, regardless of where they came from, were greeted by cheering crowds at the airport and given lavish receptions. Their visits frequently included tours of Chinese farms, cities, and factories that could demonstrate the progress that the PRC was making in its economic reconstruction. Foreign leaders were ultimately expected to gain an appreciation of China's commitment to peaceful development that they would convey to their own people. Zhou Enlai expressed this forcefully when Pakistani prime minister Huseyn Shaheed Suhrawardy visited China for the first time in October 1956. "After visiting all of the places that you wish, you can see that the Chinese people have devoted themselves to peaceful reconstruction and are willing to face all other countries of the globe with friendship; you can also see that the different ethnic groups within China are equal and that the Chinese people enjoy democracy and freedom," the premier explained.[4] Zhou intended his words to reinforce the impression that other officials had worked diligently to convey.

The PRC Foreign Ministry paid similar attention to detail when arranging international tours by Chinese officials. It tried to assure that such visits received as much favorable publicity as possible both in the host country and throughout Asia. Although border disputes and disagreements over the status of overseas Chinese sometimes plagued the PRC's relations with its neighbors, these issues were downplayed during state visits to make sure that neither side suffered any embarrassment. When senior CCP officials traveled abroad, host countries were expected to provide the same pomp that China afforded its guests.

American officials understood the symbolic importance that the PRC attached to these state visits and did what they could to discourage them or restrict their meaning. Everett F. Drumright, a leading China expert who served as the consul general to Hong Kong during the early 1950s, made several suggestions along these lines in a memo to the State Department in February 1955. The Chinese government had made it an "established practise [*sic*]" to provide "conducted tours" in which foreign visitors were shepherded to "a limited number of places to see certain designated things." Although Washington would look overbearing if it tried to block Asian leaders from visiting China, he argued, the United States should not simply allow Beijing to score political points. Drumright suggested that Asians traveling to China be "cultivated by our staffs in the various countries." Efforts could be made to "provide them with simple, direct background information about the Chinese Communists, and with specific questions to ask during their stay in China." After these visitors returned, American officials should hold meetings with them "to get information about conditions in Communist China, and . . . to give the returned visitor a better perspective on what he was not allowed to see and information he was not permitted to gather."[5] American officials assumed somewhat condescendingly that if they helped Asian leaders to see the true nature of Communist China by providing the right kind of information, they could disabuse them of whatever positive impressions of the PRC they had formed.

Much to the vexation of Drumright and like-minded American officials, the number of state visits paid by foreign dignitaries to China increased dramatically after the Bandung Conference while Zhou Enlai remained indefatigable in his eagerness to make goodwill tours of other Asian countries. The year 1956 was in many ways a banner one for Chinese diplomacy in Asia. Heads of state from Cambodia, Laos, Indonesia, and Pakistan all visited the PRC within a span of ten months, and Zhou Enlai capped off the year with a highly visible five-country Asian trip. But 1956 was also a year of intensive Sino-American competition at the diplomatic level. American officials let almost none of these state visits go forward without complications. They

Prince Norodom Sihanouk of Cambodia being greeted by crowds
on his arrival to Beijing in 1956. (Xinhua News Agency)

pressured nearly all of the Asian leaders involved to delay or cancel their visits and, once the visits themselves became faits accomplis, worked to ensure that little was achieved.

The first Asian leader to visit the PRC in 1956 was Cambodia's strong-willed and sometimes temperamental prince, Norodom Sihanouk. The prince would travel to China on many occasions during his long political career, and he would eventually take refuge there when his government was overthrown in 1970. In 1956, however, Sihanouk seemed closer to Washington than to Beijing. Cambodia had not extended official recognition to the PRC, and it received military and economic assistance from the United States.[6] The visit led to a significant improvement in Sino-Cambodian relations, however. Shortly after its completion, Beijing initiated an economic aid program in Cambodia, paving the way for both the normalization of relations between China and Cambodia in 1958 and a second visit to the PRC by Sihanouk shortly thereafter.[7]

When Sihanouk's plans to travel to Beijing became known, State Department officials quickly registered their disapproval. Before his visit, American officials warned Phnom Penh that the trip would confer undeserved legitimacy on Communist China. Three days before Sihanouk's departure, Walter S. Robertson, the assistant secretary of state for Far Eastern affairs, met with the Cambodian ambassador to inquire about the visit and make known American objections. Robertson "sincerely regretted that Cambodia had embraced a policy of neutrality." The assistant secretary believed that "such action, if not supporting Communism at least gave the impression of such support and assisted a regime which was dedicated to the suppression of individual liberties and the institution of a system of enslavement of the individual." The American's protests were to no avail. Nong Kimny, the Cambodian ambassador, insisted that Cambodian neutrality was "a matter of state," and although he expressed gratitude to the United States for its assistance, he made it clear that Sihanouk would carry through with the visit.[8]

As American officials tried to dissuade Sihanouk from the trip, Chinese officials prepared carefully for the prince's arrival. They did everything they could to draw attention to the event, assure that China made a favorable impression on the visiting dignitary, and create opportunities to further develop Sino-Cambodian ties. The PRC Foreign Ministry even drew up detailed plans for Sihanouk's welcome reception at the airport—a practice that would remain salient in CCP diplomacy toward Afro-Asian countries throughout the Cold War. The plan called for Zhou Enlai, CCP Vice Chairman Chen Yun, and several other leading party officials to form a receiving line to greet the prince and shake his hand. Bands played Chinese and Cambodian songs, and female students presented the prince and other members of his entourage with flowers. When he arrived at his hotel, Sihanouk was greeted by crowds chanting slogans such as "Ten thousand years of Sino-Cambodian Friendship!" and "Ten thousand years of peace in Asia!"[9] During Sihanouk's six-day visit he was feted with multiple banquets and given the opportunity to meet several times with Mao Zedong and Zhou Enlai. A highly respectful tone prevailed at nearly all of these meetings, with each side commending the other for its commitment to peace, anticolonialism, and playing a constructive role in Asian politics. Zhou praised Sihanouk lavishly. "The policy of peaceful neutrality that you have implemented in Southeast Asia has been influential," he told Sihanouk. "It has helped to elevate your position in Asia."[10] Sihanouk fondly remembered the atmosphere of these meetings: "In China, although I was a prince and a Buddhist, and [Zhou Enlai] a communist revolutionary, and despite the enormous disparity in the size of our countries, I was treated as an equal. There was a total absence of pressure of any sort, and a genuine interest in Cambodia's problems."[11]

The Cambodian prince happily reciprocated Chinese praise, reinforcing the image that the PRC had hoped to foster through inviting him. Before a scheduled visit to Guangdong, the prince gave a speech praising Zhou Enlai as "an able, intelligent and sincere statesmen" and thanking the PRC for adopting "the most perfectly correct attitude" in its diplomacy toward

Mao Zedong meets with Prince Sihanouk of Cambodia. (Xinhua News Agency)

Cambodia after the Geneva Conference.[12] At the end of the trip, Sihanouk presented Mao Zedong and Zhou Enlai with a special medal of honor from his father, King Norodom Suramarit. The two sides also signed a joint communiqué calling for continued efforts to improve the bilateral relationship and promote greater economic and cultural exchange.[13]

Perhaps the best testimony to the success of Chinese summitry with Cambodia is that Sihanouk visited again in just two years later to equal if not greater fanfare. On Sihanouk's return Zhou Enlai proclaimed that the warming ties between the two countries marked "the turning of a new page in the tradition of friendly Sino-Cambodian relations" and signified "the consolidation and victory of the Five Principles of Peaceful Coexistence."[14] Further efforts were made to impress Sihanouk with the PRC's progress and dynamism. On 17 August, the premier escorted Sihanouk on a tour of a steel plant in Beijing and the Beijing Steel and Iron Institute (today known as the University of Science and Technology) while proffering advice on how Cambodia could develop its own iron and steel plants. Afterward, Zhou accompanied the prince to Hebei Province so that he could view the expansion of rice paddies there.[15] The visit ended with another joint declaration expressing satisfaction with Sino-Cambodian exchanges and calling on all nations to respect Cambodia's neutrality policy and resolve conflicts according to the Five Principles of Peaceful Coexistence.[16]

American officials met with Sihanouk both before and after his visits to China but found that they could do little to alter the favorable impression created by the PRC. To Washington's frustration, the prince generally defended China as an important, responsible country with peaceful intentions. When the U.S. ambassador warned of the dangers posed by Chinese expansionism, Sihanouk retorted, "China is [a] great country nearby and a reality." He also criticized America's position on recognition explaining that, from Cambodia's perspective, "Taiwan was only a small island and mainland China is actually China."[17] After the visit, Sihanouk continued to insist that Beijing's intentions were peaceful. He reportedly told the American ambassador that through his conversations with Zhou Enlai he had been convinced that there was "no basic reason for antagonism" between the United States and China other than Taiwan.[18]

Given Beijing's success at influencing Sihanouk's outlook, it is not surprising that Americans put even greater pressure on other Asian leaders planning to visit China. They were especially concerned when Laotian prime minister Souvanna Phouma announced in June that he too would accept an invitation from the PRC. The situation that American policy makers confronted in the run-up to Phouma's visit was more delicate than the one in Cambodia. Souvanna was more vulnerable than Sihanouk politically. Whereas the self-confident Cambodian prince's authority appeared well established, in Laos an uneasy truce prevailed between the government and the insurgent Pathet Lao. Shortly before his trip to the PRC, Souvanna had reached a temporary agreement with the leader of the Pathet Lao, his half-brother Souphanouvong. The agreement may have allayed Souvanna's fears, but American officials viewed it as a form of surrender and became more critical of the prime minister.[19]

Americans had anticipated that the PRC would invite the prime minister and issued repeated warnings that such a trip could pose dangers to Laotian security.[20] Beijing confirmed American suspicions in June by issuing a formal invitation, which Souvanna immediately accepted. When Vientiane announced that the prime minister would visit the PRC in August, American diplomats urgently pressured him to delay or cancel the visit. Secretary of State Dulles instructed the American embassy to "get across [the] idea that [the] U.S. Government . . . would consider such [a] hurried visit to [Beijing] as endangering security and creating difficulties for U.S. efforts to support Laos."[21] The American embassy in Vientiane also tried but failed to persuade its French and British counterparts to put similar pressures on the Laotian government.[22] When J. Graham Parsons, the newly appointed U.S. ambassador to Laos, arrived in the country in July he made a last-ditch effort to persuade Souvanna to abandon the visit, claiming that such a trip would "make headlines" in the United States and affect the "voting of funds for aid" by Congress. But Parsons could not get the Laotian to forsake his plans.[23]

When American officials finally realized that Souvanna would not be dissuaded from the trip, they tried to make sure that the PRC gained little from it. The State Department instructed Parsons to try to "prevent Lao commitments to Chinese Communists during [his] trip." Because the Laotian prince's basic objective seemed to be to "please everyone," Parsons should offer "low-keyed friendly advice reminding him of U.S. position and support for Laos commitments to [the] West." They hoped that these efforts might reduce Souvanna's susceptibility to Chinese blandishments. The State Department also cabled the ambassador that it would prefer that no representative of the American embassy be present at Souvanna's airport sendoff before his trip.[24] It was customary for the embassy to have officials present at these events, but Washington's reasons for breaking with the norm are easy to discern. By ignoring protocol, the State Department hoped to delegitimize the trip, limiting the prestige that Laos or the PRC could accrue from it.

While Washington sought to minimize the significance of Souvanna's trip, Beijing tried to make sure that it commanded international attention. CCP officials believed that the visit could be an important boon for Sino-Laotian relations and enable the PRC to broaden its peace offensive. One Foreign Ministry report written as the visit drew near contended, "Phouma's visit to China truly has an important meaning because it can not only lead to an immediate breakthrough in Sino-Laotian relations but also advance Lao's policy of peaceful neutrality, broaden the area of peace in Asia, influence Thailand and Vietnam, and strike a blow against American imperialism."[25] Chinese officials believed that Souvanna's visit was part of a major shift in Asian politics that favored China. To continue this momentum, they needed to make a concerted effort to impress the Laotian. "When it comes to the task of receiving Phouma," the Foreign Ministry's report continued, "we should go all-out to implement a policy of being sincere, friendly, warm, and ceremonious." When Chinese diplomats approached Souvanna they were to do so "in a spirit of seeking common ground while retaining differences (*qiutong cunyi*) and seeking truth from facts (*shishi qiushi*)." They should also "encourage Laos to walk the road of peaceful neutrality, respect the opinions of their counterpart and avoid Great Power chauvinism."[26] They hoped that Souvanna would come away from the visit with an appreciation of the PRC's commitment to peace and its respect for Laos's right to choose its political destiny.

The Foreign Ministry knew that sensitive issues might surface during talks between Souvanna and Chinese leaders and it made plans to handle them in a way that would avoid embarrassing either side. In particular, Vientiane's failure to normalize relations with Beijing loomed as a thorny issue. The Chinese were, of course, eager to establish formal diplomatic ties and the imprimatur of legitimacy they conveyed. Nevertheless, the Foreign Ministry recognized that it might be difficult for Phouma to offer Beijing recognition immediately, given the difficult circumstances his nation faced on both the domestic and international fronts. Chinese officials therefore made plans to raise the issue subtly without pressuring the prime minister too much. "The circumstances of the Laotian prime minister are still not completely stable and Phouma's visit will have a ceremonial character. Therefore the chances that Phouma will conclude an agreement for diplomatic relations are not great," the Foreign Ministry reported. It added, however, that the issue could be "raised by our side for the Laotian side to consider."[27] By presenting the issue of recognition for consideration and future discussion rather than risking a conflict over it, Beijing sought to assure that it would not poison the overall atmosphere of the visit.

The PRC welcomed Souvanna with a level of fanfare that was quite similar to what it had arranged for Sihanouk. His itinerary strongly resembled that of the Cambodian. The Foreign Ministry made sure that mass rallies would greet Souvanna in every city that he visited. This included crowds of three thousand in Guangzhou, five thousand in Shanghai, and seven thousand at the Beijing airport. He attended several banquets during his weeklong stay and met with both Zhou Enlai and Mao Zedong. Foreign ministry officials also arranged for Souvanna to tour factories, agricultural cooperatives, state-managed farms, and Buddhist temples. Press coverage was arranged for Souvanna's speeches and the joint declaration that he made at the end of his visit with Zhou.[28] Once again, Beijing rolled out the red carpet for a foreign dignitary with the objective of fostering an image of the new China as a peaceful and tolerant nation concerned first and foremost with its own economic development.

During his conversations with Souvanna, Zhou echoed the general guidelines suggested by the Foreign Ministry. "China is a large and populous country; this makes it even more important that we should respect other countries, especially our neighbors, and pursue friendly relations," the premier explained. Zhou recounted the two countries' shared history of colonial oppression and expressed his belief that this "common misfortune" should make it easier for the two countries to understand each other. Seeking to make China appear more reasonable and flexible than the United States, the premier also told Souvanna, "The Chinese government is not opposed to you visiting America. . . . We also want to go to America but they won't let us."[29] Both leaders affirmed their commitment to the ideas of peace and national autonomy in a joint statement made before Souvanna's departure on 25 August. They agreed to observe the Five Principles and "develop good-neighbor relations between the two countries." China would respect Laos's policy of peace and neutrality, and the two countries would seek to "develop their economic and cultural relations for the greatest benefit of their peoples."[30]

Souvanna Phouma willingly played the role of sincere and grateful guest, enabling Beijing to score a significant coup in the courts of world and Asian opinion. Yet Souvanna himself was probably not completely persuaded by Chinese blandishments. According to historian Seth Jacobs, his primary motive for the trip was not so much to improve ties with Beijing as to seek concrete assurance that the PRC would not intervene in the Laotian civil war and strengthen his hand in negotiations with the Pathet Lao.[31] During the visit, Souvanna did bring up the related problem of North Vietnam interfering in his country's internal politics, although Zhou did little more than advise him to visit Hanoi to discuss the problem with Vietnamese leaders.[32] Moreover, not all members of Souvanna's entourage become enamored of Communist China. The Laotian crown prince Savang Vathana told American officials that the PRC had not made an altogether positive impression on the delegation. In a later visit to the United States, he told several American officials that Laotians had "had their eyes opened" and understood that "aid and well being for Laos could not emanate from Communist China." They had concluded that because the PRC itself was a poor country, it would be immoral to accept aid from it.[33]

Whatever protestations Souvanna or other Laotian officials made about the meaning of the visit, however, both Beijing and Washington believed that it had redounded greatly to the PRC's benefit. For the CCP, of course, this was good news. A report by the Foreign Ministry was highly positive about the visit's overall impact. It noted that on returning to Laos, Souvanna had told the Pathet Lao leaders that he was "most satisfied that China would respect Laotian independence." The prime minister was also reported to have praised the results of China's reconstruction.[34] Even if some difficult issues such as establishing normal diplomatic relations still needed to be resolved, Beijing was optimistic—and not completely without good reason—that its influence and profile in Laos were improving in the aftermath of Souvanna's trip.

American officials, however, were determined to prevent China from enhancing its prestige in Laos through any favor that it had curried with Souvanna. The Eisenhower administration took immediate measures to punish the prime minister for defying the United States and contain Chinese influence. "Laos' receptivity to the Communist peace offensive means the nearly exclusive Western role in Laos has come to an end," Kenneth T. Young, the director of the Office of Southeast Asian Affairs, wrote in a memo to the State

Department. "The achievement of any Western success in the U.S.-Chinese confrontation in Laos" would "demand not conceding the field to the Communists." American officials blamed Souvanna and his decision to visit Beijing for the ostensible rise of Chinese influence in Laos. Young claimed that "Souvanna's vanity, weakness of character and supreme faith that he can control the Chinese Communists, the Viet Minh and the Pathet Lao" could eventually lead to the loss of Laos to communism.[35]

It is not surprising that Souvanna soon became subject to subtle forms of reprisal by Washington. In a cable to the State Department written shortly after the prime minister's China trip, Secretary of State Dulles called for the United States to "build up [a] restraining influence on Souvanna" in the Laotian assembly and cabinet. American representatives in Laos were to use their contacts with Laotian officials to "create awareness [of the] dangers [of] being 'neutralized' and generate opposition to Souvanna's hasty actions and one way concessions." They needed to make Laotians aware of "the real ChiCom intent in neutralizing Laos," which was "in classic Chinese imperial manner, to paralyze and reduce to vassalage [a] small well-intentioned neighbor." In carrying out this "education campaign," the United States would also "continue to give behind-scenes support to influential Lao leaders . . . who before [Beijing] pilgrimage appeared skeptical and uneasy over hazardous course charted by vacillating Souvanna Phouma." Dulles even asked the embassy for its views on "who might be [a] likely successor to Souvanna if general criticism [of] his actions developed in Lao circles."[36]

Seeking to diminish Souvanna and the significance of his China trip, the United States invited Crown Prince Savang Vathana to Washington in September. The visit gave the Eisenhower administration an opportunity to increase the stature of another Laotian leader at Souvanna's expense as well as to reemphasize its warnings about the danger of Communist China. When Savang explained to President Eisenhower that China had recently shifted toward a policy of "open arms and smiles" toward Laos and that it had put the country in an awkward position, the president cautioned him about Beijing's true intentions, explaining that "anyone who knows the Communists knows that while their final goals have not changed, their tactics had." The Crown Prince assured Eisenhower that he agreed with this view.[37]

Washington's efforts to discredit Souvanna and strengthen other Laotian leaders who shared American views of Communist China did not end with Savang's visit. At Dulles's instruction, the CIA began funding a Laotian civic group known as the Committee for the Defense of National Interests (CDNI). The new organization undermined Souvanna's position in the 1958 National Assembly election, forcing him to resign and enabling the more conservative Phoui Sananikone to ascend to the premiership.[38] Washington also drew up general plans to counter the potential expansion of Chinese influence in Laos. Kenneth Young called for several "long-term courses of action" to reduce Communist influence. He argued that Washington should give top priority to "increasing the effectiveness of the countersubversive and intelligence services of the police, Army, auto-defense and propaganda organizations to combat inevitably stepped-up Chinese Communist, Viet Minh and Pathet Lao subversion." In addition, the United States needed to "minimize Laos' contacts with the Communist Bloc, stave off recognition of Communist China and the Viet Minh and dissuade Laos from accepting Communist aid."[39] These recommendations were based on a broad analysis of how China might seek to strengthen its influence in Laos once it gained Souvanna's trust and designed to inhibit the effectiveness of any potential Chinese maneuvering.

But the United States was not in a position to pressure and undermine all Southeast Asian leaders as it had Souvanna. One case in point was Indonesia's respected president, Sukarno, who visited Beijing in October 1956. Sukarno's political party had scored an important victory in parliamentary elections held a year earlier, and the Indonesian leader's stature had grown significantly as a result.[40] Sukarno already enjoyed a high degree of prestige among newly independent Afro-Asian countries, and his triumph only made both the Free World and the Communist Bloc more eager to court him. A dedicated neutralist, Sukarno believed Indonesia's interests would best be served if it maintained good relations with both East and West. He therefore decided to makes visits to both the United States and its Communist rivals in 1956, enabling him to cast his trip as an effort to be balanced rather than as a new opening to Beijing.[41] Nevertheless, Beijing and Washington vied for his trust.

When the Eisenhower administration considered inviting Sukarno to visit the United States, it was well aware that he was also being courted by the PRC. Indeed, countering the impact of a potential Sukarno visit to Beijing figured prominently in discussions of whether to invite him. After Sukarno's triumph in the parliamentary elections, the White House called the U.S. ambassador, Hugh S. Cumming Jr., back from Jakarta to discuss American strategy. The ambassador recalled that when the question of a state visit was brought up, "The query in our minds was should we invite him first to this country hoping that it would have an influence on him . . . or should we ignore him and let him go to Communist China?" Believing that if Sukarno "turned out to be influenced by the Communists . . . we would never know whether it had been our failure to invite him here or not that had been the cause," Cumming recommended that a visit be arranged.[42]

Washington did not need state visits from well-known foreign leaders to serve as a signifier of legitimacy in the same way that Beijing did. But it nevertheless wanted to make any visit to China appear relatively unimpressive.

Sukarno thus received treatment usually reserved for important foreign dignitaries. According to Paul F. Gardner, who held several diplomatic posts in Indonesia over his career, Sukarno received "a tickertape parade in New York, honorary degrees at Columbia and the University of Michigan, visits to the General Motors, Ford, and Chrysler plants in Detroit, and a tour of Disneyland conducted by Walt Disney himself." Sukarno also made a highly publicized and well-received speech to Congress.[43] Americans were confident—perhaps a bit too confident—that they had made a favorable impression on Sukarno and that he would now hew closer to the United States and its allies. Satisfied with the visit, the Eisenhower administration even decided to offer Sukarno twenty-five million dollars in development aid.[44]

Despite Washington's favorable estimation of Sukarno's trip, concerns about the Indonesian's visit to China persisted. The U.S. embassy worried that the visit would likely serve as an "occasion for the Communists to mount an enormous propaganda campaign both in Djakarta and [Beijing]."[45] American officials did not pressure Sukarno overtly, but they did subtly try to limit the propaganda value of his trip for the PRC. The State Department was especially worried about what Sukarno would say and do once he arrived in China. When he traveled to Moscow in August, Sukarno had agreed to a joint statement that was implicitly critical of NATO, angering both the United States and some of his rivals in the Indonesian government.[46] Americans used what leverage he had to prevent a recurrence of this sort of event in Beijing. The United States decided to delay the official announcement of its planned twenty-five-million-dollar credit for Indonesia until after the Indonesian returned from the PRC. Ambassador Cumming hoped that the aid credit would thus operate as a "brake" on Sukarno's actions and prevent the "ill-advised behavior in Beijing" that the Indonesian had engaged in during his visit to the Soviet Union.[47] Cumming's strategy does not appear to have been successful. Much to the ambassador's surprise and embarrassment, Indonesian officials that he spoke to ahead of Sukarno's trip already had detailed knowledge of Washington's intended aid offer, although the source they had gotten the information from was unclear.[48] Cumming acknowledged that this weakened any leverage that the timing of the aid announcement would have provided.

Ultimately, the State Department could do little to prevent either Sukarno or Beijing from exploiting the visit for political gain. As always, high-ranking CCP officials reveled in the opportunity to play the role of senior statesmen and gracious hosts. Mao Zedong and Zhou Enlai were both part of the coterie of senior Chinese leaders who greeted the Indonesian at the airport. During Sukarno's stay in the PRC, the Chinese leadership arranged for several banquets to be held in his honor. On one evening Mao and Zhou accompanied Sukarno and Nepali prime minister Tanka Acharya, who was also visiting the

PRC at the time, on a trip to see the Beijing Opera.[49] By appearing in public with two other prominent Asian leaders at one of Communist China's signature cultural institutions, Mao and Zhou could create a spectacle that would legitimate the culture of "new China" in the eyes of other Asian countries.

Before Sukarno's arrival, the Chinese state-run media loudly sang his praises—focusing on the Indonesian's commitment to peace and his credentials as an anticolonialist leader. The press credited him with "promoting peace in the Asian and African regions" and making "outstanding contributions to the victorious struggle of the Indonesian people against colonial rule." An article in *People's Daily*, the leading party newspaper, heralded the Indonesian's arrival as an event of "paramount importance in the friendly relations and cooperation between China and Indonesia."[50] By underscoring the significance of the visit while emphasizing the two countries' common struggle against colonialism and pursuit of peace, Beijing sought to bolster its own visibility as an advocate of these causes both domestically and internationally.

American officials were once again chagrined that the CCP achieved many of its objectives. In a report on Sukarno's visits to the Soviet Union and the PRC, Ambassador Cumming expressed particular concern about the CCP's impact on the Indonesian. He called Sukarno's "expressions of approval" for both Communist China and the Soviet Union "more enthusiastic than required by [an] appreciative guest." The visit seemed to have confirmed Indonesia's preexisting "sense of kinship with Communist China as [a] fellow Asian country in alleged struggle against 'colonialism and imperialism' and admiration for what Indonesians conceive to be Chinese success in economic development." The statements and speeches that Sukarno had made during his visit "largely endorse Chinese Communist policies," and the Indonesian had been "especially impressed by the confidence displayed by the Red Chinese in their leadership." Cumming also worried that the ideas and policies that Sukarno had gained exposure to in the PRC and elsewhere would find their way into Indonesia's political life. As a "result [of] Sukarno's exposure to Tito and [Mao Zedong]," the ambassador reported, "he may well try to play more active role as 'revolutionary president' . . . to unify and concentrate Indonesia's political and economic efforts."[51]

Although Cumming was certainly concerned about the aftereffects of Sukarno's visit, he by no means believed that the situation in Indonesia was desperate. He was sure that many Indonesians would retain their anti-Communist orientation and that even if Sukarno had been impressed by China he still maintained a favorable view of the United States. "I am confident," he wrote, that there were also "lasting effects of his [Sukarno's] visit to U.S. which will produce results beneficial to U.S."[52] Some other American diplomats—notably the American ambassador to the Netherlands, H. Freeman Matthews—called for punitive measures to avoid "rewarding Sukarno's lawlessness."[53] But both Cumming and the State Department rejected this approach. They recognized that canceling the aid agreement would likely only play into Beijing's hands by confirming its claims that American aid had "political strings."[54] If China had gained prestige with Sukarno and in Indonesia through pursuing summitry, then the best strategy for the United States was to remain involved in the country and contest it rather than reducing its presence.

Zhou Enlai's Grand Tour

After playing host to several of Asia's most prominent neutral leaders over the course of 1956, Beijing dispatched Zhou Enlai and Vice Premier He Long on a tour of eleven Asian and European countries between November 1956 and February 1957. At the time, it constituted the most extensive trip abroad ever made by a CCP official. The tour occurred in the immediate aftermath of the Soviet Union's brutal suppression of the Hungarian uprising, and the three European destinations on Zhou's tour—Poland, Hungary, and the Soviet Union—reflected Beijing's desire to play the role of unifier in the Communist camp.[55] Beijing chose the eight Asian countries on the premier's itinerary— North Vietnam, Cambodia, India, Pakistan, Burma, Afghanistan, Nepal, and Ceylon—as part of an effort to reaffirm the importance of the Five Principles among its neighbors. It was no accident that seven of the eight Asian countries that Zhou visited bordered directly on the PRC. Having watched the Soviet Union invade Hungary with China's tacit consent, these neighbors were now anxious that Beijing might one day use similar means to settle its differences with them. Aware of these sentiments, Zhou set the official purpose of his trip as "to seek friendship, to seek peace, and to seek knowledge."[56]

Predictably, Washington used all of the resources at its disposal to prevent Zhou's venture from succeeding. Far in advance of the trip, American officials began pressuring their Asian counterparts not to confer the legitimacy on the PRC that would be implied by welcoming its statesmen. When Robert McClintock, the American ambassador in Phnom Penh, learned that Sihanouk planned to extend an invitation to the Chinese premier, he told Cambodian diplomats that he was "deeply disturbed by the news." The ambassador added that this would "impose [a] severe strain on those friends [of] Cambodia who wished to see this country immune from [the] Communist menace."[57] McClintock's protests were to little avail, however; Cambodia would be the second country Zhou visited (after only North Vietnam) when his tour began eight months later.[58]

Zhou as always proved a magnet for publicity wherever he went on his tour. The premier received rousing welcomes from large crowds in many

Zhou Enlai is greeted during his visit to Burma in 1956 as
part of his tour of Asia. (Xinhua News Agency)

cities, mirroring the grand receptions the PRC had afforded dignitaries from
his host countries when they visited Beijing. Geng Biao, an eminent CCP
official who was PRC ambassador to Pakistan during Zhou's visit, recalled:
"Not only in Pakistan's largest city, Karachi, its second largest city Lahore,
and historical cities such as Rawalpindi, Peshawar, and Hyderabad but also
in the East Pakistan (which is now Bangladesh) capital city Dakar and the
Narayanganj business district, wherever the delegation went, warm and
kind local people came smiling to welcome it."[59] In some places, according
to Geng, thousands of people lined the roads waving banners and chanting
slogans such as "Sino-Pakistani Friendship!"[60] Similar crowds greeted the
premier in Cambodia. With a hint of envy, the U.S. embassy in Phnom Penh
reported: "Elaborate festivities and excursions were organized for Chicom
Premier [Zhou Enlai], more elaborate than anything that has ever been seen
in post-war Cambodia."[61]

Zhou strove to maximize his visibility throughout the tour by visiting
important historical and cultural sites in each country and meeting with representatives of key groups. During his stay in Nepal, the premier visited an

Zhou Enlai visiting the Naval Training School in Pakistan in 1957.
(Xinhua News Agency)

orphanage in Katmandu, where he gave a donation of five thousand rupees and then moved on to see a Buddhist school and monastery.[62] In Pakistan, Zhou brought his entire delegation to visit the tomb of Muhammad Ali Jinnah, who had played a pivotal role in bringing about Pakistan's partition from India in 1947 and was viewed as the father of the country.[63] Through demonstrations of generosity and respect for the religions, cultures, and histories of neighboring countries, Zhou sought to build on what he had done to improve China's image at Bandung. He wanted the PRC to be admired for its commitment to peace and be seen as a sympathetic friend to other Asian nations with which it shared not only a continent but also a history of anticolonial struggle.

This is not to say that the trip was without hitches. In India, it became clear that the mutual enamorment that had prevailed between Zhou and Nehru since 1954 was wearing thin. Frictions surfaced between them over two issues. When the leaders discussed events in Hungary, Zhou defended the Soviet invasion, claiming that Washington and its allies had incited the uprising against a legitimate government, while Nehru argued that Moscow's behavior violated the Five Principles.[64] The two leaders also struggled to find common ground on the issue of Tibetan autonomy. Tibet's spiritual leader, the Dalai Lama, was in India to attend the celebration of the 2,500th anniversary of Buddha's birthday during Zhou's trip. The premier worried that the Dalai Lama would be persuaded to stay in India by other Tibetan leaders who had fled there. Zhou met twice with the Dalai Lama in India and discussed the issue with Nehru. Ultimately, Nehru urged the Dalai Lama to return to Tibet and work to strengthen Tibetan autonomy from within China.[65] Zhou promised that in the future China would welcome religious exchanges between India and Tibet but warned Delhi against political involvement.[66] Although both sides remained eager not to allow Tibet to threaten Sino-Indian accord, Zhou's warning reflected a growing Chinese sensitivity toward foreign meddling in the region. For the time being, however, Zhou's rapport with Nehru remained largely intact. The premier received a "hearty welcome" in India, to use Nehru's words, and the disagreements between the two leaders did not diminish what Zhou had accomplished during the trip.[67]

During Zhou's tour, American officials emphasized the need to disabuse Asian leaders of their illusions about the PRC. Some American allies in the region, especially Pakistan, were disappointed that Washington adopted such a hard line. The Pakistanis had harbored ambitions to bolster their own position by helping to open lines of communications between the United States and the PRC and serve as a mediator between them. The Eisenhower administration made it clear that Karachi would gain no benefits through associating with Communist China. When Pakistani prime minister Suhrawardy wrote to Eisenhower on 12 December informing him of Zhou's forthcoming visit to Pakistan and asking if he might talk to the premier on the administration's behalf, Eisenhower and Dulles made it clear that they would not afford the premier another opportunity to show his moderation.[68] The president responded by urging the Pakistani to see through Zhou's deceptions and maintain Karachi's alignment with SEATO and the Free World. He explained that Beijing's insistence on its right to attack Taiwan coupled with "the standing Communist Chinese threat to the Republic of Korea and all Southeast Asia" was a "source of instability in the area and a constant threat to peace."[69]

The Eisenhower administration also sought to mitigate the impact of Zhou's tour by inviting Nehru to visit the United States on 16–20 December, less than a week after Zhou had left India for Burma. The administration likely saw the invitation as a way to divert attention from the premier and refute some of his claims. Washington suspected that Nehru had doubts about the long-term prospects for Sino-Indian entente and the Five Principles and tried to use this to its advantage. Frederic P. Bartlett, the counselor at the U.S. embassy in India, advised the president to draw parallels between the Five Principles and the Kellogg-Briand Pact, the notoriously ineffectual 1928 international agreement that outlawed war, in order to demonstrate why the United States needed to maintain a strong deterrent capability in Asia. He also suggested that American officials remind Nehru of what he termed Washington's "tedious efforts" to extract a pledge from China not to use force in the Taiwan Strait.[70]

Although Americans felt certain that Nehru privately feared Chinese expansion, publicly the Indian prime minster continued to argue that the world needed to accept the PRC as a legitimate power. Rather than heeding the warnings of his American interlocutors on China, Nehru continued to criticize U.S. policy—even on American soil. In a speech at a banquet held at the Indian embassy he praised Zhou as "a great Communist leader" and during a press conference with American journalists he called the premier "a rather remarkable man."[71] Asked about his views of the two Chinese governments, Nehru replied, "Obviously, the Formosan Government, at the most, is the Formosan Government. Let me say, the map will show you it is not China, whatever else it is."[72] Ironically, Washington's decision to invite Nehru to the United States may have helped to deepen rather than diminish the impact of the premier's trip.

Ultimately, American diplomats acknowledged that they had been unable to derail Zhou's tour in any significant way. Often their reports admitted that they could not but be impressed with the premier's diplomacy. "[Zhou] comported himself masterfully as [a] genial friend," a report by the U.S. embassy in Phnom Penh noted. "On balance," it continued, the premier's visit had "yielded Chicoms considerable propaganda benefit and introduced new cordiality into relations between Phnom Penh and Peking."[73]

A report filed by the American consul general in Dhaka was remarkably similar. "Elaborate and extraordinary preparations were made for [Zhou]'s visit," it noted. The visit on the whole was "a highly successful public relations operation by the Chinese Communists," which "must have worked to develop in the public mind a feeling that [Zhou] and the Chinese Communists are respectable, attractive, and perhaps also worthy of emulation."[74]

Americans recognized that Beijing had scored another important symbolic victory through Zhou's trip. The premier had once again successfully donned the mantle of international statesman and visited neighboring countries that no high-level CCP official had previously ventured to. Even if Zhou's tour was tarnished slightly by occasional disagreements with his hosts, it had given New China a great deal of visibility and lent further credibility to the PRC's peace campaign. Yet even if the PRC's stature was growing, its triumph was far from complete. Many neutral states in both Asia and the Middle East still had no official relations with the PRC and some recognized Taipei instead. This was a constant, nagging challenge to Beijing's legitimacy—one that it took on with some success during the late 1950s.

Achieving Recognition

Many Asian and Middle Eastern nations eagerly sought greater economic and cultural contacts with the PRC after the Bandung Conference, but offering Beijing diplomatic recognition was a far more difficult and delicate matter. The United States brought its influence and power to bear on this issue very directly, warning neutral and allied states of repercussions for establishing relations with Communist China. Moreover, countries such as Egypt, Syria, and Ceylon had recognized Jiang Jieshi's government in Taipei, and they were reluctant to break relations with the ROC. Beijing was sensitive to the challenges involved and worked patiently but persistently to persuade newly independent countries in Asia, Africa, and the Middle East to move toward official relations.

After the Bandung Conference, Beijing saw the Arab world as the most promising target of opportunity on this front. Zhou's meetings with Nasser had yielded a major diplomatic breakthrough for the PRC, and Beijing now looked to capitalize on this more concretely. At the same time, Washington's relations with Nasser and much of the Middle East had become deeply strained over a variety of issues. The Eisenhower administration primarily blamed Egypt for its failure to broker a settlement between the Arab states and Israel, though it acknowledged that the Israelis contributed to the problem. It was furious about Cairo's decision to buy Soviet weapons through Czechoslovakia and its support for anti-French forces in Algeria.[75] Nasser was equally disillusioned with the United States and its allies. He denounced the Baghdad Pact, a mutual defense agreement among Great Britain, Turkey, Iraq, and Pakistan, and organized Egypt, Syria and Saudi Arabia into a rival pact.[76] With Nasser and his supporters in the Middle East increasingly alienated from the West and sympathetic toward the PRC, Beijing sensed an opportunity.

As tensions developed between Washington and Cairo in early 1955, American officials became anxious that radicalizing Arab governments would establish relations with the PRC and called for proactive measures to prevent it. In February, the American embassy in Jordan took note of a report by an Israeli newspaper that Egypt had plans to recognize the PRC. Although the counselor at the U.S. embassy in Cairo believed Nasser was not yet contemplating this step, Secretary of State Dulles instructed the embassy that if there was "reason [to] believe [the] report [to be] true," then it should "within limits of propriety exert its influence . . . to discourage Egyptian recognition [of] Communist China."[77] In October, Washington made a more concerted effort to persuade its allies in the region to form a unified front against China on the issue. Waldemar J. Gallman, the U.S. ambassador to Iraq, asked Iraqi prime minister Nuri as-Said what he thought about the possibility of "Arab states working together to block" China but Said's response was unenthusiastic. He thought that Egypt and Saudi Arabia would not be interested and that Lebanon was too weak. There was thus little that Iraq could do to weaken Beijing's momentum.[78]

American officials watched apprehensively over the next few months as Beijing made entrees into the Arab World through cultural and economic diplomacy. When the Chinese Cultural Mission to the Middle East led by Burhan Shahidi arrived in Cairo to great fanfare in February 1956, the counselor at the U.S. embassy could read the writing on the wall. He noted that the PRC had already exchanged "delegations of scientists, journalists, and artists" with Egypt and that the "trend appears to lead to recognition of Communist China."[79] China built on this success by inviting high-profile delegations from Egypt, Syria, and other Arab states to Beijing. Often, Zhou Enlai himself met with these visitors, stressing the need for Afro-Asian unity in overcoming the legacy of colonialism. "We are very sympathetic toward the independence movements of the Arab peoples," the premier told a Syrian legal delegation visiting the PRC in May 1956 and offered assistance in helping Arab countries to sever economic ties with their former colonizers.[80] By slowly building informal but sympathetic contacts with Arab nations, Beijing hoped to create an air of inevitability about formal diplomatic recognition.

Beijing's first major success came when Egypt decided to recognize the PRC on 16 May 1956. The sudden decision likely reflected both Cairo's warming relations with Beijing and Nasser's growing alienation from the United States. Roughly six weeks earlier, the Eisenhower administration had decided to take a tougher approach toward the recalcitrant nationalist Nasser, which included freezing funds for the Egyptian's coveted Aswan Dam project.[81] Nasser's decision nonetheless infuriated the State Department, leading Secretary of State Dulles to dress down the Egyptian ambassador in Washington, Ahmed Hussein. "Recognition of Communist China has brought about an almost impossible situation," Dulles told Hussein. Nasser "could hardly have found anything that would make it harder for us to continue good relations with Egypt."[82] Of course, there was little chance that Cairo would reverse its decision, but by scolding and threatening foreign officials when their governments recognized the PRC, Dulles hoped at least to deter others from following suit.

After Cairo's decision, fears that China could use Egypt as a stepping-stone for establishing relations with other Arab countries plagued American officials. They were most immediately concerned about Syria. When Shahidi's cultural mission arrived in Damascus on 21 May, rumors swirled that the Syrian government was about to recognize Beijing.[83] According to one report,

Syria's acting foreign minister had promised that his country would recognize the PRC in the "near future."[84] At roughly the same time, a member of the Syrian parliament was meeting with Zhou Enlai in China, where the premier urged the expansion of trade and cultural exchanges between the two countries.[85] Attuned to these events, the U.S. embassy in Syria cabled Washington recommending that the ROC delegation in the United Nations approach the Syrian representative and "point out that Syrian recognition of Communist China would result in giving up a proven friend who has consistently supported the Arab point of view in the UN."[86] These measures were unsuccessful, however. Damascus recognized Beijing in July, and by October the U.S. embassy in Syria was reporting that relations between China and Syria had developed swiftly beyond their initial emphasis on trade and culture.[87]

Washington's efforts to isolate the PRC were somewhat more successful regarding the more conservative governments in the Middle East with deeper ties to the United States. Americans discouraged their closest friends in the region from pursuing contacts or exchanges that might pave the way for official relations. When Saudi Prince Faisal received an invitation to visit Beijing in 1955, for instance, U.S. officials were concerned that he would accept the invitation and that it might lead the Saudi government to consider establishing relations with the PRC. Dulles instructed the U.S. ambassador in Riyadh not to raise the issue directly but to be prepared with talking points if the Saudi ruler brought it up. He was to emphasize that Prince Faisal should think very carefully "before associating himself with [a] regime where Moslems are under persecution and where [the] Haj is utilized as a propaganda weapon to hide true facts." If the Saudis gave serious consideration to normalizing relations with Beijing, then the ambassador was to take a "more positive line, stressing . . . that we do not feel Communist China has recognized obligations in international relations."[88] Such pressures were not without effect. Saudi Arabia did not establish official relations with Beijing until 1990—long after even the United States had done so.[89]

In the Middle East, China's efforts to establish relations with Egypt and Syria had been aided by frictions between Nasser and the Eisenhower administration, but in other areas the PRC needed to exercise greater patience. In Cambodia, it took Beijing several years of steady diplomacy and engagement before the right opportunity to pursue normalization arose. Beijing understood that Phnom Penh was under tremendous pressure from Washington to brush aside Chinese entreaties on the issue. Nonetheless, after Sihanouk's successful 1956 visit to the PRC, cultural and economic delegations designed to foster goodwill sallied back and forth between the two countries. In November 1957, for instance, a Chinese art troupe visited Cambodia, where it made several performances and received a warm reception by the royal family.[90] These activities sustained momentum toward normalization even if they did not produce it immediately.

Ultimately, it was Beijing's strong support for Phnom Penh during a conflict with neighboring South Vietnam that strengthened Sihanouk's resolve to exchange ambassadors. In June 1958, Republic of Vietnam (RVN) forces infuriated the Cambodian prince when they launched an incursion into Cambodia and set up a border two kilometers inside its territory. The Cambodian government initially asked Washington to intervene in what it considered a flagrant violation of its sovereignty, but American officials refused to get involved in what they termed a dispute between two friendly nations.[91] Beijing, by contrast, had little to lose by strongly supporting Phnom Penh. Such a gesture, it realized, could build trust not only among Cambodians but also among other neutralist Asian countries whose sympathies lay with Sihanouk. At a reception for visiting Cambodian economic and religious delegations on 30 June, the PRC foreign minister Chen Yi announced, "We firmly believe that justice is on the side of Cambodia." He was confident that Phnom Penh would "gain the support of all of the peace loving peoples and nations" and achieve victory in the end.[92]

American officials understood that Beijing's unqualified support for Cambodia would stand in contrast to Washington's restraint. On 9 July, Elbridge Durbrow, the American ambassador to South Vietnam, warned, "Sihanouk may be moving closer to Communist China" and counseled against efforts to "appease" the prince because they would only "encourage him in his game of playing both ends against the middle." Sihanouk needed to be told that if he moved closer to Beijing, he "must not expect us to enter bidding contest with Communists but rather must expect that U.S. would be obliged to abandon its aid policy."[93]

Durbrow's recommendations were ineffectual. Sihanouk quietly arranged to establish partial bilateral ties with the PRC through a phone call to Zhou Enlai on 17 July.[94] Although Cambodia formally recognized the PRC on 19 July via an exchange of letters, American officials did not become aware of the decision until Sihanouk announced it in a speech before the cabinet and some members of the National Assembly on 21 July. Before the announcement, Carl W. Strom, who had taken over as the American ambassador in Phnom Penh, had urgently requested a meeting with Sihanouk in an effort to "head off" recognition. The State Department encouraged the ambassador, instructing him to "express this Government's concern" and remind the prince that his "decision affects [the] whole area [of] Southeast Asia and is of concern to all his neighbors." If Sihanouk decided to establish relations with the PRC, then Strom was to seek an audience with the king and queen to "insure [that the] U.S. viewpoint [was] thoroughly understood at [the] palace."[95] These strategies were all scuttled, however, when Washington realized that it was already too late to prevent what it considered the worst-case scenario from playing out.

Once Cambodia's recognition of the PRC became a fait accompli, Washington reevaluated its policy toward the small, neutralist country. It decided to issue vague warnings without taking actions that would push Phnom Penh closer to the PRC. The State Department called Ambassador Strom back to Washington, where he met with the assistant secretary of state for Far Eastern affairs and other relevant officials to discuss U.S. policy. Strom argued that the United States should not reduce military or economic aid to Sihanouk's government or punish it since cuts would "simply cause projects to be shifted to the Communist aid programs." Nevertheless, the military wanted to make stronger efforts to discourage Phnom Penh from establishing deeper ties with Beijing. The U.S. Pacific Command called for the administration to issue a warning that American aid policy was being reconsidered and that the United States would be watching Cambodia closely.[96] The Joint Chiefs of Staff made a similar plea in a memo to the secretary of defense, arguing that "the U.S. must obviously indicate to Cambodia and its neighbors our displeasure over that country's recognition of Communist China." It proposed that Washington inform Sihanouk "that the U.S. is compelled by his action in recognizing Communist China, to consider that future U.S. aid programs must be related to the direction in which Cambodia moves."[97] Americans were of course well aware that their warnings were unlikely to get Sihanouk to undo his actions. They more likely intended to subtly let other Afro-Asian nations contemplating ties with Communist China know that they could not recognize the PRC without consequences for their relations with the United States.

By the late 1950s, Washington's campaign to prevent postcolonial nations from recognizing the PRC expanded into Sub-Saharan Africa. Although much of the region remained under colonial rule before 1959, Washington was nevertheless intent on preventing Beijing from gaining recognition from countries that had the authority to grant it. American diplomats stationed in Africa used their influence in small and sometimes subtle ways to isolate the PRC. Often, they reacted against preliminary, informal contacts between China and Africa to ensure that Beijing could not establish a foothold that would enable it to gain the recognition of new states when the continent decolonized.

After Bandung, Liberian sympathy for the PRC became a cause for concern among American officials. Washington was naturally loath to see this country that had been established by former American slaves move toward better relations with its rival. In April 1956, the State Department learned that Monrovia had offered its initial support for China's admission to the Inter-Parliamentary Union (IPU), an organization that promoted dialogue between parliaments and legislatures from around the globe. Before the final vote at the IPU's annual meeting was cast, however, U.S. ambassador Richard Lee Jones met with Liberian president William Tubman to discuss the issue. Jones told Tubman that the United States would have to "walk out" if Red China was admitted and that Liberia's closest political allies in the United States would be disappointed. Tubman first responded that "the U.S. was making too much over Red China" and that the PRC's position would be "enhanced by the opposition being shown." Eventually, however, he cabled the Liberian delegation attending the IPU Congress to change its vote to "no" on China's admission. Jones also strongly cautioned Tubman about accepting an invitation recently tendered by Beijing to establish diplomatic relations. He warned, "Many governments are watching Liberia, and especially the President, to see what he will do toward Red China." But simply declining the offer was not enough; Tubman also needed to word his reply so that it would "not give Red China or the USSR any diplomatic advantage from the situation."[98] Liberia followed Washington's lead and did not establish relations with Beijing until 1977.

As colonialism in Africa began to collapse during the late 1950s, Americans strove to prevent China from gaining recognition from the newly emerging states. A tug of war between Beijing and Washington occurred over the loyalties of Ghana, the first country in the region to acquire independence. In February 1957, Ghana, then still known as the Gold Coast, prepared to hold a ceremony to celebrate its independence from Great Britain, and on 19 February, Beijing announced that it would dispatch the famous Marshall Nie Rongzhen, one of the deputy premiers of the State Council, as its special envoy. When American officials learned that the PRC had been invited but that the ROC had not, they "brought the matter forcefully to the attention of both the British Government and the authorities of the Gold Coast," according to Robert C. Hill, the assistant secretary of state for congressional relations. Hill worried that because of their "Asian origin," the Chinese could become "more effective purveyors of Communism in Africa than the Russians or other European Communists." If the PRC was represented at the ceremonies, he feared, it would also be able to invite Ghana's future leaders to visit Beijing, propose the establishment of cultural and trade relations, and engage in other activities that could help to boost China's profile in Africa. Washington's strategy was to lobby for the extension of an invitation to the Republic of China in the hopes that this would "result in a decision of the Chinese Communists not to appear."[99] This approach failed, however, and a Chinese delegation led by Marshall Nie attended the ceremonies as planned.[100] Ghana did not recognize the PRC until 1960, but its leadership's sympathy for Communist China reflected a broader sentiment among neutralist African leaders that would become increasingly problematic for the United States during the 1960s when more new states on the continent gained their independence.[101]

In general, while Washington was able to prevent staunchly anti-Communist governments that relied on American assistance from recognizing Beijing, many of the more contestable neutral states empathized with China. Between 1955 and 1959, the PRC normalized relations with twelve new Afro-Asian countries and concluded trade agreements with several others.[102] Such successes, American officials believed, would help "to advance [Beijing's] continuing strenuous efforts to gain fuller international recognition both as the Government of China and as a major world power."[103] By 1958, American officials had become pessimistic about their chances of arresting Beijing's peace campaign and preventing the PRC from enlarging its status in Asia. A National Intelligence Estimate prepared in May predicted that "if Communist China continues its present international policy . . . its prestige in Asia will continue to grow during the next five years." This would occur whether or not the PRC secured official diplomatic recognition from other countries.[104] What Americans were not considering was the possibility that Beijing would change its policy and completely reverse course.

During the three years after the Bandung Conference, Beijing launched an extensive diplomatic campaign in the Afro-Asian World that was based largely on the Five Principles. Through arranging state visits and seeking to resolve disagreements, the PRC raised its visibility in Asia and the Middle East and, in many instances, paved the way toward formal recognition. Washington attempted to prevent Beijing from making inroads into these areas, but in most cases its combination of cajolery and coercion could not delay the inevitable. Yet Beijing's diplomatic campaign also had limitations. Chinese diplomacy in Asia and the Middle East never led the United States to reconsider its hard-line position against the PRC, and it did nothing to change the PRC's status at the United Nations and in other international organizations. Moreover, although it may have created a general atmosphere of goodwill with its neighbors, China's peace offensive did not always solve outstanding issues—notably boundary disputes. Finally, diplomacy was an important tool for improving Beijing's ties with foreign leaders, but it did not always have as broad an impact on Afro-Asian peoples. Yet the PRC's efforts to bolster its status in the Third World could not be complete if it did not also improve popular perceptions of New China. By the mid-1950s, the PRC had begun seeking to achieve this objective through an extensive propaganda campaign targeting newly independent Afro-Asian peoples. On this front, too, it was fiercely contested by the United States.

Chapter 5

The Cultural Competition, 1955–1964

No tool of statecraft is used more directly to enhance a nation's status and prestige than cultural diplomacy. Through developing films, publications, radio broadcasts, and exchange programs advertising their virtues, states strive to fashion positive images of themselves in other parts of the world. At the same time, propaganda can also be used to weaken the status of an adversary. Publicizing the failings and vulnerabilities of rival states can be a powerful mechanism for containing their influence.

The political competition between the United States and the PRC in the Afro-Asian world during the 1950s was accompanied by an equally contentious cultural competition. By 1955, the United States Information Agency, which was responsible for America's overseas propaganda programs, had identified Chinese propaganda as a serious threat—especially in Asia. The agency worried that Beijing would build on its successes in Korea and Vietnam to enhance its standing. One report written several months after the Bandung Conference described the growing threat:

> Red China, as the dominant Communist power in the Far East, has
> assumed the leadership of Communist propaganda in that area. Moscow,
> apparently confident of [Beijing's] loyalty, has shown little reluctance in
> allowing the latter to share this role. Communist China is well-equipped
> for this task. Having captured the mainland, it has established a firm base,
> much closer than Moscow, for wider operations throughout East Asia
> and particularly, among the Overseas Chinese. Its enhanced international
> prestige, arising from military adventures in Korean and Indochina, has
> given it tremendous influence over local communist movements. More-
> over, [Beijing]-sparked propaganda drawing upon three decades of suc-
> cessful experience offers other Asian Communist parties ways and means
> of seizing power in their own countries.[1]

The growing pervasiveness of Chinese propaganda in Asia and American anxieties about it gave rise to all-out cultural warfare that persisted throughout the 1950s and 1960s.

To compete against each other, Beijing and Washington deployed virtually every available medium of propaganda while seeking to create new identifications and new boundaries in the minds of Afro-Asian peoples. They promoted ideologically determined visions of global community with clearly defined adversaries that needed to be excluded. The United States urged the citizens of newly independent countries to envision themselves as part of a society of Free World nations while representing China as a threat. National Security Council guidance on U.S. policy in the Far East called, among other things, for efforts in the field of information to "increase the understanding and ori- entation of Asian peoples toward the Free World" and "expose the menace of Chinese Communist imperialism and world Communism pointing out to Asian peoples that their self-interest, welfare and freedom will be furthered by opposition to Communism."[2] Chinese cultural policy, in contrast, worked to advance the peace offensive launched at Geneva into the realm of mass politics, creating a united front against imperialism that incorporated both the governments and the peoples of newly independent nations. It sought to realize Zhou Enlai's vision of the "unity of friendly, peaceful nations and people."[3] Much as U.S. propaganda encouraged a sense of Afro-Asian identity that embraced the Free World and excluded the PRC, Chinese propaganda encouraged identification with the causes of anti-imperialism and Afro-Asian unity while casting the United States as an outsider.

To foster such identifications, American and Chinese propagandists repeatedly lauded their own society and maligned the other's. Washington promoted an image of the United States as a prosperous, free, and dynamic country. CCP propaganda boasted of China's triumph over Western coloni- alism and its rapid economic progress in the face of hardship. At the same time, the PRC and the United States continuously depicted each other as lands rife with racial and religious conflict. Both the United States and the PRC struggled with internal social discord during the 1950s and 1960s, and each sought to make the international community aware of the other's problems.

Although the ideological content of Chinese and American propaganda contrasted starkly, the instruments that the two used to disseminate their messages had more similarities than differences. Cultural exchanges and mass media such as films, magazines, and pamphlets were generally the most sophisticated forms of propaganda available during the 1950s. Beijing and Washington made prolific use of all of them. The key instruments of cultural policy were inexpensive, especially when viewed in comparison to the mas- sive sums invested in defense or economic assistance. It was, in fact, the low relative cost of these instruments that enabled the PRC to compete so vig- orously with the United States. In many Afro-Asian countries Chinese and American propagandists used propaganda to engage in an almost constant blitz of attacks and counterattacks. American and PRC officials stationed on the ground in different Afro-Asian countries tended to be highly alert to the constant drone of psychological warfare that surrounded them and often added diplomatic pressure by protesting and seeking to curtail the activities of the other side. Although this competition took on many forms, it often started with interactions between peoples.

Exchanging People

At the heart of both Chinese and American cultural policy in the Third World was the forging of new bonds between people. Beijing and Washington regularly dispatched entertainers and cultural delegations to different Afro-Asian countries while inviting artists, religious leaders, and students from the region for visits. Both nations viewed these exchanges as a way of reaching out to ordinary people and demonstrating cultural vitality. Through promoting face-to-face contacts between their own citizens and those of newly independent countries, Washington and Beijing hoped to convince others of their good intentions and counter criticisms of their societies. During the mid- and late 1950s both the Eisenhower administration and the CCP devoted significant attention and resources to developing exchange programs and undermining those of their rivals.

The CCP initiated what it termed People's Diplomacy during the Korean War, using it to level accusations of biological warfare against the United States. The party assembled elaborate displays of equipment and weapons that had allegedly been used by American forces on the battlefield and invited teams of scientists and investigators from other countries to observe its evidence firsthand. These efforts succeeded to some degree in convincing visitors from Communist and non-Communist nations that the United States was violating international conventions.[4] During the years after the Korean War, People's Diplomacy expanded its scope while gaining greatly in sophistication. Chinese dance troupes and theater ensembles traversed the globe, and more specialized religious and trade delegations visited targeted countries where the CCP hoped to encourage progress on specific issues. A growing number of visitors from around the world also traveled to Beijing during the 1950s. Important guests were feted with lavish receptions and granted audiences with high-ranking CCP leaders such as Liu Shaoqi or Zhou Enlai. On occasion the PRC either sent cultural delegations to or welcomed visitors from countries with which it had still not established formal relations, including Japan and several countries in Latin America.[5] The tacit motive behind such exchanges was to encourage countries that had not yet recognized the PRC to acknowledge its legitimacy and pave the way for more formal ties.

The CIA kept close tabs on People's Diplomacy—in part because it was in direct competition with many U.S. policy objectives—and drew up a detailed report on the scope of the program, based in part on the CPP's claims. According to the CIA, the PRC sent 5,833 of its citizens to thirty-three countries in 1955 and 5,400 to forty-nine countries the following year. Placing an equal priority on enabling citizens of other countries to see China firsthand, the PRC welcomed 4,760 visitors from sixty-three countries in 1955 and more than 5,200 guests from seventy-five countries in 1956. The vast majority of participants in these exchanges were engaged in either culture and the arts or scientific and educational programs. The CIA estimated that during the eighteen-month period from January 1955 to June 1956 China spent between ten million and twenty million dollars on these programs.[6]

Seeking to foster a sense of collective purpose among Asian and African countries, Beijing invested heavily in these exchange programs. The Chinese government worked to make sure that its cultural troupes were well received and their performances well attended. Chinese performers made deliberate efforts to emphasize that the PRC shared much with other Afro-Asian countries both historically and in terms of aspirations for the future. They combined artistry and propaganda in ways that created both excitement and controversy.

Chinese cultural delegations often became widely viewed spectacles as they traversed regions whose citizens were deeply curious about the PRC. This was clear to many U.S. officials who kept tabs on Chinese activities. In December 1954, when a Chinese cultural troupe visited Bombay (now known as Mumbai), the American consulate reported on the event in great detail. The delegation had presented "four scheduled performances and rendered special items of music, dance and song at various functions." Officials in Bombay had shown great eagerness for the delegation's visit and arranged "nine receptions, including one given by the Mayor of Bombay, nine planned visits to local institutions and places of interest, and a tea, which was given at the Governor's House by the Acting Governor of Bombay." Bombay's citizens and media greeted the performers with enthusiasm. The delegation's performances had all sold out before it had arrived, and the "performances and the activities of the Delegation were given extensive favorable publicity in the local press."[7]

Throughout its time in Bombay, the troupe dramatized the ideals of peaceful coexistence and Sino-Indian Friendship that Zhou and Nehru espoused through the Five Principles. The American consulate reported that "every opportunity for propaganda was exploited," with the Chinese delegation frequently regaling guests with its version of the popular song "Hindi-Chini Bhai Bhai," meaning "China and India Are Brothers." In one evening performance, a choral group performed a song praising Sino-Indian friendship that had been prepared especially for the occasion. The song's lyrics pronounced:

"Both China and India are great nations, both have ancient civilization[s] . . . the Five Principles express hundred millions of peoples' desire, the close unity of the Chinese and Indian peoples is a great front of peace."[8] The lyrics promoted a new historical narrative of Sino-Indian relations that glossed over past conflicts and emphasized that China and India were both nations with glorious pasts that had been victimized by the West. At the same time, they assuaged audiences about the PRC's intentions. As Chinese officials aimed to enhance the PRC's standing among neutral Asian nations through diplomacy, Chinese cultural troupes sought to do the same through music.

Beijing's politicization of cultural exchanges did not favorably impress all spectators. Some with discerning tastes viewed these efforts to infuse performances with political messages as heavy-handed. Raghunatha Iyer, a Brahmin cultural critic and editor who saw one of the PRC cultural troupe's performances in Madras, was a case in point. He wrote a review that called the recital of "Hindi-Chini Bhai Bhai" "rather brash" and complained that "the metallic march of the tune and the mechanical pumping of arms reminded me of the long forgotten torture of action songs at school." Iyer praised dances performed by the troupe, calling them a "feast for the eye" that reflected Chinese artists' "wistful eye for the shimmering beauty of nature." But, on the whole, he was distressed by the overtly ideological tone of the performance. "Why, oh why," he asked, did China seek to "ruin this superb if limited art by weighting the feet of the Angel of Grace with the lead of ideology."[9] Ironically, in attempting to show what was most admirable about its culture and diplomacy, the PRC had also shown what many considered to be its least attractive characteristic—the dominance of Maoist ideology over virtually every sphere of activity.

Even if Chinese cultural delegations did not always sway audiences to accept their political message, they served a powerful legitimating function. Beijing often used cultural delegations to raise its profile in newly independent Afro-Asian countries where it was vying for recognition with Taipei. When Sudan gained its independence in 1956, the two Chinese governments competed for its loyalties. After Taipei dispatched an economic delegation, Beijing responded by sending a cultural troupe in April 1956. At least according to Chinese accounts, the performers received a warm response from Sudanese audiences and many of the country's newspapers praised Chinese arts. A report sent to the Foreign Ministry boasted that the Sudanese public could "genuinely appreciate Chinese art" while it "despised American mass culture." Moreover, Sudanese enthusiasm for the troupe seemed to carry over into the political realm. The success of the visit had helped to "throw the activities organized by the GMD in Sudan into confusion" because after it ended, the Sudanese would "not dare to invite a GMD delegation to visit."

During the visit, Sudan's foreign minister had even promised that "it was only a matter of time before Sudan would establish formal diplomatic relations with China."[10] The Sudanese government did not actually establish diplomatic relations with Beijing until three years later, and when it did so, the relevance of the 1956 PRC cultural troupe was at best unclear. Nevertheless, through cultural diplomacy the PRC established a symbolic presence in a country that paved the way for a more official status.

Beijing considered the official greetings received by Chinese cultural delegations especially important, and diplomats often reported on them to the Foreign Ministry. When dignitaries in other Afro-Asian countries made speeches welcoming Chinese cultural troupes, they contributed indirectly to the development of a new sense of regional identity that embraced Communist China. During a visit by Chinese performers to Rangoon, Burma, in 1956, for instance, the city's mayor praised Beijing for its commitment to peace. "China's relations with Burma have been harmonious since ancient times and they have been further strengthened since the premiers of our two countries confirmed the Five Principles," the mayor claimed.[11] A Chinese art troupe that visited Afghanistan in 1956 received a similar greeting from King Mohammad Zahir Shah: "Our countries were both participants in the Bandung Conference. We are both striving and cooperating for peace. Cultural relations between our two countries began early and evidence of this can be found in our poems and songs."[12] The PRC, of course, had little control over how foreign leaders greeted its performers, but the chance that they would elicit praise from key dignitaries undoubtedly figured into Beijing's motives for sending them.

Washington recognized that People's Diplomacy was not simply an innocuous effort to demonstrate the virtues of Chinese culture. It feared that Beijing would use cultural diplomacy to expand its prestige in Afro-Asian countries at the expense of the Free World. The United States worked to limit the impact of these Chinese performers and, at times, block them from travelling altogether. Washington was particularly vexed at the arrival of a team of fifty Chinese acrobats in Ghana in March 1958. When the State Department learned about the activities of the acrobatic troupe, it became eager to make sure that the acrobats did not visit neighboring Liberia. Secretary of State Dulles sent explicit instructions to the American embassy there to foreclose such a possibility. The troupe was "one of [Beijing's] chief weapons in [its] cultural-psychological campaign for prestige in [the] non-Communist world," the secretary wrote. The department had already pointed out to other friendly countries in the region the "undesirability of [a] visit by such [a] large group [of] indoctrinated Chinese Communists." Dulles instructed the ambassador in Monrovia to keep apprised of the acrobats' itinerary. If the troupe made plans to visit Liberia, then the embassy was to "inform the

Foreign Office [of the] character [of the] troupe and attempt [to] forestall [the visit] through such informal representations as it considers appropriate."[13] The idea was to curtail China's cultural activities in Africa subtly and informally so that the United States did not come across as domineering.

The Eisenhower administration realized, however, that blocking Chinese cultural delegations was not the only way to limit their influence. During the 1950s, the United States dramatically expanded its own cultural exchange programs and used some of them specifically for the purpose of countering People's Diplomacy. During the summer of 1954, Eisenhower asked Congress to create a President's Special Emergency Fund whose main purpose was to support presentations by private industry and tours by American artists and musicians. The president's desire to expand the range of more informal contacts between Americans and people worldwide led to the creation of the People to People program—one of the major policy initiatives of the Eisenhower administration in 1956.[14] By the late 1950s, an increasing share of U.S. exchange programs were devoted to Afro-Asian countries, where the success of People's Diplomacy was becoming a major concern. In 1959, the number of performances abroad by cultural groups supported by the president's fund totaled 1,183, but only 169 of these were in Europe. Washington sent 343 groups to the Far East, 221 to the Middle East and South Asia, 287 to South America, and 158 to Africa.[15] These numbers reflected Eisenhower administration's belief that winning over neutralist countries needed to be a higher priority than wooing those—such as Western Europeans—who already aligned with the Free World.[16]

When American diplomats stationed in neutral Asian countries noticed that Chinese exchange programs were having an impact, they often called on Washington to act. Sometimes even minor Chinese successes occasioned an American response. A Chinese circus troupe that swept through Burma in 1956 was one of many such successes to catch the attention of American officials. The troupe, one official reported, "had performed to 'full houses' in Rangoon and outlying posts" in more rural areas. The Communists had avoided targeting "sophisticated Western-oriented Asians," but this had enabled them to connect with groups that the United States could not. These concerns found their way into an annual State Department report on exchange programs. "Russian and Chinese circuses and the Chinese opera, reached an audience as yet untouched by American presentations," according to the report. To respond effectively the United States needed to have more attractions supported by the president's fund "with greater appeal for simple unsophisticated people" and "more popular music attractions."[17] Even in some of the most remote parts of Asia, Washington was unwilling to let its rivals gain prestige without a response.

By the late 1950s, both Beijing and Washington had, in ways that were often intended to undermine each other, boosted contacts between their own peoples and those of newly independent countries. Yet these exchanges had a clear limitation: no matter how large or ambitious the delegations sent abroad or invited, many important audiences still could not be reached. Both sides looked to mass media, which could more deeply penetrate societies in these contested nations. Increasingly, they began to rely on newspapers, books, radio broadcasts, and, what was perhaps the fastest growing propaganda medium at the time, film.

Film Propaganda and Sino-American Competition

By the end of World War II almost the entire world had come to recognize the power of the cinema. Because of its unique capacity to capture the imagination, film had become highly attractive to propagandists; both the CCP and the United States Information Agency produced propaganda films for distribution throughout the world.[18] At the same time, the domestic film industries in China and the United States churned out large numbers of new productions that were heavily ideological in content and fit in well with the overall propaganda programs of their respective governments.[19] Conflicts between Chinese and American diplomats over the screening and distribution of films arose frequently in Afro-Asian countries. The United States strove to maximize access to American films and prevent Chinese films from being screened. The PRC combated Washington's efforts by finding increasingly sophisticated ways to distribute its films while applying diplomatic pressure to protest showings of some American movies.

The CCP's interest in film propaganda dated back to the 1930s, when its members had formed an underground cell in Shanghai specifically devoted to penetrating the film industry. Although Communist intellectuals cooperated with Jiang Jieshi's government in the production of propaganda films during the war against Japan, after the war ended, the CCP immediately set up its own film studio. Once it had consolidated control over the Chinese mainland, the party nationalized the film industry and put the newly created Central Film Bureau in charge of all matters relating to film production, exhibition, and distribution. The new government allowed private film studios to operate for a short time, but it eventually forced them to merge with the state-controlled Shanghai Film Studio.[20] High-ranking Chinese officials paid attention to and often dictated the tone and ideological content of films produced in the PRC. They gave explicit instructions to directors and producers on many occasions. When Zhou Enlai attended a 1958 symposium for film directors, he lectured the audience on what content should be incorporated:

"The central problem is how to improve the style of our films. As the chairman [Mao] said, the class nationalist style and thought must be improved and our art perfected."[21] The government's scrutiny of filmmakers assured that their final products reflected the domestic and international objectives of the CCP.

As Chinese films increasingly reflected the party's agenda, Beijing became eager to promote them abroad, especially in neutral countries. By the late 1950s, the PRC had a particularly sophisticated operation in place in Cambodia. One report on propaganda operations drawn up by a Chinese official in Phnom Penh reported with satisfaction that "movies were an effective means of communist propaganda" in the country. A servicing company known as "Huada"—with characters meaning "China" and "extend"—arranged for Chinese films to be shown in theaters in Phnom Penh with Khmer-language soundtracks. Huada arranged showings of brief, ten-minute propaganda films such as *China Today* as well as longer full-length features. Most of these films represented the PRC as a paragon of socialist modernity while glossing over its internal hardships. According to the report, the themes of movies shown included "the growth of China's economy and industry, the rapid expansion of production and construction, the strength of the Chinese military, and anti-feudalism." Beijing also used special advertising companies in Cambodia to promote its films. These companies provided special discounts for students and workers—groups that tended to be the most receptive to Communist influence throughout Asia.[22]

The vast majority of feature films shown in Cambodia were a predictable assortment of dramas that glorified the revolutionary spirit of the Chinese people in one way or another. They included *Reconnaissance across the Yangtze*, an action-adventure film produced in Shanghai in 1958 that had won a major award from the Ministry of Culture.[23] The film detailed the exploits of a small CCP reconnaissance team assigned to inspect the buildup of GMD forces along the Yangtze River during the Chinese civil war. The team's heroics ultimately led to a major victory for CCP forces.[24] Cambodian moviegoers also turned out to see the biographical film *Huang Baomei*, whose title character was held up as a model female worker.[25] The "heroic laborer" Huang Baomei played herself in the film, which told the story of Huang's relentless efforts to raise productivity at a Shanghai factory and inspire her colleagues to work harder.[26] By painting a picture of a people and a society transformed through devotion to revolutionary ideals, these films sought to sell socialism as a way of life and foster admiration for the achievements of the PRC.

Beijing's efforts to promote its films in Cambodia seem to have achieved some success. An American report on Communist propaganda activities in Southeast Asia in 1959 noted with some sense of dismay that: "Bloc films, particularly from Communist China, dominated film distribution among overseas Chinese and to a considerable extent the Cambodian-language film market as well."[27] Cambodian audiences and reviewers also formed favorable impressions of China after viewing the films—at least based on PRC reports. After watching *Reconnaissance across the Yangtze* one Cambodian spectator marveled at the fact that "in 1949 the People's Liberation Army did not have appropriate weapons, a navy or an air force but the enemy had the most modern weapons." He came away impressed with how PLA forces had used "their resourcefulness, their courage and their dauntless spirit of self-sacrifice" to score a victory over their adversary.[28] It is difficult to ascertain how typical such responses were in Cambodia or, more broadly, in the Afro-Asian world. Yet at least some spectators likely appreciated the revolutionary spirit that could be found in these Chinese films.

By the late 1950s, Americans responsible for cultural programming were increasingly alarmed by the pervasiveness of Chinese Communist films throughout the world. A report by the USIA's Office of Research and Analysis cited PRC statistics claiming that sixty-nine countries and regions had organizations engaged in the import and export of Chinese films. The report estimated that a total of more than four hundred Chinese Communist films had been displayed abroad to two hundred million moviegoers annually. Moreover, in 1959, Beijing had sponsored Chinese film weeks in eleven countries as part of the worldwide celebration of the tenth anniversary of the PRC. Many of these were held within the Communist Bloc, but Iraq and Ceylon also hosted events.[29] Although the PRC may not have been able to compete with Hollywood when it came to resources, it had forged a formidable overseas operation in a short time.

Washington soon began to take countermeasures. The USIA's general policy toward film distribution around the globe was one of "exposing as many foreigners as possible to appropriate U.S. films and denial of screen facilities to Communist material."[30] The United States attempted to deny Chinese films access to foreign audiences in two ways. First, it used diplomatic pressure to persuade some Asian leaders to prohibit the films from being shown. Second, it sought to monopolize theaters for its own films, thereby denying opportunities to Beijing.

Blocking the exhibition of Chinese films was sometimes a delicate task. On the one hand, the United States could deny the PRC a powerful mechanism for reaching foreign audiences. On the other hand, the effort at censorship sometimes seemed to contradict the ideals that the United States was ostensibly promoting. These challenges became apparent in 1957 when the State Department learned that Chinese Communist films were going to be shown in Thailand under the sponsorship of the Thai armed forces.[31]

Although Thailand was a member of SEATO and perhaps America's closest ally in Southeast Asia, the country had recently taken measures to improve its ties with the PRC after Bandung, and this troubled Washington.[32] The State Department wrote to the American embassy in Thailand that even "non-political Communist films have propaganda purpose and form part [of the] Communist cultural offensive." If these films were shown they were "certain [to] promote Chinese Communist interests." The department therefore instructed the embassy to "take [the] earliest opportunity [to] express U.S. concern [about] this subject to [the] Prime Minister."[33] But the American embassy was reluctant to raise the issue with the Thai government at what it considered a "time of political unrest." It feared that suppressing the films would only raise resentments against the United States and did not immediately follow through on the instructions.[34] Nevertheless, American efforts to contest the PRC's film propaganda persisted.

In addition to closing off potential inroads for Chinese films, Washington worked to make sure that the United States would dominate the global film market. Hollywood and the State Department continued their long-standing cooperation to promote the export of American films and gain ascendance in as many foreign markets as possible.[35] The USIA also bolstered its production of propaganda films during the 1950s. The agency's film operations became a significant part of American cultural policy in Asian and African countries. Films produced by the USIA made a more overt effort to disseminate more specific messages than those coming out of Hollywood and dealt more directly with policy issues. They presented a positive image of American life that countered Communist depictions of the United States as a land dominated by crass materialism and social inequality.[36] At the same time, they warned of the dangers of communism, sometimes singling out Communist China for criticism.

During the Eisenhower administration, the USIA film program often targeted countries in East and Southeast Asia where Washington was most worried about the possibility of Chinese expansion or subversion. One memorandum on the program written in early 1954 explained that all motion pictures produced by the agency were either "hard-hitting anti-Communist films calculated to expose Communist lies and distortions or are designed to support and clarify American foreign policy." For "maximum effect," the USIA generally "arranged for these films to be distributed theatrically, *without USIS attribution.*"[37] *This Is Quemoy* was typical of the USIA films distributed through these channels. It focused on Beijing's role in the Taiwan Straits Crisis and the heroism of the forty-five thousand islanders on Jinmen who, according to the film, courageously carried on with their daily lives in the face of regular PRC bombardment.[38] Another "unattributed" film, entitled

Unconquerable Tibet, told the story of "how the Communist Chinese, forcing the Dalai Lama to flee into India, took control of his country."[39]

The State Department's ongoing efforts to create opportunities abroad for Hollywood film producers often proved a superb complement to the activities of the USIA in the campaign to maximize America's cinematic influence and limit China's. In some instances, American distributors managed to monopolize theaters in particular areas—piquing their CCP adversaries. In Rangoon, a Burmese city where Americans and Chinese competed intensely for cultural influence, CCP diplomats complained that the United States had established a virtual stranglehold on local movie theaters. A Foreign Ministry report on the American cultural "invasion" of Burma lamented that a U.S. movie company had "strict control over cinemas in Rangoon." It maintained its grip over the city's theaters by threatening to cancel its contract with them "if even one of its demands was not satisfied." According to the report, U.S. companies demanded that American films be screened in theaters forty weeks a year, thereby "reducing the chances for Burmese films to play."[40] Of course, if opportunities for indigenous films were curtailed by American predominance, films from China were almost entirely cut off from the Burmese market.[41]

Although CCP diplomats resented American dominance of local theaters in neutral countries, they were more vociferous in protesting showings of American films with blatantly anti-Chinese content. By the late 1950s, Hollywood producers had already made a significant number of Korean War movies that inevitably represented American soldiers as heroes and their Chinese or North Korean adversaries as treacherous villains. One such film, *Battle Flame*, found its way into theaters in Ghana in 1963. The film told the story of a group of American nurses captured by Chinese forces during the war and the efforts of American marines to rescue them. Although *Battle Flame* was not noteworthy for its production values or capacity to inspire audiences, Chinese diplomats were irate that it would be screened in a purportedly neutral country. Huang Hua, the PRC ambassador in Ghana, wrote a letter to the deputy minister of information and broadcasting complaining that the film was "aiming at deliberately and venomously vilifying Chinese people, especially the Chinese People's Volunteers who fought shoulder by shoulder with Korean people in their patriotic war against American aggression." Huang expressed his hope that the film would not be shown in Ghana because it would not be "helpful to the promotion of mutual understanding and friendship between our two peoples and countries."[42]

Although the PRC was unable to have the film removed from theaters in Ghana, Huang did at least partially achieve his objective. Several Ghanaian officials viewed the film with members of the PRC embassy staff. As a result, although the Ghana Film Production Corporation, which was responsible for distributing *Battle Flame*, refused to take the film out of circulation, it did agree to remove "certain offensive parts from the film, the brochure and poster."[43] Whether Chinese diplomats were satisfied with this solution is unclear from available records. But these negotiations over the screening and content of a relatively minor American film demonstrate how the struggle between the United States and China over cultural terrain extended down to the level of small segments of individual films. Given the intensity of this competition, it is not surprising that it encompassed not only film prints but also the printed word.

Print Propaganda

Even with the advent of new, more technologically advanced mass media such as radio, television, and film, the printed word retained a unique power to influence the worldviews of people around the globe. It remained one of the most significant weapons in the arsenals of American and Chinese propagandists seeking to advance their agendas in the Third World because it could be rapidly produced and disseminated to wide audiences. Washington and Beijing barraged contested areas with a vast array of journals, books, and leaflets while dispatching special operatives to monitor and influence the coverage of events by local news media. Both American and Chinese propagandists used print media to turn the celebratory narratives they had constructed about their own societies into a part of popular discourse in postcolonial countries. Through trumpeting the successes of their nations in overcoming problems that plagued humankind, Americans and Chinese hoped to convince the peoples of the Third World that their societies were worthy of emulation. At the same time, each portrayed the other as a dangerous adversary of newly independent peoples that sought to subvert or control progress.

Print propaganda developed swiftly in the PRC after the Korean War. By the late 1950s, the Foreign Language Press in Beijing was churning out numerous journals that targeted selected audiences throughout the world. An American intelligence report estimated that the circulation of some of the most important of these journals "reached into the millions" and extended to more than eighty countries. The report also noted that the "technical quality" of magazines printed for distribution in foreign countries was significantly higher than it was for the domestic market. Part of the reason for this was likely Beijing's determination to "compete in the foreign field with the quality product available from both the West and the other more advanced members of the Communist Bloc."[44] At the same time, CCP leaders also likely saw these relatively high quality publications as a demonstration of China's rise to modernity. Sophisticated, flashy magazines with pictures of China's factories and villages could serve as evidence that the party was bringing prosperity to the PRC even if they almost literally papered over a much grimmer reality.

Among the best known of these Chinese journals was *Peking Review*, which was originally published in English but eventually appeared in other languages such as Indonesian and Swahili. Created in 1958, the review's announced purpose was to "provide timely, accurate, first-hand information on economic, political and cultural developments in China and her relations with the rest of the world."[45] Seemingly geared at more knowledgeable readers, the *Peking Review* printed a combination of statements by CCP officials, translated articles by Chinese scholars, and news articles. Another widely circulated journal, *China Reconstructs*, focused on similar themes but used illustrations and other features to cater to popular audiences. *China Reconstructs* reached more than one hundred countries—including many that had no formal diplomatic relations with Beijing—and appeared in both English- and Spanish-language editions. Other more specialized propaganda journals such as *Chinese Literature* and *Women of China* strove to educate interested readers about more specific aspects of life in the PRC.[46]

One of Beijing's most successful techniques in print propaganda was the use of subsidies to support publications that hewed close to its views on imperialism and Afro-Asian solidarity. After the Sino-Soviet split in the early 1960s, the PRC began providing extensive assistance to a journal known as *Revolution*, which was published in Paris and tailored specifically toward Africa. The USIA reported: "Revolution denounces the Soviets and champions the Chinese as leaders in the 'struggle' against 'neocolonialism and imperialism.'"[47] Appearing in both English and French editions, the journal had a circulation in the tens of thousands and was popular in Morocco and Nigeria, among other places. Radical African students in Paris and elsewhere were particularly keen readers of the journal.[48]

In addition to printing and sponsoring journals, the PRC worked to influence media coverage in Communist and neutral nations through the activities of the New China News Agency (NCNA). Originally established in 1932, the agency opened its first foreign bureau in 1949 and had thirty-one international offices by 1960.[49] During the late 1950s the NCNA moved aggressively into African and Middle Eastern countries such as Ghana, Iraq, Morocco, and Tunisia. The agency's global offices focused on placing Chinese Communist press materials with local newspapers while generating stories for domestic consumption from their posts. Its operations grew more sophisticated over time and by 1959 included "Western-style straight news reportage," which had a less propagandistic feel than the agency's earlier work.[50] The NCNA did not always act with great political acumen. In 1960, for instance, the Indian government forced the NCNA's New Delhi bureau to close down after it gave extensive coverage to a strike by government employees. Despite the occasional faux pas, however, Washington considered the NCNA "a formidable organization charged with an expanding role in the conduct of Communist China's political warfare."[51]

The most important objective of Chinese print propaganda was to foster a positive image of life in the PRC. Articles in the *Peking Review* during the 1950s and 1960s painted a broad narrative of national progress and rising levels of prosperity among different segments of society. The reality of wide-scale devastation and misery brought on by the Great Leap Forward was a world apart from the roseate view of life in the country painted by the journal. Its June 1958 issue boasted of the PRC's "bursting granaries" and reported the "richest summer harvest in living memory."[52] Other issues described the achievements of the PRC and its people in similarly optimistic tones. Some boasted of the successes of Chinese factories and industries such as steel plants in Shanghai, which, according to the review, had "better and cheaper steel pouring out faster for the whole country."[53] The review also printed numerous stories praising the achievements of peasants and workers made possible by the PRC's new egalitarian society. One piece entitled "Peasant Wang Goes to College" told the story of how Wang Pao Ching, a young peasant from an impoverished family, had been able to attend a university and thrive there through hard work and commitment to revolutionary principles.[54]

When Chinese journals were not trumpeting the achievements of the PRC, they were most often either making the case for Afro-Asian solidarity or denouncing American imperialism. The *Peking Review* included articles on topics such as the "Spirit of Bandung" and meetings of various Afro-Asian solidarity organizations, especially when these meetings criticized the United States.[55] In 1961, it reported on resolutions passed by the Afro-Asian People's Solidarity Council, claiming that they had demonstrated that the "ferocious, aggressive activities of U.S. imperialism in Asia and Africa have enabled more and more people to recognize its ugly face."[56] And, of course, the review often printed relatively generic critiques of American imperialism and the capitalist system. Typical was an article that appeared in 1961 on "The Economic Origins of U.S. Imperialist Policies of Aggression and War."[57] Through emphasizing these themes in print propaganda directed toward Asia and Africa, Beijing aspired to enhance its image while promoting a shared Afro-Asian identity that was hostile toward the United States.

Washington did not take Beijing's verbal assault lying down. It had a powerful print propaganda apparatus at its disposal that could be used to counter Chinese attacks. The USIA had a strong presence in Asia. By the late 1950s, the agency published roughly thirty-three periodicals in seventeen Asian languages totaling more than twenty-four million copies while translating more than five hundred American books into twenty-three languages.[58] Much of this propaganda output was devoted to warnings about the threat posed by Communist China. But the USIA did not assume sole responsibility for printing and distributing anti-PRC materials. The CIA produced its own "black propaganda," which was designed not to be attributable to the United States.[59]

Earl J. Wilson, a career USIA officer who was stationed in Shanghai during the Chinese civil war, played a pivotal role in launching new publications that focused on China. Troubled by what he had seen of the Chinese Revolution, Wilson determined to share his views of the CCP with the rest of Asia. In 1950, the USIA dispatched Wilson to its Manila office, where he stayed for much of the Korean War. Wilson set up a magazine known as *Free World*, which was translated into almost every Asian language and became the most widely circulated USIA publication in the region during the 1950s and 1960s. The magazine's title and pan-Asian circulation reflected American ambitions to promote a shared sense of identity among nations in the region. The magazine took pains to define the PRC as an adversary of the community of free Asian nations. Wilson remembers that during *Free World*'s early years, it "had anti-Communist material, of course, against China, particularly and the North Korean invasion." Articles condemning Chinese aggression were paired with stories about "American support for the building of democracy" and American economic assistance programs.[60]

During the early 1960s, Wilson was assigned to Hong Kong, where the United States Information Service (USIS, as USIA was known overseas) program had become deeply entrenched in the worldwide propaganda struggle against the PRC. At the time, Hong Kong was the United States' main post for acquiring and disseminating information about Communist China. As such, the post played a key role in devising print propaganda that could be used against the PRC. During the Korean War, it had launched the China Reporting Program, which printed its own publications about China and supplied materials for use by newspapers in other countries. The most significant of the program's publications was *Current Scene*, a news serial that usually devoted entire issues to analyzing particular problems and issues of Communist China. Wilson recalls that *Current Scene* was "unattributed" and "mailed to a selected audience around the world." The articles in the journals were serious in tone and scholarly in nature, generally including formal citations for the information provided. Eventually the publication was translated into several languages and was widely cited in scholarly books and articles dealing with Chinese affairs.[61]

In addition to publishing *Current Scene*, the China Reporting Program reached out to reporters and broadcasters throughout the world. The service wrote its own newspaper column, which was sent out weekly to press services in more than one hundred countries. During the two years that Wilson worked in Hong Kong, the service also produced "five to ten original books and a lot of pamphlets dealing with Communist China."[62] These books and pamphlets were often printed under the auspices of the "Union Press" to avoid direct USIS attribution.[63] On other occasions, the China Reporting Program collaborated with the University of Hong Kong, whose publications on China frequently contained material highly critical of the PRC. In 1956, it arranged for copies of the university's journal, *Contemporary China*, to be sent to universities throughout Asia and the Middle East without attribution to the USIS.[64]

In individual countries, both Washington and Beijing worked at the local level to monitor, disrupt, counter, or undermine each other's print propaganda. Available Chinese documentation of Beijing's efforts on this front is limited but nevertheless telling. In 1957, the Chinese embassy in Burma reported on what it termed Washington's "cultural invasion" of the country. The USIS post there, it alleged, was engaged in translating American novels and anti-Communist books into Burmese and holding various cultural events such as movie screenings in its modern facilities. The embassy complained that the news agency used the slogan of "cultural communication" to "buy cultural elites and cultivate secret agents." Some of the authors who became close to the United States would then write articles criticizing China and the Soviet Union or "stirring up trouble" between Burma and the PRC. The report warned that the Chinese should "pay attention to America's cultural invasion and also seize opportunities to strengthen cultural interchange between China and Burma" and "weaken American influence."[65]

American efforts to monitor and undermine Chinese publication programs were equally vigorous. The China Reporting Program was especially attentive to the expansion of PRC propaganda operations in Africa during the mid-1960s. In 1965, it dispatched one of its public affairs officers, William K. Payeff, on a tour of thirteen African countries to assess the effectiveness of Chinese programs on the continent and devise a counterstrategy. His report, filed at the end of the tour, noted that there had been a growing number of Chinese books and magazines available in Africa and that NCNA offices in various African countries were pumping out a "steady stream" of materials that found their way into local media outlets. Not all of these Chinese initiatives had been successful, but they still demanded a concerted response on the part of the USIA. Payeff called for "a steady flow of factual, credible materials from Hong Kong and other sources to key African targets pointing out the dangers of Chinese subversion, and the incompatibility of [Beijing's] policies with African aspirations." In the future, he hoped that USIS posts in

Africa would supply the China Reporting Program with ideas and raw materials to give its stories a local African angle.[66]

As American and Chinese propagandists went toe-to-toe in Asian and African countries, they dissected each other's weaknesses and vulnerabilities to find themes they could use in their materials. They considered which issues could cause their rivals to lose prestige and tried to expose each other's social problems and internal contradictions. Both proved mercilessly astute in identifying and highlighting issues that their adversary preferred not be publicized. Amid the constant hum of propaganda attacks and counterattacks, certain themes struck a particularly powerful chord among Afro-Asian audiences and proved especially effective as weapons of cultural warfare. These themes were critical to how Beijing and Washington strove to define both themselves and each other and merit special attention.

Attacking Vulnerabilities: Race and Religion

As they competed for the loyalties of nonwhite peoples, Chinese and American propagandists often focused on racial and ethnic minorities. Problems of race hindered both Beijing and Washington's efforts to gain prestige among Afro-Asian countries. Although the two rivals represented themselves as steadfast opponents of imperialism, they had, in very different ways over the course of their histories, built continental empires that forcefully integrated racial, ethnic, and religious minorities. During 1950s and 1960s both countries struggled—again in very different ways—with the ramifications of their mistreatment of their minority populations. The unrest that occurred in the American Deep South during the 1950s and 1960s found a parallel of sorts in the unrest that occurred in Tibet and Xinjiang during the same period. The CCP exploited the civil rights struggle to highlight the racism that prevailed in the United States and make the case that Washington would never regard Asians or Africans as equals. At the same time the USIA and CIA made use of the discontent among Chinese Muslims and Tibetans to undermine China's claims that as a nonwhite country it was more capable of forming a genuine partnership with newly independent Afro-Asian nations.

The vexing difficulties faced by Washington due to the intersection of decolonization in the Third World and desegregation in the American South have been noted by other historians. As Thomas Borstelmann has written, the simultaneous emergence of anticolonialism and civil rights activism during the early Cold War presented a dilemma for a country trying to prove that a liberal capitalist and democratic order "represented a more open and humane society than that of the communist states."[67] When events in Montgomery, Alabama, or Little Rock, Arkansas, drew international attention,

U.S. officials always needed to worry about their impact on America's image abroad. Other scholars have focused on American efforts to mitigate this impact by sending jazz musicians and other prominent African Americans abroad as cultural ambassadors.[68] Much less attention has been devoted to how and why America's rivals such as the PRC came to attack it on racial issues.

For Chinese propagandists, the ongoing struggle for civil liberties waged by African Americans during the 1950s and 1960s was an irresistible target. Beijing made facile connections between racial segregation in the United States and American support for colonialism abroad. The PRC saw itself as a nonwhite power that had suffered at the hands of foreign imperialism and therefore could criticize the United States on this front with much greater authenticity than the Soviet Union or other members of the Communist Bloc. As the civil rights struggle wore on in the United States, the CCP rarely missed an opportunity to make racism in the American South an issue in the Global South. The PRC used public statements, periodicals, and, perhaps most effectively, African Americans sympathetic to Communist China in its attacks on the United States.

Throughout the 1950s and 1960s, Beijing courted disaffected African American radicals who were willing to publicly criticize segregation and American imperialism. These efforts yielded a few notable successes. Deeply alienated by racial discrimination in the United States, both prominent and lesser known black radicals found China's utopian promises of universal social equality appealing. Several African American dissidents traveled to or lived in the PRC for extended periods of time and contributed voluntarily to Beijing's efforts to use racial issues as a propaganda weapon. Their cooperation gave the PRC highly visible symbols that it could use to connect the civil rights struggles in the United States to the anti-imperialist internationalism espoused by Mao in the Third World.[69]

Perhaps the most illustrious African American visitor to the PRC during the 1950s was W. E. B. Du Bois. A legendary figure in the civil rights movement, Du Bois joined the Communist Party toward the end of his life and became a fierce critic of U.S. foreign policy during the Truman and Eisenhower administrations. Although his willingness to praise Joseph Stalin and the Soviet Union long after the two had lost favor with the American left had been partially responsible for a decline in his influence within the United States, he remained respected abroad partially for the critical role he had played in the development of Pan-Africanism. Du Bois visited China in 1959 on his ninety-first birthday and made a return visit three years later, shortly before his death. On both occasions he received red carpet treatment from his hosts in Beijing.[70]

Guo Moruo greets W. E. B. Du Bois during his 1962 visit to China. (Xinhua News Agency)

Du Bois's 1959 trip to Communist China lasted nearly two months. During this extensive tour he spent more than four hours meeting with Mao Zedong and dined twice with Zhou Enlai. The elder scholar also traversed the country, visiting Beijing, Shanghai, Nanjing, Guangdong, and other major cities. In his autobiography, Du Bois lavished praise on the PRC. "I have never seen a nation which so amazed me and touched me as China in 1959," he wrote.[71] Du Bois was unquestionably prone to see the CCP though rose-tinted glasses, and some of the speeches that he gave during his tour provided excellent grist for the CCP's propaganda mills. In speaking about "China and Africa," the legendary scholar and activist addressed himself directly to Africans, offering up praise for China, criticizing the United States, and ultimately calling for greater Sino-African friendship. He depicted the PRC as a nation that, like much of Africa, had struggled to break the bonds of colonialism. Du Bois explained that China had "burst its shackles not by boasting and strutting, not by lying about its history and its conquests, but by patience and by suffering." Americans, in contrast, could not be trusted. "Beware Africa," Du Bois warned, "America bargains for your soul." Americans "would have you believe . . . that African Americans are full American citizens, treated as equals, paid fair wages as workers, promoted for desert and free to learn and earn and travel across the world." All of this, of course, was "not true." Du Bois argued that the best course for Africans was to seek deeper political and economic ties with the PRC. He appealed to Africans on China's behalf, telling them that "China is flesh of your flesh and blood of your blood. China is coloured and knows to what a coloured slave in this modern world subjects its owner." Du Bois's flowery language may have harkened back to an earlier day, but for CCP leaders seeking to win over African nations his message carried an almost urgent relevance. His speech was swiftly printed in the *Peking Review*, where international audiences could read it.[72]

Beijing strongly publicized its relationship with Du Bois. Chinese newspapers played up the significance of his visit. An article in the *People's Daily* published during his time in China praised Du Bois for his "righteous struggle," which had "given progressive forces in America and Latin America powerful support" and "had a great influence on African independence movements."[73] In subsequent years, Chinese leaders and media sometimes cited the renowned scholar when they discussed Africa or decolonization, thereby subtly connecting American racism in the domestic context with U.S. support for imperialism.[74] When Zhou Enlai traveled to Ghana in 1964, Du Bois's widow, Shirley Graham Du Bois, who had emigrated there with her husband several years earlier, was among the people who welcomed the premier at the airport.[75] Through continuously associating itself with one of the most dignified figures in the U.S. civil rights movement, the PRC aimed to persuade people of color throughout the globe that it was more worthy of their trust than the United States.

Du Bois was perhaps the most illustrious African American to lend his voice to Beijing's propaganda offensive in the Third World, but he was not the only one. The PRC's efforts to boost its prestige among Africans also benefited from the activities of Clarence Adams, a member of the small group of American POWs who had refused repatriation at the end of the Korean War and opted instead to live in Communist China. Having grown up in the American South, Adams had concluded that his life in the United States was a "dead end" and hoped that in China he might be "treated like a human being instead of something subhuman."[76] After earning a degree in Chinese language and literature from Wuhan University, Adams took a position at the Foreign Language Press, where he assisted with translations and the production of propaganda materials.[77]

In Beijing, Adams spent time with diplomats from African countries such as Ghana, Guinea, and Mali. He became particularly close with diplomats at the Ghanaian embassy, where he was considered a "trusted friend" and at times used as an "unofficial advisor." In his autobiography, Adams claims that this was a result of his own initiative and the fact that these embassies had accepted him "with open arms."[78] Nevertheless, given that the CCP decided Adams's schooling and occupation and managed its relations with African countries so carefully, it is difficult to imagine that the party did not play a significant role in brokering Adams's contact with African diplomats. At a minimum, it is clear that Adams confirmed the negative impressions that some Ghanaian diplomats had of the treatment of blacks in the United States. He recalled that when he met the ambassador from Ghana, he was told, "Do not feel so great about your country. You do not even have a flag. We may be poor in Ghana, but we have our own flag and we're our own boss. What do you Negroes have? All the stars in your flag are white." Adams recalled that he had to admit that the ambassador "was right" because he could "not say that the stars and stripes in any way represented me."[79] Through encouraging such interactions between Adams and African officials, Beijing provided living proof of its assertions that the PRC was genuinely devoted to racial equality, whereas the United States remained a land of discrimination and segregation.

As the civil rights struggle in the United States intensified, so did the CCP's determination to use it for propaganda in the Third World. In August 1963, when more than two hundred thousand Americans assembled at the Lincoln Memorial as part of the famous March on Washington, the effect on Mao and his comrades was almost electrifying. To the CCP leadership, the march was part of a larger revolutionary struggle being waged by the oppressed peoples of the world against American racism and imperialism. Three weeks before the crowds gathered in Washington, Mao Zedong knew of the planned event and issued a statement supporting African Americans in their "just struggle against racial discrimination by U.S. imperialism." The chairman character-ized the civil rights struggle as a "demonstration of the intensifying class and national struggle within the United States." He called on the "workers, peas-ants, revolutionary intellectuals, enlightened bourgeoisie and other enlight-ened peoples of all colors whether white, black, yellow, or brown to unite and oppose American imperialism and racism."[80] Through offering strong public support for black protests, Mao sought to raise his own profile among Afro-Asian peoples while capitalizing on the struggle to damage his rival's prestige. During the next few weeks, the CCP publicized Mao's statement throughout the globe. Before he even issued the statement, the chairman sent a draft to Pu Shouchang, a senior interpreter and translator in the Foreign Ministry, and ordered that English and French versions be prepared immediately.[81]

Perhaps the most ostentatious of all of the CCP's activities on the issue was the mass rally held in Beijing on 10 October 1963. The rally occurred only five weeks after the March on Washington and Martin Luther King's "I Have a Dream" speech had shown to the entire world the deep yearnings for equality harbored by African Americans. The CCP orchestrated a rally of more than ten thousand people in Beijing for a daylong event where they listened to speeches by high-ranking party officials and performed Chinese renditions of well-known African American songs. Among the songs translated into Mandarin for the occasion were the civil rights anthem "We Shall Not Be Moved" and "Ol' Man River," a song from the musical *Show Boat* that described the hardships faced by Negroes in the South. Along with these went performances of CCP standards such as "People of All the World Unite" and "Song of the Motherland" in a bizarre fusion of Chinese Communist and African American culture.[82]

Speeches given at the rally made an explicit effort to connect the struggles of African Americans in the United States with those of other Afro-Asian peoples fighting against imperialism. Liu Ningyi, a CCP luminary who occupied a variety of important positions in the party over his career, proclaimed: "The fascist-like policy and the policy of intensified suppression of the Negroes pursued by U.S. imperialism at home is closely linked with its policies of aggression and war abroad." He even contended that the civil rights struggle in the United States was a "component part of the revolutionary struggle of the oppressed people and nations the world over." While fiercely condemning the racism of the Kennedy administration, Liu represented the PRC as a friend and supporter of the struggles of African Americans and liberation movements. "We regard their struggles as our own struggles and their victories as our own victories."[83]

Among those present at the rally was Robert F. Williams, an African American civil rights leader who had been living in exile in Cuba. Williams fled the United States after the Federal Bureau of Investigation (FBI) had issued a warrant for his arrest on trumped-up charges of kidnapping. From Cuba, he had launched a radio program known as "Radio Free Dixie" aimed at black people living in the southern part of the United States.[84] Williams had reacted favorably to Mao's August statement, sending the chairman a letter expressing gratitude for China's support.[85] Aside from inviting the controversial activist to attend the rally, Beijing arranged for him to meet with diplomats from Afro-Asian countries to discuss the plight of African Americans. During the course of his visit, Williams recalled, "The Chinese people also gave me a world platform." He "met leaders, businessmen, trade unionists, and journalists by the scores from Africa, Latin America and Asia" and found that they were often "shocked to learn about the true plight of our people in

America." Williams also boasted that he had been given the opportunity to "freely express" his "impressions about American democracy."[86]

Beijing maximized publicity for the rally both domestically and internationally. Official Chinese newspapers such as *Renmin Ribao* gave the event extensive coverage the following day.[87] Moreover, a videotape of the rally that included the speeches dubbed over into English was broadcast in many parts of the world.[88] Williams lent further assistance to the PRC on this front by boasting about his visit and the rally on his radio program when he returned to Cuba. In a "Report on China" he claimed that during his meetings with Zhou Enlai and Mao Zedong, the two pledged "all out support." Williams also reported that in China "even little children express great concern for their little black brothers and sisters in America."[89] By holding and publicizing the rally along with Williams's visit, CCP leaders sought to use the issue of race to proselytize their vision of a radical, anticolonial world community that the United States could not be a part of at least until it drastically changed its political and economic system.

Beijing's regular skewering of racial inequality in the United States immensely frustrated officials in Washington, and they were eager to respond. American propaganda tried to mitigate the damage in part by emphasizing that the United States was making rapid strides on these issues.[90] Merely defending the nation's image was not enough, however. Washington also hoped to undermine the PRC's claims to be a champion of racial equality by highlighting Beijing's struggles with dissent from the roughly forty million non-Han national minorities who lived within China's borders. In 1964, the CIA supplied "propaganda guidance" to several government agencies summarizing the American approach. It explained that "Communist China poses, both in its quarrel with the Soviet Union and its hostile belligerence to the Free World as the foremost opponent of 'white imperialism and colonialism' and the self-appointed saviour of the non-white peoples of the world." The reality, however, according to the CIA, was that "the Chicoms are not only guilty of aggression against their non-white neighbors in India and Southeast Asia, but they persecute the national minorities within their own borders and are arrogant toward other colored races." The guidance went on to list some specifics about the PRC treatment of Mongolians, Uyghurs, and other ethnic groups that could be used in propaganda directed against China.[91] Much as Beijing attempted to link the U.S. government's treatment of African Americans with its hostility to national liberation and independence movements, Washington claimed that the CCP's mistreatment of its national minorities reflected Communist China's aggressive intentions toward its neighbors.

The most damaging conflicts between the CCP and ethnic minority populations were derived from the PRC's occupation and incorporation of Tibet and Xinjiang as "autonomous regions" between 1949 and 1951. Both were ethnically heterogeneous areas where non-Han peoples constituted a majority. Ethnic Tibetans were the largest group in Tibet, while Uyghur Muslims were in the majority in Xinjiang. Over the centuries these two regions had often not been completely controlled or directly governed by the various dynasties that ruled the Chinese mainland. Nevertheless, through a combination of coercion and persuasion, the PRC had extended its sovereignty over both by 1951. People's Liberation Army forces had marched into Xinjiang and pronounced it a Chinese province in November 1949. They overwhelmed Tibetan forces at Chamdo in October 1950 and subsequently forced the Dalai Lama to negotiate the Seventeen-Point Agreement, which acknowledged the PRC's sovereignty over Tibet but allowed the region to maintain some autonomy.[92]

During the early and mid-1950s, the new Chinese government pursued a fairly accommodating policy toward these two autonomous regions so that it could focus on waging war in Korea and consolidating its rule throughout the country. Initially the CCP did not attempt to impose sudden or drastic reforms in Tibet or Xinjiang and was cautious about resorting to suppressive measures when small-scale protests and revolts broke out in remote areas.[93] The CIA began looking for evidence of anti-Muslim activities in China such as "atheistic publications" or "articles urging Moslems to adopt attitudes contrary to Islamic doctrine" in the mid-1950s with the hope that it could turn up materials that could be used in propaganda but failed to find significant evidence that Muslims in Xinjiang or elsewhere were being persecuted.[94]

The 1959 uprising in Lhasa was a gift to American propagandists, however. The CCP had first stirred resistance to its policies in the region as early as 1954 when it began to force ethnic Tibetans living in Sichuan and other provinces outside of Tibet proper to participate in collectivist reforms. The CIA sought to take advantage of this discord by encouraging armed insurgency; it provided training and weapons for Tibetan guerrilla fighters from 1957 onward.[95] Finally, in March 1959, an antigovernment rebellion erupted and engulfed the province. Beijing hesitated but eventually ordered PLA forces into the region to suppress the rebels and restore order. During this brutal crackdown, Tibet's spiritual leader, the Dalai Lama, fled to India, where he took refuge and created a new base for criticizing Chinese policy toward Tibet.[96] The CCP subsequently launched a more intensive effort carry out reform programs in Tibet that included shutting down monasteries and suppressing religious expression.[97] All of this was a public relations nightmare for the PRC that damaged its relations with India and fostered misgivings about the CCP in neighboring Buddhist countries.

Washington took immediate advantage of the situation. Tibet received extensive but subtle treatment in American propaganda targeting Afro-Asian countries, especially those with large Buddhist populations. State Department officials were delighted to find that many Asian media condemned Beijing's handling of the Tibetan rebellion without prompting. One report filed in April 1959 noted that the "non-Communist press in Asia has universally condemned China's suppression of the Tibetan uprising in forceful terms." It guessed that the "depth and strength of the Asian reaction may be due to the fact that both the Tibetans and their Chinese oppressors are 'fellow Asians' and Buddhists and to the lack of any Western involvement which would put the Tibetan situation in a 'cold war' context." With phrases such as "another Hungary" and "betrayal of Bandung" being used frequently to describe what had occurred, the USIA and other agencies involved in cultural policy reasoned that a hands-off policy that quietly encouraged such reporting would be highly effective.[98]

The USIA's approach in Ceylon, a small neutralist nation whose population was predominantly Buddhist, typified its approach. A report written by the USIS post in Colombo at the end of 1959 relished that it had been a "good year." The CCP's actions in Tibet had "clearly illustrated Communist aggressive intentions which many Ceylonese had previously felt did not exist." An official from the Ceylonese Ministry of External Affairs even told one USIA officer that "the Communist Chinese are the best propagandists you have in Asia." After the Tibetan uprising, USIA activities were "designed to support local editors and others who wanted to publicize the facts about Tibet." These efforts were all "kept unattributable" but were nevertheless significant in scope. They included placing more than a thousand column inches of unattributed material in the press, assisting a popular magazine with the production of an eight-page supplement on Tibet, and arranging for a USIS-produced film entitled *Unconquerable Tibet* to play in commercial theaters.[99] By making condemnations of China's treatment of Tibetans appear to be a reflection of Ceylonese attitudes, the USIA fostered mistrust between Beijing and Colombo while appearing to remain above the fray.

Of course, Washington did far more than simply publicize the Tibetan rebellion. It also encouraged and prolonged it by rendering a broad array of support to Tibetan dissidents. John Kenneth Knaus, a former CIA agent, has written a detailed account of how he helped to organize special training operations for Tibetan rebels in Colorado and sustain a base of two thousand guerrilla fighters in Nepal throughout the 1960s.[100] Some of the reasoning behind the operation was clearly strategic. The CIA hoped that through aid to Tibetan rebels it could weaken Beijing's hold on the region and destabilize the PRC. At the same time, American officials recognized that if Tibetan resistance persisted it would continue to draw international attention and have tremendous propaganda value. John Kenneth Galbraith, the Kennedy administration's ambassador to India, summarized that the purposes of the operation were to "prevent the consolidation of the hold of the Chinese on Tibet, draw off Chinese resources into the insurrection there, and keep in the public eye the image of Chinese aggression in the area."[101] Galbraith didn't believe that the operation was succeeding and urged its cancellation. But Washington could not give up the possibility of keeping a resistance movement so damaging to China's international image "in the public eye."

Throughout the Kennedy and Johnson administrations, aid continued to flow to support the Tibetan rebels and their cause, and propaganda remained a significant component of the operation. In 1963, the CIA brought 133 Tibetans to the United States for training in "political, propaganda and paramilitary techniques." The agency also allocated seventy-five thousand dollars for the support of two "Tibet Houses" in New York and Geneva. These houses were intended to "serve as unofficial representation for the Dalai Lama to maintain the concept of a separate Tibetan political identity." The Tibet House in New York City was to "work closely with Tibetan supporters in the United Nations, particularly the Malayan, Irish, and Thai delegations."[102] Through keeping the issue of Tibet alive in international organizations that many Afro-Asian states participated in such as the United Nations, the CIA recognized that it could tarnish China's image as a champion of racial equality in addition to weakening its government.

The USIA eagerly supplemented the CIA's activities. Throughout the 1960s, the China Reporting Program in Hong Kong prepared news summaries and articles about the situation in Tibet that it placed in foreign media. Often these pieces focused on the plight of Tibetan Buddhists and their heroic challenge to Chinese rule, much as CCP propaganda praised the heroism of the African American struggle. One article that the service sent out to USIS posts around the world in 1963, for instance, focused on Tibetan guerrillas fighting against Red Army occupation and reforms being imposed on their homeland by the CCP. According to the article, Tibetan resistance fighters were "joined in prolonged mortal struggle against the crack mountain troops of Communist China's Red Army of occupation." The reason for the struggle was that the CCP had carried out "a basic attack on the religious structure of Tibetan society." In implementing reforms China had broken earlier promises not to alter traditional religious and economic practices, targeting monks and monasteries. The article also cited a report by the International Commission of Jurists equating the CCP's actions in Tibet with genocide because it had acted with "intent to destroy a religious group."[103]

Beijing did attempt to counter American propaganda on the Tibet issue. In January 1961, the *Peking Review* ran an article on "Tibet in 1960" that explained Chinese views of Tibet. The article made no mention of the 1959 rebellion and its suppression by the PLA. Instead it boasted of the successes of the Great Leap Forward and socialist construction in improving the fortunes of Tibet. Before the Great Leap Forward serf-owners in Tibet had "plundered the serfs and slaves to satisfy the needs of their debauched and licentious life." By contrast, under Chinese rule, the serfs were "displaying soaring revolutionary enthusiasm."[104] To many Asians, however, the PRC's almost frantic efforts to whitewash the discord that existed in Tibet likely came across as heavy-handed. Soft-pedaling a portrait of Tibet as a land progressing toward the CCP's utopian goals was, to say the least, challenging when China's version of events was contested so vigorously by the Dalai Lama and other figures.

Even as Beijing sought to defend itself against international criticism on the Tibetan issue, the increasingly visible disaffection of Chinese Muslims with Communist rule was becoming a convenient new target for the USIA. During the 1950s, the CCP's increasingly radical efforts to restructure China's economy and society gradually alienated the Muslim community. The CCP sometimes confiscated land belonging to mosques, and its demands for greater emphasis on Marxism-Leninism in the educational system seemed to come at the expense of Muslim culture and tradition. When the CCP briefly allowed criticism of the party during the Hundred Flowers Campaign, many Muslims seized on the chance to attack government policy. Occasional revolts by Hui Muslims erupted, including one in spring of 1958 that reportedly sought to establish a Chinese Muslim republic.[105]

The China Reporting Program in Hong Kong immediately exploited these developments by publishing and distributing a brief informational book entitled *Moslem Unrest in China*. The book depicted the Chinese state as inexorably committed to the destruction of Islam and Muslim culture in the PRC. In Communist China, it explained: "Only such customs and traditions—and the Communists classify Islam as a matter of custom and tradition—as are 'compatible with socialism' may be preserved. Other customs and traditions, and the distinct racial entities that produce them, are to be gradually suppressed and eliminated."[106] The likely targets of the book were the Islamic countries of the Middle East and Africa whose friendship and recognition Beijing was seeking. By documenting Muslim unrest in China and fostering an image of Chinese Communists as hostile to Islam, the USIA hoped to destroy the trust the PRC had gained in the region through its diplomacy at Bandung and elsewhere.

After the publication of *Moslem Unrest in China*, USIA officials became interested in sponsoring a more comprehensive, scholarly account of tensions between the CCP and China's Muslim population for international distribution. In 1959, the agency contracted with the Council on Islamic Affairs, a short-lived think tank that focused on the role of Islam in the world, to produce a book dealing with events in the "Moslem and Buddhist regions of China." John C. Wiley, a retired ambassador who served as president of the council, tried to arrange for collaboration between Supreme Court Justice William O. Douglas and Ram Rahul, a well-known Indian scholar, on the project. Wiley argued that such a book would be "most effective in establishing in the Middle Eastern and Asian mind the fact that the policy of Red China toward its ethnic and religious minorities is no whit better than other forms of 'colonialism' which the Asians abhor."[107] For reasons that are not entirely clear, the Council on Islamic Affairs had folded by 1963, and most of the publications that it had been expected to produce were never delivered.[108] Nevertheless, the USIA's interest in producing and disseminating information on the issue would only grow over time.

Disturbances that flared in Xinjiang in 1962 revived international interest in the fate of Chinese Muslims and precipitated a fresh round of USIA reporting on the issue. The main cause of the disturbances was Beijing's effort to impose a new grain-rationing system on the region that was similar to others set up by the CCP throughout China. In April and May, as many as sixty thousand residents of Xinjiang who belonged primarily to the Kazakh and Uyghur ethnic groups crossed the border into Kazakhstan, then part of the Soviet Union. On 29 May, a riot erupted at a bus station near the Soviet border, with protestors eventually breaking into the offices of party officials and shouting such slogans as "Xinjiang Is Ours" and "Down with the Communist Party." Although the riots were quelled, covert organizations committed to Xinjiang's independence were formed after these events.[109]

American propagandists soon capitalized on news of the riots. In 1962 and 1963, the China Reporting Program in Hong Kong issued press releases and devoted increasing attention to events in Xinjiang in *Current Scene*. The USIS generally emphasized that the vast majority of refugees fleeing into the Soviet Union were Muslim with deep-seated hostility toward Chinese rule. One press release issued shortly after the riots occurred reported on "Islam Agony in Central Asia." After briefly summarizing news reports that had come out of Xinjiang, the article claimed that what had transpired there marked "but one brief episode in a long history of clashes between Moslems and Chinese." It added, "Since their very first encounter in the remote hinterlands of China, Islamic faith and communist politics have been locked in a prolonged, historic struggle." China's policies in Xinjiang were depicted as a function of communism's innate hostility toward all religions. "Communists in China, as elsewhere, are atheists by conviction, and proud of it," one USIS report claimed. "Current attacks against religion in the Peking press indicate that long-term peaceful coexistence between Islam and communism in China is highly improbable."[110] At virtually the same time that Beijing was intensifying its attacks on racial bigotry in the United States, Washington was stepping up its criticisms of religious intolerance in China, undermining the PRC's efforts to represent itself as a champion of equality and social justice.

Washington and Beijing continued seeking to exploit each other's internal difficulties with ethnic and national minorities until relations between the two thawed during the 1970s. This kind of propaganda remained an effective tool for arousing mistrust and suspicion among Afro-Asian countries toward outside powers—be they capitalist or Communist. As they vied for cultural influence in the Third World at each other's expense, Beijing and Washington also found that certain groups within newly independent countries merited particular attention. Perhaps the most important among them were the overseas Chinese communities in Southeast Asia.

Diasporic Chinese and Sino-American Cultural Competition in Asia

Formulating policy toward Chinese living overseas, especially in Southeast Asia, was one of the most challenging issues faced by Beijing as it tried to convince nations of the region of its peaceful intentions. On the one hand, the PRC believed that it was critical that these diasporic Chinese communities recognize the legitimacy of the new Communist government and continue to admire their motherland. But this was a delicate balancing act. Overt efforts to inculcate these communities with any particular viewpoint could easily arouse suspicions in their host countries. In some instances, as mentioned in Chapter 3, Beijing sought to resolve these potential issues through treaties and protocols. Yet even after these treaties were signed, Beijing remained acutely sensitive to how overseas Chinese perceived the PRC and was deeply concerned about attempts to attract them to the capitalist camp.

And of course, Washington made explicit efforts to win over diasporic Chinese from the mid-1950s onward. The United States became interested in the large numbers of overseas Chinese living in Southeast Asia not so much out of respect for their cultural influence but out of fear that they could become a tool for subversion. According to one American report, significant populations of Chinese lived in Thailand (3 million), the Philippines (3.4 million), Indonesia (2.5 million), and Malaya (2.2 million). The situations of these overseas Chinese varied greatly from one country to the other, as did their political sentiments, with some communities maintaining loyalties to the Nationalists and others becoming supportive of the CCP. Americans recognized that these diasporic Chinese were "far from being the key to SEA [Southeast Asia] for either the free world or the Communists." Yet even as the United States acknowledged that little could "be expected of the overseas

Chinese as a positive instrument of U.S. policy objectives," the Operations Coordinating Board worried about their "negative capabilities for impairing our effort." In particular, the "localized subversive strength" of overseas Chinese communities had the potential to become "the deciding factor in a close situation." It therefore became important for the United States to "deny [the] exploitation of the overseas Chinese to [Beijing]."[111]

The CCP, however, was willing to work hard to win the loyalties of what it considered overseas brethren. Beijing devised preferential measures for relatives of overseas Chinese living in the PRC, exempting them from some internal policies with the hope that it would encourage Chinese living abroad to send remittances.[112] But soft power and culture were really at the core of CCP efforts to win the hearts and minds of the Chinese diaspora. Beijing made extensive efforts to influence Chinese newspapers in Southeast Asian countries; its Xinhua News Agency enjoyed a high success rate at placing materials with overseas Chinese media.[113] Policy makers in Washington also characterized the PRC's efforts in this area as a success. One report noted that in numerous countries the Communists had "secured control over Chinese language and vernacular newspapers" that typically mixed local and foreign news with editorials about "[Beijing's] friendship with the local government, Asian-African solidarity," and the "aggressive character" of SEATO, among other topics.[114]

In selecting films for distribution in Southeast Asia, Chinese propagandists made a special effort to find movies that could create a sense of kinship between diasporic Chinese and the motherland. During the late 1950s, they gained a wide showing for *Liang Shanbo and Zhu Yingtai*, a love story set in premodern China, described by American sources as "ostensibly free from any Communist message other than the implied criticism of arranged marriages contained in the story." Even U.S. officials acknowledged that the film did an excellent job of promoting the CCP's cause because its story and genre helped to "stimulate interest in China's past, strengthen [Beijing's] claim to be the guardian of Chinese traditions, and create an impression of affluence and peace under the Communist regime."[115] By demonstrating that mainland China (not Taiwan) was the real center of modern Chinese life and culture, Beijing hoped to foster a lasting affinity for the PRC among Chinese living abroad.

Cultural delegations sent abroad became another important element in the CCP's efforts to capture the loyalties of overseas Chinese. When performers from the PRC visited Rangoon in 1955, it held a special engagement for the city's Chinese population. The group played to a full house. According to a report filed by the delegation's leader with the Foreign Ministry, the "welcome was unusually warm." One audience member who had long lived in Burma claimed that he had "never seen such a good performance since the day he was born." He added that he felt "honor and pride that the rich and splendid art of his mother country had received such a warm welcome abroad." When the Burmese foreign minister and other high-ranking officials held banquets for the delegations, they invited leaders from Rangoon's Chinese community. Chinese leaders in the country believed that this was because the delegation had helped to elevate their status.[116] The fact that a Chinese cultural delegation could command Rangoon's respect for both the PRC and Burma's own Chinese community doubtless fostered sympathy for Beijing.

American propaganda sought to undermine CCP efforts to bond overseas Chinese to the motherland. It encouraged diasporic Chinese to "increase their orientation toward their local governments and toward the free world" and to "organize and activate anti-Communist groups" in their communities.[117] The USIS in Hong Kong established a special Chinese Language Program focusing on the Chinese diaspora. One of its magazines, *World Today*, became the largest non-Communist Chinese-language magazine in the world during the early 1960s. The service also translated well-known American books into Chinese. Earl Wilson remembers helping to create "miniature bookshelves" of about thirty titles each in fields such as history, economics, and literature. Many of these books were eventually sent to libraries in Chinese schools throughout Asia.[118] In 1956, the USIS even created a Chinese-language calendar that was distributed in all Southeast Asian countries with large Chinese minorities. According to the official description, each page carried "a story of some event in Chinese history or mythology emphasizing traditions and virtues that the Communists would destroy such as filial piety, love of religion, respect for the individual, love of freedom, etc." The calendar proved popular everywhere that it was distributed, and more than 125,000 copies were eventually printed.[119]

The OCB sought to coordinate the activities of the USIS in Hong Kong with those of USIS posts in other countries, the State Department, and private foundations. It advocated new State Department programs that would invite overseas Chinese leaders to visit the United States "and view the showcase of democracy and Free World stability." Local USIS branches assumed responsibility for establishing "Chinese Youth Centers incorporating various features of YMCA and 4-H Club activities." The OCB also suggested that the Asia Foundation become active in assisting overseas Chinese schools through enlarging its textbook program, which supplied Chinese translations of American books, and supporting new programs for middle schools.[120]

The ultimate outcome of this competition for the loyalties of overseas Chinese was ambiguous. Beijing faced limitations in appealing to this group;

but these were due to the inherent contradictions in PRC propaganda rather than American efforts to counter it. The essential problem for the PRC was that a central justification for its existence was that it had supposedly swept away feudal Chinese "traditions" and replaced them with a more just social order. It was therefore often critical of Confucianism, the lunar calendar, and other Chinese festivals. Yet these were precisely the traditions that created a sense of kinship between diasporic Chinese and the motherland. Some Chinese propaganda praised overseas Chinese for making progress in forsaking these traditions.[121] Nevertheless, appealing to the Chinese diaspora on these terms was not ideal for fostering and sustaining its loyalty and undoubtedly alienated those with deep attachments to the institutions and customs that Beijing condemned. The result was that overseas Chinese, like many of those whose loyalties Beijing and Washington vied for through their propaganda, did not line up neatly behind either rival.

————————

Cultural competition between Beijing and Washington was neither a triumph nor a disaster for either side. It was a zero-sum game. The competition spread across a range of countries and languages, so measuring reception is difficult. Nevertheless, it is clear that in many places, neither side allowed the other to gain an upper hand. When Beijing sought to raise its profile by sending cultural delegations and displaying its arts, Washington tried to minimize the impact of these activities. When the PRC attempted to gain credence as a champion of social justice by advertising its support for the civil rights struggle in the United States, Washington countered by highlighting frictions between the CCP and China's national minorities. Moreover, scattered anecdotal evidence suggests that the propaganda campaigns waged by both sides could often be counterproductive. One of the ironic aspects of propaganda is that as it seeks to show the best side of a country or leader, it often ends up exhibiting the bad along with the good. The PRC's efforts to infuse its cultural exhibitions with political ideology often reduced rather than enhanced admiration for the arts in China. By the same token, in constantly seeking to disseminate their own media while blocking those of their rival, both Washington and Beijing often seemed to contradict their claims that they would respect the independent judgment of postcolonial nations and their leaders.

Nonetheless, during the 1950s and early 1960s, the PRC was, for the most part, able to hold its own in propaganda battles against the United States through selling itself as a peaceful nation and a successful example of postcolonial nation building. Beijing's situation was already starting to become more challenging by the early 1960s, however. Growing frictions with both India and the Soviet Union would soon lead to the Sino-Indian War and the

Sino-Soviet split. These conflicts had a transformative impact on Beijing's foreign policy and the way the PRC presented itself to the world. The PRC would have to contend not only with the United States but also with India and the Soviet Union in the realm of international public opinion. Chinese efforts to unify the Third World would place a growing emphasis on militancy, radicalism, and other themes that could differentiate the PRC from its rivals. These changes in China's foreign policy would greatly intensify its competition with the United States.

Chapter 6

China's Radicalization and the American Response, 1958–1963

"When I review the past seven or eight years, I see that this nation of ours has a great future," Mao Zedong proclaimed at a speech at the Supreme State Conference in January 1958.[1] And indeed, if one surveyed the PRC's accomplishments over the previous seven years, there was cause for optimism. The CCP leadership had implemented a Five-Year Plan with guidance from Moscow and attained the plan's objectives ahead of schedule.[2] Moreover, Beijing had established relations with many of its neighbors and broken out of the isolation that Washington had sought to impose on it. But this was not enough for Mao; a utopian thinker, he wanted the PRC to overtake the West economically and gain a central position in world affairs. For the chairman, the way to achieve this objective was a renewed emphasis on carrying out revolution. Mao's "revolutionary outburst" of 1958 would have a transformative impact on China's domestic and foreign affairs, giving rise to the Great Leap Forward at home and a more confrontational posture toward American imperialism abroad.[3]

The impetus toward the radicalization of China's diplomacy created by Mao during the late 1950s was strengthened by the sudden decline in China's relations with its two most critical neighbors, India and the Soviet Union. Between 1959 and 1962, disagreements between Beijing and Moscow over peaceful coexistence and other issues gradually escalated until the split between the CCP and the CPSU in 1962. The decline in Sino-Indian relations began after Chinese forces crushed the Tibetan rebellion in 1959. Frictions over Indian support for the Dalai Lama and the Sino-Indian border created the context for the 1962 Sino-Indian War, which dealt the final blow to the entente that had prevailed between the two countries since 1954.

Chinese policy toward the Third World between 1958 and 1963 evolved for two main reasons. First, the PRC believed that the Soviet Union and India had both become obstacles to its efforts to gain status in the Third World and in the international community more broadly. Second, the Sino-Soviet split and the Sino-Indian Border War compelled China to adjust its strategy for enhancing its prestige among Afro-Asian countries. The CCP abandoned some aspects of the Five Principles of Peace Coexistence and embraced more autarkic and militant notions of Afro-Asian solidarity. For its part, the

United States viewed Beijing as more rather than less dangerous as a result of its break with Moscow and Delhi and its subsequent efforts to organize the Third World in opposition to Great Power hegemony. Although Americans foresaw some possibilities of cooperating with the Soviets after the Sino-Soviet split and hoped that India could be built up as a political alternative to the PRC in Asia, they also believed that the United States would have to do more to contest Chinese influence. By 1963, both Beijing and Washington were stepping up their involvement in the Third World in ways that made even greater competition inevitable.

The Great Leap Forward and the Second Taiwan Strait Crisis

When Mao Zedong decided to launch the Great Leap Forward during the summer of 1958, it quickly made a powerful impact on China's foreign relations. Driven by Mao's radicalism, the Great Leap sought to achieve the chairman's most cherished goals: constructing a socialist utopia on the Chinese mainland while enabling the PRC to reclaim its rightful status in world affairs. Domestically, this meant that China would accelerate its socialist transformation through rapidly improving industrial and agricultural production and the introduction of a new system of communes. Dramatic increases in the production of steel and other products would enable China to overtake its Western adversaries within fifteen years or less. By mobilizing the people in pursuit of these goals, Mao was not only seeking to raise living standards but also to make sure that his country would no longer be counted inferior to the West. "Our country produces too little steel," the chairman explained at the Conference of World Communist and Workers Parties held in Moscow in 1957. "We have to do everything we can to increase our material strength. Otherwise people will look down on us."[4]

A more confrontational approach to foreign policy was handmaiden to the Great Leap Forward's radical domestic agenda. The relaxation of international tensions was no longer seen as useful for China's reconstruction. More saber rattling and harsher rhetoric against the PRC's adversaries could increase the people's zeal to make the sacrifices demanded by the chairman's new economic programs. "Tension is good for us," Mao stated shortly before launching the Great Leap Forward. "It keeps our country united."[5] In an effort to repudiate the foreign policies of the previous five years, Mao forced Zhou Enlai to make a comprehensive self-criticism in March 1958 that included his handling of China's relations with both the West and the Soviet Union.[6] Beijing still wanted good relations with its neighbors and continued to refer to the Five Principles, but it took a more confrontational posture toward the United States and the West.

The most immediate manifestation of Beijing's changing strategic priorities was the second Taiwan Strait Crisis, which Mao precipitated in August by again ordering PLA forces to shell Jinmen. The crisis lasted for two months before the CCP, believing that it had attained its objectives, suspended the shelling. The decision to manufacture a new crisis over Taiwan was based on several considerations, all of which reflected the belief that a more hostile stance toward the United States would ultimately strengthen China and enhance its prestige. In meetings with other CCP officials in the run-up to the crisis Mao emphasized that international tensions would facilitate the Great Leap Forward. When the chairman suddenly announced his decision to shell Jinmen at an enlarged politburo conference on 17 August, he argued, "To have an enemy in front of us, to have tension, is to our advantage."[7] At the same time, by making things more difficult for the United States, the PRC could, at some level, redeem its past history of humiliation at the hands of the Great Powers. "The Americans have bullied us for many years, so now that we have a chance, why not give them a hard time?" Mao explained.[8]

Mao also had a watchful eye on the situation in the Middle East when he provoked the crisis. In July 1958, the Eisenhower administration dispatched thousands of marines to Beirut at the request of Lebanese president Camille Chamoun.[9] The intervention was highly unpopular through much of the Middle East, and Chinese leaders wanted to demonstrate their solidarity with Arab nationalists.[10] The chairman hoped that a limited conflict would "prove that China supports the national liberation movements in the Middle East with not only words but also deeds."[11] He predicted in August that if the PRC shelled Jinmen and Mazu, "the people in the Arab world will be delighted, and the vast masses in Asia and Africa will take our side."[12] When Mao ordered the bombardment of Taiwan to begin on 23 August, other considerations loomed larger.[13] Yet he never doubted that the PRC's actions would be regarded as heroic among Arab nations. In September, with Chinese artillery still bombarding Jinmen and a vast armada of U.S. ships assembled off China's coast, Mao told the Supreme State Council, "The countries in the Middle East, especially Egypt and Iraq, warmly welcomed [our artillery bombardment] this time. They praise us every day, saying that we have done the right thing."[14]

The reaction to Beijing's actions in the Taiwan Strait among Afro-Asian countries was not universally enthusiastic, however. Most of the PRC's neighbors agreed with its general position on Taiwan but were nervous that the crisis would escalate. Moreover, when neutral Asian countries offered to mediate, they were disappointed with how Beijing brushed aside their efforts. The Indian ambassador to the United Nations, V. K. Krishna Menon, drew up a plan to address the General Assembly about the crisis in early October. Beijing, however, made it clear that it would not see this as a friendly gesture unless the speech completely reflected Chinese positions. "If friendly countries want to support us they should . . . acknowledge that Taiwan and the coastal islands are Chinese territory and that U.S. forces should withdraw from Taiwan," Zhou told the Indian ambassador in Beijing.[15] India's leadership continued to argue publicly that Taiwan was part of China, but Prime Minister Nehru nonetheless expressed regret that "rather rigid attitudes have been taken up by every side, and threats and the like are thrown at each other."[16] Zhou also rebuffed a similar effort by Indonesia to introduce a UN resolution calling for an end to the conflict, explaining that any such resolution needed to cite "the American occupation of Taiwan was the source of the trouble."[17]

Although Mao represented the Taiwan Strait Crisis as a victorious campaign in which China had stood up to the United States and championed national liberation movements in the Middle East, it did more harm than good for China's international image. It fostered skepticism among some Afro-Asian partners about Beijing's claims that it wanted to focus on peaceful development and avoid conflict with the United States. The influence of the Great Leap Forward on Chinese foreign policy would extend far beyond Taiwan, however. By the time the crisis erupted it had already caused tensions between China and its most important ally, the Soviet Union.

Sino-Soviet Frictions, the Third World, and the United States

Beijing's foreign policy had been closely coordinated with Moscow's between 1953 and 1957, but the Great Leap Forward frayed the bonds between the two Communist giants. Part of the reason for the sudden Sino-Soviet discord was the sheer audacity of what Mao was attempting. As he tried to propel China into a utopian Communist future, the chairman made it clear that he would no longer settle for playing second fiddle to Nikita Khrushchev or any other Soviet leader within the Communist Bloc. Vice Foreign Minister Zhang Wentian summarized the change in China's outlook in his notes on a message Mao had sent to a small group of foreign policy leaders in June 1958: "In the past, out of consideration for the Soviet Union, we did not discuss the Chairman's thinking very clearly in our propaganda. Now we need to give a greater role to the Chairman's thinking. In international relations and foreign policy we need to openly set our direction as an example."[18] With its ambitious plans to leapfrog the West and surpass even the Soviet Union as a model of socialist modernity, Beijing naturally took it upon itself to determine the future direction of the international Communist movement—a position that Moscow found absurd if not outright insulting.

At the precise moment when Beijing was coming to see itself as a rightful leader of the Communist Bloc, Moscow's devotion to peaceful coexistence seemed to relegate the PRC to secondary status. Although "peaceful coexistence" remained an important slogan in Chinese foreign policy, Beijing and Moscow were talking about fundamentally different things when they used the term. For China, peaceful coexistence meant harmony and cooperation among postcolonial, Afro-Asian nations that had different political and economic systems. For the Soviets, however, peaceful coexistence really meant peaceful competition with the capitalist West. Moscow's understanding of the concept was worrisome to Mao and his colleagues because it seemed to afford Washington an opportunity to isolate China further. Indeed, after 1956, when Khrushchev shook up the Communist world with his "secret speech," the Eisenhower administration's general approach had been to test Moscow's sincerity while having nothing to do with the PRC.[19] Washington's efforts to divide and conquer enabled Khrushchev to gain recognition as an international statesman but denied China any measure of legitimacy. To make matters worse, the Soviet leader seemed oblivious to his ally's feelings and inadvertently sharpened its disappointment through his actions. When Khrushchev visited Beijing to celebrate the PRC's tenth anniversary in 1959, he was still elated from his recent historic meeting with Eisenhower at Camp David one month earlier. Mao was deeply insulted when the Soviet lauded Eisenhower and the "Spirit of Camp David" in a public address; he complained that Khrushchev "attacked us on our own rostrum."[20]

In several key instances, Moscow's clumsy handling of the alliance heightened Mao's sensitivity toward Great Power chauvinism, which the Soviets suddenly found themselves being accused of. One case in point occurred during the summer of 1958 when the Soviets asked the PRC to agree to joint radio transmitter station in southern China and a joint submarine fleet that would use Chinese ports. After hearing about the submarine proposal, Mao angrily lectured the Soviet ambassador in Beijing: "I believe that some Russians look down upon the Chinese people," Mao complained, finding Moscow's proposal unacceptable because, if enacted, "we would have to let you have the entire coast."[21] When Khrushchev visited Beijing to assuage the chairman, Mao sought to humiliate him by proposing that they both take a swim at the CCP headquarters in Zhongnanhai. An expert swimmer, the chairman moved gracefully through the water while Khrushchev paddled and floundered.[22] Mao likened the joint flotilla proposal to past efforts by foreign imperialists to carve up China: "The British, the Japanese, and many other foreigners stayed on our territory for a long time but we drove them away. . . . We never again want to let any others use our territory for their own purposes."[23] Mao framed the issue of the proposed joint radio transmitter in similar terms. "We cannot accept your proposal," he told Khrushchev. "For so many years China's sovereignty was disregarded. This would be an infringement on our prestige; it would be a blow against our sovereignty."[24]

As the bonds between Beijing and Moscow began to fray, China made subtle adjustments in how it represented itself among Afro-Asian countries. The PRC gradually distanced its policies from Moscow's in the Third World while reasserting itself as a potential leader for the region. Although the PRC continued to publicly endorse Soviet leadership of the Communist Bloc, it also called for the intensification of national independence struggles in ways that subtly contradicted Moscow's policies. The speech given by the Chinese writer and statesman Guo Moruo during the first meeting of the Afro-Asian People's Solidarity Organization (AAPSO) in Cairo in December 1957 exemplified this somewhat paradoxical approach. He explained, "In the Afro-Asian countries, the struggle for national independence and against imperialism and colonialism forms an integral part of our movement for safeguarding peace. We must first obtain independence and equality, then we can live in peace."[25] Beijing was not negating peaceful coexistence, but it was asserting that anticolonial struggle and national independence needed to come first and implying that violence might sometimes be required to achieve a lasting peace. Though Beijing and Moscow were certainly not feuding openly, careful observers could discern that their priorities were not completely aligned.

Over the next two years, Beijing became more vocal in its support for revolutions and, in some instances, made clear its dissatisfaction with Moscow's hesitance about confronting imperialism. When the Algerian National Liberation Front declared the establishment of the Provisional Government of the Republic of Algeria in September 1958, the PRC wasted no time in offering recognition. The Soviets, however, were hoping that Charles de Gaulle's government in Paris would facilitate negotiations with the West and did not immediately offer the Algerians recognition.[26] Moscow's reluctance to support a bona fide anticolonial struggle elicited indirect but pointed criticisms of Soviet policy from Beijing. The *People's Daily* lauded the "armed struggle of the Algerian people" as a "source of great inspiration for the other African people under the yoke of colonialism." It added: "Compared with the excitement and rejoicing over the proclamation of the Algerian Republic in the Asian and African countries and of the progressive forces in every corner of the world the 'non recognition' of the colonial powers is trifling and impotent. By promptly recognizing the P.G.R.A. the Chinese people and government demonstrate once again their sympathy and support for the Algerian people and all other people fighting for their national independence."[27] Nowhere did the article explicitly criticize the Soviets, but it nevertheless put the PRC at the forefront of the global struggle against imperialism while making

Moscow's position appear weak and backward-looking. It was a strategy that allowed Beijing to gain prestige among Afro-Asian countries not through acting in unison with Moscow but through striking out on its own.

By 1959, the Eisenhower administration was sensing the tensions that had surfaced between its two Communist rivals. But what was to be done? And which side if any should the United States favor? Americans determined quickly that the Soviet Union, with its emphasis on peaceful competition, represented a lesser evil than the People's Republic of China, which seemed bent on setting the world aflame with revolution. Although the Eisenhower administration did not initially address the nascent competition between China and the Soviet Union in Afro-Asian countries, the general strategy that it adopted toward the Sino-Soviet rift would continue to inform U.S. policy toward Beijing's Third World activism. In particular, Americans looked for ways to manipulate the Soviet Union into exercising a restraining influence on the PRC and dissuade it from promoting violent struggle.

The September 1959 summit between Khrushchev and Eisenhower at Camp David seemed an ideal venue for testing this approach. One briefing paper submitted to the president in preparation for the visit explained the stance he might take. "Communist China," it began, "has pursued aggressive policies in the Far East since 1949." It had "constantly engaged in subversive, and at times openly aggressive, activities beyond its borders." Khrushchev, in contrast, had called for the relaxation of international tensions, a policy that seemed to contradict the PRC's more radical agenda. The paper contended that it was "clearly in the United States interest to seek to exploit the differences between the Soviet Union and Communist China." The president should thus make the point that "if the Soviet Union is genuinely interested in relaxing world tension it must restrain the aggressive acts of the Chinese Communists."[28] Eisenhower never really had the opportunity to make this point, however. Despite the overall success of the summit, a rather testy exchange occurred over China and Taiwan in which the Soviet premier asserted the PRC's right to take Taiwan by force. The president was so dismayed by the exchange that he later wrote Khrushchev asking for a clarification of his views.[29] At least initially, it seemed unlikely that détente with Moscow would be of any use for reining in China's growing assertiveness in Asia.

Yet Washington did not immediately give up on the idea that the Soviets could help to moderate China's behavior. After Khrushchev's visit, officials in the Eisenhower administration continued to discuss the idea of "partial responsibility." Their basic premise was that, since Moscow was the leader of the Communist Bloc, it should be assessed with some degree of responsibility for the PRC's actions. It would thus be incumbent on Khrushchev to demonstrate his commitment to peace by preventing Chinese aggression.

According to J. Graham Parson, the assistant secretary of state for Far Eastern affairs, if the premier tried and failed, "he must either imply criticism of a China that will not submit to his bidding or he must face having to accept responsibility for a partner whose conduct shows the hollowness of the Communist peace offensive."[30] The policy would create a win-win scenario for the United States because even if the PRC could not be contained, it would still exacerbate tensions within the Communist Bloc and provide Washington with propaganda that could weaken China's prestige.

The Eisenhower administration never got an opportunity to test this policy because of the infamous U-2 incident of May 1960. The episode brought an abrupt end to the spirit of Camp David and made it impossible for Washington and Moscow to discuss or coordinate on highly sensitive issues such as China. Although the Eisenhower administration failed to capitalize on early frictions between Beijing and Moscow, however, the decline of Sino-Indian relations presented a much more promising opportunity. Sino-Soviet frictions had limited propaganda value because the United States could not win either state as an ally. India, by contrast, was not only a country that could be wooed into closer alignment with the United States but also a highly significant actor in the Afro-Asian world that could help to turn opinion in the region against the PRC.

Tibet and the Beginning of Sino-Indian Conflict

Even during the heyday of the Five Principles, from roughly 1954 to 1958, Beijing and Delhi had underlying disagreements about two interrelated issues: Tibet and the Sino-Indian border. Although China and India signed an agreement on Tibet in 1954, they had very different ideas about the future of the region. Beijing was willing to allow Tibet some autonomy but nonetheless hoped to deepen its authority there. Delhi instead encouraged Tibetans to seek a greater degree of independence.[31] As described earlier, India granted asylum to the Tibetan spiritual leader, the Dalai Lama, when he fled Chinese territory in 1959 and offered him a base from which he could criticize China. Delhi's generosity toward the Dalai Lama infuriated Beijing and abruptly ended the era of Sino-Indian entente. The two also disputed the legitimacy of the McMahon Line, a boundary established between Tibet and India in 1914 through the Simla Agreement. Britain had negotiated the agreement with Tibetan leaders when the Chinese government was in disarray. Beijing therefore regarded it as a product of imperialism while Delhi insisted on its legitimacy.

Beijing's rhetoric on Delhi, Nehru, and the Five Principles changed drastically after the Dalai Lama's flight to India in 1959. The PRC no longer depicted

India as an Asian country whose struggle against foreign imperialism paralleled China's but as an ally of the imperialists intent on intervening in the PRC's domestic affairs. Beijing was incensed that Delhi had afforded the Dalai Lama a platform from which he could publicly criticize China and thus damage its prestige among neighboring countries. Chinese leaders were aware of covert U.S. support for the Tibetan guerrillas, and they naturally assumed that Delhi and Washington were conspiring against them. Mao laid out these grievances in a report he issued to the Intelligence Department of the PLA's General Staff Headquarters in September 1959. "Since independence," the chairman claimed, "India had always intended to inherit imperialist Britain's expansionism." Now it was taking advantage of the situation in Tibet to criticize the PRC in the United Nations and accuse China of expansionism. Delhi "joined the U.S. in slandering China and has not hesitated to publicly act as the vanguard of the anti-China [movement]."[32] From the PRC's prospective, India had abandoned its commitment to peaceful coexistence and was now doing as much to damage Chinese prestige in Asia as Beijing's rivals.

The ill will created by events in Tibet soon spilled over into another lingering dispute between the two countries—the demarcation of the Sino-Indian border. Chinese and Indian officials had long disagreed over where the boundary should be drawn, but Tibetans had been given the right to patrol their own border with India before the 1959 uprising. After suppressing the revolt, the CCP wanted to tighten control over what it considered to be Chinese territory and make it more difficult for Tibetans to cross over to India. From the Chinese perspective, the boundaries of the Chinese state needed to be defined more clearly and Tibetan separatists needed to be exiled or controlled.[33] On 25 April, Mao ordered Chinese border patrols into the Himalayas, and Nehru responded by implementing a military-forward policy.[34] In the weeks that followed, India adopted a confrontational posture that exacerbated frictions. By July 1959, Chinese intelligence had discovered instances of Delhi offering different forms of assistance to Tibetan rebels.[35] Finally, two armed clashes between Chinese and Indian forces followed along the increasingly militarized border; the first occurred on 25 August and the second on 21 October.[36]

After these events, Beijing launched major propaganda offensive against India in Afro-Asian countries. Communist Party officials held meetings with several Asian and Middle Eastern leaders in which they repeatedly cast Indian support for Tibet as an extension of Western colonialism. "The dispute over the Tibet issue has a very particular reason," Zhou told the ambassador from the United Arab Republic on 31 May. A number of Indian elites held a viewpoint that "had been left over from the time that British colonialism governed India and [later] spread." By way of contrast, the premier stressed, "Asian,

African, and Latin American countries . . . need to understand, support, sympathize, and cooperate with each other."[37] Zhou offered a similar explanation for the clash along the Sino-Indian border in August. After the event, he held meetings with Afghan vice premier Mohammad Naim and Ceylonese ambassador to China William Gopallawa, among others.[38] "Tibet is a part of China," he stated plainly in a discussion with the visiting Afghan vice premier, "but our Indian friends have exactly the opposite impression." This was because "the British imperialists had implemented colonial education for a long time and influenced a portion of the Indian people." The real cause of the border issue was that the British had drawn Tibet within their sphere of influence; according to Zhou, "the so-called McMahon line was a creation of imperialism and a plot to invade Tibet." Even as he criticized India's behavior as imperialistic, however, the premier also repeatedly stressed that China wished to retain its friendship with India and resolve the dispute peacefully.[39]

The PRC's efforts to sway Asian opinion were not immediately successful. Many nonaligned Asian countries became more critical of the PRC in international forums, voicing skepticism about its peaceful intentions. When delegates from twenty-one Asian nations assembled in Jogjakarta, Indonesia, to attend a Colombo Plan conference in October 1959, the *New York Times* reported that many had become deeply concerned about the course taken by the PRC. "Not a word of approval of the Chinese actions was voiced," the paper reported, adding: "The critical attitude disclosed was in sharp contrast to the feeling about Communist China among many Asians who attended the last international gathering in Indonesia." Delegates interviewed during the conference made statements such as "The Chinese Communists must be out of their minds" and "Like it or not. [Beijing] must be criticized for its actions along the Indian border."[40]

Having struggled for years to undermine China's growing stature in Asia, American officials were suddenly optimistic that they could exploit the damage that the Tibetan uprising and ensuing clashes with India had done to China's image. In September 1959, President Eisenhower approved NSC 5913/1, which covered American policy in East Asia. Rather than forecasting that Chinese Communist prestige in Asia would continue to grow—as U.S. intelligence agencies had previously believed it would—the NSC now predicted: "The ruthless character and aggressiveness which the Chinese Communist regime has displayed in domestic programs, in the Tibetan situation, and in foreign policy have increased apprehension in Asia of Communist China's strength and intentions and much of the admiration and sympathy which it enjoyed has been lost."[41]

The administration sought to encourage Delhi to keep up its resistance to China on Tibet and border issues by arranging a presidential visit to India in December 1959. Before the trip, the U.S. ambassador to India, Ellsworth Bunker, briefed Eisenhower on how to handle the Tibetan situation and Sino-Indian frictions. He advised the president to avoid "any visible attempts to draw Tibet and Sino-Chinese problems into a cold war context." Instead Bunker called for subtle intimations of American support that might increase India's willingness to take on the PRC and widen the political gulf between Beijing and Delhi: "It would be very helpful if you could indicate inferentially that in the case of a widening Sino-Indian conflict our support would go beyond simple moral backing." He also urged Eisenhower to offer "private support" on the border issue and urged the president to tell Nehru, "I agree completely with you that India should not yield any territory you consider belonging to India as a result of military occupation or threat."[42]

For Beijing, Eisenhower's visit to India confirmed that Washington and Delhi were colluding against China. After Eisenhower returned home, the PRC's International Affairs Research Institute produced a detailed report that was circulated among Foreign Ministry officials. "Eisenhower's visit to India had an obvious purpose," it explained. Washington wanted to "use the Sino-Indian border issue to sow discord in Sino-Indian relations, isolate our country, and encourage Indian-Pakistani joint defense in order to gradually lay a foundation for India and Pakistan to be incorporated into a military clique." Eisenhower's visit was not entirely successful, according to the institute. "Both sides had evil intentions to use each other but neither side had their wishes completely fulfilled through Eisenhower and Nehru's meetings." Nevertheless, the PRC had to acknowledge that the visit had unquestionably improved America's image in India, even among some of Beijing's allies in the country. India's Communist Party, for instance, had "welcomed Eisenhower's visit" and praised it for "making a new contribution to the cause of world peace."[43]

China countered during the spring of 1960 with an effort to resuscitate the Five Principles by negotiating new border agreements with two other neighbors—Burma and Nepal—and dispatching Zhou Enlai to India for several days of talks. The premier's negotiations with Rangoon and Kathmandu were efficient and successful. By 28 January, Zhou had arrived at an agreement with Burmese premier Ne Win that provided the basis for reaching a settlement.[44] When Nepal's prime minister B. P. Koirala visited Beijing in March, he left having signed not only a preliminary boundary agreement but also an economic aid agreement in which the PRC pledged to provide one hundred million Indian rupees in unconditional assistance.[45] By giving generous terms to both Burma and Nepal and settling long-bothersome border issues, Beijing hoped to demonstrate to the rest of Asia that it remained committed to the Five Principles.

Zhou could not salvage the Sino-Indian relationship, however. When the premier visited Delhi in April 1960, he went with a willingness to make concessions on boundary issues but also made it clear that he viewed Nehru's decision to grant refuge to the Dalai Lama as a hostile act. "The Dalai Lama and his followers in India have gone far beyond the scope of religious activities," Zhou complained in a meeting with the Indian defense minister. "They basically want Tibet to be independent, and they put forward accusations in the UN. All of this is occurring on Indian territory. This cannot but make the Chinese people feel deeply shaken and make us feel pained because it is interference in our internal affairs."[46] In meetings with Nehru, Zhou put forward several proposals for settling the boundary disputes, but he refused to recognize the McMahon Line. He seemed at times willing to establish the actual border at or near the line but not without an acknowledgment—one that Nehru was unwilling to provide—that the treaty creating the boundary was an illegitimate product of imperialism.[47] Ultimately, Zhou's visit to India ended in acrimony. No progress was made toward fixing the boundary, and although the Dalai Lama does not appear to have been discussed between Zhou and Nehru, obvious disagreements over the issue created a palpable tension.[48] The failure of Zhou's diplomacy in India was a major blow to China's peace campaign and the Five Principles. Whereas Delhi had previously helped to convince the rest of Asia that China's intentions were good, Beijing now had to struggle against its erstwhile partner to maintain any semblance of solidarity with its neighbors. With mutual recriminations flying forth between Beijing and Delhi, appeals for Afro-Asian unity on the basis of the Five Principles could only ring hollow. If the PRC was ever going to gain a position of leadership in the Third World, it would need a new platform.

Americans, for their part, were hopeful that Sino-Indian frictions would diminish Beijing's standing in Asia. The CIA cooperated with other official intelligence organizations to produce NIE 100–2–60 in May 1960. The document cheerily sounded the death knell of the Five Principles and predicted that China's relations with other Asian nations would not be the same after its border clash with India. "Communist China's growing strength and its aggressiveness have caused a more somber assessment of Chinese Communist motivations among Asian leaders," the report noted. Beijing had irreparably damaged its reputation. "Even if the Sino-Indian border dispute is resolved through negotiations," the report continued, "the more apprehensive Asian view of China that has recently developed probably will not be erased."[49] The PRC's suppression of the Tibetan uprising and the resulting Sino-Indian tensions had done what no amount of American coercing and cajoling had been able to accomplish: tarnish the PRC's image as a peaceful and responsible Asian state.

The demise of Sino-Indian entente raised Washington's hopes for an even broader implosion of PRC foreign policy. American officials anticipated that many of China's other friends would abandon it because of the increasingly uncompromising tone it was striking with its neighbors. Such hopes would not be completely realized, but China's relationship with India was not the only one that suffered as Beijing shifted the emphasis of its diplomacy. It was almost inevitable that as Sino-Indian ties frayed, China would also come into conflict with what was perhaps India's closet ally in the Afro-Asian world—Egypt.

Alienating Egypt

After the Bandung Conference, warming Sino-Egyptian ties had lent new credibility to the Five Principles, and Nasser had facilitated Beijing's engagement with the Arab world. The emergence of frictions between Beijing and Cairo in 1958–59 was an equally significant factor behind the unraveling of China's peace campaign. Through 1958, Beijing had continued to hold a sympathetic view of Nasser's Egypt. Chinese officials saw his Pan-Arabism as an important opponent of American imperialism; one Foreign Ministry report denounced what it claimed were U.S. efforts to "isolate, weaken, limit, and even overthrow the Pan-Arab nationalism and governments represented by Nasser."[50] But even though Nasser was a zealous nationalist, he was often suspicious of Communist parties within the Middle East and of political leaders with more radical political inclinations than his own. It was virtually inevitable that strains in the Sino-Egyptian relationship would eventually appear.

Beijing's perception of Nasser began to change after Egypt's 1958 union with Syria, which formed the United Arab Republic. Fearful that socialist internationalism would undermine his efforts to promote Pan-Arab unity, the Egyptian president launched a campaign against the Communist parties in both Egypt and Syria. Nasser also shut down several printing houses that translated and distributed Chinese and Soviet publications in Arabic. Beijing avoided direct criticism of Cairo, but Chinese rhetoric sometimes betrayed a measure of disappointment with Nasser's policies.[51]

Cairo's hostility toward the new revolutionary government that gained power in Iraq deepened Beijing's disappointment with Nasser. In July 1958, Abd al-Karim Qasim overthrew the Iraqi monarchy in a coup d'état and installed himself as prime minister. Qasim sympathized with Iraqi Communists and was wary of pro-Nasser elements in his government. He quickly purged those he viewed as a potential threat from his army and cabinet. Nasser responded by supporting a campaign to destabilize Qasim's fledgling regime.[52] Beijing, which was among Qasim's strongest supporters, worried that Cairo's sub rosa actions would undermine Afro-Asian unity. Zhou Enlai intimated as much when he met with the UAR ambassador on 25 February and told him that, although ideological differences existed, these "differences must not obstruct our common long-term goal."[53] The premier's warning had little effect, however. In early March, Egypt engineered a failed coup against Qasim. Unable to hold back its frustration with Nasser any longer, Beijing lashed out through an editorial in state-run media claiming that the Egyptian leader's "frenzied abuse against" Qasim's government was "in harmony with the imperialist tune."[54]

Egypt soon answered Beijing's hostile rhetoric with equally severe condemnation of the PRC. Angered by Chinese meddling in Iraq, Nasser sharply denounced the CCP's handling of the Tibetan crisis, siding with Nehru. Under Nasser's orders, the Cairo press claimed that the PRC had violated the Bandung spirit by invading Tibet and supporting Communists in the Arab world.[55] Zhou met with the UAR ambassador again on 31 May to explain Chinese policy and make a plea for the restoration of Afro-Asian unity. Sino-Indian tensions were temporary, he explained, and Delhi's viewpoint on Tibet was one that had been "handed down from the period of British colonial rule in India." Afro-Asian countries still had a "common fate" and needed to support each other.[56] But again Zhou's words were insufficient. Cairo withdrew its ambassador from the PRC several days later.[57]

China's relations with the UAR almost collapsed during the fall of 1959. In September, the CCP allowed Khālid Bakdāsh, secretary general of the Syrian Communist Party, to give a speech at the celebration of the PRC's tenth anniversary in which he denounced Nasser and criticized Cairo's policies toward both Syria and Iraq.[58] The Cairo press lambasted the PRC for allowing the speech and allegedly forsaking its pledge not to intervene in the affairs of other Afro-Asian countries. According to one editorial, the Chinese had forgotten that Egypt "was the first to break the boycott of their republic by Arab countries" and incurred the wrath of the West for doing so. The UAR had "treated all countries . . . without discrimination" on the basis of the Bandung principles, but Beijing had been "consorting with renegades who had left our country to launch attacks on us."[59] The Egyptian government followed with a strongly worded memorandum to the Chinese ambassador condemning the PRC for abandoning the principles of peaceful coexistence.[60]

In subsequent months, the crisis faded and more normal relations were restored, but not before the credibility of the Five Principles suffered further damage. The war of words between China and the UAR in 1958–59 destroyed the sense of mutual enamorment that had prevailed since the Bandung Conference. Beijing believed that the UAR had abandoned its commitment to progressive neutralism by intervening in Iraq, while Cairo asserted that China's suppressive campaign in Tibet and support for the Syrian Communist Party were tantamount to forsaking the Five Principles. Even if the PRC's relations with the UAR were not shattered, China's peace campaign in the Middle East was unquestionably losing steam. During the next few years, the number of Chinese delegations traveling to the UAR dropped, as did the volume of Sino-Egyptian trade.[61] For China, this meant a reduced profile in both the UAR and the Middle East overall. As in South Asia, promoting the Five Principles no longer seemed to offer the PRC a strong platform for enhancing its prestige.

Washington did not need to play an active role in encouraging this estrangement between the PRC and the UAR. American officials did, however, keep an eye on developments in Sino-Egyptian relations, reporting on disputes between Nasser and Communist China.[62] Cairo's deteriorating relations with Beijing during the late 1950s, along with its growing hostility toward communism, no doubt contributed to a rapprochement between Nasser and the Eisenhower administration. With antagonisms between Egypt and the Communist world on the rise, Eisenhower offered Nasser $150 million in surplus wheat through the Food for Peace program. The two men had a conciliatory meeting when the Egyptian visited the United Nations in September 1960. Differences over Israel and other issues were aired, but Nasser insisted that he had always wanted good relations with the United States while Eisenhower was sympathetic and accommodating.[63] At least according to American reports, Nasser left the United States highly satisfied with the results of his visit.[64]

The UAR's position in PRC diplomacy was never as pivotal as India's or the Soviet Union's. Nonetheless, the chill in Sino-Egyptian relations undermined Beijing's efforts to promote the Five Principles and sell itself as a champion of peaceful cooperation. Nasser, with his stature and influence in the Middle East, had been a valuable supporter of the PRC's peace campaign. When relations between Beijing and Cairo soured, China lost some of the luster that had earlier enabled it to win over countries in the Arab world. The problem was not that Egypt and other countries in the region turned hostile but that they no longer viewed China as a unifying force worthy of emulation. This created a dilemma for the PRC: if the Five Principles could no longer capture the imagination of Afro-Asian countries, then how could China enlarge its influence among them? The solution would be shaped greatly by Beijing's escalating conflicts with Moscow and Delhi.

The Sino-Soviet Split and Sino-American Competition in the Third World

New frictions had surfaced in the relationship between Beijing and Moscow during the late 1950s, but there had been a limit to how far either of the two Communist giants was willing to go in attacking the other. Even if China tried to establish a role for itself in the Afro-Asian world that was separate and independent from Soviet influence, it almost never directly attacked its fraternal socialist ally. All of this changed during the early 1960s as a range of domestic political factors and international developments converged, pushing the CCP toward a split with the CPSU. The breakdown of Sino-Soviet relations would have implications for both the PRC's policy in the Third World and Sino-American competition in the region.

The Twenty-Second CPSU Congress, held in Moscow in October 1961, magnified tensions between the PRC and the Soviet Union and led to a more overt rivalry in the Third World. Although Khrushchev attacked not China but Stalin and Albania at the congress, Beijing found the positions taken by the CPSU deeply troubling. The CCP still held Stalin in higher regard than Khrushchev and disliked Moscow's efforts to diminish the former leader's standing in the pantheon of international socialism without consulting the CCP. Beijing also likely felt threatened by the attack on another fraternal Communist country. After the congress Chinese diplomats working in Afro-Asian countries often sought to elicit criticisms of the CPSU's positions on Stalin and Albania while monitoring Soviet activities more closely.[65] As the two countries moved closer to open hostility, the PRC was keen to know where the sympathies of nationalists and revolutionaries in the Third World lay.

In 1962, several developments caused Beijing to jettison the relative restraint it had shown in its policy toward Moscow and move toward a definitive break. The first was Mao's political resurgence. The economic catastrophe wrought by the Great Leap Forward had forced Mao to accept a reduced role in policy making, but during the summer of 1962, the chairman used the Central Work Conference held at the beach resort Beidaihe to reassert himself. Criticisms of the Soviet Union played a major role in Mao's comeback; he argued that Moscow was veering toward revisionism if not capitalist restoration and that the PRC therefore needed to reaffirm its commitment to revolution.[66] During the fall, Moscow's handling of the Cuban Missile Crisis prompted the reenergized Mao to step up his attacks on the Soviets. The chairman complained that Khrushchev had capitulated to the American imperialists and shown inadequate support for Cuba's struggle when he withdrew Soviet ballistic missiles from the island.[67] A series of five European party congresses held in late 1962 and early 1963 was characterized by fierce mutual recriminations over Cuba and other issues. The Chinese bristled at the humiliating treatment they received at these conferences. Wu Lengxi, director of the New China News Agency, accompanied the Chinese delegation and recalled that the other parties "attacked us on the one hand and told us to discontinue the public debate on the other hand; they criticized us and then told us not to respond."[68]

During the summer of 1963, the Soviets and Chinese made one final effort to mend fences in a round of high-level talks in Moscow.[69] Differences over the Limited Nuclear Test Ban Treaty being negotiated by the United States, Great Britain, and the Soviet Union were one of the key reasons the talks failed. The treaty, which was signed on 5 August, banned nuclear tests underwater, in space, or in the atmosphere. Beijing saw the agreement—not completely inaccurately—as an effort by the superpowers to constrain China's nuclear development program and had been fiercely critical of Moscow's willingness to work with Washington on the issue.[70] The CCP viewed having a nuclear arsenal as an important signifier of global status and thus considered the treaty a manifestation of Great Power chauvinism. In October 1963, Chinese vice premier and foreign minister Chen Yi explained that atomic bombs, missiles, and aircrafts were all "reflective of the technical level of a nation's industry." China needed to conduct a successful nuclear test in the near future or it would "degenerate into a second class or third class nation." Chinese officials also accused Moscow of "band[ing] together" with the American imperialists to carry out "a policy of nuclear blackmail."[71]

The PRC responded with more vigorous efforts to promote itself as a leader in the Third World at Moscow's expense. It made anti-imperialism, support for national liberation movements, Afro-Asian unity, and the rejection of Great Power chauvinism its platform while fiercely criticizing the Soviets for appeasing the West through peaceful coexistence. At international conferences and other venues, Beijing actively strove to supplant Moscow's influence. During the third biennial conference of the Afro-Asian People's Solidarity Organization held in Moshi, Tanzania, in February 1963, the Chinese emphasized repeatedly that the Soviets would always align with "other white nations" in conflicts with nations of color.[72] The CIA believed that this constituted a "turning point in Chinese tactics" and that Mao and his comrades were "setting the stage for the next act: the establishment of new front organizations from which the USSR would be excluded from the start."[73]

By the summer of 1963, Beijing was attacking Moscow more sharply and directly. Between September 1963 and July 1964 the CCP published nine polemics lambasting the Soviet Union as an enemy of revolutionary forces in Asia and Africa and then ordered them to be translated and distributed throughout the world.[74] The fourth polemic, scathingly entitled "Apologists of Neo-Colonialism," hit Soviet policy in the Third World especially hard. A "revolutionary storm," it claimed, was sweeping through Asia, Africa, and Latin America, and this required "every political force in the world to take a stand." True Marxists-Leninists would "firmly side with the oppressed nations and actively support the national liberation movement," but "modern revisionists in fact side with the imperialists and colonialists and repudiate and oppose the national liberation movement in every possible way." The CPSU was particularly devious because Soviet leaders "dare not completely discard slogans of support for the national liberation movement" and would at times "take certain measures which create the appearance of support." On examination, however, the Soviet position on the "liberation struggles of the oppressed nations of Asia, Africa and Latin America" was "a passive or scornful or negative one," and the Russians were nothing more than "apologists for neocolonialism."[75]

Mao encapsulated this critique of the Soviet Union into a more formal doctrine when he promulgated a new version of Intermediate Zone Theory. Mao had first described an intermediate zone during the 1940s, but the concept had then reflected China's growing allegiance to the Soviet Union. He had previously claimed that there existed a vast intermediate zone between the United States and the Soviet Union consisting of oppressed, non-Western countries. Mao had argued that the American imperialists could not attack the Soviet Union unless it could control the intermediate zone.[76] After the Sino-Soviet split, however, Mao revamped this theory, now claiming that there were two intermediate zones, both of which contested superpower dominance. Mao explained that "the intermediate zone has two parts. One part is the vast, economically backward countries of Asia, Africa, and Latin America. One part, which is represented by Europe, is the imperialist and developed capitalist countries. These two zones both oppose American control. In every country of Eastern Europe the problem of opposing Soviet control has appeared."[77] Beijing no longer aspired to play an important role within the socialist camp but sought instead to position itself as a leader in a different group of nations that struggled against both Washington and Moscow.

What did the burgeoning rivalry between Beijing and Moscow in the Third World mean for American policy? Sewing divisions within the Communist camp had long been an important U.S. objective, and Americans were not unhappy to see a falling-out between their two most formidable adversaries.[78] On certain issues they anticipated new opportunities for consultation and even cooperation with the Soviets. But they could also perceive that the split would serve as a catalyst for more radical Chinese activism in the Third World and this was troubling. American officials were particularly fearful that Beijing would capitalize on its image as a non-white power and mobilize Afro-Asian countries against the United States and the Soviet Union. Under such circumstances, they believed, America needed to toughen rather than relax its efforts to contain the PRC.

One of the first efforts to delineate a comprehensive policy toward China after the Sino-Soviet split was a thirty-five-page paper submitted by Policy Planning Council chairman Walt W. Rostow in April 1962. Rostow predicted that frictions between Beijing and Moscow would impel the PRC to take a more militant approach, especially in Southeast Asia. "Aside from the fact that [Beijing] appears genuinely convinced that its proposed strategy of 'struggle in all forms' is best for the communist cause," he wrote, "the Chinese are under compulsion to demonstrate that, as against Soviet claims, low cost successes can be achieved through local aggression." The United States needed to be prepared to deal with Chinese adventurism. Rostow called for Washington to "make particularly clear" to Beijing "that its high risk policy, wherever it finds expression, will be countered resolutely and effectively and that greater risks will ensue than the USSR, or [Beijing] without Soviet support should care to accept."[79]

In subsequent months, as PRC attacks on Soviet policy burst into the open, American officials analyzed the impact of the Sino-Soviet split in greater detail. They forecasted that Beijing's status as a nonwhite power would give it an advantage in its struggle with Moscow for influence in Afro-Asian countries and ultimately enable it to emerge as a more formidable competitor for the United States. The CIA predicted in July 1963 that as a result of the split, there would be "an increase in the Chinese presence and in Chinese-sponsored racialism and radicalism in Asia, Africa and Latin America." Such PRC activities had been "harming Soviet influence in these areas for some time," and the rupture would only "further stimulate [Beijing] to these ends in the belief that the situation in the underdeveloped countries gives them a number of advantages over the Soviets." The CIA believed in particular that China stood to benefit from "economic and revolutionary situations much more akin to those of China than of the Soviet Union, antiwhite sentiments, histories of grievances against the colonial powers and—perhaps, most telling—a proclivity for irresponsible action which [Beijing] can encourage much more than can Moscow."[80]

Marshall Green, a leading State Department expert on East Asia serving as consul general in Hong Kong in August 1963, had even more dire predictions. Green, too, feared that the PRC would intensify its efforts to use the issues of race and colonialism to its advantage. He called China the "world's leading underdeveloped, non-white nation" and explained that with the gap between poor and wealthy nations continuing to widen, "China may have expanded opportunities for exploiting Afro-Asian-Latin American resentment, disillusionment and race consciousness in bidding for leadership of the underprivileged world majority." From Green's perspective, Beijing's split with Moscow made it a more formidable political threat because it was now unencumbered by the demands of fraternal socialism. He explained that Beijing's "separation from Moscow places it in a better position to exploit the hard to handle, white-versus-colored racial antagonisms and differences between poor and prosperous nations."[81]

Although both the Soviet Union and the PRC would remain America's rivals, Green believed that Moscow would become increasingly amenable to working with the United States to contain China and encouraged Washington to look for such opportunities. "In pursuing a triangularized cold war, where we and the USSR are pursuing separate goals and yet both are anxious to curb Red Chinese expansionism and influence (particularly in underdeveloped countries)," he explained, "there may be instances w[h]ere a certain parallelism of U.S. and Soviet-bloc effort, if only for tactical reasons, may occasionally emerge." He called for a "careful evaluation of Soviet designs worldwide and particularly in areas around China in order to ascertain whether and how the limited mutuality of interest . . . might be extended on a conscious basis to other countries or to regional problems, to the net advantage of U.S. interests."[82] Green's analysis echoed the views of Rostow and several other high-ranking officials in the Kennedy administration that the USSR was the more "responsible" of the two Communist giants and more likely to reduce its belligerence toward the West.[83]

But although Green saw limited opportunities to cooperate with the Soviets, he believed that the split would ultimately require the United States to devote more resources and energy to contesting the PRC in the Global South. Because the demise of the Sino-Soviet alliance had increased Chinese activism in the region, the areas where Washington and Beijing would come into conflict were also bound to increase. He explained, "The widening of the split tends to lend further justification" for America's strategy of seeking to contain China and "force it in upon itself." Yet Green did not stop at advocating a reinvigorated containment policy. He believed that meeting the growing Chinese threat in the Third World would require the United States to rethink its approach to the region more broadly. In the conclusion to his lengthy report Green explained, "We must make it clear by deeds, not just words, that our future is dependent upon the prosperity and social progress of less developed countries." He recommended that the United States do everything it could to promote economic development in these nations, including opening its markets to their goods. "Otherwise," he explained, "we stimulate hope which, frustrated, plays into [Beijing's] hands." Similarly, America needed to deal more "courageously and effectively" with civil rights issues so that it could put itself in "a better position to frustrate Chinese efforts to magnify the racial issue world wide."[84]

Americans ultimately viewed the Sino-Soviet split and competition between Beijing and Moscow in the Third World more as a source for concern than as an opportunity. They feared more than ever that the PRC would be able to present itself as a model of revolutionary nationalism and anti-imperialism that other Afro-Asian nations would follow. American officials like Green viewed promoting economic development in the Global South as the best way to prevent the PRC from enhancing its influence. Washington also hoped that a successful counterexample to the PRC—one that adopted more moderate foreign and domestic policies—could be promoted as an alternative to Communist China. During the early 1960s, Americans increasingly came to focus these hopes on India.

The Sino-Indian War and Sino-American Competition in the Third World

The 1962 Sino-Indian border conflict was a brief and limited war, but its impact on Asian politics was broad and deep. The border between China and India had remained a potential flashpoint after the flight of the Dalai Lama to India and the subsequent clashes that occurred.[85] After these events, both Beijing and Delhi expanded their military presence in disputed areas. Communist Party officials were alarmed by the Nehru government's implementation of the so-called forward policy in November 1961. Under this new policy, the Indian government instructed its forces to widen their patrols and set up additional posts that could prevent the PRC from staking out more ground along the frontier. The PRC argued that this policy encroached on its territory and violated its sovereignty.[86] In October 1962, PLA forces launched a full-scale attack against Indian troops stationed in disputed areas and, by 21 November, had cleared the borders of enemy divisions. After one month of fighting that took 8,700 Indian and 2,400 Chinese casualties, Beijing declared a unilateral cease-fire.[87]

The war was fought not only on remote and mountainous Himalayan battlefields, however, but also in the court of international public opinion. Military conflict with India further radicalized Chinese foreign policy and helped to define a new Chinese militancy that would become prominent from 1963 onward. Both Delhi and Beijing started to accentuate rather than downplay their differences, often using each other as foils to emphasize their own distinctive visions of Afro-Asian solidarity. And both made extensive efforts to peddle their respective visions of international order to other countries in the Third World.

India stressed its commitment to peace and neutrality and its preeminent position in the Non-Aligned Movement. Nehru wanted to persuade the rest of Asia that whereas his nation was committed to reducing the threat of global conflict, the PRC's main objectives were to bring about greater polarization and violence.[88] In April 1963, he published an article in *Foreign Affairs* praising Delhi's policy as being "of service to the cause of world peace." Beijing, in contrast, believed that the world was "divided essentially between imperialists and Communists, between whom war not only is inevitable in the end, but between whom tension in some form must be kept alive and even intensified as opportunity occurs." China believed, according to Nehru, that nonaligned nations occupied "an unstable, anomalous position from which, if they could be dislodged, either by cajolery or coercion, the result would be to accentuate the polarization of world forces." By contrast, he boasted, "India is such an outstanding member of the non-aligned community that her defection, whether voluntary or enforced, cannot fail to bring grave and far-reaching consequences in its train."[89] India was thus a peaceful, disinterested nation whose claim to status in the Afro-Asian world lay in its ability to stand above the Cold War.

China aimed to prevent the Indian view of the war from gaining ascendance. Beijing's narrative elevated China as a leader of world anti-imperialist forces and rebutted Delhi's accusations. Much as Nehru had contrasted India with China to emphasize India's commitment to peace, Mao and his comrades contrasted themselves with India to emphasize the PRC's unflagging resistance to Great Power hegemony. They depicted India as a tool of American imperialism and argued that following the Indian model would lead to reliance on the Great Powers rather than greater autonomy. Even as India accepted aid and advice from the United States and the Soviet Union, China was pursuing greater self-sufficiency. The PRC could therefore champion the Afro-Asian struggle against imperialism while India was holding it back.

In an address to the Standing Committee of the National People's Congress on 20 November, Zhou Enlai gave a sweeping defense of the war against India that would also serve as a basis for Chinese strategy in the months ahead. He dismissed concerns that Beijing was taking on too many adversaries at once, arguing instead that they were all connected and that it was Beijing's task to defend revolution against them:

> There are people who ask, given that we oppose imperialism, reactionary nationalism, and modern revisionism, whether we have too many enemies. We don't think so. . . . We should always strike the main enemy so that we can isolate him and win over the broad masses of people who are waging revolution, about to wage revolution or sympathetic to revolution. . . . We must see American imperialism as our main enemy because it is always hostile to us. In this instance, by attacking the Indian reactionary clique we are also exposing the United States.[90]

By linking the Sino-Indian border conflict to the struggle against American imperialism, Zhou sought to stigmatize India for its willingness to invite greater American involvement in Asia while elevating the PRC as the champion of revolution in the region.

The critical question facing Afro-Asian states was whether to use the Chinese or Indian criteria for making moral judgments about the conflict. During and immediately after the brief war, Beijing worked hard to sell them on its view of things. Chinese diplomats vigorously put forward their explanation of the conflict among Third World leaders and tried to destroy India's credibility as a peaceful, nonaligned state. In exchanges with other Afro-Asian officials they repeatedly emphasized the dangers of India's alignment with American imperialism and its requests for U.S. military assistance during the war. Chinese officials recognized that mistrust of India was as great or greater than mistrust for the PRC in some Asian countries. They opportunistically used the war to play on these fears and highlight the positive distinctiveness of China's role in the Third World.

Beijing's efforts to control the political impact of the war began almost as soon as the PLA launched its offensive. It was particularly eager to head off criticisms from Nasser and Egypt. Although Cairo had not officially condemned China, it had leaned toward India, and Nasser's influence in the Arab world made his statements and policies a matter of the utmost concern. Shortly after the fighting broke out, the Egyptian presidential council issued a statement expressing its dismay and urging mediation. Then on 8 November, Muhammad Hasanayn Haykal, the editor in chief of *Al-Ahram* and an influential figure in Nasser's government, published an editorial more bluntly critical of China. He called on the PRC to explain its stubbornness toward India and warned that Beijing would alienate itself from the rest of the Afro-Asian world.[91] On the same day that the editorial was published, Lin Zhaonan, the PRC ambassador in Cairo, met with Egyptian secretary of state Ismal Fahmy. He contended that the conflict was a byproduct of Great Power meddling and repeated the frequently asserted but nevertheless inaccurate Chinese claim that Washington sought to use the war as a pretext to set up military bases in India. The ambassador argued, "If the United States sets up military bases in India, this is the nature of an American imperialist invasion. We should first condemn America. Next we should criticize the Indian government, which allows the United States to establish military bases. The blame should not fall on China." Using an argument that was skillfully tailored to the Egyptian context, he likened India's decision to seek military aid from the United States to Saudi Arabia's claims that it allowed American bases on its territory because of the threat posed by "Nasser's Arab socialism" and accused Nehru of adopting the "U.S. imperialist policy of Asians fighting Asians."[92]

Egypt did not embrace the Chinese viewpoint but instead joined a multinational effort to mediate the conflict. With five other nonaligned nations—Ghana, Indonesia, Cambodia, Burma, and Ceylon—it participated in a conference in Colombo that lasted between December 1962 and February

1963. The conference participants tried to persuade Beijing and Delhi to negotiate, but the PRC refused. In letters sent to Prince Sihanouk in Cambodia and Ceylonese premier Sirimavo Bandaranaike before the conference, Zhou Enlai thanked his fellow Asian leaders for their involvement but continued seeking to turn sentiment against India. He explained that even though the PRC was now implementing a cease-fire, this action alone could not guarantee that renewed conflict along the border would not erupt. Once again, India and its subservience to American imperialism were to blame. "The American imperialists are still going all out to instigate anti-Chinese sentiment and to implement its scheme of Asians attacking Asians," Zhou complained; this was the true reason why India had not responded to China's proposals and remained critical of Beijing despite the cease-fire.[93]

When Indonesian foreign minister Subandrio and Bandaranaike traveled to Beijing for talks with Mao, Zhou, and Liu Shaoqi in January 1963, their hosts made the same points even more forcefully. Throughout the discussions, Liu highlighted the critical differences between an India full of "Great Power chauvinism" and other Afro-Asian nations. Like the Americans and the British, the Indians "always felt that they were a head taller than us." They had "tossed aside non-alignment but Britain and the United States had told them not to abandon the 'non-alignment' slogan." In fact, Liu argued, "India had already aligned itself with the United States and Great Britain." Zhou Enlai then recited a long list of complaints about Delhi's lack of support for anticolonial struggles. "In which of the wars for national independence did India stand on the front lines?" the premier asked. He lambasted Nehru's government for its weak positions on the Algerian civil war, the Suez Crisis, the situation in Laos, and—perhaps most pointedly, given Subandrio's presence—the West Irian conflict in Indonesia. "Right now," Zhou concluded, "India is not the leader of an alliance of peaceful neutral Afro-Asian countries and it is not at the forefront of Afro-Asian nations."[94]

Beijing may not have convinced all Afro-Asian states that its cause was just, but its soft-pedaling of the conflict worked on some key players. According to the Foreign Ministry's report on Subandrio and Bandaranaike's visit, the CCP leadership was persuasive. While Subandrio had urged China to "make an expression of generosity" and "give the Colombo nations a chance to strengthen Afro-Asian unity," he had privately criticized Nehru and India. He told Liu and Zhou that "India will never again be the leader of anti-imperialism and anti-colonialism" and that he hoped China would "support Indonesia's efforts to uphold Afro-Asian unity."[95] After the meetings had ended, the Foreign Ministry boasted to diplomatic posts in Asia that "Ceylon and Indonesia had progressed in their understanding of India's Great Power chauvinism and our fair, equitable position."[96] In the Middle East,

Egypt remained sympathetic to Delhi, but Iraq hewed closer to Beijing's position. The Chinese embassy in Baghdad reported that key Iraqi officials were making statements condemning India. The planning minister had stated that the Sino-Indian war had "completely exposed the hypocrisy of India's non-alignment policy." Moreover, Iraqi newspapers had become more sympathetic toward China; those that had once been critical of the PRC now remained quiet.[97] These were precisely the political effects that Beijing hoped its diplomacy would achieve: the rejection of nonalignment, the denunciation of India as an American tool, and a willingness to embrace Beijing's more radical anticolonial agenda.

India, in contrast, often expressed strong dissatisfaction with Afro-Asian reactions to what it perceived as naked Chinese aggression. During the 1963 Colombo Conference it became clear that while some nations, such as Egypt, were relatively sympathetic toward India, others such as Burma and Cambodia continued to regard the PRC with admiration and sympathy. They refused to endorse resolutions that directly criticized the PRC or identified China as the aggressor.[98] In the end the proposals that emerged from the conference were weak and, at least to Delhi, infuriating. Nehru lamented, "What is obvious to us does not seem to be obvious to the world."[99]

Nehru's government became deeply worried about Beijing's success at spinning the Sino-Indian conflict and realized it had few alternatives but to turn to Washington for help. In May 1963, the Indian Ministry of External Affairs produced a report on "China's Bid for World Power" that was supposedly "top secret" but nonetheless found its way into American hands. Summarizing developments in the Sino-Indian border conflict and evaluating the effectiveness of Beijing's strategy in the Third World, the report explained that China's struggle to gain support within the international Communist movement and the "regrouping of Afro-Asian countries under the Chinese banner of militant friendship" were helping to "isolate and weaken India." Beijing's campaign against India in the Third World was succeeding because "the Afro-Asian countries . . . would for diverse reasons prefer to follow the winning side—a strong protector and ally—and a militant ideology which promises to bring them added luster and concrete material gains." Although Delhi continued to seek Soviet assistance, it also believed that the Soviets would remain reluctant to aid India in its predicament because "they would face the prospect of denunciation if they go to the support of a bourgeois capitalist country struggling against a socialist country."[100]

American officials shared many of Delhi's fears and believed that they had both an opportunity and an obligation to step in and help India. With its vast population and territory, India seemed a natural counterbalance to Chinese influence in Asia. By bolstering India's status in the region, Americans believed, they could stymie the growth of China's. Whereas in the past U.S. officials had constantly expressed frustration with Nehru's nonalignment, after the war, they encouraged it under the assumption that it would help Delhi maintain an independent posture and thus strengthen its credibility among its neighbors.[101] As Secretary of State Dean Rusk later explained to the president, "It was not in our interests to 'compromise' Indian non-alignment, lest we promote Soviet-Chinese rapprochement."[102] Americans increasingly looked for ways to aid India militarily and economically that would strengthen its positions vis-à-vis China without compromising its reputation for integrity and independence.

While the military conflict was ongoing, the Kennedy administration tried to make sure that India did not suffer a devastating defeat. The fighting broke out during the same week that the Cuban Missile Crisis threatened the entire world with nuclear annihilation. The last thing that the United States wanted to do was get involved in another high-risk, prestige-engaging confrontation. Nonetheless, Washington still managed to lend Delhi some support. After Nehru requested Western assistance on 1 November, the United States moved swiftly to send military supplies to India's beleaguered forces. A State Department memorandum prepared on 3 November contended that the United States should "assure that the Indians not be so humiliated or overwhelmed as to eliminate the Indian example of the free world way of industrializing in an underdeveloped country, as a model for other underdeveloped nations."[103] By that date the United States had already sent an initial shipment that included forty thousand personnel mines, more than a million rounds of ammunition, and 750 radios. The administration also issued a public statement that it recognized the MacMahon Line as the accepted international border and offered the Indian government greater access to U.S. intelligence information.[104]

After the Sino-Indian conflict had ended, the CIA, the State Department, and the Defense Department collaborated on a study of its potential ramifications. Their report expressed optimism that conflict would reconfigure India's nonalignment in a way that benefited the United States and weakened Chinese influence. It noted that Indian leaders were "being forced to re-examine some of the basic assumptions that had been central to Indian life and attitudes." India, "the great exponent of peaceful coexistence," had "been attacked by another nation which ostentatiously shared this attitude." As a result, "the effectiveness of non-alignment as a policy" had been "brought into question." At the same time, American goals with respect to India remained modest. The report explained that the United States had provided military assistance to India during the crisis "to help a friend, not win an ally." American officials believed that they could "expect the Indians to redefine their non-alignment policy" but not to abandon it.[105] Nevertheless, they hoped that a redefined version of nonalignment would not enhance the PRC's image as the Five Principles had.

Delhi understood American anxieties well and skillfully cast its requests for U.S. diplomatic and economic support in terms of the larger contest for influence in the Third World. On 11 August 1963, Nehru wrote a letter to President John F. Kennedy explaining the challenges India faced from China and Pakistan, two countries that he claimed were increasingly working together to weaken India. Nehru warned that the Chinese were "making a bid for leadership not only in Asia but of the Communist world and this too only as a first step in their bid for world leadership." He explained later on, "The Chinese want people in Afro-Asian and Latin American countries to adopt militant, aggressive and revolutionary attitudes and are against democratic evolutionary practices and stable regimes."[106] India remained committed to non-alignment, but its leaders nevertheless shared with the United States a common interest in preventing the Afro-Asian world from aligning under the banner of Chinese militarism.

American officials proved responsive to Delhi's appeals. In subsequent months, Washington built up India as a positive example for Afro-Asian nationalists that could diminish the appeal of Chinese radicalism and militancy. After the cease-fire, Washington dispatched Averell Harriman to Delhi and Karachi to discuss future American assistance to India and offer reassurances to Pakistan, whose leadership had reacted with suspicion to the sudden increase in U.S. support for its rival. At the end of his mission, Harriman explained, "The U.S. has long sought to build a close relationship with India on grounds of its long-run potential as a principal force in Asian affairs" and that the "present situation provides a unique opportunity to advance this aim." Harriman made no concrete recommendations for expanded U.S. military assistance, but he did call for immediate allied efforts to help India achieve its political objectives. His report explained that "India's diplomatic and propaganda efforts have been inept" but that Indian government officials were "taking steps to correct their shortcomings." He called for the United States and Great Britain to "discretely assist" the Indian government in making sure that these steps succeeded.[107] Through offering India quiet assistance, Washington hoped to enhance India's prestige at Beijing's expense without leaving the nation vulnerable to Chinese accusations that Delhi was becoming an American puppet.

American economic aid to India also increased after 1962 and was often governed by the same logic that Harriman articulated. In a 1963 country plan, the U.S. Agency for International Development (USAID) explained that India was "the most powerful non-Communist Asian mainland nation." Its voice was "the most powerful among unaligned nations in world councils," and it was "the leading exponent of democracy among the unaligned and emerging countries." For these reasons, the plan argued, it was "essential that India remain free and independent" and "be able to resist the current and future pressures of Communist China." The agency wanted India not only to resist China but also to challenge the PRC's influence. The USAID hoped to "see India more closely associated with the free world, a showpiece of democracy in Asia, with a rate of economic growth which would make India under democracy more attractive to the underdeveloped world than China under the Communists." With this objective in mind, the United States committed $935 million in aid for India over two years and helped to coordinate more grants and loans from the World Bank and the International Development Association (IDA) to support Delhi's five-year plan.[108]

The depth of this sudden amity between India and the United States should not be exaggerated. Various issues such as American support for Pakistan, Moscow's continued courting of Delhi, and Indian criticism of some U.S. policies persisted and plagued the relationship. By February 1964, Robert Komer, a member of the NSC staff, was complaining to the president that America's Indian affairs were "sliding backwards from the high point" reached in 1962.[109] Nevertheless, Washington's vigorous support for India during and after its conflict with the PRC had by then already contributed to the intensification of Sino-American competition in the Third World. Initial U.S. support for Delhi had sharpened the criticisms China leveled against American imperialism in its justifications for the war. American officials, in contrast, had seen the conflict as an opportunity to tarnish China's image among Afro-Asian states, and they simply could not refuse to take advantage of it. Even if U.S.-Indian relations did not return to the high point they reached right after the Sino-Indian War, India remained a valuable tool that the United States could and did use against Chinese initiatives in the Third World.

———

The Sino-Soviet split and the Sino-Indian border conflict might have been expected to produce a more chastened PRC with greater interest in negotiating with the United States. But Beijing believed that such compromises would seriously weaken Chinese prestige, especially in the Third World. Instead, the PRC cast aside the idea of peaceful coexistence and made resistance to the Great Powers at all levels the new basis of its policy toward Asia and Africa. Washington could perceive the shift in Beijing's foreign policy during the early 1960s and, almost invariably, looked on this development as a threat. American officials committed themselves to preventing China from gaining influence among Afro-Asian states through any available means.

They attempted to strengthen India as a symbolic counterweight to the PRC in Asia and even discussed the possibility of limited cooperation with the Soviets in some instances.

Beijing's adjustments to its foreign policy between 1958 and 1963 created new areas of conflict with the United States. With its ties to India and the Soviet Union severed, the PRC would embark on a new crusade to unify nationalist and revolutionary elements in the Third World behind the principles of Afro-Asian solidarity, support for revolutions, and opposition to Great Power hegemony. This included a diplomatic campaign to find new allies and avoid isolation, more direct efforts to encourage and support wars of national liberation, and a stepped-up program of economic aid to newly independent countries in Africa. The United States would vigorously contest each initiative, seeking to undermine Beijing's diplomacy, suppress the insurgencies that it supported, and prevent China from making inroads with its economic aid programs. Sino-American competition in the Afro-Asian world reached a new intensity during the early 1960s as Americans used almost every tool at their disposal to stymie China's bold but sometimes desperate drive for influence and status in the region.

Chapter 7

The Diplomatic Campaign, 1963–1966

The early 1960s were the best of times and the worst of times for Chinese diplomacy. On the one hand, Beijing's relationship with what had once been its most important benefactor—the Soviet Union—lay in tatters, the United States and the West remained hostile, and conflict with India added to China's insecurity. On the other hand, the era was rife with new opportunities. The PRC was not the only Asian country that was frustrated with Great Power dominance in world politics. While remaining neutral, nations such as Indonesia, Cambodia, and Pakistan had become sufficiently disgruntled with Moscow and Washington to create potential allies for Beijing. Moreover, the process of decolonization in Africa was still unfolding. As new states that shared China's hostility to colonialism gained their independence, new possibilities were created for the PRC to win friends and attract sympathy.

The CCP's response to these changing international circumstances was, by necessity, bold and ambitious. Beijing sought to assemble the largest possible united front of Afro-Asian countries and use it to create a radical, militant, anti-imperialist alternative to the two Cold War camps. Through building their own institutions, hosting their own conferences, and supporting common principles and goals, Beijing hoped that these nations could create a new locus of power in international politics. China could then enhance its status both by staking out a position of leadership within this coalition and by strengthening the prestige and influence of the coalition itself. During the early 1960s China infused its diplomacy in Asia and Africa with a heavy dose of consciousness-raising activities to foster a sense of unity among potential allies. High-ranking Chinese officials visited critical countries in Asia and Africa, lobbied for a second Afro-Asian conference that would exclude the Soviet Union, and made the case for Beijing's positions on Vietnam, India, and others issues that concerned Third World leaders.

China's campaign to supplant Great Power influence in Asia and Africa was an obvious cause for alarm in both Washington and Moscow. The Kennedy and Johnson administrations struggled to disrupt Beijing's efforts at coalition building. They devoted both time and resources to pushing wavering Asian and African leaders to embrace more moderate conceptions of nonalignment. American officials also made subtle efforts to mobilize public opinion against Chinese leaders when they visited Asian and African countries and strove to undermine Beijing's efforts to hold a second Afro-Asian conference. Efforts on this front were sometimes parallel and sometimes at cross-purposes with those of the Soviets. Like Washington, Moscow wanted to see PRC diplomacy fail, and it, too, tried to weaken support for Beijing's agenda. Yet the two superpowers never fully cooperated.

Beijing enjoyed initial success in promoting its vision of Afro-Asian unity. Feeling disadvantaged in a world dominated by Washington and Moscow, some Asian and African leaders found Beijing's criticisms of Great Power hegemony appealing. At the same time, the coalition of nations that the PRC brought together was fragile; its members aligned with Beijing for diverse and sometimes competing reasons. China suffered a series of setbacks in 1965–66 that crippled its efforts to bring about an enduring change in world politics. The overthrow of its ally Sukarno in Indonesia and the cancelation of the Second Afro-Asian Conference, which Beijing had strongly supported, weakened China's prestige in the Third World and showed the limitations of its influence.

Asia: New Allies, Old Neighbors

China's quest to unify the Afro-Asian world and dethrone Great Power hegemony began with its Asian neighbors. Before 1965, the other two Asian Communist countries, North Korea and North Vietnam, generally leaned closer to the PRC than they did to the Soviet Union, and sustaining their loyalty was one important component of Chinese policy.[1] But Beijing could hardly claim to be an important leader in Asia solely on the basis of its friendship with what were traditionally its closest allies. It needed to win support for its new agenda in South and Southeast Asia, and in these regions it was contested by the United States and the Soviet Union.

After the Sino-Indian border conflict and the Sino-Soviet split, the PRC focused on improving ties with three Asian nations in particular: Pakistan, Cambodia, and Indonesia. All three states had amicable relations with the PRC during the 1950s, but during the early 1960s they moved closer to China and further from the Great Powers, supporting Beijing on major issues. China sought to parlay these enhanced relations into greater prestige in Asia and in the international arena. As in the 1950s, Beijing emphasized diplomatic visits, although now these visits were designed not only to give the PRC the imprimatur of legitimacy but also to produce strong statements of support for China's radical global agenda. The PRC also worked together with these new allies to organize international conferences and other highly visible events that could promote Afro-Asian solidarity.

Pakistan began to strengthen its ties with China during the 1962 Sino-Indian War. Americans were thrilled that the brief conflict had alienated Delhi from Beijing, but the reconfiguration of U.S. policy in South Asia that followed did not sit well with Karachi. For Pakistan, which had been a founding member of SEATO and had allowed the United States to build facilities for espionage against the Soviet Union on its territory, America's growing largesse toward its archenemy felt like a betrayal. Karachi's insecurity in turn engendered frustration with the White House. As Kennedy explained, "Everything we give to India adversely affects the balance of power with Pakistan."[2] The Soviets, for their part, had long been solicitous of India and openly hostile toward Pakistan. Khrushchev had once called the Pakistani government a "rotten and unpopular" regime.[3] Faced with Soviet and Indian hostility and uncertain about Washington's reliability, Pakistan naturally found that it had much in common with the PRC from a geostrategic standpoint.

Yet the new ties that developed were not entirely a product of circumstance. Beijing had long held a fairly sophisticated understanding of Karachi's motives. It tended to view Pakistan—to some degree correctly—not so much as a Free World nation that maintained normal relations with the PRC for strategic reasons but as an Afro-Asian nation that accepted alliance and aid from the United States because of security concerns about India. In 1956, the Foreign Ministry reported that even if Pakistan relied heavily on American assistance, it was not completely satisfied with Washington "because American aid has been small and cannot meet Pakistan's needs." Karachi was also "not happy with the American policy of 'appeasing' India."[4] At the same time, the Pakistanis found themselves on the same side as China on some major international issues. Pakistan had "generally adopted a favorable attitude towards the struggle against colonialism" and was "especially supportive of the struggle against colonialism in Africa and the Middle East." After the Bandung Conference, Pakistan had maintained a friendly attitude toward China. One leading Pakistani official had stated publicly that he did not believe that China had any intention of invading other Afro-Asian countries and that he could "sufficiently understand China's demands about authority over Taiwan."[5] Detecting a degree of ideological consanguinity underneath the veneer of Pakistan's participation in SEATO, Beijing had continued to cultivate ties with Karachi.

After the Sino-Indian War, Beijing launched a concerted effort to draw out what it considered latent tendencies in Pakistan's foreign policy. Communist Party leaders commingled new offers to settle outstanding disputes and provide assistance with exhortations to hew closer to Chinese positions on Afro-Asian solidarity, imperialism, and revisionism. In early 1963, for instance, Beijing and Karachi negotiated a frontier agreement that settled lingering boundary disputes. During negotiations, the PRC made significant concessions, and many have considered the terms of the agreement favorable to Pakistan.[6] Beijing ceded 750 square miles of territory while gaining no territory under previous Pakistani control.[7] Party officials viewed the agreement as more than a simple trust-building measure between China and Pakistan, however. They tried to use the occasion of negotiating the agreement to promote anti-American sentiment in Karachi and integrate Pakistan into a united front.

Talks between Pakistani foreign minister Zulfikar Ali Bhutto and CCP officials in February and March 1963 became an important venue for Beijing to press its agenda. The foreign minister's conversations with Zhou, Mao, and other leading CCP officials were wide-ranging. The Chinese reminded Bhutto that the Kennedy administration had been befriending India and Pakistan's expense. "Right now India is not on the side of Afro-Asian countries, it is on the side of the West," Zhou told Bhutto. "Because of this the United States chooses India and it does not choose Pakistan."[8] Party officials also tried to instill in the Pakistani leadership a sense of commitment toward Afro-Asian causes while pledging diplomatic support for Karachi's efforts to strengthen its relations with Indonesia, Cambodia, and other radical Afro-Asian countries. In discussions with Bhutto, Zhou made it clear that he was willing to use China's influence to reduce Pakistan's isolation: "In Asia, Africa, and Latin America we have a few friends, therefore we can increase your friends. We will not only support the Second Afro-Asian Conference together but we will support each other in the movement for Afro-Asian unity."[9] If Pakistan supported China's efforts at building a united front, Zhou promised, then Karachi, too, would gain stature in the region.

In subsequent months Beijing drew considerable support from Pakistan for its positions on Afro-Asian issues.[10] To the chagrin of American officials, Karachi created new ties with Beijing while becoming increasingly vocal in its praise for China. In July 1963, President Ayub Khan made a speech arguing that the smaller nations of Asia should look to China for protection against Indian aggression. Then in August, Pakistan and China signed a civil aviation agreement despite strong protests from numerous high-level American officials. In April 1964, the Pakistani foreign minister skipped a SEATO foreign ministers' meeting in Manila so that he could travel to Jakarta and attend a preparatory meeting for the second Bandung Conference.[11] At the same time, Karachi echoed Chinese criticisms of the Soviet Union, which continued to vie with the United States for India's loyalty. Nawabzada Raza, the Pakistani ambassador to the PRC, told Chen Yi in May 1964 that from Karachi's perspective, the Soviets were siding with India and his government had come to favor excluding them from Afro-Asian conferences.[12]

Washington tried to undercut burgeoning ties between Karachi and Beijing with little success. In September 1963, the Kennedy administration dispatched Assistant Secretary of State George Ball to Pakistan for talks with Ayub Khan. Ball was instructed to obtain a "clearly stated definition of Pakistan policy towards the Chinese Communists and an assurance that the Government of Pakistan will not adopt a posture towards or extend further its involvement with the Chinese Communists to the detriment of the alliance relationship."[13] After Kennedy's assassination, Ayub Khan hoped that the new president, Lyndon B. Johnson, would be more understanding of Pakistan's situation and sent a letter to the White House in July 1964 explaining that American aid to India "imperils the security of Pakistan, your ally." This policy, he explained, could "force India's smaller neighbors . . . to seek the protection of China."[14] Johnson was unimpressed by Ayub Khan's pleading. Rather than providing a written response, he instructed the U.S. Ambassador in Pakistan to convey his disappointment that the Pakistani president should "want to give the attention he has given to Communist China" at a time when Washington was "having all sorts of trouble with China in Southeast Asia."[15]

The president's warnings were of little avail. Washington continued to feel betrayed and embarrassed by Karachi's growing support for Beijing. In July 1965, Harold (Hal) Saunders, a Middle East expert on the NSC, summarized America's growing discontent with its ostensible ally in a memorandum that was circulated among high-level officials. Saunders excoriated the Pakistanis because during the previous two years they had "knowingly undercut U.S. and Free World interests by supporting Chinese Communist positions and giving the Chicoms an aura of respectability in Afro-Asia." Pakistan's political leaders had "endorsed the jargon of 'anti-imperialism,'" and had done so with "enthusiasm and fanfare" accompanied by "crude invective" directed against the United States.[16] Of course, Saunders was writing only weeks before the Indo-Pakistani War, which would shift the situation somewhat in Washington's favor. Nevertheless, in 1963 and 1964, improving ties between Beijing and Karachi unquestionably strengthened the PRC's standing in Asia and facilitated its efforts to assemble a coalition of radical Afro-Asian states.

Beijing's diplomatic gains in Cambodia were even deeper and more dramatic than in Pakistan. Much as Washington's support for India had created frustrations in Karachi, America's deepening commitment to South Vietnam had led to disillusionment with the United States in Phnom Penh. By 1962, South Vietnamese forces were frequently crossing into Cambodian territory on the basis of often faulty intelligence about hidden Vietcong camps, and Sihanouk feared getting drawn into the conflict.[17] Sihanouk wanted the United States to take action to guarantee Cambodia's territorial integrity and neutrality, but American policy did little to placate the anxious prince. Once again the PRC proved highly adept at capitalizing on the situation. It offered Phnom Penh strong support when the United States would or could not, ultimately leading Sihanouk to cast his lot with the PRC.

Relations between Washington and Phnom Penh began their precipitous decline in August 1962 when Sihanouk called for an international conference to guarantee Cambodia's neutrality. The Kennedy administration demurred because it believed that Sihanouk's proposals would ultimately confer greater legitimacy and authority on Beijing and its allies. A position paper prepared for the president claimed that Sihanouk's proposals would "invite the legal extension of Bloc influence and interference into affairs entirely outside the Bloc, requiring South Vietnam and Thailand to admit the jurisdictional authority over their Cambodian frontiers of the Geneva powers including Communist China and North Vietnam." The paper recommended placating Sihanouk without accepting his proposals. Although the prince's terms were not acceptable, "outright rejection" was "not advisable in view of the likelihood of an irrational reaction by Sihanouk possibly including carrying out his threat to call in Communist Chinese troops for protection against his neighbors." Washington should therefore help Cambodia to negotiate "bilateral protocols" with Thailand and South Vietnam, thereby obviating the need for Sihanouk's proposed conference.[18]

Kennedy's approach was inadequate, however, and U.S.-Cambodia relations deteriorated. Angered by President Ngo Dinh Diem's inept handling of the Buddhist crisis during the spring of 1963 and South Vietnamese air raids on a Cambodian village, Phnom Penh broke relations with Saigon. When Sihanouk asked Washington to support his request to station UN observers along the Cambodian-Vietnamese border in September, the United States refused, creating the impression that defending Cambodia's neutrality was not a high priority.[19] But the issue that completely wrecked Washington's relationship with Phnom Penh was the sudden resumption of secret radio broadcasts from South Vietnam by the Khmer Serei, an anti-Communist guerrilla group that opposed Sihanouk. The prince immediately suspected that Washington was somehow involved and on 5 November threatened that if all Khmer Serei broadcasts did not cease by the end of the year, he would terminate Western aid programs and turn to China for assistance in setting up a "new form of socialism."[20] When the broadcasts did not stop, Sihanouk convened a special meeting of the National Assembly and terminated American aid programs. All U.S. aid personnel received orders to leave the country by 15 January 1964. Sihanouk subsequently closed the Cambodian embassy in Washington, and the United States reduced its own diplomatic presence in Phnom Penh. America's relationship with Cambodia lay in shambles.[21]

The PRC moved quickly to replace American influence. In rejecting American assistance, Cambodia had, from the Chinese perspective, joined the ranks of Afro-Asian nations that were struggling against Great Power hegemony. On 4 December 1963, the Foreign Ministry sent a telegram to all diplomatic posts describing the news in almost ecstatic language. Sihanouk's decision to reject future American aid was at one time "a great blow against America's aggressive policies" and "a powerful exposure of America's use of aid to launch schemes to control and subvert" other nations. In the international community, Cambodia's actions "had a great influence, especially for a few Afro-Asian nations." The PRC now saw Cambodia as an example for the rest of the region to follow. Cambodia was praiseworthy because it "carries out a resolute struggle under the pressure of imperialism and revisionism, does not fear brute force and upholds the spirit of justice." Sino-Cambodian relations had of course "developed greatly" as a result of Sihanouk's decision. The Foreign Ministry drew up plans to send economic specialists and military assistance to Sihanouk's government in the near future.[22]

During the next two years, Beijing stepped up its assistance to Cambodia with the goal of bringing Sihanouk completely on board with its agenda. By the fall of 1964, the PRC had already provided Cambodia with twenty-eight thousand weapons, which Sihanouk noted was sufficient to completely replace American military aid.[23] Although Beijing could not supply all of the forms of military aid that Cambodia requested, when Sihanouk visited the PRC in September 1964, Zhou promised to continue supplying guns and shells and assist in the construction of a firearms repair factory.[24] During the next two years, China also launched new economic aid projects in light industry, health, and sanitation. The PRC built textile factories and hospitals for Sihanouk's government and planned to dispatch technical advisers to provide training for Cambodian specialists on the ground.[25]

At the same time that it showered Sihanouk with military and economic largesse, Beijing also advertised the deepening Sino-Cambodian friendship. During the prince's 1964 visit to the PRC, Liu Shaoqi held a banquet in his honor and lavished him with praise for resisting American imperialism and strengthening Afro-Asian solidarity. The royal prince had "waged resolute struggles against U.S. imperialism and its lackeys" while the Kingdom of Cambodia had "worked for the strengthening of Afro-Asian solidarity and supported other Afro-Asian peoples in their struggles against old and new colonialism." As a result, Cambodia was "enjoying an even higher international prestige and exerting an even greater influence on international affairs."[26] The closer Sihanouk moved to Beijing's positions on anti-imperialism and Afro-Asian solidarity, the more Chinese officials sought to highlight Cambodia's position and strengthen its influence. By trumpeting the achievements and anti-imperialism of its allies, Beijing hoped to enhance the status of its entire coalition.

To the outside world, including the United States, Chinese efforts to woo Cambodia seemed very successful. Phnom Penh began toeing the Chinese line not only on the need for unity against imperialism and revisionism but also on an array of issues where it had once adopted a more neutral posture. With American influence fading, the Soviet Union tried to offset some of the PRC's success in Cambodia through offers of limited military aid—notably a grant of four MIG-17 fighters and air defense equipment—but Phnom Penh remained closer to Beijing. Although Sihanouk preferred not to be drawn into the Sino-Soviet conflict, in 1963, the Cambodian media occasionally began to run articles critical of the Soviets while avoiding similar criticisms of the PRC.[27] By November 1963, the U.S. embassy in Cambodia reported that Sihanouk had begun referring to China as "our great friend to the north," refused to sign the Limited Nuclear Test Ban Treaty, and taken positions on the Sino-Indian dispute that "tended more and more openly toward the Communist Chinese."[28]

Throughout 1964, the United States sought reconciliation with Cambodia in the hopes of preventing the country from moving completely into the Chinese camp, but its efforts failed. Washington offered to send Dean Acheson as a confidential emissary to Phnom Penh, but Sihanouk publicly rejected this. When the United States made proposals for four-power talks, Sihanouk declined to participate. Last, Washington dispatched a new ambassador, Randolph Kidder, who was known to be sympathetic to Phnom Penh on key issues, but the prince refused to receive him.[29] In continuing to embarrass Washington while offering praise and support for the PRC, Cambodia soon became one of the most reliable backers of PRC's diplomatic campaign.

It was Indonesia, however, that would become China's closest and most reliable partner. Before 1963, Sino-Indonesian relations had, for the most part, been amicable, but Washington had been far more concerned about Soviet than Chinese influence in the country.[30] The leadership of the influential but nonruling Communist Party of Indonesia (PKI) had generally acknowledged that the Soviet Union should remain the leader of the world Communist movement. Moreover, the overseas Chinese community in Indonesia continued to arouse mistrust and sometimes found itself the subject of discriminatory government edicts, despite earlier agreements about its status.[31] During the early 1960s, however, several issues—notably the creation of Malaysia—caused Jakarta to become deeply frustrated with its treatment by the international community. Like the PRC, Indonesia came to reject the bipolar world order dominated by Washington and Moscow, and this created grounds for stronger ties with Beijing.[32]

Indonesia's disillusionment with the Great Powers had its roots in Great Britain's 1961 decision to create a new political entity through merging Malaya and Singapore with its territories on Borneo, a small island that belonged partially to Britain and partially to Indonesia. Jakarta initially greeted London's scheme with quiet resignation. But after the United Nations conducted a questionable "ascertainment" determining that the people of Borneo supported the proposed Malaysia federation, Sukarno came to suspect that Britain's scheme was targeted against Indonesia. Frustrated that the international community seemed to be siding with Britain, the Indonesian president announced his "confrontation" or *konfrontasi* policy on 23 September 1963. His government would attempt to weaken and undermine the newly created Federation of Malaysia through a variety of measures—including the dispatch of armed bands into Borneo—that were geared at fomenting rebellion and forcing a renegotiation of the issue.[33]

Beijing shared Jakarta's hostility to Malaysia, which it saw as part of a broader Western effort to encircle the PRC with a ring of anti-Communist regimes, and encouraged *konfrontasi*. Washington, for its part, used what leverage it had over Sukarno to promote negotiations and discourage the Indonesian government from resolving the situation by force. In January 1964, the Johnson administration dispatched Attorney General Robert F. Kennedy to mediate the crisis. Kennedy seemed at first to be making progress, but Sukarno later reneged on some of the things he had ostensibly agreed to and the confrontation continued.[34] The Johnson administration also put pressure on Sukarno by scaling down military and economic assistance and instructing Howard P. Jones, the U.S. ambassador to Indonesia, to engage in a dialogue with Indonesia's top leaders on the issue.[35]

As Americans encouraged Sukarno to reach a settlement, China sought to encourage conflict. Certain that the views of Washington and Jakarta were ultimately irreconcilable, Beijing waited as Americans struggled to find a diplomatic solution to the crisis. In late January, when Kennedy got Sukarno to promise to halt the attacks on Malaysia and hold trilateral talks with the Philippines and Malaysia, the Chinese embassy in Indonesia complained that "Sukarno's cease-fire order catered to the interests of American imperialism." Nevertheless, it predicted that Indonesia ultimately would not benefit from holding trilateral negotiations. According to the embassy's report, it was "unlikely that Sukarno will go on backing down," and "a return to confrontation" was "more likely to happen due to the obstacles to compromise."[36]

The PRC's prediction was accurate. Negotiations failed, and the views of Beijing and Jakarta on Malaysia became more closely aligned. During trilateral negotiations in Bangkok in February 1964, Indonesia flatly rejected Malaysian demands for the withdrawal of its guerrilla fighters from Borneo and questioned the legitimacy of the Malaysian government. Frustrated with Jakarta's intractability, the Malaysian prime minister took the issue to the United Nations.[37] Recognizing that their views about Malaysia were irreconcilable with those of the rest of Southeast Asia, Indonesian officials increasingly turned to Beijing for political support. As the talks in Bangkok floundered, several high-ranking Indonesian officials held meetings with the Chinese ambassador in Jakarta, where they received further encouragement for their increasingly confrontational posture. According to one Chinese report, Sukarno expressed his hope "to work together with China to destroy Malaysia and requested us to mobilize the people of Singapore and Malaysia to fight."[38]

By mid-1964, all international efforts to moderate Indonesian policy seemed to be failing as ties between Beijing and Jakarta deepened. One paper presented for consideration by the NSC in May explained that American efforts to mediate had only brought about a "heightening of the [Sukarno] regime's anti-American orientation" and "contributed somewhat to closer Indonesian ties with Communist China."[39] Along similar lines, a National Intelligence Estimate on the "Prospects for Indonesia" prepared in July 1964 expected to see a "continuation of confrontation and the drift to the left that has accompanied it" and predicted that "Indonesia's growing cordiality toward Communist China will probably continue." The swift rapprochement that had occurred between the two countries was based on "a near identity of short-term interests in the Afro-Asian world and Sukarno's admiration for Mao." The report also forecasted that the two were likely to collaborate to encourage subversion in Malaysia.[40]

Beijing and Jakarta's growing alignment was by no means confined to Malaysia or other geostrategic issues, however. They came to embrace a shared vision of Afro-Asian community and worked together to promote it. The two countries planned high-profile events designed to garner international attention and raise their prestige in the Third World. Through facilitating Afro-Asian cooperation, encouraging independence from the Great Powers, and offering strong mutual support, they sought to create a new force in international politics that could stand in opposition to the existing power structure.

One of their first efforts to bring this vision to fruition was the Games of the New Emerging Forces (GANEFO), a sporting event open only to athletes from Asia, African, and Latin American countries. By the Cold War era, international sport had already become an important signifier of legitimacy and stature. Historian Barbara J. Keys notes that during the early twentieth century "participation in international sport competitions became a statement of membership in a community of nations," thanks to the development of the Olympics and other major sporting events.[41] In the eyes of many, raising flags and playing anthems at international athletic competitions boosted national prestige.

By the early 1960s, both Beijing and Jakarta had come into conflict with international sports commissions over political issues and had withdrawn from the Olympics. It was the policies of Avery Brundage, the American president of the International Olympic Committee (IOC), that led to the PRC's estrangement from the international sporting community. Under Brundage's leadership, the IOC carried out a version of the two-China policy, inviting both the PRC and the ROC to send delegations to the 1956 Olympics. When he learned that the ROC had been invited, Dong Shouyi, the Chinese member of the IOC, wrote Brundage a letter calling him a "faithful menial of the U.S. imperialists" and suspending China's participation.[42] The Indonesian government had similarly run afoul of the IOC in 1962 when, under pressure from the PRC and its allies, it had refused to allow athletes from Taiwan and Israel to participate in the Asian Games in Jakarta.[43]

Disgruntled by the IOC's policies, China and Indonesia worked on creating an alternative where their athletes would be able to carry forth their national flags with pride. It was Sukarno who came up with the idea for GANEFO in February 1963, but from the outset the PRC lent invaluable support to the endeavor. The PRC Foreign Ministry told its ambassador to Indonesia that the two countries should "strive for the GANEFO to become founded on a gradual realization of the African-Asian-Latin American strength and a world competition face-to-face with the IOC."[44] During his visit to Jakarta in April 1963, Liu Shaoqi issued a joint declaration with Sukarno denouncing the IOC and reiterating strong support for GANEFO. Beijing later offered to pay the expenses of any emerging nation that wished to attend the games but could not do so due to financial difficulties.[45] China's ultimate purpose in supporting the games, Zhou Enlai later explained to the Indonesian minister of sports, was "to foster support for the new emerging forces and oppose imperialist domination, and to support all of those who are pressured, discriminated against and held in contempt by imperialism."[46]

When GANEFO opened in November 1963, the PRC widely advertised its role in the event and made sure that the games promoted Afro-Asian solidarity. Aside from Indonesia, China sent the largest of the fifty-one delegations that participated in the games and won the most medals. Its contribution received special recognition from Sukarno, who made a highly visible effort to shake hands with He Long, the Chinese vice premier and head of the PRC National Sports Commission, during the opening ceremonies.[47] When the games were in progress, the PRC gave them the widest possible publicity, emphasizing the new bonds being forged between Chinese athletes and those from other Afro-Asian countries. China's leading newspaper, the *People's Daily*, included both detailed reporting on the event and numerous photo spreads of Chinese athletes happily posing alongside their competitors from North Korea, Cuba, Guinea, and other countries. The paper even printed a cartoon of a Chinese athlete leading a delegation of athletes from other Afro-Asian countries and holding a GANEFO banner.[48]

For their part, Americans tried to diminish the games as much as possible. The IOC was a more immediate antagonist for GANEFO than Washington, but the official U.S. response to the games was generally in harmony with that of the IOC's American president. Brundage's chief strategy was to punish athletes and countries that participated in GANEFO by threatening to ban them from the Olympics and other international sporting events. Arguing that GANEFO was "unquestionably the first move in a campaign to take over international sport," he persuaded international sports federations to join the IOC in implementing a twelve-month ban on athletes who competed in Jakarta.[49] Secret U.S. propaganda supplemented the IOC's campaign to undermine the games. When Sukarno's government issued a decree curbing subversive activities briefly before GANEFO began, the CIA issued a propaganda directive that warned nations planning to send delegations about Indonesia's new policy: "In those countries that will send teams to Ganefo, we warn the participants that they must under no circumstances discuss politics unless they want to run the risk of execution or spending years in Sukarno's jails."[50] The CIA likely recognized that such exaggerated warnings would not dissuade countries from attending, but the agency hoped that it might poison the atmosphere.

GANEFO was, in the end, a mixed success. On the one hand, athletes from fifty-one nations attended, thereby enabling Beijing and Jakarta to boast that they had organized a major international event showcasing Afro-Asian solidarity. On the other hand, it was clear that GANEFO could not compete with the Olympics for prestige. Brundage's stipulation that athletes competing in GANEFO would be ineligible for the 1964 Tokyo Olympics had a clear impact. Aside from Indonesia and the PRC, only North Korea sent its best athletes to participate.[51] Despite the limitations of GANEFO, it represented only the first joint initiative that Beijing and Jakarta would undertake. By the time the games took place, the two nations were already discussing a variety of other potential areas for cooperation, including the Second Afro-Asian Conference. For this agenda to succeed, however, Beijing realized that it needed support not only from neighboring Asian countries but also from newly independent African countries. It was the PRC's determination to bring Africa on board with these efforts that provided the impetus for Zhou Enlai much-heralded visit to the continent.

Zhou Enlai's Africa Visit

In December 1963, Zhou Enlai embarked on a dramatic two-month tour of fourteen countries. The heart of this grand international voyage was Zhou's visit to Africa. Accompanied by Vice Premier Chen Yi, Zhou traversed ten countries in a little over six weeks.[52] It marked the first time that a high-ranking CCP official visited Africa, and Zhou's meetings with African leaders naturally elicited much fanfare and curiosity. The trip was an ambitious effort to raise China's profile in Africa while countering American and Soviet efforts to undermine Chinese diplomacy. Zhou and his entourage aimed to accomplish this objective by voicing support for Africa's anticolonial struggle, promoting Afro-Asian unity, and improving relations with individual countries.[53] The premier would establish an image of China as a major power while building solidarity between Africa and the PRC. Americans saw Zhou's venture into what was hitherto unchartered territory for China as troubling. Whenever possible, they took subtle measures to reduce the impact of Zhou's trip and prevent China from gaining ground.

At every stage of Zhou's African tour, his entourage paid attention to the image of China being presented. Great pains were taken to assure that Zhou was greeted with the pomp and circumstance merited by a high-ranking foreign dignitary. Guinea's president Ahmed Sékou Touré and Ghana's leader Kwame Nkrumah had visited the Middle Kingdom in 1960 and 1961, respectively, and received lavish welcomes; Chinese officials believed it important that the same be done for Zhou when he arrived in Africa.[54] The premier did in fact receive red carpet treatment in several destinations. In Guinea, Zhou was given a twenty-one-gun salute and greeted by cheering crowds as his motorcade left the airport. As a show of respect, President Touré escorted Zhou to his lodging, a beachside villa built in traditional African style, where the premier found a giant picture of Touré and Mao Zedong hung in the living room. Zhou's entourage received a similar reception in Mali, where crowds lined up along the street to cheer the arriving premier, and President Modibo Keïta hosted a banquet for more than a thousand guests in Bamako. In Morocco, King Hassan II made a special exception to normal protocol for the visiting premier. Rather than waiting for Zhou to be escorted to the royal palace to greet him, the king waited in the doorway at the "peace palace," where the Chinese guests were scheduled to stay.[55] China's state-run newspapers eagerly publicized the enthusiasm generated by Zhou's visit in an effort to show that the PRC was swiftly emerging as an important and trusted new actor in African affairs.[56]

Throughout his tour, Zhou proved skilled as always in playing the part of the dignified statesman who represented a nation deserving of a prominent

Zhou Enlai being greeted by President Sékou Touré during his 1964 visit to Guinea. (Xinhua News Agency)

position on the world stage. Traveling through neutral countries such as Egypt and Tunisia gave the premier a rare opportunity to talk to Western reporters. Although Mao was preaching revolutionary violence and Zhou himself would emphasize the need for struggle in some of his meetings, the urbane diplomat put on a more moderate face when necessary and emphasized that the PRC was guided by reasonable leaders who remained committed to peace. During a press conference in Cairo, for instance, a reporter from *Time* magazine asked the premier why Beijing was opposed to peace talks between East and West. Zhou responded that China was willing to negotiate and that Washington was the main obstacle to peace: "Right now America still occupies China's territory Taiwan; the U.S. 7th Fleet still threatens China from the Taiwan Strait. Despite these circumstances, China continues to hold discussions about the way to solve Sino-American disputes and does not resort to force. How can you say that China opposes peace negotiations?"[57] The premier's careful but firm rebuttals show a statesman who relished the opportunity to give American journalists a dressing down before an international audience.

Zhou took great care to show respect for African leaders and their culture. In Morocco, Zhou and Chen Yi both appeared delighted when King Hassan II invited them to drink tea at the royal palace and taught them about his country's traditional tea ceremonies. During his visit to Sudan, Zhou toured the city of Khartoum and paid his respects at the grave of Muhammad Ahmad bin Abd Allah, a revered hero who had led a military campaign against foreign domination during the late nineteenth century. The premier was also deeply impressed by the nearby Khalifa House Museum, which contained relics from both the Sudanese independence struggle and its more distant past. He was perhaps at his most relaxed in Mali, where he even partook in some of the traditional dances performed during his stay.[58] Zhou knew well that his actions on the African continent reflected not only on him personally but on China as a whole. By exhibiting cultural sensitivity and genuine interest in Africa's heritage, Zhou sought to project an image of China as a power that could understand the situation of Africans in ways that the United States or the Soviet Union could not. He hoped that Africans would make reciprocal gestures of respect.

During discussions with African heads of state, Zhou worked to improve China's image and win over key leaders to Beijing's cherished causes. In particular, he sought to dispel doubts about China's intentions that lingered from its conflict with India, make the case for participation in the Second Afro-Asian Conference, and garner admiration for the PRC. He did not always succeed, but he remained poised in tense moments and offered strong support for African leaders who appeared sympathetic to his agenda. The net effect was to deepen some friendships and undercut criticisms from African nations that had been less sympathetic toward the PRC. Moreover, Beijing was able to depict nearly every stop on Zhou's tour as an impressive triumph for Chinese diplomacy.

Reversing the damage done to China's image by the Sino-Indian War proved especially important in northern Africa. Nehru and Egyptian president Nasser had a history of mutual support and cooperation that extended back to the early 1950s.[59] Yet what was perhaps Zhou's testiest exchange on his African tour occurred during a conversation with the relatively pro-Western Tunisian president Habib Bourguiba.[60] The Tunisian questioned Zhou aggressively and expressed skepticism about Beijing's commitment to peace. "The Chinese government made African countries feel alarmed," Bourguiba claimed. "What made them feel alarmed is that . . . you know that you are a large, powerful country and despite that used military force to settle border disputes with Third World countries and occupied India's territory." Bourguiba's accusations barely ruffled the imperturbable Zhou, who had anticipated such criticisms and was eager to respond. "It is not us who occupy India's territory but India who occupies our territory," the premier explained before blaming the conflict on the legacy of European colonialism and launching into a detailed explanation of the Chinese position.[61] Zhou could not fully persuade the Tunisian during the meeting, but it is unlikely that he expected to. The chance to make the case personally on African soil was in many ways as important as the result because doing so fostered the impression of a reasonable PRC eager to build friendships on the African continent.

Zhou sung a slightly different tune when he visited left-leaning African countries. The premier hoped that the governments in Guinea, Mali, and Ghana would stand with Beijing at the vanguard of its united front condemning American imperialism and Soviet revisionism while endorsing China's call for the Second Afro-Asian Conference. Thus, during his conversations with Kwame Nkrumah in Accra, he simultaneously criticized American imperialism and Khrushchev's policy of peaceful coexistence by asserting that "as long as imperialism and colonialism exist, the threat of war will not disappear."[62] A militant approach was sometimes inevitable; Zhou explained later, "We cannot plead for peace. Only through struggle can we achieve a few of our objectives."[63] As he did throughout his tour, Zhou made his case for holding another Afro-Asian conference forcefully, arguing that this would be the best venue for Asian and African countries to pursue their common goals of attaining true independence and ending colonialism. The premier's visit to Ghana ended with a joint communiqué endorsing Chinese views on several international issues and appealing for another Afro-Asian conference.[64] Endorsements from venerable African statesman such as Nkrumah added to the impression of rising Chinese influence on the African continent.

The premier enjoyed several other important successes during his trip. Sékou Touré of Guinea and Modibo Keïta of Mali also published similar joint communiqués endorsing China's proposal to hold a Second Afro-Asian Conference and expressing sympathy for Chinese positions on Taiwan, UN representation, and other key issues.[65] African countries that did not recognize Beijing before the visit, including Congo-Brazzaville and Burundi, established relations with the PRC during Zhou's travels.[66] Nations such as Ethiopia that had previously endorsed the Indian version of nonalignment now joined the PRC in calling for an Afro-Asian conference. Because Ethiopia had not established formal relations with the PRC at the time, Americans considered this a significant victory for Beijing.[67]

Zhou's successes in Africa fueled anxieties in Washington. Americans foresaw the visit's potential to improve China's image in Africa and stir up anticolonial resentments. From the time that Zhou's trip began, the State Department received warnings about its potential symbolic and political ramifications. In December 1963, as the premier was traversing North Africa,

Zhou Enlai visits Ghana during his 1963–64 visit to Africa. (Xinhua News Agency)

Jean-Marie Soutou, the head of the African Department at the French Foreign Office, warned the American ambassador in Paris that Zhou's trip would
bolster Chinese influence on the continent. He was certain that Chinese diplomats would be able to "exploit to [the] fullest" the "fascination and curiosity of Africans over Chen Yi and Zhou Enlai." Soutou predicted that Zhou and
Chen would "meet with great success on [their] trip and we must anticipate
[a] considerable expansion [of] their influence in Africa." He elaborated that
while the Russians "have fallen on [their] faces in Africa in many respects
and in ways familiar to Western countries," the Chinese were "in African eyes
[a] fresh new element with problems and experiences closer to African heart
than those of [the] U.S. and USSR." Moreover, the Chinese appeared "inno-
cent of racism," which had tarnished the images of both the United States
and the Soviets. In the end, Soutou concluded that although some African
leaders harbored no illusions about Beijing, many would be susceptible to
the "carefully calculated approaches which Chinese will know how to make
even though they have only modest material resources." The result would be
a "new challenge to [the] West."[68]

Washington did not sit idly by but actively sought to weaken the impact
of Zhou's trip. Before the premier set foot in Africa, the State Department

sent talking points covering China's "advocacy of violence" and rejection of the Limited Nuclear Test Ban Treaty to its diplomatic posts in Africa. In the meantime, the CIA compiled documents about "Chinese Communist subversion efforts" that could be presented to African leaders. Seeking to coordinate America's response to Zhou's visit, Marshall Green, one of the State Department's foremost Asia experts, called a meeting with representatives from the Office of Intelligence and Research and the Office of Asian Communist Affairs. They decided that "overt United States involvement is undesirable" but planned several subtler measures. These included approaching India and suggesting that their ambassadors in Africa "explain the Indian side of the border war and describe Chinese Communist policy in Tibet" as well as asking the CIA to "place suitable articles in the African press" on issues such as China's trade with South Africa and its rejection of nonalignment.[69] The American strategy here was to plant doubts about Beijing's intentions in the minds of Africans, persuading them that China's vision of Afro-Asian cooperation would lead not to unity but to subversion.

After Zhou returned to China, the United States sought to prevent Beijing from realizing any political gains from the trip. Americans put especially heavy pressure on Ethiopia. The Johnson administration counted Ethiopia and its emperor Haile Selassie as one of its closest allies in Africa and provided the regime with significant military and economic assistance.[70] In early 1964, Washington subtly sought to leverage this aid to make sure that Zhou's brief visit would be the limit of Ethiopia's engagement with China. The State Department warned that in the event that Addis Ababa recognized Beijing, it would "find it extremely difficult [to] understand" the deep concerns that the emperor had voiced about Soviet assistance to its neighbor and rival Somalia. The American government would be forced to believe that Ethiopia preferred to "encourage Soviet and Chinese presence next door rather than that of [the] West."[71] Although Washington issued no direct threat to cut off assistance, such warnings insinuated that continuing to support Ethiopia would be difficult if the African nation moved closer to China. In the Ethiopian case, American pressure tactics proved effective. Ethiopia did not establish relations with the PRC until November 1970, when the Nixon administration, itself looking to improve relations with China, had stopped pressuring many allies on this issue.[72]

The Soviets shared American fears about the impact of Zhou's visit. Moscow and Washington did not coordinate their activities, but they seemed to act almost with a common purpose. With the premier simultaneously condemning both imperialism and revisionism, the Soviets did not want to see the PRC gain ground. Before Zhou's arrival in Mali,

Soviet propagandists hired local youths to distribute leaflets touting the benefits of Moscow's aid to the country and criticizing Beijing for undermining socialist internationalism.[73] One of Zhou's biographers has even contended that the Soviet pressure was behind one of the few perceived snubs that the premier received on his tour: Nasser's failure to go to the airport to greet him. According to Han Suyin, who conducted several interviews with Zhou, Nasser was under pressure from the Soviet ambassador not to give the premier's visit too much fanfare. With a major Soviet loan pending, the Egyptian president told the Chinese that urgent business elsewhere would prevent him from greeting Zhou on his arrival.[74] Such Russian machinations likely grew out of a shared understanding with Washington about what Zhou wanted to achieve and how he might be undermined.

Despite these efforts to limit the impact and meaning of Zhou's trip, Chinese officials still boasted that the tour helped to establish the PRC's presence in Africa. Several months after the visit's completion, the Foreign Ministry drafted a top-secret report describing the premier's achievements in almost ecstatic language. The visit to fourteen countries had achieved a "perfect success." It had "consolidated and developed the united front against imperialism and expanded the influence of our party and our country." Ultimately, the trip had been a "great event in China's foreign relations and had an important meaning internationally."[75] American analyses did not completely agree with the Chinese view of the trip as an unqualified success. Some saw the lukewarm reception that Zhou received in northern Africa as evidence that Beijing's appeal on the continent was limited.[76] Nevertheless, the rousing welcomes that Zhou had received through much of his trip and the fact that he had seemingly opened up an entirely new vista for Chinese diplomacy further emboldened Beijing on the international stage.

The key question that remained to be answered, however, was whether China would be able to parlay the goodwill generated by Zhou's visit to Africa into a position of real leadership in the Afro-Asian world. The key proving ground for this would be the Second Afro-Asian Conference. Lobbying for the conference had been a key objective of Zhou's trip, and the statements of support for it made by African leaders were a main reason that Beijing counted the trip a success. When Zhou returned from the trip, China's revolutionary diplomatic offensive seemed to be gaining momentum despite the odds stacked against it. But China still needed an event that could show the rest of the world that Asia and Africa were uniting under the PRC's leadership. And the United States, of course, remained committed to preventing Chinese influence from gaining ascendancy.

Chinese Setbacks: Bandung II

The plan launched by Beijing and Jakarta to hold a Second Afro-Asian Conference gave rise to a series of often-frenzied diplomatic maneuvers and counter maneuvers. Competing Chinese and American visions for the political direction of the Afro-Asian world turned this maneuvering into a significant Cold War battleground. Chinese statesmen believed that the conference would be a critical step toward realizing their vision of an Afro-Asian community that held the PRC in high esteem while rejecting American imperialism and Soviet revisionism. In the words of one Foreign Ministry official, the conference could be a "rostrum for the trial of American imperialism."[77] Americans, for their part, saw the conference as an embodiment of some of their greatest fears: a radicalized block of Afro-Asian states, rising Chinese influence, and a platform where anti-American views could be propagated.[78]

Although Beijing had been cooperating with Jakarta to promote a Second Afro-Asian Conference since 1961, the period between late 1963 and mid-1965 marked the high point in the political and diplomatic intrigues surrounding this venture. The two countries had broached the possibility of holding such a conference when Liu Shaoqi visited Indonesia in 1961, and the idea had gained momentum in 1962–63 as Sino-Indonesian ties deepened. By 1963, Pakistan had also become a strong supporter because it hoped to create an alternative to the Non-Aligned Movement in which India remained influential.[79] From 1963 onward, Chinese diplomats lobbied their Afro-Asian colleagues intensively to participate in the conference while American concerns about the political ramifications of such an event intensified.

Initially, however, the most significant opposition to convening the Second Afro-Asian Conference came not from Washington but from Delhi. Nehru's government viewed a conference that primarily reflected Beijing's agenda as a threat to its own aspirations for leadership in the Non-Aligned Movement. It therefore sought to preempt the proposed Second Afro-Asian Conference through organizing a Second Non-Aligned Conference or Belgrade II, which would be more similar to the relatively moderate gathering held in Belgrade in 1961.[80] In October 1963, India, Egypt, and Ceylon issued a joint communiqué calling for the convocation of the Second Non-Aligned Conference within a year. At a preparatory meeting attended by twenty-six countries in February 1964, it was decided that the Second Non-Aligned Conference would be held in October in Cairo.[81] India's purpose in supporting this rival enterprise was not necessarily to destroy the possibility of another Afro-Asian conference but to draw attention from it and diminish its potential significance.

Even with a place and date for the Second Non-Aligned Conference set, however, India remained concerned about possibility of an Afro-Asian conference where Beijing could determine the tone. Delhi participated vigorously in the preliminary discussions of Bandung II and tried to steer the conference away from militant Afro-Asianism. When a preparatory meeting charged with making initial plans for Bandung II convened in Jakarta in April 1964, Delhi sought to delay the conference and control its meaning. As John W. Garver, a leading expert on Sino-Indian relations, has explained, India "submitted a series of proposals carefully designed to sabotage the radical Chinese-Indonesian forces." It proposed that the conference be held in Africa—as it eventually was—in order to assure that China, Indonesia, or Pakistan did not gain the prestige that would come with hosting. India also insisted on inviting Indonesia's adversary Malaysia and the Soviet Union, which it argued was partially located in Asia. These highly disputed issues were ultimately deferred to a foreign ministers' meeting that was to assemble immediately before the actual conference.[82]

As Delhi sought to undermine Beijing by advocating for a conference of nonaligned nations, Chinese leaders strove to persuade Afro-Asian leaders that the conference they envisioned was more important. Through much of 1964, Chinese diplomats worked to assure that countries attending Belgrade II remained enthusiastic about the Second Afro-Asian Conference. When Zhou Enlai met with the Indonesian ambassador to the PRC on 19 March, he focused on making sure that the Second Afro-Asian Conference would be an impressive event that adhered to Beijing's positions on important issues. "The Afro-Asian conference does not necessarily have to clash with the Non-Aligned Conference," the premier explained. Avoiding direct confrontation would enable Indonesia and the PRC to "invite even more Afro-Asian countries, reduce obstacles, and begin preparations smoothly." The important thing was that Bandung II have a great impact. "The effect of the Second Afro-Asian Conference," Zhou told the Indonesian, "should be even greater than that of the First Afro-Asian Conference."[83]

Throughout 1964, Beijing continued seeking to differentiate the two conferences and to make sure that the one it supported would be a grand success. On 24 March, Zhou told a group of ambassadors from several Middle Eastern and African nations that "the Second Afro-Asian Conference and the Second Non-Aligned Conference were not alike in nature; they are not alike in scope and they are not completely alike in their tasks. You cannot substitute one for the other."[84] Beijing's support for the conference was not merely rhetorical, however. It also provided generous economic incentives. In July, when Algiers was chosen as the site for the conference, China offered four million dollars to assist the Algerian government with construction costs.[85] China hoped that this would enable Algeria create an impressive new venue that would benefit both the conference and the host government.

Chinese lobbying on behalf of Bandung II continued throughout the summer and fall of 1964, with key CCP officials repeatedly explaining the importance of the event. On 17 July, while an Organization of African Unity meeting in Cairo was discussing, among other things, the conference's location, Chen Yi and Zhou Enlai called a meeting with ambassadors from several African nations where they explained the meaningful contribution the conference would make to the cause of Afro-Asian unity.[86] On 12 October, Zhou Enlai promised the Pakistani ambassador that the conference would help to "advance economic collaboration, abolish the special privileges of imperialism and stabilize prices for the export of goods from Afro-Asian countries on a basis of equality, mutual assistance, and cooperation."[87] In November, Foreign Minister Chen Yi went on a six-week tour of several nations in South Asia, Southeast Asia, and the Middle East and emphasized throughout the trip that the Afro-Asian Conference would "make a step forward on the front of anti-imperialism and anti-colonialism."[88] Through this diplomatic blitz in support of the conference, Chinese diplomats hoped to build enthusiasm for the event and secure commitments to attend from as many leaders as possible. All of this could ultimately raise the profile of the conference and endow it with a stronger sense of meaning and purpose.

Back in Washington, the Johnson administration watched China's campaign to mobilize support for the event with alarm and was, from the outset, eager to preempt the Chinese on the issue. In fact, when the possibility of holding such a conference was broached in 1961, high-ranking American officials were already planning measures to stop it from being held and, in the case that the conference became inevitable, prevent China from controlling the agenda. In October 1961 Robert Komer wrote a memo to McGeorge Bundy explaining that it was "not too soon to start" worrying about the "proposed second Bandung." Komer believed that such a conference would be "far more likely than [the] Belgrade [Conference] to produce noises highly adverse to our interests." Komer suggested that the United States inform Indonesia, which harbored aspirations to serve again as host, that "having [Beijing] at the conference automatically creates an East-West issue and tends to force us into opposition." He then recommended a "three-pronged strategy." The United States, he wrote, should first try to "discretely block the conference." If this was impossible, then America needed to "at least try to keep Red China out." Last, if Chinese participation became inevitable, the United States should at least make plans to get its "case presented as favorably as possible." This might include an attempt to quietly "apprise India of our knowledge of Indo [Indonesian] efforts and help them in their opposition."[89]

In early 1964, the Johnson administration started to devote more attention to Bandung II in general and the Chinese role in particular.[90] Analyses of the planned conference emphasized the likelihood that it would benefit Chinese prestige and damage American interests. A report by the State Department's Bureau of Intelligence and Research predicted that another Afro-Asian conference would produce "a withering drumfire" of anti-American propaganda while bolstering the PRC in its competition with the Soviet Union. The memo raised the possibilities of encouraging U.S. allies in the region to attend with the hope that they could limit the anti-American rhetoric.[91] By the fall of 1964, Washington was engaged in highly surreptitious efforts to undermine the conference and limit Chinese influence. In November, W. Averell Harriman reported to Komer that the State Department had "begun quietly encouraging friendly governments to select the most competent representation possible" at the conference because "only able delegates will be able to cope with the kind of pressure and tactics we can anticipate from the other side and to make sure that our viewpoints get a hearing."[92]

Yet Washington's subtle maneuvering seemed insufficient to slow Beijing's political momentum. Although the PRC could not attend the Second Non-Aligned Conference, the proceedings at Cairo played out in a way that was far more favorable to China than many had anticipated. Beijing's strategy toward the Cairo conference was not dissimilar to Washington's strategy toward Bandung II; it worked behind the scenes and quietly encouraged friendly countries to advocate for its agenda. One instance of such lobbying occurred in Ghana, where Ambassador Huang Hua met with President Nkrumah in the run-up to the event and expressed hope that, although Beijing could not attend, the gathering would "make positive contributions to opposing imperialism, supporting national independence movements and protecting world peace." He warned that Delhi might try to bring up the Sino-Indian War and use it to criticize China and argued that such issues should not be discussed since the PRC could not participate.[93]

During the months before the Cairo Conference, Beijing was in the final stages of preparation for conducting its first nuclear test, which it carried out successfully shortly after the conference ended. Chinese officials anticipated that this might become an issue and devoted great energy to persuading other Afro-Asian nations that the PRC's nuclear program deserved support if not admiration. They made it clear that they had the technology to conduct the test and that other countries had no right to interfere. Deng Xiaoping forcefully made the point during a discussion with the Cambodian ambassador to the PRC in February: "America and the Soviet Union have atomic weapons in hand to intimidate people. Of course, they are rich; we are poor. Have they decided that we are inferior because of our skin color? Because another person has nuclear weapons, does that mean that we shouldn't make efforts?"[94]

Beijing's persuasiveness on this issue ultimately derailed a major effort by Delhi to censure China at the Non-Aligned Conference. India put forward a resolution condemning China's plans to carry out a nuclear test, but African nations voted against it. Indian delegates openly complained about the receptiveness of some of the newer African delegations toward Beijing's militant positions.[95] For the PRC, the failure of this resolution represented a significant triumph. Moreover, throughout the Cairo conference, Beijing's allies such as Indonesia generally made a greater impression than its more moderate adversaries.[96]

Moving into 1965 and the final months of preparation for Bandung II, the PRC's position seemed to be strengthening, and the conference appeared likely to serve its purposes. Suddenly, however, Chinese plans for the event suffered setbacks that ultimately led to major humiliation. Ironically, these setbacks had little to do with either American or Chinese policies but resulted from developments in Algeria and elsewhere that could not be controlled by either country. For China, the first snafu—and still a relatively minor one—came in February 1965. The participating nations had originally agreed to convene in Algiers on 10 March 1965, but as February rolled around, the Algerian government found itself far behind in the construction of the conference facility. Ultimately, the standing committee had little choice but to postpone the date of the conference until 29 June.[97]

This delay seemed to create an opportunity for more problems to crop up. Although the conference itself was postponed, participants still gathered for a preparatory meeting in March. During the meeting, frictions erupted between China and some of the more moderate Afro-Asian nations over such issues as whether the conference should invite South Vietnam or, as Beijing insisted, the National Liberation Front.[98] Perhaps sensing the divisions that existed between Beijing and other Afro-Asian states on the issue, the Soviets suddenly stirred the pot by revisiting the question of their own possible attendance. When India had raised the possibility a year earlier, the Soviets had issued statements rebutting the Chinese argument that the USSR should not be considered an Asian nation. But such arguments failed to gain an enthusiastic response and Moscow halted its efforts to lobby for an invitation. In the spring of 1965, it revived this campaign with a vengeance. TASS, the official Soviet news agency, reported in April that former Indian defense minister Krishna Menon had "demanded" Moscow's participation on the basis of its territory in Asia and long-standing opposition to imperialism.[99] This was followed by official declarations from high-level Soviet officials that the USSR would attend the conference if invited and the dispatch of several deputy foreign ministers to critical Afro-Asian countries to lobby for the Soviet position.[100] Moscow's efforts achieved some notable successes. In addition to India, other nations including the United Arab Republic, Iraq, Laos, Senegal, and Nigeria announced their support for Soviet attendance.[101] As the time for the conference neared in June, it remained unclear whether the Soviets had enough support to carry the day.

Confronted with unanticipated difficulties, Beijing redoubled its efforts to ensure that the conference would not only succeed but also advance the CCP's agenda. Between March and June 1965, Chinese officials worked persistently to encourage attendance and reaffirm the anti-imperialist tenor of the conference. In the spring of 1965, Zhou Enlai and Chen Yi both embarked on foreign tours to soft-pedal their views. In late March and early April, Zhou visited Algeria, Egypt, Pakistan, and Burma, where he lobbied for Afro-Asian unity.[102] At roughly the same time Chen Yi visited Afghanistan, Pakistan, and Nepal, emphasizing the critical significance of Algiers. In a meeting with the king of Nepal, Chen explained that the conference was "of great importance" and could "have a great impact on the reduction of international tensions." He argued that newly independent Afro-Asian nations wanted to "oppose imperialism, oppose colonialism, and make imperialism subject to restraints" and that they "wanted the Afro-Asian conference to stand higher than the Non-Aligned Conference in solving these problems." Chen Yi also continued to make the case against Soviet participation. He explained that "if the Afro-Asian Conference invites a European power, then the meeting will have no meaning." It would signify that "Afro-Asian nations themselves are not politically mature and that they needed to ask the European Great Powers to come and take over."[103]

In the final weeks before the conference, a steady drumbeat of impassioned pleas for Afro-Asian nations to participate emanated from Beijing. In early June, the premier visited Pakistan and Tanzania and devoted a meeting with Tanzanian president Julius Nyerere to discussing the conference. Shortly after returning home, Zhou held a meeting with Mao in Hangzhou to discuss strategy. Then on 15 June, he met with Ho Chi Minh, a key Chinese ally, to explain preparations for the event.[104] In the meantime, Vice Premier Chen Yi remained occupied in a series of extensive talks with an Algerian envoy sent to China by President Ahmed Ben Bella specifically to resolve issues surrounding the conference.[105] Finally, Beijing sent Vice Foreign Minister Ji Pengfei to Guinea and Mali in late May to discuss the PRC agenda and encourage participation.[106]

As CCP officials struggled to assure that the Algiers conference would further their objective, Washington continued mobilizing its allies in an attempt to spoil the conference for Beijing. On 14 April 1965, the State Department issued guidance to all diplomatic posts in Asia and Africa assessing Chinese intentions and detailing the U.S. strategy. The State Department warned that Beijing's "first and foremost objective at [the] conference" would be the "consolidation of Afro-Asian states as [a] bloc, either real or apparent, against [the] U.S. on [the] subject of neo-colonialism, using [the] U.S. role in Vietnam as [the] focal point of their attack." It predicted that Beijing would "undoubtedly try [to] flood Afro-Asian world with this concept during [the] period leading up to [the] conference" so that the delegations attending would be "conditioned sufficiently to see [a] 'neo-colonialist U.S.' as [an] uncontested fact of life."[107] Last, the department circular suggested that diplomatic posts urge non-Communist Afro-Asian countries "not only to participate but [to] be prepared to send [the] strongest possible delegation equipped to combat communist-type aims and tactics." The objective of this policy would be to "encourage those countries friendly to [the] U.S. to organize themselves to prevent ostensibly anti-U.S. resolutions from passing" and to "ensure that both our purposes and the likely efforts of hostile elements are made widely known to those attending."[108] American officials hoped such efforts could moderate the tone of the conference and minimize identification with the PRC's radical agenda.

Ultimately, Washington's efforts proved less necessary than American officials could have predicted. By May, matters seemed to be turning against both Bandung II and Beijing. Construction of the physical facilities for the conference was far behind schedule, forcing Algiers to abandon plans for an elaborate meeting hall and throw its energy behind an effort to construct a much smaller "makeshift" facility outside of Algiers.[109] For Beijing, which was intent on assuring that the conference be a grand international event, such developments were ominous. Moreover, Chinese politicking had been unable to overcome the reservations harbored by some Afro-Asian leaders. Although China's radical allies continued to be supportive, American intelligence reports noted a lack of enthusiasm among moderate African leaders stemming in part from the squabbles over which nations could attend and the overall agenda. Togo, Upper Volta, and Ivory Coast, among others, decided not to attend. The CIA remained aware of China's plans to dominate the conference and use it to attack American imperialism but was less convinced that the conference would be the influential event Beijing hoped for. Indeed, the agency thought that, on the whole, Bandung II was shaping up to be "an unwieldy and confused gathering."[110]

Even Washington could not guess at just how much of a disorganized mess the Second Afro-Asian Conference would actually be. Events that occurred in Algeria in June 1965 dealt a fatal blow to the Chinese agenda and came as great relief to the anxious Americans. On 19 June, just ten days before the conference was scheduled to assemble, Algeria's defense minister, Houari Boumédienne, overthrew Ben Bella in a bloodless coup d'état. American intelligence initially reported that plans for the event had not changed and that Boumédienne was "clearly most anxious that the conference be held on schedule."[111] But over the next few days, demonstrations against the new regime spread over Algiers and other cities in Algeria. Against this background, the new

Algerian government announced that the preparatory meeting of African and Asian foreign ministers, scheduled for 24 June, would be delayed until 26 June, casting doubt on whether the conference would still be held.[112]

In the days after the coup, Chinese officials exerted themselves to make sure that the conference was not postponed or canceled. On 20 June, Vice Foreign Minister Zeng Yongquan called a meeting with the Algerian ambassador in Beijing and explained that it regarded the coup as Algeria's internal affair and would not interfere. At the same time, he announced that China "enthusiastically supports holding the Second Afro-Asian Conference on time."[113] When Premier Zhou Enlai first heard the news about the Algerian coup, he had already arrived in Cairo, where he had planned to hold a series of meetings with Nasser in preparation for the conference. Throughout his weeklong stay in Egypt, Zhou repeatedly announced China's strong support for starting on time and lobbied other Afro-Asian nations not to back away from their prior commitments to attend. Determined to shape the meaning of the conference even as other nations were coming to question whether it should be held, Zhou met face to face with Nasser and pushed for a radical agenda that would undermine Great Power hegemony. "The anti-imperialist and anticolonialist tone of the Second Afro-Asian Conference should not be lower than that of the Second Non-Aligned Conference," he told the Egyptian "otherwise it will be a soft, weak, meaningless conference."[114] Over the next several days Zhou lobbied as many Afro-Asian countries as he could from his makeshift base in Cairo. After his meeting with Nasser on 22 June, he sent a cable to the heads of state of all countries attending the Afro-Asian conference urging them not to entertain the possibility of canceling the conference.[115]

But a tumultuous series of events and maneuvers that occurred in Algeria on 25–26 June postponed the conference until 5 November. On the evening of 25 June, a bomb allegedly planted by saboteurs exploded in the Club des Pins, the venue for the critical Foreign Ministers Conference slated to occur the following day. The explosion caused new apprehensions among the delegations in attendance and prompted some that had been uncertain about whether to go ahead with the conference to come down more firmly on the side of postponement. On Saturday, roughly half of the forty-delegations scheduled to attend the Foreign Ministers Conference had been seated when an Algerian government spokesman suddenly announced that their session was canceled and that the Standing Committee of Ambassadors would meet later that day at a different location. This abrupt change likely reflected the backstage maneuverings of Egypt along with several of the other moderate Afro-Asian states that wanted the conference to be postponed. The Standing Committee of Ambassadors voted to delay the conference before the foreign ministers could reconvene.[116]

By then, the conference was shaping up to be a major embarrassment for the PRC and its allies. Worried about conditions in Algiers and unenthused about the conference's radical agenda, numerous African nations slated to attend had simply failed to show up.[117] The conference hall, which Ben Bella had made the showpiece of Algeria's extensive preparations for the event, had still not been completed and delegates who arrived at the hall for the foreign ministers' conference were forced to walk through puddles of water as they were seated. Some of the Afro-Asian diplomats who journeyed to Algiers called the whole event "undignified" and a "circus."[118] What Chinese leaders hoped would be the crowning achievement of their efforts to forge a new united front had turned into an unmitigated disaster.

Both American officials and moderate Afro-Asian leaders reveled in the debacle, which they saw as a major setback for Beijing. The day after the conference's cancellation, the *New York Times* reported one "conservative Arab delegate" stating that the "Chinese have come off badly" and claimed that at a luncheon for prime ministers, downcast PRC diplomats had exchanged "only the briefest and most formal courtesies with the other delegates." The newspaper also cited "conference sources" who believed that "the Chinese, by their intransigence on opening the conference . . . and their efforts to tar those who opposed them with the 'imperialist' label offended several delegations."[119] In the end, rather than serving as a platform for a unified front, the bungled effort to convene a conference in Algiers only underscored disagreements between radical and moderate Afro-Asian countries and alienated the PRC from the very nations that it aspired to lead. Beijing's stubborn insistence on carrying through with the conference had made it look desperate rather than dignified.

American officials echoed this analysis, cheering the delay and eventual cancellation of Bandung II. After the conference was postponed for a final time in October, Robert Komer wrote a memorandum for the president that was almost exultant in its analysis of the way things had worked out. He explained that the demise of the Second Afro-Asian Conference was "the best possible outcome from our point of view. Not only did it postpone a confab made to order for anti-U.S. voices, but the dickering over postponement got a lot of the moderates thoroughly irritated at the Chicoms." For the foreseeable future, Komer believed, the best tack for the United States to take was to continue to quietly "commiserate with the moderate Afro-Asians on how the Chicoms wrecked their conference."[120] American officials like Komer recognized the failed conference as a golden opportunity to strengthen what they deemed the moderate Afro-Asian voices and isolate Beijing and its allies.

For its part, Beijing initially refused to concede defeat. The conference was rescheduled for 5 November, and Chinese diplomats worked with growing desperation to resuscitate it. The PRC invited the Algerian foreign minister to visit Beijing and dispatched Vice Premier Chen Yi on another diplomatic tour of several Asian and African countries.[121] But Beijing eventually scuttled the entire undertaking when it became apparent that many Afro-Asian nations would not support its positions. On 29 September, Chen Yi convened a press conference in which he stated that Beijing's attendance at the conference would be contingent on excluding both the Soviet Union and UN secretary general U Thant.[122] On 26 October, China announced that it would no longer be involved with the conference when a Preparatory Committee meeting in Algiers officially rejected its demands.[123] By that time, the other Afro-Asian states had already grown significantly less inclined to line up behind Beijing. Chinese prestige in the region was waning not only due to the failure of Bandung II but also due to developments in Pakistan and Indonesia.

The Indo-Pakistan War

In September 1965 the long-standing tensions in Kashmir burst into war between India and Pakistan and created a prestige-engaging showdown for China and the United States. Beijing and Washington were caught up in the maelstrom that swept the South Asian subcontinent and threatened to create a global crisis. Sovereignty of Kashmir had been disputed between India and Pakistan since the two nations gained their independence in 1947. A new conflict began in August 1965, when the government of Ayub Khan in Karachi infiltrated irregular Pakistani forces into parts of Kashmir occupied by India. Delhi retaliated in early September by sending its divisions across the international border near Lahore, a major urban center in Pakistan.[124] As the conflict escalated, the competing objectives of Beijing and Washington in South Asia raised the possibility that a much larger conflagration would draw in the major powers.

When Indian forces moved across the international boundary line in the Punjab on 6 September, high-level American officials immediately worried that China would interfere. Secretary of State Dean Rusk cabled the American ambassador in India with instructions to seek an appointment at the highest possible level to convey the views of the U.S. government. The secretary explained, "The danger of involvement (politically or militarily) of Communist Chinese" was "of great concern." Washington wanted to see the two sides reach a swift settlement. Rusk worried that if fighting continued, India would be drawn more deeply into the "cross currents of cold war and Communist bloc conflicts." The Chinese Communists would be "certain winners," whereas it was "difficult to see how either India or Pakistan could benefit regardless of [the] outcome." The State Department planned to call on both combatants to accept the UN Security Council's call for an immediate cease-fire.[125]

The PRC began to up the ante on 7 September. Zhou Enlai called a meeting with the Pakistani ambassador in Beijing, and the Chinese government later in the day issued a statement condemning India and warning Delhi that it "must bear all the consequences of its criminal and extended aggression."[126] China's vaguely threatening announcement caused confusion and anxiety in Washington. Two days after Beijing issued its statement, an exasperated President Johnson called a meeting with B. K. Nehru, the Indian ambassador to the United States, and complained that the question of China's potential involvement was "giving us gray hairs right now." [127] The problem for American officials was that they couldn't know how far Beijing would be willing to escalate the conflict. Did it already have an agreement to come to Pakistan's assistance? Was it willing to risk turning this local conflict into a major military confrontation? Or was it making a gambit to expand its influence in Karachi at U.S. expense? As Washington turned to this somewhat distant but potentially disastrous situation, Chinese intentions proved frustratingly difficult to read. The president remained preoccupied with assuring that Pakistan did not align itself more deeply with China even as he hoped that American diplomacy carried out through UN auspices could end the conflict before Beijing could turn it into something more dangerous. He told Ambassador Nehru that the "cardinal point" was to "keep Pakistan from going the Chinese route."[128]

The same day, Secretary of State Rusk warned the president that Chinese involvement in Kashmir would have broader ramifications for the geostrategic position of the Free World in Asia. The secretary feared that "the whole Western power position in Asia may shortly be at stake." The conflict could lead to "collapse and communal chaos" that "would call into question the future of the subcontinent itself" and "negate our effort to build there a viable counterweight to Communist China." The secretary then reeled off a list of negative consequences that might follow from such a collapse. First, "latent Japanese neutralist tendencies could bloom disturbingly in the wake of a major humiliation of India and of what would be seen as a Chinese Communist victory over the U.S." Moreover, Chinese involvement would "make South Asia and Vietnam actually two parts of the same basic problem: that of containing [Beijing's] outward thrust." Finally, if the PRC got involved and the conflict was allowed to simply run its course, then Pakistan would "wind up deeply committed to China."[129] From Rusk's perspective, Washington and Beijing had both staked their credibility on the outcome of the conflict and a symbolic triumph for the PRC could mean the expansion of Chinese political influence throughout Asia.

On 16 September, after several days of inconclusive fighting between Indian and Pakistani forces, China issued an ultimatum that put the United States and India squarely on the defensive. In essence, Beijing threatened to divert Indian forces by stirring up trouble along the Sino-Indian border. The PRC demanded that India dismantle "military structures of aggression" that it had built along the India-Tibet border within three days or face "grave consequences."[130] China's bellicose rhetoric led to urgent appeals to the Johnson administration by the Indian government. On 17 September, the Indian ambassador requested that the United States make a formal statement warning that Washington would come to Delhi's assistance if the PRC attacked.[131] The request put the Johnson administration in an awkward position. With thousands of American combat forces deployed in Vietnam, Washington was loath to risk getting dragged into another Asian war. At the same time, Americans realized that a successful Chinese intervention would not only weaken India but also enhance Beijing's credibility on the Asian mainland at Washington's expense.

The administration's fears of rising Chinese influence proved unfounded, however. The situation in South Asia never turned into the catastrophe that U.S. officials had dreaded. Over the next few days, Washington slowly realized that Beijing had overplayed its hand. The Chinese would soon suffer another significant setback. Americans had been worried that Pakistan had a prearranged understanding that the PRC would come to its assistance if the war went poorly. It soon became clear, however, that the Pakistanis—despite their occasional resort to anti-imperialist rhetoric—were no more eager to see China escalate its involvement than the Indians or the Americans. On 18 September, the Pakistani minister of finance Mohammed Shoaib called U.S. ambassador McConaughy for a meeting and privately conveyed a message from President Ayub Khan. Shoaib claimed that the president wanted to "reject Chinese overtures and come down on [the] U.S. side" but that American policy seemed "designed to push" him "toward the Chinese." He asked for only some gesture from the United States that could be a "basis for his decision."[132] Ayub Khan really hoped for an American statement blaming India for the war. Washington was unwilling to abandon its neutral posture, but Ayub's plea also implied that the danger of a new Sino-Pakistani alliance had been exaggerated.

With a stronger sense of the limitations of Sino-Pakistani friendship, the Johnson administration pressured the Pakistan government to agree to a cease-fire and avoid actions that could lead to greater Chinese intervention. On 18 September, the State Department cabled the U.S. embassy in Pakistan that it should communicate several critical points. It was to warn high-ranking Pakistani officials that if Ayub Khan "should encourage, or even—by failing to agree to a cease-fire—create the situation that produces Chicom intervention, he will have alienated himself from the West." Moreover, the State Department subtly encouraged the Pakistani government to resolve the crisis in a way that would weaken Beijing's credibility. It suggested that

Ayub Khan "take the position that the dangers of escalation involved in these moves make it imperative that the Indo-Pak conflict be stopped."[133] Pakistan could then end the crisis while saving face.

Ambassador McConaughy made these points clear when he met with the Pakistani president two days later. He warned Ayub Khan firmly about Pakistan's dalliance with the PRC and again encouraged it to seek a resolution to the conflict. The ambassador said that the "ChiComs have it within their power to put Paks in [an] impossible situation unless [the] GOP [Government of Pakistan] moves before [the] expiration of [the] Chicom ultimatum to reject [a] threatened Chinese intervention and implement [an] unconditional cease-fire with India." If the Pakistanis did not act precisely as the ambassador recommended, then they would be put in a "position of seemingly abetting or at least passively benefiting from ChiCom aggression against India." Such a position, McConaughy warned, would be virtually impossible to justify to the American government and people.[134] The purpose of McConaughy's efforts was to end the crisis in a way that drove a wedge between Beijing and Karachi.

These pressure tactics ultimately served their purpose. After a period of wavering, the Pakistani government agreed to the UN cease-fire resolution on 22 September.[135] The cease-fire was hardly a boon for relations between the United States and Pakistan, however. Both the government and general population of Pakistan were angered by what they perceived as an American betrayal. Ayub Khan did little to quell the anti-American sentiment fueled by this perception. Bob Komer noted the Pakistanis were "allowing the almost wholly government-controlled media to feed the growing anti-U.S. and pro-Chicom sentiment" and that American prestige in the country had sunk to an "all time low."[136] And of course, the outcome of the war did little to break up Pakistan's growing strategic alignment with China against India.

But even if the war and the cease-fire had contributed to Pakistan's disenchantment with Washington, Americans judged that they had been damaging for the PRC in many ways as well. First, during the conflict, the Chinese had backed away from their ultimatum to India, possibly because of Pakistani doubts about Beijing's capabilities and credibility. On 19 September, the PRC had announced its decision to extend the ultimatum for three days and on 24 September, nullified it completely, claiming that India had met its key demands. American intelligence speculated that the Ayub Khan government had urgently asked Beijing on 17 September not to intervene because it doubted that a Chinese diversion would be enough to "salvage the situation." Regardless of the motive behind this sudden shift in China's position, the CIA believed that retreating had been a "humiliating process" for the CCP. Moreover, it seemed likely to American analysts that the brief war had also created new strains in the relationship between China and Pakistan. Although the CIA predicted that "outwardly Sino-Pakistani relations are likely to remain as warm as ever," it also conjectured that the war had "probably created friction and raised serious doubts on both sides."[137]

The Indo-Pakistani War of 1965 was no triumph for the United States, but it was a disaster for Beijing and its international agenda. China had lost prestige through issuing an ineffectual ultimatum while watching its close ally accept a UN-sponsored solution. The zealous enthusiasm for China that had been readily apparent in official Pakistani rhetoric during the previous year now seemed to be waning. And the conflict itself, by underscoring political and ideological divisions in Asia, further damaged the idea of a united Afro-Asian front that the PRC had been so steadfastly promoting. Perhaps the only positive note for the PRC was that it had not altogether lost a critical ally. The same could not be said after power changed hands in Indonesia a little more than one week later.

The Indonesia Coup and Sino-American Competition

On 1 October 1965, a group that came to be known as the September 30th Movement kidnapped and executed six generals from the Indonesian army. The movement claimed that its actions had blocked a planned coup by a CIA-backed "council of generals" that it alleged was to take place a few days later. Within a week, however, Major General Suharto, the commander of the army's Strategic Reserve Command, assumed control over the entire army and destroyed the forces behind the September 30th Movement. Suharto charged that the movement was in fact a coup attempt that had been under the direction of the Indonesian Communist Party, the PKI. With treason as his justification and tacitly backed by the United States, Suharto mounted a massive purge of the PKI over the next five months. Under Suharto's command, the army slaughtered hundreds of thousands of PKI members and in March 1966 forced Sukarno to surrender his office.[138]

Competition with China in the Third World was a critical factor in shaping American policy toward Indonesia during this crisis. Washington viewed the rise of Suharto and the destruction of the PKI as an opportunity not only to sever Jakarta's deepening ties with Beijing but also to weaken Chinese claims to leadership in the postcolonial world. A radicalizing Indonesia was a lynchpin of CCP strategy in Asia. By changing the political trajectory of the country, Washington hoped to strike another blow against the crumbling edifice of Afro-Asian solidarity that the Chinese were desperately seeking to hold together.

American efforts to moderate Indonesian politics and create a rift between Beijing and Djakarta had begun long before Suharto seized power. Some of these were later described in a highly sensitive memorandum about covert action in Indonesia submitted to the 303 Committee, a special group responsible for overseeing all covert operations carried out by government agencies. Key parts of the document remain classified, making it difficult to ascertain all of the agencies and individuals that were involved. The document does disclose that during the summer of 1964, the State Department began a coordinated effort with another agency, whose name is redacted, to develop "an operational program of political action in Indonesia." In February 1965, the program was submitted to the 303 Committee for formal approval. The program's objective was to "reduce the influence on Indonesian foreign and domestic policies of the PKI and the Government of Red China and to encourage and support non-Communist elements in Indonesia." To achieve these objectives, it sought to "emphasize traditional Indonesian distrust of Mainland China and to portray the PKI as an instrument of Red Chinese imperialism." Activities envisaged by the program included providing covert assistance to individuals and organizations that opposed the PKI, developing new propaganda themes, and cultivating political leaders "for the purpose of ensuring an orderly non-Communist succession upon Sukarno's death or removal from office." The 303 Committee approved this program of action on 4 March 1965.[139]

The program's objectives and policies, for the most part, needed to be achieved and implemented over the long term. It is therefore doubtful that the United States had made much headway in carrying them out by the fall of 1965. By most accounts, American officials were genuinely surprised, albeit pleasantly so, by Suharto's coup.[140] Nevertheless, as events unfolded, American officials worked quietly to assure that Sino-Indonesian relations suffered. They sought in particular to link the September 30th Movement to the PRC by spreading stories that caches of weapons stamped with the hammer and sickle had been discovered. Marshall Green, the recently appointed American ambassador to Indonesia, wrote enthusiastically to the State Department, "We have bonanza chance to nail chicoms on disastrous events in Indonesia." The ambassador called for the "continuation [of] covert propaganda" as a "means of spreading idea of chicom complicity."[141] As the Indonesian army sought to use the September 30th Movement against the PKI, Washington subtly sought to piggyback on these efforts to discredit the Chinese with the Indonesian people.

Secretary of State Rusk agreed that the conflict between the army and the PKI provided a chance to enhance American prestige in Indonesia at China's expense. Rusk foresaw that "Chinese Communist open hostility toward Indonesian Army" was "bound to increase as [the] Army moves against [the] PKI." If Moscow and Beijing criticized Suharto as he moved against the party, then the army would be "forced to examine its attitude toward China and Russia." In this context, Indonesia's new leaders were likely to approach the "Japanese, other powers, and, no doubt, us." The situation, Rusk believed, would "offer unprecedented opportunities for us to begin to influence people and events as the military begin to understand [the] problems and dilemmas in which they find themselves." The United States should "get across that Indonesia and [the] Army have real friends who are ready to help."[142] Over the next few months, Washington did indeed offer the Indonesian army its friendship, overlooking its campaigns of mass violence against suspected PKI members and providing it with invaluable supplies and equipment.[143] As Suharto consolidated his control over national politics, Washington's influence in Indonesia grew swiftly and that of the PRC declined precipitously.

By the spring of 1966, American intelligence was exultant about the defeat that China had suffered in Indonesia. A CIA report on "[Beijing's] Setbacks in Indonesia" reported that an "exodus of Chinese Communist diplomats and technicians" was under way, the "pro-Chinese policies of Sukarno" were "being discontinued," and "[Beijing's] staunch supporter, Foreign Minister Subandrio," had been arrested. The CIA saw the demise of the Sino-Indonesian partnership as significant not only for what it meant in the specific context of Indonesia but also for what it portended for China's ambitions in the Third World. It noted that without the anti-Western Sukarno, Beijing had lost the most important proponent of its Afro-Asian agenda. Indonesia could "no longer front for the Chinese in the international arena or run interference at international meetings." The report also remarked that because of the demise of Sukarno's government, Indonesia's plan to set up a Conference of New Emerging Forces (CONEFO) that could serve as an alternative to the UN "never got off the ground and the close working relationship in other front groups and international forums where the Chinese and Indonesians were associated has come to an end. This has been a serious loss to China."[144] With the overthrow of Sukarno and the PKI, Beijing's aspiration to establish an international order in which radical Afro-Asian states rather than the Great Powers were the most significant force now seemed virtually impossible to fulfill, even to the PRC.

———

With the collapse of the Second Afro-Asian Conference and the downfall of Sukarno's government, Beijing's diplomatic offensive in the Third World was swiftly losing steam. Although China had scored significant victories in this campaign, it had never been able to establish a firmly united front of Afro-Asian countries or mount an effective challenge to the Great Power–dominated international order. By 1966, disunity in the Third World was far more in evidence than solidarity—especially the radical ideal of solidarity espoused by the PRC. Mao would soon launch the Great Proletarian Cultural Revolution, which would only exacerbate the PRC's growing isolation. Washington remained concerned with some dimensions of Chinese influence in the Third World, but it also perceived that the PRC was, in general losing its luster. In June 1966, William Jorden, a longtime journalist and diplomat who assisted the Johnson administration in shaping its Asia policy, sent a memo to Walt Rostow cheerily proclaiming that "Communist China, suffering reverses around the world (especially in Indonesia) and up against U.S. determination in Vietnam[,] is no longer regarded as 'the wave of the future.'"[145] American officials such as Jorden and Rostow were by then much less concerned that China would make sweeping gains with its diplomatic offensive than they had been three years before.

Though Americans exulted in Chinese failures, U.S. diplomacy had not been the most important factor in producing this outcome. Part of the reason for the collapse of Beijing's diplomatic offensive was simply misfortune. Shifting politics in Asia and Africa proved too complex and unpredictable for the PRC to forge the enduring alliances it needed to genuinely challenge American and Soviet influence. But Chinese leaders also had themselves to blame for the sudden collapse of their position in the Third World. Initially, Chinese diplomats had handled rising tensions in Southeast Asia and the ongoing decolonization of the African continent with care and subtlety that enabled the PRC to gain prestige. But in their stubborn insistence on having their way during the Second Afro-Asian Conference and their brinkmanship in the Indo-Pakistan War, they showed a degree of uncompromising radicalism that alienated their purported Afro-Asian brethren. Diplomacy was not the only realm in which Beijing made such damaging miscalculations, however. The radicalization of Chinese foreign policy during the early 1960s contributed not only to the development of a more radical international posture but also to a more vigorous effort to support and influence revolutionaries in places ranging from Southeast Asia to Africa. Beijing's support for wars of national liberation would bring about equally disastrous results, although in this instance the United States would share fully in reaping the whirlwind.

Chapter 8

Insurgency and Counterinsurgency, 1961–1968

Briefly after President John F. Kennedy assumed office in 1961, *Life* magazine published an article on the voracious reading habits of the new commander in chief. According to the article, JFK had requested, among other things, "two books written by Chinese Communist leader [Mao Zedong] and a photostatted translation of Cuban 'Che' Guevara's 1960 book on guerrilla warfare."[1] Not long after, according to many popular accounts of the Kennedy administration, the new president began asking his top civilian and military advisers to adopt the same reading list.[2] Why was the new president so eager to immerse himself in the philosophies of America's self-proclaimed adversaries? For Kennedy and his closest advisers, this preoccupation with the era's most famous revolutionaries was more than the simple need to know their enemies. It reflected their sense of the changing nature of the challenge they faced in the Third World. When Kennedy assumed office in 1961, insurgencies and guerrilla wars threatened to topple friendly regimes through much of the Global South.

Mao Zedong soon learned that the young American president was studying his writings but was neither flattered nor impressed. In September 1962, when Mao met with representatives of the National Liberation Front (NLF), an insurgent movement that aimed to topple U.S.-backed President Ngo Dinh Diem in South Vietnam, one of the Vietnamese informed him, "It is not only we who study the chairman's works but also our enemies." Mao did not see this as great cause for concern. "They want to destroy you; including Kennedy, they are all studying out things. But they will not learn; they are imperialists," the chairman predicted.[3] Mao believed that the United States and its allies were powerless to stop the rising tide of revolution in the Third World. The chairman saw the success of insurgencies in Afro-Asian countries as victories not only for the people who waged them but also for China. Revolutionaries in South Vietnam, Laos, the Congo, and elsewhere often cited Mao's writings and the Chinese Revolution as their inspiration. Their triumphs therefore seemed, at least to Beijing, to attest to the validity of Maoist doctrines, establish the PRC as a model for oppressed peoples waging wars of national liberation, and cement China's status as the world's leading revolutionary force. The size and scope of these struggles varied greatly, as did the quantity and quality of Chinese assistance. Nevertheless, Beijing consistently sought to help revolutionaries emulate the Chinese experience and offered weapons and guidance to those who tried to do so.

Washington's view of what was at stake in these guerrilla wars was not altogether different from Beijing's. Americans, too, believed that victories for insurgents, especially those the PRC supported, could enhance China's prestige. The key difference, of course, was that the PRC welcomed such an outcome, whereas the United States dreaded it. China's rising influence in the Third World was not the only reason for America's embrace of counterinsurgency during the Kennedy-Johnson era, but it was often a major factor and, in some instances, a dominant consideration.[4] Much as Washington used diplomatic pressure to undermine China's efforts to promote Afro-Asian political unity, it used military training programs and, at times, its own forces to counter Chinese support for revolutionaries that aimed to overthrow allied governments.

Sino-American competition had an unquestionable impact on many guerrilla struggles, though in most cases it did not determine their outcome. Often Chinese and American involvement made these struggles more violent and more protracted than they would have been without outside meddling. In the end, however, neither Chinese hopes nor American fears were realized. Some guerrilla movements failed either because they lacked sufficient popular appeal or because they suffered military defeats. And even when insurgencies triumphed, it was not necessarily understood as a victory for either Maoism or the PRC. The leaders of most guerrilla movements were, in the end, fierce nationalists with their own agendas. They did not wish to be perceived as protégés of Communist China any more than Beijing wished to be perceived as an adjunct of Soviet power. Although revolutionaries eagerly praised Mao's teachings and accepted Chinese aid, they ultimately disappointed their would-be mentors.

Chinese and American Views of Insurgencies

Support for other revolutions—especially in Asia and Africa—had been a part of the CCP's foreign policy since the earliest days of the party, but during the early 1960s China's willingness to commit itself both rhetorically and materially to this objective increased markedly. In the 1950s, the CCP had often subordinated promoting revolution abroad to the tasks of consolidating its rule at home and stabilizing its relationships with neighboring countries. As Chinese foreign policy transitioned during the early 1960s, however, Mao and his colleagues became more proactive in identifying revolutionary forces that might benefit from Chinese guidance.

As described in Chapter 6, the Sino-Soviet split spurred the PRC toward more enthusiastic support for revolutionaries in Asia and Africa. Chinese officials were optimistic that support for insurgencies would embarrass the Soviet revisionists who, in their efforts to seek peaceful coexistence with the United States, had become more reluctant to support such struggles. Zhou Enlai explained the connections among revolution in the Third World, American imperialism, and Soviet revisionism during a conversation with the Albanian leader Enver Hoxha in March 1965. Like the PRC, Albania had split with the Soviet Union, so its leaders tended to be sympathetic.[5] Zhou launched into a lengthy criticism of Soviet policy: "A characteristic of modern revisionists . . . is that they are afraid of American imperialism and a world war. They are afraid that some local war might escalate, with American interference, into a large scale world war. They do not want the peoples of the world to wage an armed war for their national independence. They are afraid of the peoples of the world revolution. Hence they are trying to discourage and stop such revolutions." [6] The premier also accused the "Soviet revisionists" of "trying to bring the socialist countries, the sister parties, and the national liberation struggles under their control and use them to make compromises with the USA."[7] While Moscow hedged in offering its full support to wars of national liberation, China could gain credibility and trust among revolutionaries by making known its unwavering commitment to their cause.

China's growing enthusiasm for national liberation struggles was also inspired by the triumph of revolutionaries in Cuba and Algeria. Its leaders formed strong ties with the leaders of both struggles and offered them glowing praise. Beijing had made known its support for Fidel Castro's government in Cuba very early and sought to build on this during the early 1960s. The *People's Daily* published an editorial praising the victory of Castro's forces shortly after Fulgencio Batista fled Havana in January 1959. China and Cuba established normal diplomatic relations in September 1960, making Castro's government the first in Latin America to recognize the PRC. Shortly after normalization, Che Guevara led an economic delegation to the PRC and was awarded an interest-free five-year loan for sixty million dollars.[8] On the second anniversary of Castro's triumph in January 1961, Mao Zedong visited the Cuban embassy to offer his congratulations and a strong statement of support for Cuba's "just struggle." The chairman issued an even more ardent statement in support of Cuba after Kennedy's failed Bay of Pigs Invasion in April 1961. Successive protests and demonstrations against the United States occurred throughout the PRC.[9]

Chinese leaders lauded the victory of the National Liberation Front (FLN) in Algeria with similar publicity and enthusiasm. Throughout the FLN's eight-year struggle against French colonialism, Beijing had long been one of its strongest supporters. In September 1958, China had extended immediate diplomatic recognition to the Provisional Algerian Government set up by the

FLN in Cairo. In the months that followed, Beijing supplied weapons to the Algerian rebels through third countries and trained some of the FLN's guerrilla forces.[10] When Paris agreed to talks with the front's leadership, Chinese leaders treated it as a victory not only for Algerians but also for the PRC and the cause of world revolution. Zhou Enlai called the head of the FLN delegation in the PRC for a meeting on 20 February 1962, two days after a lengthy negotiating session in Evian, France, had yielded an agreement for a ceasefire and eventual Algerian independence.[11] After dispensing some advice on how to conduct negotiations, the premier told the Algerian, "The victory of the Algerian people is also the victory of the Chinese people and the victory of all Afro-Asian peoples." He hoped that the FLN would achieve "an even greater victory" through the negotiations and "realize Algeria's complete independence."[12]

With revolutionaries triumphant in Cuba and Algeria, Chinese leaders scouted the globe for other places where wars of national liberation seemed likely. They became increasingly interested in Africa as a new frontier for revolution. "Africa is on the front line of the struggle," Mao told a delegation of African guests during an April 1961 meeting. The chairman emphasized that "it was possible for revolutions to win" and cited the Chinese Revolution, which had waged "a twenty-two-year armed struggle against imperialism and its running dogs" as an example. Mao explained that the lessons of the Chinese Revolution are "not only our own but could also provide an international experience study reference for friends who are in the midst of struggles against the imperialists and their running dogs."[13] Mao offered similar encouragement to a small party of African visitors from Lesotho, Comoros, and Rhodesia two years later. "All of Africa is now in the midst of a wave of anti-imperialism and anticolonialism," the chairman contended. He introduced China's revolutionary struggle and cited it as evidence that "a people's revolution could win." Mao called for Afro-Asian peoples to unite and promised support for their liberation movements. "People who have already won their independence should help those who are now waging wars of liberation; this is our international obligation," he explained.[14]

The CCP also sought to introduce its revolutionary experiences to other Afro-Asian countries by disseminating Mao's military writings. By January 1962, *The Selected Military Works of Mao Zedong* had been translated into English, French, Spanish, and Russian, with plans in place to distribute copies throughout Asia, Africa, and Latin America.[15] The party had devoted a great degree of thought and attention to this task and modified some of Mao's seminal texts slightly to make sure they could inspire revolutionaries in all of these regions. Points that might discourage potential insurgents were edited or deleted. For instance, Mao's 1938 essay "The Problem of Strategy in Guerrilla War against Japan" was modified to make it more applicable to liberation struggles in small countries. The essay had argued that one of the conditions necessary for establishing a guerrilla base was a large territory and that in its absence the odds for waging guerrilla war were not as good. But the CCP wanted to distribute Mao's writings in small and large countries alike, including some in which guerrilla wars were already in progress. Mao's secretary, Tian Jiaying, therefore suggested an addendum explaining that "the conditions under which the people of each country wage revolutionary war are not completely the same as those under which our country fought its war of resistance against Japan." Therefore, "the size of a country was not the decisive factor in determining whether a guerrilla war would succeed." Mao instructed Tian to proceed with the revisions.[16] The party's eagerness to ensure that the chairman's ideas could be applied in different contexts reflected its broader concern with gaining a leadership position among the rising generation of revolutionaries.

Three years later, Defense Minister and Vice Premier Lin Biao's widely read essay "Long Live the Victory of the People's War" encouraged insurgents in Afro-Asian countries to emulate the Chinese struggle even more explicitly. Lin argued that the revolutionary experiences of the CCP could defeat American imperialism and ultimately transform the world. The United States, he contended, was "repeating on a world-wide scale the actions of the Japanese imperialists in China and other parts of Asia." It was therefore an "urgent necessity for the people in many countries to master and use people's war as a weapon against U.S. imperialism and its lackeys." Lin believed that the specific doctrines of "people's war" that had been crafted by Chairman Mao were well suited to revolutionaries in the colonial world in their struggles against imperialism. He explained, for instance, that Mao's "theory of the establishment of rural bases and the encirclement of the cities from the countryside" was of "universal practical importance for the present revolutionary struggles of the oppressed nations and peoples and particularly . . . in Asia, Africa and Latin America."[17]

For Washington, articles like Lin Biao's raised the nightmarish prospect of Maoist-inspired guerrilla wars spreading throughout the Afro-Asian world. Such protracted, low-intensity conflicts posed a critical challenge for American policy. Soon after Kennedy took office, his deputy national security adviser Walt Rostow prepared a paper on counterinsurgency explaining that "the primary problem of American foreign policy for well over a decade" had "centered on the revolutionary process going forward in the underdeveloped areas."[18] Kennedy wasted little time in launching a systematic effort to grapple with the problem. The president and his military representative General Maxwell D. Taylor created a cabinet-level counterinsurgency committee to monitor revolutionary movements in the Third World. The administration also called for a broad effort to educate military personnel and Foreign Service officers about the problem.[19]

Kennedy's top advisers almost immediately identified Beijing as a prime instigator of guerrilla conflicts and feared that the PRC would gain in prestige if the insurgencies prevailed. In 1962, when the White House called on the NSC to draw up a comprehensive policy for dealing with the problem of insurgency, an interdepartmental committee drafted a thirty-page document entitled Overseas Internal Defense Policy of the United States (OIDP).[20] The OIDP analyzed the threat posed by "communist inspired, supported or directed insurgency." It examined the major causes of insurgencies abroad and assigned roles to specific agencies in controlling or containing them.[21] The OIDP viewed Maoism as a major driving force behind guerrilla movements and warned about the likelihood of continuing Chinese support for revolutions. The committee explained, "In one generation Chinese communists conquered the world's most populous state from within." The lessons of the CCP's "long and complex struggle" had then been "applied by various political movements in different parts of the world." According to the report, "Chinese communist techniques" had already been used by successful revolutionaries in Indochina, Cuba, and Algeria.[22] The OIDP predicted that both Moscow and Beijing would seek to instigate and support "subversive insurgencies" but warned that the PRC would be the more militant of the two Communist giants. While the Soviets still maintained that in some instances revolutionaries could take power "without resorting to armed violence," Chinese Communists believed that "the control and/or support of the rural population is an indispensable step toward the seizure of power," which was not possible "by peaceful means."[23]

The committee made wide-ranging recommendations to thwart insurgencies. It advocated subtle but extensive efforts to support friendly governments and undermine the appeal of radicalism through social and economic programs. Every American country team stationed in Asia, Africa, and Latin America would have to "involve itself constructively and acceptably in the local situation." This meant helping the local government to "see the relations of insurgency to socioeconomic development, and the blend of political and military measures required for an adequate internal defense." Country teams would also provide resources and devise techniques tailored to the local context to strengthen internal defense, including land reform, civic action, community development programs, and social projects.[24]

By the time Johnson took office, the OIDP's predictions about China seemed to be coming to fruition. In December 1964, the CIA prepared a more focused study of the subject for LBJ's national security adviser McGeorge

Bundy. The report, entitled "[Beijing's] Views on Revolutionary War," warned again of the PRC's ambitions to promote revolution and pointed to China's desire to gain prestige as its key motive. China's inability to liberate Taiwan had "compelled the Chinese Communist leaders to shift their strategy from confrontations or near-confrontations with the U.S. in the strait to a more indirect strategy requiring pressures on U.S. positions elsewhere in the world." The report argued that promoting "small wars ('armed struggle') in underdeveloped areas" was "the most distinctive element" of this new strategy. But liberating Taiwan and tying down the United States was not the PRC's only goal. The Chinese stressed these wars "in order to increase Mao's already considerable prestige as the guerrilla leader and Communist who creatively developed Leninist doctrine on revolutionary war."[25]

Some American analysts even identified Chinese support for insurgencies as the most critical threat to American interests in the Third World. A study of China prepared by a special joint state-defense department study group in 1966 contended that, "the most likely peril to the peace of nations in Asia, Africa and Latin America during the next decade is the whole range of militant dissidence fomented, encouraged or supplied by Communist China." Party leaders would not "simply relax and let victory come to them," the study warned, but would "get out and work to make sure" that revolutions occurred. It would use a combination of "subversion" and support for different nations, parties, and factions to achieve its objective. The study added that Lin Biao's doctrine of "people's war" was "essentially destructive rather than constructive" and had a reasonable likelihood of producing "unrest, chaos, dissidence or subversive insurgency" in China's neighboring countries.[26]

The team that prepared the study called for a multifaceted American response to CCP-supported insurgencies. Echoing the ground rules for counterinsurgency that had been laid out in the OICD, it explained, "The response of the free world to Chinese initiatives that would further their subversive objectives" would have to include nation-building measures to improve the internal and external defense capacities of threatened countries. The United States needed to "assist in developing out of unpromising elements viable nations capable of defense against a wide spectrum of threats, in an area close to China and in which China has ambitions antithetic to those of the U.S."[27] Concerns about Chinese-supported insurgencies became an important factor behind some of Washington's most critical policy choices. Throughout the 1960s, the Kennedy and Johnson administrations supported expansive nation-building programs and made extensive military commitments to counter the perceived Chinese threat. Nowhere was this more evident than in Vietnam.

Vietnam

Beijing and Washington had starkly different visions for the future of Southeast Asia. One envisioned a region swept by a wave of revolution and aligned with a radical Afro-Asian agenda. The other envisioned Southeast Asia as a bulwark against communism and a source of markets and raw materials for other Free World countries. Despite the wide gulf that separated their visions, the two could agree on one thing: South Vietnam would be a critical test case. Both sides understood what was at stake. Secretary of Defense Robert McNamara thought that "South Vietnam is both a test of U.S. firmness and specifically a test of U.S. capacity to deal with 'wars of national liberation.'"[28] Much as Americans believed that the Chinese were testing U.S. resolve, the Chinese believed that Washington was testing their dedication to fomenting revolution. "The United States has made South Vietnam a testing ground for the suppression of people's wars," Lin Biao wrote in "Long Live the Victory of the People's War."[29] It was inevitable that both sides would become deeply invested in the outcome of the war over South Vietnam's future.

The story of how the NLF emerged in South Vietnam and how Washington became committed to its defeat is well known. It began with the 1954 Geneva Agreements, which divided Vietnam at the seventeenth parallel but stipulated that general elections for the entire country would be held in July 1956. The Eisenhower administration, however, had almost immediately begun looking for ways to build an anti-Communist state in the south. Over the next two years Washington forged a close relationship with Ngo Dinh Diem, who had been appointed prime minister by the French-supported Bao Dai government in 1954. Rather than allowing elections to proceed, the United States helped Diem to build up an independent, anti-Communist South Vietnam through providing hundreds of millions of dollars' worth of military and economic aid.[30] By 1959, it had become increasingly clear that Vietnam would remain divided, and local Communist groups launched a series of uprisings against Diem's government. In 1960, the Democratic Republic of Vietnam (DRV) government in Hanoi worked together with southern insurgency leaders to form the NLF, an organization devoted to mobilizing the South Vietnamese population against the Republic of Vietnam government in Saigon both militarily and politically. Aided by growing dislike for Diem's rule, membership in the NLF grew swiftly and, by some estimates, controlled as much as half of the South Vietnamese population by 1963.[31]

China's enthusiasm for the insurgency in South Vietnam increased gradually during the late 1950s and early 1960s as its foreign policy continued to radicalize. After the conclusion of the Geneva Conference in 1954, Beijing had taken a more moderate line in its policies toward Indochina. It had endorsed the neutralization of Laos and Cambodia and sought good relations with the Laotian government rather than backing the Pathet Lao. The PRC had also encouraged the DRV to remain patient when it came to overthrowing Ngo Dinh Diem.[32] In 1958, when the VWP had sought Chinese advice about its plans for reunification with the south, the CCP leadership had responded that the "most urgent task" was carrying out socialist reconstruction in the north. Chinese leaders believed that conditions in the south were not yet right for revolution. They consequently urged the VWP to "wait for opportunities."[33]

Mao and his colleagues began to jettison this cautions approach from 1959 onward. Beijing's changing posture could first be seen in its growing encouragement for North Vietnamese efforts to support the NLF. In May 1960, CCP and Vietnamese Workers Party leaders held meetings in Hanoi and Beijing to discuss the situation in South Vietnam. During his visit to Hanoi, Zhou Enlai promised that China would "adopt an attitude of firm support for people's wars in the intermediate zone."[34] Chinese leaders also admitted that they had not fully understood the struggle being waged in South Vietnam and agreed that DRV support for armed struggle there was the correct strategy.[35] At the same time, Beijing retained a measure of caution during these discussions and did not encourage rapid escalation of the fighting.[36]

During the early 1960s, as competition with Moscow intensified, Chinese support for the NLF became more overt. In September 1962, the PRC welcomed a delegation representing the NLF for the first time. High-level Chinese officials had sometimes discussed the situation in South Vietnam with comrades from Hanoi, but they had not met with those most directly responsible for leading the insurgency.[37] Party officials handled the visit carefully, advising the NLF leaders on the relevance of Mao's writings on guerrilla warfare. The Foreign Ministry began drawing up its plan for receiving the four-person NLF delegation several months before its arrival. The CCP hoped that the visit would enable the NLF to "further expand its political influence in the international arena." The plan recommended that the delegation be given a "cordial, warm, and grand reception" and receive higher political treatment than delegations representing other mass organizations. It called for a welcome ceremony at the airport to be led by Liao Chengzhi, the vice director of the CCP Central Committee's Foreign Affairs Office, and attended by representatives from the Sino-Vietnamese Friendship Association and several other groups. The ministry also planned large receptions where the Afro-Asian Solidarity Committee and other relevant departments issued strong statements of support for the NLF. Last, the CCP arranged press conferences that invited both domestic and international media to publicize the visit.[38] These activities could increase global awareness of the NLF while fostering an association between the organization and the PRC, thus cultivating the image of China as a revolutionary mentor.

During the visit, members of the delegation had extensive meetings with both Chen Yi and Mao Zedong. They spoke in grandiose terms about the relevance of the Chinese experience, the potential global impact of an NLF victory, and the need for a united front against imperialism. When the delegation met with Chen Yi, both sides discussed their common experiences as guerrillas and revolutionaries, expressing a strong mutual admiration. Chen boasted, "China has experience in fighting guerrilla war. We fought for twenty-two years against Japan and Jiang Jieshi. Therefore we have more experience than any other party when it comes to guerrilla war." At the same time, Chen also believed that the South Vietnamese revolutionaries could change the world if they succeeded. "If you defeat American imperialism, it will serve as a model for the peoples of Asia, Africa, and Latin America," he predicted. The delegation praised China as a mentor. Its leader told Chen, "In the struggle of the South Vietnamese people today, much of our experience comes from things that were studied in China."[39] This mutual adulation heightened Beijing's enthusiasm for the NLF because it convinced CCP leaders that the insurgents were devout Maoists and that their triumph would lead other guerrillas to emulate the PRC.

This point became even more apparent when the delegation met with Mao himself several days later. Mao engaged them in a lengthy discussion of strategy that was framed in part by his own struggles. After describing the tactics used by the CCP in its wars against Japan and Jiang Jieshi, Mao emphasized several times that the South Vietnamese struggle was highly similar to the CCP's and that the NLF could benefit from studying the Chinese experience. He told them, "Our situation and your situation are more or less the same. In both cases weapons were few and inadequate while the enemy's weapons were more numerous and superior; they had airplanes and tanks." Mao was doubtless pleased to learn that the NLF's leadership was already using his tactics on the ground. The leader of the delegation told Mao that the NLF had "applied the principles of Chairman Mao and the Communist Party of China summarized in 'On Guerrilla Warfare'" to oppose one of Ngo Dinh Diem's offensives. Later on, they described how they had studied some of Mao's speeches and other writings that had been translated into Vietnamese. Hoping that the Vietnamese revolutionaries would emulate every detail of China's experiences, Mao even encouraged his guests to write poetry as he had done during the most desperate days of the CCP's struggle against the GMD.[40]

Ties between the CCP and the NLF continued to deepen over the next year, prompting a visit to Beijing by NLF party secretary Nguyen Van Linh in August 1963. Nguyen met with both Zhou Enlai and Mao Zedong. His discussions with the two elder statesmen reconfirmed the CCP's faith that the South Vietnamese insurgency would not only defeat American imperialism but also glorify Maoism. During Nguyen's meeting with Mao, the Vietnamese offered the chairman a long summary of the NLF's history, objectives, and tactics. Much of his narration was couched in Maoist terms. He spoke in great detail about how the "armed struggle" in South Vietnam was being carried out in conjunction with the "political struggle," a strategy that bore great similarity to the one Mao had deployed against the GMD during the Chinese civil war. "Our armed struggle has not departed from the basic principles about people's war and guerrilla war that Chairman Mao and the Chinese Communist Party summarized," Nguyen explained at the conclusion of his briefing.[41]

These expressions of indebtedness to Maoism elicited great enthusiasm from Chinese officials and strengthened PRC support for the NLF. "By persisting in your struggle," Zhou Enlai told Nguyen, "you have protected the security of the socialist camp and the peace of Asia" and "supported the revolutionary struggle of peoples throughout the world."[42] Several days after his meeting with Nguyen, Mao expressed the same sentiment publicly in a speech commemorating the eighteenth anniversary of the founding of the Democratic Republic of Vietnam. Claiming that the PRC and the DRV "relied on each other like lips and teeth," Mao called for the two countries to "genuinely respect each other, treat each other equally, aid each other, and support each other." The chairman offered special praise for the NLF which, he contended, was "waging a heroic and tenacious struggle for self-preservation against the American invaders and their running dogs." They had "set up a glorious example of daring to fight and daring to win for oppressed peoples and nations throughout the world."[43]

Beijing's assistance to the NLF extended far beyond rhetoric. While records detailing the exact quantities and types of aid the PRC supplied to Vietnam are difficult to access, enough information is available to be certain that several types of aid, including special assistance to the NLF, grew dramatically during the early 1960s. In July 1962, Mao met with Ho Chi Minh and agreed to give the DRV 90,000 rifles that could be used to equip insurgents in South Vietnam.[44] Over the next four years, Beijing supplied Hanoi with a total of 270,000 guns, 5,400 cannon and artillery pieces, 200 million rounds of ammunition, 900,000 artillery shells, and 200,000 military uniforms.[45] Although some of this aid went to equip North Vietnamese forces, it is hard to imagine that a great deal did not flow to the insurgency in the south, given the high priority that Mao attached to struggle there. In 1965, the chairman instructed the State Council that "whatever the materials the South requests, so long as we are capable of giving these, should be provided by us unconditionally."[46] When Nguyen Van Linh met with Mao Zedong in 1968, he made clear just how critical Chinese assistance had been for the NLF. Calling the chairman "Uncle Mao," he reported that "the spiritual support offered by China is most important. Even in the most difficult situations, we have the great rear area of China supporting us, which allows us to fight for as long as it takes. Materiel assistance is also important. That we force the American troops to the underground shelters [is] also because of pieces of artillery that China gave us."[47]

Beijing also provided diplomatic support to the NLF to enhance the organization's legitimacy and associate the PRC with its cause. In September 1964, the NLF established a new permanent mission in China. Almost immediately after its arrival, the mission became a whirling dervish of activity—meeting with other foreign delegations and various Chinese citizens' groups and gaining an audience with Mao Zedong, Zhou Enlai, and other top party leaders. The mission planned to "use Beijing as a base to launch propaganda and communication activities in order to gain as much support as possible."[48] It also asked for Beijing's assistance in gaining admission to the Second Afro-Asian Conference and the Non-Aligned Conference. The People's Committee for World Peace, an organization set up by the CCP for informal diplomatic activities, recommended that the PRC offer strong backing for the Vietnamese cause. "We should begin with firm support for the Vietnamese people's struggle and unity between our two parties and two countries," the committee wrote. In their dealings with the NLF delegation, Chinese officials should "strictly avoid any sort of great power chauvinism."[49] By allowing the NLF to set up a mission in China and use Beijing as its base, the PRC was doing more than simply aiding the organization. It was connecting itself and its guiding ideology to the Vietnamese insurgency so that the international community would view the NLF as a Chinese protégé.

As Beijing became more deeply committed to aiding the NLF, the United States became more deeply committed to defeating it. Americans understood that Beijing was seeking to use Vietnam as a vehicle for demonstrating the validity of Maoist doctrines, and this was one of the key reasons that they eventually chose to intervene on a massive scale. Through a series of critical decisions made between 1963 and 1965, the United States committed itself at great cost to ending the insurgency in South Vietnam. The process through which Washington arrived at these decisions was a complex and took into account many factors ranging from security to economic interests to personal credibility. Much ink has already been spilled on sorting out the motives that informed these decisions, and some scholars have noted the impact that general fears of China had on U.S. policy.[50] But with the exception of one well-argued journal article by Mao Lin, less attention had been played to how the PRC's broader support for insurgencies factored into American decision-making.[51] Although a history of American intervention or detailed review of U.S. policy toward Vietnam is outside the scope of this book, many of the most fateful choices made by the Kennedy and Johnson administrations about expanding U.S. involvement in Vietnam cannot be understood without reference to Sino-American competition and, more specifically, American fears that revolutionaries throughout Asia would emulate the Chinese model.

The Kennedy administration worried about Chinese intentions in Southeast Asia from its inauguration. The president's fears of retaliatory Chinese aggression in Vietnam led him to be cautious about escalating the American presence there.[52] At the same time, many in Kennedy's entourage recognized that China's international prestige was linked to the victory of the NLF, the Pathet Lao, and other insurgents. They recognized that Beijing saw Indochina as a test case of whether its brand of revolution could be spread abroad and strove to deny the PRC any evidence that its agenda could succeed. Walt Rostow wrote Kennedy that it was a "moot point whether [Beijing] is directly responsible for Communist insurgency efforts in Southeast Asia . . . . The force of circumstances if nothing else deeply engages Communist China's prestige and even its confidence in these efforts."[53]

By 1963, Kennedy administration policy toward Vietnam had become deeply conflicted. The president sometimes expressed skepticism about whether the United States could ever win in Vietnam and ordered a minor reduction in the number of American advisers stationed there.[54] Yet Kennedy did not reduce the U.S. presence significantly, in part because of his perception of what was at stake. From diplomats stationed on the ground in Southeast Asia to the highest-ranking members in the administration, American officials feared that the fall of South Vietnam would enhance China's status in Asia. Frederick Nolting, the U.S. ambassador to South Vietnam, explained in July 1963 that "if there was a political collapse in Vietnam and the U.S. had to withdraw, the Chinese would say that this proved that the right way to expand Communism was to use force."[55] As Kennedy wrestled with tough decisions regarding Vietnam during his last months in office, he was plagued by similar concerns. In September 1963, when journalist David Brinkley asked him whether he had any reason to doubt Eisenhower's domino theory, JFK replied that he believed it. "China is so large, looms so high just beyond the frontiers, that if South Viet-Nam went, it would not only give them an improved geographic position for a guerrilla assault on Malaya, but would also give the impression that the wave of the future in southeast Asia was China and the Communists," the president explained.[56]

Kennedy, of course, would not live to make the difficult choices about Indochina that so desperately needed to be made. Before his assassination in

November 1963, the president had ramped up the U.S. presence in Vietnam significantly, increasing the number of American advisers from around six hundred when he took office to more than sixteen thousand by the time of his assassination.[57] Nevertheless, when Lyndon B. Johnson assumed the presidency, the possibility to avoid greater entanglement was still open. Johnson would bear responsibility for the fateful decision to commit large numbers of American combat forces.

Johnson did not share Kennedy's hesitance about American involvement in Vietnam. His tendency to link the war to his personal credibility was doubtless a critical factor behind the Americanization of the conflict after 1965.[58] At the same time, however, some overarching concerns about what was at stake in Indochina remained much the same. LBJ, too, was deeply concerned about Beijing's fervor for supporting guerrilla wars. He recalled in his memoir how the PRC wanted to expand its influence through promoting insurgencies and humiliate the United States: "In October 1964 . . . Peking was promising Hanoi full support and urging 'wars of national liberation' as the solution to all the problems of the non-Communist underdeveloped nations." Johnson believed that a new "Djakarta-Hanoi-Peking-Pyongyang axis" devoted to "South Vietnam's collapse and an ignominious American withdrawal" was taking shape. "That was the prospect we faced as we determined what to do in Vietnam and Southeast Asia," he remembered.[59]

In the period between Johnson's inauguration and the Americanization of the war in 1965, both the American intelligence community and U.S. diplomats continued to connect the insurgency in Vietnam to Beijing's global ambitions. They argued that the insurgency needed to be defeated because its triumph would validate China's strategy promoting armed conflict. One report on Communist China prepared by the American consul general in Hong Kong in 1964 explained that Beijing had "an almost compulsive need to bring about a recognizable and reasonably early victory for 'people's revolutionary struggle' in South Vietnam to offset Khrushchev's 'capitulationist' line and prove a whole set of Mao's axioms." If the NLF prevailed, then Beijing would "certainly press even more strongly toward complete victory on its own terms and the unconditional withdrawal of the United States." In contrast, the survival of the South Vietnamese government would deliver a serious blow to the PRC's agenda. According to the report, "the stabilization of the country under an independent non-Communist government and international acceptance of South Vietnam's viability would all constitute a profound setback not only to Communist Chinese objectives . . . but [also] to the 'thought of [Mao Zedong] from which [Beijing's] entire approach to international affairs derives its inspiration."[60]

One month after the Gulf of Tonkin Incident—an alleged North Vietnamese attack on U.S. warship that led to a well-known congressional resolution authorizing the president to do whatever was necessary to defend America's allies in SEATO—the Central Intelligence Agency analyzed the situation in similar terms. The agency assessed possible Chinese reactions to the dispatch of additional American forces to the Vietnamese theater. "The Chinese Communists have always had much to gain from a North Vietnamese victory," the CIA claimed. According to the agency, "Success for the Chinese formula of armed resistance to 'imperialism' would greatly strengthen [Beijing's] position in the Sino-Soviet struggle" and prove that the "U.S. is a 'paper tiger' in any contest with the 'people.'"[61] During the critical period between 1964 and early 1965, when the Johnson administration fatefully decided to commit American forces to defending Saigon, intelligence agencies joined in a chorus of American official agencies warning about the benefits that would accrue to China if the National Liberation Front triumphed.

Once the president had dispatched the first American combat forces to South Vietnam and initiated bombing campaigns against the North, high-ranking officials continued to cite Chinese ambitions as a reason to increase U.S. troop commitments. Secretary of Defense Robert S. McNamara was perhaps the most explicit in making this case. On 7 November 1965, he sent the president a memo that became an important basis for discussions of whether the administration should seek to escalate the conflict. McNamara argued that previous decisions taken by the Johnson administration to intensify the war made sense only if they were "in support of a long-run United States policy to contain China." The secretary explained that "China—like Germany in 1917, like Germany in the West and Japan in the East in the late 30's, and like the USSR in 1947—looms as a major power threatening to undercut our importance and effectiveness in the world and, more remotely but more menacingly, to organize all of Asia against us." McNamara himself later deeply regretted his thinking, which "took no account of the centuries old hostility between China and Vietnam . . . or of the setbacks to China's political power caused by the recent events in India."[62] Although McNamara later recanted his views, his recommendations to the president in 1964–65 immediately influenced American policy. He recommended that the number of American troops be increased from 275,000 to 350,000 by the end of 1966 on the grounds that doing so would defeat the insurgency and prevent China from determining the future of Asia.[63]

McNamara understood in hindsight what neither American nor Chinese leaders seemed to comprehend at the time. During the 1960s, Beijing hoped for what Washington feared: an NLF triumph that would boost Chinese prestige around the world. But both sides were working under the assumption that a victory for the Vietnamese Communists would mean a victory for the PRC. The underlying realities were more complex. For one, although the NLF leaders persuaded Chinese officials that they were committed Maoists, their professed intention to emulate the Chinese Revolution was likely, to some degree, an effort to win sympathy and support from Beijing. Historian Robert Brigham has even argued that the NLF's praise for Mao was a cynical ruse. According to Brigham, "The NLF purposefully reinvented its ideological roots and manipulated its public image to make it more acceptable to Peking." Intellectuals in the Vietnamese Workers Party privately argued that the Vietnamese struggle was unique in world history, but the NLF's touring diplomats assured Beijing that they were devout Maoists.[64] Brigham did not have access to the recently declassified Chinese records of conversations used here, and it is possible that he goes to far in downplaying Chinese influence on the NLF. Nevertheless, his fundamental point about Vietnamese priorities is sound. Both the NLF and the VWP were not fighting a crusade to glorify Maoism or China; they were first and foremost struggling for the independence and unification of their country.

This explains why the Soviets were able to improve their relations with Vietnam at the PRC's expense when they turned their attention to Southeast Asia. Moscow began providing the North Vietnamese with greater amounts of aid after Khrushchev's ouster in October 1964 and became more generous throughout 1965.[65] Beijing encouraged the Vietnamese to be skeptical of Soviet support, but Hanoi proved very much the opposite.[66] Although the VWP leaders continued to praise Maoist doctrine during their visits to Beijing, by 1967 they were readily accepting Soviet aid, training and technical assistance.[67] In subsequent months, Moscow's influence on Vietnamese military strategy grew stronger while Beijing's faded to some degree. In 1968, the VWP leadership decided that guerrilla war should no longer form the basis of South Vietnamese resistance and started to show greater attraction to Russian strategies, which emphasized large-scale assaults on urban centers.[68] Whereas the VWP had initially sided with the PRC in the Sino-Soviet split, by the late 1960s, the party was trying to be more even-handed. When a dispute erupted between Chinese and Soviet military advisers in 1968, Hanoi sided with the Soviets and accused the Chinese of violating Vietnam's sovereignty.[69]

The fall of South Vietnam ultimately constituted perhaps the worst U.S. defeat of the Cold War, but it was never recognized as a great Chinese victory. By the time the Paris Peace Agreement was signed in 1973, Beijing and Hanoi had drifted far apart on some issues and the PRC had come to fear Vietnam and the Soviet Union would dominate Indochina.[70] Ironically, after improving ties with the PRC, the Nixon administration would be grateful that Beijing still had enough influence to bring Hanoi to the negotiating table.[71] When the war ended, however, there could be little question that Sino-American competition had greatly escalated its overall level of violence. China's eagerness to support guerrilla wars and America's determination to suppress them turned what might have been a limited civil war into a horrific conflagration that inflicted a heavy toll in casualties and left Vietnam devastated. The effects were not limited to Vietnam, however, but also extended to neighboring Southeast Asian countries.

Insurgency and Counterinsurgency in Vietnam's Shadow

While Beijing and Washington both saw Vietnam as the most critical testing ground for the viability of revolution in Asia, the war inevitably spilled over into the surrounding states, and these too became theaters for guerrilla wars of varying magnitudes. In Laos, Thailand, Burma, and elsewhere, Beijing sought to associate itself with and provide guidance for indigenous insurgencies seeking to overthrow neutral or pro-Western governments. Washington often took an exaggerated view of China's influence over these conflicts. Nonetheless, the possibility that a triumphant insurgency would bolster China's prestige in the region provided a powerful incentive for the United States to get involved. Even if there were no American troops outside of Vietnam, the Johnson administration eagerly provided weapons and training to police and other indigenous forces that promised to maintain stability.

The impact of the war in Vietnam was felt most directly in Laos, where the Pathet Lao, a leftist insurgency with deep links to Hanoi, strove to topple the government of Souvanna Phouma. In 1962, Beijing, Hanoi, and Washington had reached a tenuous compromise about the future of Laos at the Second Geneva Conference. The conference established Laos as a neutral state and created a tripartite government in which conservatives, neutralists, and the Communist Pathet Lao all had representation.[72] But geography proved to be destiny for the small, neutralist country because it provided an almost ideal base of operations for North Vietnamese forces seeking to transport weapons to the NLF in the south. None of the parties who signed the agreement took it very seriously. China and Vietnam continued to aid the Pathet Lao while the United States supported the country's fragile neutralist government.[73]

Competition between Beijing and Washington was far more indirect in the Laotian theater than it was in Vietnam, primarily because of the close relationship between the Vietnamese Workers Party and the Pathet Lao. The VWP had exercised a dominating influence over the Pathet Lao since the earliest days of the two organizations in the 1930s, and the Vietnamese jealously guarded their controlling position in Laos. Before 1963, Hanoi refused to allow the Pathet Lao to establish direct contacts with the PRC and insisted that any Chinese aid to the organization flow through the Democratic Republic of Vietnam. Beijing generally did not take issue with this and, during the 1950s and early 1960s, made it clear that it considered its policy toward Laos to be part of its policy toward North Vietnam.[74] But even if the VWP had the greatest influence on the Pathet Lao, Beijing could still envision the Laotians as part of a broader Eastern revolution emanating from and inspired by China.

The PRC started to support the Pathet Lao more actively in April 1963. It did not deliberately subvert Vietnamese influence over the organization, but it did establish more formal contacts and provide aid and advice more directly. The increase in Chinese involvement was precipitated by collapse of the coalition government established at the Second Geneva Conference and the subsequent resumption of fighting between Pathet Lao and government forces in the Plain of Jars. The Kennedy administration began offering covert support to all non-Communist groups in Laos, and Beijing adopted a more radical stance.[75] On 4 April, a report by the PRC Foreign Ministry argued that the Pathet Lao should be "prepared to give a strong counterattack against military provocations from any quarter" and that the organization should "increase its military strength."[76]

With Laos spiraling into all-out civil war, Kaysone Phomvihane, the leader of the Lao People's Party (LPP), visited Beijing in October 1963 and asked the CCP leadership for more assistance. Although Zhou Enlai initially told the visiting party leader that Beijing lacked familiarity with the situation in Laos, the two agreed that the PRC would send a secret work team to the Pathet Lao headquarters in Sam Neua. Beijing selected Duan Suquan, a distinguished Red Army general with experience in teaching and training, as its leader. Duan's mission stayed in Laos for four years, offering advice in military operations, intelligence gathering, the treatment of captured U.S. pilots, and land reform.[77]

After its arrival in Laos, the mission began reporting enthusiastically on what it saw there. Duan's team sent a memo to the Foreign Ministry explaining that during the last year "the Lao People's Party has taken a firm attitude in its struggle against American imperialism; it increasingly emphasizes China's revolutionary experiences." One LPP leader told the mission that "China had abundant experience in armed struggle, creating a united front, and fighting against imperialism and feudalism. This has great meaning for the struggles of poor, oppressed, and enslaved agricultural countries." Another Laotian party leader offered similar praise: "Mao's military thought is part of the universal truth of Marxism; for the people of every country currently engaged in armed struggle, it is exceptionally important."[78] During Duan's time in Laos he provided Kaysone with individual tutelage on Mao Zedong's works.

Hu Zhengqing, a member of Duan's team, recalled that when the two men studied Mao's 1946 essay "Concentrate a Superior Force to Destroy the Enemy Forces One by One," the Laotian had "listened while taking notes with rapt attention," underlining and circling the parts he thought were especially relevant and important.[79]

Duan's mission was equally pleased with the Pathet Lao's stance on the Sino-Soviet split. According to the report, the Soviets had "not only pressured the Pathet Lao by threatening to cut off aid but also provided films and publications seeking to spread the influence of revisionism." The Laotians, however, had "withstood all of the pressure applied by the Khrushchev revisionist clique to forestall Laos's revolution and insisted on the revolutionary path." The report also noted that although the LPP had initially hesitated to take sides in the Sino-Soviet split, in recent months the three countries of Indochina were "united behind the Chinese position and agreed with China's analysis of the Laotian situation."[80] What Beijing regarded as the increasing ideological purity of the Pathet Lao doubtless contributed to the CCP's support for the organization.

Beijing's growing conviction that the Pathet Lao wanted to emulate the PRC's revolutionary path led CCP officials to open the aid spigot for their Laotian comrades. Chinese aid to the Pathet Lao was irregular before 1964 but rose drastically from that summer onward. In October, Beijing assumed full responsibility for providing equipment and supplies to Pathet Lao forces. According to historian Xiaoming Zhang's carefully compiled statistics, the PRC provided 115,000 guns, 34 tanks and armored vehicles, 170 million bullets, and 920,000 grenades during the Pathet Lao's long and eventually successful struggle for power. Moreover, the PRC offered special training for more than seven hundred Lao officers. This assistance enabled the Pathet Lao to develop into a full regular military that included infantry, artillery, and engineering divisions, among others.[81] Although the VWP continued to have the strongest influence over the Pathet Lao's day-to-day operations, Beijing hoped that providing large-scale assistance would associate the PRC with another important national liberation movement and strengthen its claim to be the leader of Asia's revolutionary forces.

The U.S. response to the growing strength of the Pathet Lao was as confused as it was tragic. During the early 1960s, the Kennedy administration had decided not to send combat forces to the small, landlocked country and to forego the type of transformative nation-building programs being carried out in South Vietnam. The main reason for this decision was that Kennedy did not believe Laos possessed the kind of political leadership that would enable the creation of a reliable anti-Communist bulwark.[82] Efforts by the Kennedy and Johnson administrations to prevent the Pathet Lao from gaining power were nevertheless substantial. They included recruiting and arming Hmong tribesmen for a clandestine army supported by the CIA, a massive bombing campaign against targets on the Ho Chi Minh Trail, and an assistance program for the Lao National Police. Several historians and former government officials have covered these activities, generally focusing on the sordid details of covert U.S. operations without fitting them into the larger context of American foreign policy.[83] To be sure, many American actions against the Pathet Lao were related to specific military objectives in Vietnam. At the same time, U.S. officials also viewed the Laotian insurgency as part of the PRC's broader campaign to incite revolutionary violence in Asia.

The period between 1963 and 1964 was a turning point in American involvement in Laos, much as it was in Vietnam. At the same time that the PRC was ramping up its support to the Pathet Lao, Kennedy's advisers began urging the president to take new measures in support of the Laotian government.[84] Administration officials argued that the United States should step up its involvement in Laos for a variety of reasons, but the PRC often figured among them. Some argued that Laos required American action because it would otherwise become a prime target of Beijing's campaign to promote revolution. In July 1963, Roger Hilsman, the assistant secretary of state for Asian affairs, wrote the secretary of state explaining likely Chinese initiatives in the aftermath of the Sino-Soviet split and suggesting countermeasures. He put Laos at the top of his list of places where the PRC was likely to spread subversion and called for measures to "assure that the Chinese Communists do not underestimate the risks involved in raising the level of activity in Laos."[85] Such concerns were by no means the only factor that influenced Kennedy's policy, but they certainly weighed on the minds of high-ranking officials during the summer and fall of 1963, when the president approved new plans to strengthen the neutralist Laotian government through providing military supplies and economic assistance.[86]

In 1964, as U.S. involvement in Laos deepened and the Johnson administration authorized large-scale bombing raids against Pathet Lao positions, the larger problem of Chinese-inspired insurgencies in Southeast Asia continued to figure into American thinking. Secretary of State Rusk explained the meaning of the Laotian conflict in a commencement address at Williams College in June. After summarizing the history of the civil war in Laos and the 1962 Geneva Agreement, Rusk described what he saw as the broader problem: "The Communist assault on Laos, like that on South Viet-Nam, involves the larger question of whether anyone is to be permitted to succeed in aggression by terror, and the infiltration of arms and military personnel across national frontiers. If they are allowed to gain from these assaults in Southeast Asia, the Communist advocates of militancy everywhere will feel encouraged." As in South Vietnam, American officials believed that the key issue was containing the rising threat of guerrilla warfare and argued that Washington needed to teach a lesson to those who encouraged violent insurgencies. "It is," the secretary continued, "in the vital interest of the free world that [Beijing] and Hanoi—and all Communists everywhere—learn, once and for all that they cannot reap rewards from militancy, aggression, by seepage, and duplicity."[87]

As American involvement in Vietnam grew, interdicting the flow of supplies from Hanoi to the NLF over the infamous Ho Chi Minh Trail became the most pressing issue in Laos policy. By 1966, Washington identified Hanoi as the key backer of the Pathet Lao, and some American intelligence even referred to the Laotian insurgency as a North Vietnamese "puppet," downplaying the Chinese role to some degree.[88] But officials continued to claim that the PRC was orchestrating North Vietnamese aggression in Laos and thus the activities of the Pathet Lao. One State Department assessment written up in 1968 contended that "the present Chinese leadership probably regards NVN [North Vietnam] as a transmittal belt for wars of national liberation in SEA [Southeast Asia]." Beijing was therefore likely to "press Hanoi to move vigorously in Laos so as to facilitate Communist control of the country and broaden support for insurgent efforts in Thailand."[89]

American support for the ineffectual Laotian government ultimately proved futile, yet the success of the Pathet Lao never became a validation of Mao Zedong Thought. To the contrary, as the confidence of the Pathet Lao in their eventual victory grew, they increasingly pushed the PRC aside. As Hanoi sought greater autonomy from Beijing during the late 1960s, North Vietnam worked quietly to reduce the Chinese presence in Laos. Incidents that worsened party relations between the LPP and CCP began during the late 1960s, apparently due to Vietnamese pressure on the Laotians. In September 1968, Beijing withdrew a team of advisers from Laos when the LPP leader Kaysone Phomvihane suggested that they take a vacation. The Chinese interpreted this as a signal that, with relations between Beijing and Hanoi worsening, they were no longer wanted in Laos.[90] China's aspiration to be venerated as a revolutionary model by the Pathet Lao was not completely extinguished by this incident. Beijing continued road-building programs in northern Laos, where Americans speculated that the PRC might have been trying to prevent its influence from being eclipsed by Hanoi.[91] Nevertheless, by the early 1970s, outside observers noted that the PRC's influence over the Laotian revolutionaries seemed small. The Rand Corporation published a report on Laos in 1972 arguing that there was "no distinctly pro Chinese faction in the (Communist) People's Party of Laos (PPL)" and its leadership was "not subservient to China."[92]

Whereas revolutionaries in Laos and Vietnam turned away from the PRC once they gained power, other insurgencies in Southeast Asia supported by Beijing were defeated altogether. Chinese support for guerrilla war in Thailand, a member of SEATO and America's staunchest ally in the region, alarmed Washington, but the insurgency never gained much traction. Beijing had paid little attention to the Communist Party of Thailand (CPT) before 1964, when Thailand's willingness to serve as a base for American combat operations in Vietnam invited greater Chinese hostility. In January 1965, Foreign Minister Chen Yi allegedly made a widely quoted statement that there would be "a guerrilla war going in Thailand before the year is out."[93] At roughly the same time, the CPT established two front organizations—the Thai Independence Movement and the Thai Patriotic Front—that would bear primary responsibility for launching insurgent operations against the government. These organizations, whose membership consisted primarily of ethnic Chinese, set up offices in Beijing and received constant PRC encouragement in the form of media propaganda and, allegedly, the infiltration of CCP agents into Thailand.[94]

Because the PRC did not fully support the Thai insurgency until 1965—the end of the period covered by the PRC Foreign Ministry Archive—documentation that can suggest Chinese motives for doing so is limited. Nevertheless, official PRC statements about the CPT often depicted the Thai insurgents as another group of revolutionaries who had been inspired by the Chinese example. Like the guerrillas in Laos and South Vietnam, their victory would glorify the Maoist cause. An article that appeared in *Renmin Ribao* in October 1967 asserted that the "CPT guided by Marxism-Leninism and the thought of Mao Zedong has dauntlessly led the Thai people in taking up arms and making a courageous fight against the U.S. aggressors and their running dogs."[95] Moreover, the CPT itself regularly affirmed its allegiance to and admiration for China. In 1967, the party issued statements calling for its members to "study conscientiously Mao Zedong's thought, the acme of Marxism-Leninism in the present era." Thai guerrilla organizations also echoed the CCP's line on "Soviet revisionism" on numerous occasions.[96]

To American officials, it seemed obvious that the Thai insurgency was yet another revolutionary movement under PRC guidance. "The Thai insurgency unquestionably was a Maoist insurgency inspired by Mao Zedong and his followers," argued William N. Stokes, an American Foreign Service officer who counseled the Thai government on counterinsurgency. Stokes added: "The insurgents were trained in China, they were Chinese or Sino-Thai. The little red book was everywhere in their camps, and pictures of Mao were worn on caps by the insurgents when they wore uniforms or insignia of any kind, and the insurgency was supported from China by a clandestine radio broadcast that put the whole thing clearly in a Maoist context."[97]

In February 1965, the Johnson administration's counterinsurgency group convened a meeting to discuss Thailand. Central Intelligence director John McCone pointed to "signs that Thailand [was] becoming a prime target for ChiCom infiltration and subversion." The U.S. ambassador to Thailand, Graham Martin, worried that Chen Yi's statement that an insurgency would break out in the country within a year, along with the establishment of Thai national front groups, constituted a "preliminary preparation for an all out subversive movement in Thailand." The group discussed taking precautions to secure the Thai government, such as offering additional training for the country's provincial police.[98]

In 1966, the U.S. Army published a study of the insurgent threat to Thailand that more explicitly linked subversion there to the expansion of Chinese influence in Southeast Asia. The study argued that the "existence of a resurgent China," which had "the potential, and probably the aspiration to become the dominant single power in East Asia," constituted a major threat to America's objective of creating an "open free society of nations in Southeast Asia." The army worried that after Vietnam, Thailand might become the next venue where Beijing would promote insurgency. It explained that even if the United States defeated the NLF in South Vietnam, it was "very unlikely" that Beijing would "regard that event as final proof of the infeasibility of guerilla warfare." This was because "Maoism prepares Asia's communists to accept some defeats—as in Vietnam—and move elsewhere." The report finished with a call for American action: "The nature of the insurgency threat in Thailand must be recognized as of prime importance and U.S. support of Thai programs in this area should be increased accordingly."[99]

The United States never committed its forces to suppressing the insurgency in Thailand but still invested significantly in bolstering indigenous resistance. This meant both training Thai forces and launching infrastructure programs that facilitated Bangkok's efforts to defeat the insurgents. After the Thai government established the Communist Suppression Organization Command (CSOC) in November 1965, the USAID funded the Accelerated Rural Development Office to provide support.[100] Americans also worried that rural areas in northeastern Thailand needed to be better integrated with Bangkok, the country's capital. During the late 1960s, the USAID provided the Thai government with forty-nine million dollars for a road-building program deigned to make the northeast more accessible to both commercial enterprise and government security forces.[101] Seeking to facilitate the movement of government troops and supplies into regions that could become targets for guerrillas, Washington also provided a small number of helicopters and supported a pilot training program.[102] Finally, American advisers helped the

Thai government with modernizing its police forces and setting up a school to train district officers.[103]

In Thailand, the insurgency was ultimately far less successful than in Vietnam and Laos, but its failure spoke less to the effectiveness of American assistance than it did to the somewhat mistaken view of the Thai situation held by Beijing and Washington. They saw the insurgency as a manifestation of the same kind of radical anticolonial nationalism that was driving the Pathet Lao and the NLF. The underlying reality was quite different. Insurgents in Thailand never gained the support of a large number of peasants, as they did in Indochina, and failed to broaden their small, provincial, ethnic Chinese base. Thus, although the NLF was on the verge of triumph by the early 1970s, Americans no longer felt a sense of urgency about developments in Thailand. One Foreign Service officer stationed in rural Thailand remembered that, by 1973, "the insurgency was down to a whimper, it was clearly not a significant threat."[104] Although the Thai insurgency enjoyed a short-lived resurgence during the mid-1970s, Americans never saw it as a danger to the staunchly anti-Communist Thai government after the late 1960s.[105]

Mao and his comrades were similarly unsuccessful with their efforts to stir revolution elsewhere in Southeast Asia. Much is still unknown about Beijing's support for insurgencies in Burma, Malaysia, the Philippines, and other Asian countries. After the failure of the Second Afro-Asian Conference, Beijing felt more isolated and less reluctant to aid guerrillas seeking to overthrow neighboring governments.[106] Burma, for example, had enjoyed cordial relations with the PRC since the 1950s but found itself the target of Beijing's ire in 1967. The cause of the frictions was a series of anti-Chinese riots that erupted after Chinese diplomats violated prohibitions against propaganda activities by distributing Mao Zedong buttons and other materials to overseas Chinese students in Rangoon. Beijing responded by announcing its support for the Burmese Communist Party and encouraging Burmese Communists to work together with other ethnic insurgent groups.[107] The PRC also increased its support for the Malayan National Liberation League and allowed it to maintain a mission in Beijing. The organization was known to espouse a Maoist, anti-Soviet line.[108]

Although Washington kept tabs on Chinese support for these insurgencies, it did not feel an urgent need to intervene. In July 1967, the State Department's Bureau of Intelligence and Research sent a report to the secretary of state entitled "China's Encourages Violence in Asia." Despite its alarmist title, the report reflected the bureau's growing confidence that China would gain little from its ventures outside Indochina. It argued: "Apart from the Cultural Revolution, the Chinese no doubt hope that the various insurgencies they support eventually will develop into successful revolutionary movements that ultimately will lead to the establishment of Maoist regimes. But, with the exception of Laos and Vietnam, this goal is clearly a distant one." The report added that although Beijing continued to proclaim its support for insurgencies in Malaysia, the Philippines, and elsewhere, it provided limited material support.[109] In some cases, such as Burma, Washington offered assistance, but the host government preferred that the United States not get involved. Although Rangoon initially accepted some weapons from the United States, in 1970 it terminated the military assistance program and shunned all forms of American aid in subsequent years.[110]

Ultimately, neither Beijing nor Washington benefited from meddling with the revolutionary forces sweeping in Southeast Asia during the 1960s. By the end of the decade, they were both clearly trying to flee from their mistakes in the region as quickly as possible. Beijing abandoned many of the revolutions it had once supported as it started to improve relations with Southeast Asia while Washington began asking its allies there to assume greater responsibility for their self-defense through the Nixon Doctrine. Their failures were in part because, despite their different objectives, they shared a perception of what was at stake in Southeast Asia that differed significantly from that of the revolutionaries they supported or opposed. These experiences should have been instructive, but they were not. Similar motives fueled Chinese and American involvement in conflicts that they had even less understanding of—most notably in Africa.

Zanzibar

Africa carried neither the critical strategic significance nor the symbolic importance of Southeast Asia in the minds of most American and Chinese policy makers. Nevertheless, during the 1960s, as the continent emerged as a new frontier in the Cold War, Washington and Beijing became more focused on developments there. China believed in Africa's revolutionary potential and sought to support wars of national liberation on the continent even if it lacked the resources and expertise to provide the extensive, on the spot guidance that it offered the Vietnamese. In Africa, too, the CCP sought to introduce Maoist doctrines on guerrilla wars and supported those groups that they deemed likely to emulate the Chinese experience, though the kind of assistance the party could provide was limited. Americans found China's role in African insurgencies confusing and often grossly exaggerated the PRC's potential impact. Even vague hints that the Chinese were gaining traction in Africa sometimes led Americans to advocate getting involved.

The revolution that swept Zanzibar in January 1964 was one of the first episodes to spark American apprehension about Chinese subversion in Africa. A small island nation with a population of three hundred thousand, Zanzibar had been governed by an unpopular pro-Western sultan whom the British had left in power when they relinquished colonial rule. The island's population had long suffered from ethnic and racial frictions. Arab and South Asian minorities dominated economic life, fostering resentment among the African majority. During the years before the revolution, Communist involvement with the island's nationalist groups and organizations had been extensive. As part of their growing competition in Africa, both China and the Soviet Union had started funding different political factions in Zanzibar in 1959. The Soviets had focused their efforts on the African-led Afro-Shirazi Party (ASP), whose politics were driven by the yearnings of Zanzibar's African majority for greater political power. The PRC, on the other hand, cultivated a group of leftist Arab nationalists who broke away from the ruling Zanzibar National Party (ZNP) to form the Umma Party in 1963.[111]

Zanzibar's revolution began on 12 January 1964, when John Okello, an obscure African militant, led an armed revolt that swiftly gained access to the police armory and seized control of government facilities. Within twelve hours, the fighting was over, and within a day, the leaders of the rebellion announced a new government. Members of the ASP and Umma Party swiftly staked out positions of influence. Okello was a political neophyte, and the more experienced politicians from the two parties were able to push him aside and divide the key posts in the new government among themselves. Abeid Karume, a moderate member of the ASP, became president while some members of the Umma Party, whose support for the revolution had also been important, received appointments.[112]

Members of the ASP and Umma Party competed for influence, making Zanzibar's international orientation seem uncertain. But the individual who would eventually gain the strongest voice on foreign policy was Abdulrahman Muhammad Babu, a member of the Umma Party with long-standing ties to Beijing. Babu, who assumed the position of minister for external affairs, was unabashed in his admiration for China. In 1959, he had been one of the first African leaders selected to visit there and immediately became enamored of the CCP. He remembered, "The meetings with the Chinese leadership and the late night discussions with them on all questions of the anti-imperialist struggle were most inspiring and helped to mold my outlook."[113] Beijing knew of Babu's growing influence and his pro-Chinese view. A Foreign Ministry dispatch written briefly after the revolution praised Babu for his "definite Marxist-Leninist way of thinking, . . . resolute opposition to American and English imperialism," and "clear position against revisionism."[114]

Washington's understanding of Zanzibar's political dynamics was hazy, but Babu's rise in the government triggered suspicions that China had instigated the coup, though it had not. The concerns Americans raised about Zanzibar differed somewhat from those that they raised about Southeast Asia. Rather than worrying about Chinese support for an active insurgency, in Zanzibar they worried that Beijing would take advantage of a successful insurgency to establish a base for spreading revolution throughout Africa. On 30 January, Secretary of State Rusk sent a cable to all diplomatic posts on the continent explaining that there had been "indications of probable Chicom involvement in [the] Zanzibar revolt." Most of the connections that Rusk pointed out between Beijing and the insurgents were tenuous and speculative. They included a report that two of the leaders of the revolt had met with Chen Yi in Nairobi in December when the vice premier had attended Kenya's independence day celebration. Rusk believed that this was when the timing of the revolt had been determined. The secretary also viewed as suspicious the fact that a New China News Agency correspondent had arrived in Zanzibar a few days before the sultan's overthrow and made a "number of phone calls in Chinese." As Rusk himself admitted, these reports scarcely constituted hard evidence that Beijing had fomented the rebellion. Nevertheless, he was convinced that the PRC wanted to use Zanzibar as a base to encourage more revolutionary activity on the African continent. It seemed "obvious" to the secretary that the Chinese were "seeking [to] exploit fragile political situations for their own ends and in particular to establish [a] base in Zanzibar for further subversive activities, particular in East Africa."[115]

Even if the PRC had not played a direct role in Zanzibar's revolt, China recognized that its own struggle had inspired some of the revolutionaries and saw an opportunity to deepen its influence in Africa. Chinese diplomats stationed in other African countries immediately reported on the revolution in glowing terms and argued that, with China's assistance, Zanzibar could inspire similar events. The PRC ambassador in Kenya elatedly called the revolution a "new phenomenon on the African continent" and claimed that "the Chinese Revolution had an exceptionally broad and deep impact on the people of Zanzibar." But the country still needed international assistance and "especially Chinese support." The report urged the Foreign Ministry to render assistance to the new government not only to consolidate a relationship with a potential new ally but also because it might foster opportunities for insurgency and revolution in Africa. Beijing, the report argued, should consider visits by high-ranking Chinese officials because they would be a "great encouragement to the people of Zanzibar" and have a "deep influence on all of East Africa."[116]

Over the next few weeks, the Chinese scrambled to raise their profile in Zanzibar even as Washington did what it could to thwart them. Babu was keen to help China become the most influential foreign actor in the country. On 18 January, he invited Tu Peilin, the Xinhua News Agency correspondent in Zanzibar, to his home and briefly discussed relations between his government and the PRC. Babu claimed that both the United States and the Soviet Union were making aid proposals to Zanzibar. Nevertheless, he hoped that China would be the "first to give us aid and dispatch specialists" because that would give him an excuse to "postpone Soviet and American aid." He also hoped that Zanzibar's new president would be able to visit China so that he could see a Communist country firsthand.[117]

Americans believed that Babu's rapport with Beijing was dangerous and started looking for ways to undermine him. In March, William Leonhart, the U.S. ambassador to Tanganyika, held a series of meetings with Frank Carlucci, the U.S. consul in Zanzibar, and Stephen Miles, the British high commissioner to Tanganyika. All agreed that Babu's "elimination" was their "prime objective." The diplomats also talked about the possibility of harnessing their influence over Kenyan president Jomo Kenyatta and other East African leaders to pressure President Karume to move against Babu.[118] Though nothing came of these discussions, fears about Babu's China connection persisted. On 24 March, the Indian high commissioner for East Africa warned Leonhart that the situation in Zanzibar had "swung sharply and obviously in Babu's favor." The high commissioner feared that Zanzibar would end up as a "Communist showcase" and "export both 'Socialist success' and subversion to entire east and southern Africa." He was convinced that the Chinese were the "main instigators and backers of Babu," whom he called a "dangerous and intelligent man who knows what he wants."[119]

The critical question was what precisely Washington could do to change Zanzibar's political trajectory. Revolution had triumphed, and using force or covert operations to supplant the new government was unrealistic. Americans did find one convenient if imperfect solution to their dilemma. They lobbied Julius Nyerere's government in Dar es Salaam to consider a union between Tanganyika and Zanzibar in the hope that subsuming the island into its larger, somewhat more moderate African neighbor would limit the overall influence of Babu and his allies. Nyerere has claimed in his speeches that the idea of Tanzania, the new country created through the union of Tanganyika and Zanzibar, was born out of Pan-African sentiments shared by the political leaders of both nations.[120] He is probably right to assert that such sentiments facilitated the process. At the same time, American policy documents demonstrate that Washington pressured Nyerere to propose the union and that the initiative for it might well have come from the United States. Especially revealing is a cable that Secretary of State Dean Rusk sent to several American embassies in Africa on 30 March 1964. Rusk worried that Babu would "lead Zanzibar into [the] Commie camp" and thought that the "long range solution" to the problems created by the pro-Chinese Babu might "lie in some form of federation." The secretary then asked specifically if it would "be useful to raise again with Nyerere despite his previous objections [the] idea of [a] Tanganyika-Zanzibar federation as [a] possible way [to] strengthen Karume and reduce Babu's influence."[121] Rusk's question makes it clear that the United States had not only brought up the possibility of a federation between the two countries but also that it had raised the issue several times despite Nyerere's ambivalence.

American officials ultimately got what they wanted. On 26 April 1964, Tanganyika and Zanzibar officially merged to form the United Republic of Tanzania with Dar es Salaam as the capital and Julius Nyerere as president. The precise motives of Zanzibar's leaders for agreeing to the union remain murky. Nyerere was one of the most influential African nationalist politicians and his iconic status within the Pan-African movement may have made the leadership of what was still a small, vulnerable island nation willing to go along with him. It is also possible that the new Zanzibari president, Abeid Karume, had misgivings about Babu and other radicals in his government; he may have seen union with Tanganyika as the best ways to prevent them from becoming too influential.[122] Even after the union, the Chinese remained highly influential in Zanzibar, but Americans generally viewed the outcome with relief.

Chinese officials, for their part, had reservations about the merger despite the growing ties between Beijing and Dar es Salaam. Under Nyerere's leadership, Tanganyika had established its independence, recognized the PRC, and consistently aligned itself in favor of national liberation movements on the African continent.[123] At the same time, however, the PRC was initially not as enthusiastic about Nyerere as it was about the political leadership in Zanzibar, which it characterized as revolutionary rather than just nationalist and anticolonial. Several weeks after the Tanzanian union was finalized, Meng Ying, who had served as PRC ambassador to Zanzibar, wrote a sweeping analysis of what he saw as the "contradictions" between Tanganyika and the island. As Meng saw it, the Zanzibari people wanted to "continue the development of their nationalist democratic revolution" and were "not willing to be held back by Tanganyika." Tanganyikan authorities, however, "wanted the revolution to stop" and were "pulling it back." [124]

Yet Chinese policy in Zanzibar was not nearly as disastrous as its assistance to insurgents elsewhere. Supporting a revolution that had already gained power rather than insurgents trying to topple a sovereign government made Beijing's actions seem far more benign both in Zanzibar and in surrounding countries. After the merger, Zanzibar retained some autonomy and, as described in the next chapter, became an important venue for Chinese development projects. Assistance to other revolutionaries in Africa did not earn the PRC nearly as much goodwill.

The Congo

Even as the flames of revolution in Zanzibar seemed to be flickering out, a more troubling series of events had begun in the Belgian Congo. Chinese involvement—both real and suspected—during the crisis that unfolded in 1964 once again aroused American anxieties. Beijing's material support for the Congolese insurgency was modest. It provided training for guerrillas and small quantities of arms and assistance. But China and the United States read a symbolic value into this assistance that greatly exceeded its monetary worth. Despite Beijing's limited ability to support the rebellion financially, China aspired to create a Maoist vanguard on the African continent. Its advice and analysis of events often reflected this objective. Americans sensationalized China's impact in the Congo even though it was in fact limited. Nevertheless, alleged connections between Beijing and the Congolese insurgents became an important factor in pushing the Johnson administration to intervene.

The Congo had been in turmoil since it gained independence in 1960. When Katanga Province seceded in July 1960, the country fell into a civil war, and Prime Minister Patrice Lumumba appealed to the United Nations for assistance in restoring order. Although the Union Nations dispatched a peacekeeping mission, it refused to take action to reverse Katanga's secession. This led Lumumba to ask the Soviets for assistance. On 5 September, Congolese president Joseph Kasa-Vubu suddenly announced that he had dismissed Lumumba from his post as prime minister, but Lumumba argued that this was illegal and responded by attempting to depose Kasa-Vubu. With both domestic and international observers uncertain of who the Congo's legitimate leader was, Army chief of staff Joseph Mobutu seized power in a military coup on 14 September.[125] In November, Lumumba escaped from house arrest and fled to Stanleyville, where he set up a rival government with Antoine Gizenga, his former deputy prime minister. China recognized and supported the new government in Stanleyville, which persisted in its claims to legitimacy after Lumumba's assassination in January 1961. After Gizenga succumbed to pressure to merge with Leopoldville, however, the PRC was left without a viable leader to support.[126]

Beijing nonetheless remained hostile toward Leopoldville and looked for opportunities to subvert the new government. In late 1963 and early 1964, the PRC found new avenues for creating mischief when it established relations with two of Congo's neighbors—Congo-Brazzaville and Burundi. These newly independent nations were small and, even by African standards, poor. Through a combination of economic aid offers and skilled diplomacy, China swiftly increased its influence and began seeking to use its new allies to undermine the detested Congolese government. Before long, CCP officials were speaking brazenly of the possibilities for promoting insurgency in the Congo by creating base areas where they could train and arm guerrillas. Mao was even reported to have called Burundi "a stepping stone for reaching the Congo."[127]

In the meantime, the CCP had already started to provide training in guerrilla warfare to other Congolese insurgents in China. Perhaps the most important of these was Pierre Mulele, who would eventually lead a major uprising against the government from Kwilu Province. Disillusioned by Gizenga's decision to seek compromise, Mulele spent fifteen months in the PRC and attended a Chinese military school between April 1962 and July 1963. He returned to his native Congo in August 1963 determined to launch an armed struggle and began training partisans.[128] Mulele's forces would enjoy some spectacular successes when they launched their guerrilla campaign in January 1964. They gained control over a large portion of Kwilu and killed the army colonel of the expeditionary force that had been sent against them. Despite these initial triumphs, however, Mulele's men never captured a major urban area or expanding beyond Kwilu.[129]

Even as government forces managed to contain Mulele's revolt, other groups of Congolese revolutionaries were preparing for armed struggle in different regions of the country. Leaders of the Congo's National Liberation Council (Conseil National de Liberacion, CNL) had moved into neighboring Congo-Brazzaville, where they began planning a more general guerrilla campaign. The CNL dispatched Gaston Soumialot to Burundi with the mission of organizing a rebellion in the Congo's eastern provinces. After recruiting thousands of supporters through his activities along the Congo-Burundi border, Soumialot prepared to launch what would soon become a surprisingly successful uprising.[130] Beginning in April 1964, his forces scored a series of stunning victories. The guerrilla fighters captured the city of Uvira in May and soon swept into other cities in Kivu and neighboring provinces. Within a few months, these revolutionaries, who came to be known as Simba (lion in Swahili), had gained control of almost half of the Congo and set up a rival government in Stanleyville.[131]

The Simbas had an energizing effect on Chinese officials. For Beijing, the success of the CNL seemed to afford a new opportunity to spread Mao's revolutionary doctrines. Beijing was among the earliest supporters of the CNL, and some of the organization's leaders cited Chinese aid as instrumental in its initial successes. When Soumialot visited the PRC in August 1965, he recalled that African governments had been hesitant to support him. During his visit to Bujumbura, the capital of Burundi, however, he had "heard Chinese representatives talking about the strategies for armed struggle such as seizing weapons from the enemy." The CNL had launched its own struggle shortly after learning about these Chinese tactics but had been beset by problems. A lack of funds had made it impossible for the CNL to dispatch operatives to the Congo's interior. Shortly thereafter, however, "Chinese comrades in Bujumbura had assisted us with 100,000 Burundi francs and on 13 April we liberated Uvira and this opened up a path to the entire country."[132] Given that Soumialot was in China to ask for more assistance, it is likely that he was trying to play up Chinese influence on his movement. Nevertheless, there is no reason to doubt that Beijing tried to offer the CNL funding and guidance at a critical juncture.

Beijing's enthusiasm for the CNL continued to grow as the army's offensive scored impressive victories on the battlefield. Chinese officials were eager to make sure that the Congolese insurgency would follow the Maoist road to victory. In October 1964, with the Simbas in control of roughly half of the country but locked in combat with mercenaries hired by the government, two leading CNL officials traveled to the PRC on a trip arranged by the Chinese People's Institute of Foreign Affairs. Before their arrival, the institute drew up a detailed plan for their visit, calling for the PRC to "receive them warmly" and "exert influence on them on the basis of an understanding of the situation in the Congo." At the same time, the insurgents would be encouraged to adopt Mao's revolutionary ideals and tactics: "In accordance with the principle of Mao Zedong's thought, which explains that without the people's army and armed struggle there can be no victory, we should encourage them to stick to armed struggle and eliminate the fantasy of reconciliation. On this basis, we will strengthen their confidence, help them to recognize that their struggle will be difficult and long-term, and emphasize the creation of a way of thinking based on domestic struggle."[133]

While visiting the PRC, the CNL representatives continued to impress the CCP leadership with their earnest commitment to revolution and their professed admiration for Mao Zedong Thought. Much to the delight of his hosts, the CNL's foreign secretary expressed particular interest in China's history of struggle against colonialism. A report circulated by the Chinese People's Institute of Foreign Affairs noted that his "interest in our experience was very great; he studied diligently; he asked many fundamental questions and took detailed notes; his desire to study our experience is very urgent." During his visit, the foreign secretary also told his hosts, "American imperialism is the common enemy of the Chinese and Congolese people and we have a common duty. China's experience is very important and useful to the Congolese people." The institute was less enthusiastic in its characterization of Egide-Davidson Bocheley, the first secretary of the CNL, who it noted "in reality did not have a great interest [in our experiences] and asked very few questions when we introduced our revolutionary experience and during discussions of ballistics." Even if Bocheley failed to feign interest in Mao Zedong Thought, however, he lavished praise on his hosts. "Mao Zedong is not only the liberator of China, he is the liberator of the entire world," he told the Chinese.[134] For CCP officials, these discussions were critical. Beijing was taking the measure of the CNL to see whether the insurgency would bolster Chinese prestige if it triumphed.

When they returned to Africa, the Congolese revolutionaries continued to profess an interest in Maoism, at least during their discussions with Chinese diplomats. After a meeting with Abdoulaye Yerodia Ndombasi, one of the CNL's leading advisers, the Chinese ambassador in Burundi sent an enthusiastic report about the development of the Congolese insurgency to Beijing. He wrote that "after visiting China, researching China's revolutionary experiences, and reading the works of Chairman Mao," the leaders of the CNL had "started to emphasize and summarize their own revolutionary experiences." Moreover, "they all said that China's revolutionary experience was their model." This, the ambassador could only conclude, "was an important development and improvement for the Congolese revolution."[135]

American officials did not know all the details of Chinese efforts to encourage the Congolese insurgency, but they were convinced that the turmoil sweeping the Congo had been orchestrated by an outside power. Although a contingent of Cuban forces led by Che Guevara would ultimately aid the Simbas more significantly and more directly than the PRC, American policy documents about the Congo made few mentions of Cuba and more often expressed concern about China's role.[136] The Simba uprising reached its crescendo just as the Johnson administration was ratcheting up American involvement in Vietnam, making the dispatch of a significant contingent of U.S. forces to a distant African country unthinkable.[137] Nevertheless, several important American officials paid keen attention to Chinese activities in the Congo, and their concerns about Beijing's influence led the United States to become more deeply involved.

The spectacular defection of a Chinese diplomat working in Burundi and his subsequent claims about Beijing's ambitions in Africa played an important role in triggering American suspicions. The episode began on 26 May 1964, when Dong Jiping, the assistant cultural attaché to Burundi, sought sanctuary at the American embassy only a day after his arrival in Bujumbura. The Chinese embassy demanded that Dong be returned and the government of Burundi threatened to cut off relations with Washington, but the United States kept him under its protection. In August, Dong suddenly turned up in New York on a flight from Rome and was granted refugee status in the United States. Both the State Department and the American embassy in Burundi denied playing any role in his escape. On his arrival in the United States, Dong warned Americans about Chinese ambitions in Africa, claiming that China was determined to take over the Congo and use it as a springboard to extend its influence over the entire continent.[138] Dong's alarming testimony sparked other journalists to investigate Chinese activities in Africa. In December, *Life* magazine devoted a major spread to the subject. After traveling to Bujumbura, Roy Rowan, an assistant managing editor for the magazine, reported that Communist China was "turning Burundi into its own subsidized control center from which it can keep Congo boiling." He claimed that the PRC had set up training camps for Tutsi refugees who would be used in both Rwanda and the Congo.[139]

After Dong's defection, several key U.S. officials, notably Undersecretary of State for Political Affairs Averell Harriman, started to worry about Beijing's activities in the Congo and surrounding countries. Harriman asked the director of intelligence and research to prepare a report on the subject. The report itself pointed to the presence of Chinese personnel and advisers in neighboring countries and to linkages between Beijing and leaders of the insurgency. Nevertheless, its authors understood that diverse factors contributed to the uprising in the Congo and did not believe that Beijing's meddling played a major role in precipitating the crisis. They speculated that "while the Chicoms may have contributed an element of sophistication to insurgent activity, the eastern Congo fundamentally collapsed from within. In comparison with indigenous causes of dissidence, the Chicom contribution to the collapse of central government authority probably has nowhere been more than marginal."[140] But rather than accept the report's conclusion, Harriman continued to emphasize the dangers of Chinese involvement. On 13 August, he met with several American diplomats and intelligence officers who worked in different regions of Africa and came away convinced that the Chinese were the key backers of the Congolese insurgency. He reported:

> We have found a number of instruction handbooks on guerilla warfare which are of Chinese origin, translated into French and English, and which were only published in May 1964. It would appear that the success of some rebel groups reflected a higher degree of organization than had characterized earlier rebel operations in the Congo. The tactics they used followed the teachings of [Mao Zedong] which stressed sending in agitators to stir up the young warriors to attack police and security forces. The aim was to destroy central authority in the Congo and create chaos from which only the Communist would benefit.[141]

Harriman's understanding of the Congo crisis overstated China's influence. But this does not change the fact that high-ranking officials genuinely believed Beijing to be the driving force behind Soumialot's revolt.

Washington and its allies soon began taking measures to disrupt Chinese activities in the Congo. When Harriman met with Belgian foreign minister Paul-Henri Spaak in Brussels to discuss the rapidly deteriorating situation in the Congo, the two spoke about the problem of PRC influence in Burundi and agreed to put pressure on Bujumbura to curtail the Chinese presence. Spaak explained that his government was prepared to take specific measures in this regard. He said that the Belgian ambassador would approach the Burundi government, "point out heavy CHICOM involvement in Burundi," and "flatly pose" the choice of either "ceasing to give support to CHICOMS or rebels or having Belgians cease technical and economic aid." Spaak was eager for Washington to adopt the same approach, according to Harriman, who promised American support even though he noted that U.S. influence over the small African country was limited.[142]

Officials in Washington also kept a close eye on Congo-Brazzaville, another country where they believed Chinese advisers were consorting with Congolese revolutionaries. An intelligence estimate written about the country in 1965 likened it to Zanzibar before the creation of Tanzania in that there was "little effective control by any individual or group, but Communists, such as Babu, and pro-Communist toughs have considerable power." The report described what it termed the "militant radicalism" of the country's new political leadership and believed that one manifestation of this was "its apparent willingness to permit the Congo to be used as a base, staging area and transit point for African revolutionary movements against colonial regimes and moderate African states." Although the estimate voiced fears that Moscow as well as Beijing would use Congo-Brazzaville as a staging ground for insurgency, it clearly viewed China as a potentially dangerous adversary in Africa. It noted that "about 10 Chinese officers are instructing Congolese troops in the use of [Beijing]-supplied arms" and that another eighteen officers were reputed to be en route to the country. The CIA suspected that insurgents from other African countries were receiving training in Congo-Brazzaville. It reported that "some recruits of the [Beijing]-backed Union of the Cameroonian population (UPC) have entered the Congo and may be undergoing clandestine warfare training." Eventually, the CIA believed, Congo-Brazzaville was likely to become a "staging area of Soviet and Chinese Communist-supported subversion against colonial or moderate African countries."[143]

American concerns about Chinese influence remained a consideration when the Johnson administration began taking measures to put down the insurgency in mid-1964. In July, the United States and Belgium engineered the replacement of Congolese prime minister Cyrille Adoula with Moïse Tshombe, a skilled tactician who had the virtues of being pro-Western and anti-Communist. Congo's president Joseph Kasa-Vubu, entrusted Tshombe with suppressing the insurgency, and the CIA strengthened the new prime minister's hand through coordinating extensive paramilitary operations with Brussels. American military transports arrived in Leopoldville soon after Tshombe took office with weapons for the mercenary forces he had recruited. The United States intervened most spectacularly in the Congo in November 1964, when the Johnson administration ordered the U.S. Air Force to lift Belgian paratroopers into Stanleyville with the ostensible purpose of rescuing Western hostages. In what came to be known as Operation Dragon Rouge, Belgian soldiers fought alongside Congolese forces freeing dozens of hostages, killing hundreds of insurgents and dealing a serious blow to Soumialot and his allies.[144]

In the weeks leading up to the airlift operation, Harriman had remained watchful of Chinese subversion in the Congo and exerted a significant influence on U.S. policy. In October, he met with the British foreign secretary Gordon Walker to discuss African issues and, during the meeting, "underlined the importance we place on understanding the activities of the Chicoms and the necessity to develop a plan to counter their machinations."[145] Harriman's obsession with Beijing's role in the Congo was important because he played a critical role in lobbying for American intervention in the Congo and drawing up the plans for Operation Dragon Rouge. He pressed for reconnaissance planes to fly over Stanleyville in preparation for a possible paratrooper drop and got Secretary of State Dean Rusk to approve it over the objection of others in the State Department. When Defense Secretary Robert McNamara spoke to the president seeking to persuade him that the paratrooper drop should be carried out, he explained that it was his understanding that the entire operation "evolved out of [Harriman's] talks in Belgium."[146] Harriman, Rusk, and other key officials who pushed Johnson to intervene in the Congo had all expressed deep concern about Chinese involvement in Africa on different occasions.

The operation did not eliminate the insurgency, however, and as long as it persisted, Beijing remained involved—meeting with CNL leaders, offering advice and making limited offers of support. Zhou Enlai met with Soumialot during a June 1965 visit to Tanzania. By that time, CNL forces had suffered serious setbacks. "In every region of the Congo, the situation is very grave," Soumialot told Zhou. "Our country is threatened by imperialism," he continued, explaining that there were "mercenaries and regular forces from the United States, Belgium, Israel, and South Africa" fighting the insurgents. Under such adverse circumstance, the premier encouraged Soumialot and his fellow revolutionaries to emulate China's model of revolution. He predicted that as the United States dispatched forces to Vietnam, its pressure on the Congo would decrease. The CNL should "use this opportunity to mobilize the masses, carry out guerilla warfare, encircle the cities from the countryside, weaken enemy forces, seek assistance from the outside, and strengthen your own forces." Zhou also pledged that if the insurgency persisted in the face of adversity, Beijing would continue to support it. "As long as there is an actual armed struggle, regardless of what region, and how long it lasts, we will spare no effort to provide aid," he told Soumialot.[147]

At the same time, Zhou did not completely approve of the direction that the Congolese insurgency had taken; he hedged his bets to some degree when it came to offering support. The CNL had established a new revolutionary government and Soumialot asked Zhou to recognize it and endorse its participation in international conferences. But Zhou was critical of what he saw as the CNL leadership's tendency to put political and diplomatic issues ahead of waging armed struggle. The premier recommended that the CNL seek recognition from friendly African governments first and approach the PRC again afterward. In the meantime, he urged Soumialot to focus on winning military victories. "Political struggle depends on armed struggle," he advised. "If the armed struggle does not develop then you will be taken advantage of at the negotiating table."[148] A seasoned revolutionary, Zhou recognized that the insurgency in Congo would never follow the Chinese model completely, but he worried that it was deviating from too many of the principles of guerrilla warfare as the CCP understood them.

China's continuing involvement in the Congo remained a source of anxiety for the Johnson administration despite the success of Operation Dragon Rouge. Fears of a Chinese victory in the Congo drove American officials to advocate further intervention to crush the insurgency once and for all. In February 1965, the Counterinsurgency Group invited the U.S. ambassadors to Kenya, Tanzania, and Uganda for a meeting in which they discussed the situation in the troubled African country. The group laid out strategies for enhancing the legitimacy of the Congolese government and containing the insurgency. Cord Meyer Jr., a CIA operative in attendance at the meeting, argued that "if chaos [in the Congo] alone were all we had to fear, then a strong case could be made for our disengagement." But Meyer believed that the struggle in the Congo was linked to a broader Chinese campaign to spread revolution around the world. He explained that "the Chinese Communist[s] saw in the Congo rebellion a great opportunity and were determined if possible to gain a position of commanding influence by support to the rebels." Also present at the meeting was Averell Harriman, who, as could have been expected, struck on the same theme.[149]

A pivotal showdown between the Congolese guerrillas and U.S.-backed forces occurred in the fall of 1965. During the previous summer Cuba had also gotten involved, dispatching a column of volunteers led by the famous revolutionary Che Guevara to train Simba forces. But the Cubans were not able to sufficiently improve the organization or combat effectiveness of the Simbas before a renewed U.S.-led offensive began in September. The CIA assembled 3,000 soldiers and 350 mercenaries and backed them with its own flotilla and air force. Guevara found that the Simbas themselves were losing their will to fight. The insurgents had been intimidated by the strength of the mercenary forces but also placated somewhat by political gestures made in Leopoldville.[150] The result was that by early November, government forces had retaken control of most of the country. Rebel activity continued, but from the perspective of the PRC, the insurgents' failure constituted a serious defeat.[151]

Chinese officials reassessed the situation in the Congo after the government had recaptured most major cities and the Cuban volunteers fled to Tanzania. They were disappointed by the turn of events but not completely discouraged. They blamed the Cubans rather than Mao's ideas for the setbacks. The Chinese embassy in Tanzania argued that the Simbas had faltered because they had been too heavily influenced by other foreign contingents and not gained a sufficient comprehension of Maoist doctrines. The Congolese insurgents had still "not completely accepted our thinking on guerrilla war." He complained that the Simbas had been "unwilling to give up already occupied areas" when necessary and added parenthetically that "the Cuban advisory group had exerted a bad influence on them in this respect." The recent difficulties did not mean that all was lost, however, it simply meant that the PRC would have to redouble its efforts to promote revolution there. "The general situation in the Congo is still beneficial for the development of revolution," the embassy reported. In the future, the PRC would have to help them "sum up the lessons of experience" and "find a more correct military and political path."[152]

Ultimately, of course, the PRC failed to resuscitate the Congolese insurgency. The revolutionary cause was dealt another serious blow on 25 November 1965, when Joseph Mobutu, a right-wing general supported by the United States, seized control of the government. Mobutu used a combination of cooptation and force to quiet dissent and was, at least from the U.S. perspective, highly successful. By 1968, the State Department reported that "the Congo has gone off the list of critical foreign policy headaches" and now enjoyed "excellent" relations with the United States.[153] During the early 1970s, Mobutu's Congo—renamed Zaire—became one of the growing number of conservative Afro-Asian countries that Beijing decided it would be easier to recognize than to overthrow. The two countries established formal relations in 1972, and a year later Mobutu visited the PRC and met with Mao Zedong. During his meeting with the Congolese president, the chairman sheepishly admitted that the PRC had "lost much money and arms attempting to over-throw" him.[154] Like many of Beijing's other efforts to support wars of national liberation in Asia and Africa, it had been an exercise in futility.

———

Beijing's support for insurgencies in Asia and Africa was perhaps the most disastrous element of its Third World activism during the 1960s. Any gains in influence or prestige that the PRC made through its efforts to mentor and aid revolutionaries were ephemeral. Rather than enhancing its stature among revolutionaries, Beijing's efforts to overthrow internationally recognized governments created an enduring legacy of suspicion toward Chinese motives. At the same time, American counterinsurgency programs were, if anything, even more ineffectual. Revolutionaries gained power in Vietnam and Laos, and when they failed in other places, it was more often a result of indigenous circumstances than American policy. By the late 1960s, it was becoming painfully clear that both Chinese and Americans had foolishly chosen to play with the fire of revolutionary nationalism, and in the end, both had gotten burned.

Chapter 9

The Economic Competition, 1962–1968

In 1964, a traveler venturing into the southeastern highlands of the newly independent West African nation Guinea who came on the small town of Macenta would have likely encountered a surprisingly large international contingent. A cadre of young, idealistic American Peace Corps volunteers might be seen working with local farmers, introducing new breeds of poultry and teaching ways to improve vegetable production. Not too far away, a group of highly disciplined Chinese technicians might also be found setting up a tea plantation that could help Guinea become self-sufficient in tea processing. Despite ostensibly pursuing a common objective—the economic development of Guinea—the American and Chinese teams working in this remote, mountainous locale would have avoided virtually any form of contact with each other and remained seemingly oblivious to the other's existence.[1]

Maintaining this physical separation was crucial to both Americans and Chinese working in poor African countries such as Guinea. During the 1960s, the United States and the PRC sought to showcase two distinctive and competing visions of Africa's future through their development projects. Setting up model villages and farms, constructing new factories, and building new systems of roads created highly visible symbols of modernity that could foster admiration for the donor country. These showcases introduced new technologies and new ways of thinking, but they did so in a highly ideological way, inviting people to choose between one vision of development and the other.[2]

Such showcasing figured prominently in China's growing economic involvement in Africa during the 1960s. Driven by its rivalries with Moscow and Washington, Beijing launched a host of aid projects on the continent. Much of this was focused on a few relatively small, poor nations that were formally neutral but had left-leaning political leadership. Before 1968, the bulk of Chinese aid went to Guinea, Tanzania, Mali, Ghana, and Congo-Brazzaville. It most often included building textile mills, matchstick factories, and other facilities that enabled African countries to manufacture essential commodities independently and reduce their reliance on their former colonial masters.[3] Chinese and Africans typically worked side by side on these projects, promoting the idea that the PRC was an anticolonial economic power genuinely devoted to helping Africa achieve economic independence. The PRC derived scant economic benefit from its aid programs, and this was generally not its objective in funding them. The more important goal was to enhance China's status in the region by raising its overall profile and promoting an ideal of Afro-Asian economic cooperation that excluded Moscow and the West.

Although the countries that China focused its aid programs on were small and impoverished, they were not unimportant to Washington. When John F. Kennedy took office, he was determined to engage neutralist African leaders and invested a great deal of time and effort into courting Guinean president Sékou Touré, Tanzanian president Julius Nyerere, and Ghanaian president Kwame Nkrumah, among others. Lyndon B. Johnson carried forward many of these efforts.[4] Even if Africa was not America's top priority, Washington was loath to see Beijing expand its influence on the continent and strove to counter impact of Chinese assistance with its own. American aid programs in Africa were designed to show the benefits of integration into the world economy and liberal, market-driven models of growth. They included projects designed to promote the development and export of natural resources and to transform individual villages into models of commercialized agriculture. Americans hoped that the judicious implementation of these programs would demonstrate the superiority of capitalist development and undermine the appeal of Chinese programs.

Ultimately, Chinese economic aid in Africa bore far less disastrous consequences than the PRC's other efforts to win influence in the Third World. Beijing's aid projects were, in fact, often greeted more favorably than those of its rivals. Africans could discern that Beijing was not entirely wrong to point to the underlying motives behind Western and American assistance. Moreover, the egalitarian ethos of the PRC's aid projects, in which Chinese personnel adapted to African living standards rather than requiring special arrangements, had a strong appeal in impoverished countries such as Guinea and Tanzania. American officials were often frustrated when Beijing's aid projects were received more enthusiastically than Washington's. At the same time, the PRC's victory in this arena was modest. Its projects made a positive impression and enhanced China's prestige, but their influence generally did not extend beyond the small group of African nations where they were implemented. And China was, in the end, no more able to bring economic abundance and prosperity to Africa than its rivals were.

Chinese and American Approaches to Economic Aid in Africa

An atmosphere of cautious optimism prevailed in much of the African continent during the early 1960s as European colonialism collapsed, energetic nationalist leaders gained power, and Africans spoke of rapid progress and building new societies. Many leaders espoused "African socialism," but there was no consensus on what the term meant and its application varied tremendously from country to country.[5] Despite the general optimism about Africa's future, the challenges faced by its new leaders were immense; they included the formidable task of dismantling the structures of economic dependence created by their former colonizers.[6] These leaders craved economic aid projects that could help to liberate their nations from the lingering influence of colonial rule both materially and symbolically. China stepped into this vortex of problems, needs, and ambitions with distinctive answers to the questions Africa faced. Beijing strove to persuade African nations that it could offer a path to economic development and self-reliance that was more suited to their needs and less exploitative than the ones proposed by Washington and Moscow.

The significance that the PRC attached to its economic aid programs is evident from the fact that it maintained them throughout the 1950s and 1960s despite dire economic hardships at home. The PRC remained a relatively poor country during this period with a per capita income of roughly $600.[7] In most cases, its economic circumstances were little better than those of the countries it lavished aid on. Between 1958 and 1962 in particular, the egregious failures of the Great Leap Forward caused massive poverty and famine. Yet, in 1961, a year in which millions of Chinese died of starvation, the PRC doled out more than $100 million in economic aid, including $84 million for Burma and $11 million to Cambodia. In the same year, Beijing exported ten thousand tons of rice to Guinea.[8] Under such circumstances, China's aid programs obviously hurt its economy and people. But CCP officials continued the programs because they believed that economic aid was a responsibility China would need to shoulder if it was to assume a leadership position in the Third World.

After Zhou's visit to Africa in 1963–64, the continent became the focal point of Chinese aid programs, and the PRC eventually surpassed the United States dollar for dollar in aid to some countries. According to an American intelligence estimate, the PRC committed $200 million in aid to Sub-Saharan Africa between 1960 and 1968, excluding its massive $350 million commitment to building a railway linking Tanzania and Zambia. During the same period the Soviet Union committed $450 million while the United States committed $2.1 billion.[9] But in countries that Beijing prioritized, such as Tanzania, Guinea, and Ghana, China and the United States offered comparable aid. In Tanzania, for instance, the United States managed a relatively small aid program that provided roughly $6 million per year.[10] Beijing, by contrast, extended $54.4 million in aid to Dar es Salaam between 1960 and 1968, so the amounts were likely similar on a year-by-year basis.[11] Nevertheless, if it were simply the dollar value of aid that determined its success, American programs would likely have outshined Chinese ones throughout Africa. But this is not what happened.

The reason that Beijing could compete successfully against Washington despite the latter's vastly superior resources was that it understood how to make its aid programs appealing to Africans. The PRC made the most of every aid dollar it spent by strategically devising projects that combined symbolic meanings and political objectives. All Chinese personnel involved in these projects were expected to embody the ideal of Afro-Asian solidarity in handling their tasks and interacting with Africans on the ground. Whether helping to construct factories or establish state farms, the PRC tried to ensure that its projects gained maximum visibility as embodiments of China's commitment to Africa's development and independence. None of these projects could bring Africans self-sufficiency, but they could shape an image of the PRC as a supporter of the cause.

Zhou Enlai gave the clearest articulation of China's aid objectives in Africa during his tour of the continent in 1963–64 when he announced his Eight Principles of Economic and Technical Aid. The announcement came during the premier's visit to Ghana in January 1964 and was given additional publicity elsewhere on the trip. To confer a more official status on the principles, they were formally written into the joint communiqué that Zhou signed with Malian president Modibo Keïta later the same month.[12] Beijing advertised the Eight Principles widely during and after Zhou's trip. The choice to announce them in Ghana had probably been deliberate; its president, Kwame Nkrumah, was perhaps the most influential nationalist leader in sub-Saharan Africa at the time. In an effort to garner further international attention, Chinese propaganda journals such as the *Peking Review* devoted numerous articles to the principals in subsequent weeks.[13]

The Eight Principles were more than a set of guidelines; they were an effort to create a symbolic architecture for aid that would enable China to exert a political as well as economic impact on Africa. Each principle specified varying conditions and terms of Chinese economic assistance, promising in one way or another that Chinese aid projects and the personnel involved in them would be different from those of the PRC's rivals. Zhou's first principle was that Chinese aid would be based on "equal and mutual benefits." It should not be seen "simply as a one-sided grant but as something mutual." Second, Zhou promised that in awarding aid, the PRC would "strictly respect the sovereignty of the receiving country and would not attach any conditions or request any special privileges." The third principle stipulated that Chinese aid would be awarded in the form of interest-free loans with a flexible time period for repayment. The purpose of such aid, the premier explained in the fourth principle, would not be to encourage dependence on China but rather to help recipient countries "embark on the road toward self-reliance and independent economic development." The fifth, sixth, and seventh principles described the nature and form that Chinese development programs would take, and, last, the eighth principle stipulated that experts sent by the PRC to help administer aid projects would have the same living standards as those of the recipient country. They would not make any special requests or enjoy special privileges.[14]

Each of these principles was carefully calculated to appeal to African sensitivities. The premier's insistence that aid should be mutually beneficial reminded Africans that China was not a rich country but a newly independent one with which they waged a shared struggle to overcome the economic legacy of colonialism. Zhou's promise to respect the sovereignty of recipient countries was a not-so-subtle barb at the United States and the Soviet Union, whose aid programs, CCP officials charged, were guided by self-interest. By stressing "self-reliance" and "independent economic development," the premier not only touched on a raw nerve for African countries that had only recently cast off European colonialism but also promoted a system of economic exchange that could exclude the Great Powers. Last, by insisting that Chinese technical experts adapt to local living standards, PRC aid projects would aspire to create a highly visible symbol of China's consanguinity with African nations.

As Chinese aid programs in Africa expanded in the wake of Zhou's visit, Washington took notice. Yet Americans showed little concern about the economic impact of these programs. They knew that China was unlikely to transform the continent into an autarkic sphere. But Americans did worry about the political impact of these programs, and it was often toward countering this impact that Washington directed its efforts. Even before China stepped up its involvement in Africa, U.S. officials had come to recognize that "African states, with few exceptions, are prepared to accept economic aid, regardless of the source, provided that no strings are attached" and that the Communist Bloc was "bound and determined to expand the scale of its economic activities in Africa." According to a widely circulated paper prepared for President Kennedy by the Policy Planning Council in 1961, rather than "futilely trying to outbid bloc aid offers," Washington needed to "concentrate on trying to limit their political impact." This could be accomplished only if the United States carried out a "more vigorous and imaginative aid effort in Africa responsive to the peoples' needs."[15]

American officials argued that a similar approach should be used in response to the sudden expansion of Chinese aid programs in Africa during the mid-1960s. In August 1964, David Dean, deputy director at the Office of

Asian Communist Affairs, circulated a memorandum among several State Department officials working on Asian and African issues with recommendations on the subject. Communist China, he noted, had "more fully emerged over the past several months as a force of some significance in Africa" and that CCP efforts to gain influence on the continent could "be expected to continue and probably increase." But Dean believed that growing CCP involvement in the African region was inevitable. He argued that the "[U.S.] Government must accept the fact that there is relatively little we can do to stop or even curtail such programs." Dean felt strongly that the United States should avoid pressuring African leaders to reject Chinese assistance because doing so would ultimately give the PRC exactly what it wanted—more attention and more status in the region. "U.S. over-reaction to Chinese Communist aid" would "make greater political gains for [Beijing] than the modest aid program that Communist China can afford."[16]

Instead of resorting to overt pressure, Dean advocated a campaign of persuasion to convince African leaders that Chinese assistance was not as altruistic or effective as advertised. Dean suggested that American diplomats "point to the lack of success of some Chinese Communist aid programs elsewhere, to highlight the problems inherent in accepting such aid." Such "educational efforts" could take the form of "discussions with sympathetic or understanding local officials, and, in some cases, through gray propaganda efforts." But Dean recognized that despite their relative subtlety, these negative methods had their limitations. His memo explained that Beijing's aid programs were gaining in popularity vis-à-vis those of the United States because of the "alacrity with which requests for technicians are met by Communist China" and the "modest manner in which Chinese Communist aid personnel live in the host country." These facets of Chinese aid appealed to Africans because they represented "a degree of efficiency and willingness to consider the problems of the host country which recipients sometimes complain is lacking in our programs." He believed that "the most effective means of countering Chinese Communist aid efforts over the long run is, of course, by carrying out our own efforts in as impressive fashion as possible."[17] In short, Americans did not need to eliminate Chinese aid programs in Africa so much as it needed to upstage them.

Although Washington attempted to follow through on Dean's recommendations, it was easier said than done. The reality was that most American technical experts were not willing to live in Africa without special privileges as the Chinese were. Moreover, when it came to devising and implementing aid projects, the American imagination could never seem to transcend the combination of economic interests, excessive bureaucracy, and insensitivity toward indigenous circumstances that so often hampered U.S. development programs elsewhere. The simple and earnest approach taken by Beijing's aid projects often benefited from comparison. In countries such as Guinea, Mali, and Tanzania, American officials themselves testified to this fact.

The Radical States of West Africa

As the CCP identified parts of Africa where its economic aid programs might have a big impact, it saw particularly good prospects in the radical new states of West Africa. These included the former British colony Ghana, as well as two of the poorest new nations in Francophone Africa, Mali and Guinea. The Soviets had first made their presence felt in the region, establishing diplomatic ties with Accra, Bamako, and Conakry by 1960 and providing assistance to all three. Known for their Marxist proclivities, the political leaders of these nations—Sékou Touré, Modibo Keïta, and Kwame Nkrumah—had been shunned by the Eisenhower administration, allowing the Soviets to fill the void left by the end of imperialism. But it was not long before the Soviets began to suffer setbacks in their dealings with this highly nationalistic group of leaders. In Guinea, President Sékou Touré publicly announced his dissatisfaction with Soviet aid programs in August 1961 and expelled the Russian ambassador, Daniel Solod, several months later on charges that he had helped to incite an antigovernment protest. Events in Mali were less dramatic, but frictions surfaced between Soviet and Malian leaders over the direction of Keïta's economic policy and Moscow's reluctance to support some of the programs that Bamako wanted.[18] As the Soviets stumbled, an opportunity presented itself to their rivals.

Both the United States and China were eager to capitalize on the Soviet Union's missteps in West Africa. When the Kennedy administration was inaugurated in 1961, a key foreign policy objective was to replace Eisenhower's antipathy for neutralist African leaders with engagement through personal diplomacy and limited economic assistance. Sékou Touré and Kwame Nkrumah both received invitations to the White House soon after Kennedy took office. Moreover, despite objections from some of his advisers, Kennedy provided funding for the Volta River Project in Ghana and a smaller dam in Guinea.[19] Beijing, for its part, had enjoyed good relations with the radical West African states before they became disillusioned with Moscow. In 1960 alone, it had signed treaties of friendship with both Guinea and Ghana, along with an agreement on technical and economic cooperation with Guinea.[20] The decline of Soviet influence in the region occurred just as tensions between the PRC and the USSR were beginning to escalate. Beijing hoped that it could pry these newly independent West African countries out of the grasps of the two superpowers.

Guinea was an early venue for Sino-American competition in Africa. Both the CCP and the Kennedy administration were interested in winning the loyalties of its young, nationalistic president, Sékou Touré. In Washington, Kennedy expressed a genuine admiration for Touré and viewed him as a great potential influence over the rest of Africa. One intelligence report informed the president that Guinea "occupied a symbolic position which gives it a political importance out of all proportion to its size."[21] Guinea carried symbolic importance to Beijing as well. In 1960, Touré had become the first African head of state to visit the PRC, and his country was the first in Africa to receive economic and technical assistance from China. "Your status and our status is the same; our destiny is the same," Mao Zedong had told Touré during his visit.[22] Guinea's early recognition of the PRC and made it an important proving ground for Beijing's approach to the continent.

The Macenta tea factory, one of the earliest Chinese aid projects in Africa, was emblematic of Beijing's overall approach. The Chinese provided both financing and advisers for this project because they were confident that, if carried out correctly, it would reflect favorably on the PRC and boost its prestige. A survey team dispatched to Macenta in April 1962 and charged with assessing the feasibility of the project recommended support because "although the amount of money spent would be small, the influence would be big." The project could meet an urgent requirement of the host country, which had called for increased tea production in its three-year economic plan, and therefore earn China the gratitude of the country's leadership.[23]

Simply offering the aid was not enough, however; it would also be critical that Chinese personnel working on the project embody the ideals of the Eight Principles. The team reported: "In our interactions with the Guinean government and officials we often felt that they did not pay attention to manners and did not understand etiquette." Sometimes it was "easy to become angry" because their indigenous counterparts had the habit of arriving a half-hour or an hour late for meetings. Chinese working in the country would need to understand that such habits had "arisen from a long period of imperialist rule" and to "maintain a friendly, forgiving attitude." Although a hint of condescension may be detected in Chinese attitudes, PRC officials were determined to make sure that such sentiments did not seep into their dealings with the people they worked with there. The leader of the survey team emphasized that technicians sent to Macenta would need to "exercise patience and cannot become irritable."[24]

The survey team cited its experiences in dealing with Guineans as worthy of study and emulation by other Chinese technicians bound for the country. Its report boasted that the team had left a favorable impression on the Guinean masses and that it had been told by people around the country that "in the past white advisers only talked about theory, they never lifted a hand, they didn't understand us, they also derided and ridiculed us." But the Guineans offered praise for the Chinese specialists who "worked with their own hands and could learn about things when there was a question that needed an answer." This was proof, according to the team's report, that "our work had already left a definite influence on the masses and increased the friendship between our two countries."[25] These experiences made the Chinese optimistic that Guinea was a country where their approach would bear fruit.

Within a few years, Chinese aid projects such as the tea plantation were increasingly drawing praise from Guinean officials and being implemented successfully in several regions. In January 1966, the economic minister gave a speech offering praise for the tea plantation as well as several other projects the PRC had recently completed, including match and cigarette factories in Conakry and a tobacco plantation near Beyla, a small southeastern town.[26] The match and cigarette factories employed more than six hundred people and, even according to American reports, performed well. By 1968, Beijing had also financed the construction of the two-million-dollar Kinkon Dam in Pita prefecture.[27] As Chinese aid to Guinea rose dramatically, American officials saw the need for an American assistance program that could undercut Beijing's appeal. One U.S. embassy official in Conakry pushed for "the continuance of American sympathy for Guinea's non-alignment policy" and a "thoughtful aid program designed to aid Guinea's economic development" because they would "probably over-balance any communist activities currently being carried out in Guinea."[28]

Washington attempted to woo Conakry with a very different style of aid project. It made a major effort to encourage both American and Guinean private enterprise to participate in the country's economic development. The USAID administered an investment guaranty program specifically to assuage the concerns of American firms about moving capital into a country where the prospects for instability appeared high and whose government had been prone to nationalistic economic measures. The program guaranteed investments by U.S. entities that could develop the "economic resources and productive capacities of Guinea."[29] Whereas Chinese aid projects sought to put on display the virtues of self-reliance and Afro-Asian solidarity, the USAID hoped that its projects would exhibit the benefits of economic integration and private entrepreneurship.

Among the first ventures receiving support from this program was a partnership between the Harvey Aluminum Company and Touré's government to mine and sell bauxite from the country's well-endowed Boké region. Under the arrangement that was worked out, the two became co-owners of the Guinea Bauxite Company with Harvey acquiring a 51 percent share and the Guinean government acquiring a 49 percent share. Such a project, the American ambassador believed, had the potential to provide a new source of foreign exchange, raise the value of Guinea's exports, and help it make the first step toward the development of an integrated aluminum industry.[30] It would not only extract a strategic mineral but also link Guinea to the world market while having a liberalizing impact on its economy. Of course, the project served America's economic and strategic interests, but at the same time, it was intended to show Guineans a version of "mutually beneficial" aid that was very different from the one espoused by the Chinese.

Other U.S. assistance programs in Guinea focused on agricultural resource development and rice land rehabilitation. These programs aimed to increase agricultural productivity through experimenting with different seeds and crops and distributing the most successful varieties to farmers. The USAID and Peace Corps volunteers worked with Guinea's Ministries of Rural Economy and Economic Development and local research institutes to find which seeds would be most successful in Guinea's different regions and climates and then promote their widespread use.[31] At the heart of these projects was a technocratic vision of how Guinea could be modernized. American science and technology would help Guinean farmers to grow more prosperous while transforming the landscape through the introduction of higher-yielding seeds and crops. America's technological prowess would be put on display, inspiring admiration for the United States.

The problem with American aid projects in Guinea was not that they were completely unsuccessful but that they were often less effective as showcases than were Chinese projects. The Chinese tended to labor intensively on turnkey projects that produced visible results in a short time. American aid programs, in contrast, often took more time to create benefits that Guineans could see. By 1966, the Harvey Aluminum Company had still not gotten mining operations under way in Boké owing to a variety of contractual and technical issues.[32] Agricultural assistance projects were welcomed by Touré's government and sometimes led to fruitful collaboration between USAID agronomists and local farmers. At the same time, these projects required a period of trial and error, and some of the seeds and crops that were tried failed to produce results.[33] At the broader level, the USAID's efforts to inspire faith in American technological prowess did not capture the imagination of Guinean officials as well as the somewhat more earnest vision of mutually beneficial Afro-Asian economic cooperation that undergirded Chinese aid projects.

American officials working on the ground in Guinea found that although U.S. assistance was appreciated, Guineans were not shy about telling them whose approach they thought was having a greater impact. Cables from the

U.S. embassy in Conakry to the State Department reported on the favorable reactions that Chinese aid was eliciting. In November 1964, the embassy noted that Guinea's attitude toward the Soviets and European Communist countries was "correct but somewhat cool," while its relations with China appeared "increasingly friendly." The Chinese, it continued, had "been successful in presenting themselves as a 'revolutionary' nation fighting for economic independence and development." In part as a result of Beijing's aid programs, Conakry had come to endorse Communist China's entry into the United Nations, and Guineans "constantly praise[d] the working techniques of the Chicoms."[34] One USAID official who made a field trip to Macenta in late 1964 found that Guinean officials were full of praise for Chinese aid projects but less enthused by American ones. He was told by local officials that Guineans "have more respect for Chinese know-how than they do for American know-how." This was attributable to the fact that "the Chinese live[d] in Macenta, whereas the Americans work[ed] from Conakry—which seems so far removed from everyday life."[35]

Some American officials later acknowledged that Beijing had simply possessed a better grasp of the projects Guinea wanted and needed. Robinson McIlvaine, who served as the U.S. ambassador in Conakry between 1966 and 1969, remembered that the Chinese were "very unobtrusive." He added: "They had a big group there, because they were doing major projects. They were building a big cultural center, had built a tobacco plant and a hydroelectric project up-country." During meetings with the ambassador, President Touré praised the Chinese for being "very discreet" because they did not "come around and rape our women and get drunk on the streets and so forth." By contrast, McIlvaine believed that Americans were "trying to do too much" and that Guineans had not been "ready for any of the kind of projects we were trying to do."[36]

Although American aid programs in Guinea were foundering by the mid-1960s, a bizarre incident in October 1966 led to their termination and gave the Chinese the opportunity to strengthen their influence. In Ghana, a military government had recently overthrown Kwame Nkrumah, and the deposed president fled to Guinea. Seeking to force Conakry to turn Nkrumah over, the new military regime ordered the kidnapping of the Guinean foreign minister, Louis Lansana Beavogui, when his Pan-Am flight landed in Accra en route to an Organization of African Unity meeting. Possibly because the flight was operated by Pan-Am, Touré's government immediately blamed the United States for the incident and detained the ambassador for a week in the American embassy.[37] Although American diplomats resolved the situation, suspicions lingered that Washington had been involved, in part because the CIA was widely rumored to have played a role in Nkrumah's ouster.[38]

The damage done to U.S.-Guinean relations by the kidnapping had immediate ramifications for American aid programs. On 8 November, Touré told the American ambassador that the seventy-five Peace Corps volunteers working in Macenta would have to leave Guinea within a week. He demanded that Pan-Am cease all flights to and from Conakry and called for the immediate deportation of any "provocative" U.S. nationals. Last, he announced that the United States was "welcome to reduce aid" and that his government would not tolerate "economic blackmail." After receiving a report from Ambassador McIlvaine about the episode, Walt Rostow recommended not only that the Peace Corps be withdrawn but also that the ambassador "advise all private U.S. citizens and AID contract personnel to leave" and "make arrangements to cut Embassy and AID mission personnel to essential minimum."[39] While Chinese aid programs thrived, the USAID had virtually capitulated in Guinea.

Economic aid competition between Beijing and Washington in neighboring Mali followed a similar course, with the PRC ultimately becoming the small, landlocked nation's most significant benefactor. With a population of four million and a literacy rate of only 3 percent, Mali had virtually no skilled manpower, infrastructure, or natural resources. Its major cash crop, peanuts, had to be transported over difficult terrain because the railroad that once connected landlocked Mali to the coast via Senegal had fallen into disrepair.[40] After it gained independence in 1960, the country's circumstances were dire, and Bamako was eager for aid from both the East and the West.

Although Mali was neither economically nor strategically vital to the United States, President Kennedy took an interest in it as he tried to win over newly independent African nations. During his first year in office, the president held two meetings with high-ranking Malian officials, with Minister of State Jean-Marie Kone in July 1961 and with President Modibo Keïta in September. At both meetings, Malian officials brought up the subject of American development aid. Kone told the president that Mali was about to launch a three-hundred-million-dollar Five-Year Plan and that "his government was counting on U.S. help." Kennedy assured Kone that he was "very sympathetic to Mali's development aspirations" and that the United States "would do what it could to help."[41]

Beijing, for its part, carefully assessed the situation in Mali in 1962 and concluded that a real opportunity existed for its aid programs to have an impact there. The Soviets, it noted, continued seeking to disrupt Sino-Malian relations but had become increasingly unpopular. "Unreconciled to their failure in Guinea," the Soviets "invested even more money in Mali in order to cultivate an example of peaceful transition [to socialism] and combat our [Chinese] influence." But the Soviet Union's "great power chauvinism, unscrupulousness, and double-faced saying without doing had left a bad impression on every group in Malian society." President Keïta had complained openly that when Soviet technicians came to Mali, they "want refrigerators, air conditioners and cars . . . you can see the vestiges of colonialism on them." Because of this, "Soviet prestige had already begun to decline and the people's faith in the Soviets had been shattered."[42]

The United States was a more troublesome foe. American imperialists, it explained, "feigned benevolence but employed insidious two-faced methods that were crafty and covert." Although U.S. aid commitments to Mali were not large, Washington was "throwing out a long line to catch a big fish" or, in other words, adopting a patient, long-term strategy with the hope that it would reap a big reward. Under its strategy of "awarding small favors," the United States was "giving a few commodities as gifts and using them as bribes to curry favor." Unfortunately, the report continued, Malians "did not clearly recognize the danger" of American imperialism and "lacked vigilance." Instead, they "looked forward to the United States and West Germany giving them more aid and their fantasy about American imperialism was especially great."[43]

But even if the Americans were more formidable adversaries than the Soviets, Beijing realized that the conditions driving Bamako to seek U.S. aid also made Chinese assistance valuable. The CCP could accept Mali's eagerness to have aid from any source as a necessary evil. Its "three-sided aid requests" to the West, the Communist Bloc, and other Afro-Asian countries were part of its unavoidable strategy to "salvage its livelihood from the cracks." Nevertheless, Bamako still needed China's "unselfish aid," which would help Mali "to solve its difficulties and set up a model that the Malian government can show to the public as an example to follow."[44] The Chinese hoped that setting up visible aid projects as models would draw attention to the benefits of Sino-African cooperation.

When they selected and implemented aid projects for Mali, Chinese officials astutely recognized that producing tangible results swiftly would be important. "Mali is an important point of struggle between us and the revisionists and imperialists," the Chinese embassy in Bamako reported to Beijing in February 1964. Mali's most "basic" need in terms of aid projects was, of course, "quality," but its most "urgent" need was "speed," meaning projects that would have an immediate impact. "If we cannot surpass the revisionists and imperialists in terms of speed," the embassy wrote, "we will have many difficulties in the struggle against imperialism and in winning the trust of the Malian people." It therefore recommended that a range of proposed aid projects, including a glass factory, a cement plant, and a food-processing plant, be launched soon.[45]

Seeking to outstrip and outshine its rivals in Mali, the PRC set up new aid projects with great speed and efficiency. Its successes received wide publicity from both the Chinese and Malian governments. In 1967, the *People's Daily* boasted that a cigarette factory, a sugar factory, and a matchstick factory had been completed ahead of schedule and that a spinning factory and movie theater were under construction. The paper included numerous quotations from Malian factory workers praising the patience and dedication of Chinese technicians.[46] By 1968, China had completed its largest project in Mali, a $7.8 million textile complex that reduced Mali's textile imports by $1 million annually.[47] These projects could not lift Malians out of poverty or improve the country's economic growth rate. They did, however, provide powerful symbols of rapid progress that were readily visible to indigenous workers and government officials. And Beijing seemed to recognize that the symbolic power of aid projects, more than anything else, boosted the prestige of the donor nation.

Ensuring the proper comportment of Chinese specialists was a concern for the PRC in Mali as it had been in Guinea. In Mali, too, Beijing demanded that its teams foster solidarity with native workers and farmers by adapting to their culture and living conditions. One report covering Chinese agricultural specialists described the group's living conditions: "Chinese specialists lead a plain, hardworking life; they bear the burden willingly. They persevere in their work in the field while braving 50-degree [Celsius] heat. When they go on trips they often go on foot, they endure hunger, at night they endure mosquito bites completely without complaint. They never make requests about their living conditions; they didn't ask for fans, air conditioners, or refrigerators."[48] Even if the report exaggerated the hardships, Beijing unquestionably prided itself on the ability of its personnel to endure difficult conditions and reject the privileges demanded by the Soviets and Americans.

The activities of these Chinese specialists commanded the attention not only of Malians, according to the report, but also of neighboring African countries: "They received positive evaluations throughout Mali and caused people in neighboring countries to pay attention. In the hinterland of West Africa, they used industrious labor and first-rate work and behavior to give publicity to Marxism-Leninism and Mao Zedong Thought, embody the spirit of proletarian internationalism, and exerted a relatively large influence."[49] Although the report obviously emphasized positive contributions, it was nevertheless a clear statement of Beijing's goals and the image it wished to project. Through enduring travails while remaining sensitive to the needs of Malians, Chinese specialists personified the ideological agenda of the PRC and advertised the idea of Sino-African solidarity.

Concerned about growing Chinese influence in Mali, Washington took measures to undercut the appeal of Beijing's aid programs, but they were largely ineffective. American officials did not pressure Bamako to reject

Chinese aid, aware that doing so could easily backfire. They did, however, try to persuade Malians that the Chinese model was not as well suited for their country as Beijing would have them believe. When the Malian government sent a goodwill delegation to the United States to discuss American assistance and other issues in June 1965, the secretary of state and other high-ranking American officials met personally with members of the delegation. The Americans were quick to bring up the upsurge in Chinese influence that had occurred in Mali during the previous two years. Governor Averell Harriman, the U.S. ambassador-at-large, told the delegation that if Mali "wishes to accept Chinese aid, it is free to do so and we will not complain." He subtly cautioned them, however, asking why they thought that they "could get good advice from the Chinese Communists who have had so little success in the field of agriculture." He reminded them that "Karl Marx was a city boy" and that Japan and Taiwan, both of which had systems of private landownership, had achieved much higher rates of agricultural productivity than Communist China had.[50] By comparing the PRC with Japan and Taiwan, Harriman sought to persuade the Malians that the Chinese model would not succeed in Africa and prevent them from being seduced by the PRC.

Malian officials, for their part, tried to use American concerns about growing Chinese influence to goad Washington into providing more aid. When Secretary of State Rusk brought up the issue of China's growing presence in Mali during a meeting with Hamacire N'Doure, the minister of cooperation, N'Doure explained that his country was "like a person who is drowning and grasps at anything that is thrown at him which might help." During the meeting he tried to make Rusk understand the appeal of the PRC. He told the secretary that on gaining independence, Mali "had very little to work with and everything remained to be done." The government had drawn up a development plan and requested aid from every diplomatic mission stationed in Bamako. N'Doure told Rusk that the "Chinese moved in very quickly and agreed to accept responsibility for many of the projects." According to the minister, Malians had no particular affinity for Chinese aid; they in fact wanted "nothing better than that the United States come in to take the place of the Chinese."[51] It was Beijing's speed, initiative, and responsiveness to Mali's needs that was giving its aid projects such great luster.

The United States made a modest commitment to providing Mali with economic assistance, in part to contest Chinese influence. American aid projects were also intended to have a demonstration effect. One of the USAID's most ambitious efforts in Mali was its Village Development Project. The agency selected Djoliba, a village of 1,500 inhabitants located near the capital, Bamako, as its model village. The purpose was to show the benefits of planning, self-help, and improved village facilities. Some of the villagers were trained in self-help techniques and construction. The USAID also encouraged the development of village handicrafts and small industries that could generate profits and instill a sense of commercialism. Djoliba was made to stand apart physically from other villages through the destruction of its old dwelling compounds and the construction of modern, new houses. The model village with its "open spaces and broad landscaped avenues" stood in contrast to the "traditional" villages, which were strewn with "mud huts and narrow, unsanitary twisting lanes." Ultimately, American officials hoped, the renovated village would take "on an aspect of the new emerging Africa," becoming a symbol of the benefits of Western technology and entrepreneurial values.[52]

Although the Village Development Project might have created a mini-spectacle of capitalist modernity, it did not produce the intended results and did not draw great praise from either Malian officials or the local population. Originally, the USAID had intended to use Djoliba as a model for renovating and transforming other villages throughout the country. But the Malian government was unenthused by such plans and did not apply for funds to continue the program after 1965.[53] While USAID reports—at least the ones that have been declassified—did not include many details about the long-term reception and impact of the program, reasons for the lack of enthusiasm can be surmised. Although reports claimed that the villagers in Djoliba eventually felt a sense of pride in their new houses, this apparently occurred only after much persuasion. Initially, the destruction of traditional dwellings was "a very solemn occasion and one met with an air of sentimental reluctance."[54] Overcoming such sentiments in village after village would have likely proved a difficult task. Moreover, American technicians never lived in the village; instead they tried to secure the most comfortable possible working conditions for themselves. They initially planned to construct a special building with an "avant garde plastic structure" to house the program's headquarters and technicians.[55] Although this plan was abandoned when it became clear that more model villages would not be constructed, U.S. technicians never really got their hands dirty.[56]

American officials could often sense, much to their frustration, that the PRC's approach to aid was winning more hearts and minds. They sometimes attributed this to the defects of Malian officials rather than to the flaws of USAID programs. C. Roberts Moore, who served as the U.S. ambassador to Mali between 1965 and 1968, recollected that it "was very difficult to deal with anybody in the government below the level of the secretary general of a minister, simply because they weren't equipped, either educationally or, let's say, psychologically to deal with problems that required responsibility or decisions."[57] According to Moore, this often made the implementation of American aid projects highly inefficient. He remembered that the United

States had agreed to give Mali several million dollars to build a school, which had been designed by a prominent architectural firm. But for the United States asking the Malians to "examine the plans" and "give us their suggestions" proved difficult and time-consuming. The result, the ambassador remembered, was that "three years after my arrival, the project was still pending." But in "the meantime, the Chinese had come in, built a textile factory, had it opened and operating, and we still hadn't turned the first shovel on our school." Eventually, USAID abandoned its plans to build the school because it realized that "the maintenance on the buildings that we had in mind would have been so great that the Malians would never have been able to meet it out of their budget."[58]

Moore attributed Beijing's success to the Chinese having simply constructed their factory without "troubling the Malians to get their views on whether the construction ideas were sound or not."[59] What Moore failed to understand was the intrinsic and understandable appeal of aid projects that could be completed swiftly in an impoverished country like Mali. And Malians quite understandably were more inspired by Chinese technicians who patiently imparted them with new expertise and skills than they were with American diplomats who could only communicate with high-ranking officials in the government. By 1965, American intelligence reported flatly that China was gaining prestige swiftly in Mali as a result of its aid programs. In February, the CIA issued a report entitled "Mali—[Beijing]'s Leading African Booster," which explained that the "major leaders of Mali's Marxist-oriented regime view Chinese aid and example as particularly suited to their country's needs." These leaders had consequently become more supportive of Beijing in the arena of international politics. Seydou Kouyate, the minister of economic and financial coordination, was quoted as saying that "it is inconceivable to speak of Chinese neo-colonialism." The CIA also reported that Bamako had "already become the continent's most enthusiastic public backer of [Beijing], even hailing the Chinese nuclear weapons program, despite its own adherence to the test ban treaty."[60]

By the mid-1960s Beijing had rapidly emerged rather unexpectedly as an influential force in left-leaning West African countries. The PRC garnered goodwill in Guinea and Mali through implementing relatively small-scale projects that had an immediate impact while keeping an eye on how its personnel operated in the field. Despite superior resources, Americans failed to persuade Africans that Western models of development had more to offer. At the same time, the relatively small scale of Chinese projects made it difficult for the PRC to completely sideline its rivals, which were capable of much grander schemes. In Tanzania, however, Beijing offered more diverse forms of aid on a larger scale.

Tanzania

Tanzania would become perhaps the most significant venue for competition between Chinese and American aid programs in Africa. The Tanzanian president Julius Nyerere was a highly regarded African nationalist with leftist tendencies and modernizing ambitions. Despite the occasionally radical tone of his speeches and writings, Nyerere always maintained an interest in receiving aid from both the Free World and the Communist Bloc and thought that Tanzanians needed to study both sides. He wrote, "We would be stupid to reject everything or everyone coming out of the West because that is the home of capitalism; we would be stupid to reject everything the communists do." Nyerere argued that African socialism was "neither of these things." His citizens could "learn from both—and from other political systems—without trying to copy or seek their approval."[61] Beijing and Washington both believed that swaying an important but wavering African leader like Nyerere to their side would carry symbolic value even if it did not produce economic or strategic benefits.

The Kennedy administration unquestionably felt a sense of urgency about establishing American influence in Dar es Salaam. Samuel H. Butterfield, a Foreign Service officer working with USAID in Tanzania during the 1960s, remembered that "Nyerere was one of the African leaders for whom there were great expectations for level-headed leadership inspired by a vision of an important future and important changes on the African continent."[62] Some American officials argued that extending U.S. influence over Nyerere and Tanzania would be crucial to shaping the economic trajectory of the African region. William Leonhart, the U.S. ambassador to the country, explained that the influence of the country's "successful example could importantly affect prospects for the new states of East, Central and Southern Africa likely to emerge in the next few years for more integrated development and political or economic federation in the area; and for the influence of the U.S. in those events."[63]

Early in his presidency, Kennedy courted Nyerere and began American aid programs in Tanganyika, which, as described in the previous chapter, shortly merged with Zanzibar to form Tanzania. The president invited Nyerere to the White House soon after he took office, and the two met on 15 July 1961, making Nyerere one of the first foreign guests to meet with the new president. At the time, Tanganyika had still not formally achieved its independence from Great Britain, but Kennedy promised that once it did so, U.S. aid would be forthcoming.[64] During the visit, the United States made a $10 million aid commitment to Tanzania, which, one USAID officer working in Africa explained, was "a substantial amount of money for a tropical African country" in the early 1960s.[65]

But the Chinese were equally drawn to Nyerere and hoped to prevent Washington and its allies from controlling the economic destiny of newly independent Tanganyika. Beijing and Dar es Salaam normalized diplomatic relations on the day that Tanganyika gained its independence from Great Britain in December 1961.[66] In subsequent months Chinese diplomats began cultivating its leaders and making tentative offers of aid. He Ying, the first PRC ambassador to Tanganyika, made an effort to meet with Julius Nyerere in 1962 even though Nyerere had resigned from the office of prime minister and held no official position in the government at the time.[67] In May 1962, Ambassador He met with Oscar Kambona, Tanganyika's foreign minister and a well-known African nationalist. Although the two did not discuss economic aid explicitly, their four-hour conversation put Beijing in a supportive frame of mind toward Dar es Salaam. One of the more radical members of Nyerere's cabinet, Kambona voiced his support for national liberation movements in Africa and denounced American imperialism. Afterward, the ambassador enthusiastically reported to Beijing on Kambona's independent posture and hostility toward colonialism. Given the country's important position in Africa, "maintaining a certain degree of contact and cooperation" would "not only be useful for winning over and influencing Tanganyika but also for the development of our work in the region."[68] Like the United States, the PRC perceived newly independent Tanganyika as a critical player in shaping the future of Africa and was keen on establishing a meaningful presence there.

Several prominent Tanzanians participated in new Chinese programs that brought African guests to tour the PRC's cities and communes launched after Zhou's 1963–64 trip to the continent. The goal of these visits was to put the achievements of Chinese Communism on display and convince African leaders that the CCP's models of agricultural and industrial development had relevance to Africa. The Tanzanian response appears to have been highly favorable. In June 1964, Tanzania's vice president, Rashidi Kawawa, spent eleven days in the PRC touring the mainland with Chinese leaders. Party officials arranged a tour of Chinese industry and agriculture for Kawawa and his entourage, accompanying them on visits to several factories and a commune. The tour seems to have produced its intended effect. According to a report filed with the Foreign Ministry, members of the Tanzanian delegation had told their hosts that the results achieved by the PRC since 1948 were "astonishing" and "a great encouragement to us." Vice President Kawawa added that he had "learned many things from China's experiences that would be useful for Tanzania." The visit boosted the Tanzanians' enthusiasm for Chinese aid, and they requested assistance from Beijing before their visit ended. Kawawa explained, "Tanzania has coal and iron, but right now it needs technical assistance." He hoped that Chinese experts "could start work in Tanzania soon."[69]

During Kawawa's visit Chinese officials also labored to dissuade the Tanzanians from accepting American assistance, arguing that Washington did not understand the predicament of postcolonial societies. For evidence, he pointed to a recent struggle between Beijing and Washington to win over another newly independent Afro-Asian country—Burma—by aiding in the construction of cotton-spinning factories. According to Zhou, the factory built by the United States had been planned based on American cotton. Thus, even after the factory was finished, the Burmese government still had to buy cotton from the United States. When the American factory continued to lose money, Burma's leader Ne Win approached the PRC for aid in building another factory. In contrast to America's self-serving approach, Zhou explained, the PRC had helped the Burmese to build a new factory that was "based on indigenous circumstances," and the result was that the factory earned profits.[70] Zhou's ingeniously crafted allegory of Chinese success and American failure in another postcolonial society was also an argument for favoring Chinese aid.

Yet Zhou knew that the proving grounds for his claims would be in Tanzania itself. American and Chinese aid programs in Tanzania often sought to win over the same segments of the country's population, albeit through very different approaches. In Tanzania, agriculture, which included both subsistence and commercial farming, was the most significant sector of the economy, and improving living standards without paying attention to this area was unimaginable.[71] Beijing and Washington both made agricultural assistance a top priority. They competed for the loyalties of the Tanzanian farmer through aid projects emphasizing distinctive priorities and values. Washington sought to demonstrate the benefits of reorganizing agricultural production to meet the demands of the market while Beijing devised projects that could showcase the advantages of greater collectivization. The conflicting guidance offered by American and Chinese advisers on this issue fit squarely within broader debates throughout the Third World at the time between advocates of commercial and planned farming.

The American approach was to build Tanzanian agriculture from the ground up. It sought to empower and educate small farmers, thereby enabling them to produce and sell their products more efficiently. Samuel Butterfield recalled that Kennedy era aid projects were "aimed primarily at helping the rural engine of growth in Tanzania, which was the small farm family." He believed that the typical Tanzanian small farmer was a "real entrepreneur" who "responded to market opportunities."[72] Americans inevitably held that the best way to assist these farm families was to strengthen their connections to the market. Building and improving the country's limited system of roads was critical to this objective. Thus, a significant portion of Kennedy's

$10 million commitment to Tanzania went toward the construction of "farm to market feeder roads." In addition, the USAID imported some $1.5 million worth of road culverts and trained Peace Corps volunteers to install them in critical areas.[73] The new roads would enable farmers in selected areas of the country to profit more easily from commercial enterprise and create a model for the rest of the country to follow.

The PRC's aid program created agricultural models of a very different kind. Beijing sought to demonstrate that collective farming informed by the Chinese experience was more likely to enable Tanzania to achieve self-sufficiency. It sponsored the construction of several large state farms during the 1960s and 1970s. The first of these, the Ruvu State Farm, came about as a result of agreements signed during Vice President Kawawa's visit to the PRC in 1964. The farm spanned seven thousand acres along the Ruvu River and had areas dedicated to paddy rice, fruit trees, and livestock. Like Chinese cooperatives, the Ruvu State Farm was designed to mobilize large numbers of workers to carry out projects that were considered too difficult or complex for smaller individual farms. It contained laborers' camps that could accommodate two hundred workers and clubs and schools for the workers and their families.[74] Beijing also assisted with the construction of the Upenja State Farm in Zanzibar. Chinese technicians arrived on the island in 1965 and assisted with the tasks of clearing thirteen hundred acres of wilderness and converting it into farmland. By providing training for Zanzibari technicians, including harvester operators, machine repairmen, and tractor drivers, China helped to establish Tanzania's first mechanized farm.[75]

Although Tanzanians were willing to listen to American advice, the PRC had a deeper influence. Zhou Boping, who became the chargé d'affaires at the Chinese embassy in Dar es Salaam in 1966 and ambassador in 1967, remembers accompanying Nyerere on a visit to Ruvu. He found the president "extremely satisfied and proud" that the Ruvu farm project had "succeeded in reclaiming land, planting rice, and enabling Tanzania to become self-sufficient in rice production."[76] Other Tanzanians were impressed by how Chinese technicians embraced a standard of living that was harsh and simple compared to those of their European competitors. Ali Sultan Issa, who served as the minister of education, youth, and culture in Zanzibar, remembered that the "Chinese cultivated rice with the people but the Europeans would not." Although "each country helped in its own way," Issa explained, "the Chinese were more akin to us; they lived in the fields, planted with us, and won the hearts of the people."[77]

By the late 1960s, as growing numbers of Tanzanian officials gained exposure to the PRC, they became even more enamored of its agricultural model. In 1966, a team of Tanzanian officials that included Nyerere's older brother toured the PRC and found much to commend. They were reported to have said that "China was truly amazing," in that its agriculture had developed so swiftly and was set up so well. They had been, at least according to official reports, "greatly inspired" by the farming machines they had seen in an agricultural exhibition. Ultimately, they attributed the success of Chinese agriculture to Mao Zedong's leadership and expressed their conviction that Tanzania had much to learn from China's experience.[78]

Roughly one year after the visit, President Nyerere made his Arusha Declaration and began implementing his much-studied *ujamaa* program.[79] Under *ujamaa*, the government nationalized industries, banks, and raw materials. The program's most important objective, however, was the transformation of the Tanzanian countryside. The government planned to resettle the country's agricultural population into model villages with planned housing layouts and designs. The villages would be characterized by collective ownership of property and communal farming.[80] Some aspects of *ujamaa* bore a clear resemblance to Maoism: it saw the peasantry as the most important agent for national reconstruction, it employed sharp anticolonial rhetoric, and it sought to inculcate citizens with its own distinctive variety of socialism.[81]

By the late 1960s, American aid officials felt impotent to stop what they considered Tanzania's unfortunate move toward collectivized agriculture. American officials greeted the Arusha Declaration with great dismay. The USAID director in Tanzania, Samuel Butterfield, believed that the plan reflected "another fundamental flaw in Nyerere's vision for his centrally-planned African socialism." He criticized Arusha as a "very sad thing."[82] Although American officials could see that Arusha was not simply an effort to replicate Chinese agricultural policies, they rightly noted—often with predictable remorse—that Beijing had exerted a good deal of influence on the policy. Francis McNamara, an economic officer at the U.S. embassy in Dar es Salaam during the 1960s, thought that Nyerere's *ujamaa* villages "were not quite rural communes but the Chinese influence was obvious." Nyerere's agricultural policies eventually became one of several factors that contributed to American disillusionment with his government. McNamara further reflected, "Nyerere lost my sympathy (because I really did have a high regard for him) when he forced people into Ujamaa villages."[83]

Chinese aid to Tanzania was not confined to agriculture, however. It gained popularity in other areas as well, sometimes despite its negligible economic impact. One of the most famous Chinese aid projects carried out in Tanzania was the Friendship Textile Mill, whose construction was funded by a £2,500,000 interest-free loan from the PRC. Erected in Dar es Salaam's industrial area, it was completed in 1968. The mill would eventually form the basis for the Tanzania China Friendship Textile Company when China started to invest aggressively in Africa during the 1990s.[84] What made the mill so appealing during the 1960s was that it promised to sever one of the most enduring sources of Tanzania's economic dependence on Europe. Although the country had been a significant producer of cotton as a British colony, Great Britain had simply extracted raw materials, never constructing any facilities where cotton could be spun into cloth. Instead, processing occurred overseas and finished cloth was sold in Tanzania at prices that were much higher than those obtained for the cotton. With the mill, Tanzania could produce its own textiles and—at least hypothetically—reduce its need for integration with the Western capitalist economies.

As always, China sought to maximize the political and symbolic value of the project. Beijing dispatched 150 of its own technicians and workers to labor side by side with the mill's 3,000 indigenous employees in the opening stages of its operation. Both Chinese and Tanzanians involved with the project hoped that mixing workers from the two countries could create a visible example of friendship and progress. Tanzanian finance minister Amir Jamal pledged that his people "would follow the example of the Chinese to work hard in the spirit of socialism and self-reliance" at the opening of the mill.[85] The factory, however, was not a long-term economic success. When the Chinese workers returned home, the Tanzanians had difficulty managing the factory on their own and, in 1984, were forced to ask Beijing for help in rehabilitating the mill. During the 1990s, the PRC again sought to revitalize the factory through a new program that offered concessional loans for joint ventures, but despite its assistance, the factory never became self-supporting.[86] This result would have been difficult to guess from the attention the factory garnered when it opened. Articles praising the Chinese role and emphasizing Sino-African cooperation appeared in Tanzanian newspapers such as the *East African Standard*.[87] Even the African American newspaper the *Black Panther* published a glowing description of the factory. According to the article, the most important thing was that Tanzanians would manage the factory "themselves and consequently they are learning from their own mistakes." This, of course, stood in contrast to the Western imperialists, who had been interested only in cheap labor and raw materials.[88] Although the Friendship Textile Mill was a failure in terms of its contribution to Tanzania's economic development, from the standpoint of Chinese prestige and status in East Africa, it was a great success.

Despite Tanzanian enthusiasm for factories and industrial development, the USAID generally shied away from such projects. Samuel Butterfield remembered that Washington was unwilling to "finance the construction of state-owned enterprises such as tire manufacturing or that sort of thing, which the Tanzanians were keen to do, to develop their industrial base."[89]

Americans believed that the country's greatest deficit was not its lack of factories but the "desperate shortage of skilled Africans." The USAID therefore decided to give "first priority" to activities "which rapidly upgrade or maintain skills most broadly needed by the country, especially within the public service."[90] The majority of the aid projects described in USAID country plans for Tanzania focused on education and training. They included providing advisers and funding the construction of Tanzania's Institute of Public Administration as well as assistance to agricultural schools and colleges.[91] Some American officials have claimed that these projects were well received by Tanzanians but the USAID also complained that they did not garner as much attention as competing projects launched by the Communist Bloc, especially those sponsored by the PRC. One agency report noted with chagrin that "publicity on AID projects has tended to be overshadowed by the fanfare given to large-scale projects . . . from other sources, in particular those of the Chinese Communists and the Bloc."[92] The problem was that technical training and educational programs did not produce a dramatic, immediate impact on either production or the imagination. American aid projects may well have been more realistic, but realism did not create a very appealing symbol, and this made Washington's approach to aid a harder sell.

Although Americans were dissatisfied with the relative lack of attention their assistance programs received in Tanzania, they nevertheless remained a factor in most parts of the country. On the island of Zanzibar, however, China became particularly influential, and the American presence was virtually eliminated by the late 1960s. On Zanzibar, more than anywhere else, Beijing had the opportunity to implement and demonstrate its vision of Sino-African cooperation.

The Zanzibari Showcase

Zanzibar lost its status as an independent state when it merged with Tanganyika in 1964, yet the island remained an important cynosure for Chinese aid programs in Africa. After a revolution on the island brought to power a radical new leadership in January 1964, Chinese diplomats moved in swiftly with promises of aid. The PRC offered to support the construction of a "revolutionary university," send teams of doctors, and dispatch military, technical, and economic advisers.[93] Shortly after Zanzibar merged with Tanganyika, the PRC ambassador to the island, Meng Ying, recommended that China continue to provide Zanzibar with the economic and technical aid that it had promised.[94] The island's political leadership had not abandoned its radical proclivities, and this allowed Chinese advisers and technicians to influence economic policy there in ways that went beyond the scope of Beijing's activities elsewhere in Africa, including the Tanzanian mainland. In Zanzibar, the PRC extended its influence into banking, planning, and other areas, shaping the political economy of the entire island. By April 1964, Undersecretary of State George S. Ball was voicing fears that Zanzibar was becoming a "Communist 'showcase' of development" that was "welcoming, even soliciting, Bloc and Chicom economic assistance; while rejecting or ignoring offers U.S. and UK assistance."[95] The question was whether the showcase would succeed.

One of Beijing's first endeavors in Zanzibar was helping the island reorganize its finances. Chinese diplomats stationed in Zanzibar believed that the lingering presence and influence of European financiers was a central obstacle to economic autonomy on the island. Advisers sent by Beijing argued that Zanzibar needed to place foreign exchange under government control in order to eliminate the special privileges retained by the Europeans. In the months immediately following the revolution, Chinese financial advisers advocated the creation of an indigenous bank. "Only after an independent nationalist government establishes its own bank and issues its own currency under the leadership of a revolutionary government could it truly shake off imperialist control," they reported to the Finance Ministry.[96] Chinese officials remained committed to the project after Zanzibar merged with Tanganyika. By 1966, Beijing had provided £800,000 to capitalize the new People's Bank of Zanzibar and to renovate the building in which it would be housed.[97]

In addition to funding the bank, Beijing dispatched economic advisers who worked diligently to steer the island toward nationalistic economic policies that promoted self-reliance. The team noted, for instance, that Karume's government had an "aspiration to nationalize trade" and thought this was understandable in light of the fact that the island had long been a victim of "imperialist exploitation and oppression."[98] Chinese advisers recommended that Zanzibar establish government-operated trade stores. Their purpose included "strengthening the power of the government over the economy, . . . demonstrating the impact of state-run industry, and encouraging agricultural and industrial production."[99] Beijing's guidance had an unmistakable impact on trade and finance policy. By 1968, one American intelligence report about conditions on the island noted, "government efforts to control all aspects of the economy." A government-run export-import corporation had been created, and Karume had seized control over the island's retail trade network.[100]

Washington soon came to see Zanzibar as a lost cause. Official American reports glumly conceded that Chinese aid projects on Zanzibar were being greeted with almost unbounded enthusiasm. In June 1966, the U.S. consulate reported that the "medical teams, Chicom agricultural technicians, their well drilling project, and to a certain extent their military advisors have all made a favorable impact in Zanzibar." Chinese sent to work in Zanzibar had "lived frugally, and in some areas close to the people." These projects had enabled Beijing to gain "a position of considerable power and influence in Zanzibar government circles." Moreover, the consulate predicted, the Chinese seemed likely to "continue to play the dominant role among the foreign states represented in Zanzibar."[101]

A 1968 report by the CIA reached similar conclusions. The agency believed that Chinese aid programs in Zanzibar had come to occupy a preeminent position and seemed likely to stay there. China had faced competition from its rivals in the Communist Bloc, especially East Germany, whose efforts were encouraged by the Soviets. But the Chinese had "worked assiduously at undercutting the East Germans" and ultimately fared very well by comparison. Zanzibari officials had become "increasingly dissatisfied and disillusioned with the East German projects," which had been plagued by "poor planning and progress" and the use of "overpriced" equipment that was "not suited to Zanzibar's needs." The CIA estimated that there were four hundred Chinese on the island supervising a diverse variety of aid projects that included a state farm, a leather and shoe factory, an agricultural implement repair facility, and a small pharmaceutical plant. Chinese technicians were also assisting with well-drilling projects and irrigation and rice-growing schemes. By contrast "only a handful of Westerners" remained on the island, and the "sole U.S. aid project" was the construction of a small technical school.[102]

The CIA credited the triumph of PRC aid programs in Zanzibar to their efficient and strategic implementation. The Chinese had "gradually become the dominant force because of their well-managed, relatively-inexpensive aid, their ability to live frugally and work hard, and their extensive and well-financed contacts—both overt and covert—with many influential Zanzibaris." The agency predicted that, partially because of the success of their aid programs, the Chinese were "likely to remain influential in Zanzibar for the foreseeable future."[103] On Zanzibar, Americans resigned themselves to China's special influence. Nevertheless, they remained vigilant about Beijing's efforts to expand its aid programs in Tanzania and the rest of East Africa. After 1965, they made a concerted effort to undermine China's most ambitious development project of all—a railway to connect Zambia's copper mines with the port city of Dar es Salaam.

The TAZARA Railway

The construction of the Tanzania-Zambia Railway (TAZARA) was the most ambitious, expensive, and well known of Beijing's efforts to aid Africa during the 1960s and 1970s. Completed in 1975, the railroad eventually stretched 1,060 miles from Dar es Salaam across the frequently difficult terrain of southern Tanzania and ended in the small Zambian city of Kapiri Mposhi. From the outset, the railway embodied the fundamental tenets of China's developmental approach in Africa. It cut Zambia's economic linkages with parts of Africa that remained under the control of European colonialism or white settler minorities. It had the potential to enhance the self-sufficiency of two newly independent states that had made clear their sympathy toward Afro-Asian causes. And it was a highly visible symbol of both short- and long-term Sino-African friendship. For all of these reasons, Washington worked to blunt the political and psychological impact of this project.

Scholars have looked this experiment in Sino-African cooperation from a variety of perspectives, often placing it in the context of Beijing's expanding involvement in Africa during the late 1960s and 1970s.[104] Most recently, Jamie Monson's *Africa's Freedom Railway* has shed new light on the subject by examining how the train reshaped social boundaries during and after its construction.[105] Here, the focus is on understanding the railway project and the surrounding controversies in the framework of Sino-American competition in East Africa. The PRC initially proposed the project because it hoped to show up its competitors in the region. When Beijing signed the agreement to build the railway with Dar es Salaam and Lusaka, it stunned American officials and led to U.S. efforts to undercut the project's appeal.

The ambivalence of Washington and its allies about the railway was, above all, what drove Dar es Salaam and Lusaka into Beijing's arms. When Nyerere first requested American help with the project in the early 1960s, he put the United States in an awkward position. Americans recognized that East Africa desperately needed to improve its transportation infrastructure and did not want rivals to sweep in and capture the prestige and visibility that would come with building new projects in this area. At the same time, however, the costs were far in excess of America's aid budget for the two countries, and many aid experts doubted that the railroad would ever be financially viable. A briefing paper prepared for President Kennedy before Nyerere's 1963 visit to the White House predicted that the African nationalist might ask for "assistance in establishing a rail link with Northern Rhodesia [called Zambia after 1964] in order to lessen the latter's dependence on Portuguese ports for its copper ore" but cautioned that the railway would cost between $150 and $200 million, far in excess of what the United States was willing to consider.[106]

Dar es Salaam and Lusaka had little luck in persuading other potential donors. In mid-1964, the World Bank published a negative feasibility study and subsequently refused any involvement with the project. With potential Western donors spooked by the bank's analysis, Nyerere decided to approach Moscow, but the Soviets showed little more enthusiasm than their rivals on the other side of the Iron Curtain.[107] Just as the prospects of getting assistance from the Soviets or the West were dimming, however, Beijing showed interest in the project. When Nyerere visited the PRC in February 1965, the CCP leadership expressed an eagerness to help and discussed sending a team of specialists to conduct a survey.[108]

Why was Beijing so willing to fund an extremely costly aid project in East Africa that most of the other major powers competing for influence in the region viewed as overly ambitious and unworkable? To begin with, the PRC used a very different financial calculus than the United States or its allies. Rather than profitability, it emphasized the degree to which Chinese assistance could contribute to self-sufficiency and counter the economic legacies of imperialism. At the same time, expanding Beijing's prestige and status among African nations remained an important consideration. Associating China with this expansive symbol of modernity—one whose construction the West had refused to take part in—had the potential to inscribe Beijing's vision of Sino-African partnership permanently across a broad swath of the East African landscape.

Zhou Boping, a former Chinese diplomat stationed in Tanzania during the 1960s who was deeply involved in the project, recalls that competition with the West—especially the United States—and Beijing's determination to foster greater economic autonomy in the African continent both figured prominently in Zhou Enlai's rationale for green-lighting the project. In a meeting with several other high-ranking officials in early 1965, Premier Zhou listed the reasons why assisting with the construction of the railroad represented a unique opportunity for China in Africa. Tanzania and Zambia were two countries that "supported national independence movements in southern Africa regardless of the threat from the West," and the railway constituted an "urgent need" of both countries. China, he explained, should therefore support them. But African needs were far from Zhou's only concern. The premier also thought about the potential impact that the railroad might have and how it would affect China's status vis-à-vis that of the West. He explained: "Focusing our efforts on this kind of large work would have a bigger effect and influence than a few medium- and small-sized projects in other African countries." Best of all, China's decision to build the railroad would "certainly incite panic among a few Western countries." It was possible that Beijing's rivals would respond by offering to take on the project after all. But this, too, would "leave a bad taste" in the mouths of the Tanzanians. At a minimum, Nyerere would be able to use China's offer as a "trump card" to oppose the "harsh conditions" that the Westerners might seek to impose in return for their assistance.[109]

Despite the expense, Chinese officials saw offering to build the railroad as a win-win proposition. If Tanzania and Zambia accepted Beijing's offer, the

PRC would gain an opportunity to undertake a project that would receive extensive publicity and strengthen China's visibility in Africa. Even if the United States and its allies made a counteroffer, they would merely confirm African impressions that Western aid was self-interested. Moreover, with the confidence that came with having a Chinese offer in hand, Nyerere would be far less tractable in his dealings with Washington or London. He would be grateful for the offer of Chinese aid even if he chose not to accept it.

Zhou's analysis of how the United States and its allies might respond to China's offer was on the mark. Having learned that the premier would make a formal offer to Tanzania and Zambia during a planned visit to Dar es Salaam in June 1965, American officials scrambled to alert Washington and find a way to stymie the Chinese. A State Department intelligence report written briefly before Zhou's visit expressed deep, albeit exaggerated concerns about the dangers of allowing Beijing to build the railroad. It warned that Beijing's offer could "dramatize Communist China's role in Africa, . . . increase Chinese influence and leverage among southern African liberation movements" and give the PRC "the initiative in East-Central Africa's highest priority, most politically sensitive development project." The report then weighed the costs and benefits of different potential American responses. Washington could "refuse on principal to be rushed or maneuvered into countering [Beijing's] politically-motivated proposal." But this approach would afford the Chinese Communists "an unprecedented opportunity to expand their foothold in East and Central Africa." The expansion of Chinese influence would in turn "produce a polarization of forces in Southern Africa along cold war and racial lines." A second alternative was "ruling out Tanzania as 'lost' to the Communists" and focusing on promoting stability in Zambia. Doing so, however, would imperil if not destroy Washington's ambitions to promote African integration. The report suggested that America's best alternative was to "organize a consortium of Western interests to build the rail link." Such an offer would be cast as part of a broader effort to construct a "Zone of Peace design for an integrated East-Central African economic complex," thereby avoiding the appearance of "yielding to 'communist-threat' blackmail."[110]

In contemplating their response to China's offer, Americans focused on preventing Beijing from reaping any political benefits or expanding its influence. Absent from the report was even the slightest consideration of how China's involvement would affect Africa's economic development. The most important objective for Washington was assuring that Beijing could not convert its support for the railway into political or symbolic currency. With this goal in mind, the United States and its allies worked over the next year to discourage Tanzania and Zambia from accepting China's offer.

The focal point for Washington's efforts to block the potential Chinese-built railway was Zambian president Kenneth Kaunda. More moderate in his politics and less enamored of the Chinese than Nyerere, Kaunda was—at least until 1967—not inclined to jump at Beijing's offer. The Zambian president preferred Western financing and was cautious of Chinese influence. Realizing this, Washington and its allies played on his fears. In the days before Zhou's June 1965 visit to Dar es Salaam, during which U.S. intelligence predicted the premier would put forward a proposal, American diplomats led a hasty effort to preempt China's offer by promising Kaunda that they would provide an alternative. William Leonhart, the U.S. ambassador to Tanzania, urged the State Department to devise a proposal for a conference of nations interested in funding the railway that could be put to Kaunda immediately. The purpose of this proposal would be "to give Kaunda's hand enough strength to prevent GURT [Government of the United Republic of Tanzania] acceptance [of the] Chicom construction offer."[111] Leonhart hoped that dangling a more serious offer of Western aid could prevent or at least delay China from gaining the opportunity that it coveted.

Washington's strategy succeeded, but only in the short term. Hoping for Western aid, Kaunda and Nyerere dithered about accepting Chinese funding. Party leaders were forced to bide their time as Western efforts to put together an offer played themselves out. Shortly after Zhou's visit to Tanzania, the United Kingdom and Canada funded a feasibility study carried out by a British consulting firm. When the firm issued a highly favorable report in August 1966, Lusaka was optimistic that the next step would be a new consortium of the United States, Great Britain, Germany, Japan, and the World Bank that would pay for an engineering survey and, eventually, for the construction of the railroad. Zambia's optimism was unfounded, however. When the firm's report was submitted to the African Development Bank and the World Bank, the two banks agreed to reevaluate the project. Once again, however, the verdict was negative: the two banks called for further technical and economic investigation before conducting an engineering survey.[112]

The second negative report from the World Bank finally convinced Kaunda that the United States and its allies had no intention of financing the railroad. American maneuvering had only delayed the inevitable. The deal was more or less sealed in June 1967 when Kaunda finally traveled to Beijing for tête-à-tête meetings with the CCP leadership. By all accounts, Zhou and his colleagues masterfully assuaged any remaining doubts that might have lingered in Kaunda's mind. He Ying, the PRC ambassador to Tanzania who was summoned to Beijing to take part in the discussions, recalled that Kaunda had a fierce sense of self-respect and was too proud to take the initiative in requesting China's assistance. But Zhou "showed sympathy for his self-esteem and hardships and brought up the question of the railroad in a straightforward manner." The premier strove to coopt the Zambian president into his vision of mutual assistance and cooperation among Afro-Asian states by explaining that "this is to support Africa's national independence and its struggle against colonialism; it is also to help you develop a national economy and consolidate your independence."[113]

Jubilant from China's recent success at detonating a hydrogen bomb, Chairman Mao was, if anything, even more affirmative than Zhou: "The railroad you are building is only 1,700 kilometers [1,050 miles] and requires an investment of only 100 million British pounds, that is nothing." Like Zhou, Mao emphasized solidarity among newly independent Afro-Asian countries. China would help Zambia with the railroad because "the nations that became independent first have an obligation to help the nations that gained their independence later on." At least according to Chinese accounts, Kaunda was genuinely moved by Mao's display of generosity and goodwill.[114] After Zambia's frustrating experiences seeking assistance from the West, the CCP's enthusiasm doubtless went a long way toward convincing Kaunda that, in a world divided between rapacious imperialists and new nations struggling to sustain their independence, Beijing was a more trustworthy friend than Washington or Moscow.

Before Kaunda returned home, Zhou discussed his plan to send a team of specialists to survey the conditions for building the railroad. Once again, the CCP leadership did all that it could to assure that the manner and attitude of its technicians would cement Sino-African friendship and enhance Beijing's status among Africans. Premier Zhou outlined three principles that would govern how the survey team conducted its work. First, the team would not interfere with the internal politics of the host country; it would "devote itself wholeheartedly to the welfare of the people." Second, after providing sufficient training, the workers would quickly return home. Finally, their wages and treatment would be the same as that of workers in the host country. They would not enjoy any "special privileges" and "must not have any great power chauvinism."[115] Much like the Chinese technicians who had been dispatched to Guinea and Mali, the railroad survey team was meant to differentiate China from the other Great Powers. It would enhance the PRC's reputation in Africa as a country bent on cooperation rather than exploitation. The main point of distinction in the case of the Tanzania-Zambia railway is that they would seek to fulfill these objectives on a much grander scale.

Before Beijing formally agreed to finance the entire railway project through an interest-free loan in September 1967, some Americans had been skeptical that the Chinese could manage such an expensive undertaking. Once the agreement was announced, American officials were left wringing their hands. They almost universally perceived the railroad agreement as a political triumph for China and an embarrassment for the United States. David Shear, an assistant program officer at the USAID in Dar es Salaam, recalled that the agreement was "seen as a huge coup for the Chinese."[116] Similarly, John Hummon, another officer who served with the USAID in Tanzania during the 1960s, remembered that the railway agreement was "major and depressing news in Washington."[117]

Stunned by China's audacity, Washington strove to diminish the recognition that Beijing could gain through building the railroad. The most direct U.S. counter maneuver was a massive road improvement and construction project covering a route that lay parallel with the proposed railway. Americans argued that building what came to be known as the Tanzam Highway or the Great North Road would be a quicker, more efficient mode of transport than the train system. "The key point," recalled Edward Marks, an economic and commercial officer stationed in Lusaka during the late 1960s, "was that the road would be ours and could pre-empt the Chinese invasion."[118] To assist Zambia with exporting copper and acquiring fuel—a desperately needed commodity because its hostile southern neighbor, Rhodesia, had cut off the newly independent nation's access to oil—Washington and London even mounted an airlift operation flying C-130s between the Zambian copper belt and Dar es Salaam.[119]

Ultimately, however, the Great North Road failed to inspire Africans in the same way that the railway did. The highway did facilitate transport of some materials, but neither Tanzania nor Zambia had enough trucks to enable it to become a major artery of commerce. According to one U.S. estimate, Zambia would have required $100 million to purchase the 3,500 trucks necessary to carry its annual imports and exports. Moreover, both countries lacked enough personnel with the technical expertise and organizational skills to operate and maintain such a massive system of trucks and roads.[120] Although Nyerere and Kaunda welcomed the construction of the highway, they tended to view it as a complement to rather than as a replacement for the railroad. Ironically, because the road was completed before the railway, it was often used as an avenue for transporting needed materials for building the railroad tracks. Thus, it ended up facilitating rather than trumping Chinese Communist efforts.[121] Once again China had gained recognition through a major aid project and American efforts to contest it had proven futile.

———

By the late 1960s, Chinese economic assistance programs in Africa had proven surprisingly successful. Through highly visible projects infused with an egalitarian ethos, Beijing appealed to the nationalistic sensitivities of newly independent Africans in ways that Washington and Moscow never quite seemed to manage. American, Chinese, and African sources all confirm that the PRC enhanced its status in Africa through its well-conceived aid programs.

Yet despite this success, Chinese aid to Africa never produced the transformative victory for the PRC that CCP leaders envisioned. For one thing, only a handful of African countries received significant amounts of aid from Beijing. This reflected both the limits of the PRC's resources and a lack of interest in receiving Chinese aid in more conservative African countries. Beijing had been optimistic about its prospects in Kenya, whose leadership was nationalist but relatively pro-Western.[122] Yet President Jomo Kenyatta ultimately chose, with Western encouragement, to curtail Chinese influence, and he never allowed the PRC to operate a significant aid program in his country. In Kenya, Nigeria, Ethiopia, and numerous other moderate or conservative newly independent African states, the PRC did not become influential until after the Cold War ended.

The volatile nature of postcolonial African politics also limited the long-term impact of Chinese aid programs in some countries. In February 1966, the Ghanaian military launched a successful coup against President Kwame Nkrumah just as he had left for a state visit to Beijing. One Johnson administration official thought this was a "windfall" for the United States because a left-leaning government had been replaced by one that was "almost pathetically pro-Western."[123] This development inevitably had a negative impact on the overall Sino-Ghanaian relationship, including Chinese aid programs. In Mali, where Chinese aid projects had been especially well received, Beijing suffered a significant setback in 1968 when President Modibo Keïta was overthrown in a military coup. Beijing had been in negotiations with Conakry and Bamako to assist in the construction of a second major railroad project in Africa connecting Guinea and Mali, but these discussions came to a halt in the wake of the coup.[124]

Even in countries where Chinese aid programs achieved popularity, the broader failure of foreign assistance to raise the level of prosperity often caused disillusionment with the whole enterprise of development. In Guinea, for instance, Beijing may have gained status and recognition, but Guineans did not gain the higher living standards that they craved. Despite aid from both Washington and Beijing and rich natural resources, Guinea made little progress during the 1960s, and many grew cynical toward all forms of foreign support. According to the *New York Times*, a joke about how aid projects typically worked was widely repeated in Conakry at the time: "West Germany will do the feasibility study. The Americans will furnish the equipment, the Russians will take payment in bananas, the Chinese will supply the labor.

Touré will take the credit and the Guineans who take over will see to it that nothing works."[125] Guinea's failed economic policies were not China's fault, but at the national level, neither Guinea nor China's other closest allies in Africa ever became effective showcases that could persuade the rest of the continent that Sino-African economic cooperation offered the best road to development and growth. This, too, is a reason that the goodwill generated by Chinese aid never extended beyond a few countries.

Despite these limitations, China's experiences as an economic benefactor in Africa during the 1960s were instructive for both the PRC and the United States. Although the characteristics of Beijing's economic involvement in Africa have evolved greatly over time, the PRC has continued to couch its appeals to Africans in similar terms, arguing that it can understand the continent's problems in ways that Westerners cannot. Such ideals continue to figure subtly but frequently in Chinese discourse about the region. Washington, for its part, learned that in some places it had no choice but to accept Chinese influence as an unalterable reality and that an uneasy coexistence could prevail without direct conflict. It was America's growing resignation to the fact that Communist China would survive and remain an influential actor on the world scene that eventually forced it to reconsider its unrelenting hostility toward the PRC.

Chapter 10

Competition and Cooperation, 1968–1979

When President Richard M. Nixon left Andrews Air Force Base for Beijing on 17 February 1972, he had an almost palpable sense of the forces of history moving around him. "We were embarking," he wrote, "upon a voyage of philosophical discovery as uncertain, and in some respects as perilous, as the voyages of geographical discovery of a much earlier time."[1] The president had a keen awareness not only of the epochal nature of the journey that he was undertaking but also of the more specific role the trip could play in restoring U.S. prestige around the world. For Nixon, the success of the trip hinged on whether America's new relationship with the PRC would enable it to strengthen its position in world politics and keep its pride intact as it withdrew from Southeast Asia. Several days before departing, Nixon had scrawled down a few pages of talking points for his visit. They were littered throughout with terse, straightforward sentences that highlighted the priority the president attached to maintaining and restoring national honor during his trip. There was a "need for the U.S. to act honorably in Vietnam," he wrote on one page. On another he jotted down, "We must be honorable or our friendship was worthless."[2]

Few presidents understood the significance of honor, prestige, and status in international politics better than Richard Nixon. Through much of his political career, Nixon harbored an almost obsessive animosity toward East Coast elites who, he believed, looked down at him because of his relatively modest origins. When he assumed the presidency, Nixon's complex about his social standing in elite society translated readily into a powerful fixation with America's standing in the world. Much as the president had been disrespected and shunned by the liberal Ivy League establishment, the United States was unfairly getting beaten up on in world politics. America, he believed, needed to stop allowing itself to be pushed around like a "pitiful helpless giant" and not be afraid to demonstrate its strength.[3]

Yet Nixon's constant attention to national prestige and status could be a virtue as much as a flaw when it came to U.S. diplomacy. If the president was zealously protective of American honor, his Quaker upbringing had also instilled in him a sense of fairness, which made it possible to recognize that other nations—including America's adversaries—were guided by similar sensitivities. Washington could not constantly look to undermine the prestige of its rivals without expecting them to return the favor. It was Nixon's understanding of this basic reality of international relations that made it possible for him to transform America's relationship with China and bring about a shift from competition to cooperation when it came to the Third World.

Geostrategic considerations—especially a common desire to contain the Soviet Union—were unquestionably critical in drawing Beijing and Washington closer together during the early 1970s. This has been covered in great detail elsewhere.[4] But the two nations might never have acted on their common interests if Nixon had not taken a radically different view of China's international status than his predecessors. Whereas previous administrations had all struggled to isolate China and destroy its prestige in the Third World, the Nixon administration wanted to reintegrate the PRC into the international community and afford it the respect due to a major power. This made it easier for Beijing to square its ideological convictions with the perceived strategic necessity of better relations with Washington. It also wrought significant changes in China's approach to the United States. Although Beijing's denunciations of American imperialism in the Third World continued, Mao and his colleagues often took subtle measures to make sure that its new partner did not lose credibility.

As the Sino-American relationship transformed itself between 1972 and 1979, status proved both an enabling and complicating factor. In the direct and thorough discussions that took place between Washington and Beijing during the first two years of détente, the two came to recognize that it was no longer in their interests to embarrass each other. Between 1971 and 1973 rapprochement was facilitated by the flexibility that each showed in accommodating the other's desire to maintain its credibility on key issues. But after this initial euphoric period, the two sides faced difficult choices between deepening their cooperation and enhancing their status. China could not move to close to the United States without appearing to abandon revolutionary causes while the United States could not recognize the PRC without appearing to abandon its allies. For some time the dialogue continued but was fraught with tensions over these issues. After 1976, however, both Beijing and the United States made significant changes in their foreign policies as Jimmy Carter assumed the presidency in the United States and Deng Xiaoping consolidated his power in China. With Soviet adventurism on the rise, the global priorities of the two countries became more deeply aligned. In this shifting international environment, they often looked for ways to cooperate and enhance each other's status so that they could more effectively pursue common goals.

Toward Rapprochement

The first faint signs of change in Sino-American relations appeared during the late 1960s. More than anything else, the decline of Beijing's global influence would create opportunities for American diplomacy. By 1966, Americans had far less reason to fear a dramatic increase in Chinese prestige in the Third World. Beijing's hopes of fostering political unity among radical Asian and African states had died with the failure of the Second Bandung Conference and the demise of radical leaders in Indonesia, Ghana, and Algeria. Although China was reaping considerable success through its aid programs, it also becoming clear that these could not reverse the collapse of Chinese influence in the Afro-Asian word. Ultimately, however, internal developments in China would prove most damaging to the country's global ambitions.

In May 1966, Mao Zedong launched the Cultural Revolution, a broad political, social, and cultural attack on what he termed "capitalist roaders," or those pursuing the capitalist path. In reality, Mao's so-called revolution was a tool to purge those who, in the chairman's increasingly paranoid mind, constituted a political threat or deviated even slightly from Maoist orthodoxies. High-ranking officials in the CCP, including Liu Shaoqi and Deng Xiaoping, were forced to make self-criticism and sent into political exile. But the Cultural Revolution did not stop with political purges against a few party elites. Red Guard groups formed throughout the country and sought to purge revisionists in all sectors of society through carrying out violent class struggle. The result was a nightmare of political brutality, economic hardship, and social turmoil.[5]

During the revolution's most intense and radical phase—between 1966 and 1969—Chinese xenophobia led to a series of bizarre diplomatic episodes both in Beijing and in PRC embassies abroad that seriously damaged China's international standing. Long-standing allies such as North Korea suddenly found themselves denounced as revisionists and faced with little choice other than to move closer to Moscow.[6] In August 1967, Mao's Red Guards carried out a series of attacks on the Indian, Burmese, and Indonesian embassies and burned the British legation to the ground with flaming gasoline torches. In some instances, Beijing either replaced or supplemented its diplomatic representation in Afro-Asian countries with new officers charged with propagating Mao Zedong Thought. Inexperienced in diplomacy and highly sensitive toward any perceived slight against China, these new officers exacerbated frictions with indigenous governments and provoked unnecessary incidents. The PRC closed its embassies in Tunisia, Dahomey, Ghana, and several other Afro-Asian countries after conflicts erupted between Chinese diplomats and host governments. Zhou Enlai tried to shelter the Foreign Ministry from some of the worst excesses of the Cultural Revolution and ensure that Chinese foreign policy operated with as little interference as possible. But even Zhou's influence had limits in the frenzied atmosphere that gripped China during the late 1960s.[7] China soon found itself more isolated from the international community than at any other point since its founding.

As Chinese politics descended into chaos during the late 1960s, Americans began to contemplate a change in China policy. With its attention riveted on the war in Vietnam, the Johnson administration could never stay focused on the subject for very long. But American rhetoric shifted during Johnson's last two years in office. Although Washington continued to see Beijing as a threat on many levels, key American officials and agencies also began to foresee the possibility that China would moderate its policies and that areas of Sino-American conflict could be reduced.

In June 1966, just after the Cultural Revolution had gotten under way, a State-Defense study group prepared a report on Communist China's long-term prospects. To some degree, the report reflected long-standing American beliefs that the Chinese agenda in Asia was fundamentally opposed to U.S. interests. It explained that the CCP's "objectives of regional hegemony and world revolution clash with our own fundamental interests in preventing [the] domination of Asia by any single power and in developing a peaceful and open world society of free nations." But the report concluded on a more hopeful note. It argued that containment was likely to succeed and that when it did so the United States would have an opportunity to draw China into the community of nations. In particular, American diplomacy would have to help the Chinese to find new ways of gaining status and prestige in a different international environment. As "Chinese policy moderates," the report argued, "we should try to draw China into activities on the broader world scene where, through exposure to outside reality and successful assumption of international responsibility, she might gain a degree of status and respect which could substitute in part for the unattainable goals of regional domination and super-power status."[8] The report did not usher in a transformation in policy, but it did indicate a modest shift. China's efforts to raise its global standing was no longer seen only as part of a zero-sum game where Chinese gains were inevitably U.S. losses. Instead, the report saw the possibility of steering Beijing's yearning for status in a more constructive direction.

President Johnson made some of these points more bluntly one month later during a nationally televised address delivered from the White House theater to the American Alumni Council. Although he warned that there was no end in sight to the conflict engulfing Vietnam, Johnson spoke of the possibility for reconciliation with Communist China in the future. He argued that "reconciliation between nations that now call themselves enemies" was "essential for peace in Asia." According to the president, a "misguided China must be encouraged toward understanding of the outside world and toward policies of peaceful cooperation." He hoped that in the future a more moderate Beijing would be more susceptible to cooptation because, ultimately, "lasting peace" could "never come to Asia as long as 700 million people are isolated by their rulers from the outside world."[9] Johnson followed through on this speech with a few minor gestures to ease Sino-American tensions. Washington proposed exchanges in scientific and cultural fields during the ongoing ambassadorial talks in Warsaw and unilaterally lifted the travel ban on journalists, writers, and doctors seeking to visit the PRC.[10] The president recognized that the United States and China would continue to clash over Vietnam and numerous other issues, but it had dawned on him that a permanent campaign to isolate China would not serve long-term U.S. interests.

But LBJ was not the right man to open China. The blunt and plainspoken southerner was a masterful political operator in the domestic context, but he lacked the subtleness and sensitivity to approach a country with such a deeply rooted mistrust of American imperialism. Moreover, it was still an awkward and inopportune time for improving Sino-American ties. With the Cultural Revolution at its height and CCP leaders fearful and angry about the Americanization of the war in Vietnam, the Chinese firmly rebuffed U.S. proposals. Seeking to demonstrate its commitment to confrontation rather than compromise with the American imperialists, Beijing decided in 1966 that ambassadorial talks in Warsaw should be held less rather than more frequently and unilaterally lengthened interval between meetings from three to five months.[11]

Over the next few years, however, the fire of Sino-Soviet conflict melted away the icy recalcitrance that greeted Washington's first efforts to improve relations with the PRC. The events of 1968–69 took the rivalry between the Chinese and the Soviets to a new level and convinced Beijing that Moscow was its most dangerous adversary. During the late 1960s, as mistrust between the two Communist giants grew, they had both deployed hundreds of thousands of troops along their shared border. In March 1969, clashes broke out between Chinese and Soviet border guards at Zhenbao Island in the Ussuri River, which had been the subject of territorial disputes. A similar conflict erupted in Xinjiang Province in August, raising fears of a larger war with the potential to inflict significant damage on both sides. Large-scale conflict was averted, but not before Beijing's perception of its geostrategic situation went through a fundamental transformation. After the border skirmish, Chinese leaders denounced the Soviet Union as a "social-imperialist country" and claimed that Moscow had now become the center of world reactionary forces.[12] This ratcheting up of China's conflict with its northern neighbor gave

Mao a strong incentive to entertain "unconventional thoughts" about the PRC's relationship with the United States.[13]

Within China, the ideological fervor that had accompanied the Cultural Revolution was abating. Mao dismantled the Red Guards and slowly allowed the rehabilitation of some officials who had been exiled. Beijing also ordered many of the diplomats and ambassadors who had been recalled at the height of the Cultural Revolution to return to their posts, and Chinese diplomacy began to take a more moderate tone.[14] Over the next few years, the PRC strove to mend fences with other socialist countries that it had alienated during the Cultural Revolution and to establish relations with more Afro-Asian and Latin American countries. Between 1968 and 1972, it normalized relations with twenty-five countries in Asia, Africa, and Latin America, including some that leaned toward the West in the Cold War, such as Turkey and Iran.[15] Beijing's willingness to deal with governments that it had not long ago considered lackeys or reactionaries fostered a much more propitious environment for improved Sino-American ties.

These changes were not in themselves sufficient to end long-standing Sino-American hostility, however. Leaders who had the commitment and skill to take advantage of the new situation needed to emerge. It was Richard M. Nixon's determination to open China that would ultimately transform the relationship and begin a shift from competition to cooperation in the Third World. The new president wanted to extricate the United States from Vietnam, reduce American commitments in Asia, and achieve a stable balance of power in world politics. He believed that improving relations with Beijing could give the United States an extremely valuable card to play in the game of international diplomacy. A friendlier Beijing might pressure the Vietnamese to negotiate and give the United States more leverage in its efforts to pursue détente with the Soviet Union. Almost immediately after taking office, Nixon moved forward with small measures designed to demonstrate his sincerity. He called for the immediate relaxation of economic controls that had been in place since the Korean War and loosened the restrictions on Americans traveling to China, allowing them to bring home one hundred dollars' worth of Chinese goods.[16]

Nixon's approach to China reflected some of the ideas that Johnson had conveyed during the final years of his presidency, but Nixon was more willing to grapple with the implications of a new Sino-American relationship. He called for the United States to be firm in countering Chinese efforts to spread revolution, but he also believed that it was dangerous for the PRC to remain isolated from the international community. China policy was by its nature a delicate task that needed to steer between the Scylla of appeasement and the Charybdis of discouraging Beijing from greater engagement with the West. Nixon understood that U.S. policy would be most successful if it offered the Chinese leadership an alternative means of gaining status in world affairs while discouraging its ambitions to do so through promoting revolution. He explained his positions in a 1967 article on "Asia after Vietnam" in *Foreign Affairs*. The world, Nixon argued, "simply cannot afford to leave China forever outside the family of nations" where it would "nurture its hates, cherish its fantasies and threaten its neighbors." In the long term, peace could be assured only if the PRC evolved and assumed a more constructive role in Asia. The United States needed to "persuade China that it *must* change: that it cannot satisfy its imperial ambitions, and that its own national interest requires a turning away from foreign adventuring and a turning inward toward the solution of its own domestic problems." Ultimately, Nixon believed that the United States would have to pull "China back into the world community—but as a great and progressing nation not as an epicenter of world revolution."[17] As a president, Nixon was by no means loath to see Beijing enhance its global stature. He recognized the importance of international prestige to Chinese leaders and thought carefully about how they could achieve it in a manner that was conducive to American interests. He envisioned China as a major power but hoped that when it came to Asia and the rest of the world Beijing would be a great progressive force rather than a great revolutionary one.

But how could the PRC be drawn out of its growing isolation from the international community? And how could it come to trust the United States, which had sought to contain it since its inception? Nixon and his national security adviser Henry Kissinger understood from the outset that they needed to avoid doing anything to damage Chinese prestige. China, they recognized, would never accept any offer to hold talks with the United States if the Nixon administration made it look like a show of charity or American benevolence.

The Nixon administration put this approach into practice during its first two years by sending out tentative feelers that slowly expanded and paved the way for Kissinger's secret trip to the PRC in July 1971. Throughout this period the president and his national security adviser feared that if too much publicity surrounded preliminary negotiations, it would be difficult to move ahead without worrying about how every minor gesture would be perceived around the world. So the administration began its campaign to open China not through bold public proclamations but through subtle and often secret communications relayed by private backchannels, with Pakistan being the one Nixon ultimately favored.

Kissinger laid out the rationale for this approach in a memorandum to President Nixon in February 1970 that covered his discussions of U.S.-China relations with the Pakistani ambassador to the United States. The ambassador had emphasized that the Chinese were encouraged by the Nixon administration's early efforts to improve ties but warned that the Chinese would be "very sensitive if the U.S. were to show its belief that their willingness to conduct a meaningful dialogue with the U.S. is a sign of Chinese weakness or fear of U.S.-Soviet collaboration against China." Beijing needed a new relationship with the United States to strengthen its geopolitical position vis-à-vis Moscow, but it did not want to look weak in pursuing it. Kissinger explained that a "direct White House channel to Beijing which would not be known outside the White House on which we could guarantee total security" was the best way to allay Chinese concerns.[18] An obsession with secrecy was one of the hallmarks of the Nixon administration and one of the ingredients that would ultimately bring about the president's downfall. But in the case of Sino-American rapprochement it was necessary. Erasing Beijing's deep-seated mistrust required that Washington take into account China's preference for handling delicate issues behind closed doors without creating the kind of diplomatic theater where Chinese leaders might lose face.

In October 1970, President Nixon initiated a series of covert messages that led to Kissinger's visit. He asked Pakistani president Yahya Khan to convey to Beijing Washington's desire to send a high-level emissary to China. During the next few months, negotiations over procedural details, including when the emissary could be sent, proceeded through the Pakistani backchannel. The major bone of contention was what subjects the potential American emissary could discuss with Chinese leaders. Beijing insisted that any meeting focus on the question of Taiwan and normalization, whereas the Nixon administration hoped for a broader exchange of views on a panoply of issues. After several months of intermittent exchanges, the White House received a note written by Zhou Enlai on 27 April accepting Nixon's proposal for high-level talks. The note subtly conveyed to Washington Beijing's seriousness about establishing the right environment for the meeting. Kissinger was impressed by Zhou Enlai's "warm tone," which he regarded as an indication that "we needed to fear no humiliation."[19] Nevertheless, Beijing was still insisting that the subject of the talks be Taiwan. Nixon responded with a counterproposal on 10 May stating that he was willing to visit the PRC for direct conversations in which "each side would be free to raise the issue of principal concern to it." On 29 May, three days after convening a Politburo meeting to lay out the principles that would govern China's dealings with the United States, Zhou sent a note that Nixon would call "the most important communication that has come to an American president since the end of World War II." The missive promised to give the Nixon administration the meeting it wanted—a summit between the two countries' heads of state in which a range of critical issues could be discussed.[20]

Throughout this period of back-and-forth exchanges, each side took extreme care to make sure that all correspondence remained strictly sub rosa and to reassure the other that it would not lose face. The Nixon administration monitored its public statements about the PRC to ensure that none of them conveyed the wrong impression. Nixon and Kissinger were quick to correct a blunder made by Secretary of State William Rogers days after they received Zhou's 27 April note. The secretary of state had been asked about the possibility of Nixon's visiting China. But Rogers's answer showed that he had been kept in the dark about communications through the Pakistani back-channel and knew only of a more offhand statement that Mao had made seven months earlier in an interview with the American journalist Edgar Snow. He told a reporter that Mao's invitation to Nixon had been "fairly casually made" and was not "serious" and added almost gratuitously that the Chinese were still "fairly paranoic in their attitude toward the rest of the world."[21] Nixon and Kissinger immediately worried that when Mao and his comrades saw the statement, they would "conclude that we thought China was susceptible to pressure despite its warnings months earlier not to treat its opening toward us as a sign of weakness."[22] Nixon hastily convened a press conference to correct the State Department's faux pas by announcing that he did hope to visit China in the future in an unspecified capacity.[23]

While the negotiations over sending a high-level American emissary to China proceeded, the Nixon administration took other less noticeable yet significant steps to boost Beijing's confidence in preparation for the meeting. Nixon worked to assure that the Sino-Soviet conflict did not leave the PRC even more isolated from the rest of the international community. After the Sino-Soviet border clashes, Moscow had been working vigorously to stymie Beijing's efforts to normalize and improve relations with European and Afro-Asian countries, frequently bringing diplomatic pressure to bear on governments that entered into negotiations with the Chinese. When Kissinger sent the president a memo describing these Soviet efforts, Nixon suggested that the United States should "subtly encourage" the countries being pressured by the Soviets not to establish relations with the PRC to proceed.[24] One reason for this was to make the Soviets more willing to come to the negotiating table. But the maneuver also reflected Nixon's eagerness to break with Washington's long-standing approach to China.

The Nixon administration's keen sensitivity to Chinese prestige both in its general policies and in its handling of detailed negotiations played a critical role in softening the hard-line views of CCP leaders and smoothing the way for high-level visits. A little more than a month after receiving Zhou Enlai's invitation, Kissinger would be on his way to Beijing, taking the first tentative steps toward normalization. As the dialogue began, a major challenge the two sides confronted was carrying over their mutual regard for each other's status to broader discussions about world politics.

The New Sino-American Dialogue and the Third World

Henry Kissinger's secret trip to the PRC in July 1971 began a new era of dialogue between Chinese and American officials. The visit gave rise to a series of increasingly extensive and wide-ranging discussions. Geopolitical imperatives—notably, a common desire on the part of Washington and Beijing to contain the Soviet Union—were a pivotal driving force in bringing the national security adviser to the other side of the bamboo curtain. At the same time, it was the delicacy and tact of statesmen on both sides that made early summitry between the United States and China successful.

American officials recognized that the very act of visiting the PRC would afford China a greater status in world affairs. In the period before Henry Kissinger's July 1971 visit, the national security adviser instructed his staff to prepare briefing books estimating what Beijing's objectives for the summit would be and describing American objectives. John H. Holdridge, a senior staff member for the Far East on the NSC and a key figure in early Sino-American negotiations, took the lead in drafting an assessment that Kissinger eventually signed off on and sent to Nixon.[25] The final briefing book reported that the Chinese were "expecting to make major political gains." They anticipated that the PRC's "prestige" would "increase enormously" and that China would "unequivocally become one of the 'big five'" as a result of the Kissinger and Nixon visits.[26]

The high-level meetings between the United States and the PRC during the initial rapprochement were calibrated to protect both American and Chinese credibility in the world. Beijing and Washington made few commitments to each other and—at least initially—did not even consider any joint or coordinated action regardless of whether parallel interests were involved. Instead they held frequent, long discussions where they spelled out their understandings of international events in great detail and strove to refine each other's worldviews. Henry Kissinger wrote in his memoir that there "were no reciprocal commitments, not even an attempt to define coordinated action." Instead, he explained, the two "great nations sought cooperation" through "harmonizing their respective understandings of international issues and their interests in relation to them. Cooperation thus became a psychological, not merely a legal necessity."[27] The rationale behind such discussions seemed to be that as the two sides came to better understand each other's priorities and limitations, they would be less likely to take positions that could cause the other party embarrassment.

Nixon-Kissinger diplomacy sought above all to link the top priorities of each side—Taiwan for the PRC and Vietnam for the United States. For Zhou and his comrades, the refusal of much of the international community, including the United Nations, to recognize Beijing rather than Taipei as the legitimate government of all of China remained the most critical barrier to the PRC enlarging its status in world politics. For the Nixon administration, extricating America from Vietnam without suffering humiliation that would damage its credibility in the Free World stood as the most pressing objective. Nixon and Kissinger hoped that if they promised to move toward recognizing Beijing, the PRC would subtly pressure Hanoi to compromise in peace negotiations with Washington. At the same time, they recognized that the PRC could not simply abandon the Vietnamese and wanted Chinese leaders to understand that switching official recognition from Taipei to Beijing would be a complicated and tortuous process for the United States.

Zhou Enlai quickly recognized what Kissinger was trying to do. During the first meeting he asked the national security adviser point blank whether he was linking Taiwan and Vietnam. Impressed by Zhou's alacrity, Kissinger bluntly admitted that he was.[28] Rather than creating friction, this exchange seemed to leave both men with an appreciation for the other's frankness, helping them reach common understandings. They came to recognize that they could take separate positions without seeking to weaken each other's prestige.

The two statesmen demonstrated a keen understanding of this during their discussions of Indochina. Kissinger and his staff recognized that "for ideological reasons," his counterpart "clearly had to support Hanoi."[29] Sensitive to the damage to China's image if it suddenly shifted its approach toward Vietnam, the Americans never pushed Zhou and his colleagues to change their policies toward the war-stricken country. At the same time, Zhou made it clear that the PRC had no interest in using the Vietnam conflict to weaken America's international standing. He strongly encouraged Washington to withdraw its forces, but he always emphasized—with what comes across as great sincerity in transcripts of the discussions—that doing so would bring honor rather than humiliation to the United States. The premier listened carefully as Kissinger expressed the Nixon administration's determination to withdrawal honorably from Vietnam. He then recommended that the United States "forthrightly withdraw and completely withdraw all forces and leave the problems of Indochina to be determined by the people of these three countries." He promised that this "was the most honorable and glorious way to withdraw from Indochina."[30] Kissinger left China strongly encouraged by his discussions with Zhou on Indochina. On their final day of talks Zhou had brought up the issue in what the national security adviser considered an "astonishingly sympathetic and open manner" and promised to talk to the Vietnamese. Kissinger believed that Zhou might "be able to exert some influence."[31]

In their give and take on the pivotal but delicate question of Taiwan, Zhou and Kissinger again arrived at mutual understandings that could facilitate progress while leaving the prestige of both sides intact. For Mao and his colleagues, Kissinger's and Nixon's willingness to travel to Beijing and negotiate face to face represented a long-sought-after acknowledgment of the fundamental legitimacy of their government. But Zhou still insisted that the United States needed to recognize that Taiwan was a part of China and that the PRC was the only legitimate Chinese government. Washington would also have to draw down its forces in Taiwan and invalidate its defense treaty with the ROC. Much as the Nixon administration wanted to withdraw from Vietnam in a measured way that did not diminish American prestige, however, it also wanted to reduce U.S. commitments to Taiwan slowly so that it did not appear to be caving in to Beijing's demands. Here, too, Zhou showed flexibility and was able to work out an understanding with his American counterpart. "If you need some time," the premier told Kissinger during their first meeting, "we can understand."[32] Washington, for its part, was willing to promise the PRC that it would move gradually toward recognizing Beijing. In the meantime, the United States would not adopt a "two Chinas" policy or support the indigenous Taiwanese independence movement.[33] This informal agreement promised to confer on Beijing a long-desired international legitimacy while enabling Washington to ease away from its commitments to Taiwan.

When the question of the PRC's admission to the United Nations came up several months later, both sides stuck to their ends of the bargain. In the past, partially because of American influence, China had never been able to muster the votes needed in the General Assembly to gain admission. But with Sino-American relations on the mend, international sentiment in favor of Beijing's admission had increased substantially. For the PRC, joining the organization represented a significant opportunity to strengthen its legitimacy. The Nixon administration recognized that it could no longer impede this process if it was intent on pursuing rapprochement. For Washington, however, the critical question was how to enable the PRC's admission without appearing to abandon Taipei. Kissinger and Zhou had touched on the issue in July. Kissinger had raised the possibility that Washington would support a formula that admitted the PRC and gave it Taipei's seat on the Security Council but nevertheless did not expel Taiwan. Although the premier explained that China would "have to oppose the U.S. position," he also agreed "smilingly" to "mute the rhetoric" when the issue was being debated.[34] Thus, Beijing's overall effort to gain UN admission would be aided by Washington's lack of resistance while China would not unduly seek to embarrass the United States if it tried to maintain a role for Taiwan in the organization.

Nevertheless, Nixon administration officials agonized over how to maintain American credibility as a decisive vote approached. Washington had agreed readily that it would not try to keep Beijing out by using its veto power or threatening to cut financial support.[35] The issue was complicated, however, because the vote was scheduled to take place during Kissinger's second visit to Beijing in late October, and Washington did not want to appear to be abandoning Taipei owing to pressures from the PRC. Ultimately, the administration adopted a somewhat Janus-faced approach. On the one hand, it encouraged Taipei to accept the possibility of dual representation in the United Nations. The State Department—which remained relatively sympathetic to Taipei—along with the American ambassador to the United Nations, future president George H. W. Bush, lobbied nations in the General Assembly to adopt this formula. On the other hand, the United States deliberately strove to avoid making the UN vote a reflection of American power or influence. An influential study on China policy prepared for the president by the Rand Corporation had explained that the administration "should not stake too much prestige nor arouse the United States public on an issue this risky." Pushing too hard for dual representation might alienate Beijing and damage Sino-American rapprochement.[36] In the absence of strong American pressure, the United Nations voted to admit the PRC and expel Taiwan.[37] For Washington, this outcome was not optimal, but it had enabled the United States to avoid forsaking Taipei while satisfying one of China's most critical demands.

After China's admission to the United Nations became a fait accompli, the Nixon administration anticipated using the organization to redirect Beijing's ambitions. In November, the president ordered the formation of an ad hoc committee to study the implications of Chinese participation in the United Nations and other multilateral institutions.[38] The committee's report anticipated that the PRC would continue to attach importance to upholding its status in the Third World as a champion of anti-imperialism. This would of course mean rhetorical attacks against the United States. Beijing's "desire to become the leader of the 'Third World' and its antagonistic posture vis-à-vis the U.S., USSR and Japan" assured that it would be "especially radical on colonial and economic issues, placing ideology and propaganda ahead of practicability." At the same time, the report foresaw that Beijing's radicalism would be tempered through participation in international organizations. Ultimately, "to succeed in the leadership role it seems to be intent on asserting," the PRC would "have to demonstrate that multilateral diplomacy can, with PRC participation, produce results and reach agreements more satisfactory to the Afro-Asian states than those reached prior to PRC entry into the UN." China would need "to adopt more pragmatic bargaining positions and become more willing to reach compromise settlements."[39] In other words, now that China had joined the United Nations, it might continue to espouse the radical causes that it had long considered critical to its prestige, but it could also gain stature through compromising with the United States and its allies on some issues.

Given these alternatives, Washington determined to hasten Beijing's integration into the United Nations and other international bodies with the hope that doing so would lead it toward greater moderation. The committee recommended in particular that the United States "facilitate an early and active participation by the PRC in a wide variety of UN activities where its presence is inevitable or where a basis for cooperation with it exists." It should also "discourage the PRC from looking at these institutions from a purely political and propaganda point of view."[40] Such efforts to co-opt Beijing would also dominate the Nixon administration's thinking during the president's visit to China in February.

As Nixon's visit to Beijing approached, the administration became increasingly determined to collaborate with the Chinese to strengthen the prestige of both nations. Meetings, Nixon believed, would need to be conducted in an atmosphere of mutual respect. In notes that he jotted down for his talk with Mao, the president determined to:

Treat him (as Emperor)

1 Don't quarrel.
2 Don't praise him (too much).
3 Praise the people—art, ancient.
4 Praise poems.
5 Love of country.[41]

At the same time, Nixon's advisers were eager to ensure that the Chinese would not try to take advantage of the summit to launch a propaganda attack against the president. In January, Alexander Haig, then serving as deputy national security adviser, met with Zhou Enlai to go over final preparation for the summit. During the meeting, Haig warned Zhou that "most American journalists are shallow idiots" who tended to "draw their editorial line from the atmospherics of the situation." It was therefore "crucial that there be no public embarrassment of the president as a result of his visit to Beijing." It was in their "mutual interest that the visit reinforce Nixon's image as a world leader." Zhou assured Haig that his side had "taken into consideration the fact that you have certain internal problems which we see from the press."[42]

Nixon hoped that Beijing and Washington would come to share a reciprocal concern for each other's standing that extended to some of the more intractable issues in Asian politics. He repeatedly emphasized that neither country would benefit if they sought to force each other to back away from existing commitments. The president explained in his notes what he presumably hoped to get across to Chairman Mao:

We must be honorable to old friends or our friendship is worthless to new friends.

1 We don't ask them to give up their ideology or their friends.
2 They must not ask us to do so.[43]

Nixon believed that such trade-offs would enable the two sides to pursue rapprochement without appearing weak before their long-standing allies.

Perhaps the most significant trade-off that the president sought was on the issues of Taiwan and Vietnam. He followed up on Kissinger's efforts to link the two in a way that would not damage the prestige of either side. Elsewhere in his handwritten notes, Nixon expressed this quite bluntly:

Taiwan=Vietnam=trade off

1 Your people expect action on Taiwan.
2 Our people expect action on Vietnam. Neither can act immediately—But both are inevitable—Let us not embarrass each other.[44]

The president realized that China had little choice but to continue to support Hanoi even as Americans continued to die in Vietnam. He hoped that if he showed understanding for the Chinese position on the issue, Beijing would tolerate gradual progress toward normalization rather than immediate U.S. derecognition of Taipei.

Sometimes tacitly, sometimes explicitly, the two sides agreed not to force each other to abandon their principles or their allies. Nixon, for instance, fully expected Chinese rhetorical attacks on American imperialism to continue. Just before leaving China, the president expressed his hope that although disagreements might continue to arise between Beijing and Washington, the two sides would "avoid personal references" and "keep the rhetoric cool." In his final conversation with Zhou, Nixon tried to explain how this might work: "You have a position, in your country and in the whole socialist movement and the world, a position of principle which we, of course, expect you to maintain. We have a position on our side which is a different one. We will avoid giving any indication that either of us changed our principles. The only indication we will give is that we tried to find here common ground, and as time goes on, we will try to find more common ground."[45] This approach to Beijing differed starkly from that of Nixon's predecessors. Whereas Eisenhower, Kennedy, and Johnson had attempted to diminish the PRC's status as a champion of revolutions, Nixon had no problem with the Chinese maintaining their credibility in this regard. The important thing was that neither side appear to be wavering in its support for long-held positions as a result of the summit.

Zhou and his colleagues demonstrated a similar concern for American prestige even if they differed with their counterparts on the nature of the most honorable courses of action for the United States. This came across most clearly in some of Zhou's criticisms of the U.S. position in Vietnam. Whereas Nixon discussed at length why the demands of "peace with honor" might require the United States to maintain a military presence in Indochina for some time, Zhou encouraged Nixon to withdraw American forces sooner rather than later. But he did not do so simply to express his opposition to U.S. policy. Zhou recognized as much as Nixon did how the Vietnam War was sapping America's strength and prestige in international politics. The premier told Nixon flatly, "The later you withdraw from Indochina, the more you'll be in a passive position and although your interests is to bring about an honorable conclusion to the war, the result would be to the contrary."[46] Zhou might have simply been trying to influence Nixon's thinking about Vietnam by using the president's own terms and logic. But more likely—especially when one considers Beijing's overall motives for agreeing to the Nixon visit—the premier sincerely did not want to see the United States greatly weakened.

The text of the Shanghai Communiqué, a joint statement issued at the end of Nixon's visit, codified the administration's approach. Both sides inserted clear statements of their principles. The United States reaffirmed its support for "individual freedom and social progress for all the peoples of the world, free of outside pressure or intervention." It also pledged to maintain close ties with South Korea and Japan. The PRC, for its part, was eager to ensure that the Nixon-Mao summit did not tarnish its image as a revolutionary leader in the Third World. Beijing reiterated its firm support for "the struggles of all of the oppressed peoples and nations for freedom and liberation," referring in particular to the "peoples of Viet Nam, Laos and Cambodia." The United States did not explicitly promise to switch its recognition from Taipei to Beijing but made it clear that American policy would move in that direction. The communiqué stated that "progress toward the normalization of relations between China and the United States is in the interest of all countries." Washington acknowledged that Taiwan was part of China and expressed its intention gradually to withdraw its forces from the island.[47] What made the communiqué "excellent" in the words of one high-ranking American official who worked on it was a sense of progress in Sino-U.S. relations that was readily apparent to the rest of the international community.[48] At the same time, the language adopted in the communiqué protected the standing of both sides among their respective allies.

Nixon's China visit reconfigured both Sino-American relations and international politics. Nowhere was this more apparent than in the Third World. With Beijing and Washington now seeking to strengthen rather than destroy each other's prestige in the region, allegiances shifted and new opportunities appeared. Both countries benefited from the summit—not only because of the euphoric atmosphere that it created but also because the two could now subtly support each other in obtaining key objectives.

As Sino-American relations warmed, the tone and content of Beijing's advice to Hanoi changed. Chinese leaders were no longer eager to see America humiliated by the war in Indochina. In some ways, the PRC soon became almost as interested in bringing about an honorable U.S. exit from Vietnam as the Nixon administration was. During their conversations with Vietnamese leaders, Zhou and Mao encouraged Hanoi to negotiate with the United States and even to concede to some American demands. On 12 July 1972, Le Duc Tho, the DRV's chief negotiator in the peace talks in Paris, traveled to Beijing to consult with Zhou Enlai. The premier encouraged the Vietnamese to remain vigilant in their struggle but also pushed them to mix confrontation with negotiation. He told Le, "On the one hand, it is necessary to prepare for fighting. On the other hand, you have to negotiate," and he related the CCP's experiences in talking while fighting during the Chinese civil war and the Korean War. He recommended that Hanoi grant Washington a concession by allowing South Vietnamese president Nguyen Van Thieu to serve as a representative in a future coalition government. Zhou admitted that Nguyen was a "puppet of the US" but believed that if Washington saw him sharing power in the future Vietnamese government, it would "find it easier to accept a political solution."[49] Zhou and Mao offered their Vietnamese allies similar advice leading up to the signing of the Paris Peace Accords in January 1973.[50]

American officials were pleased with Beijing's efforts on Vietnam. In a memo to Henry Kissinger, one high-ranking member of the NSC staff explained that the PRC had "taken a low-key and two-sided approach to the Vietnam situation, at once expressing verbal support for their Vietnamese allies, but keeping the tone of their rhetoric against the USG [U.S. government] quite cool." Chinese public statements had "continued to call for a peaceful resolution of the Vietnam war" and "avoided attacking the President by name."[51] This was exactly what the Americans hoped for from Beijing. They knew that China would continue to support the Vietnamese but believed that by encouraging negotiation and not casting too much verbal abuse on the United States, Beijing could facilitate the honorable exit that the president sought.

As the PRC helped to revitalize America's standing in the world through encouraging progress in Vietnam, the United States strengthened Beijing's prestige in two key ways: it reduced its support for Taipei, and it did not obstruct China's efforts to expand its relations with the more conservative Afro-Asian nations where American influence was strong. The most immediate manifestation of Washington's diminished support for Taiwan was the drawing down of U.S. forces on the island. Although errors made in counting personnel meant that the initial reductions were less than anticipated, the number of U.S. troops in Taiwan did fall from 8,735 in fiscal year 1972 to 7,139 the following year.[52] When Kissinger traveled to China in November 1973, he privately offered Zhou further assurances on this front—promising that total U.S. forces in Taiwan would be halved by 1974 and that American F-4 Phantom jets, which were capable of delivering a nuclear payload, would be removed.[53] These gestures were important to the Chinese not only because they signified the sincerity of America's intent to normalize relations but also because they weakened Taipei's standing relative to Beijing's.

The Nixon administration's willingness to see Chinese diplomacy reinvigorated had been apparent from the time the president took office. But this left open the question of how the United States would respond when Beijing tried to improve its relations with American allies. The nations of Southeast Asia—especially the more conservative ones such as Malaysia, Thailand, and Indonesia—were attuned to developments on the mainland and, as Beijing began seeking to end its isolation, naturally contemplated improved relations with it. Washington could have pressured its allies in the region to shun contacts with Beijing by threatening to withhold military or economic assistance. Even before Nixon visited China, however, this was not the U.S. approach. The American consulate in Taiwan, for instance, had predicted that countries in the region would eventually move toward varying degrees of accommodation with Beijing. Despite some concerns, the consulate nevertheless called for the United States to take a hands-off position. It explained that "the enhancement of [Beijing's] diplomatic influence through the pursuit of détente would probably not be so harmful to U.S. interests as to justify our intervention" and concluded that "U.S. efforts to prevent or deter accommodation between [Beijing] and these nations are not warranted."[54]

In this more permissive international context, China was able to normalize and improve relations with numerous countries that had previously regarded it with suspicion. Chinese diplomats often returned to the rhetoric of Afro-Asian unity and peaceful coexistence although they did not target it against the United States as they had in the past. In Latin America, Beijing maintained normal relations with Chile after Augusto Pinochet seized power from Salvador Allende's socialist government in a military coup that was tacitly encouraged by Washington. Although the PRC came under criticism from some progressive countries for supporting a military dictator, CCP leaders blamed

Allende's pro-Soviet policies for his demise and cited the Five Principles of Peaceful Coexistence as the basis for its dealings with the new government in Santiago.[55] Beijing's maneuvering in Africa followed a similar pattern. Here, too, the PRC embraced numerous governments that it had once ostracized. China normalized relations with Ethiopia in November 1970 and then invited its emperor, Haile Selassie, for a state visit in October 1971. During the visit Zhou emphasized that their two countries could cooperate despite the differences in their governing philosophies: "The Afro-Asian peoples should unite and support each other under the banner of the Bandung Conference and observe the Five Principles of Peaceful Coexistence toward countries with different social systems."[56] Zhou used similar rhetoric when he entertained Mobutu Sese Seko, the staunchly pro-American, highly autocratic president of Zaire, in January 1973. The premier explained to Mobutu that "our social systems and ideologies are not alike. But this should not impede us from developing peaceful friendly relations on the basis of the Five Principles of Peaceful Coexistence."[57] Over the next few years, cooperation between Beijing and Zaire increased as both countries strove to weaken the Soviet presence in Africa. Between 1972 and 1980, Zaire received more than $130 million in economic aid from the PRC.[58]

Within a year of Nixon's China visit, Beijing and Washington recognized that they shared some objectives in the Third World. Their mutual opposition to Soviet expansionism made America willing to support Beijing's efforts to restore its influence in Asia and Africa; for its part, Beijing needed a strong United States that could confront Moscow and did not want to see America humiliated. Although Americans continued to harbor suspicions about China, they found by the end of 1973 that it was not difficult to harmonize their views when it came to some developments in the Third World. Americans waxed optimistic about the future of Sino-American relations and the opportunities that might present themselves for cooperation in Asia and Africa.

After subsequent visits to China in February and November 1973, Kissinger filed upbeat reports that highlighted not only the growing warmth in the relationship but also a convergence of interests in the Third World. Washington and Hanoi had reached a settlement roughly one month before the February visit, and this contributed to what Kissinger described as a "frank and cordial" atmosphere during his twenty hours of meetings with Zhou. He wrote to Nixon, "With the Vietnam settlement behind us, the reception was the warmest and easiest ever," and "the Chinese are bent on accelerating our relationship." He added that evidence of a shared worldview had appeared in earlier meetings, but the Vietnam War "inhibited Chinese moves." With the conflict over, the "floodgates opened."[59] Kissinger called his November visit "a positive success on all planes" and boasted that the United States and China had become "tacit allies" in that they agreed on the "necessity of a strong American world role" to counter the Soviets and the "strategic importance of Europe, Japan, the Middle East and the Near East-South Asia axis."[60]

But even as the Sino-American relationship appeared to be improving on the surface, potential troubles bubbled underneath. Despite his optimistic tone, the secretary of state raised several caveats. One was the political future of Nixon himself. The Watergate scandal was weakening the president's position, and this concerned Beijing. "Our domestic situation clearly troubles the Chinese," Kissinger explained. They worried that internal political turmoil would undercut U.S. leadership in world affairs, and the secretary understood well that Washington would lose its "principal value" to the Chinese if it did not "act as a major force on a global scale." Kissinger also worried about China's domestic politics. He noted that Mao and Zhou appeared healthy, but they were "old" and appeared to face domestic political challenges. "We have no assurance," he worried, "that the PRC will continue its policy toward us when Mao and Zhou depart."[61] Kissinger's memo should probably have struck a far more ominous tone. Many of the developments that caused him concern would accelerate during the next year, destabilizing the fragile Sino-American rapprochement and lessening the euphoria about China that prevailed in Washington.

Competition within a Cooperative Framework

The early successes of Sino-American détente made it appear that reconciliation would be an unexpectedly easy process. The period between 1974 and 1976 proved otherwise. China and the United States continued to share the strategic objective that had brought them together—containing the advance of an increasingly assertive Soviet Union. But persistent ideological and strategic differences made it difficult for each to maintain its own prestige, especially in the Third World, without undermining or disappointing the other. Leaders from the two sides still met frequently and continued seeking to harmonize their interests through broad discussions of international politics. Cooperation, however, often proved elusive, and areas of disagreement soon resurfaced.

The domestic political turmoil that swept both countries during this period was unquestionably a complicating factor. As the Watergate scandal destroyed the Nixon presidency, an increasingly assertive Congress imposed constraints on U.S. policy that made Washington appear a less dependable partner. At the same time, a power struggle between radicals, led by the so-called Gang of Four, and pragmatic reformers, led by Deng Xiaoping, occurred within the CCP. After 1974, Deng Xiaoping replaced Zhou Enlai as the PRC's chief diplomat in discussions with Kissinger. But Deng's position was tenuous during this period and Americans were often baffled by the inconsistent tone of Chinese policy.

Sino-American rapprochement began to veer off course during the fall of 1973. By that time Beijing was growing disenchanted with the United States for two key reasons. First, it was suspicious of Washington's efforts to pursue détente with the Soviet Union, which it feared could be directed against China. General Secretary Leonid Brezhnev's June 1973 visit to Washington stoked Chinese fears that the Americans were planning to collude with the Soviets. Second, it was frustrated at the Nixon administration's slow progress in drawing down its commitments to Taipei and moving toward full recognition of Beijing. Although Nixon had explained the political and bureaucratic hurdles that needed to be scaled before Washington could formally establish ties with the PRC, party leaders became impatient.[62] Both sources of Chinese dissatisfaction stemmed to some degree from anxieties about the PRC's status in international politics.

American summitry with Moscow concerned China primarily because it seemed to put them in an inferior position vis-à-vis the United States. One of the key objectives of the so-called triangular diplomacy pursued by the Nixon administration was to make sure that Washington maintained lines of communication with both Beijing and Moscow even as the two remained locked in bitter enmity. In his memoirs, Kissinger explained: "American's national interest required us to maneuver in a way that would position us closer to each of the Communist giants than they were to each other." Washington tilted toward Beijing because it was "the weaker and the more exposed," but Nixon and Kissinger feared that they would lose leverage if they simply cast their lot with Beijing.[63]

Ironically, it was the very success of this strategy that contributed to the cooling of Sino-American relations. Mao, a masterful strategist and tactician, understood all too well the diplomatic advantages that Washington was accruing and didn't like it. The Chinese naturally wanted to be the most central and important players in the triangle and envied how Nixon-Kissinger diplomacy had put the United States in an ascendant position. Kissinger remembered that the chairman "understood our design far better than our domestic critics did" and would "surely have preferred to be on the side of the strategic triangle that had the greater options."[64] When Kissinger visited Beijing in October 1975, an ailing Mao pointedly vented his frustration; he accused the Americans of "leaping" to Moscow "by way of our shoulders."[65] What made American summitry with Moscow so difficult for Mao to stomach was not simply that it raised the prospect of U.S.-Soviet collusion but that it seemed to give Washington a more elevated role in international affairs while making Beijing a less critical player.

It is therefore not surprising that Chinese officials attempted to discourage the thaw in U.S.-Soviet relations. During talks with their American counterparts, they railed constantly against the threat posed by an expansionist Soviet Union and accused Washington of being too soft. Such accusations reached an angry crescendo during a series of talks in late 1975. In October, Kissinger journeyed to China to help prepare for an upcoming visit by President Gerald Ford. Deng Xiaoping repeatedly warned the secretary of state that the "polar bear" was "out to fix the United States." It could do so because it had "a greater military strength than the United States and the European countries put together."[66] Mao also chastised the United States for its passive posture vis-à-vis the Soviets, albeit in a more obscure tone. The chairman warned somewhat cryptically, "The world is not tranquil and a storm—the wind and rain—are coming. And at the approach of the wind and rain the swallows are busy."[67] Winston Lord summarized the meeting as "on the whole disturbing, signifying a cooling of our relationship linked to the Chinese perception of the U.S. as a fading strategic power in the face of Soviet advance."[68]

Washington's handling of the Taiwan question fueled Chinese disillusionment. Although the United States promised that normalization was on the horizon, CCP officials believed that American policy contradicted the spirit of the Shanghai Communiqué. In February 1974, the Nixon administration appointed Leonard S. Unger, a seasoned Asia expert, as its new ambassador to the ROC. The move upset Chinese officials while seeming to provide reassurance to Taipei that Washington was not ready to abandon it. The United States had also agreed to construct a new embassy building in Taiwan, allow the establishment of new ROC consulates in the United States, and furnish Taiwan with new military technologies.[69] At the same time, a host of minor problems and perceived slights made it difficult for the new liaison offices that Beijing and Washington had set up for dealing with each other to operate smoothly.[70] One of Beijing's central motives for pursuing rapprochement with Washington in the first place was to strengthen its stature and weaken Taipei's. When American diplomacy bolstered Taipei's confidence, it naturally became a source of frustration.

The combination of Chinese disappointment with the United States and intensifying Sino-Soviet rivalry triggered a renewed emphasis on the Third World in PRC diplomacy. Seeking to recoup in Asia and Africa what it believed it had lost in its relations with the superpowers, Beijing vigorously reasserted itself as a leader in the Third World. In early 1974, Mao and Deng began to espouse Three Worlds Theory. The chairman first articulated a rough version of the theory during a meeting with Zambian president Kenneth Kaunda in February 1974.[71] With Mao's instruction, Deng Xiaoping gave a much fuller elaboration during a speech to the UN General Assembly in April. He explained that the two hegemonic superpowers constituted the First World, the developing countries of Asia, Africa and Latin America belonged to the Third World, and that the developed countries of Europe and Asia made up the Second World. The two superpowers were the "biggest international exploiters and oppressors" of the day, continuously seeking to bring the nations of the Third World under their control and bully the countries in the Second World.[72]

Three Worlds Theory in essence enabled Beijing to reclaim the mantra of champion of Asia, Africa, and Latin America against superpower ambitions. The theory avoided labeling nations as enemies by virtue of their governing ideology—a fact that would enable the PRC to normalize relations with Thailand and other pro-Western nations in the Third World. Nonetheless, it returned to the theme of south-south cooperation as a means of undermining Great Power hegemonism, using the very fact that the PRC was not a Great Power to foster a more favorable image of China. The new theory may have been directed more against the Soviet Union than the United States.[73] Nevertheless, in asserting itself as a champion of the Third World and calling for unity against the superpowers the PRC was unconcerned about whether American prestige suffered collateral damage.

The theory informed much of Beijing's diplomacy toward Asian, African, and Latin American nations over the next two years. Party officials regularly lectured foreign dignitaries about American and Soviet intentions while exhorting them to resist Great Power hegemony. When the prime minister of Congo-Brazzaville, Henri Lopès, visited China and met with Deng Xiaoping in February 1975, Deng told him that "the socialist camp no longer exists." The vice premier went on to encourage unity among Third World nations. "The problems of the Third World," he explained, "can only be solved through cooperation. The most important thing is to prevent the two hegemonists from benefiting."[74] After agreeing to normalize relations with Thailand, Deng welcomed the country's prime minister, Kukrit Pramoj, to China with similar rhetoric. "The basic problem of today's international situation," he complained, "is the rivalry of the two hegemonists. Many problems are created by the U.S.-Soviet struggle for hegemony." He also called for Third World unity and the creation of a "zone of peace" in Southeast Asia.[75] Through much of the period between 1974 and 1976, Deng continued this somewhat Janus-faced approach toward the United States—holding multiple rounds of high-level talks with Kissinger even as he publicly excoriated American hegemonism. It was a delicate balancing act through which China sought to strengthen its influence in the Third World by attacking United States without freezing the ongoing Sino-U.S. dialogue.

Washington understood what the CCP was up to, although some American officials were more troubled by Beijing's toughening rhetoric than others. Among those most piqued by the PRC's strategy was future president George H. W. Bush, who spent fourteen months in China as Chief of the U.S. Liaison Office. In his *China Diary*, Bush simultaneously captured the thrill of immersion in a rich but long-isolated culture and the frustrations of conducting diplomacy in a nation whose leaders still sat on the opposite side of an ideological chasm. And he did it all in the characteristic mangled syntax that would later become a hallmark of his presidency. Many of his diary entries reflected an understanding of China's motives but conveyed a deep chagrin at the nearly constant drumbeat of harsh rhetoric against American imperialism. In a diary entry from December 1974, Bush complained of the Chinese, "They are sensitive to affronts—their being concerned about the opening of the consulates and putting an ambassador in Taiwan. But they think nothing of slamming us hard in public. I say they think nothing of it. I am sure they balance it out and decide they have to do this to maintain their revolutionary credentials and to clearly establish themselves as the leader of the Third World."[76]

Bush did try to persuade the Chinese to tone down their rhetoric. As the United States began to reassess its policy in Southeast Asia after its withdrawal from Vietnam, Bush wrote a somewhat jumbled diary entry that described what he saw as his agenda: "Southeast Asia. Total reassessment of policy, summing up with China. Probing more in depth what they mean about hegemony. Convincing them that we are not hegemonic; insisting to them, more than we do, that the rhetoric of the Third World, which is causing an unraveling at the United Nations[,] . . . is no good for world peace."[77] Ultimately, for Bush, China's sharp criticisms of the United States posed a bewildering predicament. He recognized that China wanted and even needed rapprochement to continue but that it also needed to assume a radical, anti-American posture in the Third World. "Obviously China wants us strong and wants us involved in many places," he wrote, "and yet publicly they must be on us as imperialists. A dilemma."[78]

Other American officials, notably Henry Kissinger, took a more benign view of Beijing's frequent verbal attacks. During his meetings with Chinese officials, the secretary of state sometimes joked with his counterparts about "firing empty cannons"—a Chinese phrase referring to the PRC's use of essentially empty rhetoric to put its position on record without entailing concrete commitments. Kissinger and Nixon came to expect that Chinese officials would resort to this practice from time to time but keep their criticisms of the United States within certain predictable limits. The relatively light-hearted manner in which Kissinger typically approached this issue can be gleaned from one conversation that he had with PRC vice foreign minister Qiao Guanhua in October 1974. Qiao had just given a speech at the United Nations replete with the usual Chinese denunciations of the two hegemonists, and Kissinger believed that he had gone a little too far. Kissinger remarked that the "Vice Foreign Minister fired full cannons today, no empty cannons," and "established a degree of equivalence" between Moscow and Washington instead of making it clear that the Soviets were the greater evil as he usually did. Qiao protested that he had in fact criticized the Soviets more but that he needed to include some criticism of Washington to give his denunciation of Moscow greater credibility. He told Kissinger: "I have to give you some criticisms. If I don't, then I'm not on good grounds for criticizing our neighbor [the Soviet Union]." Laughter broke out when the secretary of state laconically replied, "I just want you to know that we won't feel offended if you don't."[79] To be sure, Kissinger was also trying in a subtle way to change the tone of Chinese discourse. But he nevertheless accepted that Beijing would have to publicly adhere to certain positions to maintain its own credibility.

But even if the goals of Beijing's attacks on American hegemony were to enhance the PRC's prestige and reflected no real animosity toward the United States, they had very real implications when it came to possibilities for cooperation in the Third World. During Gerald Ford's tenure in office there were two places in particular—Cambodia and Angola—where the United States hoped for Chinese support but came away disappointed and ultimately suffered setbacks. In his memoirs, Kissinger attributes these failures largely to growing congressional activism, which, he insists, constrained American actions at critical junctures. But in both cases, China's concern about its standing in the Third World proved an obstacle to fuller Sino-American cooperation.

In Cambodia, Beijing and Washington had found themselves on opposite sides in yet another civil war beginning in 1970, but by 1973 their interests in the country had some areas of convergence. In 1970, the Cambodian military had ousted Prince Sihanouk while he was on a visit to the Soviet Union and replaced him with the general Lon Nol. The Nixon administration supported the general because Sihanouk's absence made it easier for the United States to carry out plans to launch an invasion into Cambodian territory with the goal of wiping out hidden North Vietnamese sanctuaries.[80] On the heels of the invasion, the United States launched a massive bombing campaign in the Cambodian countryside in a further effort to extirpate the Communists. But far from weakening Communist forces, Sihanouk's removal and the U.S. invasion bolstered the popularity of indigenous insurgents known as the Khmer Rouge, who were supported by Hanoi. A civil war between the Lon Nol government and the Khmer Rouge erupted, and over the next three years, the Khmers steadily increased the proportion of Cambodian territory under their control.[81]

China's initial strategy was to encourage unity between its old ally Sihanouk and the Khmer Rouge. The prince would remain in China while the insurgents liberated Cambodia from Lon Nol and the U.S. imperialists. Sihanouk established a government in exile known as the Royal Government of National Union Kampuchea that used Beijing as a base and received extensive Chinese funding and advice.[82] At the same time, the PRC sent several million dollars over the Ho Chi Minh Trail for the Khmer Rouge to purchase weapons from corrupt government officials.[83] Beijing's likely motive was to gain the trust of both Sihanouk and the Khmer Rouge. Which of the two would be the more important force in Cambodian politics if Lon Nol was defeated was uncertain, but this strategy seemed to maximize Beijing's chances of reestablishing a strong influence over its former ally. Yet the CCP remained uneasy about the situation in general and the Khmer Rouge in particular. Though strains between the Khmer Rouge and the Vietnamese were becoming apparent, Hanoi's influence over the Cambodian insurgency remained paramount, and the Vietnamese continued to move closer to the Soviets. As the struggle progressed and Sino-Vietnamese solidarity weakened, Beijing worried that Moscow would use its ties to Hanoi to enhance its influence in Cambodia.[84]

Washington shared Beijing's interest in assuring that the Soviets did not strengthen their presence in Phnom Penh. When Kissinger traveled to Beijing for talks with Zhou Enlai in February 1973, the two discussed the possibility of working together to establish a coalition government in Cambodia that would not be subservient to Moscow or Hanoi. The problem was that they disagreed on the configuration of the coalition government. The Chinese encouraged the United States to improve relations with Sihanouk and promised the Americans that a government under the prince's leadership would remain neutral and not be subject to outside control. Zhou explained to Kissinger that Beijing did not want to turn Sihanouk into "someone that would heed our beck and call" because it "would be like hegemony." Moreover, it was "impossible for Cambodia to become completely red now" and that if it "were attempted, it would result in even greater problems."[85] Washington, however, wanted Beijing to open contacts with Lon Nol, which Zhou flatly refused.[86] In the end, no firm agreement was reached. Kissinger assured Zhou that he agreed with him on basic principles—that Cambodia should be independent, neutral, and peaceful—but explained vaguely that they would have to find "some framework for achieving them in a way that takes account of all the real forces."[87]

Over the next few months, however, the two seemed to move closer to an agreement on Cambodia. In May, Kissinger offered significant concessions, including the withdrawal of U.S. personnel and a halt to American bombings. He also expressed a willingness to proceed with discussions between Ambassador David Bruce (the chief of the U.S. liaison office in Beijing) and Sihanouk while stating that the United States would not oppose the prince's return to Cambodia. Washington would arrange for Lon Nol to leave the country for medical treatment in the United States. But the secretary of state also tried to make it clear that such compromises would be acceptable only if implemented in a way that did not weaken American credibility. The process of easing Lon Nol out of power and returning Sihanouk had to "extend over some time" and could "not be conducted in a way that" did not "take into account" American "necessities."[88]

By mid-June, Kissinger was optimistic that a settlement was in reach. But then on 18 July, Han Xu, the deputy director of the PRC liaison office in Washington, delivered a highly disconcerting note to Brent Scowcroft, who served as military assistant to the president. The note lambasted Washington for continuing its bombing campaigns and supporting Lon Nol. It then explained that under such circumstances, it was "obviously inappropriate to communicate to Samdech Sihanouk the tentative thinking on the settlement of the Cambodia question as set forth by the U.S. side last May." Kissinger correctly read the note as "an opting-out by the Chinese of any involvement in negotiations for a Cambodian settlement."[89] Beijing's about-face on Cambodia left the Nixon administration surprised and disappointed. Despite American pleading, China's position on the issue hardened in subsequent months. When Kissinger approached the Chinese about the issue again in June 1974, the PRC liaison chief told him bluntly that "we support the Cambodian people in continuing their struggle; we do not want to involve ourselves in peace negotiations."[90] In the absence of negotiations, the Khmer Rouge scored repeated victories on the battlefield until Phnom Penh fell in April 1975.

Americans could never completely understand the reasons that Chinese policy toward Cambodia had switched so rapidly. Was it a reaction to something specific that Washington did? Or did it reflect China's changing domestic political situation? More important than either of these explanations was Beijing's evolving view of the Khmer Rouge.[91] Before mid-1973, the CCP leadership had been deeply concerned that if the Khmer Rouge triumphed, it could cement the domination of all of Indochina by a Soviet-Vietnamese axis. But by the summer of 1973, tensions had already surfaced between the Vietnamese politburo and the Khmer Rouge leadership. Hanoi had been pressuring the Cambodians to begin peace talks, which Khmer Rouge leaders refused. When the Communist Party of Cambodia (CPK) held its annual plenum in July, its delegates decided that Vietnam should now be treated as a "friend but a friend with conflict."[92] As Vietnamese influence over the Khmer Rouge faded, the PRC saw an opportunity to advance its interests.

During the period between mid-1973 and 1975, China's support for the Khmer Rouge grew in generosity and enthusiasm. Beijing's motives reflected a combination of realpolitik and lingering aspirations to be viewed as the leader of revolutionary forces in Asia. As CPK general secretary Pol Pot and the Khmer Rouge leadership improved ties with the PRC, Beijing saw one last opportunity to mentor other Asian revolutionaries. After 1974, Khmer Rouge leaders began to make more frequent and lengthy visits to the PRC. During the visits, they often expressed a sense of revolutionary camaraderie with the Chinese that unquestionably endeared them to the aging CCP leaders. American officials took notice when Khieu Samphan, the deputy prime minister of GRUNK, visited Beijing in April 1974 and "offered unstinting praise for the PRC."[93] By the time Khieu left China in late May, he had received a pledge from Mao that Beijing would supply his forces with weapons free of charge. China also provided the Khmer Rouge with important tactical assistance during the final stage of their struggle by helping to mine the Mekong River and shut off enemy supply lines.[94]

After the Khmer Rouge triumphed, Mao positioned himself as both a mentor and a key supporter of the new Cambodian government. Pol Pot visited China in June 1975, shortly after his forces had taken Phnom Penh, and was one of the last foreign leaders to meet with the ailing leader. Although Mao's comments were somewhat obscure, no doubt due to his poor condition at the time, the chairman's excitement at once again offering advice to another revolutionary nevertheless comes across. Pol Pot told Mao that he had studied the chairman's writings on people's war from his youth and used them as a road map for the CPK.[95] The chairman replied with a somewhat rambling statement on the nature of socialism, Leninism, and communism and told the younger revolutionary that he "should not completely copy China's experience" and think for himself because Marx's theory was "a guideline for action but not a doctrine."[96] Two months later, Beijing promised the Khmer Rouge one billion dollars in aid over the next five years.[97] The CCP had clearly forsaken the possibility of cooperation with Washington in order to support the Khmer Rouge. Chinese policy reflected the fact that the PRC was still struggling to set its priorities. It unquestionably wanted to continue its dialogue with the United States, but it still desired to be seen as a leader in the Afro-Asian world, especially among revolutionaries. It faced a tough choice but in the end was willing to forego cooperation with its erstwhile rival if doing so enhanced its status in a strategic neighboring country.

In Angola, Beijing and Washington had an even stronger incentive to cooperate, but here, too, China proved unwilling to sacrifice its revolutionary credentials for the sake of détente. Since 1961, Angolan revolutionaries had waged an armed struggle for independence against Portugal, which had countered with a fierce counterinsurgency campaign. The long war for independence ended in January 1975, not through a victory on the battlefield but owing to a change of power in Lisbon. A military coup in Portugal the previous year led to the formation of a new government that wanted to end Portuguese involvement in Africa and grant Angola its independence. The problem for Angola was that its independence movement had never been unified; it was the product of an uneasy alliance among three groups—each with strengths in different tribes and regions. The first of these, the National Front for the Liberation of Angola (FNLA), was characterized by a strong sense of indigenous nationalism that was mistrustful of both communism and Western imperialism. The Popular Movement for the Liberation of Angola (MPLA) adhered to a Marxist agenda that stressed the need for social revolution. Finally, the National Union for the Total Liberation of Angola (UNITA) differentiated itself from the other two primarily by its enthusiastic embrace of militarism and emphasis on national unity and self-sufficiency.[98] No sooner had Angola gained its independence than these three movements began to struggle among themselves for dominance.

The divisions within the Angolan liberation movement soon turned the newly independent country into a theater for Great Power conflict. The MPLA's closest allies were Cuba and the Soviet Union, with Moscow providing weapons and funds and Havana sending troops to train MPLA forces in guerrilla warfare. Chiefly to prevent the Soviet-backed MPLA from gaining control, the Ford administration authorized nearly twenty-five million dollars for the CIA to conduct covert operations in support of the FNLA and UNITA.[99] Beijing's strategy toward the civil war in Angola was the most complicated. During the 1960s, Beijing had played host to leaders from both the MPLA and FNLA and veered back and forth in its estimation of these organizations.[100] When the Portuguese empire collapsed, China was torn between its desire to burnish its reputation as an ally of liberation movements and its equally powerful determination to limit opportunities for Soviet expansion. The result was a schizophrenic policy. With the encouragement of its new ally in the region Mobutu, Beijing sent weapons and advisers to Zaire, where it provided training for FNLA forces.[101] At the same time, the PRC kept lines of communication open to all three liberation movements and encouraged unity among them.[102]

During the spring and summer of 1975 China repeatedly sought to hedge its bets in Angola as the military conflict between the three movements intensified. Beijing hosted visiting delegations from all three movements within a three-month time span. A visit by representatives of UNITA in May was followed one month later by a visit from an MPLA delegation. The UNITA group received a promise for small-scale assistance while the envoys from the MPLA likely pleaded with Beijing to cut off its rivals.[103] Last, in July, Deng Xiaoping met with an FNLA delegation. The vice premier offered advice that seemed deliberately to avoid favoritism. He told his guests that "in the end the support of the people will decide who wins" and that the people would back whoever stood by the principles of independence, unity, and progress.[104] This was not a promise that China would help the FNLA but instead hinted that the PRC would maintain good relations with whoever emerged triumphant in Angola. Toward the end of the year, Beijing began to cut back its aid to the FNLA and joined the Organization for African Unity (OAU) in calling for an end to the conflict. What was the purpose of this involved yet noncommittal diplomacy? Part of it might have been an adjustment to the realities on the battlefield where the MPLA was making gains. But American intelligence reports also believed that through lowering its profile and aligning its views with those of the OAU, Beijing hoped to "score propaganda points at Moscow's expense."[105] By calling for unity and an end to conflict Beijing could position itself as an opponent of Great Power hegemony in Africa rather than as a partisan supporter of one side or the other.

For the Ford administration, which had decided to throw its resources behind UNITA and the FNLA, Beijing's shift toward neutrality came as a disappointment. When President Ford and Kissinger visited China in December, they subtly pressured Mao and Deng to take a more active posture in opposing the MPLA. Speaking about Angola and Africa, Ford explained: "We are taking forthright actions to prevent the Soviet Union from getting a stronghold in that part of that great continent." Skeptical about the efficacy of American efforts, Mao told the Americans bluntly: "You don't seem to have any means. Nor do we." But Ford was unwilling to give up the possibility of cooperation on an issue where Chinese and American strategic interests seemed to be so closely aligned. "We both could do better," he told Mao, and argued that "if there is broad action by ourselves, the People's Republic and others, we can prevent the Soviet Union from having a very important naval facility and controlling substantial resources in Angola." Later on, Kissinger hinted at the potential division of labor for joint Sino-American action. He told the Chinese that UNITA and the FNLA "need training from those who understand guerilla war. We can get them the equipment if others give them the training." But the Chinese did not want to be enlisted in support of a cause that they were increasingly ambivalent about in public. In the closing minutes of the meeting, Mao responded to Ford's suggestions about how the PRC could help in Angola by repeatedly promising vaguely to "make a try" while avoiding specific agreements or promises.[106]

Ultimately, of course, Angola was a disaster not only for Sino-American cooperation but also for American foreign policy. Just two weeks after Ford's visit to China, an increasingly assertive Senate passed the Tunney Amendment banning the use of funds for Angola and effectively ending covert American support for UNITA and the FNLA. Kissinger has claimed that Congress legislated a defeat for the United States in Angola when it was on the "verge of success."[107] But it is difficult to assess whether continuing CIA operations in Angola would have been sufficient to counter the decisive support that the MPLA received from Moscow and Havana even if the Ford administration had convinced Beijing to get more involved. Within months of the passage of the Tunney Amendment, the civil war in Angola was over and the Soviets had scored a significant victory.

The Ford administration's failed attempt at enlisting Chinese cooperation in Angola made the limits of the new Sino-American relationship painfully clear. The two countries' shared geostrategic interest in thwarting the Soviet Union was still not enough to trump Beijing's concerns about its prestige among national liberation movements. And even though the outcome of the civil war in Angola was less than ideal to Mao and his colleagues, China still fared significantly better than the United States in that it maintained some semblance of influence. One American intelligence report noted that although the Soviets were the MPLA's most significant supporters, the movement had "carefully avoided closing the door on" Beijing, and the group had "resisted Soviet pressures to side in the ideological dispute with China."[108] Thus although Moscow won a victory in Angola, Beijing was able to avoid a total defeat.

In the end, China's decision not to consider closer cooperation in Angola likely reflected two things: its assessment of the situation on the ground and its dissatisfaction with the American approach to détente. Things were already going badly for UNITA and the FNLA on the battlefield, and Beijing could likely recognize that they would only get worse without American funding. But this decision also continued a trend toward impartiality in Beijing's Angola policy that had been noticeable months before. The policy was part of a broader swing back to the Third World in the period between 1974 and 1976 that sought to strengthen China's identification with Afro-Asian nationalism. At the same time, Beijing's unhappiness about Washington's summitry with Moscow and failure to normalize relations with the PRC must have made it question whether the United States would be a trustworthy partner in Africa. Fortunately for Washington, the discord between China and the United States stemmed mainly from issues that could be rectified through incremental changes in American policy. When political change came to Beijing and Washington in 1976, many obstacles to closer Sino-American cooperation were removed.

Deng Xiaoping and the Carter Administration

The year 1976 marked the end of an era in Chinese politics and foreign policy. The deaths of China's two most prominent statesmen, Zhou Enlai and Mao Zedong, occurred in January and September. China would never be the same again. In a nonviolent leadership struggle that lasted roughly two years, Deng Xiaoping slowly eased Mao's hand-picked successor, Hua Guofeng, out of power and gained control over domestic and foreign policy making. During his tenure in power Deng would preside over dramatic reforms that transformed and opened China's economy. Deng brought the same characteristic pragmatism that governed his domestic policy to foreign affairs. Beijing would still seek status in all areas of the globe—including the Third World—and it remained preoccupied with countering the Soviet threat. But its strategies for acquiring social recognition changed. Under Deng, Chinese diplomacy would be weighted far more heavily toward creating a favorable environment for the country's economic development. The PRC still sought to foster a sense of solidarity with Third World countries, but support for revolution and promoting anti-Americanism faded from its agenda.

Jimmy Carter's narrow victory in the 1976 presidential election assured that American foreign policy would change as well. The new president brought a different team of advisers with their own distinctive view of America's role in the world with him to the White House. Although the Chinese viewed the political misfortunes of the principal architects of Sino-American detente with concern, the Carter administration's approach would strengthen rather than fray the new ties between Washington and Beijing. To a greater degree than his predecessors, Carter was willing to give the Chinese what they really wanted: normalization, cooperation in new areas, and, most important, assurances that the United States would stand firmly with the PRC in resisting Soviet expansion. Rather than trying to establish a diplomatic triangle that gave Washington leverage over both Moscow and Beijing, the Carter administration leaned more heavily toward the PRC as a counterweight to the Soviets. As a result, Beijing could embrace its new relationship with the United States more enthusiastically and without the suspicion that the Americans would use it to strengthen themselves at China's expense.

Carter's national security adviser Zbigniew Brzezinski was perhaps the most pivotal figure in promoting closer cooperation with China. Whereas Secretary of State Cyrus Vance tended to be wary of alienating Moscow and jeopardizing arms control negotiations, Brzezinski believed that pursuing détente with the Soviets had emboldened the Kremlin in Africa and elsewhere. He was insistent on playing the China card against Moscow and lobbied the president not only to offer the Chinese diplomatic recognition but also to build military ties and share sensitive intelligence information.[109] Brzezinski journeyed to Beijing in May 1978 as the bearer of good tidings. He told Deng Xiaoping that Carter was intent on normalizing relations and vowed that Washington intended to make no concessions to the Soviet Union. When Deng asked Brzezinski whether normalization had been delayed because Washington had a "fear of offending the Soviet Union," the national security adviser strongly insisted that this was not the case. "I would be willing to make a little bet with you," he told Deng, "as to who is less popular in the Soviet Union—you or me."[110]

During the months that followed, negotiations over normalization took place. Although his diplomacy was a world apart from that of Nixon and Kissinger on most issues, when it came to negotiations with the Chinese, Carter, too, recognized that secrecy was vital to assuring that neither side suffered embarrassment. When the president received a plan for holding discussions on the issue from the State Department he wrote comments on it that made this point clear: "Leaks can kill the whole effort. . . . Avoid any public hints of degree of progress. I don't trust: 1) Congress, 2) The White House, 3) State, or 4) Defense to keep a secret."[111] After six months of high-level negotiations, the two sides released a joint communiqué on December 15 stating their intention to recognize each other. Beijing did not get everything that it wanted; the United States was still unwilling to promise that it would discontinue arms sales to Taiwan.[112] But normalization with the United States unquestionably conferred a new degree of legitimacy on the PRC while weakening that of its rival across the Taiwan Strait.

The two sides celebrated Sino-American normalization with an official visit by Deng Xiaoping to the United States in January 1979. The visit afforded Deng a valuable opportunity to strengthen his political legitimacy at home and to boost the PRC's prestige internationally. During the visit, both sides downplayed their differences on key issues to avoid causing each other a loss of face. Deng showed particular diplomatic aplomb on the Taiwan question. Despite the generally favorable reaction that the Carter administration's decision to recognize Beijing had garnered, Taipei still had its share of extremely vocal supporters both in the halls of Congress and among the general public. The vice chairman chose his words on the issue carefully to avoid inciting a popular backlash against normalization. During one banquet sponsored by the Asia Society and several of its partners, Deng explained first that "how the problem of Taiwan's return to the motherland will be solved is an internal matter." But even as he strongly asserted Beijing's sovereignty over Taiwan, Deng strove to make it clear that the PRC was not intent on military conflict. "We absolutely wish to use peaceful methods to solve this problem," he explained, and added, "After Sino-American normalization the possibility of this kind [of solution] is greater."[113] Deng's willingness to strike a conciliatory tone minimized the domestic backlash against the Carter administration for abandoning Taiwan.

The administration demonstrated a similar flexibility on the issue of human rights. During his presidential campaign, Carter had been a crusader on the issue—he had pledged that Washington would play a leadership role in promoting social justice throughout the world. After assuming office Carter indiscriminately criticized America's allies and adversaries alike on human rights issues. China, however, would prove the exception. Before his visit to the United States, Deng stated publicly that he did not wish to discuss human rights, and Carter's advisers strongly encouraged him to avoid confrontation on the issue. Secretary of State Vance wrote to Carter that when media queries surfaced, "We should explain our world-wide commitment to the human rights issue in terms of our overall foreign policy." Such an approach would of course spare the PRC from specific criticism. Vance suggested that if Carter wanted to raise the issue, it "would be an appropriate topic for a private discussion in the car or at dinner."[114] The president's willingness to set aside what had become a central tenet of his foreign policy signified his commitment to helping the vice premier maximize the public relations benefits of his trip.

Improved relations with Washington led the PRC to tone down the anti-American component of its rhetoric in its dealings with other Afro-Asian countries. Deng continued to emphasize China's kinship with the region but did not condemn Washington. Few records of Deng's conversations with Afro-Asian leaders from the late 1970s onward have thus far been declassified. But those discussions that have been released reflect an unmistakable shift in Beijing's priorities. During a conversation with a special envoy from Algeria in May 1978, Deng explained that "our foreign policy is based on Mao Zedong's strategic thinking about the Three Worlds" and called for Third World unity. Even while criticizing imperialism and hegemonism, however, he did not single out the United States or any other country as an adversary or oppressor. At the same time, there was a new dimension to these conversations. Deng often spoke about China's past mistakes and its need for reform in highly pragmatic terms. He criticized the Gang of Four for closing China's doors so that the people "did not even know what the world was like." The country had become "technologically backward," and its "level of managerial ability was low." In the future, Deng explained, China needed to "attract the world's most advanced technology and use it as a starting point for its development."[115] Such statements likely signaled several things: that China would be focusing on its own economic development rather than spreading revolution in the coming years; that Beijing would no longer provide the same levels of military and economic aid it had in the past; and that China would still seek cooperation with other Afro-Asian countries in the shared pursuit of higher living standards.

Even as Beijing increasingly stressed pragmatic cooperation in its relations with many Afro-Asian countries, however, it worried about the "polar bear." And it was Deng's obsession with Moscow that most often guided him when he discussed the geopolitics of the Third World with his American interlocutors. Rather than contesting American influence, Deng and his colleagues frequently warned the United States that it needed to play a bigger role in the region to counter the Soviets. Throughout Zbigniew Brzezinski's May 1978 visit to the PRC, the Chinese constantly criticized American policies for not being active enough. One region where Beijing wanted the United States to contest the Soviets more vigorously was Africa. Moscow's recent triumph in Angola had engendered deep angst in China and America alike about the future of the continent. "In southern Africa the Soviet Union is energetically pushing forward its policy of expansion and infiltration," PRC foreign minister Huang Hua complained. "In the face of this expansion of Soviet-Cuban forces in Africa, the U.S. response is too weak."[116]

When the Chinese were not complaining about American passivity in Africa, they were encouraging its activities in other parts of the Third World—notably the Middle East. Mao and Zhou had repeatedly advised Kissinger and Nixon that in their dealings in the Middle East they should "use two hands," one supporting the Israelis and the other supporting the Palestinians or Egyptians. The Chinese were generally more sympathetic to the Arabs than the Israelis, but they considered peace brokered by Washington vastly preferable to any scenario in which the Soviets expanded their influence. Deng's affirmative attitude toward American diplomacy in the region was equally apparent. "I hope you succeed," he plainly told Cyrus Vance after the secretary had described American plans to find "a constructive way to shape events" in the Middle East.[117] Ironically, the combination of changing geopolitical circumstances and the Carter administration's greater willingness to accommodate Chinese concerns had, by 1979, turned the PRC into one of the strongest supporters of American policy in the Third World.

During the Carter years, Sino-American rapprochement extended beyond high-level dialogues to encompass more concrete forms of cooperation. The two sought in particular to coordinate their activities when confronted with aggressive moves by the Soviet Union or its allies. As always, the PRC was particularly zealous in guarding against new threats to its security in South and Southeast Asia. Soon after Beijing and Washington finally normalized relations, two major crises in this strategic region—the Vietnamese invasion of Cambodia and the Soviet invasion of Afghanistan—grabbed their attention. Beijing and Washington collaborated far more explicitly and extensively in the case of Afghanistan, but key officials in the Carter administration were fundamentally sympathetic to Chinese concerns in both cases.

The crisis in Cambodia began in December 1978, when Vietnamese forces marched across the border and installed a new government in Phnom Penh. The Pol Pot regime, which the Vietnamese forced out, had gained international notoriety for the murderous tactics it had used to consolidate its rule. But Vietnam's intentions were not beneficent. Once the Khmer Rouge gained power in Phnom Penh, they had tilted heavily toward the PRC in its conflict with Vietnam and the Soviet Union. The Vietnamese action was therefore intended not only to improve conditions in Cambodia but also to allay geostrategic concerns about the Sino-Cambodian entente.[118] It was a bold move that directly challenged the PRC's position in Southeast Asia and reflected Hanoi's confidence in Soviet support if conflict with China ensued.

Troubled by Hanoi's assertiveness, Deng Xiaoping ordered a brief invasion against Vietnam in February 1979, destroying any remaining semblance of Communist solidarity. Chinese forces decimated Vietnam's border defenses, moved into six provinces, and occupied three provincial capitals. In March, several weeks after the invasion had begun, Deng Xiaoping ordered the withdrawal of Chinese forces. Publicly Deng expressed satisfaction that the PRC had, in his oft-repeated phrase, "taught the Vietnamese a lesson," but the war was not a clear-cut military victory. Chinese forces had occupied Vietnamese territory but encountered firm resistance and suffered as many as twenty-five thousand casualties. Moreover, the invasion did not end Hanoi's occupation of Cambodia, which would continue for another decade. At the same time, the offensive demonstrated to the other nations of Southeast Asia that Beijing did not fear to take the initiative against Soviet allies. Moreover, Moscow had remained on the sidelines during the incursion—disappointing the Vietnamese and weakening its own credibility in the region.[119]

Launched just two months after Beijing and Washington had normalized relations and less than two weeks after Deng's visit to the United States, the invasion put the Carter administration in an awkward position. It did not want to condone a relatively straightforward case of one country invading another but was equally cautious not to alienate or embarrass the Chinese. Differences between Brzezinski and the State Department over how to handle the situation made the administration's reaction seem confused and disjointed. Nevertheless, American policy ultimately did far more to facilitate than to impede Chinese actions.

Deng had given the Carter administration fair warning. He requested a private meeting with the president during his January visit to the United States and, in Zbigniew Brzezinski's words, "dropped a small bombshell" at the feet of the president and his advisers. The national security adviser remembers that, in a "deliberate and resolute tone," Deng explained his plans for a brief, punitive expedition against the Vietnamese that would be similar in size and scope to the Sino-Indian conflict seventeen years earlier. Deng made it clear that China was prepared for the possibility of Soviet involvement and that it did not expect any support from the United States.[120]

Deng's announcement forced Carter and his advisers to consider how they would respond if the Chinese went ahead with the invasion. The White House was eager to avoid any appearance of collusion in a blatant act of military aggression, but it also did not want to disrupt the normalization process. The solution was a handwritten note from Carter to Deng urging restraint and expressing American concerns about the possible consequences of the invasion. The Carter administration likely understood that such a note was not enough to dissuade the highly resolute Chinese leadership. In fact, Brzezinski has explained that their intention was to avoid locking "the United States into a position which could generate later pressure to condemn China in the UN."[121] By going on the record against the invasion, Carter could silence domestic and international critics without having to censure the PRC in international organizations.

With the prospect of military conflict between China and Vietnam on the horizon, the White House determined that it would seek to remain neutral while keeping attuned to Chinese sensitivities. Brzezinski laid out the basis for such a policy in a memorandum to the president on 6 February. The national security adviser argued that the United States should not explicitly endorse or condemn the invasion; instead, it should demand the removal of all troops from Indochina—meaning the withdrawal of both Vietnamese and PRC forces to their own territories. He contended that this approach was "tenable on both political and moral grounds." Moreover, it would enable the crisis to be resolved in a manner that did not make the parties appear to be surrendering. Brzezinski hoped that these demands would lay the groundwork for Prince Sihanouk to return to Cambodia after the Vietnamese withdrew. American policy would "thus give everyone the face saving basis for accommodation."[122]

Once the invasion began Brzezinski continued to work—sometimes in opposition to the State Department—to strengthen China's position and avoid signaling American disapproval. On the basis of an interview with a senior intelligence official, China scholar James Mann has claimed that the national security adviser met with the Chinese ambassador daily during the conflict to share highly sensitive intelligence information about Soviet deployments.[123] No records of such meetings have been released, but if they occurred, they would not have been inconsistent with Brzezinski's broader approach during the conflict, which prioritized Washington's relationship with Beijing. Throughout the three-week long invasion, the national security adviser and his staff successfully opposed efforts by the State Department to censure the PRC. Before meetings of the Special Coordinating Committee of the NSC they sometimes strategized about how to undercut Secretary of State Vance's positions. In preparation for one critical meeting held three days after the invasion, two members of the NSC staff sent Brzezinski a secret memorandum laying out a plan for countering the State Department's likely efforts to punish the PRC. They would first promote "an implicit linkage between the withdrawal of Chinese and Vietnamese to their own territories" so that they would not "get sucked into a situation in which we press the Chinese for a withdrawal but do not press the Vietnamese for withdrawal." The memorandum also predicted that Cyrus Vance would try to cancel or delay a scheduled trip by Treasury Secretary Michael Blumenthal to the PRC as a punishment for the invasion. Brzezinski's goal, it contended, "should be that it takes place." If the visit was canceled, it would signal that the president's China policy was "vacillating and inconsistent" and had "suffered a setback."[124] Of course, Brzezinski's unflagging advocacy for the PRC in this situation did little to assist Beijing on the battlefield. But it did limit international criticism.

While American policy toward the Sino-Vietnamese conflict proved more of a help than a hindrance to China, it was the Soviet invasion of Afghanistan that gave rise to direct military ties and explicit, publicly acknowledged cooperation between Washington and Beijing. American and Chinese leaders began to confer on the issue months before the Soviet invasion. Afghan politics had long been a vortex with the tendency to draw in neighboring countries, but the events that led to the Soviet invasion began in the spring of 1978. On 28 April, a military coup installed the strongly pro-Soviet Nur Muhammad Taraqi as prime minister. Taraqi swiftly turned to Moscow for aid and guidance. But the new government's efforts to implement an ambitious program of socioeconomic reform based in part on Soviet models encountered significant resistance throughout the country. The threat posed by this resistance to the pro-Soviet regime had become obvious by March 1979 when a rebellion led by an alliance of local townspeople and Islamist guerrillas erupted in the city of Herat.[125]

Americans were quick to perceive that the Chinese were just as troubled by growing Soviet involvement in Afghanistan as they were. The coup took place a few weeks prior to Brzezinski's visit to Beijing. Before the national security adviser departed, his deputy Paul B. Henze wrote him a preparatory memo on South and Central Asia. "I would expect the Chinese to be much more upset about the recent turn of events in Afghanistan than about anything that has happened in the Horn [of Africa] in the past year," he wrote.

"It would be interesting to see whether our views and the Chinese view are very far apart."[126] Henze proved more or less correct. During Brzezinski's meeting with Deng Xiaoping, the two discussed Afghanistan only briefly, but the vice premier made it clear that he viewed the coup as an unwelcome development. "I think the coup was created singlehandedly by [the] Soviet Union," he told Brzezinski, and added that it would claim to be nonaligned but "all these are false statements."[127]

Afghanistan figured still more prominently in Sino-American discussions when Vice President Walter Mondale visited China in August 1979. By that time, Carter had already initiated Operation Cyclone, which allocated half a million dollars to support the growing anti-Soviet rebellion. Americans were also aware that Beijing had begun supplying the Islamic insurgents—called the mujahedeen—with antiaircraft missiles that were being used effectively against Russian jet fighters. During his visit, the vice president helped to bring about a significant upgrade in the Sino-American relationship. Mondale later recalled, "I brought information . . . about Soviet locations across the border. I brought listening devices. We agreed to the sale of satellite and other equipment that they hadn't had before, and I told them we were going to [modify] export control rules [for] them."[128] Back in Washington, Brzezinski recognized that Mondale's visit had fundamentally altered Sino-American relations. "We have moved significantly into the beginnings of a genuine security relationship with China," he wrote two of his key staff members.[129]

Moscow's decision to up the ante and intervene militarily in order to strengthen the flagging Afghan government came on 25 December. Americans immediately drew up plans to counter what they deemed an act of naked aggression. Security cooperation with China was an important element of the American strategy. One NSC memo for Brzezinski called for Washington to "offer to sell the Chinese anti-tank guns and over the horizon radar." The radar would give the PRC early warning of a Soviet attack. The administration, it recommended, should also announce that future arms sales to the PRC were possible and would be "decided on a case by case basis."[130] For the first time, American policy sought explicitly to rebalance the strategic equation in Asia by tilting publicly toward the PRC.

In January 1980, the Carter administration made another important symbolic gesture that had long been sought by Beijing. It arranged for Secretary of Defense Harold Brown to visit the PRC. The visit signified that the United States was ready to go beyond diplomatic exchanges and move toward a broader strategic partnership. Cooperation in Afghanistan ranked at the top of the secretary's agenda. In approaching the Chinese, Americans were sensitive not only to the geopolitical import of the Soviet invasion but also to its impact on China's regional status. Brown's "talking points" on Southwest

Asia saw the Soviet "move into Afghanistan as aimed at Chinese prestige in Pakistan and India, as well as U.S. interests in the Gulf."[131] Americans therefore believed that cooperation with China against the Soviets would help to restore Beijing's status in South Asia in addition to weakening Moscow.

The Carter administration authorized Brown to make some highly specific proposals to the Chinese encompassing both military and political collaboration. At the military level he asked for formal intelligence exchanges and discussed the possibility of setting up an over-the-horizon detection system. The United States and China both had a vested interest in strengthening Pakistan, which allowed Afghan rebels to take refuge and set up training camps in the mountainous border region that divided it from Afghanistan. Brown promised that the United States would delink the sale of arms to Pakistan from the nuclear issue—in effect promising to sell weapons to Karachi despite its ambitions to acquire nuclear weapons—and added that "it would help if China could provide arms for Afghan nationalists and for Pakistan also."[132] Deng Xiaoping agreed vigorously with Brown's proposals. "The correct way for other countries to handle the Afghanistan problem is to aid the resistance forces," he told the secretary of defense. "The aid should not just be symbolic."[133] With both sides eager to arm the mujahedeen, it did not take long for them to find ways to collaborate. They soon came to an arrangement whereby the CIA paid the Chinese for weapons that it shipped through Pakistan to the Afghan rebels.[134]

At the political level, the United States wanted to mobilize international opinion, especially among Islamic countries, against the Soviet invasion. American officials believed that Beijing was in a position to help it with this objective. Brown's talking points explained that the United States would "press for action in Muslim Arab and international bodies" but that it was "not well placed in all these to take the initiative." On the other hand, "Chinese calls for action could be very helpful." Washington also recognized that the Non-Aligned Movement would be a "crucial forum for debating this invasion." It wanted to see "Cuban leadership blunted, and Soviet Third World appeal dimmed by the Afghan initiatives." Americans wanted to "consult with China on how to approach this question."[135] Washington's eagerness to work with the Chinese to mobilize opinion in Muslim and nonaligned countries against the Soviets certainly stood in stark contrast to the way Americans had not so long ago directed a vast propaganda effort against Chinese communism in these very same places.

The Soviet invasion of Afghanistan brought about an unprecedented unity in Chinese and American policy toward the Third World. Intelligence sharing, joint covert operations, and agreements to take almost identical positions in international organizations fostered a mutual sense of goodwill between these erstwhile rivals. Along with the Vietnamese invasion of Cambodia, the war in Afghanistan transformed the Sino-American relationship in the Third World. But it did not transform it completely.

Despite their shared hostility toward the Soviet Union and their pursuit of common purposes in other areas such as trade and scientific exchange, China and the United States remained very dissimilar countries with different histories and perceptions of their roles in the Third World. Residual ideological differences still cropped up from time to time and deflated the ballooning sense of jubilation that Brzezinski and others felt about the new relationship. Beijing continued to see itself as a Third World country that held much in common with other nations in Asia and Africa, including goals and circumstances that its new Great Power ally could never understand. Although the two now found it easier to cooperate—at least tacitly—when mutual strategic interests were at stake, even after normalization Americans continued to perceive limits as to where and when they could work together with the Chinese toward a common goal.

Deng certainly softened his criticism of the United States when he met with other Afro-Asian leaders, but he continued to pursue China's more long-standing mission of fostering solidarity between the PRC and the Third World. By the early 1980s, socialism and Three Worlds Theory figured less prominently in Deng's rhetoric than the economic challenges that China confronted. But he continued to sound such familiar themes as the need for cooperation among developing countries and the evils of imperialism. Addressing a visiting Algerian delegation in January 1982, he likened the efforts of Third World countries to "develop themselves" to a "field of battle." The vice premier still believed that the "Great Powers, the imperialists, and the new and old colonialists do not want us to develop." The countries of the Third World therefore needed to "strengthen friendly cooperative relations and open up a wider realm of cooperation." He advocated "North-South dialogue and South-South cooperation."[136] Although far less radical and more accommodating than that of his predecessors, Deng's positions were still not compatible with American objectives.

Carter administration officials recognized that despite the rapid improvement of Sino-American relations, China's continuing identification with the Third World limited the possibilities for cooperation in some regions even if it proved useful in Afghanistan and other issues. Early on in Carter's administration, the same obstacles to working with Beijing in Africa that had plagued Nixon and Ford persisted. One presidential review memorandum on the Horn of Africa prepared in 1977 noted that China was increasing its influence in parts of Africa such as Sudan and Ethiopia at the expense of the Soviets. The Chinese wanted to see the United States "function as a counterweight to the Soviets," but their principle goals remained "weakening the Soviet position" and "enhancing" their "own position as champion of the Third World." Americans understood that the "longer term thrust" of Beijing's policy in Africa would continue to lie in "demonstrating commonality with the Africans on major North-South issues and in defining the Third World interests as basically opposed to those of both the U.S. and the USSR." Beijing's strategy, the report added regretfully, "limits the cooperation which we can anticipate with the PRC even though we have a parallel interest in opposing the Soviets in Africa, particularly in Angola."[137]

Even after Beijing and Washington had normalized relations and moved toward broader cooperation, Americans noted that the PRC still sought to enhance its status in the Third World independent of its diplomacy with the United States. One intelligence assessment prepared briefly after normalization explained, "The Chinese have taken special pride in assuming a leading role in the 'third world' and despite their limitation have sacrificed on occasion to build influence for themselves."[138] Of course, this did not necessarily mean that there would be points of conflict between the two nations in the Third World, only that China had its own motives for expanding its influence there. Indeed, the report generally waxed optimistic about Sino-American relations.[139] For the time being, both countries' top priority was containing the expansion of the Soviet Union, which fostered a convergence of interests in many parts of the world. But Chinese ambitions in the Third World would prove a far more enduring hallmark of international politics than Soviet expansionism. After the Soviet Union collapsed, much of the basis for Sino-American collaboration in the Global South would swiftly unravel, leading Americans to take a far less benign view of China's continuing efforts to define a more important role for itself in the region.

Conclusion

During his first trip abroad as general secretary of the CCP in March 2013, Xi Jinping visited four countries, three of them in Africa. After stopping in Russia, the PRC's new leader visited Tanzania, South Africa, and the Republic of Congo. Echoes of the past could clearly be heard as Xi arrived in Tanzania to a rousing welcome that no doubt highlighted China's growing presence on the continent. They could also be heard in the speech that he delivered at the Julius Nyerere Convention Center on 25 March. "The friendly exchanges between China and Africa date back a long time," Xi said, and reminded his audience that

> in the 1950s and 60s the first-generation leaders of New China—Mao Zedong, Zhou Enlai and others—and African statesmen of the older generation ushered in a new epoch in Africa-China relations. Since then, the Chinese and African people have sincerely supported and closely cooperated with each other in the endeavor to fight against colonialism and imperialism and achieve national independence and liberation, in the pursuit of development and national revival. A fraternal bond has been formed in this process, which has seen us through thick and thin.[1]

Of course, China had undergone an astounding transformation since the era that Xi spoke of, as had Sino-African relations. The economic reforms initiated by Deng Xiaoping in the 1970s had brought about rapid industrialization and a swiftly expanding middle class. The privileged position in Chinese thought once enjoyed by Maoism had long ago been ceded to scientific advancement and commercialism. The scope and nature of Chinese involvement in Africa had gone through an equally dramatic change. The relatively modest textile mills and matchstick factories that China built during the 1960s had been replaced by multi-million-dollar investments in natural resources and special support for state-owned multinational corporations.

And yet, Xi made it abundantly clear that China's Africa policy would continue to be governed by long-standing tenets. The PRC continued to see itself as part of a broader community of Afro-Asian nations that had once struggled under colonialism. Moreover, much of Beijing's growing involvement in Asia, Africa, and Latin America was still buttressed by an underlying belief that China had something to offer the people of these regions that the West did not. Xi sprinkled his address with phrases such as "mutual benefit" and "friendship and cooperation" that sounded remarkably similar to the promises that Zhou Enlai had made when he laid out his Eight Principles of aid to African countries.[2]

In the intervening years, the Sino-American relationship had evolved into a complex mixture of competition, consultation, and cooperation on a wide spectrum of issues. Yet more than a hint of the anxiety with which Americans once perceived China's forays into Africa could be detected. By the time of Xi's visit, the notion that Beijing's growing involvement in Africa was a threat to U.S. interests had already become widespread in the American media. Perhaps seeking to dissipate some of the favorable publicity that Xi's visit generated, President Barack Obama visited Africa three months later, stopping in both South Africa and Tanzania. At the same time, Washington's overall posture toward China's growing influence in what had once been called the Third World was far more diverse and varied than it had been during the Cold War. Some Americans worried, but others held out the possibility that Beijing could emerge as a "responsible stakeholder" in Asia and elsewhere.[3] But even if the resurgence of Sino-American competition in the Global South during the twenty-first century has not completely validated Karl Marx's dictum that "history repeats itself," it has at least reminded us that, as Mark Twain is reputed to have said, history "rhymes."

China, Status, and the Third World

Throughout the Cold War, enlarging the status of the PRC in the Third World was an overriding goal of Chinese foreign policy. The idea that China should naturally play a leadership role among newly independent Afro-Asian peoples was an article of faith in Maoist China and a foundation of the country's identity. Beijing sought to enlarge its status in newly independent countries through a variety of techniques that included diplomacy, economic assistance, propaganda, and support for revolutionaries. Although its emphasis and tactics changed over time, the underlying message was always the same: the people of the Third World should unite under Beijing's leadership and create a new order that would stand firmly against foreign domination. This message proved flexible enough to use not only against the United States but also against the Soviet Union and, to a lesser degree, India after 1962.

How successful was Beijing at achieving this objective? As I have described in the Introduction, status is difficult to quantify or measure. It is impossible to say exactly how much status China gained and lost among Afro-Asian countries at different times. Nevertheless, when the record of Chinese involvement in the Third World is examined, clear themes emerge. The first is that the peoples of Asia, Africa, and, to a lesser degree, Latin America were not without admiration for the PRC. When China appealed to other new nations on the basis of their shared legacy of suffering and exploitation at the hands of European imperialism, it tapped into one of the most powerful discursive forces in the Cold War world—a force that Washington often underestimated. Communist China could effectively sell itself and its revolution to Asians and Africans because it *had* succeeded in creating a powerful new state that could mobilize its vast population. This was something that many leaders in postcolonial nations were struggling to do. The intrinsic appeal that China's vision had to Afro-Asian peoples could be seen in Zhou Enlai's well-received diplomatic performances at the Geneva and Bandung Conferences, in the eagerness with which some revolutionaries embraced Maoist doctrines, and in the limited success the PRC enjoyed through its aid programs in Africa during the 1960s.

A second pattern that becomes equally clear with the benefit of hindsight is that China's actions often did more to damage its prestige than did those of its rivals. China's decisions to brutally suppress dissent in Tibet in 1959, allow frictions with India to climax in a border war in 1962, and blindly insist on holding a Second Afro-Asian Conference when it was clear that support was waning were all disastrous choices that alienated Beijing from some of the very countries it was courting. These decisions all stemmed from the same fundamental problem in Chinese foreign policy. Although the revolutionary nationalism that guided Beijing's engagement with the Afro-Asian world during the Cold War could at times lead to self-confident displays of China's achievements, it could also lead to an overzealous defensiveness when it came to either domestic problems or challenges to its leadership on sensitive issues. This made it virtually impossible for Beijing to bring unity and direction to the disparate group of Asian and African nations whose esteem it craved.

Yet not all of Beijing's failings were of its own making. A third characteristic of China's relations with the Third World was their unpredictability. The PRC often struggled to uphold its status in the region because of unforeseeable events and rapidly changing circumstances. The overthrow of friendly leaders such as Sukarno in Indonesia and Kwame Nkrumah in Ghana, economic decision making in countries that received Chinese aid, and the fate of some of the insurgencies that the CCP supported were all beyond the PRC's control. Yet all of these developments had a profound influence on China's status in the Third World. Although the United States and the USSR both feared that China might be able to appeal to the Afro-Asian world in ways that they could not, the reality was that the politics of the Third World frustrated the PRC just as much they did its rivals.

In the twenty-first century, alignment with the Global South remains an important part of Chinese diplomacy. According to Zheng Wang's work on historical memory in Chinese politics, PRC officials continue to emphasize that "China and the Third World have a better mutual understanding and share good relationships due to the fact that they went through similar experiences throughout history and were similarly subjected to colonial aggression."[4] In their public rhetoric, Chinese leaders continue to subtly assert the idea that China has a responsibility to play a leadership role in the developing world. In his report to the Seventeenth Party Congress in 2007, Hu Jintao, the general secretary of the CCP, remarked: "For other developing countries, we will continue to increase solidarity and cooperation with them, cement traditional friendship, expand practical cooperation, provide assistance to them within our ability, and uphold the legitimate demands and common interests of developing countries."[5] What Hu's remarks make clear is that Chinese leaders continue to believe not only in China's "solidarity" with other Afro-Asian countries but also that the PRC has an obligation to provide them with aid and uphold their interests. Party leaders today do not express these ideas as boldly as their predecessors did, but they nevertheless continue to express them.

During the early twenty-first century, the PRC's growing engagement with African countries was especially noticeable to outside observers. The Forum on China-Africa Cooperation, a triennial event that brings together CCP leaders and African heads of state, has drawn significant media attention in part because the PRC often uses it to announce major loans or other initiatives. The *New York Times* called the 2006 forum held in Beijing a "huge diplomatic event" and noted sweeping efforts to showcase China's virtues. Posters calling Africa a "land of myths and miracles" were easy to spot throughout the city, construction had been halted, and the government had even managed to turn Beijing's usually gray sky blue.[6] The confidence of Chinese scholars and officials about China's ability to offer Africans something new was readily apparent. "The Western approach of imposing its values and political system on other countries is not acceptable to China. We focus on mutual development not promoting one country at the expense of the other," one Chinese scholar was quoted as having said.[7]

The combination of enthusiasm and apprehension that has greeted Beijing's investment in Africa in the twenty-first century is not altogether dissimilar to the mixed feelings engendered by China's Cold War forays into the Third World. The rapid economic growth that has turned China into a major force in international politics has stirred admiration among many Africans, and some have even come to see the PRC as a model. Meles Zenawi, the prime minister of Ethiopia from 1995 until his death in 2012, was among Africa's most outspoken supporters of China. He was known for advocating development models that emphasized economic growth over democracy and political freedom. Lauding Beijing for its aid to Ethiopia, he once claimed, "The people of China and Africa share similar backgrounds that helped them to stand for one goal today, which is economic development."[8] Rwandan President Paul Kagame has also openly praised the PRC for its role in Africa. "The Chinese bring what Africa needs: investment and money for governments and companies," he told one newspaper. By contrast, Western firms "have to a large extent polluted Africa and they are still doing it."[9]

Not all African countries are equally enamored of the PRC. As China's involvement in the region increased, concerns about the scope and nature of its activities surfaced in both Africa and the West. Chinese firms engaged in commercial activities on the continent came under increasing scrutiny. Many complained that Beijing needed to do more to ensure that its companies complied with stricter environmental standards.[10] Others voiced concerns that Chinese firms doing business in Africa as part of Beijing's "Going Out" strategy had demonstrated a lack of corporate social responsibility.[11] Deeply concerned about China's environmental and labor practices, some African leaders became increasingly hostile toward the Chinese presence. For Lamido Sanusi, the respected governor of the central bank of Nigeria, Beijing's policies toward Africa were scarcely better than those of European imperialists. "The days of the Non-Aligned Movement that united us after colonialism, are gone," he wrote in the *Financial Times* in 2013. "China is no longer a fellow under-developed economy—it is the world's second-biggest, capable of the same forms of exploitation as the west. It is a significant contributor to Africa's deindustrialization and underdevelopment."[12] What should concern the PRC about Sanusi's views is not whether they are accurate but the inescapable reality that they are becoming more common. The more widespread such sentiments become, the more difficult it will be for the PRC to achieve its long-standing ambition to be seen as a leader of the Afro-Asian community.

The growing disenchantment with China in Africa paralleled the deepening mistrust with which some Asian countries regarded the Middle Kingdom in recent years. Much as the excesses of nationalism sometimes caused China's neighbors to view it as a threat during the Cold War, so too has Beijing's turn toward a more assertive posture on the South China Sea, Tibet, and other issues contributed to rising tensions in Asia. China had initially been fairly successful at charming its neighbors into believing that it was earnestly committed to a "peaceful rise."[13] By 2010, however, several countries in South and Southeast Asia were encouraging a more robust American role in the region to counter growing Chinese assertiveness. In 2011, the highly regarded journalist Robert D. Kaplan interviewed "a high-ranking official of a South China

Sea littoral state" about territorial disputes with the PRC and was told, "The Chinese never give justifications for their claims. They had a real Middle Kingdom mentality, and are dead set against taking these disputes to court." The official quietly hoped that the United States would remain a counterbalance to China in the region. "An American military presence is needed to countervail China, but we won't vocalize that," the official added.[14] China seemed once again to be at risk of isolating itself through its hypernationalistic policies.

There are of course many dimensions of politics in developing countries over which China has no control. At the same time, however, Beijing does control the environmental and social regulations it places on firms doing business abroad. Chinese leaders can also choose whether to project a generous, self-confident nationalism that will make other Afro-Asian countries more inclined to admire China or a more defensive and jingoistic nationalism that will cause its neighbors to fear it. If the PRC should take away any lesson from its experiences in the Third World during the Cold War, it is how swiftly it can undermine its own status in the region through unwise choices. Only by making itself accountable to global environmental and labor standards and tempering its nationalism can China ever regain the Middle Kingdom status that it once enjoyed.

The United States and China

Throughout the Cold War, the United States met China's efforts to gain standing in the Third World with stubborn resistance. American administrations viewed international politics as a zero-sum game in which any gain for the PRC invariably meant a loss for the Free World. In Asia and Africa, U.S. diplomats constantly pressured neutral countries to shun the PRC diplomatically and to reject its offers of assistance. Washington made expensive commitments to counterinsurgency in numerous Southeast Asian and African countries solely to prevent outcomes that could be construed as a triumph for Maoism. The United States even tried to diminish, if not outright wreck, international conferences that might give the PRC a platform for advancing its agenda. Yet none of these tactics turned Afro-Asian nations against Beijing. In some instances, they simply made the United States look every bit the global bully that the PRC depicted it as. Most often, when Third World nations decided to reject Chinese influence they did so because their own values and judgments compelled them to, not because of American pressure. China's failures in the Third World often gave away the futility of American policies as much as its successes.

Many U.S. policies designed to counteract China's Third World activism were based on a very exaggerated view of Beijing's potential influence. Some of America's most disastrous policy decisions during the Cold War were made because U.S. officials took Chinese ambitions *too* seriously. The fear that Maoism would gain prestige throughout the world if the National Liberation Front triumphed in Vietnam was not the only factor that pushed the Johnson administration toward this most tragic of America's Cold War interventions, but Washington's views about what Vietnam could mean for the PRC's global influence were grossly overstated. Moreover, the United States almost always overestimated the negative ramifications of other nations extending diplomatic recognition to the PRC or accepting Chinese aid. America's approach to the PRC in the Third World went far beyond erring on the side of caution and sometimes bordered on an unjustifiable hysteria. More often than not, this distorted view of the Chinese threat compounded the difficulties the United States faced in winning the allegiance of Afro-Asian countries.

Fortunately, during the twenty-first century American officials have generally—though not always—shown a more somber and nuanced understanding of Chinese influence. They no longer categorically view China as a threat in Asia or Africa and recognize that, in some instances, Beijing's presence in these regions can have advantages as well as disadvantages. Although occasionally sensational statements by American officials have garnered media attention, in recent years the president and other key leaders have been dispassionate in their analysis of the PRC and its motives. President Obama has argued that the international relations of the Global South should not be viewed as a zero-sum game. When asked whether the United States was "frightened" by China's presence in Africa during his March 2013 visit there, the president replied, "I actually welcome the attention that Africa is receiving from countries like China and Brazil, India, and Turkey. . . . [T]he more interest they show in Africa, the more tools we have and mechanisms we have to further incorporate Africa into the global economy, which has the potential of creating jobs and businesses and opportunity. So I don't feel threatened by it. I think it's a good thing."[15]

Yet not all American officials have abandoned the tendency to exaggerate the Chinese threat. One of the most well-publicized examples was a statement made in 2014 by Assistant Secretary of State for African Affairs Johnnie Carson during a meeting with oil companies in Laos, Nigeria. Carson called China "a very aggressive and pernicious economic competitor with no morals."[16] Carson's phrasing not only took an overly simplistic view of the PRC's motives but also drew on a more long-standing discourse about China as an amoral society that has been all too prominent in the rhetoric of American foreign policy makers during the last century.[17] To make matters worse, after a cable quoting Carson became publicly available through WikiLeaks, many in the media misrepresented the assistant secretary's statement as general U.S. policy.[18] The inability of global media to differentiate between an off-the-cuff comment by one official—albeit a high-ranking one—and America's broader approach to China ultimately caused Washington a great deal of embarrassment and undermined its efforts to pursue cooperation with the PRC in other areas.

Although American and Chinese interests will unquestionably continue to diverge on key issues, American officials should avoid overstating Chinese influence and steer away from blanket condemnations of Beijing. Hysterical responses to Chinese globalism accomplished little during the Cold War and often reflected badly on the United States. In the twenty-first century such hysteria will only convince the PRC of Washington's bad intentions, rankle nationalist sensitivities, and increase the likelihood that Beijing will opt for greater assertiveness rather than moderation. Only if the United States can put aside old stereotypes about China and embrace a more balanced view of the benefits and drawbacks that its rise will have for the United States will the two countries be able to work together in areas where they have shared interests.

Competition or Cooperation?

Through much of the Cold War, competition and rivalry defined the Sino-American relationship in the Third World. The PRC viewed destroying American influence as part of its broader mission to unite the postcolonial world under the aegis of revolution. The United States, for its part, looked at even modest gains for Chinese prestige in Afro-Asian countries as a threat and contested almost every PRC effort to raise its standing. What was the ultimate impact of this competition? Although neither the United States nor China can clearly be said to have won, the competition clearly often had horrific consequences for postcolonial countries. In many instances, it reinforced or exacerbated tensions among groups that were struggling for power, leading to political turmoil and, in some instances, violent conflict. Elites in some newly independent countries tried to be savvy by playing Washington and Beijing off against each other, but this strategy seldom if ever worked out as planned. Conflicting advice and rival aid programs that undermined each other created confusion and frustration rather than economic development and rising living standards. The sad irony was that the United States and China both had much to offer the Third World, but their rivalry ultimately prevented them from delivering on their promises to bring about greater stability and prosperity.

In the twenty-first century, there remains a chance that things will be different despite occasional lapses in judgment by Beijing and Washington. Both sides have come to recognize that they have much to gain through cooperating in Africa and elsewhere instead of incessantly competing. Recently, both sides have claimed to be willing to work together. "We'll partner with the Chinese," President Obama promised in March 2013 when discussing the need to build infrastructure for trade on the African continent.[19] By the time Obama visited China in November 2014, American and Chinese medical teams were already coordinating their efforts to contain the Ebola virus. At the time, the White House announced further plans for working together. According to an official press release, the two countries intended to "discuss as soon as possible new areas for cooperation to build African energy capacity and to expand dramatically power generation and access to electricity in sub-Saharan Africa."[20] These tentative but promising first steps offered a tantalizing glimpse of what the United States and China could accomplish through collaborating for the benefit of other countries. But a great deal of work remains to be done before the promise of greater Sino-American cooperation in the Global South is realized.

There can be little question that Sino-American cooperation in developing countries and elsewhere will be critical to the resolution of many of the greatest challenges the world faces in the twenty-first century. When Beijing and Washington work together on important global issues such as climate change, counterterrorism, or promoting economic development in poor countries, their standing as the globe's two most influential actors makes it more likely that the rest of the world will follow suit. Sharing ideas and collaborating offers a far better chance of helping those nations that are still mired in poverty and political chaos to solve their problems than competition. To be sure, China and the United States have very different histories, political systems, and global outlooks. They must nonetheless realize that these differences can, in some instances, make cooperation more fruitful even if they sometimes make competition inevitable. Ultimately, greater cooperation offers both the United States and the PRC the chance to enhance their status in international politics for decades to come.

Notes

Abbreviations

AAD	Access to Archival Databases
CDF	Central Decimal File
CNL	Conseil National de Liberacion
CREST	CIA Research Tool
CWIHP	Cold War International History Project
DNSA	Digital National Security Archive
DDRS	Declassified Documents Reference Service
DXNP	*Deng Xiaoping nianpu, 1975–1997*
FRUS	*Foreign Relations of the United States*
GFL	Gerald Ford Library, Ann Arbor, Michigan
JCL	Jimmy Carter Library, Atlanta, Georgia
JFKL	John F. Kennedy Library, Boston, Massachusetts
JYMZWG	*Jianguo yilai Mao Zedong wengao*
LBJL	Lyndon B. Johnson Library, Austin, Texas
LSNP	*Liu Shaoqi nianpu*
LOC	Library of Congress, Washington, D.C.
MZWW	*Mao Zedong waijiao wenxuan*
NARA	National Archives and Records Administration II
NYT	*New York Times*
PRCFMA	People's Republic of China Foreign Ministry Archive
RFWP	Robert F. Williams Papers
RG	Record Group
RNL	Richard Nixon Library, Yorba Linda, Calif.
SWJN	*Selected Works of Jawaharlal Nehru*
USIA	United States Information Agency
WCDA	Wilson Center Digital Archive
WAHP	W. Averell Harriman Papers, Library of Congress
ZEJSWX	*Zhou Enlai junshi wenxuan*
ZENP	*Zhou Enlai nianpu, 1949–1976*
ZEWJWX	*Zhou Enlai waijiao wenxuan*
ZEZ	*Zhou Enlai zhuan,1898–1976*
ZYWJ	*Zhonggong zhongyang wenjian xuanji*

Introduction

1. There is no shortage of highly alarmist literature describing how China will change the international system in the coming years. See, e.g., Halper, *Beijing Consensus*; and

Jacques, *When China Rules the World*. Focusing more on China's strategies for gaining influence are Kurlantzick, *Charm Offensive*; and Michel and Beuret, *China Safari*.

2. Connelly, "Taking of the Cold War Lens."

3. Smith, "New Bottles for New Wine," 568.

4. On this point, see Jeremy Friedman's excellent *Shadow Cold War*.

5. On the formation and persistence of Sino-American enmity during the Cold War era, see Chang, *Friends and Enemies*; Christensen, *Useful Adversaries*; Zhang, *Deterrence and Strategic Culture*; and Cohen, *America's Response to China*, esp. 148–215.

6. The first wave of scholarship on this issue was written mostly by political scientists during the late 1960s and early 1970s. Largely based on published Chinese sources such as newspapers, some of it remains useful. See, e.g., Mozingo, *Chinese Policy toward Indonesia*; Ogunsanwo, *China's Policy in Africa*; Gurtov, *China and Southeast Asia*; and Larkin, *China and Africa*. More recently scholars writing about China's relations with Afro-Asian countries during the Cold War have made use of new Chinese materials, although the literature on the subject is still small. See, e.g., Zhai, *China and the Vietnam Wars*; and Cheng, "Sino-Cuban Relations." A small number of Chinese scholars—especially younger ones—on the mainland have also begun to use new Chinese materials to investigate this subject. Their work has begun to appear in Chinese academic journals. See, e.g., Jiang, "Nongzhi yuanfei"; and Li, "Shilun zhongguo."

7. This literature is far too vast to describe here in detail. A representative sample includes Little, *American Orientalism*; McMahon, *Limits of Empire*; and Hahn and Heiss, *Cold War and Revolution*.

8. On U.S.-Soviet competition, see Westad, *Global Cold War*; on Sino-Soviet competition, see Friedman, *Shadow Cold War*; on U.S.-Cuban competition in Africa, see Gleijeses, *Conflicting Missions*.

9. Gaddis, *We Now Know*, 284.

10. For a fuller discussion, see Larson et al., "Status and World Order."

11. Wohlforth, "Status and Interstate Conflict," 121. For a similar definition, see Johnston, *Social States*, 82.

12. This discussion is loosely based on some of the concepts laid out in Larson et al., "Status and World Order," 15–16, but I have modified the terms and definitions to fit my arguments.

13. See, e.g., Wang, *Never Forget National Humiliation*, 10; and Shambaugh, "Tangled Titans," 8. Deng, *China's Struggle for Status*.

14. Kang, *East Asia before the West*.

15. See, among others, Larson and Shevchenko, "Status Seekers"; Deng, "Better Than Power"; and Yan, "Rise of China."

16. See, e.g., Wolf, "Rising Powers."

17. Chen, *Mao's China and the Cold War*, 47; Chen, *China's Road to the Korean War*, 22, 24, 90, 214.

18. Chen, *Mao's China and the Cold War*, 11.

19. Chen, *China Challenge in the Twenty-First Century*, 5; Wang, *Never Forget National Humiliation*.

20. See, e.g., Chen, *Mao's China and the Cold War*, 10–11; and Hunt, *Genesis of Chinese Communist Foreign Policy*, 204–12.

21. On Zhou Enlai's statesmanship, see Xiong, *Zhou Enlai chu deng shijie wutai*.

22. On this point, see Friedman, *Shadow Cold War*, 2–3.

23. Gerth and Mills, *From Max Weber*, 180.

24. Jervis, *Logic of Images in International Relations*, 7.

25. The obvious allusion here is the ubiquitously cited Anderson, *Imagined Communities*.

26. Among the book-length studies in English to make use of these sources are Jerslid, *Sino-Soviet Alliance*; Xia, *Negotiating with the Enemy*; and Li, *History of the Modern Chinese Army*.

27. For an interesting perspective on the problems historians in China have faced during the last two years, see Cunningham, "Denying Historians."

28. One exception is the widely used study by Westad et al., "77 Conversations between Chinese and Foreign Leaders."

29. The National Archives of Cambodia's website, for instance, explains that Pol Pot destroyed the "majority of ministerial documents" from 1954 to 1970 when he seized power. http://www.nac.gov.kh/english/index.php?option=com_content&view=article&id=53&Itemid=65.

30. See, e.g., CIA Central Research Staff, "Chinese Communism and Latin America," 26 February 1960, DDRS; CIA, "Chinese Communist Party Advice to Latin American Revolutionary Leaders," 25 June 1964, DDRS.

31. Xie, *Zhongguo dangdai waijiaoshi*, 129–32, 270–72; Van Ness, *Revolution and Chinese Foreign Policy*, 218–21.

32. On the importance of the Soviet role in particular, see Daigle, *Limits of Détente*.

Chapter 1

1. Manela, *Wilsonian Moment*. This work has strongly influenced my analysis of Mao in 1919.

2. The literature on these events is growing. In addition to Manela's work, cited above, see the latter part of MacMillan's popular *Paris 1919*.

3. Manela, *Wilsonian Moment*, 177–96, gives a good summary of these developments.

4. *Mao Zedong zhuan*, 49–50; Hunt, *Genesis of Chinese Communist Foreign Policy*, 74–75.

5. Mao Zedong, "Poor Wilson," 14 July 1919, in Schram, *Mao's Road to Power*, 1:338.

6. Mao Zedong, "Afghanistan Picks Up the Sword," 14 July 1919, in Schram, *Mao's Road to Power*, 1:335.

7. Mao Zedong, "So Much for Self Determination!," 14 July 1919, in Schram, *Mao's Road to Power*, 1:337.

8. On Mao's growing admiration for Marxism and the Soviet Union during this period, see Hunt, *Genesis of Chinese Communist Foreign Policy*, 78–80.

9. Cited in ibid., 73.

10. Ibid., 114.

11. Mao Zedong, "Letter to Xiao Xudong, Cai Linbin and the Other Members in France," December 1, 1920, in Schram, *Mao's Road to Power*, 2:7.

12. Mao Zedong, "Letter to Zhang Guoji," 25 November 1920, in Schram, *Mao's Road to Power*, 1:604.

13. Meisner, *Mao's China and After*, 25.

14. Zarrow, *China in War and Revolution*, 196–97.

15. Among those arguing that Moscow played a robust role are Dirlik, *Origins of Chinese Communism*; Pantsov, *Bolsheviks and the Chinese Revolution*. Emphasizing indigenous elements are Van de Ven, *From Friend to Comrade*; and Schwartz, *Chinese Communism and the Rise of Mao*. For an unannotated summary, see Saich, "Chinese Communist Party during the Era of the Comintern."

16. Lenin, "Awakening of Asia."

17. Cited in Haithcox, *Communism and Nationalism in India*, 58.

18. Hunt, *Genesis of Chinese Communist Foreign Policy*, 108–10.

19. For a brief description of these events, see Spence, *Gate of Heavenly Peace*, 222–24.

20. Meisner, *Mao's China and After*, 25.

21. *ZYWJ*, 1:419.

22. Ibid., 467.

23. For a complete account of the treaties, including the protests, see Wang, *China's Unequal Treaties*.

24. Cited in ibid., 74.

25. *FRUS*, 1925, 1:800–801.

26. Cohen, *America's Response to China*, 94.

27. *FRUS*, 1926, 1:217.

28. Buhite, *Nelson T. Johnson*, 34.

29. Cohen, *America's Response to China*, 94–97.

30. These events are well covered in the basic literature. See, e.g., Meisner, *Mao's China and After*, 25–28.

31. Schram, *Mao's Road to Power*, 2:xiv–lv, gives a good description, and some of the actual essays follow in the volume.

32. *Mao Zedong nianpu*, 1:132–33.

33. Karl, *Mao Zedong and China*, 30.

34. *Mao Zedong nianpu*, 1:178.

35. Spence, *Search for Modern China*, 371–72; Zarrow, *China in War and Revolution*, 279–80.

36. Karl, *Mao Zedong and China*, 36.

37. Cohen, *America's Response to China*, 105.

38. For a good summary of these campaigns, see Jones, *Victorious Insurgencies*, 24–28.

39. "Conclusion of the Joint Conference and Announcement of the Establishment of the Front Committee," 16 February 1930, in Schram, *Mao's Road to Power*, 3:269. The "soviets" referred to other soviets that the author believed would spring up throughout the world as a result of Chinese and Russian influence.

40. On the politics behinds this, see Schram, *Mao's Road to Power*, 3:lv–lvii.

41. "Telegram of the Chinese Revolutionary Military Commission on Attacking Nanchang and Regrouping in Wuhan," 22 June 1930, Schram, *Mao's Road to Power*, 3:458–59.

42. *ZYWJ*, 9:606, 629. The significance of this speech is also noted in Hunt, *Genesis of Chinese Communist Foreign Policy*, 118.

43. Paine, *Wars for Asia*, 74–75.

44. "Proletariat and Oppressed Peoples of the World, Unite!," 30 August 1933, in Schram, *Mao's Road to Power*, 4:520–21.

45. Meisner, *Mao's China and After*, 33.

46. Ibid., 34–35.

47. "Interview with Edgar Snow on Special Questions," 23 July 1936, Schram, *Mao's Road to Power*, 5:288.

48. "Interview with Edgar Snow on Japanese Imperialism," 16 July 1936, in Schram, *Mao's Road to Power*, 5:262–63.

49. Much of this is summarized in Cohen, *America's Response to China*, 105–20. Cohen mostly emphasizes American inaction.

50. For a summary, see Buhite, *Nelson T. Johnson and American Policy toward China*, 7–8.

51. "Monthly Report for September 1930," *FRUS*, 1930, 2:46–48. I have taken this extract from Hu, *Stanley K. Hornbeck*, 215.

52. *FRUS*, 1930, 2:26–27. On Americans' tendency to view communism as unworkable in China, see also Cohen, *America's Response to China*, 134–38.

53. Hu, *Stanley K. Hornbeck*, 217.

54. O. Edmund Clubb to Nelson T. Johnson, 6 September 1932, Nelson T. Johnson Papers, box 17, LOC.

55. Johnson to Clubb, 21 July 1932, Nelson T. Johnson Papers, box 17, LOC.

56. Hu, *Stanley K. Hornbeck*, 217.

57. Cited in ibid.

58. See, e.g., "Proclamation by the Central Government of the Chinese Soviet Republic on the Selling out of North China by the Guomindang," 19 June 1934, in Schram, *Mao's Road to Power*, 4:760–61.

59. Chen, *Mao's China and the Cold War*, 20.

60. Selden, *China in Revolution*, 93–94.

61. Zarrow, *China in War and Revolution*, 303.

62. "On Resisting Japan, Democracy, and Northern Youth," in Schram, *Mao's Road to Power*, 5:667.

63. For a brief biography of Zhang Hanfu, see: http://www.fmprc.gov.cn/mfa_eng/ziliao_665539/wjrw_665549/lrfbzjbzzl_665553/t40500.shtml.

64. Cited in Goldstein, "Chinese Revolution in the Colonial Areas," 603.

65. Westad, *Decisive Encounters*, 30; Bianco, *Origins of the Chinese Revolution*, 149–53.

66. Schram, *Mao's Road to Power*, 6:liii.

67. Johnson to Roy Howard, 31 December 1935, Nelson T. Johnson Papers, box 26, LOC.

68. For a full summary of the battle and its aftermath, see Van Slyke, "Battle of the Hundred Regiments."

69. "Deputy Commanding Officer Peng Discusses the Great Significance of the '100 Regiments' Campaign," in Saich and Yang, *Rise to Power of the Chinese Communist Party*, 944.

70. Zarrow, *China in War and Revolution*, 276, 286.

71. Niu, *From Yan'an to the World*, 89–90.

72. Zarrow, *China in War and Revolution*, 330.

73. Ibid., 331.

74. Liu Shao-Ch'i, "Training of the Communist Party Member," in Compton, *Mao's China*, 129. Compton used the Wade-Giles system to romanize Liu's name.

75. Cited in Goldstein, "Chinese Revolution in the Colonial Areas," 611. I have converted Goldstein's Wade-Giles romanizations to pinyin.

76. Cited in ibid., 611.

77. Liu, *Selected Works of Liu Shaoqi*, 1:333.

78. Hunt, *Genesis of Chinese Communist Foreign Policy*, 220.

79. Goldstein, "Chinese Revolution and the Colonial Areas," 613–14.

80. *Mao Zedong nianpu*, 2:343–44.

81. "Directive of the Central Committee of the Chinese Communist Party Regarding the Pacific Anti-Japanese United Front," 9 December 1941; Schram, *Mao's Road to Power*, 6:847.

82. On this point, see Dallek, *Franklin D. Roosevelt and American Foreign Policy*, 499–500.

83. *FRUS*, 1938, 3:179.

84. *FRUS*, 1939, 3:309.

85. The literature on this is extensive. One of the most thorough sources remains Louis, *Imperialism at Bay*.

86. On Mao's evolving views of the United States during World War II, see Hunt, *Genesis of Chinese Communist Foreign Policy*, 148–57.

87. "Excerpts from Guenther Stein's Notes of Interview with [Mao Zedong]," 14 July 1944, RG 59, CDF, 1940–1944, 893.009–144, NARA.

88. "Transmitting Reports Containing Views and Statements of Communist Leaders," 14 September 1944, RG 59, CDF, 1940–1944, 893.009–144_63, NARA.

89. "Memorandum by the Second Secretary of Embassy in China (Davies) Temporarily in the United States," *FRUS*, 1943, China Supplement, 260.

90. For a full account, see Carter, *Mission to Yenan*.

91. Report by the Secretary of Embassy in China (Service), 3 September 1944, *FRUS*, 1944, 6:616.

92. Niu, *From Yan'an to the World*, 153.

93. Liu, *Recast All under Heaven*, 64.

94. For more detailed accounts, see Schaller, *U.S. Crusade in China*, 195–200; and Reardon-Anderson, *Yenan and the Great Powers*, 51–67.

95. *FRUS*, 1945, 7:223.

96. Cohen, *America's Response to China*, 145–46.

97. Report, CCP Southern Bureau, "Opinions on Diplomatic Affairs and Suggestions to the Central Committee," 16 August 1944, in Zhang and Chen, *Chinese Communist Foreign Policy*, 9–12.

98. Mao Zedong, "On Coalition Government," 24 April 1945, https://www.marxists.org/reference/archive/mao/selected-works/volume-3/mswv3_25.htm.

99. Chen, *Mao's China and the Cold War*, 27–31.

100. Ibid., 33–34.

101. Cohen, *America's Response to China*, 156.

102. On the immediate impact of the Soviet withdrawal on the civil war, see especially Westad, *Cold War and Revolution*, 140–64.

103. "Talk with the American Correspondent Anna Louise Strong," August 1946, http://www.marxists.org/reference/archive/mao/selected-works/volume-4/mswv4_13.htm.

104. Chen, *Mao's China and the Cold War*, 5.

105. Sheng, *Battling Western Imperialism*, 146.

106. *ZYWJ*, 16:709.

107. Ibid., 722–23.

108. Meisner, *Mao's China and After*, 50.

109. Cohen, *America's Response to China*, 161.

110. Lüthi, *Sino-Soviet Split*, 30, notes the unreliability of Soviet and shift in Soviet attitude.

111. Shen and Xia, "Leadership Transfer in the Asian Revolution," 198–200.

112. Cited in Chen, "Bridging Revolution and Decolonization," 144.

113. Ibid., 144–45.

114. Shen and Xia, "Leadership Transfer in the Asian Revolution," 202.

115. Cited in Chen, "Bridging Revolution and Decolonization," 145.

116. Shen and Xia, "Leadership Transfer in the Asian Revolution," 202–3.

117. Cohen, *America's Response to China*, 159–61.

118. *FRUS*, 1949, 8:44–50.

119. Westad, *Decisive Encounters*, 161.

120. *FRUS*, 1949, 8:215–16.

121. Intelligence Memorandum No. 208, "Communist Methods in Asia," 26 August 1949, DDRS.

122. *FRUS*, 1949, 8:561–64.

123. Tucker, *Patterns in the Dust*, 178–83.

124. See, e.g., Cohen, "Symposium."

125. Zhang and Chen, *Chinese Communist Foreign Policy*, 112.

126. *FRUS*, 1949, 9:168–69.

127. Ibid., 231–32.

128. "Review of the World Situation as It Relates to the Security of the United States," 18 January 1950, DDRS.

Chapter 2

1. Volgy et al., "Status Considerations," 66.

2. This point is discussed in the previous chapter, but see also Chen and Yang, "Chinese Politics," 249.

3. On this point, especially in the context of Indochina, see Niu, *Lengzhan yu Zhongguo waijiao juece*, 261–63.

4. Cited in Zhai, *China and the Vietnam Wars*, 21.

5. On the outbreak of the war and American and Chinese responses to it, see Chen, *China's Road to the Korean War*, 127–28; Stueck, *Korean War*, 31–36; and Acheson, *Present at the Creation*, 402–14. The Chinese historian Shen Zhihua covers this topic in the context of Sino-Soviet relations in *Mao Zedong*.

6. Weathersby, "'Should We Fear This?,'" 12–13.

7. Stueck, *Korean War*, 45; Chen, *China's Road to the Korean War*, 125–30.

8. Li Xiaobing puts the total number of Chinese volunteers at 3.1 million. See Li, *China at War*, 80.

9. Whiting, *China Crosses the Yalu*, was long the standard Western work on the subject. It argued that China entered the war because it believed that the United States posed a security threat. Other important works that cover the subject include Zhang,

Deterrence and Strategic Culture, which emphasizes misperceptions on both sides; Thomas J. Christensen, *Useful Adversaries*, which emphasizes domestic politics; and Shen, *Mao Zedong*, which places Mao's decision-making in the context of the Sino-Soviet alliance and emphasizes Chinese fears that the United States would invade northeastern China if North Korea fell.

10. Chen, *China's Road to the Korean War*, 214.

11. Cited in ibid., 186.

12. Cited in ibid., 202.

13. *ZEJSWX*, 72–74.

14. Zhonggong zhongyang wenxian yanjiushi, *Jianguo yilai Mao Zedong junshi wengao*, 1:235.

15. Ibid., 449.

16. This is described in Stueck, *Korean War*, 115–16, 139–40.

17. "Telegram from Zhou Enlai to Wu Xiuquan and Qiao Guanhua," Wilson Center Digital Archive, http://digitalarchive.wilsoncenter.org/document/114235.

18. Wu, *Zai waijiaobu banian de jingli*, 52.

19. For a summary, especially of considerations on the Chinese side, see Chen, *Mao's China and the Cold War*, 91–117.

20. *ZEJSWX*, 137–38.

21. Ibid., 145.

22. Ciphered telegram, Mao Zedong to Filippov (Stalin) conveying 15 July 1962 telegram from Mao to Kim Il Sung and 16 July 1952 reply from Kim to Mao, http://digitalarchive.wilsoncenter.org/document/113642.pdf?v=dbe8ea3dc941a8b10ab464151f0cde95.

23. *FRUS*, 1950, 7:1237.

24. Good on this are: Stueck, *Korean War*, 127–38; Millett, *War for Korea*, 291–332; and Beisner, *Dean Acheson*, 393–416.

25. Acheson, *Present at the Creation*, 514.

26. *FRUS*, 1950, 7:1625.

27. *FRUS*, 1951, 7:77.

28. "A Report to the National Security Council by the Executive Secretary on United States Objectives, Policies and Courses of Action in Asia," 4 May 1951, DDRS.

29. Li and Beirne, "Chinese Offensive in Korea, Fifth," 75–77.

30. Chen, *Mao's China and the Cold War*, 97.

31. Cited in Stueck, *Korean War*, 310.

32. *FRUS*, 1952–1954, 15:838–57.

33. Ibid., 849.

34. Ibid., 1012–17.

35. Ibid., 1065.

36. Ibid., 1067.

37. Ibid., 1144.

38. Gacek, *Logic of Force*, 81–82.

39. For a detailed discussion, see Stueck, *Korean War*, 313–42.

40. Cited in Zhang, *Mao's Military Romanticism*, 248.

41. Cited in ibid., 249.

42. *FRUS*, 1952–1954, 14:347.

43. Ibid., 347–8.

44. On this point, see also Niu, *Lengzhan yu Zhongguo waijiao juece*, 263.

45. *ZEWJWX*, 18–19.

46. Logevall, *Embers of War*, 282.

47. *LSNP*, 2:256.

48. *FRUS*, 1950, 6:781–84.

49. Westad, *Decisive Encounters*, 316–17.

50. Cited in Zhang, *Deterrence and Strategic Culture*, 173.

51. Zhai, *China and the Vietnam Wars*, 19.

52. Ibid., 19; Chen, *Mao's China and the Cold War*, 123–24.

53. Cited in Zhai, *China and the Vietnam Wars*, 23–24.

54. Luo, "Wuchan jieji guojizhuyi de guanghui dianfan," 5–6.

55. Ibid., 6.

56. Ibid., 9.

57. Zhai, *China and the Vietnam Wars*, 33–38.

58. Ibid., 43–49.

59. *Renmin Ribao*, 23 January 1954.

60. Ibid., 9 May 1954.

61. Zhang, *Deterrence and Strategic Culture*, 177–81.

62. "National Intelligence Estimate, Resistance of Thailand, Burma and Malaya to Communist Pressures in the Event of a Communist Victory in Indochina in 1951," 15 March 1951, DDRS.

63. "NSC Staff Study on the United States Objectives and Courses of Action with respect to Communist Aggression in Indochina," 13 February 1952, reprinted in U.S. Department of State, *United States-Vietnam Relations, 1945–1967*, 8:468–76.

64. *FRUS*, 1952–1954, 13:747.

65. For a detailed summary of these discussions, see Zhang, *Deterrence and Strategic Culture*, 163–67.

66. Luo, "Wuchan jieji guojizhuyi de guanghui dianfan," 7.

67. Chen, *China's Road to the Korean War*, 99–100.

68. *FRUS*, 1949, 9:460–61.

69. Ibid., 466.

70. *FRUS*, 1950, 7:202–3.

71. *ZENP*, 1:51.

72. "Prospects for an Early Successful Chinese Communist Attack on Taiwan," 26 July 1950, DDRS.

73. *FRUS*, 1950, 6:414.

74. *FRUS*, 1952–1954, 14:54.

75. Roy, *Taiwan*, 128–29.

76. See, e.g., *FRUS*, 1952–1954, 14:1084–85, 1248.

77. On the Guomindang perspective, see Roy, *Taiwan*, 128–29.

78. *FRUS*, 1952–1954, 14:280, 282, 284.

79. Ibid., 292.

80. Ibid., 300–301.

81. Ibid., 279–82.

82. "A Report to the National Security Council by the NSC Planning Board on the United States Courses of Action with Respect to Formosa and the National Government of China," 30 March 1953, DDRS.

83. Ibid.

84. *FRUS*, 1952–1954, 14:309–10.

85. Zhang, *Deterrence and Strategic Culture*, 202–3.

86. There is an extensive literature on this. See, among others, Chang, "To the Nuclear Brink," 96–122; Zhang, *Deterrence and Strategic Culture*, 189–224; and Accinelli, *Crisis and Commitment*.

87. On some of these points, see Garver, *Sino-American Alliance*, 54–55.

88. Zhang, *Economic Cold War*, 31.

89. Ibid., 1; Engel, *Cold War at 30,000 Feet*, 199.

90. Shimizu, *Creating People of Plenty*, 49.

91. "Intervention of the Central People's Government of the People's Republic of China in Korea," http://www.un.org/en/ga/search/view_doc.asp?symbol=A/RES/498(V)&Lang=E&Area=RESOLUTION.

92. Zhang, *Economic Cold War*, 39.

93. *FRUS*, 1951, 7:1958–59.

94. Ibid., 1960.

95. "Resolutions Adopted by the General Assembly at Its Fifth Session," http://www.un.org/depts/dhl/resguide/r5_en.shtml; American disappointment with the outcome is conveyed to some degree in "Additional Economic Measures Against Communist China," 26 December 1952, RG 59, CDF, 1950–1954, box 2209, NARA.

96. CA–Walter P. McConaughy to FE–Mr. Johnson, 31 October 1952, RG 59, CDF, 1950–1954, box 2205, NARA.

97. Resolution 500, "Additional Measures to Be Employed to Meet the Aggression in Korea," http://www.un.org/en/ga/search/view_doc.asp?symbol=A/RES/500(V)&Lang=E&Area=RESOLUTION.

98. "Additional Economic Measures against Communist China," 26 December 1952, RG 59, CDF, 1950–1954, box 2209, NARA.

99. Zhang, *Economic Cold War*, 121–37.

100. *FRUS*, 1952–1954, 14:291.

101. Ibid., 305.

102. Cited in Zhang, *Economic Cold War*, 123.

103. *ZENP*, 1:188–89.

104. See, e.g., Kang, *East Asia before the West*, 56.

105. *ZENP*, 1:261.

106. Ibid., 1:262.

107. Ibid., 1:280.

Chapter 3

1. For a complete description, see Xia, "Nixon, Mao, Kissinger and Zhou."

2. Some of this is described in MacMillan, *Nixon and Mao*, 30.

3. For an articulation of the current policy, see Zheng Bijian, "China's 'Peaceful Rise,'" 18–24.

4. Sihanouk, *My War with the CIA*, 75.

5. Borstelmann, *Cold War and the Color Line*, 105–6.

6. Zhang "Constructing 'Peaceful Coexistence,'" 510.

7. "Hand delivered note, Zhou Enlai to Stalin, conveying telegram from Mao Zedong to Zhou Enlai," 16 September, 1952, WCDA, http://digitalarchive.wilsoncenter.org/document/113030.

8. "Minutes of Conversation between I. V. Stalin and Zhou Enlai," 19 September 1952, WCDA, http://digitalarchive.wilsoncenter.org/document/111247.

9. *ZENP*, 1:261.

10. *JYMZWG*, 3:576.

11. *ZEWJWX*, 59–62.

12. Khan, *Moslem, Trader, Nomad, Spy*, 26–28.

13. *ZENP*, 1:342.

14. "India and International Situation," *SWJN*, 25:420.

15. Narayanan, "Five Principles of Peaceful Co-Existence," 10.

16. "Conversation with [Zhou Enlai] II," *SWJN*, 26:380–81.

17. "Conversation with [Zhou Enlai] IV," *SWJN*, 26:391.

18. On possible Indian motives, see Pullin, "'Noise and Flutter,'" 212.

19. *ZENP*, 1:393.

20. Ibid., 1:393–4.

21. New Delhi to Secretary of State, 27 June 1954, RG 59, CDF, 1950–1954, box 2167, NARA.

22. Circulation of First Working Draft on "Evaluation of U.S. Operating Programs Relating to India," 23 September 1954, DDRS.

23. Ibid.

24. *FRUS*, 1952–1954, 12, pt. 2:231.

25. "A Great Event in History," *SWJN*, 27:3.

26. "Voyage of Discovery," *SWJN*, 27:58–59, 67.

27. Myoe, *In the Name of Pauk Phaw*, 26.

28. *ZENP*, 1:428–29.

29. *FRUS*, 1952–1954, 14, pt. 1:1039–40.

30. This is covered in Leffler, *Soul of Mankind*, 114–22.

31. Williamson, *Separate Agendas*, 29.

32. *FRUS*, 1952–1954, 7, pt. 1:1225.

33. Ibid., 825.

34. Ibid., 883.

35. Ibid., 823.

36. Ibid., 824.

37. Chen, "China and the Indochina Settlement at the Geneva Conference of 1954," 241–42; *FRUS*, 1952–1954, 16:415.

38. *FRUS*, 1952–1954, 7, pt. 1:1042.

39. Ibid.

40. "Preliminary Opinions on the Assessment of and Preparation for the Geneva Conference," Prepared by the PRC Ministry of Foreign Affairs and Approved in Principle at Meeting of the CCP Central Secretariat, 2 March 1954, *CWIHP Bulletin* 16, 12.

41. *FRUS*, 1952–1954, 16:427.

42. Chen, "China and the Indochina Settlement at the Geneva Conference of 1954," 242.

43. From the Journal of Molotov: Secret Memorandum of Conversation between Molotov and PRC Ambassador Zhang Wentian, 6 March 1954, *CWIHP Bulletin* 16, 86–87.

44. *FRUS, 1952–1954*, 16:427.

45. *ZENP*, 1:359.

46. Ibid., 360.

47. Leffler, *Soul of Mankind*, 143–44; Immerman, *John Foster Dulles*, 81.

48. *FRUS, 1952–1954*, 16:778.

49. Minutes of conversation between Zhou Enlai and Eden, 14 May 1954, *CWIHP Bulletin* 16, 21.

50. Minutes, Meeting between Wang Bingnan and French Delegation Member Paul Boncour, 14 June 1954, *CWIHP Bulletin* 16, 43.

51. "Record of Conversation between R. G. Casey and [Zhou Enlai]," 18 June 1954, FO 371/112074, Public Records Office, Kew, England. Available online at http://www.wilsoncenter.org/sites/default/files/ReconsideringGenevaConf_2b.pdf.

52. "From Geneva Conference (United Kingdom Delegation) to Foreign Office," 22 June 1954, FO 371/112074, Public Records Office, Kew, England. Available online at http://www.wilsoncenter.org/sites/default/files/ReconsideringGenevaConf_2b.pdf.

53. *FRUS, 1952–1954*, 7, pt. 1:1225.

54. Chen, "China and the Indochina Settlement," 245–46.

55. *FRUS, 1952–1954*, 16:3.

56. Chen, "China and the Indochina Settlement," 245–49.

57. Minutes, Zhou Enlai's Meeting with Mendes-France, 23 June 1954, *CWIHP Bulletin* 16, 52–53.

58. Minutes of a Conversation between Zhou Enlai and Anthony Eden, 17 July 1954, *CWIHP Bulletin* 16, 65.

59. Cited in Chen, "China and the Indochina Settlement," 255.

60. *FRUS, 1952–1954*, 16:1175.

61. Ibid., 1331.

62. Ibid., 1189–93.

63. Chen, "China and the Indochina Settlement," 250–61.

64. *FRUS, 1952–1954*, 16:1505–42.

65. *ZENP*, 1:406.

66. Extract from protocol No. 6 of the meeting of the Soviet Union Communist Party Central Committee Plenum, 24 June 1954, Center for the Storage of Contemporary Documentation, Moscow. Also part of a collection of documents assembled for the 1954 Geneva Conference and the Cold War in Asia, Woodrow Wilson Center, 17–18 February 2006.

67. *FRUS, 1952–1954*, 16:1503.

68. Ibid., 1502.

69. Ibid.

70. Telegram, CCP Central Committee to Zhou Enlai, Concerning Policies and Measures in the Struggle against the United States and Jiang Jieshi after the Geneva Conference, 27 July 1954, *CWIHP Bulletin* 16, 83.

71. For a general overview of the conference, see Kahin, *African-Asian Conference*.

72. Anwar, "Indonesia and the Bandung Conference," 183.

73. Ghose, *Jawaharlal Nehru*, 269.

74. Anwar, "Indonesia and the Bandung Conference," 183.

75. "Memo from PRC Foreign Ministry Asia Department regarding the Question of the Afro-Asian Conference," 15 December 1954, file 207–00085–17 (1), PRCFMA.

76. *ZENP*, 1:421.

77. *MZWW*, 183.

78. "Thoughts on Afro-Asian Conference," *SWJN*, 27:110.

79. "Letter from Zhou Enlai to Ali Sastroamidjojo," 10 February 1955, Wilson Center Digital Archive, http://digitalarchive.wilsoncenter.org/document/114659.

80. *FRUS*, 1952–1954, 12, pt. 1:1084.

81. Parker, "Cold War II," 875.

82. Cited in ibid., 875.

83. "Memo by PRC Embassy in Indonesia on Viewing the Afro-Asian Conference from the Bogor Conference," 1 January 1955–31 December 1955, file 207–00001–03 (1), PRCFMA. Here and elsewhere when PRC Foreign Ministry documents are cited in English only, I am using translations provided to me by the Cold War International History Project at the Woodrow Wilson Center.

84. "Draft Proposal regarding the Initial Preparations for the Afro-Asian Conference," 16 January 1955, file 207–00004–03(1), PRCFMA.

85. *ZENP*, 1:460.

86. Ibid., 459.

87. "PRC Draft Proposal for Attending the Afro-Asian Conference," 4–5 April 1955, file 207–00004–01 (1), PRCFMA.

88. Ibid.

89. Ibid.

90. Ibid.

91. *ZENP*, 1:460–61.

92. "Afro-Asian Conference Propaganda," 10 February 1955, RG 59, Records relating to South Asia, 1947–1959, box 7, NARA.

93. "Briefing Paper for Use by the Secretary in Private Talks with Other Delegations at Bangkok Regarding U.S. Attitudes toward Afro-Asian Conference," 10 February 1955, RG 59, Records Relating to South Asia, 1947–1959, box 7, NARA.

94. Circular 491, 25 February 1955, RG 59, Conference Files, 1949–1963, box 68, NARA.

95. Afro-Asian Working Group, "The Chinese Communist Empire: [Beijing]'s New Imperialism," 3 March 1955, RG 59, Conference Files, 1949–1963, box 68, NARA.

96. "Memo, Proposal of PRC Trade Plans at the Afro Asian Conference," 4 March 1955, file 207–00070–01 (1), PRCFMA.

97. Chen, *Mao's China and the Cold War*, 168–69.

98. Tsang, "Target Zhou Enlai," 770–71.

99. Ibid., 771–82. Tsang argues that Zhou not only knew about the planned assassination attempt but tried to use it for his own political advantage.

100. Chen, "Bridging Revolution and Decolonization," 160.

101. Huang, *Huang Hua Memoirs*, 159–60.

102. *ZENP*, 1:465.

103. *ZEWJWX*, 121–22.

104. Xiong, *Zhou Enlai chu deng shijie wutai*, 228; Huang, *Huang Hua Memoirs*,160.

105. Xiong, *Zhou Enlai chu deng shijie wutai*, 230.

106. "Cable from Zhang Hanfu, 'First Daily Report on the Activities of the Delegation,'" 19 April 1955, WCDA, http://digitalarchive.wilsoncenter.org/document/114674.

107. On the developing rivalry, see Graver, *Protracted Contest*, 119.

108. "Cable from Zhang Hanfu, 'Daily Report on the Activities of the Delegation,'" 21 April 1955, WCDA, http://digitalarchive.wilsoncenter.org/collection/16/bandung-conference-1955/4.

109. *ZEZ*, 3:1060–61. Kotelawala briefly relates his version of the incident in his autobiography. The basic description is similar though Kotelawala leaves out the more conciliatory atmosphere that prevailed the next day. Kotelawala, *Asian Prime Minister's Story*, 187.

110. "Zhou zongli zai quanguo renmin daibiao dahui changwuweiyuanhui shang guanyu Ya Fei huiyi de baogao [Premier Zhou's Report on the Afro-Asian Conference at a meeting of the Standing Committee of the National People's Congress]," 13 May 1955, file 207–00014–01 (1), PRCFMA.

111. Romulo, *Meaning of Bandung*, 19.

112. Zhang, *Deterrence and Strategic Culture*, 216.

113. *ZENP*, 1:464.

114. "Cable from Zhang Hanfu, 'Daily Report on the Activities of the Delegation,'" 21 April 1955; *ZEZ*, 3:1060.

115. Shichor, *Middle East in China's Foreign Policy*, 40–45.

116. Liu, *Chinese Ambassadors*, 60.

117. "Cable from Zhang Hanfu, 'Daily Report on the Activities of the Delegation,'" 21 April 1955; "Cable from Zhang Hanfu, 'Daily Activities Log,'" 23 April 1955, WCDA, http://digitalarchive.wilsoncenter.org/document/114679; "Zhou Enlai zongli Ya Fei huiyi qijian huijian Lebanen zhu Meiguo dashi Malike tanhua jilu [Record of a conversation between Premier Zhou Enlai and the Lebanese ambassador to the U.S. Malik at the time of the Bandung Conference]," 25 April 1955, file 207–00015–02, PRCFMA.

118. Shichor, *Middle East in China's Foreign Policy*, 53–54.

119. Mao, "Sino-Muslims in Chinese Nation Building," 186–89.

120. Shichor, *Middle East in China's Foreign Policy*, 42–44.

121. "Conversation with [Zhou Enlai] and U Nu," *SWJN*, 28:123.

122. "Specific Refutations against the American Disruption of Influence of the Afro-Asian Conference," 26 April 1955, file 207–00063–10, PRCFMA.

123. For a complete text, see "Final Communiqué of the Afro-Asian Conference," http://www.bandungspirit.org/IMG/pdf/Final_Communique_Bandung_1955.pdf.

124. The text of the communiqué is available in numerous places online. See, e.g., http://franke.uchicago.edu/Final_Communique_Bandung_1955.pdf.

125. Romulo, *Meaning of Bandung*, 11.

126. "Zhou Enlai zongli Ya Fei." The quotations and capitalizations are from the English-language version that Malik sent to Zhou.

127. OIR No. 6903, "Results of the Bandung Conference a Preliminary Analysis," 27 April 1955, DDRS.

128. Ibid.

129. "Zhou zongli zai quanguo renmin daibiao."

Chapter 4

1. *ZEWJWX*, 214–15.

2. For an assessment, see McMahon, *Limits of Empire*, 65–68.

3. On the diplomatic rituals themselves, see Kang, *East Asia before the West*, 54–81. On the similarities with traditional practices, see Nathan and Scobell, *China's Search for Security*, 319–20.

4. *ZEWJWX*, 178.

5. "Suggestions for Exploiting Conducted Tours of Communist China," 6 February 1955, RG 59, CDF, 1955–1959, box 3933, NARA.

6. *FRUS*, 1955–1957, 21:409–97. Military aid is discussed more extensively than economic aid, though both are mentioned.

7. OCB, Outline Plan of Operations with Respect to Cambodia, 10 April 1957, DDRS; the 1958 meeting and recognition are discussed in greater detail below, but see "Developments in Cambodia's Recognition of Communist China," 29 July 1958, RG 59, CDF, 1955–1959, box 3936, NARA, for Washington's initial reactions.

8. *FRUS*, 1955–1957, 21:498–99.

9. "Yingsong jianpuzhai wangguo shouxiang xihanuke qinwang jichang yishi de chengxu he anpai [The order and arrangement for welcoming the Cambodian head of state Prince Sihanouk at the airport]," 9 February 1956, file 204–00198–03, PRCFMA.

10. *ZENP*, 1:548.

11. Sihanouk, *My War with the CIA*, 82.

12. "Speech to Be Delivered by Prince Sihanouk of Cambodia on the Occasion of his Pending Visit to Canton," 28 February 1956, file 204–00200–03, PRCFMA (in English).

13. PRC Foreign Ministry Diplomatic History Research Office, *Zhou Enlai waijiao huodong dashiji*, 84–85; *FRUS*, 1955–1957, 21:498n2.

14. "Zhou zongli zai jichang huanying xihanuke shouxiang de jianghuagao [Draft of Zhou Enlai's speech welcoming Sihanouk at the airport]," 15 August 1958, file 204–00297–02, PRCFMA.

15. *ZENP*, 2:161–62.

16. Ibid., 163–64.

17. *FRUS*, 1958–1960, 16:241.

18. Ibid., 250.

19. Jacobs, *Universe Unraveling*, 58–60.

20. *FRUS*, 1955–1957, 21:771.

21. Ibid., 774.

22. Ibid., 776–77.

23. Jacobs, *Universe Unraveling*, 62.

24. *FRUS*, 1955–1957, 21:791–92.

25. "Laowo shouxiang Fuma fanghua jiedai [The plan to receive Fuma during his visit to China]," 10 August 1956, file 204–00029–01, PRCFMA.

26. Ibid.

27. Ibid.

28. Ibid.

29. *ZENP*, 1:612.

30. "Zhou Enlai zongli he Laowo shouxiang Fuma de lianhe shengming [Joint statement by Premier Zhou Enlai and Laotian prime minister Phouma]," 25 August 1956, file 204–00029–03, PRCFMA (in English).

31. Jacobs, *Universe Unraveling*, 62–63.

32. "Zhongguo he Laowo de guanxi [China's relations with Laos]," 1 November 1956, file 203–00183–03, PRCFMA.

33. *FRUS, 1955–1957*, 21:816.

34. "Zhongguo he Laowo de guanxi."

35. *FRUS, 1955–1957*, 21:806–8.

36. Ibid., 804–5.

37. Ibid., 816–17.

38. This is described in Jacobs, *Universe Unraveling*, 137–42.

39. *FRUS, 1955–1957*, 21:808.

40. McMahon, *Limits of Empire*, 84; *FRUS, 1955–1957*, 22:201–4.

41. Mozingo, *Chinese Policy toward Indonesia*, 149–50; McMahon, *Limits of Empire*, 85.

42. Cited in Gardner, *Shared Hopes, Separate Fears*, 124.

43. Ibid., 126.

44. McMahon, *Limits of Empire*, 85.

45. Operations Coordinating Board, Intelligence Notes, 5 October 1956, DDRS.

46. *FRUS, 1955–1957*, 22:306, 306n.

47. Ibid., 306–7.

48. Ibid., 309–10.

49. PRC Foreign Ministry Diplomatic History Research Office, *Zhou Enlai waijiao huodong dashiji*, 97.

50. Cited in Mozingo, *Chinese Policy toward Indonesia*, 150.

51. *FRUS, 1955–1957*, 22:316–19.

52. Ibid., 318.

53. Ibid., 322.

54. Ibid., 324.

55. Chen, *Mao's China and the Cold War*, 161.

56. *ZEZ*, 3:1135–36.

57. Phnom Penh to Secretary of State, 15 March 1956, RG 59, CDF, 1955–1959, box 2629, NARA.

58. *ZENP*, 1:641.

59. Geng, *Geng Biao huiyilu*, 89.

60. Ibid., 96.

61. Phnom Penh to Secretary of State, 2 December 1956, RG 59, CDF, 1955–1959, box 3357, NARA.

62. *ZENP*, 2:16.

63. Geng, *Geng Biao Huiyilu*, 93.

64. *SWJN*, 36:621–22.

65. Graver, *Protracted Contest*, 53–54.

66. *ZEZ*, 3:1147–48.

67. *SWJN*, 36:474.

68. Enclosed in Karachi to Secretary of State, 12 December 1956, DDRS.

69. Eisenhower's response was enclosed in Dulles to Karachi, 19 December 1956, DDRS.

70. New Delhi to Secretary of State, 7 December 1956, DDRS.

71. *SWJN*, 36:474, 496.

72. Ibid., 498.

73. Phnom Penh to Secretary of State, 2 December 1956, RG 59, CDF 1955–1959, box 3357, NARA.

74. Consul General Dacca to Secretary of State, 6 January 1959, RG 59, CDF, 1955–1959, box 209, NARA.

75. "United States Policy in the Near East," 28 March 1956, DDRS.

76. Yaqub, *Containing Arab Nationalism*, 38.

77. Amman to Secretary of State, 20 February 1955, Cairo to Secretary of State, 22 February 1955, and Secretary of State to Cairo, 21 April 1955, RG 59, CDF, 1955–1959, box 2679, NARA.

78. Baghdad to Secretary of State, 11 October 1955, RG 59, CDF, 1955–1959, box 2686, NARA.

79. American Embassy Cairo to Secretary of State, 7 March 1956, RG 59, CDF, 1955–1959, box 2679, NARA.

80. *ZENP*, 1:576.

81. Little, *American Orientalism*, 169–70.

82. *FRUS*, 1955–1957, 15:647–48.

83. Damascus to Secretary of State, 23 May 1956, "Syrian Recognition of Red China," 29 May 1956, RG 59, CDF, 1955–1959, box 2686, NARA.

84. Damascus to Secretary of State, 31 May 1956, RG 59, CDF, 1955–1959, box 2686, NARA.

85. *ZENP*, 1:583.

86. Operations Coordinating Board, "Daily Intelligence Abstracts of Interest to Working Groups," 25 May 1956, DDRS.

87. American Embassy Damascus to Department of State, 26 October 1956, CDF, 1955–1959, box 2686, NARA.

88. *FRUS*, 1955–1957, 13:263–64.

89. http://www.fmprc.gov.cn/eng/wjb/zzjg/xybfs/gjlb/2878/.

90. "Yishutuan zai Jian huodong qingkuang baogao [A report on the activities of an art troupe in Cambodia]," 18 November 1957, file 106–00362–06, PRCFMA.

91. Bitar, "Bombs, Plots and Allies," 151–52.

92. Yun, *Chushi qiguo jishi*, 42–43.

93. *FRUS*, 1955–1957, 16:235–36.

94. Richardson, *China Cambodia and the Five Principles of Peaceful Coexistence*, 34–35.

95. *FRUS*, 1955–1957, 16:239–40.

96. Ibid., 244–45.

97. Ibid., 248.

98. *FRUS*, 1955–1957, 13:402–3.

99. Ibid., 18:373–74.

100. Zhou, *Nie Rongzhen nianpu*, 1605.

101. For a complete list of African countries that recognized the PRC during the 1950s and 1960s, see Larkin, *China and Africa*, 66–67.

102. Xie, *Dangdai Zhongguo waijiaoshi*, 165; "Highlights and Trends in Communist China, September through December, 1955," RG 59, CDF, 1955–1959, box 3919, NARA.

103. "Highlights and Trends in Communist China, September through December, 1955," RG 59, CDF, 1955–1959, box 3919, NARA.

104. *FRUS, 1958–1960*, 19:26.

Chapter 5

1. "Communist Propaganda in Mainland China: 1955," 16 December 1955 (draft), RG 306, Records of the USIA, Entry# P76, Far East Program Files, 1954–1959, box 1, NARA.

2. *FRUS, 1958–1960*, 16:143.

3. Zhou used this phrase on numerous occasions. See, e.g., *ZEWW*, 185.

4. Intelligence Report, "Communist China's 'People's Diplomacy,'" January 1955 through June 1956, 7 February 1957, CREST Database, NARA.

5. Ibid.

6. Ibid.

7. "Visit of Chinese Cultural Mission to Bombay," 6 January 1955, RG 59, CDF, 1955–1959, box 2264, NARA.

8. Ibid.

9. "Transmittal of Article on Chinese Cultural Delegation Written by Leading South Indian Brahmin Journalist," 12 January 1955, RG 59, CDF, 1955–1959, box 2264, NARA.

10. "Zhongguo wenhua yishu daibiaotuan fangwen Sudan [A Chinese Cultural Delegation Visits Sudan]," file 107-00043-05, PRCFMA.

11. "Wo wenhua daibiaotuan zai Miandian de huodong qingkuang he Mianfang gejie chaodai qingkuang [The activities of our cultural delegation in Burma and its reception in different areas]," 22 January 1955, file 105-00161-04 (1), PRCFMA.

12. "Guanyu wo wenhua daibiaotuan fangwen Afugan jingguo ji shoudao relie huanying de qingkuang [The situation of our cultural delegation visiting Afghanistan and receiving a warm reception]," 30 August 1956, file 105-00775-03, PRCFMA.

13. Department of State to American Embassy Liberia, 5 April 1958, RG 59, CDF, 1955–1959, box 2263, NARA.

14. Osgood, *Total Cold War*, 213–16, 222–34.

15. Robert H. Thayer, "Organizations in Cultural Relations Abroad," Robert H. Thayer Papers, box 13, LOC.

16. Osgood, *Total Cold War*, 219–20.

17. "Annual Report of the Educational Exchange Program for the Period July 1, 1956 to July 1, 1957," 5 February 1958, RG 59, CDF, 1955–1959, box 2226, NARA.

18. On the USIA, see Shaw, *Hollywood's Cold War*, 167–98.

19. On the American side, see Shaw and Youngblood, *Cinematic Cold War*, 17–36. On the Chinese side, see Clark, *Chinese Cinema*, 25–93.

20. Xiao, "Chinese Cinema," 21–24.

21. *ZENP*, 2:139; for a detailed explanation of what was meant by class nationalism in Chinese films, see Hu, *Projecting a Nation*, 75–115.

22. "Gongchanjuyi xuanchuan zai Jianpuzhai [Communist propaganda in Cambodia]," 2 October 1959, file 106–00495–01, PRCFMA.

23. Ibid.

24. Zhang and Xiao, *Encyclopedia of Chinese Film*, 278.

25. "Gongchanjuyi xuanchuan zai Jianpuzhai."

26. Zhang and Xiao, *Encyclopedia of Chinese Film*, 193.

27. "Communist Propaganda Activities in Southeast Asia: 1959," 22 March 1960, RG 306, Records of the USIA: Office of Research and Special Reports, 1964–1982, box 1, NARA.

28. "Gongchanjuyi xuanchuan zai Jianpuzhai."

29. "Communist China's Worldwide Propaganda Offensive 1959," 4 May 1960, RG 306, Records of the USIA: Office of Research and Special Reports, box 2, NARA.

30. Joint USIA-State Message to American Embassy, Rangoon, 5 May 1960, RG 59, CDF, 1960–1963, box 1080, NARA.

31. Dulles to American Embassy Bangkok, 25 February 1957, RG 59, CDF, 1955–1959, box 2264, NARA.

32. Fineman, *Special Relationship*, 233–35.

33. Dulles to American Embassy Bangkok, 25 February 1957.

34. Eric Kocher to William Sebald, 8 March 1957, RG 59, CDF, 1955–1959, box 2264, NARA.

35. There is a fairly substantial literature on this subject. Here I discuss only how it was relevant to Sino-American competition in the Third World. For background see, among others, Rosenberg, *Spreading the American Dream*, 99–103; and Shaw, *Hollywood's Cold War*; Kitamura, *Screening Enlightenment*, is a more focused case study.

36. For specific examples, see Shaw, *Hollywood's Cold War*, 167–98.

37. T. C. Streibert to C. D. Jackson, 19 January 1954, DDRS. Underlines are in the document.

38. "The USIA Program," 30 June 1959, DDRS. The film itself is available in the National Archives II. Its accession number is ARC 49916. Jinmin has often been romanized as Quemoy.

39. "USIA Program."

40. "1957 nian Meiguo dui Miandian de wenhua qinlue [America's cultural invasion of Burma]," file 105–00810–01, PRCFMA.

41. This is confirmed to, some degree, by Joint USIA-State Message to American Embassy, Rangoon, 5 May 1960, RG 59, CDF, 1960–1963, box 1080, NARA. The document speaks in passing of "an almost airtight embargo of CHICOMS" in Burmese theaters.

42. "Zhongguo waijiaobu he duiwai wenhua lianluo weiyuanhui jiu Jiana shangying Meiguo fanhua dianyingpian 'zhanhua' xiang jia zhengfu jiaoshe shi huifu zhujia shiguan [China's Foreign Ministry and Cultural Exchange Committee replies to the embassy in Ghana to negotiate about the showing of the anti-Chinese American movie 'Battle Flame']," 23 April 1963, file 108–00928–01, PRCFMA.

43. "Zhongguo waijiaobu jiu Jiana shibao he wanbao zhuanzai meiguo 'niuyue shibao' fanhua Manhua xiang jia zhengfu jiaoshe shi huifu zhujia shiguan [China's Foreign Ministry replies to the embassy in Ghana to negotiate about the reprinting of anti-Chinese cartoons from the *New York Times* in the *Ghana Times* and *Evening Post*]," June 1963, file 108–00928–03, PRCFMA.

44. "Communist China's Worldwide Propaganda Offensive 1959," 4 May 1960, RG 306, Records of the USIA: Office of Research and Special Reports, box 2, NARA.

45. *Peking Review*, 4 March 1958, 3.

46. "Communist China's Worldwide Propaganda Offensive 1959."

47. "Africa-Communist China," 4 April 1965, RG 306, Records of the USIA, Entry# P249, Office of the Assistant Director for Africa, Policy Files, 1955–1967, box 1, NARA.

48. Ibid.

49. "Communist China: Organization for the Conduct of Foreign Relations," December 1960, CREST Database.

50. "Communist China's Worldwide Propaganda Offensive 1959."

51. "NCNA Overseas Operations," 5 March 1962, RG 306, Records of the USIA, Entry# P44, Office of Policy Research, Records of the Assistant Director for Research and Analysis, box 2, NARA.

52. *Peking Review*, 24 June 1958, 4.

53. *Peking Review*, 27 January 1961, 17–18.

54. *Peking Review*, 20 January 1961, 19–21.

55. See, e.g., "The Bandung Spirit Thrives," *Peking Review*, 28 April 1958, 6.

56. *Peking Review*, 3 February 1961, 12–13.

57. *Peking Review*, 27 January 1961, 13–15.

58. Osgood, *Total Cold War*, 121.

59. Interview with Earl Wilson in *Frontline Diplomacy*.

60. Ibid.

61. Ibid.

62. Ibid.

63. See, e.g., "USIS-sponsored English Language Book: Buddhism in China," 10 July 1956, RG 306, Records of the USIA, Entry# P46 Master Files of Field Publications, 1951–1979, box 44, NARA.

64. "List of Publications and Educational Institutions," 28 November 1956, RG 306, Records of the USIA, Entry# P76, Far East Program Files, 1954–1959, NARA.

65. "1957 nian Meiguo dui Miandian de wenhua qinlue [America's cultural invasion of Burma in 1957]," file 105–00810–01, PRCFMA.

66. "Visit of DPAO USIS to 13 African Countries in Attempt to Increase understanding and Effectiveness of China Reporting Program in Africa," 22 June 1965, RG 306, Records of the USIA, Entry# P249, Office of the Assistant Director for Africa, Policy Files, 1959–1967, box 1, NARA.

67. Borstelmann, *Cold War and the Color Line*, 2; on the relation between civil rights and the Cold War, see also Dudziak, *Cold War Civil Rights*.

68. Von Eschen, *Satchmo Blows Up the World*.

69. One book that covers some of the same ground covered here from a different perspective is Frazier, *East Is Black*. Rather than focusing on how China used African-American intellectuals in its propaganda, Frazier is focused on the experiences and travel writing of these intellectuals during their time in the PRC.

70. The best recent biography of Du Bois is Lewis, *W. E. B. Du Bois*. See especially 554–72 on his later life.

71. Ibid., 28.

72. *Peking Review*, 3 March 1959, 11–13.

73. *Renmin Ribao*, 23 February 1959.

74. See, e.g., *ZEWJWX*, 396–97.

75. *Renmin Ribao*, 17 January 1964.

76. Adams, *American Dream*, 66–67.

77. Ibid., 93–94.

78. Ibid., 97–99.

79. Ibid., 99.

80. *JYMZWG*, 10:336–37.

81. Ibid., 333–34.

82. "Shoudou gejie renmin fandui meiguo diguozhuyi, zhichi meiguo heiren fandui zhongzu jishi douzheng dahui [A great meeting in the capital of the struggle of various peoples against American imperialism, in support of the American Negro and against racial discrimination]," 10 October 1963, RFWP, reel 8, LOC.

83. "Speech Delivered by Liu Ning-Yi at the Rally of People of All Circles in Peking Supporting the American Negroes in Their Struggle against Racial Discrimination," RFWP, reel 8, LOC.

84. The best book on Williams is Tyson, *Radio Free Dixie*.

85. Frazier, "Thunder in the East," 934.

86. Exclusive to Howard News Syndicate, "China Surges Ahead," November 1963, RFWP, reel 6, LOC.

87. *Renmin Ribao*, 11 October 1963.

88. "U.S. Negro Leader Cables Thanks to Chinese People," RFWP, reel 1, LOC.

89. "Report on China," RFWP, reel 6, LOC.

90. On this point, see Belmonte, *Selling the American Way*, 159–78.

91. CIA Biweekly Propaganda Guidance, "Communist China's Real Attitude toward Colonialism and the Non-White Peoples," 20 April 1964.

92. On Tibet, see Chen, "Tibetan Rebellion of 1959," 54–101. On Xinjiang, see Gao, "Call of the Oases."

93. "Chinese Communist Anti-Moslem Propaganda," 2 May 1956, CREST Database, NARA; "Tibet and China: Background Paper," 27 April 1959, CREST Database, NARA.

94. "Chinese Communist Anti-Moslem Propaganda."

95. Garver, *Protracted Contest*, 55.

96. Chen, "Tibetan Rebellion of 1959," 54–55.

97. For a complete history of Sino-Tibetan relations and a detailed account of these events, see Shakya, *Dragon in the Land of Snows*. On events in 1959, see 185–211. See also Chen "Tibetan Rebellion of 1959," 54–101.

98. William Lacy to Larue R. Lutkins, 10 April 1959, RG 59, CDF, 1955–1959, box 2718, NARA.

99. USIS Colombo to USIA, 8 December 1959, RG 59, Bureau of Cultural Affairs Planning and Development Staff, Country Files, 1955–1964, box 222.

100. Knaus, *Orphans of the Cold War*.

101. *FRUS*, 1961–1963, 22:170–71.

102. *FRUS*, 1964–1968, 30:731–33.

103. China Reporting Service, "Tibetan Guerillas Continue Fierce Resistance to Occupation, Reforms Imposed on Homeland," 11 June 1963, RG 306, Records of the USIA, Entry # 2, Magazines and Periodicals, box 5.

104. *Peking Review*, 20 January 1961, 15–17.

105. Israeli, "Muslim Minority in the People's Republic of China," 903–4.

106. *Moslem Unrest in China*, RG 306, Records of the USIA, Entry# P 46, Master File Copies of Field Publications, 1951–1979, box 44, NARA.

107. John C. Wiley to Albert Harkness, 15 April 1959, RG 306, Records of the USIA, Entry# P 2, Book Development Files, box 10, NARA.

108. Gordon Ewing to Eugene Skora, 3 January 1963, RG 306, Records of the USIA, Entry# P 2, Book Development Files, box 10, NARA.

109. Michael Dillion, *Xinjiang*, 56.

110. "Islam Agony in Central Asia," 1 July 1963, RG 306, Entry 39, box 6, NARA.

111. Operations Coordinating Board, "Guidelines for United States Programs Affecting the Overseas Chinese in Southeast Asia," 11 December 1957, DDRS.

112. Ibid.

113. Oyen, "Communism, Containment and the Chinese Overseas," 68–70.

114. Operations Coordinating Board, "Guidelines for United States Programs Affecting the Overseas Chinese in Southeast Asia," 11 December 1957, DDRS.

115. Ibid.

116. "Wo wenhua daibiaotuan zai Mian yanchu qingkuang jianbao [A summary of the performances of our cultural delegation in Burma]," 9 February 1955, file 105–00163–04, PRCFMA.

117. Operations Coordinating Board, "Guidelines for United States Programs Affecting the Overseas Chinese in Southeast Asia," 11 December 1957, DDRS.

118. Interview with Earl Wilson in *Frontline Diplomacy*.

119. "Chinese Calendar 1956," RG 306, Records of the USIA, Entry# P 46, Master File Copies of Field Publications, 1951–1979, box 44, NARA.

120. "The Overseas Chinese as an Instrument of U.S. Policy," 13 July 1956, DDRS.

121. "Wayward Ways of Overseas Chinese Stymies Peking Regime," 24 September 1964, RG 306, Records of the USIA, Entry# P64, Research Memoranda, 1963–1999, box 11, NARA.

Chapter 6

1. Mao Zedong, "Speech at the Supreme State Conference," 28 January 1958, https://www.marxists.org/reference/archive/mao/selected-works/volume-8/mswv8_03.htm.

2. There is an extensive literature on this. For a basic description, see Spence, *Search for Modern China*, 541–50.

3. This "revolutionary outburst" is described in Chen, *Mao's China and the Cold War*, 171–75.

4. Li, *Private Life of Chairman Mao*, 224.

5. Ibid., 225.

6. Chen, *Mao's China and the Cold War*, 72–73.

7. Cited in ibid., 180.

8. Cited in ibid., 183.

9. The best summary of the entire episode can be found in Yaqub, *Containing Arab Nationalism*, 205–36.

10. See, e.g., Wu Lengxi, "Inside Story of the Decision Making during the Shelling of Jinmen," *CWIHP Bulletin* 6–7, 207–14; and Ye, *Ye Fei huiyilu*, 656–57.

11. Cited in Zhang, *Deterrence and Strategic Culture*, 235.

12. Cited in Chen, *Mao's China and the Cold War*, 182.

13. See, e.g., ibid., 182.

14. "Speech, Mao Zedong at the Fifteenth Meeting of the Supreme State Council, 5 September 1958 (Excerpt)," *CWIHP Bulletin* 6–7, 214–19.

15. *ZENP*, 2:179.

16. *SWJN*, 44:98.

17. *ZENP*, 2:179.

18. Cited in Christensen, *Worse Than a Monolith*, 150. I have omitted Christensen's inclusion of some of the original Chinese phrases.

19. On this point, see Chang, *Friends and Enemies*, especially 157–65.

20. Lüthi, *Sino-Soviet Split*, 148; Chen, *Mao's China and the Cold War*, 80; Mao Zedong, "Speech at the Tenth Plenum of the Eighth Central Committee," 24 September 1962, http://www.marxists.org/reference/archive/mao/selected-works/volume-8/mswv8_63.htm.

21. "Minutes Conversation between Mao Zedong and Ambassador Yudin," http://digitalarchive.wilsoncenter.org/document/116982.

22. Lüthi, *Sino-Soviet Split*, 93–94.

23. Quan, *Mao Zedong yu Heluxiaofu*, 141.

24. Khrushchev, *Memoirs of Nikita Khrushchev: Volume 3*, 456.

25. Cited in Lowenthal, "China," 170.

26. Rey, "De Gaulle, French Diplomacy, and Franco-Soviet Relations Seen from Moscow," 28.

27. Cited in Ogunsanwo, *China's Policy in Africa*, 50–51.

28. "Khrushchev Visit," 4 September 1959, DDRS.

29. See *FRUS*, 1958–1960, 19:600–601.

30. Ibid., 622–23.

31. Garver, *Protracted Contest*, 53.

32. "Military Report on India's Anti-China Plots," 24 September 1959, file 105–00944–07, PRCFMA. English translation provided to the author by the Cold War International History Project at the Woodrow Wilson Center.

33. This argument is laid out most clearly in Khan, *Muslim, Trader, Nomad, Spy*.

34. Lüthi, *Sino-Soviet Split*, 143–44.

35. Khan, *Muslim, Trader, Nomad, Spy*, 93.

36. Chen, "Tibetan Rebellion of 1959," 89.

37. *ZENP*, 2:231.

38. Ibid., 250–51, 254.

39. Ibid., 250–51.

40. *NYT*, 30 October 1959.

41. *FRUS*, 1958–1960, 16:134.

42. "Your Conversations with Mr. Nehru," 7 December 1959, DDRS.

43. "Aisenhaowei'er fangwen yindu [Eisenhower visits India]," 31 December 1959, file 105–00946–02, PRCFMA.

44. Fravel, *Strong Borders and Secure Nation*, 86–87.

45. *ZENP*, 2:286.

46. Ibid., 307.

47. On Zhou's willingness to compromise, see Fravel, *Strong Borders and Secure Nation*, 93–96. Zhou rejected the McMahon Line multiple times; see *ZENP*, 2:307–8.

48. Though Zhou Enlai's life chronicle has a fairly detailed record of the discussions, it contains no mention of the Dalai Lama after Zhou first brought the issue up with the defense minister. See *ZENP*, 2:307–14.

49. *FRUS*, 1958–1960, 19:665.

50. "Meiguo dui Zhongdong de jiben zhengce he zuofa neirong tiyao [A summary of America's policy and methods in the Middle East]," 30 August 1958, file 107–00295–05, PRCFMA.

51. Shichor, *Middle East in China's Foreign Policy*, 77–78.

52. Barrett, *Greater Middle East and the Cold War*, 111–12.

53. *ZENP*, 2:207.

54. Cited in Shichor, *Middle East in China's Foreign Policy*, 81.

55. "Synopsis of Intelligence Material Reported to the President," 5 May 1959, DDRS.

56. *ZENP*, 2:231.

57. Shichor, *Middle East in China's Foreign Policy*, 82.

58. Ibid., 82–83.

59. "Akhbar Editorial," 1 October 1959, translation in RG 59, CDF, 1955–1959, box 2706, NARA.

60. Shichor, *Middle East in China's Foreign Policy*, 83.

61. Ibid., 98–99.

62. See, e.g., Cairo to Secretary of State, 4 October 1959, RG 59, CDF, 1955–1959, box 2706, NARA.

63. Little, *American Orientalism*, 180–81.

64. Department of State to Cairo, 5 October 1960, DDRS.

65. Friedman, *Shadow Cold War*, 86–89.

66. Lüthi, *Sino-Soviet Split*, 220–21; Chen, *Mao's China and the Cold War*, 82–83.

67. Lüthi, *Sino-Soviet Split*, 226–27.

68. Wu, *Shinian lunzhan*, 1:520.

69. Lüthi, *Sino-Soviet Split*, 266–72.

70. For a detailed account of the treaty negotiations, see Chang, *Friends and Enemies*, 228–53.

71. Both quotations are from "Status of Programs to Influence World Opinion with Respect to Chinese Communist Nuclear Detonation," 2 July 1964, http://nsarchive.gwu.edu/NSAEBB/NSAEBB38/document14.pdf.

72. The phrase "other white nations" is quoted in "The Sino-Soviet Conflict in the Fronts," http://www.foia.cia.gov/sites/default/files/document_conversions/14/esau-24.pdf.

73. Ibid.

74. For the Polemics themselves, see CCP Central Committee, *Polemic of the General Line of the Communist Movement*. On their distribution, see Friedman, *Shadow Cold War*, 96.

75. CCP Central Committee, *Polemic of the General Line of the Communist Movement*, 187–88.

76. Chen, *Mao's China and the Cold War*, 5.

77. *Mao Zedong waijiao wenxuan*, 506–9.

78. On American efforts to foster divisions between Beijing and Moscow early in the Cold War, see Chang, *Friends and Enemies*.

79. "U.S. Policy re the Sino-Soviet Conflict," DDRS.

80. "Implications of the Sino-Soviet Rupture for the U.S.," July 1963, http://www.foia.cia.gov/docs/DOC_0000384484/DOC_0000384484.pdf.

81. Green to State Department, "Trends and Prospects in Communist China: Implications for U.S. Policy," 16 August 1963, RG 59, Central Foreign Policy Files, 1963, box 3858, NARA.

82. Ibid.

83. On this point, see Chang, *Friends and Enemies*, 258–59.

84. Green to State Department, "Trends and Prospects in Communist China: Implications for U.S. Policy."

85. These are described in Chapter 4.

86. For a more complete summary of the run up to the conflict, see Fravel, *Strong Borders and Secure Nation*, 172–97.

87. Xiaobing Li, "Sino-Indian Border War (1962)," 399–400.

88. For the background and evolution of India's commitment to nonalignment, see Garver, *Protracted Contest*, 121–24.

89. Nehru, "Changing India," 460–61.

90. Zhonggong zhongyang wenxian yanjiushi, *Zhou Enlai junshi wenxuan*, 4: 469.

91. Ogunswano, *China's Policy in Africa*, 108–9.

92. "Alian guowu mishu tan Zhong Yin bianjie wenti [A discussion of the Sino-Indian border problem with the UAR secretary of state]," 8 November 1962, file 107-00488-05, PRCFMA.

93. "Faqu Zhou zongli fenbie zhi Ban furen he Xihanuke xinzhong, waiwen benshi [Foreign-language source materials from the letters sent by Zhou Enlai to Bandaranaike and Sihanouk, respectively], file 106-01398-02, PRCFMA.

94. "Xilan zongli, Yinni waizhang fang Hua huitan qingkuang [The premier of Ceylon and the Indonesian foreign minister visit China]," file 105-01792-08, PRCFMA.

95. Ibid.

96. Ibid.

97. "Xian Kasaimu deng dui Zhong Yin bianjie wenti de kanfa [The opinion of Kasim and others about the Sino-Indian border problem]," 31 December 1962, file 107-00509-03 (6), PRCFMA.

98. *NYT*, 17 December 1962.

99. *NYT*, 14 December 1962.

100. Ministry of External Affairs, "China's Bid for World Power," May 1963, box 442, WAHP.

101. For a brief summary of the evolving American attitude toward nonalignment, see Lawrence, "Rise and Fall of Non-Alignment," 147.

102. *FRUS*, 1961–1963, 19:593–96.

103. "FE Memorandum on United States Policy in the Sino Indian Conflict," 3 November 1962, box 536, WAHP.

104. *FRUS*, 1961–1963, 19: 365.

105. Ibid., 365.

106. Ibid., 632–35.

107. "Report of the Harriman Mission," box 536, WAHP.

108. "Country Assistance Program India," August 1963, PD-ACC-349, USAID Development Experience Clearinghouse.

109. Robert Komer to the President, 24 February 1964, DDRS.

Chapter 7

1. On North Korea's close relationship with China before 1965, see Cheng, "Evolution of Sino-North Korean Relations in the 1960s"; on Vietnam's tendency to lean toward China in the Sino-Soviet split, see Zhai, *China and the Vietnam Wars*, 122–29.

2. Cited in Kux, *Disenchanted Allies*, 146.

3. Department of State to American Embassy Karachi, 16 June 1961, RG 59, Central Decimal Files, 1961–1963, box 1366, NARA.

4. "Bajisitan de jiben qingkuang he dongxiang [The basic situation and tendency in Pakistan]," 25 February 1956, file 102–00055–05, PRCFMA.

5. Ibid.

6. M. Taylor Fravel, for instance, writes that the "agreement overall was more favorable to Pakistan." See Fravel, *Strong Borders and Secure Nation*, 116.

7. *NYT*, 4 March 1963.

8. "Zhou Enlai zongli, Chen Yi fuzongli jiejian Bajisitan waijiaobuzhang Butuo tanhua jilu [Record of a conversation between Zhou Enlai, Chen Yi, and Bhutto]," 3 March 1963, file 204–01502–03, PRCFMA.

9. Ibid.

10. For an excellent and somewhat more thorough discussion of these efforts, see Tang, "Beyond India," 7–9.

11. "Pakistani Transgressions of U.S. Friendship," 16 July 1965, NSF, box 151, LBJL.

12. Tang, "Beyond India," 8.

13. "Instructions for Mr. Ball's Mission to Pakistan, September 1963," 28 August 1963, NSF: NSC Histories South Asia, box 24, LBJL.

14. *FRUS*, 1964–1968, 25:129–30.

15. Ibid., 136–38.

16. "What Do We Want in Pakistan?" 16 July 1965, NSF, box 151, LBJL.

17. Clymer, *Troubled Relations*, 49–60.

18. "Kennedy-Macmillan Nassau Meeting, December 19–20, 1962, Position Paper: Cambodia," 13 December 1962, DDRS.

19. Clymer, *Troubled Relations*, 56–58.

20. American Embassy Phnom Penh to Department of State, 7 November 1963, RG 59, General Records of the Department of State, Central Foreign Policy File, 1963, box 3487, NARA.

21. Clymer, *Troubled Relations*, 57–59.

22. "Waijiaobu fadian: Jianpuzhai dangqian xingshi [Foreign Ministry telegram: The situation facing Cambodia]," 4 December 1964, file 106–01125–01, PRCFMA.

23. Richardson, *China, Cambodia, and the Five Principles of Peaceful Coexistence*, 45.

24. "Zhou zongli tong Xihanuke qinwang de tanhua jilu [Memo of a conversation between Zhou Enlai and Sihanouk]," 28 September 1964, file 204–01548–01 (1), PRCFMA.

25. "Zhou zongli yu Xihanuke di er ci dandu huitan jilu [Record of the second solo meeting between Premier Zhou and Sihanouk]," 27 September 1965, file 106–01521–04, PRCFMA.

26. "Chairman Liu Shaoqi's speech at the banquet in Honor of Prince Sihanouk," 27 September 1964 (in English), file 204–01546–02, PRCFMA.

27. American Embassy Phnom Penh to Department of State, 4 June 1963, RG 59, General Records of the Department of State, Central Foreign Policy File, 1963, box 3487, NARA.

28. Phnom Penh to Department of State, 7 November 1963, RG 59, Subject Numeric Files, 1963, box 3847, NARA.

29. *FRUS*, 1964–1968, 27:337–40.

30. On Chinese influence in Indonesia before the 1960s, see Liu, *China and the Shaping of Indonesia*, which emphasizes that Indonesians came to embrace the PRC as an alternative model of modernity. On American concerns about Soviet influence in Indonesia during the early 1960s, see *FRUS*, 1961–1963, 23:443–45.

31. Mozingo, *Chinese Policy toward Indonesia*, 156–91.

32. On this point, see also Zhou, "Ambivalent Alliance," 1, which presents an insightful analysis of the Sino-Indonesian relationship on multiple levels.

33. Mozingo, *Chinese Policy toward Indonesia*, 192–202.

34. Rakove, *Kennedy, Johnson, and the Nonaligned World*, 149.

35. "Paper for Consideration at the National Security Meeting, May 12, 1964. Subject: Indonesia and the Indonesia-Malaysia Dispute," 9 May 1964, DDRS.

36. "Guanyu Malaixiya wenti [About the problem of Malaysia]," 31 January 1964, file 110–01696–03, PRCFMA.

37. *NYT*, 4 March 1964.

38. "Guanyu Malaixiya wenti [About the problem of Malaysia]," 20 February 1964, file 110–01696–03, PRCFMA.

39. "Paper for Consideration at the National Security Meeting, 12 May 1964."

40. National Intelligence Estimate, "Prospects for Indonesia," 22 July 1964, http://www.foia.cia.gov/docs/DOC_0000012246/DOC_0000012246.pdf.

41. Keys, *Globalizing Sport*, 17.

42. Cited in Xu, *Olympic Dreams*, 85–86.

43. "Biweekly Propaganda Guidance," 7 October 1963, CREST database, NARA.

44. Cited in Shuman, "Elite Competitive Sport in the People's Republic of China," 267.

45. Xu, *Olympic Dreams*, 52–53.

46. "Zhou Enlai zongli, Chen Yi fuzongli, He Long fuzongli jiejian Yinni tiyubuzhang Maladi deng tanhua jilu [Memorandum of a conversation between Premier Zhou Enlai, Vice Premiers Chen Yi and He Long, and Indonesian minister of sports Maladi]," 29 April 1964, file 105–01240–08, PRCFMA.

47. Pauker, "GANEFO I."

48. Excellent on this is Shuman, "Elite Competitive Sport in the People's Republic of China." For a typical set of photos from the event, see *Renmin Ribao*, 23 November 1963.

49. Shuman, "Elite Competitive Sport in the People's Republic of China," 271.

50. "Central Propaganda Directive," 4 November 1963, CREST database, NARA.

51. Shuman, "Elite Competitive Sport in the People's Republic of China," 272.

52. For an overview, see *ZEZ*, 4:1529–68.

53. Ibid., 1530.

54. Diplomatic History Institute, *Zhou Enlai waijiao huodong dashi ji* 170, 189, notes that a crowd of more than three hundred thousand greeted Sékou Touré in Shanghai and that a crowd of one hundred thousand cheered on Nkrumah at a gathering in Beijing.

55. Chen, *Tanlu zai 1964*, 181, 213, 218–19.

56. Some examples are cited in *ZEZ*, 4:1529, 1531, 1536.

57. Cited in Chen, *Tanlu zai 1964*, 168–69.

58. Ibid., 183, 212–13, 226.

59. Pasha, "India and West Asia," 304–5.

60. Several scholars have noted Bourguiba's pro-Western orientation. See, e.g., Connelly, *Diplomatic Revolution*, 147.

61. "Zhou Enali zongli xiang Tunisi zongtong Buerguba zongtong huitan jilu [A record of Premier Zhou's conversation with Tunisian president Bourguiba]," 9 January 1964, file 203–00621–01, PRCFMA.

62. "Zhou Enlai zongli xiang Enkeluma zongtong di yi ci dandu huihua jilu [Record of the first solo conversation between Premier Zhou Enlai and President Nkrumah]," 14 January 1964, file 203–00623–01, PRCFMA.

63. *ZENP*, 2:610.

64. "Visit of Chicom Premier and Foreign Minister to Africa," 14 February 1964, RG 59, Subject Numeric Files, 1964–1966, box 2011, NARA.

65. *ZENP*, 2:610, 616; "Visit of Chicom Premier and Foreign Minister to Africa."

66. Arthur Dean to Ashe, undated, RG 59, General Records of the Office of Asian Communist Affairs, box 2, NARA.

67. "Visit of Chicom Premier and Foreign Minister to Africa."

68. Paris to Secretary of State, 16 December 1963, DDRS.

69. Green to Hilsman, "Chinese Communists African Tour," RG 59, General Records of the Office of Asian Communist Affairs, box 2, NARA.

70. The most complete account of U.S.-Ethiopian relations during this period is Vestal, *Lion of Judah in the New World,* especially 121–60.

71. Department of State to American Embassy Addis Ababa, 4 January 1964, DDRS.

72. "Bilateral Political Relations between China and Ethiopia," http://www.npc.gov .cn/englishnpc/Special4/2008–11/03/content_1456444.htm.

73. Scalapino, "Sino-Soviet Competition in Africa," 152.

74. Han, *Eldest Son*, 298.

75. "Shisi guo fangwen baogao dagang [The main points of a report on the visit to fourteen countries]," 17 June 1964, file 203–00607–01, PRCFMA.

76. "Visit of Chicom Premier and Foreign Minister to Africa"; Robert A. Scalpino, "On the Trail of Zhou Enlai in Africa," Memorandum RM-4061-PR, April 1964, http:// www.rand.org/pubs/research_memoranda/RM4061.html.

77. Cited in Li, "Shilun Zhongguo," 116.

78. There are two excellent recent accounts of Chinese and American diplomacy during the conference that were especially useful. For an account of Chinese diplomacy, see Li, "Shilun Zhongguo." On the American side, see Gettig, "'Trouble Ahead in Afro-Asia.'" I have drawn on both of these accounts.

79. Garver, *Protracted Contest*, 123–25.

80. Rakove, *Kennedy, Johnson, and the Nonaligned World*, 220–21.

81. Garver, *Protracted Contest*, 125.

82. Ibid., 126–27.

83. *ZENP*, 2:627.

84. Ibid., 628.

85. Li, "Shilun Zhongguo," 116.

86. *Chen Yi nianpu*, 2:1039.

87. *ZENP*, 2:675.

88. Cited in Li, "Shilun Zhongguo," 118.

89. Robert Komer to McGeorge Bundy, 19 October 1961, DDRS.

90. For a detailed analysis, see Gettig, "'Trouble Ahead in Afro-Asia,'" 129–35.

91. Cited in ibid., 134.

92. Averell Harriman to Komer, 20 November 1964, DDRS.

93. "Huang Hua dashi he Enkeluma zongtong tanhua jilu [Memorandum of a conversation between Huang Hua and Nkrumah]," 1 October 1964, file 113–00405–016, PRCFMA.

94. "Deng Xiaoping daizongli jiejian jian zhu Hua dashi Xilike Madake tanhua jilu [Record of a conversation between Vice Premier Deng Xiaoping and the Cambodian ambassador to the PRC Xilike Madake]," 7 February 1964, file 106–01467–01, PRCFMA.

95. Rakove, *Kennedy, Johnson and the Nonaligned World*, 224.

96. Ibid., 220–24.

97. Directorate of Intelligence, "The Second Afro-Asian Conference: A Status Report," 10 May 1965, DDRS.

98. This is described in ibid.

99. Ibid.

100. Central Intelligence Agency, "Prospects for the Second Afro-Asian Conference," 23 June 1965, DDRS.

101. Friedman, "Reviving Revolution," 209.

102. *ZENP*, 2:722–23.

103. "Chen Yi fuzongli fangwen Nibo'er: Huijian Niguowang, shouxiang, waijiaodaju tanhua jilu [Vice Premier Chen Yi's visit to Nepal: Record of a conversation with the king, the prime minister, and important diplomats]," 30 March 1965, file 203–00656–01, PRCFMA.

104. *ZENP*, 2:734–37.

105. Li, "Shilun Zhongguo," 122–23.

106. See "Ji Pengfei fuwaizhang xiang Mali zongtong Kaida tanhua jilu [Record of a conversation between Ji Pengfei and Malian president Keita]," 2 June 1965, file 106–01268–05, PRCFMA; and "Waijiaobu Ji Pengfei fubuzhang fangwen Jiniya qingkuang [Ji Pengfei's visit to Guinea]," 27 May 1965, file 108–00632–04, PRCFMA.

107. "Guidance Paper for the Second Afro-Asian Conference (Bandung II)," 14 April 1965, DDRS.

108. Ibid.

109. "The Second Afro-Asian Conference: A Status Report," 10 May 1965, DDRS.

110. Ibid.

111. Central Intelligence Agency, "Prospects for the Second Afro-Asian Conference," 23 June 1965, DDRS.

112. "Preparatory Afro-Asian Talks Postponed a Day in Algiers," *NYT*, 24 June 1965.

113. Li, "Shilun Zhongguo," 124.

114. *ZENP*, 2:738.

115. Ibid., 739–40.

116. For a clear summary of these events, see Pauker, "Rise and Fall of Afro-Asian Solidarity," 425–32; and Gettig, "Trouble Ahead in Afro-Asia," 144–46.

117. "Afro-Asian Summit Ends before It Starts," *NYT*, 27 June 1965.

118. Ibid.; "African-Asian Conference in Postponed until November 5," *NYT*, 27 June 1965.

119. "Algiers Parley Delay Seen as Stunning Blow to China," *NYT*, 28 June 1965.

120. Robert W. Komer, "Memorandum for the President," 1 November 1965, DDRS.

121. Li, "Shilun Zhongguo," 128–30.

122. "Chen Yi's Press Conference," 1 October 1965, DDRS; Gettig, "'Trouble Ahead in Afro-Asia,'" 148.

123. Gettig, "'Trouble Ahead in Afro-Asia,'" 149.

124. McMahon, *Cold War on the Periphery*, 327–28.

125. *FRUS*, 1964–1968, 25:366–7.

126. *ZENP*, 2:755; the Chinese statement is quoted in Armstrong, *Revolutionary Diplomacy*, 167.

127. *FRUS*, 1964–1968, 25:374.

128. Ibid.

129. Ibid., 376.

130. CIA, Intelligence Memorandum, "Sino-Pakistani Cooperation in the Kashmir War," October 14, 1965, SC no. 10519/65, DDRS.

131. *FRUS*, 1964–1968, 25:401.

132. Ibid., 406–7.

133. Ibid., 409–10.

134. Ibid., 416.

135. McMahon, *Cold War on the Periphery*, 332.

136. Ibid., 438.

137. CIA, Intelligence Memorandum, "Sino-Pakistani Cooperation in the Kashmir War."

138. Simpson, *Economists with Guns*, 172.

139. *FRUS*, 1964–1968, 26:234–36.

140. See, e.g., Rakove, *Kennedy, Johnson, and the Nonaligned World*, 236–37.

141. Cited in Simpson, *Economists with Guns*, 180–81.

142. Department of State to Embassy in Indonesia, telegram, 29 October 1965, *FRUS*, 1964–1968, 26:341–42.

143. Simpson, *Economists with Guns*, 186–87.

144. CIA, "Special Report: Peking's Setbacks in Indonesia," 1 April 1966, NSF, box 248, LBJL.

145. "Memorandum for Mr. Rostow: Elements of Progress in Asia," 24 June 1966, DDRS.

Chapter 8

1. Sidey, "President's Voracious Reading Habits."

2. Schlesinger, *Thousand Days*, 341; Friedman, *Kennedy's Wars*, 288.

3. "Mao Zedong zhuxi huijian Yuenan nanfang minzu jiefang zhenxian daibiaotuan tanhua jilu [Record of a conversation between Mao Zedong and a delegation from the South Vietnamese National Liberation Front]," file 106–00142–01, PRCFMA.

4. There is a substantial literature on American counterinsurgency efforts during the Cold War and the Kennedy administration. Much of it focuses on Vietnam, though discussion of Communist China as a factor is limited. See, e.g., Shafer, *Deadly Paradigms*; and Blaufarb, *Counterinsurgency Era*.

5. See, e.g., Lalaj et al., "'Albania Is Not Cuba,'" 187–89.

6. "Memorandum of Conversation between Comrade Zhou Enlai and Party and State Leaders of the PRA," 27–29 March 1965, *CWIHP Bulletin* 16, 274.

7. Ibid.

8. All of this is discussed at length in Cheng, "Sino-Cuban Relations during the Early Years of the Castro Regime," 78–95.

9. Xie, *Zhongguo dangdai waijiaoshi*, 220–21.

10., 216; Shinn and Eisenmann, *China and Africa*, 233

11. For the full details of these negotiations, see Connelly, *Diplomatic Revolution*, 249–75.

12. *ZEWJWX*, 322–26.

13. *MZWW*, 463–65.

14. *JYMZWG*, 10:338–39.

15. Ibid., 14–15.

16. Ibid., 14–15.

17. Lin Biao, "Long Live the Victory of the People's War," online version http://www.marxists.org/reference/archive/lin-biao/1965/09/peoples_war/index.htm, accessed 18 December 2013.

18. Walt Whitman Rostow, Draft of paper on counterinsurgency, 15 August 1961, DDRS.

19. Maechling Jr., "Insurgency and Counterinsurgency," 32–33.

20. Ibid., 34.

21. "U.S. Overseas Internal Defense Policy," 13 August 1962, DDRS.

22. Ibid.

23. Ibid.

24. Ibid.

25. "[Beijing's] Views on Revolutionary War," 14 December 1964, DDRS.

26. "Communist China Long Range Study: Military and Political Factors," June 1966, DDRS.

27. Ibid.

28. Cited in Mao, "China and the Escalation of the Vietnam War," 35.

29. Lin Biao, "Long Live the Victory of the People's War," online version http://www.marxists.org/reference/archive/lin-biao/1965/09/peoples_war/index.htm, accessed 18 December 2013.

30. For a summary, see Lawrence, *Vietnam War*, 56–67; Bradley, *Vietnam at War*, 79–89.

31. Bradley, *Vietnam at War*, 93–96.

32. Chinese efforts to achieve a compromise and encourage moderation on the Vietnamese side are noted by several scholars. See Christensen, *Worse Than a Monolith*, 128–30; Chen, *Mao's China and the Cold War*, 138–44.

33. Cited in Zhai, *China and the Vietnam Wars*, 80.

34. *ZENP*, 2:318.

35. Zhai, *China and the Vietnam Wars*, 83.

36. Ibid., 83.

37. For summaries of some of these meetings, see *ZENP*, 2:416–17; and Guo et al., *Zhong Yue guanxi yanbian sishinian*, 66–69.

38. "Guanyu Yuenan nanfang renmin jiefang zhenxian ni pai siren daibiaotuan chufangshi [About the plan of the NLF to dispatch a four-person delegation]," 13 June 1962, file 106–00995–01, PRCFMA.

39. "Chen Yi fuzongli jiejian Yuenan nanfang jiefang zhenxian daibiaotuan tanhua jilu [Record of a conversation between Vice Minister Chen Yi and an NLF delegation]," 24 September 1962, file 106–01412–02, PRCFMA.

40. "Mao Zedong zhuxi huijian Yuenan nanfang minzu jiefang zhenxian daibiaotuan tanhua jilu [Record of a conversation between Mao Zedong and a delegation from the South Vietnamese National Liberation Front]," file 106–00142–01, PRCFMA.

41. "Yuenan nanfangju Ruan Meiju tongzhi jishu jieshao nan Yue douzheng qingkuang de tanhua jilu [Record of a conversation in which Comrade Nguyen Muoi Cuc continues to introduce the situation of the South Vietnamese struggle], file 106–01411–02, PRCFMA. Nguyen Van Linh had many aliases, including Nguyen Muoi Cuc, which is being used here.

42. "Zhou Enlai zongli tong Yuennan laodongdang zhonggyang nanfangju shuji Ruan Wenling tanhua jilu [Record of a conversation between Zhou Enlai and Nguyen Van Linh, secretary of the Southern Office of the Vietnamese Workers Party], 15 August 1963, file 106–01411–04, PRCFMA.

43. JYMZW, 10:358–59.

44. Zhai, *China and the Vietnam Wars*, 116.

45. Christensen, *Worse Than a Monolith*, 167–68.

46. Cited in Zhang, "Beijing's Aid to Hanoi and the United States China Confrontations, 1964–1968," 269.

47. "Mao Zedong and Pham Van Dong," in Westad et al., "77 Conversations," 145–45.

48. "Yuenan nanfang minzu jiefang zhenxian zhu Hua daibiaotuan de qingkuang [The situation of the South Vietnamese National Liberation Front delegation]," 13 November 1964, file 106–00883–01, PRCFMA.

49. Ibid.

50. On American counterinsurgency in Vietnam see, among others, Catton, *Diem's Final Failure*; and Carter, *Inventing Vietnam*. Among the best books on U.S. decision-making are Logevall, *Choosing War*; and Gardner, *Pay Any Price*. On Laos, see Warner, *Shooting at the Moon*; Castle, *At War in the Shadow of Vietnam*; and Verrone, "Behind the Wall of Geneva."

51. Mao, "China and the Escalation of the Vietnam War." I agree with Mao on many of his major points here though I am slightly less attentive to the Sino-Soviet split and more attentive to the broader American response to Chinese supported insurgencies.

52. This is described in Kochavi, *Conflict Perpetuated*, 163–74.

53. Ibid., 175.

54. McMahon, *Limits of Empire*, 112.

55. *FRUS*, 1961–1963, 3:466–67.

56. Transcript of Broadcast on NBC's "Huntley-Brinkley Report," 9 September 1963, *Public Papers of the President*, 1963, item 349.

57. McMahon, *Limits of Empire*, 107.

58. Logevall, *Choosing War*, argues this point most explicitly.

59. Johnson, *Vantage Point*, 134–36.

60. "Communist China 1964 and Recommendations for U.S. Policy," 21 February 1964, DDRS.

61. "Communist Reaction to Increased U.S. Pressure against North Vietnam," 9 September 1964, DDRS.

62. McNamara, *In Retrospect*, 218–19.

63. Ibid., 219.

64. Brigham, *Guerrilla Diplomacy*, 61.

65. This is described in detail in Gaiduk, *Soviet Union and the Vietnam War*, 22–72.

66. For a detailed account of Sino-Soviet conflict over aid to Vietnam, see Li, "Sino-Soviet Dispute over Vietnam's Anti-American War, 1965–1972," 289–313.

67. Nguyen, *Hanoi's War*, 95. For another example of VWP leaders praising China as a revolutionary example during the late 1960s, see "Zhou Enlai and Pham Van Dong, Vo Nguyen Giap," 7 April 1967, in Westad et al., "77 Conversations," 98.

68. Nguyen, *Hanoi's War*, 95–96.

69. Chen, *Mao's China and the Cold War*, 232.

70. Zhai, *China and the Vietnam Wars*, 104–5.

71. This is discussed in more detail in Chapter 10.

72. Zhai, *China and the Vietnam Wars*, 190.

73. Fox, *History of Laos*, 135.

74. Xiaoming Zhang, "China's Involvement in Laos during the Vietnam War," 1147, 1163.

75. On Kennedy's policy, see Freedman, *Kennedy's Wars*, 353–54.

76. "Guanyu Laowo douzheng fangzhen de yijian [Opinions on policy toward the Laotian struggle]," 4 April 1963, file 106-01421-02, PRCFMA.

77. Zhai, *China and the Vietnam Wars*, 121–22; Zhang, "China's Involvement in Laos during the Vietnam War," 1147–48.

78. "Yinian lai Laowo renmindang zai fanmei douzheng he guoji gongsanzhuyi yundongzhong de taidu [The attitude of the Laos People's Party on the struggle against America and international communism in the last year]," 13 January 1964, file 106-0081-03, PRCFMA.

79. Hu, *Yige waijiaoguan de riji*, 48.

80. "Yinian lai Laowo renmindang zai fanmei douzheng he guoji gongsanzhuyi yundongzhong de taidu."

81. Zhang, "China's Involvement in Laos during the Vietnam War," 1158–59.

82. On this point, see Jacobs, *Universe Unraveling*, 235–70; and Saunders, *Leaders at War*, 114–18.

83. See, e.g., Kuzamarov, *Modernizing Repression*; and Castle, *At War in the Shadow of Vietnam*.

84. Verrone, "Behind the Wall of Geneva: Lao Politics," 128–30.

85. "Suggested United States Responses to Likely Chinese Communist Initiatives," 31 July 1963, DDRS.

86. *FRUS*, 1961–1963, 29:1036–40,1046–47.

87. Dean Rusk, "Why Laos Is Critically Important," *Department of State Bulletin* 51, no. 1306, 6 July 1964.

88. *FRUS, 1964–1968*, 27:487.

89. *FRUS, 1964–1968*, 28:777–79.

90. Chen, *Mao's China and the Cold War*, 233.

91. *FRUS, 1964–1968*, 28:775–76.

92. Paul F. Langer, "Soviet Union, China and the Pathet Lao," January 1972, http://www.rand.org/content/dam/rand/pubs/papers/2008/P4765.pdf.

93. Melvin Gurtov notes that the quotation was widely cited but casts doubt on whether Chen actually said it. See Gurtov, *China and Southeast Asia*, 19n.

94. Lovelace, *China and the "People's War" in Thailand*, 48–53; Flynn, "Preserving the Hub," 198–202. Flynn mentions Thai allegations that the PRC was infiltrating agents into rural Thailand.

95. Cited in Gurtov, *China and Southeast Asia*, 36.

96. Ibid., 37; Lovelace, *China and the "People's War" in Thailand*, 55.

97. Interview with William N. Stokes in *Frontline Diplomacy*.

98. "Minutes of the Meeting of the Special Group (CI)," 29 January 1965, RG 59, Bureau of Far Eastern Affairs, Office of the Country Director for Thailand, Records relating to Thailand, 1964–1966, box 5, NARA.

99. U.S. Army Study, "Insurgent Threat to Thailand," August 1966, RG 59, Bureau of Far Eastern Affairs, Office of the Country Director for Thailand, Records Relating to Thailand, 1964–1966, box 6, NARA.

100. Hyun, "Indigenizing the Cold War," 212.

101. Flynn, "Preserving the Hub," 204–5; interview with Philip R. Mayhew in *Frontline Diplomacy*.

102. Flynn, "Preserving the Hub," 218; interview with Stokes.

103. Interview with Stokes.

104. Ibid.

105. Marks, *Maoist Insurgency since Vietnam*, 47–48. Marks provides a detailed treatment of the Thai insurgency. He does not see counterinsurgency as very effective.

106. Chinese foreign policy during the Cultural Revolution is discussed in more detail in Chapter 10. The most detailed study of Chinese diplomacy during the period in English is Barnouin and Yu, *Chinese Foreign Policy during the Cultural Revolution*.

107. "Peking and the Burmese Communists: The Perils and Profits of Insurgency," July 1971, http://www.foia.cia.gov/CPE/ESAU/esau-52.pdf.

108. "China Encourages Violence in Asia," 14 July 1967, DDRS.

109. Ibid.

110. Holmes, "China Burma Relations since the Rift," 692.

111. Hunter, *Zanzibar*, 22–31.

112. Ibid., 55–62.

113. Cited in Babu and Wilson, *Future That Works*, xv.

114. "Guanyu Sanggeiba'er zhengbian [About Zanzibar's change in government]," 22 January 1964, file 108–00439–01, PRCFMA.

115. State Department to All AF Diplomatic Posts, 30 January 1964, DDRS.

116. "Sanggeiba'er zhengbian he muqian jushi de yijian [Opinion on the change of government in Zanzibar and the current situation]," file 108–00439–01, 23 January 1964, PRCFMA.

117. "Babu suotan jijian shi [A few issues that Babu talked about]," 19 January 1964, file 203–00410–03, PRCFMA.

118. Dar-es-Salaam to Secretary of State, 8 March 1964, DDRS.

119. Nairobi to Secretary of State, 24 March 1964, DDRS.

120. On Nyerere's claims, see Nyerere, *Freedom and Unity*, 291–94.

121. Secretary of State to American Embassy Addis Ababa et al., RG 59, Subject Numeric Files, 1964–1966, box 3043, NARA.

122. There is little scholarship on the specific dynamics of the union but for a cursory review that speculates about possible motives; see Mwakikagile, *Union of Tanganyika and Zanzibar*.

123. This is described in Yu, *China's African Policy*, 14–32.

124. "Zhongguo zhu Sanggeiba'er dashi Meng Ying bao Sanggeiba'er yu Tangannike maodun he sang muqian xingshi [The Chinese ambassador to Zanzibar Meng Ying reports on the situation in Zanzibar and contradictions between Zanzibar and Tanganyika]," file 108–00423–01, PRCFMA.

125. Nzongola-Ntalaja, *Congo*, 107–9.

126. Larkin, *China and Africa*, 181–82.

127. Weinstein, *Soviet and Chinese Aid to African Nations*, 59.

128. Ogunswano, *China's Policy in Africa*, 175; Nzongola-Ntalaja, *Congo*, 128–29.

129. Nzongola-Ntalaja, *Congo*, 129–30.

130. Ibid., 131–32.

131. Much of this is described in Villafaña, *Cold War in the Congo*, 93–111.

132. "Zhongguo daibioatuan tong Gangguo (li) geming zui gao weiyuanhui daibiaotuan di yi ci huitan jilu [A Chinese delegation meets the delegation from the Congolese National Liberation Council]," 20 August 1965, file 108–01422–01, PRCFMA.

133. "Jiedai Gangguo (li) quanguo jiefang weiyuanhui jihua [A plan to receive a delegation from the Congolese National Liberation Council]," 1 October 1964, file 106–00509–02, PRCFMA.

134. "Gangguo (li) Boxieli he Youmubu [Bocheley and Youmubu from Congo Leopoldville]," 6 October 1964, file 108–00509–01, PRCFMA. The foreign minister is rendered in Chinese as "Youmubu," but it is unclear what the English spelling of the name is.

135. Gangguo (li) jieweihui guwen lai tan qingkuang ji kanfa [A CNL adviser comes to discuss his situation], 11 January 1965, file 108–00615–01, PRCFMA.

136. On the Cuban role, see Gleijeses, *Conflicting Missions*, 101–59. Gleijeses also notes that the CIA remained oblivious to Cuban involvement. The documents in the most recent *FRUS* volume on the Congo (*FRUS*, 1964–1968, vol. 33) do not mention Cuba even once.

137. On this point, see Gleijeses, *Conflicting Missions*, 124.

138. "China Defector Says Peking to Take Over Congo," *NYT*, 5 August 1964; "World: A Model Red," *Time*, 14 August 1964.

139. "Peking Puts Up a Communist Command Post," *Life*, 18 December 1964.

140. Chinese Communist Involvement in Congolese Insurrections," 11 August 1964, NSF, box 81, LBJL.

141. "Events in the Congo," 13 August 1964, DDRS.

142. Brussels to Secretary of State, 8 August 1964, NSF, box 81, LBJL.

143. "Prospects in Brazzaville," 17 May 1965, DDRS.

144. Much of this is described in Villafaña, *Cold War in the Congo*, 93–111.

145. "Talk with Foreign Secretary Patrick Gordon Walker," 27 October 1964, DDRS.

146. Telephone conversation between LBJ and McNamara, lbj_wh6411_22_6389_mcnamara.mp3, http://whitehousetapes.nettapes/johnson/telephone.

147. "Zhou Enlai zhongli jiejian Gangguo (li) zuigao geming weiyuanhui zhixing zhuxi Sumiyaluo tanhua jilu [Premier Zhou Enlai meets Soumialot, the acting chair of Congo Leopoldville's high revolutionary committee]," 5 June 1965, file 108–01423–01, PRCFMA.

148. Ibid.

149. *FRUS*, 1964–1968, 33:578–79.

150. Gleijeses, *Conflicting Missions*, 137–44.

151. Americans continued to report on insurgent activity in the Congo. See, e.g., *FRUS*, 1964–1968, 33:669–70. On the Chinese perspective, see "Gang dongxian aiguo wuzhang muqian chujing he women de kanfa [The present unfavorable situation of patriotic forces on the eastern front of the Congo and our opinion]," file 108–00612–01, PRCFMA.

152. "Gang dongxian aiguo wuzhang muqian chujing he women de kanfa."

153. Cited in Schmitz, *United States and Right-Wing Dictatorships*, 9.

154. Cited in Shinn and Eisenmann, *China and Africa*, 291.

Chapter 9

1. This description was derived in part from Larry W. Harms, "A Peace Corps Volunteer's Adventures: Guinea I, 1963–1965," Volunteer Stories, Peace Corps Digital Library, http://collection.peacecorps.gov/cdm/singleitem/collection/p9009coll2/id/83/rec/1.

2. On showcasing, see Cullather, *Hungry World*, 159–79.

3. "Intelligence Memorandum: The New Look in Chinese Communist Aid to Sub-Saharan Africa," September 1968, DDRS.

4. On the importance of engaging Africa to the Kennedy administration, see Muehlenbeck, *Betting on the Africans*; DeRoche, "Dreams and Disappointments"; and Noer, *Soapy*.

5. See, e.g., Mohiddin, *African Socialism in Two Countries*.

6. Some of this is described in Meredith, *Fate of Africa*, 142–43.

7. Statistics derived by the quantitative macroeconomic historian Angus Maddison are available at http://www.ggdc.net.

8. Dikötter, *Mao's Great Famine*, 113–14.

9. Directorate of Intelligence, "Intelligence Memorandum: The New Look in Chinese Communist Aid to Sub-Saharan Africa," September 1968, DDRS.

10. Grubbs, *Secular Missionaries*, 156.

11. Directorate of Intelligence, "Intelligence Memorandum: The New Look in Chinese Communist Aid to Sub-Saharan Africa," September 1968, DDRS.

12. *ZEWJWX*, 388–89.

13. See, e.g., *Peking Review*, 31 January, 1 May 1964.

14. *ZENP*, 2:611–12.

15. *FRUS*, 1961–1963, 21:294–96.

16. "Our Response to Chinese Communist Efforts in Africa," 21 August 1964, RG 59, General Records of the Department of State, Subject Files of the Office of Asian Communist Affairs, box 2, NARA.

17. Ibid.

18. On Soviet policy toward the region and its limitations, see Mazov, *Distant Front in the Cold War*, 183–90, 220–26. On the Eisenhower administration's relative neglect of the region, see Muehlenbeck, *Betting on the Africans*, 17–28. Muehlenbeck does note that Eisenhower courted Nkrumah because of his prestige in the region but generally sees U.S. policy toward West Africa as indifferent before 1960.

19. Muehlenbeck, *Betting on the Africans*, 66–70, 81–90.

20. For the actual texts of these treaties, see Ogunswano, *China's Policy in Africa*, 278–81.

21. Cited in Muehlenbeck, *Betting on the Africans*, 67.

22. Chen, *Tanlu zai 1964*, 54–55. Mao is quoted on p. 55.

23. "Yuan Ji chaye zhuanjiazu gongzuo baogao [Report of the 'aid Guinea' tea specialist team]," September 1962, file 108–00805–03, PRCFMA.

24. Ibid.

25. Ibid.

26. Larkin, *China and Africa*, 98n.

27. Directorate of Intelligence, "Intelligence Memorandum: The New Look in Chinese Communist Aid to Sub-Saharan Africa," September 1968, DDRS.

28. American Embassy Conakry to Department of State, 13 November 1964, RG 59, Subject Numeric Files 1964–1966, box 2018, NARA.

29. "Guinea Country Assessment," January 1965, RG 286, USAID Mission to Guinea, Executive Office, Entry# P645: Classified Central Subject Files, 1962–1970, container 4, NARA.

30. American Embassy Conakry to Department of State, "Harvey Boke Concession," 15 November 1962, RG 286, USAID Mission to Guinea, Executive Office, Entry# P645: Classified Central Subject Files, 1962–1970, container 1, NARA.

31. This is described in Food and Agriculture Division, USAID, "Annual Progress Report: Agricultural Projects 1966," PD-AAS-128, USAID Development Experience Clearinghouse.

32. *NYT*, 31 January 1966.

33. Food and Agriculture Division, USAID, "Annual Progress Report: Agricultural Projects 1966."

34. American Embassy Conakry to Department of State, 13 November 1964, RG 59, Subject Numeric Files 1964–1966, box 2018, NARA.

35. Roy A. Harrell Jr., "Report on Field Trip, 25 November–5 December, 1964," 8 January 1965, RG 286, USAID Mission to Guinea, Executive Office, Entry# P645: Classified Central Subject Files, 1962–1970, container 3, NARA.

36. Interview with Robinson McIlvaine in *Frontline Diplomacy*.

37. Ibid.

38. See, e.g., Assensoh and Alex-Assensoh, *African Military History and Politics*, 132–33.

39. Rostow to the President, 8 November 1966, DDRS.

40. National Intelligence Estimate Number 60–62, "Guinea and Mali as Exemplars of African Nationalism," July 1962, DDRS.

41. "Call by Jean Marie Kone, Minister of State of the Republic of Mali, on the President," 12 July 1961, DDRS; "Briefing Memorandum on Mali" enclosed in "Memorandum for McGeorge Bundy," 7 July 1961, DDRS.

42. "1962 nian Mali jingji xingshi [Mali's economic situation in 1962]," file 108–00366–01, PRCFMA.

43. Ibid.

44. Ibid.

45. "Zhou Enlai zongli fangwen Mali shi Ma fang xi wo yuuanzhu de xiangmu ji wo zhu Ma shiguan xi wo yuan Ma gongye xiangmu zaori shang Ma shi [The projects that Mali hoped we will aid and the industrial projects that our embassy in Mali hoped would be aided quickly at the time of Premier Zhou Enlai's visit]," 21 February 1964, file 108–00529–02, PRCFMA.

46. *Renmin Ribao*, 5 January 1967.

47. "Intelligence Memorandum: The New Look in Chinese Communist Aid to Sub-Saharan Africa," September 1968, DDRS.

48. "Wo zai Mali nongye zhuanjia gongzuo zongjie" [A summary of the work of our agricultural specialists in Mali], 2 February 1964, file 108–01055–04, PRCFMA.

49. Ibid.

50. U.S.-Mali Relations; Mali Goodwill Mission Meeting with Governor Harriman, 23 June 1965, NSF, box 94, LBJL.

51. Ibid.

52. Country Assistance Program, Mali FY 1966, PD-ACC-734, USAID Development Experience Clearinghouse.

53. Ibid.

54. Ibid.

55. Ibid.

56. Ibid.

57. Interview with C. Roberts Moore in *Frontline Diplomacy*.

58. Ibid.

59. Ibid.

60. "Mali—[Beijing's] Leading African Booster," 12 February 1965, NSF, box 94, LBJL.

61. Nyerere, *Freedom and Socialism*.

62. Interview with Samuel H. Butterfield in *Frontline Diplomacy*.

63. "Year End Assessment 1962," 1 January 1963, NSF, box 162, JFKL.

64. Muehlenbeck, *Betting on the Africans*, 99–106.

65. Interview with Butterfield.

66. http://www.fmprc.gov.cn/eng/wjb/zzjg/fzs/gjlb/3099/.

67. Chen, *Tanlu zai 1964*, 144–46.

68. "He dashi yu Tan neizhengbuzhang tanhua neirong [The contents of a conversation between Ambassador He and Tanganyika's foreign minister], 2 May 1962, file 108–00275–06, PRCFMA.

69. "Tansang zhengfu youhao daibiaotuan zai Shanghai canguan fangwen qingkuang jianbao [A report on a visit to Shanghai by a Tanzanian government economic friendship delegation]," 19 June 1964, file 108–00456–01, PRCFMA.

70. "Zhou zongli tong Tansangniya di er fuzong Kawawa huitan jilu [Memorandum of a Conversation between Premier Zhou and Tanzanian Vice President Kawawa]," 16 June 1964, file 108–01318–06, PRCFMA.

71. Country Assistance Program, United Republic of Tanganyika and Zanzibar, FY 1966, PD-ACC-973, USAID Development Experience Clearinghouse.

72. Interview with Butterfield.

73. Interview with David Shear in *Frontline Diplomacy*.

74. *East African Standard*, 6 May 1967; Ogunsanwo, *China's Policy in Africa*, 140; Zhou, *Feichang shiqi de waijiao shengya*, 37.

75. Ogunsanwo, *China's Policy in Africa*, 203.

76. Zhou, *Feichang shiqi de waijiao shengya*, 37.

77. Burgess, *Race Revolution and the Struggle for Human Rights in Zanzibar*, 107.

78. "Tansangniya youhao daibiaotuan fang Hua jianbao [Report on the visit of a friendship delegation from Tanzania]," 29 September 1966, file 916–1-271, Shaanxi Provincial Archive.

79. The program gained both famed and notoriety as an example of failed high modernism owing to its treatment in James C. Scott's influential book *Seeing Like a State*.

80. Ibid., 223–30; Lal, "Maoism in Tanzania," 96–104.

81. On the similarities, see Lal, "Maoism in Tanzania," 97–101.

82. Interview with Butterfield. There is a sizeable literature on the Arusha Declaration and Ujamaa. See, e.g., McHenry, *Tanzania's Ujamaa Villages*; and Lal, "Between the Village and the World."

83. Interview with Francis T. McNamara in *Frontline Diplomacy*.

84. The website of the Tanzanian embassy in China gives a basic description. See http://www.tanzaniaembassy.org.cn/eng/embassy2-2.asp.

85. *East African Standard*, 6 February 1968.

86. This is described in excellent detail in Brautigam, *Dragon's Gift*, 197–99.

87. *East African Standard*, 6 February 1968.

88. Cited in Brautigam, *Dragon's Gift*, 198.

89. Interview with Butterfield.

90. Country Assistance Program Tanganyika, January 1963, RG 286, USAID Mission to Tanzania, Executive Office, Entry #P846, Central Subject Files, 1962–1965, box 3.

91. Country Assistance Program, Tanzania, FY 1967, PD-ACC-685, USAID Development Experience Clearinghouse.

92. USAID, "Country Assistance Program United Republic of Tanganyika and Zanzibar," FY 1966, PD-ACC-973, USAID Development Experience Clearinghouse.

93. "Wo zhu Sanggeibaer dashi Meng Ying furen he liren baihui qingkuang [The situation of Ambassador to Zanzibar Meng Ying going to and leaving his post]," file 108–00431–01, PRCFMA.

94. "Zhongguo zhu Sanggeiba'er dashi Meng Ying bao Sanggeibaer yu Tangannike maodun he sang muqian xingse [The Chinese ambassador to Zanzibar Meng Ying reports on the situation in Zanzibar and contradictions between Zanzibar and Tanganyika]," file 108–00423–01, PRCFMA.

95. Department of State to American Embassy Paris, 13 April 1964, NSF, box 103, LBJ.

96. "Guanyu Sanggeiba'er jianli yinhang de jianyi [Recommendations concerning the Establishment of a Bank in Zanzibar]," file 108–00437–02, PRCFMA.

97. "Chicom Influence in Zanzibar," 30 June 1966, RG 59, Subject Numeric Files, 1964–1966, box 2024, NARA.

98. "Zhongguo pai wang Sanggeiba'er jingmao zhuanjiazu zai Sang gongzuo qingkuang [The situation of the team of economic and trade advisers dispatched by China to Zanzibar]," file 108–00436–03, PRCFMA.

99. "Zhongguo fu Sanggeiba'er jingmao zhuanjia de gongzuo jianyi [The recommendation of the team of trade and economic experts in Zanzibar]," file 108–00436–01, PRCFMA.

100. "Intelligence Memorandum: The Current Disarray in Zanzibar," DDRS.

101. "Chicom Influence in Zanzibar."

102. CIA, Directorate of Intelligence, "Intelligence Memorandum: The Current Disarray in Zanzibar," 2 December 1968, DDRS.

103. Ibid.

104. This has been true of both English- and Chinese-language writing about the subject. See, e.g., Ogunswano, *China's Policy in Africa*, 204–13; and Wang Qinmei, "Tansang tielu—Zhong Fei guanxi shishang yizuo yongheng de fengbei," 272–82.

105. Monson, *Africa's Freedom Railway*.

106. "Visit of President Nyerere of Tanganyika to Washington, July 15–16, 1963," DDRS.

107. "Possible Chinese Aid to Tanzania Railway," 27 May 1965, CREST, NARA.

108. Zhou, *Feichang shiqi de waijiao shengya*, 130–31.

109. Ibid., 131–32.

110. "Chinese Communist Railroad Venture in Tanzania: Western Policy Alternatives," DDRS.

111. William Leonhart to Secretary of State, 2 June 1965, DDRS.

112. "Tanzania and Zambia: A Chinese Communist Railroad and a Western Road System?" March 1968, CREST, NARA.

113. Chen Dunde, *Tanlu zai 1964*, 284–85.

114. Ibid., 287.

115. *ZENP*, 3:163.

116. Interview with Shear.

117. Interview with John Hummon in *Frontline Diplomacy*.

118. Interview with Edward Marks in *Frontline Diplomacy*.

119. Ibid.

120. "Tanzania and Zambia: A Chinese Communist Railroad and a Western Road System?"

121. Interview with Butterfield.

122. "1964 nianshang bannian Kenniya xingshi xiaojie [A summary of the situation in Kenya during the first half of 1964]," 24 July 1964, file 108–00468–01, PRCFMA.

123. Cited in Rakove, *Kennedy, Johnson, and the Nonaligned World*, 238.

124. Shinn and Eisenman, *China and Africa*, 241.

125. *NYT*, 10 November 1966.

Chapter 10

1. Nixon, *RN*, 559.

2. Nixon's handwritten notes, Nixon Presidential Materials, President's Personal Files, box 7, RNL.

3. Richard Nixon, "Address to the Nation on the Situation in Southeast Asia," 30 April 1970, available online by Gerhard Peters and John T. Woolley, *American Presidency Project,* http://www.presidency.ucsb.edu/ws/?pid=2490.

4. See, e.g., Tudda, *Cold War Turning Point*; MacMillan, *Nixon and Mao*; and Xia, *Negotiating with the Enemy*.

5. The most definitive account of the Cultural Revolution in English is MacFarquhar and Schoenhalls, *Mao's Last Revolution*.

6. Brazinsky, "Between Ideology and Strategy," 164–65.

7. Barnouin and Yu, *Chinese Foreign Policy during the Cultural Revolution*, 72–78; *ZEZ*, 4:1734–35.

8. *FRUS*, 1964–1968, 30:332–43.

9. Lyndon B. Johnson, "Remarks to the American Alumni Council: U.S. Asian Policy," 12 July 1966, http://www.presidency.ucsb.edu/ws/?pid=27710.

10. Xia, *Negotiating with the Enemy*, 130–32.

11. Ibid.

12. Chen, *Mao's China and the Cold War*, 239–42.

13. The quotation is from Xia, *Negotiating with the Enemy*,139.

14. Ibid., 136–37; Chen, *Mao's China and the Cold War*, 243–44.

15. Xie, *Zhongguo dangdai waijiaoshi*, 265–66.

16. This is well covered in the historiography. See, among others, MacMillan, *Nixon and Mao*, 164; and Goh, *Constructing the U.S. Rapprochement with China*, 112–21.

17. Nixon, "Asia after Vietnam," 121–23.

18. *FRUS*, 1969–1976, 17:185–87.

19. Cited in Tudda, *Cold War Turning Point*, 70.

20. Both quotations are cited in Xia, *Negotiating with the Enemy*, 155–59, which also contains a much more detailed description of these negotiations.

21. Cited in Tudda, *Cold War Turning Point*, 71.

22. Cited in ibid., 71.

23. Ibid., 71–72.

24. Kissinger, *White House Years*, 219.

25. Xia, *Negotiating with the Enemy*, 163, briefly describes the process of preparing the briefing book.

26. "POLO I, Kissinger Briefing Book, July 1971 Trip to China," NSC box 850, RNL.

27. Kissinger, *White House Years*, 1263.

28. "My Talks with Zhou Enlai," 14 July 1971, available at the National Security Archive website: http://www.gwu.edu/~nsarchiv/NSAEBB/NSAEBB66/ch-40.pdf.

29. Ibid.

30. "Memcon of Your Conversations with Zhou Enlai," 29 July 1971, http://www.gwu.edu/~nsarchiv/NSAEBB/NSAEBB66/ch-34.pdf.

31. "My Talks with Zhou Enlai."

32. "Memcon of Your Conversations with Zhou Enlai."

33. "My Talks with Zhou Enlai."

34. Ibid.

35. Tucker, *Strait Talk*, 49.

36. Cited in Garver, *Sino-American Alliance*, 262.

37. For more details, see *FRUS*, 1969–1976, 5:272–455.

38. *FRUS*, 1969–1976, 17:587–88.

39. Ibid., 604–5.

40. Ibid., 605.

41. Nixon's handwritten notes, Nixon Presidential Materials, President's Personal Files, box 7, RNL.

42. *FRUS, 1969–1976*, 17:637–49.

43. Nixon's handwritten notes, Nixon Presidential Materials, President's Personal Files, box 7, RNL.

44. Cited in Xia, *Negotiating with the Enemy*, 198.

45. *FRUS, 1969–1976*, 17:816–17.

46. "Memorandum of a Conversation," 22 February 1972, http://www.gwu.edu/~n-sarchiv/NSAEBB/NSAEBB106/NZ-1.pdf.

47. *FRUS, 1969–1976*, 17:812–16.

48. The assessment is from the interview with Winston Lord in *Frontline Diplomacy*.

49. "Zhou Enlai and Le Duc Tho," 12 July 1972, in Westad et al., "77 Conversations."

50. See, e.g., "Mao Zedong and Nguyen Thi Binh," 29 December 1972; and "Zhou Enlai and Truong Chinh," 31 December 1972, in Westad et al., "77 Conversations."

51. *FRUS, 1969–1976*, 18:14.

52. Ibid., 860–61.

53. Tucker, *Strait Talk*, 63–64.

54. Amconsul Hong Kong to Department of State, 30 December 1970, RG 59, General Records of the Department of State, Subject Numeric Files, 1970–1973, box 2183, NARA.

55. Chen, "China's changing policies toward the Third World and the Global Cold War," 109.

56. *ZENP*, 3:488.

57. The Diplomatic History Institute, *Zhou Enlai waijiao huodong dashi ji*, 384.

58. Bureau of Intelligence and Research, "China's Policy toward Sub-Saharan Africa," 20 August 1985, DNSA.

59. *FRUS, 1969–1976*, 18:203–8.

60. Ibid., 431.

61. Ibid., 431–41.

62. Ibid., 447–51.

63. Kissinger, *Years of Renewal*, 151.

64. Ibid., 151.

65. "Memorandum of Conversation," 21 October 1975, DNSA.

66. "Memorandum of Conversation," 20 October 1975, DNSA.

67. "Memorandum of Conversation," 21 October 1975, DNSA.

68. *FRUS, 1969–1976*, 18:828.

69. Arthur W. Hummel Jr. to Henry Kissinger, 20 March 1974, DNSA; "Indicators of PRC Internal Dissent and Desire for Movement on the Taiwan Issue," 23 May 1974, DNSA.

70. Richard Solomon to Kissinger, 31 December 1973, DNSA.

71. *MZWW*, 600–601.

72. "Speech by Chairman of the Delegation of the People's Republic of China, Deng Xiaoping, at the Special Session of the U.N. General Assembly," 10 April 1974, http://www.marxists.org/reference/archive/deng-xiaoping/1974/04/10.htm.

73. Chen Jian argues this point in "China's Changing Policies toward the Third World and the Global Cold War," 108.

74. *DXNP*, 1:22–23.

75. Ibid., 62–63.

76. Engel, *China Diary of George H. W. Bush*, 135.

77. Ibid., 267.

78. Ibid., 225.

79. *FRUS*, 1969–1976, 18:524–25.

80. McMahon, *Limits of Empire*, 162.

81. For a summary, see Kiernan, *Pol Pot Regime*, 18–20.

82. Zhai, "China and the Cambodian Conflict," 386–87.

83. Short, *Pol Po*, 202.

84. Zhai, "China and the Cambodian Conflict," 388.

85. "Memorandum of Conversation," 18 February 1973, DNSA.

86. Zhai, "China and the Cambodian Conflict," 389.

87. "Memorandum of Conversation," 18 February 1973, DNSA.

88. "Memorandum of Conversation," 27 May 1973, DNSA.

89. "Memorandum of Conversation," 19 July 1973, DNSA.

90. W. R. Smyser to Kissinger, 6 September 1974, NSA Presidential Country Files for East Asia and the Pacific, box 2, GFL.

91. Zhai Qiang and Andrew Mertha both make a similar point. See Zhai, "China and the Cambodian Conflict," 392; and Mertha, *Brothers in Arms*, 5.

92. Cited in Short, *Pol Pot*, 251.

93. American Consul Hong Kong to Secretary of State, 2 April 1974, Central Foreign Policy Files, AAD, NARA.

94. Zhai, *China and the Vietnam Wars*, 212–13.

95. Zhai, "China and the Cambodian Conflict," 393.

96. "Mao Zedong and Pol Pot," 21 June 1975, in Westad et al., "77 Conversations."

97. Zhai, *China and the Vietnam Wars*, 213.

98. Westad, *Global Cold War*, 210–11.

99. Ibid.

100. Friedman, "Reviving Revolution," 388–436.

101. Guimaraes, *Origins of the Angolan Civil War*, 158–59.

102. Secretary of State to American Embassy Madrid, 20 November 1975, Central Foreign Policy Files, AAD, NARA.

103. "Chinese Contact with Angolan Nationalist Groups," June 1975, DNSA.

104. *DXNP*, 1:69.

105. National Intelligence Bulletin, 11 December 1975, DNSA.

106. "Memorandum of Conversation," 2 December 1975, DNSA.

107. Kissinger, *Years of Renewal*, 832–33.

108. National Intelligence Bulletin, 11 December 1975, DNSA.

109. See, e.g., Tucker, "Evolution of U.S. China Relations," 36–37.

110. "Memorandum of Conversation," 25 May 1978, DDRS.

111. Vogel, *Deng Xiaoping and the Transformation of China*, 318.

112. Tucker, *Strait Talk*, 106–7.

113. *DXNP*, 1:478–79.

114. "Scope Paper for the Visit of Vice Premier Deng Xiaoping of the People's Republic of China," 26 January 1979, NLC 15-42-5-14-9, JCL.

115. *DXNP*, 1:330–31.

116. "Summary of Dr. Brzezinski's Meeting with Foreign Minister Huang Hua," 21 May 1978, Zbigniew Brzezinski Collection, Geographic File, box 9, JCL.

117. Memorandum of a Conversation on "International Issues," Vertical File, box 40, JCL.

118. See, e.g., Khoo, *Collateral Damage*, 126–30.

119. Vogel, *Deng Xiaoping*, 531–35; CIA, "China's Vietnam War: Preparations, Combat Performance and Apparent Lessons," NLC-SAFE 17 A-9–18–1-6, JCL.

120. Brzezinski, *Power and Principle*, 409–10.

121. Ibid.

122. Brzezinski to Carter, 6 February 1979, DDRS.

123. Mann, *About Face*, 100.

124. Michael Oksenberg and William Oden to Zbigniew Brzezinski, 19 February 1979, Zbigniew Brzezinski Collection, Geographic File, box 10, JCL.

125. For a more detailed description, see Westad, *Global Cold War*, 302–10.

126. Paul B. Henze to Brzezinski, 11 May 1978, NLC-4–38–7-20–7, JCL.

127. Memorandum of Conversation, 25 May 1978, DDRS.

128. Interview cited in Kalb, *Haunting Legacy*, 77–78.

129. Brzezinski to David Aaron and Oksenberg, 4 September 1979, DDRS.

130. Marshall Brement to Brzezinski, 2 January 1980, NCL 12–1-3–3-1, JCL.

131. "Southwest Asia, Secret Talking Points," January 1980, CH 00479, DNSA.

132. Ibid.

133. *DXNP*, 1:590.

134. Mann, *About Face*, 136–37.

135. "Southwest Asia, Secret Talking Points."

136. *DXNP*, 2:795–96.

137. Presidential Review Memorandum/NSC-21, "The Horn of Africa," NLC-31–18–1-2–5, JCL.

138. "An Overview of Chinese Foreign Policy," NLC 5–2-3–6-5, JCL.

139. Ibid.

Conclusion

1. "Speech by President Xi Jinping at the Julius Nyerere Convention Center," 25 March 2013, English translation available at: http://www.china.org.cn/report/2013–04/27/content_28677171.htm.

2. Ibid.

3. See, e.g., James Swann, Deputy Assistant Secretary for African Affairs, China-Africa Relations and the Global Village: A Diplomatic Perspective, 1 April 2008, http://2001–2009.state.gov/p/af/rls/rm/2008/102946.htm.

4. Wang, *Never Forget National Humiliation*, 126.

5. "Full Text of Hu Jintao's Report at 17th Party Congress," http://english.people.com.cn/90001/90776/90785/6290148.html; also cited in ibid., 126–27.

6. *NYT*, 2 November 2006.

7. Quoted in ibid.

8. Cited in Murithi Mutiga, "Africa and the Chinese Way," *NYT*, 15 December 2013.

9. "China Praised for African Links," 11 October 2009, http://news.bbc.co.uk/2/hi/8301826.stm.

10. See, e.g., Compagnon and Alejandro, "China's External Environmental Policy."

11. On this point, see Economy and Levi, *By All Means Necessary*, 99–114. The authors describe the PRC's efforts to address these criticisms.

12. Lamido Sanusi, "Africa Must Get Real about Chinese Ties," *Financial Times*, 11 March 2013.

13. Published in 2008, Kurlantzick, *Charm Offensive*, saw the PRC's efforts to woo its neighbors as highly effective. American officials at the time took a similar view.

14. Kaplan, *Asia's Cauldron*, 11–12.

15. "Remarks by President Obama and President of Zuma of South Africa at Joint Press Conference," http://www.whitehouse.gov/the-press-office/2013/06/29/remarks-president-obama-and-president-zuma-south-africa-joint-press-conf.

16. Carson's quotation appeared in dozens of newspapers and journals. See, e.g., John Feffer, "Obama: Into Africa," *Foreign Policy in Focus*, 8 August 2014, http://fpif.org/obama-africa/.

17. On the American tendency to represent Asians as immoral, see Hunt, *Ideology and U.S. Foreign Policy*, 69–77.

18. The journalist John Feffer, for instance, called Carson's statement an "unvarnished U.S. perspective" in "Obama: Into Africa." The Agence France Presse simply reported: "The United States thinks China is a very aggressive and pernicious economic competitor with no morals.'" Its article was used widely in global media at the time.

19. "Remarks by President Obama and President of Zuma of South Africa at Joint Press Conference."

20. "Fact Sheet: U.S.-China Economic Relations," http://www.whitehouse.gov/the-press-office/2014/11/12/fact-sheet-us-china-economic-relations.

Bibliography

Archives

Dwight D. Eisenhower Library, Abilene, Kansas
Foreign Ministry Archive, Beijing
Gerald R. Ford Library, Ann Arbor, Michigan
Jimmy Carter Library, Atlanta, Georgia
John F. Kennedy Library, Boston
Library of Congress, Manuscripts Reading Room
Lyndon B. Johnson Library, Austin, Texas
National Archives and Record Administration, College Park, Maryland
Richard M. Nixon Library, Yorba Linda, California

Online Archives and Sources

China Realtime blog
Declassified Documents Reference Service (DDRS)
Digital National Security Archive (DNSA)
http://www.marxists.org
Peace Corps Digital Library (PCDL)

Published Primary Source Documents

Association for Diplomatic Studies and Training, ed. *Frontline Diplomacy: The Foreign Affairs Oral History Collection.*
The Diplomatic History Institute under the PRC Foreign Ministry. *Zhou Enlai waijiao huodong dashi ji, 1949–1975* [Important events in Zhou Enlai's diplomatic activities, 1949–1975]. Beijing: Shijie zhishi, 1993.
Liu, Shufa, ed. *Chen Yi nianpu* [Chronological record of Chen Yi]. 2 vols. Beijing: Renmin chubanshe, 1995.
Palat, Madhavan, ed. *Selected Works of Jawaharlal Nehru*, 2nd Ser. 45 vols. London: Oxford University Press, 2013–.
Schram, Stuart R., ed. *Mao's Road to Power: Revolutionary Writing, 1912–1949*. 9 vols. New York: M. E. Sharpe, 2004–.
U.S. Department of State. *The Department of State Bulletin*. Washington, D.C.: Office of Media Services, 1939–89.
———. *Foreign Relations of the United States* [*FRUS*]. Washington, D.C.: Government Printing Office, 1862–.
———. *United States–Vietnam Relations, 1945–1967* [The Pentagon Papers]. Washington, D.C.: Government Printing Office, 1971.

United Nations official documents.

Zhonggong zhongyang wenxian yanjiushi, ed. *Deng Xiaoping nianpu, 1975–1997* [Chronological record of Deng Xiaoping, 1975–1997]. 2 vols. Beijing: Zhongyang wenxian chubanshe, 2004.

———. *Jianguo yilai Mao Zedong junshi wengao* [Mao Zedong's military manuscripts since the founding of the PRC]. 3 vols. Beijing: Junshi kexue chubanshe, 2010.

———. *Jianguo yilai Mao Zedong wengao* [Mao Zedong's manuscripts since the founding of the PRC]. 3 vols. Beijing: Junshi kexue chubanshe, 2010.

———. *Liu Shaoqi nianpu, 1898–1969* [Chronological Record of Liu Shaoqi, 1898–1969]. Beijing: Zhongyang wenxian chubanshe, 1996.

———. *Mao Zedong nianpu, 1893–1949* [Chronological record of Mao Zedong, 1893–1949]. 3 vols. Beijing: Renmin chubanshe, 1993–97.

———. *Mao Zedong waijiao wenxuan* [Diplomatic papers of Mao Zedong]. Beijing: Zhongyang wenxian chubanshe, 1994.

———. *Mao Zedong zhuan, 1893–1976* [Biography of Mao Zedong, 1893–1976]. 6 vols. Beijing: Zhongyang wenxian chubanshe, 2010.

———. *Zhou Enlai junshi wenxuan* [Zhou Enlai's Military Manuscripts]. 4 vols. (Beijing: Renmin chubanshe, 1997).

———. *Zhou Enlai nianpu, 1949–1976* [Chronological record of Zhou Enlai, 1949–1976]. 3 vols. Beijing: Zhongyang wenxian chubanshe, 1997.

———. *Zhou Enlai zhuan, 1898–1976* [Biography of Zhou Enlai, 1898–1976]. 4 vols. Beijing: Zhongyang wenxian chubanshe, 2011.

Zhongyang danganguan, ed. *Zhonggong zhongyang wenjian xuanji* [Selected documents of the CCP Central Committee]. 18 vols. Beijing: Zhonggong zhongyang dangxiao, 1989–92.

Periodicals

Department of State Bulletin
East African Standard
Life
New York Times
Peking Review
Renmin Ribao [*People's Daily*]
Time

English-Language Secondary Sources

Accinelli, Robert. *Crisis and Commitment: United States Policy toward Taiwan, 1950–1955*. Chapel Hill: University of North Carolina Press, 1996.

Acheson, Dean. *Present at the Creation: My Years in the State Department*. New York: W. W. Norton, 1969.

Adams, Clarence. *An American Dream: The Life of an African American Soldier and POW Who Spent Twelve Years in Communist China*. Amherst: University of Massachusetts Press, 2007.

Anderson, Benedict. *Imagined Communities: Reflections on the Origins and Spread of Nationalism.* London: Verso, 2006.

Anwar, Dewi Fortuna. "Indonesia and the Bandung Conference: Then and Now." In *Bandung Revisited: The Legacy of the 1955 Asian-African Conference for International Order*, edited See Sang Tan and Amitav Acharya. Singapore: NUS Press, 2008.

Armstrong, J. D. *Revolutionary Diplomacy: Chinese Foreign Policy and the United Front Doctrine.* Berkeley: University of California Press, 1977.

Assensoh, A. B., and Yvette M. Alex-Assensoh. *African Military History and Politics: Coups and Ideological Incursions, 1900–Present.* New York: Palgrave-Macmillan, 2001.

Babu, Selma, and Amrit Wilson, eds. *The Future That Works: The Writings of A. M. Babu.* Trenton, N.J.: Africa World Press, 2002.

Barnouin, Barbara, and Chenggen Yu. *Chinese Foreign Policy during the Cultural Revolution.* London: Kegan Paul International, 1998.

Barrett, Roby C. *The Greater Middle East and the Cold War: US Foreign Policy Under Eisenhower and Kennedy.* London: I. B. Tauris, 2010.

Beisner, Robert. *Dean Acheson: A Life in the Cold War.* New York: Oxford University Press, 2006.

Belmonte, Laura A. *Selling the American Way: U.S. Propaganda and the Cold War.* Philadelphia: University of Pennsylvania Press, 2008.

Bernstein, Richard. *China 1945: Mao's Revolution and America's Fateful Choice.* New York: Alfred A. Knopf, 2014.

Bianco, Lucien. *Origins of the Chinese Revolution, 1915–1949.* Palo Alto, Calif.: Stanford University Press, 1971.

Bitar, Mona. "Bombs, Plots and Allies: Cambodia and the Western Powers, 1958–1959." In *The Clandestine Cold War in Asia, 1945–1965: Western Intelligence, Propaganda and Special Operations*, edited by Richard J. Aldrich et al. London: Routledge, 2000.

Blaufarb, Douglas. *The Counterinsurgency Era: U.S. Doctrine and Performance, 1950 to the Present.* New York: Free Press, 1977.

Blecher, Marc. *China against the Tides: Restructuring through Revolution, Radicalism and Reform*, 3rd ed. New York: Continuum, 2010.

Borstelmann, Thomas. *The Cold War and the Color Line: American Race Relations in the Global Arena.* Cambridge, Mass.: Harvard University Press, 2002.

Bradley, Mark Philip. *Vietnam at War.* New York: Oxford University Press, 2009.

Branfman, Fred, ed. *Voices from the Plain of Jars: Life under an Air War.* Madison: University of Wisconsin Press, 2013.

Brautigam, Deborah. *The Dragon's Gift: The Real Story of China in Africa.* New York: Oxford University Press, 2010.

Brazinsky, Gregg Andrew. "Between Ideology and Strategy: China's Security Policy toward the Korean Peninsula since Rapprochement." In *Trilateralism and Beyond: Great Power Politics and the Korean Security Dilemma during and after the Cold War*, edited by Robert A. Wampler. Kent, Ohio: Kent State University Press, 2012.

Brigham, Robert K. *Guerrilla Diplomacy: The NLF's Foreign Relations and the Vietnam War.* Ithaca, N.Y.: Cornell University Press, 1998.

Brzezinski, Zbigniew. *Power and Principle: Memoirs of the National Security Advisor, 1977–1981.* New York: Farrar, Straus and Giroux, 1983.

Buhite, Russel D. *Nelson T. Johnson and American Policy toward China, 1925–1941*. East Lansing: Michigan State University Press, 1968.

Burgess, G. Thomas, ed. *Race Revolution and the Struggle for Human Rights in Zanzibar: The Memoirs of Ali Sultan Issa and Seif Sharif Hamad*. Athens: Ohio University Press, 2009.

Carter, Carolle J. *Mission to Yenan: American Liaison with the Chinese Communists, 1944–1947*. Lexington: University of Kentucky Press, 1997.

Carter, James M. *Inventing Vietnam: The United States and State Building, 1954–1969*. Cambridge: Cambridge University Press, 2008.

Castle, Timothy N. *At War in the Shadow of Vietnam*. New York: Columbia University Press, 1993.

Catton, Philip E. *Diem's Final Failure: Prelude to America's War in Vietnam*. Lawrence: University of Kansas Press, 2003.

CCP Central Committee, ed. *The Polemic of the General Line of the Communist Movement*. Beijing: Foreign Language Press, 1965.

Chang, Gordon H. *Friends and Enemies: The United States, China, and the Soviet Union, 1948–1972*. Palo Alto, Calif.: Stanford University Press, 1990.

———. "To the Nuclear Brink: Eisenhower, Dulles, and the Quemoy-Matsu Crisis." *International Security* 12 (Summer 1988): 96–122.

Chen, Jian. "Bridging Revolution and Decolonization: The 'Bandung Discourse' in China's Early Cold War Experience." *Chinese Historical Review* 15 (Fall 2008): 207–41.

———. *The China Challenge in the Twenty-First Century: Implications for U.S. Foreign Policy*. Washington, D.C.: U.S. Institute of Peace, 1998.

———. "China's Changing Policies toward the Third World and the Global Cold War." In *The End of the Cold War and the Third World: New Perspective on Regional Conflict*, edited by Artemy M. Kalinovsky and Sergey Radchenko. London: Routledge, 2011.

———. *China's Road to the Korean War: The Making of the Sino-American Confrontation*. New York: Columbia University Press, 1994.

———. *Mao's China and the Cold War*. Chapel Hill: University of North Carolina Press, 2001.

———. "The Tibetan Rebellion of 1959 and China's Changing Relations with India and the Soviet Union." *Journal of Cold War Studies* 8, no. 3 (Summer 2006): 54–101.

Chen, Jian, and Kuisong Yang. "Chinese Politics and the Collapse of the Sino-Soviet Alliance." In *Brothers in Arms: The Rise and Fall of the Sino-Soviet Alliance, 1945–1963*, edited by Odd Arne Westad. Washington, D.C.: Woodrow Wilson Center Press, 1998.

Cheng, J. Chester, ed. *The Politics of the Chinese Red Army: A Translation of the Bulletin of the People's Liberation Army*. Stanford, Calif.: Hoover Institution Press, 1966.

Cheng, Xiaohe. "The Evolution of Sino-North Korean Relations in the 1960s." *Asian Perspective* 34 (2010): 173–99.

Cheng, Yinghong. "Sino-Cuban Relations during the Early Years of the Castro Regime, 1959–1966." *Journal of Cold War Studies* 9 (Summer 2007): 78–114.

Christensen, Thomas J. *Useful Adversaries: Grand Strategy, Domestic Mobilization, and Sino-American Conflict, 1947–1958*. Princeton, N.J.: Princeton University Press, 1996.

———. *Worse Than a Monolith: Alliance Politics and Problems of Coercive Diplomacy in Asia*. Princeton, N.J.: Princeton University Pres, 2011.

Clark, Paul. *Chinese Cinema: Culture and Politics since 1949*. Cambridge: Cambridge University Press, 1987.

Clymer, Kenton. *Troubled Relations: The United States and Cambodia since 1870*. De Kalb: Northern Illinois University Press, 2007.

Cohen, Warren I. *America's Response to China: A History of Sino-American Relations*. 4th ed. New York: Columbia University Press, 2010.

———, ed. "Symposium: Rethinking the Lost Chance in China." *Diplomatic History* 21 (Winter 1997): 71–115.

Compton, Boyd, ed. *Mao's China: Party Reform Documents, 1942–1944*. Seattle: University of Washington Press, 1952.

Connelly, Matthew. *A Diplomatic Revolution: Algeria's Fight for Independence and the Origins of the Post–Cold War Era*. New York: Oxford University Press, 2002.

———. "Taking of the Cold War Lens: Visions of North-South Conflict during the Algerian War for Independence." *American Historical Review* 105 (June 2000): 739–69.

Cullather, Nick. *The Hungry World: America's Cold War Battle against Poverty in Asia*. Cambridge, Mass.: Harvard University Press, 2010.

Cunningham, Maura. "Denying Historians: China's Archives Increasingly Off-Bounds." China Realtime blog, 16 August 2014, http://blogs.wsj.com/chinarealtime/2014/08/19/denying-historians-chinas-archives-increasingly-off-bounds/.

Daigle, Craig. *The Limits of Détente: The United States, the Soviet Union, and the Arab-Israeli Conflict*. New Haven, Conn.: Yale University Press, 2012.

Dallek, Robert. *Franklin D. Roosevelt and American Foreign Policy, 1932–1945*. New York: Oxford University Press, 1995.

Deng, Yong. *China's Struggle for Status: The Realignment of International Relations*. New York: Cambridge University Press, 2008.

———. "Better Than Power: 'International Status' and Chinese Foreign Policy." In *China Rising: Power and Motivation in Chinese Foreign Policy*, edited by Yong Deng and Fei-Ling Wang. Lanham, Md.: Rowman and Littlefield, 2005.

De Roche, Andy. "Dreams and Disappointments: Kenneth Kaunda and the United States, 1960–1964." *Safundi* 9 (October 2008): 369–94.

Dikötter, Frank. *Mao's Great Famine: The History of China's Most Devastating Catastrophe, 1958–1962*. New York: Walker, 2010.

Dillion, Michael. *Xinjiang: China's Moslem Far Northwest*. London: Routledge, 2004.

Dirlik, Arif. *The Origins of Chinese Communism*. New York: Oxford University Press, 1989.

Du Bois, W. E. B. *The Autobiography of W. E. B. Du Bois: A Soliloquy on Viewing My Life from the Last Decade of Its First Century*. New York: Oxford University Press, 2007.

Engel, Jeffrey A. *Cold War at 30,000 Feet: The Anglo-American Fight for Aviation Supremacy*. Cambridge, Mass.: Harvard University Press, 2007.

———, ed. *The China Diary of George H. W. Bush: The Making of a President*. Princeton, N.J.: Princeton University Press, 2008.

Fineman, Daniel. *A Special Relationship: The United States and Military Government in Thailand, 1948–1957*. Honolulu: University of Hawaii Press, 1997.

Flynn, James Roberts. "Preserving the Hub: U.S.-Thai Relations during the Vietnam War, 1961–1976." Ph.D. diss., University of Kentucky, 2001.

Fox, Martin Stuart. *A History of Laos*. London: Cambridge University Press, 1997.

Fravel, M. Taylor. *Strong Borders and Secure Nation: Cooperation and Conflict in China's Territorial Disputes*. Princeton, N.J.: Princeton University Press, 2008.

Frazier, Robeson Taj. *The East Is Black: Cold War China in the Black Radical Imagination*. Durham, N.C.: Duke University Press, 2015.

———. "Thunder in the East: China, Exiled Crusaders and the Unevenness of Black Internationalism." *American Quarterly* 63 (December 2011): 934.

Freedman, Lawrence. *Kennedy's Wars: Berlin, Cuba, Laos, and Vietnam*. New York: Oxford University Press, 2000.

Friedman, Jeremy. "Reviving Revolution: The Sino-Soviet Split, the 'Third World,' and the Fate of the Left." Ph.D. diss., Princeton University, 2011.

———. *Shadow Cold War: The Sino-Soviet Competition for the Third World*. Chapel Hill: University of North Carolina Press, 2015.

———. "Soviet Policy in the Developing World and the Chinese Challenge in the 1960s." *Cold War History* 10 (May 2010): 247–72.

Gacek, Christopher M. *The Logic of Force: The Dilemma of Limited War in American Foreign Policy*. New York: Columbia University Press, 1994.

Gaddis, John Lewis. *We Now Know: Rethinking Cold War History*. New York: Oxford University Press, 1997.

Gaiduk, Ilya V. *The Soviet Union and the Vietnam War*. Chicago: Ivan R. Dee, 1996.

Gardner, Lloyd C. *Pay Any Price: Lyndon Johnson and the Wars for Vietnam*. New York: Ivan R. Dee, 1997.

Gao, James Z. "The Call of the Oases: The 'Peaceful Liberation' of Xinjiang, 1949–1953." In *Dilemmas of Victory: The Early Years of the People's Republic of China*, edited by Jeremy Brown and Paul Pickowicz. Cambridge, Mass.: Harvard University Press, 2007.

Gardner, Paul F. *Shared Hopes, Separate Fears: Fifty Years of U.S.-Indonesian Relations*. Philadelphia: University of Pennsylvania Press, 1997.

Garver, John W. *Protracted Contest: Sino-Indian Rivalry in the Twentieth Century*. Seattle: University of Washington Press, 2001.

———. *The Sino-American Alliance: Nationalist China and American Cold War Strategy*. New York: M. E. Sharpe, 1997.

Gerth, H. H., and C. Wright Mills, eds. *From Max Weber: Essays in Sociology*. New York: Oxford University Press, 1946.

Gettig, Eric. "'Trouble ahead in Afro-Asia': The United States, the Second Bandung Conference, and the Struggle for the Third World." *Diplomatic History* 39 (January 2015): 126–56.

Ghose, Sankar. *Jawaharlal Nehru: A Biography*. Bombay: Allied, 1993.

Gleijeses, Piero. *Conflicting Missions: Havana, Washington, and Africa, 1959–1976*. Chapel Hill: University of North Carolina Press, 2001.

Goh, Evelyn. *Constructing the U.S. Rapprochement with China, 1961–1974: From Red Menace to Tacit Ally*. London: Cambridge University Press, 2004.

Goldstein, Steven M. "The Chinese Revolution in the Colonial Areas: The View from Yenan, 1937–1941." *China Quarterly* 75 (September 1978): 594–622.

Grubbs, Larry. *Secular Missionaries: Americans and African Development in the 1960s.* Amherst: University of Massachusetts Press, 2009.

Guimaraes, Fernando Andreson. *The Origins of the Angolan Civil War: Foreign Intervention and Domestic Political Conflict.* London: MacMillan, 2001.

Gurtov, Melvin. *China and Southeast Asia—The Politics of Survival: A Study of Foreign Policy Interaction.* Baltimore: Johns Hopkins University Press, 1971.

Hahn, Peter L., and Mary Ann Heiss, eds. *Cold War and Revolution: The United States and the Third World since 1945.* Columbus: Ohio State University Press, 2001.

Haithcox, John Patrick. *Communism and Nationalism in India: M. N. Roy and Comintern Policy, 1920–1939.* Princeton, N.J.: Princeton University Press, 1971.

Halper, Stefan. *The Beijing Consensus: How China's Authoritarian Model Will Dominate the Twenty-First Century.* New York: Basic Books, 2010.

Han, Suyin. *Eldest Son: Zhou Enlai and the Making of Modern China, 1898–1976.* New York: Hill and Wang, 1994.

Holmes, Robert A. "China Burma Relations since the Rift." *Asian Survey* 12 (August 1972): 686–700.

Hu, Jubin. *Projecting a Nation: National Cinema before 1949.* Hong Kong: Hong Kong University Press, 2003.

Hu, Shizhang. *Stanley K. Hornbeck and the Open Door Policy.* Westport, Conn.: Greenwood, 1995.

Huang, Hua, *Huang Hua Memoirs.* Beijing: Foreign Language Press, 2008.

Hunt, Michael H. *The Genesis of Chinese Communist Foreign Policy.* New York: Columbia University Press, 1996.

———. *Ideology and U.S. Foreign Policy.* New Haven, Conn.: Yale University Press, 1987.

Hunter, Helen-Louise. *Zanzibar: The Hundred Days of Revolution.* Santa Barbara, Calif.: ABC-Clio, 2013.

Hyun, Sinae. "Indigenizing the Cold War: Nation Building by the Border Patrol Police of Thailand, 1945–1980." Ph.D. diss., University of Wisconsin–Madison, 2014.

Immerman, Richard H. *John Foster Dulles: Piety, Pragmatism and Power in U.S. Foreign Policy.* Wilmington, Del.: Scholarly Resources, 1999.

Israeli, Raphael. "The Muslim Minority in the People's Republic of China." *Asian Survey* 21 (August 1981): 901–19.

Jacobs, Seth. *The Universe Unraveling: American Foreign Policy in Cold War Laos.* Ithaca, N.Y.: Cornell University Press, 2012.

Jacques, Martin. *When China Rules the World: The End of the Western World and the Birth of a New Global Order.* New York: Penguin, 2009.

Jerslid, Austin. *The Sino-Soviet Alliance: An International History.* Chapel Hill: University of North Carolina Press, 2014.

Jervis, Robert. *The Logic of Images in International Relations.* New York: Columbia University Press, 1989.

Johnston, Alastair I. *Social States: China in International Institutions, 1980–2000.* Princeton, N.J.: Princeton University Press, 2007.

Johnson, Lyndon Baines. *The Vantage Point: Perspectives on the Presidency, 1963–1969.* New York: Holt, Rinehart, and Winston, 1971.

Jones, Anthony James. *Victorious Insurgencies: Four Rebellions That Shaped Our World*. Lexington: University of Kentucky Press, 2010.

Kahin, George McT. *The African-Asian Conference*. Ithaca, N.Y.: Cornell University Press, 1956.

Kalb, Marvin and Deborah. *Haunting Legacy: Vietnam and the American Presidency from Ford to Obama*. Washington, D.C.: Brookings Institution Press, 2011.

Kang, David C. *East Asia before the West: Five Centuries of Trade and Tribute*. New York: Columbia University Press, 2010.

Kaplan, Robert. *Asia's Cauldron: The South China Sea and the End of a Stable Pacific*. New York: Random House, 2014.

Karl, Rebecca E. *Mao Zedong and China in the Twentieth-Century World*. Durham, N.C.: Duke University Press, 2010.

Keys, Barbara J. *Globalizing Sport: National Rivalry and International Community in the 1930s*. Cambridge, Mass.: Harvard University Press, 2006.

Khan, Sulmaan Wasif. *Moslem, Trader, Nomad, Spy: China's Cold War and the People of the Tibetan Borderlands*. Chapel Hill: University of North Carolina Press, 2015.

Khoo, Nicholas. *Collateral Damage: Sino-Soviet Rivalry and the Termination of the Sino-Vietnamese Alliance*. New York: Columbia University Press, 2011.

Khrushchev, Sergei, ed. *Memoirs of Nikita Khrushchev*. Vol. 3, *Statesman, 1953–1964*. University Park: Penn State University Press, 2007.

Kiernan, Ben. *The Pol Pot Regime: Race, Power, and Genocide in Cambodia under the Khmer Rouge*. New Haven, Conn.: Yale University Press, 2008.

Kissinger, Henry. *White House Years*. New York: Little, Brown, 1979.

———. *Years of Renewal*. New York: Simon and Schuster, 1999.

Kitamura, Hiroshi. *Screening Enlightenment: Hollywood and the Cultural Reconstruction of Defeated Japan*. Ithaca, N.Y.: Cornell University Press, 2010.

Knaus, John Kenneth. *Orphans of the Cold War: American and the Tibetan Struggle for Survival*. New York: Public Affairs, 2000.

Kochavi, Noam. *A Conflict Perpetuated: China Policy during the Kennedy Years*. Westport, Conn.: Praeger, 2002.

Kotelawala, John. *An Asian Prime Minister's Story*. London: George G. Harap, 1956.

Kurlantzick, Joshua. *The Charm Offensive: How China's Soft Power Is Transforming the World*. New Haven, Conn.: Yale University Press, 2008.

Kux, Dennis. *Disenchanted Allies: The United States and Pakistan, 1947–2000*. Baltimore: Johns Hopkins University Press, 2001.

Kuzmarov, Jeremy. *Modernizing Repression: Police Training and Nation Building in the American Century*. Amherst: University of Massachusetts Press, 2012.

Lal, Priya. "Between the Village and the World: Imagining and Practicing Development in Tanzania, 1964–1975." Ph.D. diss., New York University, 2011.

———. "Maoism in Tanzania: Shared Imaginaries and Material Connection." In *Mao's Little Red Book: A Global History*, edited by Alexander C. Cook. New York: Cambridge University Press, 2014.

Lalaj, Ana, et al. "'Albania Is Not Cuba.': Sino-Albanian Summits and the Sino-Soviet Split." *Cold War International History Project Bulletin* 16 (Fall 2007/Winter 2008): 187–89.

Langer, Paul F. "The Soviet Union, China and the Pathet Lao: Analysis and Chronology." http://www.rand.org/content/dam/rand/pubs/papers/2008/P4765.pdf. 5 January 2014.

Larkin, Bruce D. *China and Africa, 1949–1970: The Foreign Policy of the People's Republic of China*. Berkeley: University of California Press, 1971.

Larson, Deborah Welch, and Shevchenko, Alexei. "Status Seekers: Chinese and Russian Responses to U.S. Primacy." *International Security* 34 (Spring 2010): 63–95.

Larson, Deborah Welch, et al. "Status and World Order." In *Status in World Politics*, edited by T. V. Paul et al. Cambridge: Cambridge University Press, 2014.

Lawrence, Mark Atwood. "The Rise and Fall of Non-Alignment." In *The Cold War in the Third World*, edited by Robert J. McMahon. Oxford: Oxford University Press, 2013.

———. *The Vietnam War: A Concise International History*. New York: Oxford University Press, 2008.

Leffler, Melvyn P. *For the Soul of Mankind: The United States, the Soviet Union, and the Cold War*. New York: Hill and Wang, 2007.

Lenin, V. I. "The Awakening of Asia." https://www.marxists.org/archive/lenin/works/1913/may/07b.htm.

Lewis, David L. *W. E. B. Du Bois: The Fight for Equality and the American Century*. New York: MacMillan, 2001.

Li, Danhui. "The Sino-Soviet Dispute over Vietnam's Anti-American War, 1965–1972." In *Behind the Bamboo Curtain: China, Vietnam, and the World beyond Asia*, edited by Priscilla Roberts. Stanford, Calif.: Stanford University Press, 2006.

Li, Mingjiang. "Ideological Dilemma: Mao's China and the Sino-Soviet Split, 1962–1963." *Cold War History* 11 (August 2011): 387–419.

Li, Xiaobing. *A History of the Modern Chinese Army*. Lexington: University of Kentucky Press, 2007.

———, ed. *China at War: An Encyclopedia*. Santa Barbara, Calif.: ABC-CLIO, 2012.

Li, Xiaobing, and Daniel Randall Beirne. "Chinese Offensive in Korea, Fifth." In *China at War: An Encyclopedia*, edited by Xiaobing Li. Santa Barbara, Calif.: ABC-CLIO, 2012.

Little, Douglas. *American Orientalism: The United States and the Middle East since 1945*. Chapel Hill: University of North Carolina Press, 2002.

Liu, Hong. *China and the Shaping of Indonesia, 1949–1965*. Singapore: NUS Press, 2011.

Liu, Shaoqi. *Selected Works of Liu Shaoqi*. Vol. 1. Elmsford, N.Y.: Pergamon, 1984.

Liu, Xiaohong. *Chinese Ambassadors: The Rise of Diplomatic Professionalism since 1949*. Seattle: University of Washington Press, 2001.

———. *Recast All under Heaven: Revolution, War, Diplomacy, and Frontier China in the 20th Century*. New York: Continuum, 2010.

Logevall, Fredrik. *Choosing War: The Lost Chance for Peace and the Escalation of War in Vietnam*. Berkeley: University of California Press, 2001.

———. *Embers of War: The Fall of an Empire and the Making of America's Vietnam*. New York: Random House, 2014.

Louis, Roger William. *Imperialism at Bay: The United States and the Decolonization of the British Empire, 1941–1945*. New York: Oxford University Press, 1987.

Lovelace, Daniel Dudley. *China and "People's War" in Thailand, 1964–1969.* Los Angeles: Center for Chinese Studies, University of California, 1971.

Lowenthal, Richard. "China." In *Africa and the Communist World,* edited by Zbigniew Brzezinski. Stanford, Calif.: Stanford University Press, 1963.

Lüthi, Lorenz M. *The Sino-Soviet Split: Cold War in the Communist World.* Princeton, N.J.: Princeton University Press, 2008.

MacFarquhar, Roderick, and Michael Schoenhalls. *Mao's Last Revolution.* Cambridge, Mass.: Harvard University Press, 2006.

MacMillan, Margaret. *Nixon and Mao: The Week That Changed the World.* New York: Random House, 2007.

———. *Paris 1919: Six Days That Changed the World.* New York: Random House, 2003.

Maechling, Charles, Jr. "Insurgency and Counterinsurgency: The Role of Strategic Theory." *Parameters* 14 (Fall 1984): 32–41.

Manela, Erez. *The Wilsonian Moment: Self-Determination and the International Origins of Anticolonial Nationalism.* New York: Oxford University Pres, 2007.

Mann, James. *About Face: America's Curious Relationship with China from Nixon to Clinton.* New York: Vintage, 2000.

Mao, Lin. "China and the Escalation of the Vietnam War: The First Years of the Johnson Administration." *Journal of Cold War Studies* 11 (Spring 2009): 35–69.

Mao, Yufeng. "Sino-Muslims in Chinese Nation Building, 1906–1956." Ph.D. diss., George Washington University, 2007.

Marks, Thomas A. *Maoist Insurgency since Vietnam.* New York: Frank Cass, 1996.

Mazov, Sergey. *A Distant Front in the Cold War: The USSR in West Africa and the Congo, 1956–1964.* Stanford, Calif.: Stanford University Press, 2010.

McHenry, Dean. *Tanzania's Ujamaa Villages: The Implementation of a Rural Development Strategy.* Berkeley: Institute of International Studies, 1979.

McMahon, Robert J. *The Cold War on the Periphery: The United States, India, and Pakistan.* New York: Columbia University Press, 1994.

———. *The Limits of Empire: The United States and Southeast Asia since World War II.* New York: Columbia University Press, 1999.

McNamara, Robert S. *In Retrospect: The Tragedy and Lessons of Vietnam.* New York: Random House, 1995.

Meisner, Maurice. *Mao's China and After: A History of the People's Republic.* New York: Free Press, 1999.

Meredith, Martin. *The Fate of Africa: A History of Fifty Years of Independence.* New York: Public Affairs, 2006.

Merrill, Dennis. *Bread and the Ballot: The United States and India's Economic Development, 1947–1963.* Chapel Hill: University of North Carolina Press, 1990.

Mertha, Andrew. *Brothers in Arms: Chinese Aid to the Khmer Rouge, 1975–1979.* Ithaca, N.Y.: Cornell University Press, 2014.

Michel, Serge, and Michel Beuret. *China Safari: On the Trail of Beijing's Expansion in Africa.* New York: Nation Books, 2009.

Millett, Allan R. *The War for Korea, 1950–1951: They Came from the North.* Lawrence: University of Kansas Press, 2010.

Mitter, Rana. *Forgotten Ally: China's World War II, 1937–1945.* New York: Houghton Mifflin, 2013.

Mohiddin, Ahmed. *African Socialism in Two Countries*. London: Croom Helm, 1981.

Monson, Jamie. *Africa's Freedom Railway: How a Chinese Development Project Changed Lives and Livelihoods in Tanzania*. Bloomington: Indiana University Press, 2009.

Mozingo, David P. *Chinese Policy toward Indonesia, 1949–1967*. Ithaca, N.Y.: Cornell University Press, 1975.

Muehlenbeck, Philip E. *Betting on the Africans: John F. Kennedy's Courting of African Nationalist Leaders*. New York: Oxford University Press, 2012.

Mwakikagile, Godfrey. *The Union of Tanganyika and Zanzibar: Product of the Cold War*. Pretoria, South Africa: New Africa Press, 2008.

Myoe, Myung Aung. *In the Name of Pauk Phaw: Myanmar's China Policy since 1948*. Singapore: Institute for Southeast Asian Studies, 2011.

Narayanan, K. R. "The Five Principles of Peaceful Co-Existence: The Appropriate Code for a Globalized World." *Foreign Affairs Journal* 72 (June 2004): 9–13.

Nathan, Andrew J., and Andrew Scobell. *China's Search for Security*. New York: Columbia University Press, 2012.

Nehru, Jawaharlal. "Changing India." *Foreign Affairs* 41 (April 1963): 453–65.

Nguyen, Lien-Hang T. *Hanoi's War: An International History of the War for Peace in Vietnam*. Chapel Hill: University of North Carolina Press, 2012.

Niu, Jun, *From Yan'an to the World: The Origin and Development of Chinese Communist Foreign Policy*. Norwalk, Conn.: East Bridge, 2005.

Nixon, Richard M. *RN: The Memoirs of Richard Nixon*. New York: Grosset and Dunlap, 1972.
———. "Asia after Vietnam." *Foreign Affairs* 46 (October 1967): 111–25.

Noer, Thomas. *Soapy: A Biography of G. Mennen Williams*. Ann Arbor: University of Michigan Press, 2005.

Nyerere, Julius. *Freedom and Unity: A Selection from Writings and Speeches, 1952–1965*. London: Oxford University Press, 1967.

Nzongola-Ntalaja, Georges. *Congo from Leopold to Kabila: A People's History*. New York: Zed Books, 2002.

Ogunsanwo, Alaba. *China's Policy in Africa, 1958–1971*. Cambridge: Cambridge University Press, 1974.

Osgood, Kenneth. *Total Cold War: Eisenhower's Propaganda Battle at Home and Abroad*. Lawrence: University Press of Kansas, 2006.

Oyen, Meredith. "Communism, Containment and the Chinese Overseas." In *The Cold War in Asia: The Battle for Hearts and Minds*, edited by Zheng Yangwen et al. Leiden: E. J. Brill, 2010.

Paine, S. C. M. *The Wars for Asia, 1911–1949*. Cambridge: Cambridge University Press, 2012.

Pantsov, Alexander. *The Bolsheviks and the Chinese Revolution, 1919–1927*. Honolulu: University of Hawaii Press, 2000.

Parker, Jason. "Cold War II: The Eisenhower Administration, the Bandung Conference, and the Reperiodization of the Postwar Era." *Diplomatic History* 30 (November 2006): 867–92.

Pasha, A. K. "India and West Asia: Challenges and Opportunities." In *India's Foreign Policy*, edited by Anjali Ghosh et al. Delhi: Pearson, 2009.

Pauker, Ewa T. "GANEFO I: Sports and Politics in Djakarta." *Rand Corporation Published Research*, July 19, 2014. http://www.rand.org/content/dam/rand/pubs/papers/2009/P2935.pdf.

Pauker, Guy J. "The Rise and Fall of Afro-Asian Solidarity." *Asian Survey* 9 (September 1965): 425–32.

Rabe, Stephen G. *The Killing Zone: The United States Wages Cold War in Latin America.* New York: Oxford University Press, 2011.

Radchenko, Sergey. *Two Suns in the Heavens: The Sino-Soviet Struggle for Supremacy, 1962–1967.* Stanford, Calif.: Stanford University Press, 2009.

———. *Unwanted Visionaries: The Soviet Failure in Asia at the End of the Cold War.* New York: Oxford University Press, 2014.

Rakove, Robert B. *Kennedy, Johnson, and the Nonaligned World.* New York: Cambridge University Press, 2013.

Reardon-Anderson, James. *Yenan and the Great Powers: The Origins of Chinese Communist Foreign Policy, 1944–1946.* New York: Columbia University Press, 1980.

Rey, Marie-Pierre. "De Gaulle, French Diplomacy, and Franco-Soviet Relations Seen from Moscow." In *Globalizing de Gaulle: International Perspectives on French Foreign Policies,* edited by Christian Nuenlist, Anne Locher, and Garret Martin. Lanham, Md.: Lexington Books, 2010.

Richardson, Sophie. *China Cambodia and the Five Principles of Peaceful Coexistence.* New York: Columbia University Press, 2010.

Romulo, Carlos P. *The Meaning of Bandung.* Chapel Hill: University of North Carolina Press, 1955.

Rosenberg, Emily. *Spreading the American Dream: American Economic and Cultural Expansion, 1890–1945.* New York: Hill and Wang, 1982.

Roy, Denny. *Taiwan: A Political History.* Ithaca, N.Y.: Cornell University Press, 2003.

Saich, Tony. "The Chinese Communist Party during the Era of the Comintern (1919–1943)." http://www.hks.edu/fs/asaich/chinese-communisty-party-during-comintern.pdf.

Saich, Tony, and Benjamin Yang, eds. *The Rise to Power of the Chinese Communist Party: Documents and Analysis.* New York: M. E. Sharpe, 1996.

Saunders, Elizabeth. *Leaders at War: How Presidents Shape Military Interventions.* Ithaca, N.Y.: Cornell University Press, 2011.

Scalapino, Robert A. "On the Trail of Zhou Enlai in Africa." *Rand Corporation Published Research,* 16 July 2014. http://www.rand.org/pubs/research_memoranda/RM4061.html.

———. "Sino-Soviet Competition in Africa." *Foreign Affairs* 42 (July 1964): 640–54.

Schaller, Michael. *The U.S. Crusade in China, 1938–1945.* New York: Columbia University Press, 1979.

Schlesinger, Arthur M. Jr. *A Thousand Days: John F. Kennedy in the White House.* New York: Mariner, 2002.

Schmitz, David F. *The United States and Right Wing Dictatorships, 1965–1989.* Cambridge: Cambridge University Press, 2006.

Schwartz, Benjamin I. *Chinese Communism and the Rise of Mao.* New York: Harper and Row, 1958.

Scott, James C. *Seeing Like a State: How Certain Schemes to Improve the Human Condition Have Failed.* New Haven, Conn.: Yale University Press, 1999.

Selden, Mark. *China in Revolution: The Yenan Way Revisited.* Armonk, N.Y.: M. E. Sharpe, 1995.

Shafer, D. Michael. *Deadly Paradigms: The Failure of U.S. Counterinsurgency Policy.* Princeton, N.J.: Princeton University Press, 1988.

Shakya, Tsering. *The Dragon in the Land of Snows: A History of Modern Tibet since 1947.* New York: Penguin, 2000.

Shambaugh, David. "Tangled Titans: Conceptualizing the U.S. China Relationship." In *Tangled Titans: The United States and China*, edited by David Shambaugh. New York: Rowman and Littlefield, 2013.

Shaw, Tony. *Hollywood's Cold War.* Amherst: University of Massachusetts Press, 2007.

Shaw, Tony, and Denise J. Youngblood. *Cinematic Cold War: The American and Soviet Struggle for Hearts and Minds.* Lawrence: University of Kansas Press, 2010.

Shen, Zhiahua, and Xia Yafeng. "Leadership Transfer in the Asian Revolution: Mao Zedong and the Asian Cominform." *Cold War History* 14 (May 2014): 195–213.

Sheng, Michael. *Battling Western Imperialism: Mao, Stalin, and the United States.* Princeton, N.J.: Princeton University Press, 1997.

Shichor, Yitzchak. *The Middle East in China's Foreign Policy, 1949–1977.* Cambridge: Cambridge University Press, 1979.

Shimizu, Sayuri. *Creating People of Plenty: The United States and Japan's Economic Alternatives, 1950–1960.* Kent, Ohio: Kent State University Press, 2001.

Shinn, David H., and Joshua Eisenmann. *China and Africa: A Century of Engagement.* Philadelphia: University of Pennsylvania Press, 2012.

Short, Philip. *Pol Pot: Anatomy of a Nightmare.* New York: Henry Holt, 2006.

Shuman, Amanda. "Elite Competitive Sport in the People's Republic of China: The Games of the New Emerging Forces (GANEFO)." *Journal of Sport History* 40 (Summer 2013): 258–83.

Sidey, Hugh. "The President's Voracious Reading Habits." *Life*, 17 March 1961, 56.

Sihanouk, Norodom. *My War with the CIA: The Memoirs of Prince Norodom Sihanouk.* New York: Pantheon, 1972.

Simpson, Bradley. *Economists with Guns: Authoritarian Development and U.S.-Indonesian Relations, 1960–1968.* Stanford, Calif.: Stanford University Press, 2010.

Slyke, Lyman P. Van. "The Battle of the Hundred Regiments: Problems of Coordination and Control during the Sino-Japanese War." *Modern Asian Studies* 30 (October 1996): 979–1005.

Smith, Tony. "New Bottles for New Wine: A Pericentric Framework for the Study of the Cold War." *Diplomatic History* 24 (October 2000): 567–91.

Spence, Jonathan D. *The Gate of Heavenly Peace: The Chinese and Their Revolution.* New York: Penguin, 1981.

———. *Mao Zedong: A Life.* New York: Penguin, 2006.

———. *The Search for Modern China.* New York: W. W. Norton, 1990.

Stueck, William. *The Korean War: An International History.* Princeton, N.J.: Princeton University Press, 1995.

———. *Rethinking the Korean War: A New Diplomatic and Strategic History.* Princeton, N.J.: Princeton University Press, 2002.

Tang, Chris. "Beyond India: The Utility of Sino-Pakistani Relations in Chinese Foreign Policy, 1962–1965." *CWIHP Working Paper 64*, November 2012. https://www.wilsoncenter.org/sites/default/files/CWIHPWP64Beyond%20 IndiaTheUtilityofSinoPakistaniRelationsinChineseForeignPolicy.pdf.

Taubman, William. *Khrushchev: The Man and His Era*. New York: W. W. Norton, 2004.

Tsang, Steve. "Target Zhou Enlai: The 'Kashmir Princess' Incident of 1955." *China Quarterly* 139 (1994): 766–82.

Tucker, Nancy Bernkopf. *The China Threat: Memories, Myths, and Realities in the 1950s*. New York: Columbia University Press, 2012.

———. "The Evolution of U.S. China Relations." In *Tangled Titans: The United States and China*, edited by David Shambaugh. Lanham, Md.: Rowman and Littlefield, 2012.

———. *Patterns in the Dust: Chinese-American Relations and the Recognition Controversy, 1949–1950*. New York: Columbia University Press, 1983.

———. *Strait Talk: United States–Taiwan Relations and the Crisis with China*. Cambridge, Mass.: Harvard University Press, 2009.

Tudda, Chris. *A Cold War Turning Point: Nixon and China, 1969–1972*. Baton Rouge: Louisiana State University Press, 2012.

Tyson, Timothy. *Radio Free Dixie: Robert F. Williams and the Roots of Black Power*. Chapel Hill: University of North Carolina Press, 2001.

Van de Ven, Hans J. *From Friend to Comrade: The Founding of the Chinese Communist Party, 1920–1927*. Berkeley: University of California Press, 1992.

Van Ness, Peter. *Revolution and Chinese Foreign Policy: Peking's Support for Wars of National Liberation*. Berkeley: University of California Press, 1970.

Van Slyke, Lyman P. "The Battle of the Hundred Regiments: Problems of Coordination and Control during the Sino-Japanese War." *Modern Asian Studies* 30 (October 1996): 979–1005.

Verrone, Richard Burks. "Behind the Wall of Geneva: Lao Politics, American Counterinsurgency and Why the U.S. Lost in Laos, 1961–1965." Ph.D. diss., Texas Tech University, 2001.

Vestal, Theodore M. *The Lion of Judah in the New World: Haile Selassie of Ethiopia and the Shaping of Americans' Attitudes toward Africa*. New York: Praeger, 2011.

Villafaña, Frank R. *Cold War in the Congo: The Confrontation of Cuban Military Forces, 1960–1967*. New Brunswick, N.J.: Transaction, 2011.

Vogel, Ezra. *Deng Xiaoping and the Transformation of China*. Cambridge, Mass.: Belknap Press of Harvard University Press, 2013.

Volgy, Thomas J., et al. "Status Considerations in the Rise of International Politics and the Rise of Regional Powers." In *Status in World Politics*, edited by T. V. Paul et al. Cambridge: Cambridge University Press, 2014.

Von Eschen, Penny. *Satchmo Blows Up the World: Jazz Musicians Play the Cold War*. Cambridge, Mass.: Harvard University Press, 2004.

Wang, Dong. *China's Unequal Treaties: Narrating National Histories*. Lanham, Md.: Lexington Books, 2005.

Wang, Zheng. *Never Forget National Humiliation: Historical Memory in Chinese Politics*. New York: Columbia University Press, 2012.

Warner, Roger. *Shooting at the Moon: The Story of America's Clandestine War in Laos*. New York: Streetforth, 1998.

Weathersby, Kathryn. "'Should We Fear This?' Stalin and the Danger of War with America." *CWIHP Working Paper 39*, 31 May 2013. http://www.wilsoncenter.org/sites/default/files/ACFAEF.pdf.

Weinstein, Warren. *Soviet and Chinese Aid to African Nations*. New York: Praeger, 1980.

Westad, Odd Arne. *Cold War and Revolution: Soviet-American Rivalry and the Origins of the Chinese Civil War*. New York: Columbia University Press, 1993.

———. *Decisive Encounters: The Chinese Civil War, 1946–1950*. Stanford, Calif.: Stanford University Press, 2003.

———. *The Global Cold War: Third World Interventions and the Making of Our Times*. Cambridge: Cambridge University Press, 2005.

Westad, Odd Arne, et al., eds. "77 Conversations between Chinese and Foreign Leaders on the Wars in Indochina, 1964–1977." *CWIHP Working Paper 22*, May 1998. http://www.wilsoncenter.org/sites/default/files/ACFB39.pdf.

Whiting, Allen S. *China Crosses the Yalu: The Decision to Enter the Korean War*. Stanford, Calif.: Stanford University Press, 1960.

Wilbur, C. Martin. *The Nationalist Revolution in China, 1923–1928*. Cambridge: Cambridge University Press, 1983.

Williamson, Daniel C. *Separate Agendas: Churchill, Eisenhower, and Anglo-American Relations, 1953–1955*. Plymouth, Mass.: Lexington Books, 2006.

Wohlforth, William C. "Status and Interstate Conflict." In *Status in World Politics*, edited by T. V. Paul et al. Cambridge: Cambridge University Press, 2014.

Wolf, Reinhard. "Rising Powers, Status Ambitions, and the Need to Reassure: What China Could Learn from Imperial Germany's Failures." *Chinese Journal of International Politics* 7 (Summer 2014): 185–219.

Xia, Yafeng. *Negotiating with the Enemy: U.S.-China Talks during the Cold War, 1949–1972*. Bloomington: Indiana University Press, 2006.

———. "Nixon, Mao, Kissinger and Zhou—The Tale of Four Historical Giants." In "Nixon and Kissinger/Nixon and Mao Roundtable," edited by David A. Welsh, 23 September 2007. http://www.h-net.org/diplo/roundtables/PDF/NixonKissingerMao-Roundtable.pdf.

Xiao, Zhiwei. "Chinese Cinema." In *Encyclopedia of Chinese Film*, edited by Yingjin Zhang and Zhiwei Xiao. New York: Routledge, 1998.

Xu, Guoqi. *Olympic Dreams: China and Sports, 1895–2008*. Cambridge, Mass.: Harvard University Press, 2008.

Yan, Xuetong. "The Rise of China and Its Power Status." *Chinese Journal of International Politics* 1 (2006): 5–33.

Yang, Kuisong. "Changes in Mao Zedong Attitude toward the Indochina War, 1949–1973." *CWIHP Working Paper 34*, February 2002. https://www.wilsoncenter.org/sites/default/files/ACFB04.pdf.

Yaqub, Salim. *Containing Arab Nationalism: The Eisenhower Doctrine and the Middle East*. Chapel Hill: University of North Carolina Press, 2004.

Yu, George T. *China's African Policy: A Study of Tanzania*. New York: Praeger, 1975.

Zarrow, Peter. *China in War and Revolution, 1895–1949*. New York: Routledge, 2005.

Zhai, Qiang. "China and the Cambodian Conflict, 1970–1975." In *Behind the Bamboo Curtain: China, Vietnam, and the World beyond Asia*, edited by Priscilla Roberts. Stanford, Calif.: Stanford University Press, 2006.

———. *China and the Vietnam Wars, 1950–1975*. Chapel Hill: University of North Carolina Press, 2000.

Zhang, Bijian. "China's 'Peaceful Rise' to Great Power Status." *Foreign Affairs* 84 (September/October 2005): 18–24.

Zhang, Shuguang. "Beijing's Aid to Hanoi and the United States China Confrontations, 1964–1968." In *Behind the Bamboo Curtain: China, Vietnam and the World beyond Asia*, edited by Priscilla Roberts. Stanford, Calif.: Stanford University Press, 2006.

———. "Constructing 'Peaceful Coexistence': China's Diplomacy toward the Geneva and Bandung Conferences, 1954–55." *Cold War History* 7, no. 4 (2007): 509–28.

———. *Deterrence and Strategic Culture: Chinese-American Confrontations, 1949–1958*. Ithaca, N.Y.: Cornell University Press, 1992.

———. *Economic Cold War: America's Embargo against China and the Sino-Soviet Alliance, 1949–1953*. Stanford, Calif.: Stanford University Press, 2001.

———. *Mao's Military Romanticism: China and the Korean War, 1950–1953*. Lawrence: University Press of Kansas, 1995.

Zhang, Shuguang, and Jian Chen, eds. *Chinese Communist Foreign Policy and the Cold War in Asia: New Documentary Evidence, 1944–1950*. Chicago: Imprint Publications, 1996.

Zhang, Xiaoming. "China's Involvement in Laos during the Vietnam War, 1963–1975." *Journal of Military History* 66 (October 2002): 114–66.

Zhou, Taomo. "Ambivalent Alliance: Chinese Policy towards Indonesia, 1960–1965." *CWIHP Working Paper 67*, 14 August 2013.

Chinese-Language Secondary Sources

Chen, Dunde. *Tanlu zai 1964: Zhou Enlai feiwang Feizhou* [Finding the way in 1964: Zhou Enlai flies to Africa]. Beijing: Jiefangjun wenyi chubanshe, 2007.

Geng, Biao. *Geng Biao huiyilu, 1949–1992* [Memoirs of Geng Biao, 1949–1992]. Nanjing: Jiangsu renmin chubanshe, 1998.

Guo, Ming, et al. *Zhong Yue guanxi yanbian sishinian* [Four decades of the evolution of Sino-Vietnamese relations]. Nanjing: Guangxi renmin chubanshe, 1992.

Hu, Zhengqing. *Yige waijiaoguan de riji* [The diaries of a diplomat]. Jinan: Huanghe chubanshe, 1991.

Jiang, Huajie. "Nongzhi yuanfei (1971–1983): Zhongguo yuanfei moshi yu chengjiao de ge'an yanjiu [China's agricultural and technical assistance to Africa (1971–1983): Research about the methods and results of Chinese aid to Africa]." *Waijiao pinglun* [Commentary on Diplomacy] (January 2013): 30–49.

Li, Qianyu. "Shilun Zhongguo dui di er ci Ya Fei huiyi zhengce de yanbian [The evolution of China's policy toward the Second Afro-Asian Conference]." *Guoji zhengchi yanjiu* [International Relations Research] 4 (2010): 115–33.

Luo, Guibo. "Wuchan jieji guojizhuyi de guanghui dianfan: Yi Mao Zedong he yuanyue kangfa [An exceptional model of proletarian internationalism: Mao Zedong and the war to aid Vietnam and resist France]." In *Zhongguo junshi guwentuan yuanyue kangfa shilu: Dangshiren de huiyi* [True Stories of the CMAG in the war to aid Vietnam and resist France: Personal memoirs], edited by CCP Party History Compilation Team. Beijing: Zhonggong dangshi chubanshe, 2002.

Niu, Jun. *Lengzhan yu Zhongguo waijiao juece* [The Cold War and Chinese foreign policy decision-making]. Beijing: Jiuzhou chubanshe, 2010.

PRC Foreign Ministry Diplomatic History Research Office, ed. *Zhou Enlai waijiao huodong dashiji, 1949–1975* [Important events in Zhou Enlai's diplomatic activities, 1949–1975]. Beijing: Shijie zhishi chubanshe, 1993.

Quan, Yanchi. *Mao Zedong yu Heluxiaofu* [Mao Zedong and Khrushchev]. Beijing: Renmin chubanshe.

Shen, Zhihua. *Mao Zedong, Sidalin yu Chaoxian zhanzheng* [Mao, Stalin, and the Korean War]. Guangzhou: Guangdong renmin chubanshe, 2003.

Wang, Qinmei. "Tansang tielu—Zhong Fei guanxi shishang yizuo yongheng de fengbei [The Tan-Zam Railway: An imperishable masterpiece in Sino-African relations]." In *Tongxin ruojin: Zhong Fei youhao guanxi de huihuang licheng* [Hearts joined by a golden link: The brilliant course of Sino-African friendship], edited by Liu Miaogeng et al. Beijing: Shijie zhishi chubanshe, 2006.

Wu, Lengxi. *Shinian lunzhan, 1956–1966: Zhongsu guanxi huiyilu* [Ten years of debate, 1955–1956: A memoir of Sino-Soviet relations]. Beijing: Zhongyang wenxian, 1999.

———. *Yi Mao zhuxi: Wo qinshen jingli de ruogan zhongda lishi shijian pianduan* [Remembering Chairman Mao: A series of important historical events that I personally experienced]. Beijing: Xinhua chubanshe, 1995.

Wu, Xiuquan. *Zai waijiaobu banian de jingli 1950.1–1958.10* [My eight years in the Foreign Ministry, January 1950–October 1958]. Beijing: Shijie zhishi chubanshe, 1983.

Xie, Yixian, et al. *Dangdai Zhongguo waijiaoshi: 1949–2001.* [Contemporary Chinese diplomacy, 1949–2001]. Beijing: Zhongguo qingnian chubanshe, 2002.

Xiong, Huayuan. *Zhou Enlai chu deng shijie wutai* [Zhou Enlai goes onto the world stage]. Shenyang: Liaoning People's Press, 1999.

Ye, Fei. *Ye Fei huiyilu* [The memoirs of Ye Fei]. Beijing: Jiefang chubanshe, 1988.

Yun, Shui. *Chushi qiguo jishi: Jiangjun dashi Wang Youping* [Record of diplomatic missions to seven countries: General Ambassador Wang Youping]. Beijing: Shijie zhishi chubanshe, 1996.

Zhou, Boping. *Feichang shiqi de waijiao shengya* [The diplomatic career of an extraordinary period]. Beijing: Shijie zhishi chubanshe, 2003.

Zhou, Junlun, ed., *Nie Rongzhen nianpu* [Chronological life of Nie Rongzhen]. Beijing: Renmin chubanshe, 1999.

Index

Jiang Jieshi, 21, 28, 34, 36, 39, 44, 63–66, 68, 76, 92, 95, 125, 139, 240
Johnson, Lyndon B., 199, 224, 236, 244, 266, 271, 307–8

Kang, David C., 5
Karume, Abeid, 256, 258, 259, 294
Keïta, Modibo, 207, 210, 273, 276, 281–82, 302
Kennedy, John F., 192, 197
Khrushchev, Nikita, 169–72, 181, 197, 210, 244, 246, 249
Kim Il Sung, 48, 51, 53
Kissinger, Henry, 310–12, 316, 318, 333, 334, 336, 338; diplomacy with the PRC, 320–30; secret trip to PRC, 313–15
Korean War, 4, 10, 13, 46, 48–57, 58, 62, 64, 68, 69, 71, 74, 76, 83, 106, 134, 143, 144, 147, 152, 159, 320

Laos, 83, 88–92, 96, 108, 112–13, 115–17, 189, 218, 231, 239, 247–52, 254–55, 269, 319, 353
Lenin, Vladimir, 18
Limited Nuclear Test Ban Treaty, 182, 202, 212
Lin Biao, 235, 237–38
Liu Shaoqi, 31, 32, 40–41, 43, 47, 58, 77, 134, 189, 201, 205, 214, 306
Long March, 25, 28

MacMurray, John V., 20–21
Malenkov, Georgi, 82
Mali, 153, 207, 209–10, 212, 219, 270, 276, 281–86, 300, 302,
Mao Zedong, 6, 24–25, 32–35, 37, 43, 44, 45, 47, 48, 77, 94, 95, 110, 118, 151, 166, 189, 198, 219, 230, 231–32, 268, 277, 300, 315, 320, 324–25, 331 333–34, 338; African Americans and, 153–55; Cultural Revolution and, 306; death of, 335; early writings of, 15–18; first Indochina conflict and, 58–60; Great Leap Forward and, 166–67; Intermediate Zone Theory of, 39, 183; interviews with Edgar Snow, 25, 312;

Korean War and, 48–52; Sino-Japanese War and, 29–30; Sino-Soviet split and, 170, 174; support for insurgencies, 233–35, 239–42; Taiwan Strait Crisis and, 168–69; work with peasants, 22–23
Mao Zedong Thought, 32–33, 251, 262–63, 283
May 30th Movement, 19
Mendes-France, Pierre, 88–89
Mikoyan, Anastas, 40
Mobutu, Joseph, 268, 322, 332
Molotov, Vyacheslov, 82–83, 85, 90
Morocco, 20, 145, 207, 209
Mulele, Pierre, 261

Nasser, Gamel Abdel, 100, 102, 125–27, 178–80, 188, 209, 213, 221
National Liberation Front (NLF), 231, 238–47, 251, 253–54
National Security Council (NSC), 42, 55, 56, 57, 61, 66, 71–72, 175, 193, 204, 236, 313, 320, 341
Nehru, Jawaharlal, 77–82, 93–94, 100, 122–24, 135, 169, 173–74, 176–77, 186–92, 209, 214, 224
Nepal, 118, 120, 121, 157, 176, 219
Ngo Dinh Diem, 200, 231, 238–40
Nguyen Van Linh, 240, 242
Nie Rongzhen, 19, 130
Nixon, Richard M., 11, 57, 72, 75, 212, 246, 305; détente with China, 309–24
Non-Aligned Movement, 186, 214, 343, 351
North Korea, 2, 46, 47, 48–53, 57, 196, 206, 306
Nyerere, Julius, 219, 258–59, 271, 287–88, 290–91, 296–301

Pakistan, 12, 70, 71, 76, 93, 101, 103, 107, 108, 176, 192, 193, 195, 196, 214, 215, 216, 219, 223, 310, 312; Indo-Pakistan War, 223–27; strengthens ties with China, 197–99; Zhou Enlai's visit to, 120–23
Peace Corps, 270, 279, 281, 290
Peng Dehuai, 23, 30, 52, 56

People's Army of Vietnam (PAVN),
    59–60
People's Daily, 60, 119, 152, 171, 206,
    233, 283

Red Army, 23, 25, 28, 31, 158, 248
Roosevelt, Franklin Delano (FDR),
    34–36
Rostow, Walt W., 183–85, 230, 235,
    243, 281
Rusk, Dean, 191, 223, 224, 228–29, 250,
    257, 258, 259, 266, 284

San Francisco Peace Treaty, 65
Second Afro-Asian Conference
    (Bandung II), 214–23
Sihanouk, Norodom, 76, 109–14, 120,
    127–29, 189, 199–202, 328–30, 340
Simbas, 261–68
Sino-Vietnamese War, 339–41
Smith, Tony, 2
Snow, Edgar, 25
Soumialot, Gaston, 261–62, 264,
    266–67
Southeast Asia Treaty Organization
    (SEATO), 81, 88, 89, 93, 123, 142, 162,
    197, 198, 245, 252
South Vietnam, 96, 128, 199–200, 218,
    231, 238–53, 320
Souvanna, Phouma, 112–17, 247
Stalin, Joseph, 38, 40, 41, 43, 48, 58, 77,
    82, 150, 181
Status, 1–2; China and, 6–10, 16–17,
    47–48, 49, 75, 166, 195, 202, 348–52;
    cultural diplomacy and, 132; definition
    of, 4–5; Nixon and, 304–5
Sudan, 96, 136–37, 209, 344
Suharto, 227–29
Sukarno, 93, 117–20, 196, 203–6,
    227–29, 349

Taiwan, 10, 24, 29, 48, 51, 57, 63–68,
    73, 92, 93, 99, 112, 123–24, 168–69,
    172, 197, 205, 208, 210, 237, 284, 311,
    313, 314–16, 318, 321, 325, 327, 336–37.
    See also China, Republic of

Taiwan Strait Crisis: First, 68, 101;
    Second; 167–69
Tanzania, 7, 182, 219, 258, 265, 266, 267,
    268, 347–48; Chinese aid to, 287–92,
    295–300
Thailand, 45, 61, 96, 101, 107, 113,
    141–42, 161, 200, 247, 321, 326;
    counterinsurgency in, 251–54
Three Worlds Theory, 325–26, 337, 344
Tibet, 18, 78, 123, 143, 149, 155–59, 173–79,
    212, 345, 351
Touré, Sékou, 207, 210, 271, 276–81, 303
Truman, Harry S., 45, 54, 57, 63, 64
Tunisia, 208–10, 306

Unequal Treaties, 20–21
Union of Soviet Socialist Republics
    (USSR), 4, 10, 34, 39–40, 41, 43, 62,
    66, 69, 77, 85, 98, 182, 184–85, 198, 202,
    209, 211, 215, 217, 218, 223, 233, 245,
    256, 258, 272, 276, 281, 305, 309, 313,
    316, 323, 324, 325, 336, 338–39, 349;
    split with China, 179–84; tensions with
    China, 169–73
United States: aid to Guinea, 278–80;
    aid to Jiang Jieshi, 42; Bandung
    Conference and, 104; Berlin
    Conference and, 82–84; Cambodia
    and, 112–13, 199–200, 202; cooperation
    with China 335–44, 54–55; economic
    aid to Africa, 274–76; Geneva
    Conference and, 84–85, 89–90;
    hostility to China, 8–9, 127, 128,
    130–31; Indo-Pakistani War and,
    225–27; intervention in the Congo,
    265–67; Korean War and, 52–55; Laos
    and, 115–17; Mali and, 282, 284–86;
    rapprochement with China, 306–12;
    response to Zhou Enlai's Africa visit,
    211–12; response to Zhou Enlai's Asia
    tour, 123–24; Second Afro-Asian
    Conference and, 217, 219–20; Sino-
    Indian War and, 190–93; Sino-Soviet
    frictions and, 172–73; Sino-Soviet split
    and, 184–86; Suharto and, 228–29;
    Sukarno visit to, 117–18; support for